# SECULAR CHORAL MUSIC IN PRINT

## 1996 SUPPLEMENT

Edited by

Robert W. Cho
Elisa T. Kahn-Ellis
Donald T. Reese
Frank James Staneck

Music-In-Print Series, Vol. 2u

MUSICDATA, INC.
Philadelphia, 1996

The Music-In-Print Series to date:

Vols. 1a,b. Sacred Choral Music In Print, Second Edition (1985)
Vol. 1c. Sacred Choral Music In Print, Second Edition: Arranger Index (1987)
Vol. 1s. Sacred Choral Music In Print: 1988 Supplement
Vol. 1t. Sacred Choral Music In Print: 1992 Supplement
Vol. 1u. Sacred Choral Music In Print: 1996 Supplement
Vol. 1x. Sacred Choral Music In Print: Master Index 1996
Vols. 2a,b. Secular Choral Music In Print, Second Edition (1987)
Vol. 2c. Secular Choral Music In Print, Second Edition: Arranger Index (1987)
Vol. 2s. Secular Choral Music In Print: 1991 Supplement
Vol. 2t. Secular Choral Music In Print: 1993 Supplement
Vol. 2u. Secular Choral Music In Print: 1996 Supplement
Vol. 2x. Secular Choral Music In Print: Master Index 1996 (in preparation)
Vol. 3. Organ Music In Print, Second Edition (1984)
Vol. 3s. Organ Music In Print: 1990 Supplement
Vol. 4. Classical Vocal Music In Print (1976) (out of print)
Vol. 4s. Classical Vocal Music In Print: 1985 Supplement
Vol. 4t. Classical Vocal Music In Print: 1995 Supplement
Vol. 4x. Classical Vocal Music In Print: Master Index 1995
Vol. 5. Orchestral Music In Print (1979)
Vol. 5s. Orchestral Music In Print: 1983 Supplement
Vol. 5t. Orchestral Music In Print: 1994 Supplement
Vol. 5x. Orchestral Music In Print: Master Index 1994
Vol. 6. String Music In Print, Second Edition (1973)
Vol. 6s. String Music In Print: 1984 Supplement
Vol. 7. Classical Guitar Music In Print (1989)
Vols. XCa,b. Music-In-Print Master Composer Index 1995
Vol. XT. Music-In-Print Master Title Index 1995

Music-In-Print Series: ISSN 0146-7883

Copyright © 1996 by Musicdata, Inc.

All rights reserved under International and Pan-American Copyright Conventions by Musicdata, Inc.

No part of this work covered by the copyrights hereon may be reproduced or copied in any form or by any means—graphic, electronic, or mechanical, including photocopying, recording, taping or information storage and retrieval systems—without written permission of the publisher.

Printed by Port City Press, Baltimore, Maryland

Musicdata, Inc.
P.O. Box 48010
Philadelphia, Pennsylvania 19144-8010

Library of Congress Cataloging-in-Publication Data

Daugherty, F. Mark, 1951-
   Secular choral music in print.

   (Music-in-print series ; vol. 2)
   Rev. ed. of: Secular choral music / edited by
Thomas R. Nardone, James H. Nye, Mark Resnick.
1st ed. 1974.
   1. Choral music—Bibliography.   I. Simon, Susan H.,
1943-   . II. Nardone, Thomas R.  Secular choral
music.  III. Series: Music-in-print series ; v. 2.
ML128.V7D3  1987    016.7841    87-24749
ISBN 0-88478-041-4

# Contents

| | |
|---|---|
| Preface | v |
| Guide to Use | vii |
| List of Abbreviations | xi |
| **Secular Choral Music In Print: 1996 Supplement** | **1** |
| **Arranger Index** | **107** |
| Publisher Directory | 115 |
| Advertisements | 155 |
|     Index to Advertisers | 155 |

# Preface

The vast amount of secular choral music represented in this series is as varied as it is enormous. This genre continues to expand in all directions of scope, volume, diversity, and content. Musicdata endeavors to provide as complete a list as possible of music in print throughout the world. Included in this volume is secular choral music from all periods and in all styles. Standard choral pieces as well as concert versions of larger dramatic works are also represented here.

The series is a good source for locating the publisher of a particular work and discovering newly composed publications. With this in mind, *Secular Choral Music In Print: 1996 Supplement* should be used in conjunction with *Secular Choral Music In Print, 2nd Edition*, *Secular Choral Music In Print: 1991 Supplement* and *Secular Choral Music In Print: 1993 Supplement*.

Deciding whether a piece is secular or sacred remains a problem for us and we rely on a publisher's indications to resolve the matter. In the absence of any guidance from the publisher we have chosen to include pieces that straddle the line and may be suitable for religious worship services. Titles are organized with initial articles rotated.

The distinction between composer and arranger is often blurred and inconsistent in publishers' catalogs. Since this editorial question is impossible to resolve, we have once again included an Arranger Index enabling the user to locate a piece under both composer and arranger.

Music publishers have actively participated in the preparation for this volume by submitting catalogs marked with their new listings published since the 1993 supplementary volume appeared. Obviously, our work is dependent on the cooperation of music publishers and we wish to offer our thanks to those publishers who have generously assisted us by providing accurate, up-to-date listings.

We wish to thank Musicdata staff members Kathe Jacoby and Joseph Pluciennik who assisted us in this project with their computer expertise, and Mimi Tashiro of the Stanford University Music Library for her assistance in obtaining current composer necrology. Special thanks to Mark Resnick, whose tireless efforts and commitment to Musicdata make the Music-In-Print Series a reality.

Philadelphia, Pennsylvania    June 1996

Robert W. Cho    Elisa T. Kahn-Ellis
Donald T. Reese    Frank James Staneck

# Guide to Use

## THE MUSIC-IN-PRINT SERIES

The Music-In-Print series is an ongoing effort to locate and catalog all music in print throughout the world. The intention is to cover all areas of music as rapidly as resources permit, as well as to provide a mechanism for keeping the information up to date.

Since 1973, Musicdata, Inc. has solicited catalogs and listings from music publishers throughout the world. Using the information supplied by co-operating publishers, the series lists specific editions which are available from a publisher either for sale or on a rental basis in appropriate categories. The volumes in the series are basically organized by the primary performing force, instrument or instrumental family, such as Sacred Choral Music, Organ Music or String Music.

It is often difficult to define the boundaries between the various broad areas of music covered by the volumes in the series. The definition of sacred and secular choral music varies from publisher to publisher; some major choral works are no longer listed in Orchestral Music, reflecting changing editorial practice; some solo vocal music is in Orchestral Music; etc. The user is advised to consult the preface to individual volumes for greater definition of scope. Use of more than one volume may well be necessary to locate an edition or all editions of a work.

Editorial policy is to include as much information as the publisher supplies, within the limits of practicality. An important goal of the series is to try to bring together different editions of a composition under a single title.

## VOLUME FORMAT

The volumes of the Music-In-Print series have two basic formats: unified or structured. Reference to the editor's preface and the table of contents will assist in determining how a given volume is organized.

The unified volumes (e.g., Organ Music, Orchestral Music) are arranged in a single alphabetical interfiling of composers' names, titles of works and cross references. The title under a composer's name serves as the focus for major information on each composition. In the absence of a composer, the title in the main alphabet becomes the focal point for this information.

The structured volumes (e.g., String Music) are arranged by an imposed framework: instrumentation, time period, type of work or other categorization. Within each section, entries are alphabetized by composer name or, in the absence of a composer, by title. Entries will be repeated in all appropriate sections. A structured volume also contains a Composer/Title Index and, in some cases, other specialized indexes. The Composer/Title Index is a single alphabetical list of composers' names, composition titles and cross references, with a reference to the section(s) of the volume in which complete edition information will be found. The running heads on each page of the catalog enable the user to quickly find the proper section.

## ENTRY TYPES

Two basic types of entries appear in the Music-In-Print series: normal and collection. A normal entry describes a single piece of music. A collection consists of any two or more associated pieces.

## NORMAL ENTRY CONTENT

In order to bring together all different editions of a composition under a uniform and/or structured title, many musical form titles are translated into English (so, Konzert becomes Concerto, Fantaisie becomes Fantasy, etc.).

For each title there are two types of information: a) generic information about the composition and b) specific information pertaining to the editions which are in print. Included in the generic information category are the uniform title of the composition, a structured title for the work (e.g., Concerto No. 2 In D Minor; Cantata No. 140), a thematic catalog number or opus and number designation, the larger source from which the work was taken, and remarks.

Following the generic information about the piece is the information about the individual editions. This information includes the arranger, the published title of the edition if different from the uniform title, the language of the text (for vocal works), instrumentation required for performance, the duration of the work in minutes (') and seconds ("), a difficulty rating assigned to the edition by the publisher or editor, the format of the publication, publisher, publisher's number, and price or rental information concerning the edition.

Following is an example of a typical entry under a composer:

MOZART, WOLFGANG AMADEUS (1756-1791)
  Nozze Di Figaro, Le: Overture
    [4']
    2.2.2.2. 2.2.0.0. timp,strings
    sc,parts RICORDI-IT rental    (M1)
  "Marriage of Figaro, The: Overture"
    sc,parts BREITKOPF-W f.s.    (M2)

In this entry under the composer, Wolfgang Amadeus Mozart, the title of an excerpt, "Overture", follows the original title of the complete work, "Nozze Di Figaro, Le". It is scored for 2 flutes, 2 oboes, 2 clarinets, 2 bassoons, 2 horns, 2 trumpets, timpani and strings. Duration is approximately 4 minutes. The code RICORDI-IT indicates the publisher of the first listed edition; score and parts are offered by this publisher on rental. The sequence number (M1) marks the end of the information on this edition. The English title "Marriage Of Figaro, The: Overture" is given for the next edition which is published by BREITKOPF-W; score and parts for this edition are for sale.

The full names and addresses of all publishers or U.S. agents are given in the publisher list which follows the list of editions at the end of the book.

Following is an example of an entry with a structured title:

MOZART, WOLFGANG AMADEUS (1756-1791)
  Symphony No. 25, [excerpt]
    (Gordon, Philip) 2.1.2.1.al-
    sax. ten-sax. 2.2.1.1.timp,perc,
    strings [3'] (Menuetto, [arr.])
    PRESSER sets $7.50, and up, sc
    $1.50    (M3)

Here a structured title "Symphony No. 25," requires a different form of listing. The excerpt, "Menuetto", has been arranged by Philip Gordon for 2 flutes, oboe, 2 clarinets, bassoon, alto saxophone, tenor saxophone, 2 horns, 2 trumpets, trombone, tuba, timpani, percussion and strings. Duration is three minutes. The publisher, PRESSER, offers sets of parts priced at $7.50 and up. A separate score is available for $1.50.

## INSTRUMENTATION

Instrumentation is given in the customary order. When a work is scored for full orchestra, the number of wind players required is indicated by two groups of numbers—four for woodwinds (flute, oboe, clarinet, bassoon) and four for brass (horn, trumpet, trombone, tuba). Other instruments are listed by name, or abbreviated name. A number placed before a named instrument indicates the number of players. A slash is used for alternate instrumentation.

The common auxiliary wind instruments are not mentioned by most publishers. For example, 2.2.3.3. for woodwinds indicates the work is scored for two flutes, but it *may* include a piccolo part which can be played by one of the flutists. Similarly, it is possible that parts for English horn, bass clarinet and contrabassoon are provided but no additional players will be required. If the publisher does specify the auxiliary instruments required, this information is given either in parentheses (the number of players is not affected) or after a plus sign (an additional player is needed).

*Example:*

  2(pic).2+opt ob.3(opt bass-clar).2+contrabsn.
  4.2.3.0+opt tuba.timp,2-3perc,harp,cel/pno,
  strings

This example is scored for 2 flutes and piccolo (played by one of the flutists), 2 oboes plus an optional third oboe, 3 clarinets (one may play the optional bass clarinet part), 2 bassoons plus contrabassoon (additional player required), 4 horns, 2 trumpets, 3 trombones, optional tuba, timpani, percussion (2 or 3 players), harp, celeste or piano, and strings.

The term "orch" may be substituted for a detailed listing if the publisher has not provided the instrumentation for orchestral works.

Solo instrumental parts are listed following the complete orchestration of a work.

Choral parts are given as a list of voices (e.g., SATB, TTBB, etc.). The term "cor" (and similar terms) may be substituted when the publisher has not listed the specific voices.

Solo vocal parts are given as a list of voices followed by the term "solo" or "soli." The term "solo voice(s)" is used when the publisher does not specify the voice(s). (No attempt has been made to give equivalents for scale ranges listed by publishers.)

## REMARKS

The remarks are a series of codes or abbreviations giving information on the seasonal or other usage of the piece, the type of music, and the national origin and century for folk or anonymous pieces. (These codes also make it possible to retrieve, from the data base developed for the Music-In-Print series, specialized listings of music for particular seasons, types, etc.) Following this Guide to Use will be found a complete List of Abbreviations.

## PRICES

Only U.S. dollar prices are given, and we can give no assurance of their accuracy. They are best used for making rough comparisons. The publishers should be consulted directly for current prices.

## SEQUENCE NUMBERS

An alphanumeric number, appearing on the right margin, has been assigned to each edition represented in this catalog. These are for the purpose of easing identification and location of specific entries.

## COLLECTION ENTRY CONTENT

An attempt has been made to provide the user with access to pieces contained within collections, while still keeping the work within reasonable bounds of time and space. Accordingly, the following practices have been adopted:

If the members of a collection are published separately, they are listed individually, regardless of the number of pieces involved. If the collection is only published as a whole, the members are listed only if they do not exceed six in number. For larger collections, a code is given indicating the number of pieces and whether or not the contents are listed in the publisher's catalog. For example,

CC18L indicates a collection of 18 pieces which are *listed* in the publisher's catalog
CC101U indicates a collection of 101 pieces which are *unlisted* in the publisher's catalog
CCU indicates a collection of an unknown number of pieces

Whenever the members are listed, they are also cross-referenced to the collection. For example, consider the following entry:

FIVE VOLUNTARIES, [ARR.]
 (Davies, Peter Maxwell) 3.3.2.1, 3.3.0.0.
  timp,perc,strings,cont sc,parts
  SCHOTT 10994 f.s.
  contains: Attaignant, Pierre,
   Magnificat; Clarke, Jeremiah,
   King William's March; Clarke,
   Jeremiah, Serenade; Couperin,
   Louis, Sarabande; Croft, William,
   March Tune            (F1)

Published by Schott, edition number 10994, this collection edited by Peter Maxwell Davies contains five members, which are not published separately. Under each of the members there is a cross reference saying 'see FIVE VOLUNTARIES, [ARR.]'.

Collection entries also contain many of the elements of information found in normal entries. For example, the entry shown above contains arranger, instrumentation, format of publication, publisher and publisher number.

Collections of several pieces published as a whole, but having no overall title, create another problem. In this case the complete publication information is given under the composer or title of the first piece listed, together with the comment 'contains also,' followed by titles of the other collection members.

## CROSS REFERENCES

In order to provide the user with as many points of access as possible, the Music-In-Print series has been heavily cross referenced. In the unified volumes, the cross references are interfiled with the composers' names and the titles. In the structured volumes, cross references only appear in the Composer/Title Index.

Works may be located by title, with or without knowing the name of the composer. Using the first example by Mozart above, this composition may be located under either its Italian or English title in the main alphabet, as well as under the composer.

To make this possible the following cross references would exist in the main alphabet:

NOZZE DI FIGARO, LE: OVERTURE
 see Mozart, Wolfgang Amadeus

and

MARRIAGE OF FIGARO, THE: OVERTURE see
 Mozart, Wolfgang Amadeus, Nozze Di
 Figaro, Le: Overture

and in addition, the following cross reference would be found under the composer's name:

Marriage of Figaro, The: Overture
 *see Nozze Di Figaro, Le: Overture

Cross references are employed also to assist in the search for works frequently identified by popular names or subtitles, such as the "Surprise" Symphony of Haydn and the "Jupiter" Symphony of Mozart.

Numerous cross references have been made from unused and variant forms of composer names to assist the user in finding the form of name chosen for the series.

## COLLECTION CROSS REFERENCES

Whenever the members of a collection are listed, they are cross referenced to the collection. In unified volumes, these are interfiled with composers' names and titles. In structured volumes, these cross references only occur in the Composer/Title Index.

Using the above example, FIVE VOLUNTARIES, [ARR.], there is a cross reference under each of the composers saying 'see FIVE VOLUNTARIES, [Arr.]'. (If a collection member lacks a composer, the cross reference will occur at the title.)

When collections are also published separately, the cross references in both directions read 'see also'. If the members are only published separately (i.e., the collection were not published as a whole) then the cross reference under the collection would read 'see' and under the members, 'see from'. Thus, 'see' and 'see also' direct the user to information concerning publication, while 'see from' provides access to the collection of which a given publication is a part.

With untitled collections, which are listed under the first composer and/or title, the cross reference 'see' under each of the other collection members directs the user to the full entry under the first member, at which point complete edition information will be found.

## COMPOSER/TITLE INDEX

The Composer/Title Index is a single alphabetical listing of composer names, composition titles and cross references. This index is used to identify the location of a specific entry in a structured volume.

The actual reference is usually under the composer name, and only under a title when a work is not attributable to a person. The reference is to the chapter and/or section of the volume which contains the entry for the music sought.

For example, in String Music, IV.1 refers the user to Chapter IV, Section 1: String Quartets. Similarly, VIII refers to Chapter VIII: Music for Eight Instruments. Reference to the table of contents and the head of each page of the volume will assist the user in finding the appropriate section containing the information sought.

## ARRANGER INDEX

The Arranger Index lists in alphabetical order all arrangers and editors cited in a specific volume. The arranger's or editor's name is listed in all capital letters. In the case of multiple arrangers, the arranger names appear together, separated by semi-colons. The listing under each arranger name gives the composer and title of each arranged (edited) work, in alphabetical order. If a work has no composer, it is listed by title. In the case of uniform and translated titles, the uniform titles are the ones appearing in the index.

This arrangement allows the user to look up any desired arranger or editor and then scan for the composers and titles of desired works. Once the composer and title have been determined, the work may then be looked up in the catalog itself to obtain complete bibliographic and ordering information.

## MASTER INDEX

The Music-In-Print Master Index provides a single place to look in order to locate any composer or title listed in the Music-In-Print series. The Master Index eliminates all problems of knowing whether a specific piece of music is listed in a base volume, supplementary volumes, or not at all.

The Master Composer Index lists all composers found within the Music-In-Print series. Under each composer's name is a complete alphabetical listing of the titles of works by that composer to be found in the series. Next to each title is a number or series of numbers referring the user to the volume or volumes containing the specific piece. A key explaining these numbers and the volumes to which they correspond is to be found on the reverse side of the title page. Once the user has located the correct volume, it is easy to find the specific piece in the volume's alphabetical sequence. In the case of structured volumes, reference should be made to the Composer/Title Index in each volume.

The Master Title Index lists in a single alphabetical listing all titles of works within the Music-In-Print series. Each title is followed by a reference number or series of numbers, directing the user to the volume or volumes containing the specific title as explained above.

Additionally, as more supplementary volumes are added to the Music-In-Print series, certain volumes may update the Master Index in a specific area from time to time, through the publication of a specialized Master Index. In this way, the user can easily locate a piece of music within the volumes dealing with a specific area.

# List of Abbreviations

The following is a general list of abbreviations developed for the Music-In-Print series. Therefore, all of the abbreviations do not necessarily occur in the present volume. Also, it should be noted that terms spelled out in full in the catalog, e.g. woodwinds, tuba, Easter, Passover, folk, Swiss, do not appear in this list.

| | | | | | |
|---|---|---|---|---|---|
| A | alto | C&W | Country & Western | Dounias | thematic catalog of the violin concertos of Giuseppe Tartini by Minous Dounias |
| acap | a cappella | C.Landon | numbering of the keyboard sonatas of Joseph Haydn by Christa Landon | | |
| accomp | accompaniment | | | | |
| acord | accordion | | | Doxol | Doxology |
| Adv | Advent | camb | cambiata | | |
| Afr | African | Can | Canadian | | |
| Agnus | Agnus Dei | cant | cantata | | |
| al-clar | alto clarinet | Carib | Caribbean | | |
| al-fl | alto flute | CC | collection | ea. | each |
| al-sax | alto saxophone | CCU | collection, unlisted | ECY | End of Church Year |
| Allelu | Alleluia | CCUL | collection, partially listed | ed | edition |
| AmInd | American Indian | cel | celesta | educ | educational material |
| ampl | amplified | Cen Am | Central American | elec | electric |
| Anh. | Anhang (supplement) | cent | century | Ember | Ember Days |
| anti | antiphonal | cf. | compare | Eng | English |
| app | appendix, appendices | Chin | Chinese | enl | enlarged |
| arr. | arranged | chord | chord organ | Epiph | Epiphany |
| Asc | Ascension | Circum | Circumcision | eq voices | equal voices |
| ASD | All Saints' Day | clar | clarinet | Eur | European |
| aud | audience | cloth | clothbound | evang | evangelistic |
| Austral | Australian | cmplt ed | complete edition | Eve | Evening |
| | | Cnfrm | Confirmation | | |
| | | Commun | Communion | | |
| B | bass | cong | congregation | F. | thematic catalog of the instrumental works of Antonio Vivaldi by Antonio Fanna |
| Bald | Baldwin organ | Conn | Conn organ | | |
| Bar | baritone | cont | continuo | | |
| bar horn | baritone horn | contrabsn | contrabassoon | | |
| bar-sax | baritone saxophone | copy | ed produced to order by a copy process | f(f) | following |
| bass-clar | bass clarinet | | | f.s. | for sale |
| bass-fl | bass flute | cor | chorus | fac ed | facsimile edition |
| bass-sax | bass saxophone | cor pts | choral parts | facsim | facsimile(s) |
| bass-trom | bass trombone | cor-resp | choral response | Fest | festivals |
| bass-trp | bass trumpet | Corpus | Corpus Christi | film | music from film score |
| bds | boards | cradle | cradle song | Finn | Finnish |
| Belg | Belgian | cym | cymbals | fl | flute |
| Benton | thematic catalog of the works of Ignace Pleyel by Rita Benton | | | Fr | French |
| Bibl | Biblical | | | | |
| bk | book | | | | |
| Boh | Bohemian | | | Gd.Fri. | Good Friday |
| boy cor | boys' chorus | | | Ge. | thematic catalog of the works of Luigi Boccherini by Yves Gerard |
| Braz | Brazilian | | | | |
| Bryan | thematic catalog of the symphonies of Johann Wanhal by Paul Bryan | D. | thematic catalog of the works of Franz Schubert by Otto Erich Deutsch | | |
| | | | | Gen | general |
| | | | | Ger | German |
| | | Dan | Danish | Giegling | thematic catalog of the works of Giuseppe Torelli by Franz Giegling |
| bsn | bassoon | db | double bass | | |
| BVM | Blessed Virgin Mary | db-tuba | double-bass tuba | | |
| BWV | Bach-Werke-Verzeichnis; thematic catalog of the works of J.S. Bach by Wolfgang Schmieder | dbl cor | double chorus | | |
| | | Ded | Dedication | girl cor | girls' chorus |
| | | degr. | degree, 1-9 (difficulty), assigned by editor | glock | glockenspiel |
| | | | | gr. I-V | grades I-V, assigned by publisher |
| BuxWV | Buxtehude-Werke-Verzeichnis; thematic catalog of the works of Dietrich Buxtehude by G. Kärstadt (Wiesbaden, 1974) | desc | descant | | |
| | | diag | diagram(s) | Greg | Gregorian chant |
| | | diff | difficult | gtr | guitar |
| | | | | Gulbransen | Gulbransen organ |

| | | | | | |
|---|---|---|---|---|---|
| Hamm | Hammond organ | L | listed | Paymer | thematic catalog of the works of G.B. Pergolesi by Marvin Paymer |
| Harv | Harvest | Landon | numbering of the keyboard trios of Joseph Haydn by H.C.R. Landon | | |
| Heb | Hebrew | | | pce, pcs | piece, pieces |
| Helm | thematic catalog of the works of C.P.E. Bach by Eugene Helm | Lat | Latin | Pent | Pentecost |
| | | liturg | liturgical | perc | percussion |
| Hill | thematic catalog of the works of F.L. Gassmann by George Hill | Longo | thematic catalog of the sonatas of Domenico Scarlatti by Alessandro Longo | perf mat | performance material |
| | | | | perf sc | performance score |
| | | | | Perger | thematic catalog of the instrumental works of Michael Haydn by Lothar Perger |
| Hob. | thematic catalog of the works of Joseph Haydn by Anthony van Hoboken | Lowery | Lowery organ | | |
| Holywk | Holy Week | | | pic | piccolo |
| horn | French horn | Magnif | Magnificat | pic-trp | piccolo trumpet |
| hpsd | harpsichord | maj | major | pipe | pipe organ |
| Hung | Hungarian | man | manualiter; on the manuals alone | pno | piano |
| HWC | Healey Willan Catalogue | | | pno-cond sc | piano-conducting score |
| | | mand | mandolin | pno red | piano reduction |
| | | manuscript | manuscript (handwritten) | Pol | Polish |
| | | med | medium | Polynes | Polynesian |
| ill | illustrated, illustrations | mel | melody | pop | popular |
| Ind | Indian | men cor | mens' chorus | Port | Portuguese |
| inst | instruments | Mex | Mexican | pos | position |
| intro | introduction | Mez | mezzo-soprano | PreClass | Pre-Classical |
| ipa | instrumental parts available | MIN | Musicdata Identification Number | pref | preface |
| ipr | instrumental parts for rent | | | Proces | processional |
| Ir | Irish | min | minor | Psntd | Passiontide |
| Isr | Israeli | min sc | miniature score | pt, pts | part, parts |
| It | Italian | mix cor | mixed chorus | | |
| | | Morav | Moravian | | |
| | | Morn | Morning | | |
| | | mot | motet | | |
| | | | | quar | quartet |
| J-C | thematic catalog of the works of G.B. Sammartini by Newell Jenkins and Bathia Churgin | Neth | Netherlands | quin | quintet |
| | | NJ | Name of Jesus | Quinqua | Quinquagesima |
| | | No. | number | | |
| | | Nor Am | North American | | |
| Jap | Japanese | Norw | Norwegian | rec | recorder |
| Jew | Jewish | Nos. | numbers | Reces | recessional |
| jr cor | junior chorus | Nunc | Nunc Dimittis | Refm | Reformation |
| Jubil | Jubilate Deo | | | rent | for rent |
| | | | | repr | reprint |
| | | ob | oboe | Req | Requiem |
| | | oct | octavo | rev | revised, revision |
| K. | thematic catalog of the works of W.A. Mozart by Ludwig, Ritter von Köchel; thematic catalog of the works of J.J. Fux by the same author | offer | offertory | Royal | royal occasion |
| | | Op. | Opus | Rum | Rumanian |
| | | Op. Posth. | Opus Posthumous | Russ | Russian |
| | | opt | optional, ad lib | RV | Ryom-Verzeichnis; thematic catalog of the works of Antonio Vivaldi by Peter Ryom |
| | | ora | oratorio | | |
| Kaul | thematic catalog of the instrumental works of F.A. Rosetti by Oskar Kaul | orch | orchestra | | |
| | | org | organ | | |
| | | org man | organ, manuals only | | |
| kbd | keyboard | orig | original | | |
| Kirkpatrick | thematic catalog of the sonatas of Domenico Scarlatti by Ralph Kirkpatrick | | | S | soprano |
| | | P., P.S. | thematic catalogs of the orchestral works of Antonio Vivaldi by Marc Pincherle | s.p. | separately published |
| | | | | Sab | Sabbath |
| Kor | Korean | | | sac | sacred |
| Krebs | thematic catalog of the works of Karl Ditters von Dittersdorf by Karl Krebs | p(p) | page(s) | sax | saxophone |
| | | Palm | Palm Sunday | sc | score |
| | | pap | paperbound | Scot | Scottish |
| | | | | sec | secular |

# LIST OF ABBREVIATIONS

| | | | | | |
|---|---|---|---|---|---|
| Septua | Septuagesima | trom | trombone | Wolf | thematic catalog of the symphonies of Johann Stamitz by Eugene Wolf |
| Sexa | Sexagesima | trp | trumpet | | |
| show | music from musical show score | TV | music from television score | | |
| | | TWV | Telemann-Werke-Verzeichnis; thematic catalog of the works of G.P. Telemann by Mencke and Ruhncke | wom cor | womens' chorus |
| So Am | South American | | | WoO. | work without opus number; used in thematic catalogs of the works of Beethoven by Kinsky and Halm and of the works of J.N. Hummel by Dieter Zimmerscheid |
| sop-clar | soprano clarinet | | | | |
| sop-sax | soprano saxophone | | | | |
| Span | Spanish | | | | |
| speak cor | speaking chorus | | | | |
| spir | spiritual | U | unlisted | | |
| sr cor | senior chorus | UL | partially listed | Wq. | thematic catalog of the works of C.P.E. Bach by Alfred Wotquenne |
| study sc | study score | unis | unison | | |
| suppl | supplement | US | United States | | |
| Swed | Swedish | | | Wurlitzer | Wurlitzer organ |
| SWV | Schütz-Werke-Verzeichnis; thematic catalog of the works of Heinrich Schütz by W. Bittinger (Kassel, 1960) | | | WV | Wagenseil-Verzeichnis; thematic catalog of the works of G.C. Wagenseil by Helga Scholz-Michelitsch |
| | | vcl | violoncello | | |
| | | vibra | vibraphone | | |
| | | vla | viola | | |
| | | vln | violin | | |
| T | tenor | voc pt | vocal part | | |
| tamb | tambourine | voc sc | vocal score | | |
| temp blks | temple blocks | VOCG | Robert de Visée, Oeuvres Completes pour Guitare edited by Robert Strizich | | |
| ten-sax | tenor saxophone | | | Xmas | Christmas |
| Thanks | Thanksgiving | | | xylo | xylophone |
| Thomas | Thomas organ | vol(s) | volume(s) | | |
| TI | Tárrega Index; thematic catalog of the Preludes, Studies, and Exercises of Francisco Tárrega by Mijndert Jape | | | | |
| | | Whitsun | Whitsuntide | | |
| | | WO | without opus number; used in thematic catalog of the works of Muzio Clementi by Alan Tyson | Z. | thematic catalog of the works of Henry Purcell by Franklin Zimmerman |
| timp | timpani | | | | |
| transl | translation | | | | |
| treb | treble | | | | |
| Trin | Trinity | | | | |

# SECULAR CHORAL MUSIC

## A

A BLÜAH ÜBARN HIMML *CC43U,Austrian
(Mittergradnegger, Günther) mix cor
HEYN ISBN 3 85366 426 1 f.s.   (A1)

A CACHE-CACHE see Segard

A CAPPELLA *CC111U
mix cor HUG 7370 f.s.   (A2)

A CAPPELLA see Bainbridge, Simon

A CHANTER, RIRE ET BOIRE... see Philidor

A CHÂTILLENS, AU POINT DU JOUR see Mermoud, Robert

A DAKAR, AU SÉNÉGAL see Mermoud, Robert

A DOS D'OISEAU see Tremblot de la Croix, Francine

À GU 'DAGEN DU INGA MI see Fem Folkeviser Fra Gausdal

A LA CLAIRE FONTAINE see Boller, Carlo see Broughton see Petti see Petti, Anthony see Suter, L.M.

A LA CLAVELINA see Rodrigo, Joaquín

A LA FONTAINE see Broughton, Marilyn

A LA FONTAINE BELLERIE see Martin

A LA FONTAINE DU PRES see Willaert, Adrian

A LA FORÊT see Mendelssohn-Bartholdy, Felix

A LA MUSIQUE see Lefevre, Jacques see Liszt, Franz

A LA NATURE see De Senger,H.

A LA RENCONTRE see Henchoz, Emile

A LA SANTÉ DE NOÉ see Aubanel, Georges see Doret, Gustave

A LA SURFACE DES EAUX see Vuataz, Roger

A L'ABSENTE see Schubert, Franz (Peter)

A L'ÉMIGRANT see Zbinden, Julien-François

A LIADLE MACHT DAS HERZLE WEIT *CCU
(Streiner, Hans) HEYN f.s. mix cor
ISBN 3 85366 762 7; men cor
ISBN 3 85366 763 5   (A3)

A L'OMBRE D'UN ORMEAU see Canteloube, Joseph

A MA FAUX see Boller, Carlo

A MOLÉSON see Boller, Carlo

A MON PAYS see Lang, H.

A NOUS LE BEL ÂGE see Pillon

À PROPOS DE SAINT-DENIS GAMEAU see Dion, Denis

A QUEST'OLMO see Monteverdi, Claudio

A QUI CONTER SA PEINE? see Schubert, Franz (Peter), Wohin Soll Ich Mich Wenden?

A QUI DONNER LA ROSE? see Doret, Gustave

A TA QUENOUILLE see Bovet, J.

A TOI MON COEUR see Praetorius, Michael

A TRAVERS BOIS see Jaques-Dalcroze, Émile

A WINDSCHIEFES KEUSCHLE *CCU
(Streiner, Hans) HEYN f.s. mix cor
ISBN 3 85366 360 5; men cor
ISBN 3 85366 356 7   (A4)

ABBA FÖR DAMKÖR
(Idar, Ingegerd) SSAA SVERIG SK 778 f.s.   (A5)

ABE, RYOTARO (1962-   )
Hikari No Tamago O Migomoru-Tame Ni
mix cor,pno JAPAN   (A6)

Kiri Ni Nai Futatsu No Senritsu
mix cor,pno JAPAN   (A7)

ABEILLES, LES see Delibes, Léo

ABEND BEI PAUL LINCKE,EIN see Lincke, Paul

ABEND BEI PAUL LINCKE,EIN see Lincke, Paul

ABEND IM TAL see Bella, Rudolf

ABEND IM TESSIN see Kreis, Otto

ABEND IN SILS-MARIA see Märki, Ernst

ABENDGESANG IM LENZ see Reger, Max

ABENDLIED see Adam, Karl, Friedrich see Neuhaus, Gérard see Rusch, Peter see Schubert, Franz (Peter) see Stocker, Karl see Vollenweider, Hans

ABENDLIED (LUEGED, VO BÄRGE UND TAL) see Huber, Walter Simon

ABENDSEGEN see Studer, Hans

ÅBER DIANDLE IM TÅL *CCU,folk song, Austrian
(Drewes, Helmut) men cor HEYN
ISBN 3 85366 228 5 f.s.   (A8)

ABI GEZINT see Ellstein, Abe

ABIKO, YOSHIRO (1951-   )
Aoba-Ku Ga Suki
mix cor,pno,elec org JAPAN   (A9)

Atarashii Machi
wom cor,pno&elec org JAPAN   (A10)

Bokura No Furusato
jr cor,pno&elec org JAPAN   (A11)

Sugita Hibi Ni Yosete
mix cor,pno&elec org JAPAN   (A12)

Tooi Kagami
wom cor,woodwinds JAPAN   (A13)

Yume Three Sho
wom cor,pno&elec org JAPAN   (A14)

ABOULKER
Quatre Contes Musicaux
4pt jr cor,pno BILLAUDOT   (A15)

Vente Sur Demande
4pt jr cor BILLAUDOT   (A16)

ABOUT BEAUTY see Suzuki, Yukikazu, Utsukushii Mono Ni Tsuite

ABOUT LOVE see Kirk

ABSCHIED UND HERZELEID see Jugend Singt II

ABSCHIED VON DER HARFE see Aeschbacher, C.

ABSCHIEDSLIED see Boller, Carlo see Schmid, Walter

ABSCHIEDSLIED (HEINRICH ISSAK UM 1490) see Kratochwil, Heinz

ABSCHIEDSLIED UND LIEBESLIED see Möckl, Franz

ABSENTE, L' see Doret, Gustave

ABSTIMMUNGS-SUNNTIG see Ruprecht, Ernst

ABT, FRANZ (1819-1885)
Wanderlied
(Krenger) wom cor,acap MULLES   (A17)

ACCORDÉON see Miche, Paul

ACCUEILLEZ-MOI, FORÊTS TRANQUILLES see Haydn, [Johann] Michael, An Den Wald

ACH GOTT, WIE WEH TUT SCHEIDEN see Silcher, Friedrich

ACH SCHATZ, ICH MUSS MICH SCHEIDEN see Jeep, Johann

ACH SCHÄTZLEIN, ZART SCHÖNS JUNGFRAULEIN see Jeep, Johann

ACH, WIE IST'S MÖGLICH DANN see Silcher, Friedrich

ACHTUNG SPITFEUER see Lindroth, Peter

ACKERSONNTAG see Kaufmann, Fred

ACRE OF LAND, AN see Vaughan Williams, Ralph

ACROSS THE GREAT DIVIDE see Manners, Richard

AD VADI LIGGUR LEIDIN see Sigurbjornsson, Hrodmar Ingi

ADACHI, HIROMI (1935-   )
Hakuryu Lake, The
mix cor,orch JAPAN   (A18)

Lion In Hittite, The
jr cor,pno JAPAN   (A19)

Ten Pictures
jr cor,pno JAPAN   (A20)

Turkish Dance
jr cor,pno JAPAN   (A21)

ADAGIO see Corelli, Arcangelo

ADAM, J.
Belle, Belle Rose
men cor HUG 8491   (A22)

ADAM, KARL, FRIEDRICH
Abendlied
mix cor BUTZ 858   (A23)

ADAM DE LA HALE (ca. 1237-ca. 1287)
Minnelied
wom cor BOHM   (A24)

ADAMS, BRYAN
All For Love (composed with Lange, Robert; Kamen, Michael)
SATB WARNER 9020AC1X   (A25)
SAB WARNER 9020AC3X   (A26)
TBB WARNER 9020AC4X   (A27)

ADAMS, BYRON
Irish Airman, An
TTBB EARTHSNG EM-11   (A28)

Passerby,A
TTBB,pno EARTHSNG EM-20   (A29)

ADAMS, JONATHAN
Red, Red Rose, A
SATB,pno HERITAGE 15-1171H   (A30)

ADÉ DONZALLET see Farewell, Lad

ADIEU see Delmas, Marc-Jean-Baptiste see Tichy, O.A.

ADIEU, L' see Isaac, Heinrich

ADIEU, CHER CAMARADE see Dutilleux, Henri

ADIEU! MY NATIVE SHORE (from Insbruch, Ich Muss Dich Lassen)
(Robert Lucas De Pearsall) 4pt mix cor,acap ALLAIR   (A31)

ADIEU, PETITE ROSE see Jaques-Dalcroze, Émile

ADIEU, SYLVIE see Bovet, J.

ADIJO KERIDA
SATB,pno,opt gtr (med easy, text in Ladino) HAZÁ HZ-027   (A32)

ADIOSES see Barnes, Milton

ADLER, SAMUEL HANS (1928-   )
Farmer's Curst Wife, The
SATB,pno LAWSON 52529   (A33)

Prophecy Of Peace, A
SATB,acap LAWSON 52655   (A34)

ADORATION see Spohr, Ludwig (Louis)

ADRIFT! A LITTLE BOAT ADRIFT! see Grier, Gene

ADYU MON BI PAYI see Kaelin, Pierre

AE FOND KISS see Mayer, William Robert

AESCHBACHER, C.
Abschied Von Der Harfe
wom cor,acap MULLES   (A35)

Aroleid
men cor,acap MULLES   (A36)

D'zyt Isch Cho
2pt wom cor MULLES   (A37)

Frühling, Du Bist Da
2pt wom cor MULLES   (A38)

O Du Wunderliche Welt
men cor,acap MULLES   (A39)

Sie Kommen
2pt wom cor MULLES   (A40)

Wär Glöggelet
2pt wom cor MULLES   (A41)

AESCHBACHER, WALTHER (1901-1969)
  Grünes Blatt
    men cor,acap MULLES (A42)

  Il Est Une Maison
    men cor HUG 8235 (A43)

  Nachtreise
    men cor,acap MULLES (A44)

AESOP'S FABLES NO. 1: INTRODUCTION see
  Smith, Gregg

AFANASIEFF, WALTER
  Hero (composed with Carey, Mariah)
    (Strommen, Carl) SATB WARNER
      WBCH93178 (A45)
    (Strommen, Carl) SAB WARNER
      WBCH93179 (A46)
    (Strommen, Carl) 2pt cor WARNER
      WBCH93180 (A47)

AFANGAR see Ragnarsson, Hjalmar H.

AFRICA see Kelly, Bryan

AFRICAN CELEBRATION see Hatfield, S.

AFRICAN JIGSAW
  sc WEINBERGER 12236 (A48)

AFTERNOON ON A HILL see Bray, Julie
  Gardner see Kreutz

AFTON WATER see Fleming

AFTONTANKAR VID FRIDAS RUTA see
  Sjöberg, Birger

AGAPE SACRA, L' see Wagner, Richard

AGELESS ADMONITIONS
  (Rice, Martin) SATB,kbd MUSIC SEV.
    689 f.s.
    contains: Anonymous, Tobacco's But
      An Evil Weed; Belcher, Supply,
      Set Down That Glass (A49)

AGINCOURT SONG,THE see Henry VIII, King
  of England

AGNES see Märki, Ernst

AGUA Y VIENTO, CANCION see Sanchez,
  Damian

AH, BEHOLD-THE DARK OF NIGHT see
  Taneyev

AH! DIS-MOI DONC BERGÈRE see Lesur,
  Daniel

AH! MAUDIT SOIT L'AMOUR! see
  Canteloube, Joseph

AH! OUI QUE JE SUIS À MON AISE see
  Boller, Carlo

AH! QUE LE VIN EST BON! see Martin

AH, ROBIN, GENTLE ROBIN see Cornyshe,
  William (Cornish)

AH! SI J'ÉTAIS UN OISEAU see Arrieu,
  Claude

AH! SI MON MOINE VOULAIT DANSER see
  Patriquin, Donald

AHLIN, SVEN (1951- )
  Räkneexemplet Livet
    mix cor,acap STIM (A50)

AHROLD, FRANK A. (1931- )
  Little Boy Blue
    SATB,pno LAWSON 52512 (A51)

AI NO GRAMMATOLOGY see Fukushi, Norio

AI NO TOKI-HAKUCHO  *CCU
  ONGAKU f.s. (A52)

AICHELE, KARL
  Kleine Chorschule  *educ
    mix cor SCHUL CLS 179 (A53)

AIGUILLEUR, L' see Mermoud, Robert

AIMER LA TERRE see Kaelin, Pierre

AIMEZ-MOI BIEN, M'AMIE see Marenzio,
  Luca

AIR see Handel, George Frideric

AIR D'ARMIDE see Gluck, Christoph
  Willibald, Ritter von

AIR ON THE G STRING see Bach, Johann
  Sebastian, Aria

AIRBORNE, THE see Moses, Leonard

AIRMAILS TOWARD A HOPE, THE see Ikebe,
  Shin-Ichiro

AKI NO MICHI see Kunieda, Harue

AKIGAWA NO UTA see Suzuki, Teruaki

AL DIE WILLEN TE KAP'REN VAREN see
  Kolyada

AL LA SUISSE see Bovet, J.

ALADDIN SONG KIT #31 see Klevberg

ALBÉNIZ, ISAAC (1860-1909)
  Grana (from "Suite Espagnole")
    (Swingle, Ward) SSAATTBB,db,drums
      (gr. II) voc pt,pts UNC JP SOS-5X
      (A54)

  Sevilla
    (Swingle, Ward) SSAATTBB,db,drums
      (gr. IV) voc pt,pts UNC JP SOS-6X
      (A55)

  Tango In D Major
    (Swingle, Ward) SSAATTBB,db,drums
      (gr. II) voc pt,pts UNC JP SOS-4X
      (A56)

  Zortzico
    (Swingle, Ward) SATB,db,drums (gr.
      II) voc pt,pts UNC JP GR-6X (A57)

ALBERO see Malmlöf-Forssling, Carin

ALBERT, HEINRICH (1604-1651)
  Lob Der Freundschaft
    men cor,acap MULLES (A58)

ALBRECHT, SALLY K.
  Celebrate The Feast Of Lights
    (composed with Brownsey)
    3pt cor ALFRED 11624 (A59)
    2pt cor ALFRED 5829 (A60)

  Christmas Rush, The
    2pt cor ALFRED 11622 (A61)

  Come Let Us Sing
    2pt cor ALFRED 11647 (A62)

  Dealing With The Reindeer
    2pt cor ALFRED 5820 (A63)

  Gettin' Ready For Christmas (composed
    with Althouse, Jay)
    3pt cor ALFRED 5801 (A64)
    2pt cor ALFRED 5802 (A65)

  Jingle All The Way
    2pt cor ALFRED 11648 (A66)

  Joyeux Noel, Feliz Navidad
    3pt cor ALFRED 11620 (A67)
    2pt cor ALFRED 11621 (A68)

  Rockin' Down The Chimney Tonight!
    3pt cor ALFRED 11594 (A69)
    SSA ALFRED 11595 (A70)

  Rockin' The Baby
    2pt cor ALFRED 5814 (A71)
    3pt cor ALFRED 5813 (A72)

  Santa Wants A Brand New Bag
    2pt cor ALFRED 11396 (A73)

  Turn The Lights On
    2pt cor ALFRED 11385 (A74)
    3pt cor ALFRED 11384 (A75)

ALBUM DE FAMILLE, L' see Bron, Patrick

ALCHEMIST:, THE see Larson, Martin

ALCIVAR, BOB
  Come Rain, Come Shine
    SATBB,perc (gr. IV) UNC JP (A76)

  Tenderly
    SATBB,perc (gr. III) UNC JP (A77)

ALDERIGHI, DANTE (1898-1968)
  Filastroche
    mix cor BILLAUDOT (A78)

ALE see Schudel, Thomas

ALEGORIA BUFFA see Prado, José-Antonio
  (Almeida)

ALEM, OSCAR
  Pampa Verde, La  *CC10L
    (Olaso, Luis Maria De) mix cor
      LAGOS f.s. (A79)

ALEXANDER, JOSEF (1907- )
  Jazz Fantasia
    SATB,acap LAWSON 52490 (A80)

ALEXANDER'S RAGTIME BAND see Berlin see
  Berlin, Irving

ALEXANDROV, ALEXANDER VASILIEVICH
  (1883-1946)
  Qu'on Me Rende À Cette Terre
    mix cor HUG 8534 (A81)
    men cor HUG 8533 (A82)

ALEXANDROV, ALEXANDER VASILIEVICH
  (cont'd.)

  Vrai Marin, Le
    mix cor HUG 8534 (A83)
    men cor HUG 8533 (A84)

ALICE BRAND see Parker, Horatio William

ALIPRANDI, PAUL (1925- )
  Harmonie Du Soir
    (Bonneau) mix cor,gtr BILLAUDOT
      (A85)

  Saint Raphaël
    (Bonneau) mix cor,gtr BILLAUDOT
      (A86)

ALKAN, CHARLES-HENRI VALENTIN
  (1813-1888)
  Marche Funèbre Sur La Mort D'un
    Papagallo
    SSTB,3ob,bsn,org BILLAUDOT (A87)

ALL ABOARD!
  (Funk) 2pt cor SATB (medley
    containing People Get Ready, Love
    Train & Chattanooga Choo Choo)
    WARNER CM9511 CM9509 ipa (A88)
  (Funk) 2pt cor SAB (medley containing
    People Get Ready, Love Train &
    Chattanooga Choo Choo) WARNER
    CM9511 CM9510 ipa (A89)
  (Funk, Jeff) SATB (medley containing
    People Get Ready, Love Train &
    Chattanooga Choo Choo) WARNER
    CM9509 ipa (A90)
  (Funk, Jeff) SAB (medley containing
    People Get Ready, Love Train &
    Chattanooga Choo Choo) WARNER
    CM9510 ipa (A91)

ALL ABOUT CHRISTMAS CAROLS see
  Schwartz, Dan

ALL ALONE AT CHRISTMAS
  (Althouse) SATB (medley containing
    All Alone On Christmas, Silver
    Bells, A Holly Jolly Christmas &
    Sleigh Ride) WARNER C0310C1X
      (A92)
  (Althouse) SAB (medley containing All
    Alone On Christmas, Silver Bells, A
    Holly Jolly Christmas & Sleigh
    Ride) WARNER C0310C3X ipa (A93)

ALL ALONE BENEATH THE MISTLETOE see
  Althouse, Jay

ALL AMOUNG THE BARLEY see Stirling,
  Elizabeth

ALL AND SOME see Spedding, Alan

ALL AROUND THE WORLD TONIGHT see Estes,
  Jerry

ALL FOR LOVE see Adams, Bryan

ALL GLORY see Denbow, Stefania Björnson

ALL I ASK OF YOU see Lloyd Webber,
  Andrew

ALL I WANT FOR CHRISTMAS (IS YOU) see
  Minikel

ALL I WANT TO DO IS DANCE see Schwartz,
  Dan

ALL IN A GARDEN FAIR  *folk song,Eng
  (Francis, G.T.) SATB BANKS 878 (A94)

ALL MY TRIALS
  (Snyder) SATB WARNER SV9525 (A95)
  (Snyder) SATB WARNER SV9525 (A96)

ALL NIGHT, ALL DAY see Simms, Patsy
  Ford

ALL PEOPLE ARE CREATED EQUAL see
  McPheeters

ALL PRAISE TO THOSE WHO MAKE MUSIC see
  Marshall, Jane M. (Mrs. Elbert H.)

ALL THAT GLITTERS IS NOT GOLD see
  Strohbach, Siegfried

ALL THAT I AM see Himes, William

ALL THE LOVELY WAY HOME see Beattie,
  Donald

ALL THE THINGS YOU ARE see Kern see
  Kern, Jerome

ALL THE WORLD'S A STAGE see Maderna,
  Bruno

ALL THINGS ARE CONNECTED see Julseth-
  Heinrich, Jeanne

ALL THROUGH THE DAY see Harris, Jerry
  Weseley

ALL THROUGH THE NIGHT
  (Schram) SSA ALFRED 11302 (A97)
  (Schram) 2pt cor ALFRED 11303 (A98)

ALL YE WHO MUSIC LOVE see Donato

ALLA MATTINA see Anonymous

ALLAIN, E.J.
  Minuit Sonne Allègrement
    mix cor HUG 8205 (A99)

ALLAWAY, BEN
  Bandari
    SATB,perc SANTA SBMP 66 (A100)

  Freedom Come *Afr
    SATB, opt conga drums SANTA SBMP 67 (A101)
    TTBB,acap SANTA SBMP 68 (A102)

ALLDAHL, PER-GUNNAR (1943- )
  Gamle Man
    3pt men cor,acap/opt 4trom STIM (A103)

ALLE FRONDE DEI SALICI see Lombardi, Luca

ALLÉE, L' see Breard

ALLEGRETTO see Mozart, Wolfgang Amadeus

ALLEGRO see Beethoven, Ludwig van see Handel, George Frideric

ALLEGRO see Mozart, Wolfgang Amadeus

ALLEGRO see Mozart, Wolfgang Amadeus

ALLEGRO see Mozart, Wolfgang Amadeus

ALLELUIA see Kaelin, Pierre

ALLER AUGEN WARTEN AUF DICH see Rauch, Andreas

ALLES HAT SEIN ZEIT see Haydn, [Franz] Joseph see Haydn, [Franz] Joseph, Everyone Has His Day

ALLES ØYNE see Volle, Bjarne

ALLEZ ZU JARDIN see Doret, Gustave

ALLOBROGES, LES see Aubanel, Georges see Saint-Kopp

ALLON GAY BERGERES see Costeley, Guillaume

ALLONS AU BOIS see Martin

ALLONS, BERGERS see Bovet, J.

ALLONS DANSER LA SAINT-JEAN see Rochat, Jean

ALLONS DANSER SOUS LES ORMEAUX see Boller, Carlo

ALLONS EN VENDANGES see Boller, Carlo

ALLONS, MES COMPAGNONS! see Henchoz, Emile

ALLONS PÊCHER LE POISSON see Piaget, Ada May

ALLOUETTE
  (Bertalot) SATBB,acap PRESSER 312-41658 (A104)

ALMA LLANERA see Gutiérrez, Pedro

ALMOST LIKE BEING IN LOVE see Lerner

ALONE IN WOODS see Itoh, Mikio

ALONG THE MILKY WAY see Shibata, Minao

ALONG THE SHORE
  (Wetherell,E.) SATB BANKS ECS0203 (A105)

ALOUETTE see Mermoud, Robert

ALOUETTE, L' see Haenni, G. see Jaques-Dalcroze, Émile see Sala, Andre

ALPAGE, L' see Boller, Carlo

ALPÉE, L' see Bovet, J.

ALPEN see Schmid, Walter

ALPENGLÜHEN see Märki, Ernst

ALPENLÄNDISCHE JODLER UND VOLKSLIEDER *CCU
  (Mittergradnegger, Günther) mix cor HEYN NR. 137 f.s. (A106)

ALPENLÄNDISCHE JODLER UND VOLKSLIEDER *CCU
  (Mittergradnegger, Günther) mix cor HEYN NR. 131 f.s. (A107)

ALPENLÄNDISCHE VOLKSLIEDER *CCU,folk song
  (Mittergradnegger, Günther) mix cor HEYN NR. 138 f.s. (A108)

ALPHABET, THE see Mozart, Wolfgang Amadeus

ALPSEGEN see Krenger, R.

ALPUFZUG see Hofer-Schneeberger, Emma

ALS GHY VAN DE DOODT SULT ZIJN VERBETEN, OP. 38 see Kerstens, Huub

ALSINA, CARLOS ROQUÉ (1941- )
  Recit Oubile,D' Un
    cor,3perc ZERBONI 10379 (A109)

ÄLSKA MEJ see Andersson, Benny

ÄLT, ÅBER GUAT *CCU,folk song,Austrian
  (Wulz, Helmut) mix cor&eq voices HEYN ISBN 3 85366 687 6 f.s. (A110)

ALTE GUGGISBERGER LIED,DAS see Burkard, Willi

ALTE HERZ,DAS see Schmid, A.

ALTE HÜTLEIN, DAS see Bovet, J., Vieux Chalet, Le

ALTE KÄRNTNERLIEDER *CCU
  (Anderluh, Anton) mix cor HEYN NR. 122 f.s. (A111)

ALTE LIEBI SUNNE,DIE see Juker, A.

ALTE LIED, 'S see Märki, Ernst

ALTE LINDE,DIE see Märki, Ernst

ALTE SCHWYZER,DIE see Vollenweider, Hans

ALTE TISCH,DER see Märki, Ernst

ALTES STÄDTCHEN see Schmid, Walter

ALTHOUSE, JAY
  All Alone Beneath The Mistletoe
    SATB ALFRED 11570 (A112)
    SAB ALFRED 11571 (A113)
    SSA ALFRED 11572 (A114)

  Can Santa Make It Through Tonight?
    SATB ALFRED 1352 (A115)
    3pt cor ALFRED 11353 (A116)
    2pt cor ALFRED 11354 (A117)

  Have You Heard? (A Christmas Spiritual)
    SATB ALFRED 11336 (A118)
    3pt cor ALFRED 11337 (A119)

  Holiday Wish, A
    SATB ALFRED 11312 (A120)
    SAB ALFRED 11313 (A121)
    2pt cor ALFRED 11314 (A122)

  Let Freedom Ring
    SATB ALFRED 11625 (A123)
    3pt cor ALFRED 11626 (A124)
    2pt cor ALFRED 11627 (A125)

  Listen To The Music
    SATB ALFRED 5815 (A126)
    3pt cor ALFRED 5816 (A127)
    2pt cor ALFRED 5817 (A128)

  May Our Paths Meet Again (composed with Albrecht, Sally K.)
    SATB ALFRED 11397 (A129)
    3pt mix cor ALFRED 11398 (A130)

  May Sunshine Light Your Way
    SATB ALFRED 11641 (A131)
    3pt cor ALFRED 11642 (A132)
    2pt cor ALFRED 11643 (A133)

  One Candle Lights The Way (composed with Albrecht, Sally K.)
    SATB ALFRED 11632 (A134)
    3pt cor ALFRED 11633 (A135)
    2pt cor ALFRED 1634 (A136)

  Slow Dancing In The Snow
    3pt cor ALFRED 5799 (A137)
    SSA ALFRED 5800 (A138)
    SATB ALFRED 5798 (A139)

  Song Of Joy
    2pt cor ALFRED 5797 (A140)

  Together As One (composed with Albrecht, Sally K.)
    SATB ALFRED 5824 (A141)
    3pt cor ALFRED 5825 (A142)
    2pt cor ALFRED 5826 (A143)

ALWAYS IT'S SPRING see Pearce, Malcolm

AM BRÜNNELEIN see Bungart, Heinrich

AM BRUNNEN VOR DEM TORE see Silcher, Friedrich

AM HÖHENFEUER see Schmid, Walter

AM MÜHLBACH see Hofer-Schneeberger, Emma

AM VOLKSTAGE see Munzinger, Carl

AM WELLENSPIEL DER AARE see Koch

AM ZIRBITZEN DROBEN (HEFT 1) (from Song Book By Grani Höfler) CCU
  (Cacak-Leipert) men cor HEYN NR. 48 f.s. (A144)

AMÅL I, AMÅL DU see Mittergradnegger, Günter

AMANT DISCRET, L' see Buisson

AMARILIS see Orrego-Salas, Juan A.

AMARILLAS, LAS see Hatfield, S.

ÂME DU VIN, L' see Broquet, Louis

AME NO OTO see Kawasaki, Etsuo

AMERICA see Bloch

AMERICA, OF THEE I SING! see Strid, George L.O.

AMERICA, THE BEAUTIFUL see Bates

AMERICAN DREAM, THE see Schonberg, Claude-Michel

AMERICAN FOLK RHAPSODY see Spevacek, Linda

AMERICANS WEST see Johnson, Neil

AMES, MORGAN
  I Don't Know Why I Love You Like I Do
    SSAB,acap (gr. I) UNC JP (A145)

  I'll Never Smile Again
    SSAB,acap (gr. II) UNC JP (A146)

AMIS, C'EST MA TOURNÉE! see Bron, Patrick

AMMAN, ULRICH
  Bärgblüemli
    men cor,acap MULLES (A147)

  Es Häägli
    men cor,acap MULLES (A148)

  Lied Der Heimat
    men cor,acap MULLES (A149)

  Mähderlied
    men cor,acap MULLES (A150)

AMMANN, BENNO (1904- )
  Chanson De La Bergère, La
    men cor HUG 8315 (A151)

  Lied Vom Hirtenmädchen, Das
    [Ger] men cor HUG 8316 (A152)

  Unser Leben Gleicht Der Reise (Bersinalied)
    men cor,acap MULLES (A153)

AMOUR DE MOI,L' see Anonymous see Canteloube, Joseph see Esvan

AMOUR EST UN ENFANT MOQUEUR, L' see Mendelssohn-Bartholdy, Felix

AMOUR ET LA MORT,L' see Theodorakis, Mikis

AMOUR PASSAGER, L' see Gastoldi, Giovanni Giacomo

AMOUR TRAHI see Miche, Paul

AMOURS PERDIT LES TRAICT QU'IL ME TIRA see Maillard, René

AN DAS HERZ see Märki, Ernst

AN DEN FRÜHLING see Schubert, Franz (Peter)

AN DEN WALD see Haydn, [Johann] Michael

AN DIE FREUDE see Beethoven, Ludwig van

AN DIE HEIMAT see Schmid, Walter

AN DIE HERRSCHER DER WELT see Cerha, Friedrich

AN DIE MUSIK see Schubert, Franz (Peter)

AN DIE TULPE see Märki, Ernst

AN MEIN VATERLAND see Baumgartner, Walter

ANCIDETEMI PUR see Arcadelt, Jacob

ANCORA DELL'INFERNO see Pierucci, Armando

AND IT WAS NIGHT see Martin

AND WE SHALL SING MY SONGS OF PRAISE see Galinne, Rachel

AND WITH, AND TO see Applebaum, Edward

AND YOU KNOW THAT see Crenshaw, Randy

ANDALUZA see Granados, Enrique

ANDANTE see Mendelssohn-Bartholdy, Felix see Mozart, Wolfgang Amadeus

ANDERLUH, ANTON
  Auf, Zum Fröhlichen Jagen (Heft 1) *CCU
    men cor HEYN NR. 21 f.s. (A154)

  Auf, Zum Fröhlichen Jagen (Heft 2) *CCU
    eq voices HEYN NR. 23 f.s. hunting songs (A155)

  Es Ist Wohl A Scheane Zeit
    men cor HEYN NR. 53 (A156)

  Fröhlich Lied Zur Rechten Zeit, Ein (Heft 2)
    men cor HEYN NR. 24 (A157)

  Fünf Kärtner Volks Lieder *CC5U, folk song, Austrian
    men cor HEYN NR.56 f.s. (A158)

  Glück Auf (Heft 1) *CCU
    men cor HEYN NR. 22 f.s. mountain dweller's songs (A159)

  Hochzeitslieder *CCU
    men cor HEYN NR. 25 f.s. (A160)

  I Hàb Di Treu G'liabt
    mix cor HEYN NR. 117 (A161)

  Liebe Alte Lieder *CCU
    men cor HEYN NR. 55 f.s. (A162)

  Schön Ist Die Jugend
    men cor HEYN NR. 54 (A163)

ANDERLUH MÄNNERCHORBUCH, DAS *CC110U, folk song, Austrian
  (Anderluh, Anton-Wulz, Helmut) men cor HEYN ISBN 3 85366 505 5 f.s. (A164)

ANDERLUH VOLKSLIEDERBUCH, DAS *CC200U, folk song, Austrian
  (Wulz, Helmut) mix cor/eq voices HEYN ISBN 3 85366 381 8 (A165)

ANDERSON
  Hey Girl!, Hey Girl!
    SSA WARCH 35229 (A166)

  Lullaby Of The Little Angels
    SSA WARCH 34405 (A167)

ANDERSON, LEROY (1908-1975)
  Sleigh Ride
    SSA WARCH 34694 (A168)
    SAB WARCH 34695 (A169)
    SATB WARCH 34696 (A170)

  Small Child
    SATB WARCH 35672 (A171)

  Syncopated Clock, The
    (Ginsburg, Ned) SATB WARNER 8010SC1X (A172)
    (Ginsburg, Ned) SAB WARNER 8010SC3X (A173)
    (Ginsburg, Ned) 2pt cor WARNER 8010SC5 (A174)

ANDERSON, TOM
  Caravan
    SSATB, perc (gr. IV) UNC JP (A175)

  Cute
    SATB, perc (gr. II) UNC JP (A176)

ANDERSON, WILLIAM H.
  Lullaby Of The Little Angels
    SSA THOMP.G VEI10033 (A177)

  Piper And The Chiming Peas
    unis cor THOMP.G VG146 (A178)

ANDERSSON
  I Know Him So Well (from Chess) (composed with Rice; Ulvaeus)
    SATB NOVELLO 090430 (A179)

ANDERSSON, BENNY (1946- )
  Älska Mej
    (Ljung, Nils) mix cor, acap SVERIG SK 773 (A180)

ANDREAE, VOLKMAR (1879-1962)
  Handwerksburschen Abschied
    men cor, acap MULLES (A181)

ANDRIESSEN, JURRIAAN (1925- )
  Madonna Laura (from F. Petrarca)
    4pt mix cor, 3.2.2.2. 4.3.3.1. timp, perc, strings sc DONEMUS (A182)

ANEMOS B see Guerrero, Francisco

ANGELO DEL POVERO, L' see Gentilucci, Armando

ANGELS AMONG US
  (Schmutte, Pete) SATB (by Alabama) WARNER CH9552 (A183)
  (Schmutte, Pete) SAB (by Alabama) WARNER CH9553 (A184)

ÄNGELU see Björklund, Staffan

ANGÉLUS, L' see Bovet, J.

ANGÉLUS DU SOIR, L' see Boller, Carlo

ANGES DANS NOS CAMPAGNES, LES see Boller, Carlo

ANGES DU PRINTEMPS, LES see Bordese, L.

ANIMAL CRACKER ANIMALS see Graham

ANMUTIGER VORTAG
  3pt wom cor MULLES M&S 1199 (A185)

ANN HINI GOZ see Lesur, Daniel

ANNA FRANCK see Gamberini, Leopoldo

ÄNNCHEN VON THARAU see Silcher, Friedrich

ANNE OF GREEN GABLES see Cable, Howard

ANNIE LAURIE *Scot
  (Guibat) mix cor HUG 7671 (A186)
  see Bray see Martin, Gilbert M. see Scott, [Lady] John (Alicia Ann)

ANNIE MEDLEY
  SSA WARCH 30023 (A187)

ANNIE MEDLEY NO. 2
  SSA WARCH 30024 (A188)
  SATB WARCH 30025 (A189)

ANNIVERSAIRE DE GRAND-PAPA, L' see Bron, Patrick

ANONYMOUS
  Alla Mattina
    men cor HUG 8861 (A190)

  Amour De Moi, L'
    (Swingle, Ward) SSAATTBB, acap (gr. II) voc pt, pts UNC JP SF-1 (A191)

  Audete, Gaudete *Xmas
    (Swingle, Ward) SSAATTBB, acap (gr. III) voc pt, pts UNC JP SBS-12X (A192)

  Cantar Friulano *CC8U
    (Dipiazza, O.) eq voices&mix cor, acap ZERBONI 9639 f.s. (A193)

  Cantar Veneto *CC8U
    (Zotto, G.) eq voices&mix cor, acap ZERBONI 9331 f.s. (A194)

  Cargado De Tantos Males
    (Swingle, Ward) TTBB (gr. II) voc pt, pts UNC JP SM-12X (A195)

  Country Dances
    (Swingle, Ward) SSAATTBB, acap (gr. V) voc pt, pts UNC JP SF-2 (A196)

  De Punta Y Taco *folk song, So Am
    (Swingle, Ward) SSAATTBB, acap (gr. III) voc pt, pts UNC JP SF-8X (A197)

  Dodici Canti Popolari Friulani *CC12U
    (Dipiazza, O.) treb cor, acap ZERBONI 9206 f.s. (A198)

  È L'üselin Del Bosch..; Andremo A Strapà I Selari, L'
    (Zecca) mix cor BÈRBEN BERBEN 1686 (A199)

  El Paisanito
    (Swingle, Ward) SSAATTBB, AA soli, acap (gr. III) voc pt, pts UNC JP SF-3 (A200)
    (Swingle, Ward) TTTBB, solo voice, acap (gr. III) voc pt, pts UNC JP SF-10X (A201)

ANONYMOUS (cont'd.)
  Europa Unita Canta, L' *CCU
    (Crestani, M.) men cor, acap ZERBONI 8509 f.s. (A202)

  Five Portuguese Villancicos
    (Brito, Manuel Carlos De) 3pt cor ANTICO AE20 f.s. (A203)

  Hirondelle Messagere Des Amours, L'
    SATB WARCH 34494 (A204)

  International Folk *CC11L
    (Casagrande) mix cor BERBEN BERBEN 1825 (A205)

  Ma Belle Si Tu Voulais
    cor, solo voice, harp BILLAUDOT (A206)

  Music History 101
    (Swingle, Ward) SSAATTBB, acap (gr. V) voc pt, pts UNC JP SF-7 (A207)
    (Swingle, Ward) TTTTBBBB, acap (gr. V) voc pt, pts UNC JP SF-9X (A208)

  Nobody Knows The Trouble I've Seen
    SATB WARCH 34476 (A209)

  Pavane
    mix cor HUG 6038 (A210)

  Quattordici Canti Popolari Friulani *CC14U
    (Dipiazza, O.) wom cor, acap ZERBONI 9428 f.s. (A211)

  Quattro Elaborazioni Corali *CC4U
    (Perosa, A. - Dipiazza, O. - Russolo, G. - Nesbeda, F.) mix cor/treb cor, acap ZERBONI 8749 f.s. (A212)

  Roi Boit, Le
    see Suite Québecoise

  Romanza Espanola
    (Swingle, Ward) SSAATTBB, S&T soli, db, drums (gr. II) voc pt, pts UNC JP SOS-7X (A213)

  Rossignoletsauvage
    see Suite Québecoise

  Saints Fugue
    (Swingle, Ward) SSAATTBB, acap (gr. IV) voc pt, pts UNC JP SJ-2 (A214)

  Seven Courtly Love Songs (from Cancionero Musical De Segovia (15th Cent.))
    (Lee, Carolyn) 3pt cor ANTICO AE19 f.s. (A215)

  Suite Québecoise
    (Swingle, Ward) SSAATTBB, acap (gr. II) voc pt, pts UNC JP f.s. contains: Roi Boit, Le; Rossignoletsauvage; Tout Garcon Qui Sert (A216)

  Tes Yeux
    men cor HUG 3644 (A217)

  Tout Garcon Qui Sert
    see Suite Québecoise

  Undici Canti Poplari Friulani *CC11U
    (Liani, D.) mix cor, acap ZERBONI 8371 f.s. (A218)

  Violette, La
    mix cor HUG 7915 (A219)

ANOTHER LOVE POEM see Schudel, Thomas

ANSINK, CAROLINE (1959- )
  To A Thousand Murdered Girls (from Boumi-Pappas)
    4pt mix cor, ob, English horn, clar, bsn, perc, 2vln, vla, vcl DONEMUS sc f.s., pts f.s. (A220)

ANTHOLOGIA GRAECA see Suzuki, Teruaki

ANTHOLOGIE DE LA CHANSON PARISIENNE AU XVIE SIECLE *CC48U
  (Lesure) OISEAU OL 186 f.s. (A221)

ANTOLOGIA DI CANTI POPOLARI *CCU
  (Dipiazza, Orlando) cor, acap ZERBONI 10074 f.s. (A222)

ANTOLOGIA DI CANTI POPOLARI NATALIZI *CCU
  (Filippi, S.) mix cor/wom cor ZERBONI 10839 f.s. by various composers (A223)

ANTONIOU, THEODORE (1935- )
  Eros I (1990)
    SATB, pno, chamber orch MARGUN MP1098 (A224)

  Prometheus (1983)
    SATB, narrator, pno/org, 3.3.3.3. 4.3.3.1. 4perc, harp, strings [27'] MARGUN MP1078 SC (A225)

ANVIL CHORUS FROM "IL TROVATORE" see Verdi, Giuseppe

ANY DREAM WILL DO see Lloyd Webber, Andrew

ANYTHING GOES!
  (Schmutte, Pete) SATB (medley containing Anything Goes, Ain't She Sweet & Ma (He's Making Eyes At Me)) WARNER CM9595 ipa (A226)
  (Schmutte, Pete) SAB (medley containing Anything Goes, Ain't She Sweet & Ma (He's Making Eyes At Me)) WARNER CM9596 ipa (A227)

ANYTIME YOU NEED A FRIEND
  (Schmutte, Pete) SATB WARNER WBCH9430 (A228)
  (Schmutte, Pete) SAB WARNER WBCH 9431 (A229)
  (Schmutte, Pete) SSA WARNER WBCH 9432 (A230)

AOBA-KU GA SUKI see Abiko, Yoshiro

APOCALYPSE, OP. 40 see Kerstens, Huub

APOTHELOZ, JEAN (1900-1965)
  Chanson D'hiver
    eq voices HUG 8274 (A231)

  Chasse, La
    men cor HUG 8166 (A232)

  Fontaine Solaire
    mix cor HUG 8033 (A233)

  Grand-Guillaume
    men cor HUG 8211 (A234)

  Guerre Des Baleiniers, La
    men cor HUG 8099 (A235)

  Jabouli Boulette
    mix cor HUG 8190 (A236)

  Lune Jaune, La
    men cor HUG 6852 (A237)

  Me Plaît La Grâce
    men cor HUG 8268 (A238)

  Micromégas
    men cor HUG 8212 (A239)

  Noce, La
    mix cor HUG 6741 (A240)

  Poète, Le
    men cor HUG 8267 (A241)

  Porteur D'eau, Le
    eq voices HUG 8273 (A242)

  Ronde Sur La Falaise, La
    mix cor HUG 6741 (A243)

  Vieille Chanson
    mix cor HUG 8189 (A244)

APPEL see Boller, Carlo see Bron, Patrick

APPEL, L' see Tichy, O.A.

APPLE TREE CAROL see Lovelace, Austin Cole

APPLE-TREE WASSAIL see Hatfield, S.

APPLEBAUM
  Carols Of French Canada
    SSA WARCH 35250 (A245)

  Cherry Tree Carol
    SATB WARCH 35664 (A246)

APPLEBAUM, EDWARD (1937- )
  And With, And To
    10pt men cor sc MMB X099001 (A247)

APPRENTI FORGERON, L' see Zbinden, Julien-François

APRIKOSENTAL, DAS see Haenni, Ch. see Haenni, G.

APRIL see Ford

APRIL RAIN SONG see Bray, Julie Gardner

APRILSE GRIL see Swerts, Piet

AQUA INVOCATION see Nishimura, Akira

AQUÈLOS MOUNTAGNOS see Kaelin, Pierre

ÄRA see Björklund, Staffan

ARACIL, ALFREDO (1954- )
  Paradiso
    cor,acap ZERBONI 10391 (A248)

ARASHINO, HIDEO (1935- )
  Ten-Nyo Ga Tonda
    jr cor,pno JAPAN (A249)

ARBRE BRUYANT COMME UNE VILLE see Hemmerling, Carlos

ARBRE COMME UN OISEAU see Mermoud, Robert

ARBRE IMMENSE see Hemmerling, Carlos

ARCADELT, JACOB (ca. 1505-1568)
  Ancidetemi Pur
    see Three Madrigals By Jacques Arcadelt

  Il Ciel Che Rado
    see Three Madrigals By Jacques Arcadelt

  Io Dico Che Fra Voi
    see Three Madrigals By Jacques Arcadelt

  Margot, Labourés Les Vignes
    mix cor HUG 7837 (A250)

  Sing Out With Joy
    (Liebergen, Patrick) SAB,acap WARNER SV9417 (A251)

  Three Madrigals By Jacques Arcadelt
    (Fenlon, Iain) 4pt cor ANTICO AE8 f.s.
    contains: Ancidetemi Pur; Il Ciel Che Rado; Io Dico Che Fra Voi (A252)

ARCANO see Hoch, Francesco

ARCHER
  Christmas
    SSA WARCH 35249 (A253)

ARCHER, VIOLET (1913- )
  Children Singing
    SA THOMP.G VG259 (A254)

  Eight Short Songs For Young Singers
    unis cor THOMP.G VG1007 (A255)

  Joyful Song
    SATB THOMP.G VG476 (A256)

ARE YOU AWARE OF MY LOVE? see Schwartz, Dan

ARE YOU GOING AWAY? see Ham, Tae Kyum, Kashiri

ARGERSINGER, CHARLES
  Guess Who I Saw Today
    SSAATB/SSAATTB,perc (gr. III) UNC JP (A257)

  More Love
    SSAATTBB,acap (gr. V) UNC JP (A258)

ARIA see Bach, Johann Sebastian

ARISE, ARISE *folk song,Eng
  (Bremer, Jetse) SATB,acap LAWSON 52697 (A259)

ARISE, SWEET LOVE see Leslie, Henry David

ARISE, YOUR LIGHT HAS COME see Grotenhuis, Dale

ARLEN, HAROLD (1905- )
  It's Only A Paper Moon
    (Strommen, Carl) SATB WARNER WBCH9326 (A260)
    (Strommen, Carl) SAB WARNER WBCH9327 (A261)

ARLEQUIN ET COLOMBINE
  3pt wom cor MULLES M&S 1238 (A262)

ARMAILLI DES ALPETTES, L' see Bovet, J.

ARMAILLI DES GRANDS MONTS, L' see Bovet, J.

ARMAILLIS, LES see Jaques-Dalcroze, Émile

ARMAILLIS DE GRANDVILLARD, LES see Boller, Carlo

ARMOR see Robert-Lalouet, M.

ARMSTRONG, MATTHEW
  If A Man Does Not Keep Pace
    TTBB,acap MUSIC SEV. 727 (A263)

ARMURIER, L' see Mermoud, Robert

ARNETH-KANTATE see Bruckner, Anton

ARNOUD, J.
  Hymne Au Soleil
    3 eq voices BILLAUDOT (A264)

AROLEID see Aeschbacher, C.

ARRIEU, CLAUDE (1903- )
  Ah! Si J'étais Un Oiseau
    3 eq voices BILLAUDOT (A265)

  Aux Damoyselles Paresseuses D'écrire À Leurs Amys
    3 eq voices BILLAUDOT (A266)

  De Trois Couleurs, Gris, Tanné Et Noir
    3 eq voices BILLAUDOT (A267)

  Recueil Des Trois Chansons *CC3U
    3 eq voices BILLAUDOT f.s. (A268)

  Rondeau Du Guay
    3 eq voices BILLAUDOT (A269)

  Rondeaux De Clément Marot
    3 eq voices BILLAUDOT (A270)

ARRIGO, GIROLAMO (1930- )
  Cantata Hurbinek, La
    SSMezTBarB, soprano clar in E flat, clar,bass clar,contrabass clar, 4trom,4db sc RICORDI-IT 131834 (A271)

  Organum Jeronimus
    SSMezTTTBarB,14inst sc RICORDI-IT 131917 (A272)

ARROW AND THE SONG, THE see Lightfoot, Mary Lynn

ARS ANTIQUA see Suzuki, Teruaki

ARTMAN, RUTH ELEANOR (1919- )
  Song Of The Littlest Angel
    SA WARNER SV7710 (A273)

AS I WALKED THROUGH THE MEADOWS *folk song,Eng
  (Bremer, Jetse) TTBB,acap LAWSON 52698 (A274)

AS IMPERCEPTIBLY AS GRIEF see Snyder, Timothy

AS LONG AS HE NEEDS ME see Bart

AS THE DEER see Nystrom, Hampus Huldt

AS THE MOON ROSE see Rippentrop, Denice

AS THE MOON'S SOFT SPLENDOUR see Staton, J.F.

AS THROUGH EARTH'S GARDEN ONCE I STRAYED see Suben, Joel Eric

AS TORRENTS IN SUMMER see Elgar, [Sir] Edward (William)

ASAKAWA, HARUO (1942- )
  Hato Yo
    "Oh, Dove!" mix cor,pno JAPAN (A275)

  Oh, Dove!
    see Hato Yo

ASANT, KATSUHIKO (1960- )
  Atarashiki Komichi Yori
    men cor JAPAN (A276)

ASAOKA, MAKIKO (1956- )
  Five Songs
    wom cor,pno JAPAN (A277)

ASGEIRSSON, JON (1928- )
  Haldid Til Hallarinnar
    mix cor,pno ICELAND 010-069 (A278)
    see Islenskir Songdansar

  I Gledinni
    mix cor,pno ICELAND 010-067, 010-068 (A279)
    see Islenskir Songdansar

  I Holl Godmundar
    mix cor,pno ICELAND 010-070 (A280)
    see Islenskir Songdansar

  I Verinu
    mix cor,pno ICELAND 010-066 (A281)
    see Islenskir Songdansar

  Islenskir Songdansar
    ICELAND f.s. mix cor,orch 010-905; mix cor,pno 010-906
    contains: Haldid Til Hallarinnar; I Gledinni; I Holl Godmundar; I Verinu (A282)

ASH GROVE, THE
  (Bradley Ellingboe) SATB,2clar FOSTER MF 3050 (A283)

ASPECTS OF LOVE see Lloyd Webber, Andrew

ASRIEL, ANDRÉ (1922- )
    Frosch und der Ochse, Der
        DEUTSCHER DV 7711            (A284)

    Fuchs und die Trauben, Der
        DEUTSCHER DV 7708            (A285)

    Schlange und der Krebs, Die
        DEUTSCHER DV 7712            (A286)

ASTON, PETER G. (1938- )
    Deck The Halls
        unis cor PAVAN PBR1065       (A287)

AT DAWN see Snyder, Audrey

AT THE FOOT OF YONDER MOUNTAIN
    (Rentz) 2pt cor WARNER OCT02598
                                     (A288)
    (Rentz) 2pt cor WARNER OCT02598
                                     (A289)

ATARASHII MACHI see Abiko, Yoshiro

ATARASHIKI KOMICHI YORI see Asant, Katsuhiko

ATELIER see Vercken, François

ATMENDE KLARSEIN, DAS see Nono, Luigi

ATTEBERRY, RON
    When Lilacs Bloom'd
        SSA,pno HERITAGE 15-1192H    (A290)

ATTENHOFER, KARL (1837-1914)
    Waldkönig
        men cor,acap MULLES          (A291)

ATTENTE see Martin

AU BOIS DE LA ROSIÈRE see Rochat, Jean

AU BORD DE LA RIVIÈRE see Lesur, Daniel

AU BORD DE L'EAU see Daetwyler, Jean

AU BORD DU LAC see Boller, Carlo

AU BORD D'UN GRAND VERGER see Othmayr, Kaspar

AU BOUT DU MONDE see Henchoz, Emile

AU CLAIR DE LA LUNE see Edwards, Geoffrey

AU CLAIR DE LA TERRE see Zbinden, Julien-François

AU DIAPASON *CC100U
    mix cor HUG 8150 f.s. sacred & secular    (A292)

AU DOUX PAYS see Boller, Carlo

AU DRAPEAU see Boller, Carlo

AU FIL DES CHANTS see Aubanel, Georges

AU FOND DES YEUX see Henchoz, Emile

AU GOULOT DE LA FONTAINE see Bovet, J.

AU JARDIN DE LA VIE see Miche, Paul

AU JARDIN DE MON PÈRE see Doret, Gustave

AU JARDIN DE MONS PÈRE see Bovet, J.

AU LÉMAN see Bovet, J. see Mendelssohn-Bartholdy, Felix

AU MILIEU DES PRÉS see Bovet, J.

AU MOIS DE MAI, LA FEUILLE EST NEUVE see Mermoud, Robert

AU PAYS see Binet, Jean

AU PAYS BASQUE see Fernand

AU PETIT JARDIN see Hemmerling, Carlos

AU PIED D'UN SAULE QUI PLEURE see Brahms, Johannes

AU PRINTEMPS see Delibes, Léo

AU SEIN DE MA DOULEUR see Bach, Johann Sebastian

AU SEUIL DE L'INFINI see Gaillard, Paul-Andre

AU SOLEIL DE L'AMITIÉ see Kaelin, Pierre

AU SON DU TAMBOURIN see Rameau, Jean-Philippe

AU TEMPS DE NEIGE see Kaelin, Pierre

AU TEMPS DES CERISETTES see Miche, Paul

AU VERT BOCAGE see Delor

AU VIEUX PAYS see Boller, Carlo

AU VIEUX TEMPS see Bovet, J.

AUBADE see Pileur, G. see Schubert, Franz (Peter)

AUBADE SUR LE FLEUVE see Praetorius, Michael

AUBANEL, GEORGES
    A La Santé De Noé
        mix cor HUG 8309             (A293)

    Allobroges, Les
        4pt mix cor BILLAUDOT        (A294)

    Au Fil Des Chants *CCU
        3-4pt men cor BILLAUDOT f.s. 3 vols.    (A295)

    Auprès De Ma Blonde
        4pt mix cor BILLAUDOT        (A296)

    Batelière, La
        mix cor,SBar soli HUG 8308   (A297)

    Chantons Noël Sur La Musette
        mix cor HUG 8137             (A298)

    "Danaé", La
        men cor HUG 8147             (A299)
        see Trois Chansons De Marins

    En Passant Par La Lorraine
        4pt mix cor BILLAUDOT        (A300)

    Jambe Me Fait Mal, La
        mix cor HUG 8136             (A301)

    Jardinière Du Roi, La
        mix cor HUG 8308             (A302)

    Pêcheurs De Groix, Les
        men cor HUG 8146             (A303)
        see Trois Chansons De Marins

    Sot Petit Jeune Homme
        mix cor HUG 8309             (A304)

    Trois Chansons De Marins
        mix cor HUG f.s.
            contains: "Danaé", La; Pêcheurs De Groix, Les; Valparaiso
                                     (A305)

    Valparaiso
        men cor HUG 8145             (A306)
        see Trois Chansons De Marins

    Vecy Le May
        mix cor HUG 8138             (A307)

AUBE see Solbiati, Alessandro

AUBE CLAIRE see Gesseney, L.

AUBERGE DE LA VIE, L' see Delmas, Marc-Jean-Baptiste

AUDETE, GAUDETE see Anonymous

AUF DIE HÖHEN see Krenger, R.

AUF, FREUNDE, SINGT DEM GOTT DER EHEN see Beethoven, Ludwig van

AUF, IHR BRÜDER, SEID BEREIT see Gunsenheimer, Gustav

AUF WIEDERSEH'N see Decker, Wilhelm

AUF, ZUM FRÖHLICHEN JAGEN (HEFT 1) see Anderluh, Anton

AUF, ZUM FRÖHLICHEN JAGEN (HEFT 2) see Anderluh, Anton

AUF, ZUM TANZ see Kupp, Albert

AUFBRUCH see Schmid, Walter see Schweizer, Alfred

AUFISTEIG'N - EINESCHAU'N *CCU
    (Mittergradnegger, Günther) men cor HEYN NR. 61 f.s.    (A308)

AUFSCHWUNG see Oetiker, August

AUFTAKTEULE, DIE see Keller, Wilhelm

AUGENBLICKE WERDEN STUNDEN see Huber, Walter Simon

AUGSBURGER TAFELCONFECT, DAS see Rathgeber, Valentin

AUGURIES OF INNOCENCE see Hagen, Daron

AUGUST see Zentner, Johannes

AUPRÈS DE MA BLONDE see Aubanel, Georges

AUPRÈS DE TOI see Bach, Johann Sebastian, Bist Du Bei Mir

AURA LEE see Martin, Gilbert M.

AURIC, GEORGES (1899-1983)
    Cinq Chansons Françaises
        mix cor,acap SALABERT EAS 19088    (A309)

AUS DEN SPRÜCHEN DAS LIEDER WEISHEIT see Gasser, Ulrich

AUS DER LIEDERMAPPE DES KÄRNTNER LEHRERQUINTETTS *CCU
    (Mulle, Justinus- Mittergradnegger, Günther) mix cor HEYN NR. 128 f.s.    (A310)

AUS DER LIEDERMAPPE DES KÄRNTNER LEHRERQUINTETTS *CCU
    (Mulle, Justinus-Mittergradnegger, Günther) mix cor HEYN NR. 139 f.s.    (A311)

AUS DER LIEDERMAPPE DES KÄRNTNER LEHRERQUINTETTS *CCU
    (Mulle, Justinus-Mittergradnegger, Günther) wom cor HEYN NR. 153 f.s.    (A312)

AUS DER LIEDERMAPPE DES KÄRNTNER LEHRERQUINTETTS *CCU,Austrian
    (Mulle, Justinus-Mittergradnegger, Günther) men cor HEYN NR. 59 f.s.    (A313)

AUS DER LIEDERMAPPE DES KÄRNTNER LEHRERQUINTETTS *CCU,Austrian
    (Mulle, Justinus-Mittergradnegger, Günther) mix cor HEYN NR. 116 f.s.    (A314)

AUS DER LIEDERMAPPE DES KÄRTNER LEHRERQUINTETTS *CCU
    (Mulle, Justinus -Mittergradnegger, Günther) men cor HEYN NR. 41 f.s.    (A315)

AUS ÖSTERREICHS BERGEN see Burkhart, F.

AUS ZEIT UND LEID, EIN RÜCKBLICK? see Schweizer, Alfred

AUSGANG see Zahler, J.R.

AUSGEWÄHLTE CHORWERKE see Weismann, Wilhelm

AUSLÄNDISCHE VOLKSLIEDER 1982 (from Kärntner Chorblätter) CCU
    (Mittergradnegger, Günther) mix cor HEYN f.s.    (A316)

ÄUSSERSTE, DAS see Helmschrott, Robert M.

AUSTRALIAN CHRISTMAS CAROL MEDLEY see James

AUTOMNE see Vuataz, Roger

AUTOMNE, L' see Doret, Gustave

AUTRE JOUR, L' see Lagger, Oscar

AUTRE JOUR EN VOULANT DANSER, L' see Lagger, Oscar

AUTUMN see Bhatia, Vanraj A., Sharad

AUTUMN NIGHT SONG see Baxter, Francis H.

AUTUMN SONG see Carl

AUTUMN TINTS see Gilbert

AUTUMN VESPER see Snyder, Audrey

AUTUMNS, OP. 22, THE see Heininen, Paavo

AUX DAMOYSELLES PARESSEUSES D'ÉCRIRE À LEURS AMYS see Arrieu, Claude

AVANT L'AURORE see Beaugrand

AVARE, L' see Gesseney, L.

AVEUGLE, L' see Mermoud, Robert

AVEUX, LES see Massias, Gerard

AVIDAMENTE ALLARGO LA MIA MANO see Schiavo, Gianpaolo

AVIRON, L' see Planel, Jean

AVNI, TZVI (1927- )
    Makhelora *CC3U
        3pt jr cor/SSA,acap ISR.MUS.INST. IMI 6958 f.s.    (A317)

AVRIL see Boller, Carlo see Canteloube, Joseph see Naudier see Reichel, Bernard

AWAKE! AWAKE! THE FLOW'RS UNFOLD see Leslie, Henry David

AWARE see Blumenfeld, Harold

AWAY FROM THE ROLL OF THE SEA see
　Curti, F. see MacGillivray,
　Allister

AYAME NO UTA see Yuyama, Akira

AYE SHE KAIMED HER YELLOW HAIR see
　Whittaker, William Gillies

AYER, PETE
　Deck The Halls
　　SATB HOPE K 316　　(A318)

# B

BABY WHAT YOU GOIN TO BE see Sleeth

BACCHANALE see Pantillon, François

BACCHANTES D'EURIPIDE, LES see Xenakis,
　Yannis (Iannis)

BACH, CARL PHILIPP EMANUEL (1714-1788)
　Solfeggietto
　　(Swingle, Ward) SATB,db,drums (gr.
　　V) UNC JP GB-10X　　(B1)

BACH, JOHANN SEBASTIAN (1685-1750)
　Air On The G String
　　see Aria

　Aria
　　(Swingle, Ward) "Air On The G
　　String" SATB,db,drums (gr. I) voc
　　pt,pts UNC JP BGH-1　　(B2)

　Au Sein De Ma Douleur
　　mix cor,pno/org/orch HUG 1901　(B3)

　Auprès De Toi
　　see Bist Du Bei Mir

　Badinerie (from Suite In B-Minor)
　　(Swingle, Ward) SSAATTBB,S solo,db,
　　drums (gr. III) UNC JP GB-2X　(B4)

　Bist Du Bei Mir
　　"Auprès De Toi" [Fr/Ger] mix cor
　　HUG 7074　　(B5)
　　"Auprès De Toi" [Fr/Ger] men cor
　　HUG 8133　　(B6)

　Bourree
　　(Swingle, Ward) SATB,acap (gr. I)
　　voc pt,pts UNC JP SB-2　　(B7)
　　(Ugland, Johan Varen) men cor,acap
　　NOTON N-9148　　(B8)

　Canon
　　(Swingle, Ward) SATB,db,drums (gr.
　　I) voc pt,pts UNC JP BGH-2　(B9)

　Chorale Prelude (from "Sleepers,
　　Awake" Cantata)
　　(Swingle, Ward) SATB,db,drums (gr.
　　II) voc pt,pts UNC JP BGH-5 (B10)

　Fugue In C Minor (from Well-Tempered
　　Clavichord I)
　　(Swingle, Ward) SATB,db,drums (gr.
　　III) voc pt,pts UNC JP BGH-3
　　　　(B11)

　Fugue In D Major (from Well-Tempered
　　Clavichord)
　　(Swingle, Ward) SATB,db,drums (gr.
　　III) voc pt,pts UNC JP BGH-7X
　　　　(B12)
　　(Swingle, Ward) SATB,db,drums (gr.
　　II) voc pt,pts UNC JP BGH-12X
　　　　(B13)

　Fugue In D Minor (from Art Of The
　　Fugue)
　　(Swingle, Ward) SATB,db,drums (gr.
　　IV) voc pt,pts UNC JP BGH-6X
　　　　(B14)

　Gigue
　　(Swingle, Ward) TB,db,drums (gr.
　　III) UNC JP GB-5X　　(B15)

　Invention In C Major
　　(Swingle, Ward) TB,db,drums UNC JP
　　BGH-11X　　(B16)
　　(Swingle, Ward) TB,db,drums (gr.
　　III) UNC JP BGH-11X　　(B17)

　Largo (from Concerto In F Minor For
　　Harpsichord And Strings)
　　(Swingle, Ward) SATB,S solo,db&
　　drums (gr. II) voc pt,pts UNC JP
　　GB-4　　(B18)

　Magnolia Petals
　　(Roff, J.) 2pt jr cor oct THOMAS
　　1C0109010　　(B19)

　Nun Ruhen Alle Wälder
　　eq voices HUG 7592　　(B20)

　Organ Fugue BWV 578
　　(Swingle, Ward) SSAATTBB,acap (gr.
　　I) voc pt,pts UNC JP SB-1　(B21)

　Preambule (from Harpsichord Partita
　　No. 5)
　　(Swingle, Ward) SATB,db,drums (gr.
　　IV) voc pt,pts UNC JP GB-7X (B22)

　Prelude In C Major (from Well-
　　Tempered Clavichord II)
　　(Swingle, Ward) SATB,db,drums (gr.
　　IV) voc pt,pts UNC JP BGH-10X
　　　　(B23)

BACH, JOHANN SEBASTIAN (cont'd.)

　Prelude In F Minor (from Well-
　　Tempered Clavichord II)
　　(Swingle, Ward) SATB,db,drums (gr.
　　III) voc pt,pts UNC JP BGH-4
　　　　(B24)

　Prelude No. 9 (from Well-Tempered
　　Clavichord II)
　　(Swingle, Ward) SATB,db,drums (gr.
　　III) voc pt,pts UNC JP BGH-8X
　　　　(B25)

　Prelude No. 19 (from Well-Tempered
　　Clavichord I)
　　(Swingle, Ward) SATB,db,drums (gr.
　　II) voc pt,pts UNC JP GB-6X (B26)

　Prelude No. 22 (from Well-Tempered
　　Clavichord II)
　　(Swingle, Ward) SATB,acap (gr. II)
　　voc pt,pts UNC JP SB-3X　　(B27)

　Prelude No. 24 (from Well-Tempered
　　Clavichord II)
　　(Swingle, Ward) SATB,db,drums (gr.
　　II) voc pt,pts UNC JP GB-11X
　　　　(B28)

　Quand Viendra L'heure De La Mort
　　mix cor,opt pno/org/orch HUG 1909
　　　　(B29)

　Sinfonia (from Partita In B-Flat
　　Major)
　　(Swingle, Ward) SATB,db,drums (gr.
　　IV) voc pt,pts UNC JP BGH-9X
　　　　(B30)

　Toccata And Fugue In D Minor
　　(Burke, Howard) SSATBB,acap (gr.
　　IV) UNC JP　　(B31)

　Viens, Mon Âme, Et Contemple
　　mix cor HUG 1856　　(B32)

　Voici Les Heures Brèves
　　eq voices HUG 7592　　(B33)

BACH, WILHELM FRIEDEMANN (1710-1784)
　Fruehling, Der
　　(Swingle, Ward) SATB,db,drums (gr.
　　II) UNC JP GB-3　　(B34)

BACHARACH, BURT F. (1928-　　)
　Raindrops Keep Fallin' On My Head
　　(Cederberg, Anna) SATB,acap SVERIG
　　SK 813　　(B35)

BACK BAY SHUFFLE see Shaw

BACON, BOYD
　Loving Father, A
　　SATB&opt unis cor,inst WARNER
　　BSC00231　　(B36)

BADINERIE see Bach, Johann Sebastian
　see Naudier

BADINGS, HENK (1907-1987)
　Trois Ballades *CC3U
　　3-4pt wom cor BILLAUDOT f.s. (B37)

BAGUEUR D'OISEAUX, LE see Mermoud,
　Robert

BAILIFF'S DAUGHTER see Halley

BAINBRIDGE, SIMON (1952-　　)
　A Cappella
　　6pt cor UNITED MUS　　(B38)
　Devil's Punchbowl, The
　　jr cor,1.1.1.1. 1.1.1.0. timp,
　　strings UNITED MUS　　(B39)

BAIRD, JOHN
　Sonnet
　　treb cor,harp/kbd CAMDEN CM016
　　　　(B40)

BAISER, LE see Haenni, G.

BAISER DE MA MÈRE, LE see Bovet, J.

BAJO LA LUNA GITANA see Terashima,
　Rikuya

BAL DES INSECTS, LE see Lang, H.

BALAS, ARPAD (1937-　　)
　Due Composizioni A Tre Parti *CC2U
　　3pt jr cor,acap ZERBONI 8816 f.s.
　　　　(B41)

BALAYEURS, LES see Boller, Carlo

BALD PRANGT, DEN MORGEN ZU VERKÜNDEN
　AUS "DIE ZAUBERFLÖTE" see Mozart,
　Wolfgang Amadeus

BÅLD SCHEINT A LIACHT VON DAR HEAH
　(from Chorblätter)
　　(Streiner, Hans) mix cor HEYN (B42)
　　(Streiner, Hans) men cor HEYN (B43)

BALDVINSSON, TRYGGVI (1965-　　)
　Thar Sem Hafjollin Heilog Risa
　　SATB ICELAND 063-020　　(B44)

BALFE, MICHAEL WILLIAM (1808-1870)
   Excelsior!
    (Dicks, E.A.) SATB BANKS 377 (B45)

   Kilarney
    (Campione, A.) SATB BANKS 59 (B46)

BALISSAT, J.
   Chanson De Nöel (from Fête Des
    Vignerons 1977, La)
    mix cor HUG 8630 (B47)

   Chanson Du Blé (from Fête Des
    Vignerons 1977, La)
    mix cor HUG 8631 (B48)
    men cor HUG 8636 (B49)

   Chanson Du Merle Et De La Vigne Qui
    Pleure (from Fête Des Vignerons
    1977, La)
    mix cor HUG 8632 (B50)

   O Moisson De Mon Enfance (from Fête
    Des Vignerons 1977, La)
    mix cor HUG 8631 (B51)
    men cor HUG 8636 (B52)

BALLABILE see Ponchielli, Amilcare

BALLAD OF A KNIGHT AND HIS DAUGHTER,THE
   see Parker, Horatio William

BALLAD TO SASKATCHEWAN see Raum,
   Elizabeth

BALLADE DU LAC see Daetwyler, Jean

BALLADES, LES see Machaut, Guillaume de

BALLET FANTASIE SUIKAZURA see Niikura,
   Ken

BALLIF, CLAUDE (1924- )
   Fragments D'une Ode À La Faim
    12pt mix cor TRANSAT. TRO01428 (B53)

BALLNACHT see Tamas, Janos

BALLOU LAMMY see International Carols,
   Set 1

BALMER, LUC (1898- )
   Fahnenflucht
    men cor,acap MULLES (B54)

   Güldene Schelle, Die
    wom cor&jr cor,child solo,orch
    MULLES pno red f.s., pts ipa (B55)

   Mädchenlied
    wom cor,acap MULLES (B56)

   Mys Bärn
    men cor,acap MULLES (B57)

BALZANELLI
   Con Alas En Los Ojos
    4pt mix cor LAGOS (B58)

   Cuando Nacen Los Vientos
    4pt mix cor LAGOS (B59)

   Hombre Que No Come Caramelos, Un
    4pt mix cor LAGOS (B60)

   Jugaba La Niña Aquella
    3pt mix cor LAGOS (B61)

BALZLI-CHLEEBLATT
   3pt wom cor MULLES (B62)

BANALE, LA see Zbinden, Julien-François

BANDARI see Allaway, Ben

BÄNDELTANZ,DER see Lampart, Reinhold

BANDICOOT, THE see Jennings, Carolyn

BANK, JACQUES (1943- )
   Episodes De La Vie D'un Artiste (H.
    Berlioz, H. Smithson, D.K.
    Holoman)
    4pt mix cor&jr cor,STBar soli,
    3.3.3.3. 4.3.3.1. timp,3perc,
    2harp,pno,2acord,strings [65'] sc
    DONEMUS (B63)

BÄNKLI, 'S see Herzog, Emil

BANKS OF LOCH ERIN see Six Canadian
   Folksongs

BANKS OF THE DON see Henderson, Ruth
   Watson

BANQUET DE SAINTE CCILE see Naudier

BAPPUKU-DON see Oyama, Junko

BAPTÊME, LE see Doret, Gustave

BARBER, SAMUEL (1910-1981)
   God's Grandeur
    SATB,opt acap SCHIRM.G 50482114 (B64)

BARBLAN, OTTO (1860-1943)
   Hymne À La Patrie
    "Vaterlandshymne" men cor HUG 5419 (B65)

   Vaterlandshymne
    see Hymne À La Patrie

BARCAROLLE see Bovet, J. see Brahms,
   Johannes

BARDOS, LAJOS (1899- )
   Erik A Som
    SATB,acap SANTA SBMP 47 (B66)

BÄRGBLÜEMLI see Amman, Ulrich

BARĪNIA see Mistress

BÄRN, DU EDLE SCHIZERSTÄRN see Burkard,
   Willi

BÄRN, DU EDLE SCHWIZERSTÄRN see Furer,
   Samuel

BARNBY, [SIR] JOSEPH (1838-1896)
   Good Night
    SATB BANKS 3 (B67)

   Luna
    SATB BANKS 271 (B68)

   Sweet And Low
    (Challinor, F.A.) 2pt cor BANKS 864 (B69)

   Wife's Song,A
    SATB BANKS 64 (B70)

BÄRNER BÄR,DER see Vollenweider, Hans

BÄRNER BUEBE see Keller, Hugo

BARNERIM see Møller, Svein

BARNES, EDWARD (1957- )
   Morning Trumpet, The
    SATB sc MMB X094002 (B71)

   Union (from Zion Songster)
    SATB sc MMB X094003 (B72)

BARNES, MILTON (1931- )
   Adioses (Cantata)
    [Span] wom cor,Mez solo,fl,vcl,pno,
    perc CAN.MUS.CENT. (B73)

   Cantata
    see Adioses

   Fantasy On Jewish Themes *Yiddish
    SATB,T solo,clar,trp,vln,db,pno,
    drums CAN.MUS.CENT. (B74)

BAROQUE SAMBA see Meader, Darmon

BARRABAS see Togni, Camillo

BARRETT
   Glorious Morning
    SATB SHAWNEE A-6901 ipa (B75)

BARRETT, RICHARD (1959- )
   Green Pastures (from The Tigers)
    SATB,2+pic.2+English horn.2+bass
    clar.2+contrabsn. 4.3.3.1. timp,
    perc,cel,xylo,harp,strings,opt
    bugle UNITED MUS perf mat rent (B76)

   Two Herrick Pieces *CC2U
    SA,3(pic).2+English horn.2+bass
    clar.3. 4.0.3.0. timp,3perc,harp,
    strings voc sc UNITED MUS f.s. (B77)

BARRON, JOHN
   Nobody Knows The Trouble I've Seen
    SATB THOMP.G VG5002 (B78)

BARRY, JEFF
   Do Wah Diddy Diddy (composed with
    Greenwich, Ellie)
    (Althouse, Jay) SATB WARNER
    WBCH9310 (B79)
    (Althouse, Jay) 3pt mix cor WARNER
    WBCH9311 (B80)
    (Althouse, Jay) TBB WARNER WBCH9312 (B81)

BART
   As Long As He Needs Me
    SSA WARCH 34812 (B82)
    SATB WARCH 34818 (B83)

   I'd Do Anything
    2pt boy cor/2pt girl cor WARCH
    34801 (B84)

   Oliver
    SSA WARCH 35362 (B85)

   Where Is Love
    SATB WARCH 34796 (B86)
    SSA WARCH 34797 (B87)

BARTER see Mechem, Kirke Lewis

BARTHELME, GEORG
   Man Nehme (composed with Keller,
    Wilhelm; Klein, Richard Rudolf;
    Kukuck, Felicitas; Poser, Hans;
    Weber, Horst) *CC14U
    3-4 eq voices FIDULA 6052 f.s. (B88)

BARUCHET, JOSEPH
   Complainte Picarde
    mix cor HUG 8287 (B89)

BASANT see Bhatia, Vanraj A.

BASEBALL see Broughton, Marilyn

BASIE, WILLIAM (COUNT) (1906-1984)
   One O'clock Jump
    (Anderson, Tom) SSATBB,perc (gr.
    III) UNC JP (B90)

BASIL THE CAT see Shields, Valerie

BATEAU, LE see Broquet, Louis

BATEAU DE YANGTSÉ, LE see Falquet, Rene

BATELIÈRE, LA see Aubanel, Georges

BATES
   America, The Beautiful (composed with
    Ward)
    SATB ALFRED 11369 (B91)
    men cor oct THOMAS 1C0668911 (B92)

BATTLE CRY OF FREEDOM, THE see Poné,
   Gundaris

BAUERNKANTATE see Schlerf, L.

BAUERNLIED see Bovet, J.

BAUERNREGEL see Brun, Fritz

BAUMGARTNER, WALTER
   An Mein Vaterland
    wom cor,acap MULLES (B93)

BÄUMLEIN STAND IM TIEFEN TAL, EIN
   *CCU,folk song,Ger
   (Wulz, Helmut) eq voices&mix cor HEYN
   ISBN 3 85366 492 X f.s. (B94)

BÄURIN HAT D'KATZ VERLORN, D' see
   Mozart, Wolfgang Amadeus, Chat De
   La Mère Michel, Le

BAVARIAN YODELLING SONG see Nelson

BAXTER, FRANCIS H.
   Autumn Night Song
    see Four Ancient Chinese Paintings

   Dawn Of Spring, The
    see Four Ancient Chinese Paintings

   Four Ancient Chinese Paintings
    SATB,pno LAURN f.s.
    contains: Autumn Night Song; Dawn
    Of Spring, The; Snow On The
    River; Summer Day In The Garden (B95)

   Snow On The River
    see Four Ancient Chinese Paintings

   Summer Day In The Garden
    see Four Ancient Chinese Paintings

BAZIN, FRANÇOIS-EMANUEL-JOSEPH
   (1816-1878)
   Gloire À La France
    4pt men cor BILLAUDOT (B96)
    (Arnoud) 3 eq voices BILLAUDOT (B97)

BE JOYFUL WITH SINGING see Buxtehude,
   Dietrich

BE MY BABY TONIGHT
   (Funk) SATB WARNER 8120BC1X ipa (B98)
   (Funk) SAB WARNER 8120BC3X ipa (B99)
   (Funk) 2pt cor WARNER 8120BC5X ipa (B100)

BE THE STREAM THAT OXBOWS see Bray,
   Julie Gardner

BE TRUE TO YOUR SCHOOL
   (Funk) SATB WARNER 1506BC1X ipa (B101)
   (Funk) 3pt mix cor WARNER 1506BC3X
   ipa (B102)
   (Funk) 2pt cor WARNER 1506BC5X ipa (B103)

BEACH, [MRS.] H.H.A. (AMY MARCY CHENEY)
   (1867-1944)
   Chambered Nautilus Op.66,The
    SSA,S solo,pno/orch HILD 09435 (B104)

   Festival Jubilate
    SATB,pno HILD 09503 (B105)

BEACH PARTY see Broberg, Robert Karl
   Oskar see Broberg, Robert Karl
   Oskar

# SECULAR CHORAL MUSIC

BEADS see Kurtag, György, Klárisok

BEATI MORTUI see Mendelssohn-Bartholdy, Felix

BEATI PAUPERES II see Huber, Klaus

BEATTIE, DONALD
   All The Lovely Way Home
     2pt cor HAS HAS 007    (B106)

   In Alaska In A Major
     cor,solo voice oct HAS HAS 009    (B107)

   In Paradise
     unis cor oct HAS HAS 011    (B108)

   Kings And Queens
     2pt cor oct HAS HAS 015    (B109)

BEAU BERGER, LE see Henchoz, Emile

BEAU CHEVALIER see Broquet, Louis

BEAU PAPILLON, VIT', MARIE-TOI! see Canteloube, Joseph

BEAU PAYS, LE see Broquet, Louis

BEAU PETIT COEUR see Martin

BEAUGRAND
   Avant L'aurore
     2 eq voices BILLAUDOT    (B110)

BEAUTIFUL DREAMER see Foster, Stephen Collins

BEAUTIFUL SOUP see Fine

BEAUX DANSEURS see Mermoud, Robert

BEAUX SOUVENIRS D'ANTAN see Lang, H.

BEAUX VILLAGES, LES see Boller, Carlo

BECKER, VALENTIN E.
   Wohlauf, Die Luft Geht Frisch Und Rein
     SATB,acap BOHM    (B111)

BECKWITH, JOHN (1927- )
   Houses In Heaven
     SATB THOMP.G VEI1096    (B112)

BEEBE, HANK
   If We Love
     SATB,kbd LAURN CH-1094    (B113)

   My Driver's Test
     speaking cor HOPE K 312    (B114)

BEEP-BOP see Lyons,Bill

BEESON, JACK HAMILTON (1921- )
   Knots (Jack And Jill For Grown-Ups)
     SATB,soli,acap (diff) PRESSER 312-41629    (B115)

BEETHOVEN, LUDWIG VAN (1770-1827)
   Allegro (from Piano Sonata Op. 26)
     (Swingle, Ward) SSAATTBB,db,drums (gr. IV) voc pt,pts UNC JP GR-2X    (B116)

   An Die Freude (from Symphony No. 9, Op. 125)
     cor,SATBar soli,3.2.2.3. 4.2.3.0. timp,perc,strings RICORDI-IT    (B117)

   Auf, Freunde, Singt Dem Gott Der Ehen see Mehrstimmige Gesäng

   Bundeslied see Mehrstimmige Gesäng

   Cantata Campestre see Mehrstimmige Gesäng

   Es Lebe Unser Teurer Fürst see Mehrstimmige Gesäng

   Mehrstimmige Gesäng
     mix cor,pno HENLE f.s.
     contains: Auf, Freunde, Singt Dem Gott Der Ehen, WoO.105; Bundeslied, Op.122; Cantata Campestre, WoO.103; Es Lebe Unser Teurer Fürst, WoO.106; Opferlied, Op.121b    (B118)

   Opferlied see Mehrstimmige Gesäng

   Scherzo (from Violin & Piano Sonata Op. 24)
     (Swingle, Ward) SATTBB,db,drums (gr. III) voc pt,pts UNC JP GR-1X    (B119)

BEGEGNUNG see Helmschrott, Robert M. see Helmschrott, Robert M. see Meister, Casimir

BEGGAR'S SONG, THE see Perry

BEI MEINES BUHLEN HAUPTE see Zimmermann, Bernd Alois

BEIDERBECKE
   In A Mist
     (Swingle, Ward) SSAATTBB,acap (gr. V) voc pt,pts UNC JP RTJ-4X    (B120)

BEKEHRTE,DER see Kreis, Otto

BEKKU, SADAO (1922- )
   Light Colored Songs see Tansai-Syo

   Tansai-Syo
     "Light Colored Songs" wom cor ONGAKU 555420    (B121)

BEL ANGE, LE see Bovet, J.

BEL ASTRE QUE J'ADORE *pop
   mix cor HUG 8191    (B122)
   see Martin

BEL ÉTRANGER see Jaques-Dalcroze, Émile

BELCUM, HENK VAN
   Waarom
     SATB,acap BANK 11.900.080    (B123)

BELL
   Jazzy Rhythm Of Life
     2pt cor LESLIE 2078    (B124)

   My Balloon
     SA LESLIE 2081    (B125)

BELL CAROL see Leontovich, M.

BELL CHORUS FROM "IL PAGLIACCI" see Leoncavallo, Ruggiero

BELLA, RUDOLF (1890- )
   Abend Im Tal
     wom cor,acap MULLES    (B126)

   Ewig Jung Ist Nur Die Sonne
     wom cor,acap MULLES    (B127)

   Frühling, O Goldene Zeit
     wom cor,acap MULLES    (B128)

   Herbstgefühl
     wom cor,acap MULLES    (B129)

   Hochsommernacht
     wom cor,acap MULLES    (B130)

   Singet Leise
     wom cor,acap MULLES    (B131)

BELLE ATTENDAIT, LA see Lagger, Oscar

BELLE, BELLE ROSE see Adam, J.

BELLE FRANÇOISE, LA see Planel, Jean

BELLE JEANNETOON, LA see Lagger, Oscar

BELLE LUNE AU DOUX VISAGE see Sibelius, Jean

BELLE ROSE, LA see Lagger, Oscar

BELLMAN, CARL MICHAEL (1740-1795)
   Bellman Suite,A
     (Swingle, Ward) SATB,db,drums, synthesizer (diff) voc pt,pts UNC JP SC-4X    (B132)

   Träd Fram Du Nattens Gud
     (Sköld) SATB NOTERIA 2826    (B133)

BELLMAN SUITE,A see Bellman, Carl Michael

BELLUCCI, GIACOMO
   Polittico
     dbl cor BERBEN BERBEN 3192    (B134)

BELMONT
   If Music Be The Food Of Love
     SATB WARCH 34491    (B135)

   Roadside Fire, The
     SATB WARCH 34504    (B136)

BELMONT, JEAN
   Farewell Overture, The *Gen
     SATB,acap (med) DEAN 15-1207 R    (B137)
     SATB,acap DEAN 15-1207R    (B138)

   Invitations
     SATB,fl,perc (Choral Cycle, diff) DEAN sc 30-1092 R, pts 30-1144 R    (B139)
     SATB,fl&perc DEAN sc 30-1092R, pts 30-1144R    (B140)

BELSHAZZAR see Handel, George Frideric

BENGTSSON, BERNT
   När Ljuvt Naturen Grönskar
     SATB NOTERIA B 2776    (B141)

BENJAMIN
   Three Mystical Songs *CC3U
     SATB BOOSEY-ENG OCTB7022 f.s.    (B142)

BENNETT, [SIR] WILLIAM STERNDALE (1816-1875)
   With A Laugh As We Go Round
     SATB BANKS 150    (B143)

BENNINGHOFF, ORTWIN
   Drei Abendlieder
     mix cor NEUE NM 2065    (B144)

   Herbst *cant
     mix cor,S solo,chamber orch NEUE NM 2013    (B145)

   Il Pleure Dans Mon Couer
     cor,instrumental ensemble ((after a canon by Debussy)) NEUE NM 2066    (B146)

BENVENUTI, ARRIGO (1925- )
   Gymel E Corale
     mix cor BERBEN BERBEN 9927    (B147)

BERBEL, MARCELO
   Quimey Neuquen
     (Gomez, Eduardo) jr cor LAGOS    (B148)

BERCEAU DU PRINTEMPS, LE see Boller, Carlo

BERCEUSE (from Terre Et L'étoile, La)
   wom cor HUG 8846    (B149)
   see Brahms, Johannes, Wiegenlied
   see Bron, Patrick see Dvořák, Antonín see Vuataz, Roger

BERCEUSE DE GRAND'MAMAN, LA see Hemmerling, Carlos

BERCEUSE DE LA VIERGE see Sutermeister, Heinrich

BERCEUSE DES TOUT PETITS see Ithier

BERCEUSE PATRIOTIQUE see Bovet, J.

BERCEUSE POUR L'AN 2000 see Zbinden, Julien-François

BERCEUSE POUR LINETTTE see Bovet, J.

BERCEUSE POUR NEGRITO see Robert-Lalouet, M.

BERGER, LE see Haenni, G.

BERGER DU CIEL see Henchoz, Emile

BERGÈRE see Sala, Andre

BERGÈRE AUX CHAMPS, LA see Martin

BERGÈRE FIDÈLE, LA see Boller, Carlo

BERGÈRE SOUS LES SAULES, LA see Vecchi, Orazio (Horatio)

BERGERETTE see Miche, Paul

BERGERETTE, LA see Doret, Gustave

BERGERETTE AU BOIS JOLY see Robert-Lalouet, M.

BERGMAN, ERIK (1911- )
   Nein Zur Lebensangst
     SATB,narrator,acap (diff) PRESSER 512-00637    (B150)

   Petrarca Suite *Op.118
     SATB,acap,Bar solo (diff, contains four love sonnets) PRESSER 512-00639    (B151)

BERGSOMMER see Schmid, Walter

BERLIN
   Alexander's Ragtime Band
     (Wagner) 2pt cor,kbd (easy) PRESSER 392-41693    (B152)
     (Wagner) SATB (easy) PRESSER 392-41535    (B153)
     (Wagner) SAB (easy) PRESSER 392-41461    (B154)
     (Wagner) SSA (easy) PRESSER 392-41562    (B155)

   I Love A Piano (composed with Besig)
     (Price) 2pt cor ALFRED 5803    (B156)

BERLIN, IRVING (1888-1989)
   Alexander's Ragtime Band
     (Hood) TTBB,pno PRESSER 312-41657    (B157)

   They Say That Falling In Love Is Wonderful
     (Ames, Morgan) SSAB,acap (gr. V) UNC JP    (B158)

BERLINER LUFT see Lincke, Paul

BERNIER, RENE (1905-1984)
   Chants Incantatoires (from Ombre Et
    Les Blés, L') CCU
     mix cor BILLAUDOT f.s. (B159)

   Incantation
    4 eq voices BILLAUDOT (B160)

   Incantations
    4pt wom cor BILLAUDOT (B161)

BERNSTEIN, LEONARD (1918-1990)
   Dream With Me
    TTBB,acap BOOSEY-ENG OCTB6742 (B162)

   Maria (from West Side Story)
    SATB NOVELLO 090630 (B163)

BERR, JOSÉ
   Urlicht
    wom cor,acap MULLES (B164)

BERRY
   Joy Overflowing
    SATB SHAWNEE A-6907 ipa (B165)

BERTAUX
   Old Man Variations, The
    3pt treb cor BOOSEY-ENG OCTB6708 (B166)

BERTHOMIEU, MARC
   Joli Lapin Blanc, Le
    3 eq voices BILLAUDOT (B167)

   Kangourou Boxeur, Le
    3 eq voices BILLAUDOT (B168)

   Ronde Des Escargots
    3 eq voices BILLAUDOT (B169)

BERTOGG, CONRAD
   Slberdisteln
    wom cor,acap MULLES (B170)

BESIDE THE NODLE RIVER see Nodle
   Kangbyon

BESIG
   Get On Board This Train (composed
    with Price, Nancy)
    2pt cor ALFRED 11301 (B171)

   Regards To Broadway! (composed with
    Cohan)
    (Price) 2pt cor ALFRED 11554 (B172)

BEST IS YET-IT AIN'T NECESSARI'LY SO,
   THE see Broadley, Sharon

BEST LOVED SONGS OF RODGERS AND HART
   (Schmutte, Pete) SATB (a medley incl.
    Bewitched & Funny Valentine) WARNER
    WBCH9418 (B173)
   (Schmutte, Pete) SAB (a medley incl.
    Bewitched & Funny Valentine) WARNER
    WBCH9419 (B174)
   (Schmutte, Pete) SSA (a medley incl.
    Bewitched & Funny Valentine) WARNER
    WBCH9420 (B175)

BEST OF BOND:, THE
   (Ginsburg, Ned) SATB (medley incl.
    Bond Theme, Goldfinger, Live And
    Let Die) WARNER C0295C1X ipa (B176)
   (Ginsburg, Ned) SAB (medley incl.
    Bond Theme, Goldfinger, Live And
    Let Die) WARNER C0295C3X ipa (B177)

BEST OF GARTH BROOKS:, THE
   (Schmutte, Pete) SATB (medley incl.
    The Dance, Unanswered Prayers, &
    The River) WARNER C0312C1X (B178)
   (Schmutte, Pete) SAB (medley incl.
    The Dance, Unanswered Prayers, &
    The River) WARNER C0312C3X (B179)

BEST OF MY LOVE
   (Schmutte, Pete) SAB (medley of the
    eagles hits) WARNER WBCH9321 (B180)
   (Schmutte, Pete) SATB (medley of the
    eagles hits) WARNER WBCH9320 (B181)

BEST OF TIMES see Gilpin, Greg

BEST SELLING POPS FOR YOUNG VOICES:
   SONG KIT #15
   (Chinn-Cacavas-Snyder-Gilpin) 1-2pt
    cor WARNER cor pts C0215CSI, sc
    C0215CCI (B182)

BEST YEARS OF MY LIFE, THE see
   Jennings, Will

BESTIAIRE ET L'HERBIER, LE see Passani,
   Emile

BETRACHTUNG DER ZEIT see Studer, Hans

BETSY ROSS RAG see Campbell-Towell, Lee

BETTINELLI, BRUNO (1913-  )
   Mistero, Il
    see Poesie Di Tiziana

   Poesie Di Tiziana
    wom cor RICORDI-IT 132793 f.s.
    contains: Mistero, Il; Segreto,
    Il; Ti Innamorasti Del Fiume
     (B183)

   Segreto, Il
    see Poesie Di Tiziana

   Ti Innamorasti Del Fiume
    see Poesie Di Tiziana

BETTY BOTTER see Freedman

BEWITCHED see Rodgers, Richard

BEYOND THE BLUE SKY see Morisaki,
   Takatoshi

BEYOND THE HORIZON see Kinoshita,
   Makiko, Chiheisen No Kanata

BEZENCON, GILBERT
   Gare Au Zazou
    eq voices HUG 8863 (B184)

   Zazou Zinzin, Le
    men cor HUG 8862 (B185)

BHATIA, VANRAJ A. (1927-  )
   Autumn
    see Sharad

   Basant (from Six Seasons)
    "Spring" SATB (hindi) EARTHSNG
    ES-41 (B186)

   Grishma (from Six Seasons)
    "Summer" SATB (hindi) EARTHSNG
    ES-41 (B187)

   Harvest
    see Shishir

   Hemant (from Six Seasons)
    "Winter" SATB (hindi) EARTHSNG
    ES-41 (B188)

   Monsoon
    see Varsha

   Sharad (from Six Seasons)
    "Autumn" SATB (hindi) EARTHSNG
    ES-41 (B189)

   Shishir (from Six Seasons)
    "Harvest" SATB (hindi) EARTHSNG
    ES-41 (B190)

   Spring
    see Basant

   Summer
    see Grishma

   Varsha (from Six Seasons)
    "Monsoon" SATB (hindi) EARTHSNG
    ES-41 (B191)

   Winter
    see Hemant

BI-N-I NID E RYCHE MÖNTSCH? see
   Steiger, F.

BIALOSKY, MARSHALL H. (1923-  )
   He Came All So Still
    SSAA SEESAW (B192)

BIANCHI, ITALO (1936-  )
   Canto Alla Mia Terra
    4pt cor BERBEN BERBEN 1375 (B193)

BICYCLETTES, LES see Bron, Patrick

BIEBL, FRANZ (1906-  )
   Frülingsglaube (from Schubert)
    SATB,acap BOHM (B194)

   Glück Zum Neuen Jahr
    SATB,acap BOHM (B195)

BIENVENUE see Miche, Paul

BIERI, ALBRECHT
   Frühlingsboten
    men cor,acap MULLES (B196)

BIG FAT HAIRY VISION OF EVIL see
   Jergenson, Dale

BIG SPENDER see Coleman

BIGLER, RUDOLF
   Tulpe,Die
    wom cor,acap MULLES (B197)

BILLINGSLEY
   Feelings
    SATB SHAWNEE A-1967 (B198)

BINET, JEAN (1893-1960)
   Au Pays (from Grange Aux Roud, La)
    mix cor HUG 8107 (B199)

   Cerises, Les
    eq voices HUG 7926 (B200)

   Chanson Des Présents, La
    eq voices HUG 7908 (B201)

   Cloche Dans Le Ciel, La (from Grange
    Aux Roud, La)
    mix cor HUG 8105 (B202)

   Complainte Du Mercenaire, La
    men cor HUG 7933 (B203)

   Filles, Les
    eq voices HUG 7681 (B204)

   Maison, La (from Grange Aux Roud, La)
    mix cor HUG 8108 (B205)

   Mal Du Pays
    men cor HUG 8042 (B206)

   Ode à Diane et Apollon
    mix cor,2.2(English horn).2.2.
    4.3.3.1. timp,perc,strings HENN
    HL 606 (B207)

   Petits Glaneurs, Les
    eq voices HUG 7927 (B208)

   Pour Être Heureux (from Grange Aux
    Roud, La)
    mix cor HUG 8106 (B209)

   Terre A Reverdi, La (from Grange Aux
    Roud, La)
    mix cor HUG 8104 (B210)

BIONDA, BELLA BIONDA see Boller, Carlo
   see Furrer, Walter

BIRD DOG
   (Lawrence, Stephen) TTB WARNER CH9578
    (B211)

BIRDS see Daley, Eleanor

BIRTHDAY SONG,A see Rees-Davies, Ieuan

BISHOP
   Home, Sweet Home
    (Hunter-Shaw) TTBB LAWSON 4-533
    (B212)

BISHOP, [SIR] HENRY (ROWLEY)
   (1786-1855)
   Fisherman's Good Night,The
    SATB BANKS 102 (B213)

   Home Sweet Home
    (Dicks, E.A.) SATB BANKS 630 (B214)

BISSEL
   Summer Evening, A
    SSA WARCH 34402 (B215)

BISSELL
   Mary Ann
    SATB WARCH 35668 (B216)

   Weathers
    SA WARCH 35225 (B217)

   When I Set Out For Lyoness
    SA WARCH 35235 (B218)

BIST DU BEI MIR see Bach, Johann
   Sebastian

BISTRO, LE see Rochat, Jean

BITKIN, ZE'EV
   Mimkomcha
    2pt cor OR-TAV (B219)

BITSCH, MARCEL (1921-  )
   Complainte Du Paysan-Soldat (from
    Petite Suite Polonaise)
    mix cor HUG 8767 (B220)
    men cor HUG 8770 (B221)

   Confidence (from Petite Suite
    Polonaise)
    men cor HUG 8769 (B222)
    mix cor HUG 8766 (B223)

   Si Vous Avez Une Fille (from Petite
    Suite Polonaise)
    men cor HUG 8768 (B224)
    mix cor HUG 8765 (B225)

BITTEN BY THE BEAT
   (Funk, Jeff) SATB (rock medley incl.
    We Will Rock You, Old Time Rock &
    Roll & Rocking Pneumonia) WARNER
    C0329C1X ipa (B226)
   (Funk, Jeff) SAB (rock medley incl.
    We Will Rock You, Old Time Rock &
    Roll & Rocking Pneumonia) WARNER
    C0329C3X ipa (B227)
   (Funk, Jeff) 2pt cor (rock medley
    incl. We Will Rock You, Old Time
    Rock & Roll & Rocking Pneumonia)
    WARNER C0329C5X ipa (B228)

BIZET, GEORGES (1838-1875)
   Toreador's Song, The (from "Carmen")
     SATB,opt Bar solo,pno BOOSEY-ENG
      MET0002                 (B229)

BJÖRKLUND, STAFFAN (1944- )
   Ängelu
     SATB NOTERIA B 2779       (B230)

   Ära
     SATB NOTERIA B 2778       (B231)

BJÖRLIN, ULF (1933-1993)
   Raoul Wallenberg Portrait:, A
    *Symphony
    mix cor&jr cor,3 speaking voices,
     orch STIM                (B232)

BLACK IS THE COLOR  *folk song
   SATBB,acap UNC JP         (B233)
   (Matsuoka, Yumiko) SATBB,acap (gr.
    III) UNC JP              (B234)

BLACKBERRY WINTER see Wilder, Alec

BLAME IT ON MY YOUTH see Carlos, Glenn

BLANDADE RÖSTER 5
   SVERIG SK 792 f.s. anthology  (B235)

BLÄTTERFALL see Hug, Fritz

BLÅVEISSKOGEN see Hansen, Vidar

BLEAK MIDWINTER, THE see Ringwald, Roy

BLISS, P. PAUL (1872-1933)
   Pro Phundo Basso
     SATB (humorous quartet) BANKS 184
                                (B236)

BLOCH
   America
     SATB WARCH 40701         (B237)

BLOMMORNAS VALS see Tchaikovsky, Piotr
   Ilyich

BLOOMING IN SPRING see Ota, Sakurako

BLOW, BLOW, THOU WINTER WIND see
   Porterfield, Sherrie

BLOW OUT THE TRUMPET see Martin

BLOW THE CANDLES OUT see Smith, Gregg

BLOW YE WINDS
   (Stocker, D.) TBB,pno THOMAS
     1C0369407                 (B238)
   (Stocker, D.) men cor THOMAS
     1C0369407                 (B239)

BLUE RONDO A LA TURK see Brubeck, David
   (Dave) Warren

BLUE SKY,THE see Rippentrop, Denice

BLUEBIRD see Holman, Derek

BLUES DOWN TO MY SHOES see Shaw, Kirby

BLUMENFELD, HAROLD (1923- )
   Aware
    see Four Tranquil Poems After D.H.
     Lawrence

   Four Tranquil Poems After D.H.
    Lawrence
     TTBB sc MMB f.s.
      contains: Aware; Green; Silence;
       White Blossom, A     (B240)

   Green
    see Four Tranquil Poems After D.H.
     Lawrence

   Silence
    see Four Tranquil Poems After D.H.
     Lawrence

   Three Scottish Poems (from L.A.G.
    Strong) CC3U
     SATB sc MMB X094004      (B241)

   War Lament
     SSAATTBB,gtr sc MMB X098001 (B242)

   White Blossom, A
    see Four Tranquil Poems After D.H.
     Lawrence

BLUMENLIEDER  *CC11L
   3-4pt wom cor/1-6pt wom cor,opt pno
    MULLES f.s.               (B243)

BLUMENLIEDER, OP. 15 see Furer, Arthur

BLÜMLEIN BLÜHT AM WEGE,EIN see
   Niedermann, Gustav

BOAR AND THE DROMEDAR, DON'T EVER
   SQUEEZE see Henderson

BOAR'S HEAD CAROL
   (Shaw And Parker) [Eng/Lat] TTBB,acap
    LEONARD-US 50305010     (B244)

BOCK, JERRY (1928- )
   Grand Knowing You
    (Schmutte, Pete) SATB WARNER
     WBCH9411 ipa         (B245)
    (Schmutte, Pete) SAB WARNER
     WBCH9412 ipa         (B246)
    (Schmutte, Pete) 2pt cor WARNER
     WBCH9413 ipa         (B247)

BODY
   Petit Port Breton,Le
     4pt men cor BILLAUDOT    (B248)

BODY AND SOUL
   (Chinn, Teena) SATB,acap WARNER
    CH9532                  (B249)

BØE, BERNT (1947- )
   Seter Vise Frå Sunndalen
    3pt mix cor,kbd NOTON N-8929 (B250)

BOER EN SNIJDER see Toebosch, Louis

BOESCH, BALTHASAR
   I Der Frömdi
     men cor,acap MULLES      (B251)

   I Dr Frömdi
    (Krenger) wom cor,acap MULLES
                                (B252)

   Meine Heimat
     men cor,acap MULLES      (B253)

   O Sei Gegrüsst Mein Vaterland
     men cor,acap MULLES      (B254)

BOHÉMIEN see Volery, Francis

BOHÉMIEN, LE see Kodály, Zoltán

BOHÉMIENS, LES see Martin

BOHLY
   Chant D'automne Et De Vendange
     4pt men cor BILLAUDOT    (B255)

   France Aimée
     4pt men cor BILLAUDOT    (B256)

BOIELDIEU, FRANÇOIS-ADRIEN (1775-1834)
   Pour Toi Ma Bonne Mère
    2 eq voices BILLAUDOT     (B257)

BOÎTE À MUSIQUE see Miche, Paul see
   Piaget, Ada May

BOITO, ARRIGO (1842-1918)
   Prologue From "Mefistofele" (I-E)
    mix cor,Bar solo,orch voc sc JERONA
     JC1003 perf mat rent    (B258)

BOKURA NO FURUSATO see Abiko, Yoshiro

BOLLER, CARLO
   A La Claire Fontaine
    see Deux Chansons De France

   A Ma Faux
     men cor HUG 7475        (B259)

   A Moléson (from Images De Mon Pays)
     mix cor,opt solo voice,acap/pno HUG
      6742                     (B260)
     men cor,acap HUG 6969     (B261)
     eq voices,acap HUG 6747   (B262)

   Abschiedslied
     [Ger] mix cor HUG 7556    (B263)
     [Ger] men cor HUG 8464    (B264)

   Ah! Oui Que Je Suis À Mon Aise
     mix cor HUG 6605        (B265)

   Allons Danser Sous Les Ormeaux
     mix cor HUG 7855        (B266)

   Allons En Vendanges
     mix cor HUG 7650        (B267)
     men cor HUG 7651        (B268)

   Alpage, L'
     mix cor HUG 6824        (B269)

   Angélus Du Soir, L' (from Pastorale
    Gruérienne)
     mix cor,acap/pno HUG 7279  (B270)
     3 eq voices HUG 8736     (B271)
     men cor HUG 8737        (B272)

   Anges Dans Nos Campagnes, Les
     mix cor HUG 6954        (B273)

   Appel (from Pastorale Gruérienne)
     mix cor,T solo,acap/pno HUG 7284
                                (B274)

   Armaillis De Grandvillard, Les (from
    Pastorale Gruérienne)
     mix cor,acap/pno HUG 7283  (B275)

   Au Bord Du Lac
     men cor HUG 6645        (B276)

   Au Doux Pays
     "Soldatenlied" mix cor HUG 6681
                                (B277)

BOLLER, CARLO (cont'd.)

   Au Drapeau
     mix cor HUG 7340        (B278)
     men cor HUG 7339        (B279)

   Au Vieux Pays
     mix cor HUG 8734        (B280)
     eq voices,Bar solo HUG 7793 (B281)
     men cor HUG 7028        (B282)

   Avril
     eq voices HUG 6665      (B283)

   Balayeurs, Les (from Pays Du Lac)
     men cor,acap HUG 8603    (B284)

   Beaux Villages, Les (from Images De
    Mon Pays)
     men cor,acap HUG 6977    (B285)
     mix cor,acap/pno HUG 6871  (B286)
     eq voices,opt pno/org/orch HUG 7088
                                (B287)

   Berceau Du Printemps, Le
     men cor HUG 7452        (B288)

   Bergère Fidèle, La
     mix cor,S solo HUG 6606    (B289)

   Bionda, Bella Bionda
     mix cor HUG 6847        (B290)

   Bon Village, Le
     mix cor HUG 7156A       (B291)
     mix cor,Bar solo,opt pno/org/orch
      HUG 7156               (B292)
     men cor,Bar solo,pno/org/orch HUG
      7157                   (B293)

   Bon Voyage, Vin De Ma Vigne! (from
    Vignettes)
     mix cor,acap/pno HUG 7577  (B294)
     men cor HUG 8710        (B295)

   Cela File Avec Le Temps
     eq voices HUG 7202      (B296)

   C'est À Boire Qu'il Nous Faut!
     men cor HUG 8862        (B297)

   C'est Le Bon Lever
     mix cor HUG 6728        (B298)
     men cor HUG 7472        (B299)

   Chanson D'automne
     men cor HUG 6890        (B300)

   Chanson De La Cime, La
     eq voices HUG 6848      (B301)

   Chanson De L'armailli
     mix cor HUG 7228        (B302)
     men cor HUG 7071        (B303)

   Chanson De Mariage
     mix cor,SBar soli HUG 7765  (B304)

   Chanson De Troupe
     mix cor HUG 6904        (B305)

   Chanson Des Faneuses (from Pastorale
    Gruérienne)
     mix cor,acap/pno HUG 7277  (B306)

   Chanson Des Glaçons (from Pastorale
    Gruérienne)
     eq voices,pno/org/orch HUG 7271
                                (B307)

   Chanson Des Mayentzets (from
    Pastorale Gruérienne)
     mix cor,acap/pno HUG 7289  (B308)
     jr cor,pno/org/orch HUG 7274 (B309)

   Chanson Des Nains (from Pastorale
    Gruérienne)
     mix cor,acap/pno HUG 7272  (B310)

   Chanson Des Vieux (from Pays Du Lac)
     mix cor,opt solo,acap/pno HUG 7543
                                (B311)
     men cor,opt solo voice,opt pno/org/
      orch HUG 8335         (B312)

   Chanson Des Vignerons (from Images De
    Mon Pays)
     men cor,acap HUG 6978    (B313)
     mix cor,acap/pno HUG 6872  (B314)
     eq voices,acap HUG 6915   (B315)

   Chanson Du Dimanche (from Images De
    Mon Pays)
     mix cor,acap/pno HUG 6877  (B316)
     eq voices,opt pno/org/orch HUG 7201
                                (B317)

   Chanson Du Sol Vaudois, La
     mix cor HUG 7227        (B318)

   Chanson Espagnole
     mix cor HUG 6979        (B319)
     eq voices HUG 6590      (B320)

   Chant De La Fidélité
     men cor HUG 7476        (B321)

## SECULAR CHORAL MUSIC

BOLLER, CARLO (cont'd.)

   Chant Des Braconniers (from Pastorale Gruérienne)
      men cor,acap HUG 7280   (B322)

   Chant Du Berger (from Images De Mon Pays)
      mix cor,acap/pno HUG 6876   (B323)

   Chant Du Drapeau
      "Fahnenlied" [Fr] mix cor HUG 6887   (B324)
      "Fahnenlied" [Ger] mix cor HUG 8462   (B325)
      "Fahnenlied" [Fr] eq voices HUG 6916   (B326)
      "Fahnenlied" [Fr] men cor HUG 7552, 6883   (B327)
      "Fahnenlied" [Ger] men cor HUG 7552   (B328)

   Chant Du Lac (from Images De Mon Pays)
      mix cor,acap/pno HUG 6880   (B329)

   Chant Du Pays (from Images De Mon Pays)
      mix cor,acap/pno HUG 6886   (B330)
      men cor,acap HUG 6884   (B331)

   Chant Du Paysan (from Pastorale Gruérienne)
      mix cor,T solo,acap/pno HUG 7290   (B332)
      mix cor,solo voice,acap/pno HUG 7276   (B333)

   Château, Ta Forteresse... (from Images De Mon Pays)
      mix cor,acap/pno HUG 6881   (B334)

   Chevriers, Les (from Pastorale Gruérienne)
      mix cor,T solo,acap/pno HUG 7278   (B335)

   Choral Des Adieux
      mix cor HUG 6479   (B336)
      eq voices HUG 6480   (B337)
      men cor HUG 6464   (B338)

   Clochers, Les (from Vignettes)
      mix cor,acap/pno HUG 7580   (B339)

   Coclicôt
      mix cor HUG 7665   (B340)

   Compagnon, Hisse La Voile! (from Vignettes)
      mix cor,acap/pno HUG 7572   (B341)

   Coucou
      mix cor HUG 6748   (B342)
      eq voices HUG 6625   (B343)
      men cor HUG 6633   (B344)

   Crieur Public, Le (from Pays Du Lac)
      men cor,opt pno/org/orch HUG 8333   (B345)
      mix cor,acap/pno HUG 8192   (B346)

   Da Bist Du, Winzersmann!
      [Ger] 3pt mix cor,opt pno/org/orch HUG 7555   (B347)
      [Ger] men cor HUG 8072   (B348)

   Dans Cette Étable
      mix cor HUG 6726   (B349)

   Dans Le Jardin De La Mairie
      mix cor,opt pno/org/orch HUG 7226   (B350)

   Dans Le Verger Désert (from Pays Du Lac)
      mix cor,ST soli,pno/org/orch HUG 8221   (B351)

   De Quoi Nourrit-On Les Femmes?
      mix cor HUG 7666   (B352)

   Dedans La Cour Du Roi
      mix cor HUG 6666   (B353)

   Départ Du Soldat, Le (Addio, Mia Bell'addio)
      mix cor HUG 6680   (B354)

   Deux Chansons De France
      HUG f.s.
      contains: A La Claire Fontaine (mix cor,Mez/A solo); En Passant Par La Lorraine (mix cor)   (B355)

   Dormi, Dormi, Bel Bambin
      mix cor HUG 7629   (B356)

   En Passant Par La Lorraine
      see Deux Chansons De France

   Enfant, L'
      eq voices HUG 6848   (B357)

   Entendez La Trompette
      men cor HUG 7477   (B358)

BOLLER, CARLO (cont'd.)

   Entre Le Boeuf Et L'âne Gris
      mix cor HUG 6953   (B359)

   Fahnenlied
      see Chant Du Drapeau

   Femmes De Chez Nous, Les (from Images De Mon Pays)
      mix cor,acap/pno HUG 6874   (B360)
      eq voices,acap HUG 6965   (B361)

   File, File Au Fil De L'eau
      mix cor HUG 8243   (B362)

   Fille À Colin, La (from Pastorale Gruérienne)
      mix cor,acap/pno HUG 7287   (B363)

   Fruits Sont Mûrs, Les (from Pays Du Lac)
      mix cor,acap/pno HUG 7542   (B364)

   Galé Chudâ
      "Petit Soldat" men cor HUG 7507   (B365)

   Heimweh
      [Ger] mix cor HUG 8073   (B366)
      [Ger] men cor HUG 7554   (B367)

   Hymne À La Patrie (from Images De Mon Pays)
      mix cor,acap/pno HUG 6882   (B368)
      eq voices,acap HUG 7089   (B369)
      men cor,acap HUG 7551   (B370)

   Hymne An Das Vaterland
      [Ger] mix cor HUG 8461   (B371)
      [Ger] men cor HUG 7551   (B372)

   Il En Faut Du Temps (from Pays Du Lac)
      mix cor,acap/pno HUG 7165   (B373)

   Images De Mon Pays *ora
      mix cor,SBar&narrator,orch HUG voc pt 6980, cor pts 6981, pts   (B374)
      mix cor,SBar&narrator,orch HUG voc sc 6980, cor pts 6981   (B375)

   J'ai Quitté Ma Maison
      mix cor HUG 7649   (B376)

   Jardiniers, Les (from Pays Du Lac)
      mix cor HUG 7164   (B377)

   Jardins Secrets (from Images De Mon Pays)
      mix cor,acap/pno HUG 6875   (B378)

   Jeunes Filles De Val D'illiez, Les
      mix cor HUG 7102   (B379)

   Joli Gringot (from Pastorale Gruérienne)
      mix cor,acap/pno HUG 7288   (B380)

   Lorsque L'amour Part Pour La Chasse (from Vignettes)
      mix cor,opt S solo,acap/pno HUG 7574   (B381)

   Louange À Toi, Pays! (from Pays Du Lac)
      mix cor,acap/pno HUG 7098   (B382)
      men cor,acap HUG 7068   (B383)

   March Des Paysans (from Pays Du Lac)
      mix cor,acap/pno HUG 7456   (B384)
      men cor,opt pno/org/orch HUG 8334   (B385)

   Mariage, Le
      mix cor HUG 6742   (B386)

   Marie-Madelon
      see Trois Chansons De Marins

   Matin De Mai
      men cor HUG 6806   (B387)

   Meine Alp
      [Ger] mix cor HUG 7556   (B388)
      [Ger] men cor HUG 8464   (B389)

   Mort Du Chêne, La
      men cor,B solo,pno/org/orch HUG 7281   (B390)

   Nostalgie (from Pastorale Gruérienne)
      mix cor HUG 7282   (B391)
      men cor,acap HUG 7229   (B392)

   Notre Chalet, Là-Haut
      men cor HUG 6464   (B393)
      eq voices HUG 6480   (B394)
      mix cor HUG 6479   (B395)

   Nous Étions Trois Filles
      mix cor,S solo HUG 7439   (B396)

   O Ma Gruyère
      mix cor,opt pno/org/orch HUG 7285   (B397)

BOLLER, CARLO (cont'd.)

   O Vous Qui Reposez (from Pays Du Lac)
      mix cor,acap,pno HUG 8294   (B398)

   Ohé, Le Marié! (from Images De Mon Pays)
      mix cor,acap/pno HUG 6966   (B399)
      eq voices,acap HUG 6975   (B400)
      men cor,acap HUG 6958   (B401)

   Oiseau Du Printemps, L'
      eq voices HUG 6944   (B402)

   Old Folks At Home, The
      [Fr/Eng] mix cor HUG 8734   (B403)

   Par Ce Bleu Matin D'été (from Pays Du Lac)
      mix cor,acap/pno HUG 7449   (B404)

   Par-Dessus La Clôture
      mix cor HUG 7214   (B405)
      men cor HUG 7213   (B406)
      eq voices HUG 7342   (B407)

   Par Un Beau Jour De Mai...
      mix cor HUG 6819   (B408)
      men cor HUG 6850   (B409)

   Pastorale Gruérienne *ora
      mix cor,soli,pno/orch voc sc HUG 7270   (B410)
      cor,pno HUG 7270   (B411)

   Pauvre Homme Revenant Du Bois, Un
      mix cor HUG 7666   (B412)

   Pays Du Lac
      mix cor,pno/orch (musical) cor pts HUG 7030   (B413)

   Pays Écoute! (from Images De Mon Pays)
      mix cor,SBar soli,acap/pno HUG 7033   (B414)

   Pays, Tu Es Comme Une Coupe Claire (from Pays Du Lac)
      mix cor,acap/pno HUG 7097   (B415)
      men cor,acap HUG 7069   (B416)

   Pêcheurs, Les (from Images De Mon Pays)
      mix cor,T solo,acap/pno HUG 7032   (B417)

   Petit Gas, Le
      eq voices HUG 7202   (B418)

   Petit Soldat
      see Galé Chudâ

   Petite Chanson
      eq voices HUG 7536   (B419)

   Petite Église De Chez Nous
      eq voices HUG 6591   (B420)

   Petits Airs, Les
      eq voices HUG 7467   (B421)

   Pique La Baleine
      mix cor HUG 7988   (B422)
      see Trois Chansons De Marins

   Prenons-Le, C'est Le Blanc Chemin
      mix cor HUG 6967   (B423)

   Près De La Forêt
      mix cor HUG 6660   (B424)
      men cor HUG 6652   (B425)

   Prière Des Mayentzets (from Pastorale Gruérienne)
      mix cor,acap/pno HUG 7275   (B426)

   Prière Pour Les Morts
      [Russ/Lat/Fr] mix cor HUG 7954   (B427)
      men cor HUG 7959   (B428)

   Que Dieu Protège Ton Voyage
      mix cor HUG 7438   (B429)

   Rendez-Vous Demain Matin
      mix cor HUG 8243   (B430)

   Ronde Des Années, La (from Vignettes)
      mix cor,acap/pno HUG 7578   (B431)

   Ronde Des Chansons, La
      eq voices HUG 7571   (B432)

   Ronde Des Fleurs, La (from Pastorale Gruérienne)
      eq voices,pno/org/orch HUG 7273   (B433)

   Ronde Du Printemps (from Pastorale Gruérienne)
      eq voices,opt pno/org/orch HUG 7286   (B434)

   Saisons À La Sagne, Les
      mix cor,Bar/A solo HUG 6903   (B435)

   Seize Cantiques
      men cor HUG 7193   (B436)

## BOLLER, CARLO (cont'd.)

Sigismond Le Jardinier (from Vignettes)
  mix cor,acap/pno HUG 7576  (B437)
  eq voices,opt pno/org/orch HUG 7628  (B438)

Soldat De Guerre
  mix cor,Bar solo HUG 7579  (B439)

Soldat Qui Pars (from Vignettes)
  mix cor,acap/pno HUG 6878  (B440)

Soldatenlied
  see Au Doux Pays

Sont Les Filles De La Rochelle
  see Trois Chansons De Marins

Sous Les Platanes Du Préau (from Pays Du Lac)
  mix cor,acap/pno HUG 7153  (B441)
  eq voices,opt pno/org/orch HUG 7041  (B442)

Sur Les Routes Du Monde
  mix cor HUG 7241  (B443)
  men cor HUG 7242  (B444)
  eq voices HUG 7243  (B445)

Sylvie
  mix cor,opt pno/org/orch HUG 7084  (B446)
  men cor HUG 7083  (B447)
  eq voices HUG 7090  (B448)

Tambour, Bats Pas Si Fort! (from Images De Mon Pays)
  mix cor,acap/pno HUG 6879  (B449)

Te Voici, Vigneron! (from Pays Du Lac)
  eq voices,opt pno/org/orch HUG 7087  (B450)
  mix cor,acap/pno HUG 7042  (B451)
  men cor,acap HUG 7067  (B452)

Terre De Mon Enfance (from Pays Du Lac)
  mix cor,T/S solo,acap/pno HUG 7103  (B453)
  mix cor,solo voice,acap/pno (Simplified Version) HUG 7103A  (B454)

Terre Vaudoise
  mix cor HUG 7154  (B455)
  men cor HUG 7104  (B456)
  eq voices HUG 7180  (B457)

Tirez Vos Rideaux, Demoiselles (from Vignettes)
  mix cor,acap/pno HUG 7575  (B458)

Tout Ce Pays Aimé
  mix cor HUG 7334  (B459)
  men cor HUG 7338  (B460)
  eq voices HUG 7341  (B461)

Tout Là-Bas Près Des Rochers
  mix cor HUG 7631  (B462)
  eq voices HUG 7637  (B463)

Trois Chansons De Marins
  mix cor HUG f.s.
  contains: Marie-Madelon; Pique La Baleine; Sont Les Filles De La Rochelle  (B464)

Trois Filles En Blanc (from Images De Mon Pays)
  mix cor,acap/pno HUG 6873  (B465)
  eq voices,acap HUG 6976  (B466)

Unsere Dörfer
  [Ger] mix cor HUG 7557  (B467)
  [Ger] men cor HUG 8460  (B468)

Vent, Le
  eq voices HUG 7458  (B469)

Vient Le Jour De La Fiancée
  eq voices HUG 6592  (B470)

Vigne De Printemps, La (from Vignettes)
  mix cor,acap/pno HUG 7573  (B471)
  eq voices,opt pno/org/orch HUG 7599  (B472)
  men cor HUG 8735  (B473)

Vignettes
  mix cor,acap/pno (divertissement) HUG  (B474)

Voici Le Mois De Mai
  HUG 7440  (B475)

BON JOUR, MON COEUR see Lassus, Roland de (Orlandus)

BON SYNDIC, LE see Hemmerling, Carlos

BON VILLAGE, LE see Boller, Carlo

BON VOYAGE, VIN DE MA VIGNE! see Boller, Carlo

BONHEUR AU VILLAGE, LE see Miche, Paul

BONHEUR EST DANS LE PRÉ, LE see Robert-Lalouet, M.

BONHEUR N'EST QU'UN RÊVE,LE see Furrer, Walter

BONHOMME see Graham, R.

BONJOUR AU NOUVEAU-NÉ see Krauer, A

BONNE GRAND'MÈRE, LA see Hemmerling, Carlos

BONNES DAMES DE ST-GERVAIS, LES see Jaques-Dalcroze, Émile

BONNES GENS, APPLAUDISSEZ! see Henchoz, Emile

BONNY BOBBY SHAFTO see Walters, Edmund

BONSOIR see Martin

BOOGIE WOOGIE RHYTHM see Simms, Patsy Ford

BOOGIE WOOGIE SANTA CLAUS
  (Ames, Morgan) SSAB,acap (gr. IV) UNC JP  (B476)

BOOK BAG BOOGIE see Lawrence, Stephen L.

BORDESE, L.
Anges Du Printemps, Les
  mix cor HUG 2186  (B477)

BORISHANSKY, ELLIOT (1930- )
Pippa's Song
  SA THOMP.G VG261  (B478)

BORTNIANSKY, DIMITRI STEPANOVICH (1751-1825)
Vespergesang
  mix cor BÜTZ 176  (B479)

BOSCO, GILBERTO (1946- )
Interludio
  wom cor,fl,clar,4perc ZERBONI 9506  (B480)

BOSHKOFF, RUTH
I Will Bring You Brooches
  unis cor,rec/fl,pno BOOSEY-ENG OCTB6740  (B481)

BOSSI, RENZO (1883-1965)
Cinque Canti Popolari Sardi *CC5U
  cor,acap ZERBONI 4985 f.s.  (B482)

BOULANGER, LILI (1893-1918)
Hymne Au Soleil
  [Fr] SATB,A solo RECITAL 453  (B483)

Soir Sur La Plaine
  [Fr] SATB,STB soli RECITAL 452  (B484)

BOULEAU QUI MURMURE see Janáček, Leoš

BOUMAN
Three Rhymes
  1-2pt treb cor,pno EARTHSNG EW-13  (B485)

BOUQUETS DE ROMANDIE see Miche, Paul

BOURNEL
Chanson De Mai
  4pt men cor BILLAUDOT  (B486)

BOURREE see Bach, Johann Sebastian

BOURRÉE D'AUVERGNE see Dyck, C.

BOURRÉE DES SABOTS see Darcieux, F.

BOVET, J.
A Ta Quenouille
  mix cor HUG 7980  (B487)

Adieu, Sylvie
  mix cor HUG 6116  (B488)

Al La Suisse
  mix cor HUG 3925  (B489)

Allons, Bergers
  mix cor HUG 6189  (B490)

Alpée, L'
  mix cor HUG 7761  (B491)
  men cor HUG 6128  (B492)

Alte Hütlein, Das
  see Vieux Chalet, Le

Angélus, L'
  mix cor HUG 8582  (B493)

Armailli Des Alpettes, L'
  men cor HUG 8780  (B494)

Armailli Des Grands Monts, L'
  mix cor,solo HUG 7511  (B495)
  men cor,T solo HUG 7731  (B496)

## BOVET, J. (cont'd.)

Au Goulot De La Fontaine
  mix cor HUG 8667  (B497)

Au Jardin De Mons Père
  men cor HUG 7757  (B498)

Au Léman
  men cor HUG 6011  (B499)

Au Milieu Des Prés
  mix cor HUG 8285  (B500)

Au Vieux Temps
  mix cor HUG 8433  (B501)
  men cor HUG 8781  (B502)

Baiser De Ma Mère, Le
  mix cor HUG 8433  (B503)

Barcarolle
  "Gretchen Fein" [Fr/Ger] mix cor,T solo HUG 8437  (B504)

Bauernlied
  [Ger] mix cor,T solo HUG 7646  (B505)
  [Ger] men cor,T solo HUG 7647  (B506)
  [Ger] eq voices,solo voice HUG 7645  (B507)

Bel Ange, Le
  mix cor HUG 6110  (B508)

Berceuse Patriotique
  mix cor,solo HUG 7762  (B509)

Berceuse Pour Linettte
  mix cor HUG 8435  (B510)

Campanules, Les
  mix cor HUG 8440  (B511)

C'est Toi
  mix cor HUG 8437  (B512)

Chagrin De Madeleine, Le
  mix cor,S solo HUG 3989  (B513)
  men cor HUG 6388  (B514)

Chanson De L'alpe
  mix cor,fl HUG 8702  (B515)

Chanson Du Tir À La Rose
  mix cor HUG 8378  (B516)

Chanson Du Vent Clair
  mix cor HUG 6068  (B517)
  men cor HUG 6221  (B518)

Chant De L'aurore
  mix cor HUG 6068  (B519)

Chant De Ma Mère, Le
  mix cor,Bar solo HUG 8034  (B520)
  men cor,Bar solo HUG 8706  (B521)

Chant De Mai
  mix cor HUG 2770  (B522)

Chant Des Suisses À L'étranger
  "Lied Des Auslandschweizer" [Ger/Fr] mix cor HUG 7454  (B523)
  "Lied Des Auslandschweizer" [Ger/Fr] men cor HUG 7453  (B524)

Chèvres De Gruyères, Les
  mix cor HUG 8665  (B525)

Chez Nous
  mix cor HUG 7844  (B526)

Choeur Des Jeunes Filles
  3pt cor HUG 8068  (B527)

Cloche Du Bonheur, La
  mix cor,S solo,vcl HUG 8702  (B528)

Coglieremo Un Ramo Di Fiori
  mix cor HUG 8599  (B529)

Dedans Ma Chaumière
  mix cor HUG 8433  (B530)

Dimanche Au Soir
  mix cor HUG 8580  (B531)

Douce Nuit
  mix cor HUG 8511  (B532)
  men cor HUG 8553  (B533)

Eglantine, L'
  mix cor HUG 8704  (B534)

Faire Du Bien
  mix cor HUG 8725  (B535)

Fanfare Du Printemps, La
  mix cor HUG 7230  (B536)
  eq voices HUG 7606  (B537)
  men cor HUG 7026  (B538)

Fidélité
  mix cor HUG 8580  (B539)

**BOVET, J. (cont'd.)**

Flot Et Le Vent, Le
men cor HUG 7758 (B540)

Frühlingsmarsch
[Ger] mix cor,opt pno/org/orch HUG 7643 (B541)
[Ger] men cor,opt pno/org/orch HUG 7644 (B542)
[Ger] eq voices,opt pno/org/orch HUG 7642 (B543)

Galé Gringo
"Joli Gringot" men cor HUG 8598 (B544)

Gavotte Des Priseurs, La
men cor HUG 6161 (B545)

Gentil Coqu'licot
men cor HUG 7757 (B546)

Grand Boeufs Au Labour, Les
men cor HUG 7822 (B547)

Gretchen Fein
see Barcarolle

Helvétie, Ma Patrie
men cor HUG 6417 (B548)

Hymme À La Gruyère
mix cor HUG 8666 (B549)
men cor HUG 8706 (B550)

Hymme Nuptial
mix cor HUG 8663 (B551)

Il Est Un Vieux Pommier
men cor HUG 8432 (B552)

Il Faut Peu De Chose
mix cor HUG 8663 (B553)

Il Passa
mix cor HUG 8438 (B554)

Immortelle De Jean, L'
mix cor HUG 7980 (B555)

Instant Du Bonheur, L'
mix cor HUG 7250 (B556)
men cor HUG 7179 (B557)

Jean De La "Boillette"
men cor HUG 8780 (B558)

Jean L'éclopé
mix cor HUG 8436 (B559)

Jeannette Au Jardinet
mix cor HUG 8580 (B560)

Joli Gringot
see Galé Gringo

Joyeuse Diane
men cor HUG 6417 (B561)

Kan Y'éthé Dzouvenèta
mix cor HUG 6116 (B562)

Là-Bas, Dans Le Hameau
mix cor HUG 8434 (B563)

Là-Haut, Sur La Montagne
mix cor HUG 6116 (B564)

Là-Haut, Tout En Haut
mix cor HUG 7762 (B565)
men cor HUG 7758 (B566)
eq voices HUG 7756 (B567)

Léneli Du Simmeliberg
mix cor HUG 8285 (B568)

Lied Des Auslandschweizer
[Ger] mix cor HUG 7454 (B569)
[Ger] men cor HUG 7453 (B570)
see Chant Des Suisses À L'étranger

Lisa S'en Va Joyeuse
men cor HUG 7757 (B571)

Liseli Du Muhletal
men cor HUG 7489 (B572)

Liuba
mix cor HUG 7761 (B573)
men cor HUG 7758 (B574)

Ma Sarine
mix cor HUG 8828 (B575)

Maïentzets, Les
mix cor HUG 7811 (B576)

Maison Des Ancêtres, La
mix cor HUG 8438 (B577)

March Des Petits Oignons, La
mix cor HUG 7763 (B578)
men cor HUG 3990 (B579)

**BOVET, J. (cont'd.)**

Mariannes Kummer
[Ger] mix cor HUG 7858 (B580)

Mariette
mix cor HUG 8704 (B581)

Méli-Mélo
mix cor HUG 7862 (B582)
men cor HUG 6115 (B583)

Ménétriers De Village
mix cor HUG 8581 (B584)

Mignon Suisse
men cor HUG 6927 (B585)

Misch-Masch
[Ger] men cor HUG 8813 (B586)

Mon Coeur Est Las
mix cor HUG 8435 (B587)

Mon Petit "Chez Nous"
mix cor HUG 7761 (B588)
men cor HUG 7332 (B589)

Mon Village
mix cor HUG 8436 (B590)
men cor HUG 8707 (B591)

Montagne, La
mix cor HUG 8666 (B592)
men cor HUG 8650 (B593)

Montée À L'alpage, La
mix cor HUG 8599 (B594)
men cor HUG 8598 (B595)

Moulin, Le
eq voices HUG 7249 (B596)

Noces, Les
mix cor (Petite Suite) HUG 8068 (B597)

Notre Suisse
"Unsere Schweiz" [Fr/Ger] mix cor HUG 6694 (B598)
"Unsere Schweiz" [Fr/Ger] men cor HUG 6928 (B599)
"Unsere Schweiz" [Fr/Ger] 1-2 eq voices HUG 8149 (B600)
"Unsere Schweiz" [Fr/Ger] 4 eq voices HUG 7638 (B601)

O Mariette, Joliette
mix cor HUG 7760 (B602)

Par Jeu!
mix cor HUG 8439 (B603)

Pardon De Madeleine, Le
mix cor HUG 8664 (B604)

Pavane Des Pingouins, La
men cor HUG 6403 (B605)

Paysan, Que Ton Chant S'élève
mix cor,T solo HUG 7510 (B606)
mix cor,S solo HUG 7639 (B607)
men cor HUG 7520 (B608)
eq voices,S solo HUG 7639 (B609)

Perce-Neige, Les
mix cor HUG 8440 (B610)

Petit Coeur
mix cor HUG 8667 (B611)

Petite Marjolaine
mix cor HUG 6116 (B612)

Petits Chevriers, Les
mix cor HUG 7760 (B613)

Pourquoi N'être Pas Gai?
mix cor HUG 8378 (B614)

Poya, La (La Montée À L'alpage)
mix cor HUG 8599 (B615)

Prélude
mix cor HUG 8068 (B616)

Prière Du Pâtre, La
mix cor HUG 7863 (B617)
men cor HUG 8553 (B618)

Quand Ma Mère Chantait
mix cor,Bar solo HUG 8664 (B619)

Raclette Valaisanne, La
mix cor HUG 8703 (B620)
men cor HUG 8311 (B621)

Ramage Opportun
mix cor HUG 8433 (B622)

Ransignolets Du Bois Joli
mix cor HUG 8434 (B623)

Ranz Des Vaches, Le
mix cor HUG 6695 (B624)
men cor HUG 8650 (B625)

**BOVET, J. (cont'd.)**

Rappel Du Foyer, Le
mix cor HUG 8511 (B626)

Refrain De L'oiseau, Le
mix cor HUG 8725 (B627)

Retour Des Frontières
men cor HUG 6397 (B628)

Rêver
men cor HUG 8432 (B629)

Ronde Des Mouettes, La
mix cor/2 eq voices HUG 8725 (B630)

Roses, Les
mix cor HUG 8440 (B631)

Ruisseau, Le
mix cor HUG 8665 (B632)
men cor HUG 8707 (B633)

Salade À La "Doucette", La
mix cor HUG 8705 (B634)

Secret Du Ruisseau, Le
mix cor HUG 7844 (B635)
men cor HUG 8781 (B636)

Seulette Suis, Sans Mon Berger
eq voices HUG 7756 (B637)

Simple Histoire
mix cor HUG 7863 (B638)
men cor HUG 8553 (B639)

Souvenirs Du Temps Passé, Les
mix cor HUG 7760 (B640)
men cor HUG 7757 (B641)

Suite Fleurie
mix cor HUG 8440 (B642)

Sur Les Flancs Du Moléson
men cor HUG 7822 (B643)

Terre Où J'ai Vu Le Jour
men cor HUG 3664 (B644)

Tout Là-Haut
mix cor HUG 6116 (B645)

Unsere Schweiz
see Notre Suisse

Valse Des Feuilles, La
men cor HUG 7956 (B646)

Véroniques, Les
mix cor HUG 8440 (B647)

Vers Mon Village
mix cor HUG 8582 (B648)

Vieux Chalet, Le
"Alte Hütlein, Das" [Fr/Ger] mix cor HUG 7640 (B649)
"Alte Hütlein, Das" [Fr/Ger] eq voices HUG 7346 (B650)
"Alte Hütlein, Das" [Fr/Ger] men cor HUG 3664 (B651)

Vieux Léman, Le
mix cor HUG 3640 (B652)
men cor HUG 3641 (B653)

Vignobles
mix cor HUG 8703 (B654)

Village Au Bord De L'eau, Le
mix cor HUG 8034 (B655)

Yogueli Et Vréneli
mix cor HUG 8511 (B656)
men cor HUG 8553 (B657)

"Youtse", La
mix cor HUG 7761 (B658)
men cor HUG 7758 (B659)

**BOYCE, WILLIAM (1711-1779)**
Together Let Us Range The Fields
(Bartlett, Ian) 2pt cor BANKS ECS 227 (B660)

**BOZAY, ATTILA (1939- )**
Drei Quartette *CC3U
BREITKOPF-W CHB5249 f.s. (B661)

**BRAHMS, JOHANNES (1833-1897)**
Au Pied D'un Saule Qui Pleure
eq voices HUG 8006 (B662)

Barcarolle
eq voices HUG 8006 (B663)

Berceuse
see Wiegenlied

Canons For Women's Voices, Op. 113 (G)
wom cor JERONA JC1006 (B664)

BRAHMS, JOHANNES (cont'd.)

   Cor A Lancé Son Appel, Le
    see Ich Schwing Mein Horn

   Gypsy Song No. 5
    see Zigeunerlieder

   Hüt Du Dich
    see Three Brahms Songs For Women's Choir

   Ich Schwing Mein Horn
    "Cor A Lancé Son Appel, Le" men cor
    HUG 8096 (B665)

   Je Dois Partir
    mix cor HUG 7887 (B666)

   Jour De Grâce
    mix cor HUG 8519 (B667)

   Jour De Mai
    mix cor HUG 7943 (B668)

   Klänge #1
    see Three Brahms Songs For Women's Choir

   Klänge #2
    see Three Brahms Songs For Women's Choir

   Liebeslieder - Walzer, Op. 52
    (Hindermann, Paul) 3pt wom cor,pno
    kbd pt,cor pts MULLES (B669)

   Ma Douce Enfant
    mix cor HUG 7943 (B670)

   Madrigal
    mix cor HUG 7887 (B671)

   Sandman, The
    (Gallina) 2pt cor SHAWNEE EA-0207 (B672)

   Three Brahms Songs For Women's Choir
    (from Fünf Duette Op.66)
    SA,pno GENTRY JG218 f.s.
    contains: Hüt Du Dich; Klänge #1; Klänge #2 (B673)

   Three Brahms Songs For Womens Chorus
    *CC3U
    wom cor GENTRY JG2180 f.s. (B674)

   Walesnacht
    mix cor BUTZ 201 (B675)

   Wiegenlied
    "Berceuse" [Ger/Fr] men cor,T/S solo HUG 8423 (B676)
    "Berceuse" [Ger/Fr] mix cor,S solo HUG 8356 (B677)
    (Porterfield, Sherri) 3pt mix cor WARNER SV9435 (B678)

   Zigeunerlieder
    (Fleet) "Gypsy Song No. 5" SATB KJOS 8786 (B679)

BRAND, THEO (1925- )
   Fuchs Und Die Trauben, Der
    wom cor BOHM (B680)

BRASSENS, GEORGES
   Gastibelza
    [Fr] SATB,acap A COEUR JOIE 058 (B681)

BRAUN, YEHESKIEL (1922- )
   Duo Medii Aevi Cantica
    "Two Medieval Songs" [Lat] 3pt girl cor,acap ISR.MUS.INST. IMI 7015 (B682)

   Fifteen Passover Songs *CC15U
    3-4pt mix cor,acap ISR.MUS.INST. IMI 6486 f.s. (B683)

   King Solomon's Proverbs *CC28U,canon
    2-3 eq voices ISR.MUS.INST. IMI 6962 f.s. (B684)

   Proverbs *cant
    3pt jr cor,fl&harp ISR.MUS.INST. IMI 6957 (B685)

   Two Medieval Songs
    see Duo Medii Aevi Cantica

BRAUTCHOR AUS "LOHENGRIN" see Wagner, Richard

BRAY
   Annie Laurie
    SATB WARCH 34486 (B686)

   White Butterflies
    unis cor WARCH 35661 (B687)

BRAY, JULIE GARDNER
   Afternoon On A Hill
    SATB,opt fl HERITAGE 15-1182H (B688)

   April Rain Song
    3pt mix cor HERITAGE 15-1089 (B689)

BRAY, JULIE GARDNER (cont'd.)

   Be The Stream That Oxbows
    3pt mix cor HERITAGE 15-1185H (B690)

   Follow The Drinkin' Gourd
    3pt mix cor,opt solo,pno HERITAGE 15-1115 (B691)
    SATB HERITAGE 15-1116 (B692)

BREARD
   Allée, L'
    4pt men cor BILLAUDOT (B693)

   Chant De La Bière, Le
    4pt men cor BILLAUDOT (B694)

   Chant De La Gitane, Le
    4pt mix cor BILLAUDOT (B695)

   Chant De La Méditerranée, Le
    4pt mix cor BILLAUDOT (B696)

   Chant De La Mine, Le
    4pt men cor BILLAUDOT (B697)

   Chant De La Rose, Le
    4pt men cor BILLAUDOT (B698)

   Chant De La Terre, Le
    4pt men cor BILLAUDOT (B699)

   Chant Des Bergers Grecs, Le
    4pt men cor BILLAUDOT (B700)

   Chant Des Cimes, Le
    4pt men cor BILLAUDOT (B701)

   Chant Des Lilas, Le
    4pt men cor BILLAUDOT (B702)

   Chant Des Lys, Le
    4pt mix cor BILLAUDOT (B703)

   Chant Des Marguerites, Le
    4pt mix cor BILLAUDOT (B704)

   Chant Des Mimosas, Le
    4pt men cor BILLAUDOT (B705)

   Chant Des Oeillets, Le
    4pt men cor BILLAUDOT (B706)

   Chant Des Orangers, Le
    4pt mix cor BILLAUDOT (B707)

   Chant Des Violettes, Le
    4pt men cor BILLAUDOT (B708)

   Chant D'orient, Le
    4pt mix cor BILLAUDOT (B709)

   Chant Du Muguet, Le
    4pt men cor BILLAUDOT (B710)

   Chant Du Myosotis, Le
    4pt mix cor BILLAUDOT (B711)

   Chant Du Soir
    2pt wom cor BILLAUDOT (B712)

   Chant Du Soir, Le
    4pt men cor BILLAUDOT (B713)

   Charlatan, Le
    4pt men cor BILLAUDOT (B714)

   Chien Et Le Chat, Le
    4pt men cor BILLAUDOT (B715)

   Éléphant Blanc, L'
    4pt men cor BILLAUDOT (B716)

   Goelands, Les
    4pt mix cor BILLAUDOT (B717)

   Horloge, L'
    4pt men cor BILLAUDOT (B718)

   Hymne Au Vin
    4pt men cor BILLAUDOT (B719)
    4pt mix cor BILLAUDOT (B720)

   Hymne Aux Nations Latines
    2pt wom cor BILLAUDOT (B721)

   Lierre Et Le Thym, Le
    4pt mix cor BILLAUDOT (B722)

   Onze Novembre
    4pt men cor BILLAUDOT (B723)

   Parias, Les
    4pt men cor BILLAUDOT (B724)

   Rencontre De Fête
    4pt wom cor BILLAUDOT (B725)

   Roi De Perse, Le
    2pt wom cor BILLAUDOT (B726)

   Rossignol Et Le Prince, Le
    3 eq voices BILLAUDOT (B727)

BREATHING EARTH, THE see Ota, Sakurako

BREMER, JETSE (1959- )
   Sailor By My Right, A
    SATB,acap LAWSON 52699 (B728)

BRENTA, GASTON (1902-1969)
   Deux Choeurs Sur Un Poème De Th. Gauthier *CC2U
    3 eq voices,S solo BILLAUDOT f.s. (B729)

BRERO, CESARE (1908-1973)
   Sette Quartine D'omar Khayyâm
    cor,female solo,2.0.2.0. 4.4.3.1. perc,elec gtr,cel,2pno RICORDI-IT (B730)

BRICOLEUR, LE see Henchoz, Emile

BRICUSSE
   Gonna Build A Mountain (composed with Newley)
    2pt treb cor WARCH 34799 (B731)
    SATB WARCH 34800 (B732)

   Wonderful Day Like Today, A (composed with Newley)
    SSA WARCH 34813 (B733)

BRICUSSE, LESLIE (1931- )
   Who Can I Turn To? (composed with Newley, Anthony)
    (Althouse) SSA ALFRED 11377 (B734)
    (Althouse) SATB ALFRED 11375 (B735)
    (Althouse) SAB ALFRED 11376 (B736)

BRIGHT CAP AND STREAMERS see Sowash, Rick

BRIGHT JOURNEYS; SONGS OF LOVE AND LIGHT see Gawthrop, Daniel E.

BRIGHT LIGHTS see Kern

BRIGHTLY SHINES THE MOON
  (Sveshnikov, A.) "Svetit Svetel Mesiats" [Russ] SATB RUSSICA FS 003 (B737)

BRING HIM HOME see Schonberg, Claude-Michel

BRINGE GRÜSSE, KLEINES VÖGELEIN see Meier, M.

BRINGS, ALLEN STEPHEN (1934- )
   Mountain Song
    SATB,pno MUSIC SEV. 740 (B738)

BRITTEN, [SIR] BENJAMIN (1913-1976)
   Company Of Heaven, The
    SATB,ST&narrator,timp,org,strings pno-cond sc FABER 50481203 (B739)

   Lone Dog
    unis cor BOOSEY-ENG OCTB6738 (B740)

BRITTSOMMARMÅLAREN see Janunger, Kjell

BROADLEY, SHARON
   Best Is Yet-It Ain't Necessari'ly So, The
    cor (gr. III) UNC JP (B741)

   Happying
    SATB,perc (gr. III) UNC JP (B742)

   Steppin' Out-Puttin' On The Ritz
    3pt cor (gr. III) UNC JP (B743)

   Walkin'
    SATB,perc (gr. II) UNC JP (B744)

BROADWAY LADIES
  (Kern, Philip) SSA (medley incl. We're In The Money, Big Spender & Whatever Lola Wants) WARNER CM9586 ipa (B745)

BROBERG, ROBERT KARL OSKAR (1940- )
   Beach Party *CC3U
    (Strand, Michael) mix cor,acap SVERIG SK 769 f.s. (B746)

   Beach Party
    (Strand, Michael) TTB,pno SVERIG SK 771 (B747)

   Tre Låtar Till
    (Strand, Michael) mix cor,acap SVERIG SK 770 (B748)

BROEGE, TIMOTHY (1947- )
   Micah's Words
    SATB,pno ALLAIR (B749)

   Songs Of Walt Whitman
    SSA,pno ALLAIR (B750)

   Sun Heart
    SATB,pno ALLAIR (B751)

   Three Chinese Lyrics
    SATB,acap ALLAIR (B752)

BRON, PATRICK
  Album De Famille, L'
    see Images De Soleil

  Amis, C'est Ma Tournée!
    men cor HUG 8793                    (B753)

  Anniversaire De Grand-Papa, L'
    see Images De Soleil

  Appel
    men cor HUG 8838                    (B754)

  Berceuse
    eq voices HUG 8846                  (B755)

  Bicyclettes, Les
    see Images De Soleil

  Brune Aux Yeux Verts, La
    see Images De Soleil

  Chanson Du Croquant, La
    men cor HUG 8723                    (B756)

  Fête Des Chanteurs, La
    see Images De Soleil

  Images De Soleil
    mix cor HUG f.s.
      contains: Album De Famille, L';
        Anniversaire De Grand-Papa, L';
        Bicyclettes, Les; Brune Aux
        Yeux Verts, La; Fête Des
        Chanteurs, La                   (B757)

  Liqueur Des Mots, La
    mix cor HUG 8837                    (B758)

  Marie-Marion
    men cor HUG 8728                    (B759)

  Marie Mieux-Aimée
    mix cor HUG 8858                    (B760)

  Petite Soeur En Fleurs
    mix cor HUG 8792                    (B761)

  Pigeon Vole!
    3 eq voices HUG 8662                (B762)

  Sérénade Sans Guitare
    men cor HUG 8847                    (B763)

  Soir, Le
    men cor HUG 8845                    (B764)

  Tartarin De Tarascon
    mix cor HUG 8722                    (B765)

  Terre Et L'étoile, La
    mix cor&men cor&wom cor,narrator,
    opt pno (chorale suite) HUG         (B766)

  Tu Es Le Pays
    mix cor HUG 8859                    (B767)

BROOKS, GARTH
  River,The (composed with Shaw,
    Victoria)
    (Strommen, Carl) SATB WARNER
      2805RC1X                          (B768)
    (Strommen, Carl) SAB WARNER
      2805RC3X                          (B769)
    (Strommen, Carl) 2pt cor WARNER
      2805RC5X                          (B770)

BROOMS
  (Rubtsov, F.) "Veniki" [Russ] SATB
    RUSSICA FS 002                      (B771)

BROQUET, LOUIS (1888-1954)
  Âme Du Vin, L'
    men cor HUG 6962                    (B772)

  Bateau, Le
    mix cor HUG 7682                    (B773)

  Beau Chevalier
    men cor HUG 6960                    (B774)

  Beau Pays, Le
    eq voices HUG 7101                  (B775)

  Calme Du Soir
    mix cor HUG 7877                    (B776)

  Catherine De Finhaut
    see Deux Chansons Valaisannes

  Catherine De Finhaut, La (from Deux
    Chansons Valaisannes)
    mix cor HUG 7879                    (B777)
    men cor HUG 7073                    (B778)

  C'est La Fête Du Hameau
    mix cor HUG 7876                    (B779)

  C'est Le Vent Du Printemps
    men cor HUG 7100                    (B780)

  C'était Un Garçon Bien Sage...
    mix cor HUG 7308                    (B781)

BROQUET, LOUIS (cont'd.)
  Colin
    mix cor HUG 6449                    (B782)

  Comme Il Fait Noir
    mix cor HUG 7905                    (B783)

  Dans Les Bois
    mix cor HUG 7063                    (B784)

  Deux Chansonnettes
    men cor HUG 7197 f.s.
      contains: Ecoutez, Là-Bas...;
        Jour Est Près D'éclore, Le
                                        (B785)

  Deux Chansons Valaisannes
    men cor HUG 7073 f.s.
      contains: Catherine De Finhaut;
        Héritage, L'                    (B786)

  Ecoutez, Là-Bas...
    see Deux Chansonnettes

  Farandole
    mix cor HUG 7236                    (B787)

  Fille Du Vigneron, La
    men cor HUG 7880                    (B788)

  Fleuve, Le
    mix cor HUG 7792                    (B789)

  Gentil Coqu'licot
    mix cor HUG 6449                    (B790)

  Gloire Au Seigneur
    mix cor HUG 8465                    (B791)

  Grenouille Et Boeuf, La
    men cor HUG 7676                    (B792)

  Héritage, L' (from Deux Chansons
    Valaisannes)
    mix cor HUG 7879                    (B793)
    men cor HUG 7073                    (B794)
    see Deux Chansons Valaisannes

  Hymne À La Charité
    mix cor HUG 7664                    (B795)

  Hymne À La Sagesse
    mix cor HUG 7767                    (B796)

  Hymne Du Matin
    mix cor HUG 7387                    (B797)

  Jour, Le
    mix cor HUG 7990                    (B798)

  Jour Est Près D'éclore, Le
    see Deux Chansonnettes

  Là-Haut
    men cor HUG 7099                    (B799)

  Malbrouk
    mix cor HUG 7662                    (B800)

  Moisson, La
    mix cor HUG 7307                    (B801)

  Moissonneurs
    men cor HUG 7532                    (B802)

  Mon Pays, Sois Satisfait De Ta Beauté
    men cor HUG 6811                    (B803)

  Mon Père Avait Cinq Cents Moutons
    mix cor HUG 6448                    (B804)

  Nuits D'été
    mix cor HUG 7878                    (B805)

  Renouveau
    men cor HUG 7490                    (B806)

  Ronde Fantasque
    eq voices HUG 7064                  (B807)

  Rose, La
    men cor HUG 7883                    (B808)

  Soir, Le
    mix cor HUG 7306                    (B809)

  Soir Sur Lelac
    eq voices HUG 7470                  (B810)

  Veux-Tu De Mon Coeur
    mix cor HUG 7875                    (B811)

  Vieux Chalets, Les
    men cor HUG 7533                    (B812)

  Vieux Pays, Le
    mix cor HUG 8110                    (B813)

BROUGHTON
  A La Claire Fontaine
    SSA WARCH 34401                     (B814)

  Just Like Me-The Telephone Wires
    unis cor WARCH 35658                (B815)

BROUGHTON (cont'd.)
  My Caterpillar
    unis cor WARCH 34377                (B816)

  No Mouth
    unis cor WARCH 34378                (B817)

  Nursery Rhyme Nonsense
    unis cor WARCH 34379                (B818)

  Wheels
    unis cor WARCH 35660                (B819)

BROUGHTON, BOBBY
  I'll Carry You In My Heart
    SATB GILPIN HT9301                  (B820)

BROUGHTON, MARILYN
  A La Fontaine
    unis cor THOMP.G VG1005             (B821)
    SSA THOMP.G VG336                   (B822)

  Baseball
    unis cor THOMP.G VG1012             (B823)

  Hockey
    unis cor THOMP.G VG1014             (B824)

BROUILLARD see Gesseney, L.

BROWN, NACIO HERB (1896-1964)
  Singin' In The Rain
    (Tini, A.A.) SSATTB,acap (gr. III)
    UNC JP                              (B825)

BROWN, RAYNER (1912-    )
  Four Songs For Women's Chorus
    wom cor,fl,bsn,vcl BROWN,R          (B826)

  Letania De Nuestro Señor Don Quijote
    cor,brass,perc BROWN,R              (B827)

BRUBECK, DAVID (DAVE) WARREN
  (1920-    )
  Blue Rondo A La Turk
    (Swingle, Ward) SSAATTBB,acap (gr.
    IV) voc pt,pts UNC JP SJ-3          (B828)

BRÜCKE ZU ALLEN KINDERN,EINE see
  Schwaen, Kurt

BRÜCKENBOGEN B,DER see Kretzschmar,
  Günther

BRUCKNER, ANTON (1824-1896)
  Arneth-Kantate (from Kritische
    Gesamtausgabe, B XXII)
    SATTBB,TTBB soli,0.0.0.0. 3.2.1.0.
    MUSIKWISS. ISMN M-50025-033-3
                                        (B829)

  Entsagen (from Kritische
    Gesamtausgabe, B XXII)
    SATB,S/T solo,org/pno MUSIKWISS.
    ISMN M-50025-033-3                  (B830)

  Fest-Kantata (from Kritische
    Gesamtausgabe, B XXII)
    TTBB, Bar solo,2.2.0+2clar in D+
    2clar in A.2. 4.3.3.1. timp
    MUSIKWISS. ISMN M-50025-034-0
                                        (B831)

  Festgesang (from Kritische
    Gesamtausgabe, B XXII)
    SATB,STB soli,pno MUSIKWISS.
    ISMN M-50025-033-3                  (B832)

  Germanenzug (from Kritische
    Gesamtausgabe, B XXII)
    TTBB,solo voice,brass MUSIKWISS.
    ISMN M-50025-033-3                  (B833)

  Helgoland (from Kritische
    Gesamtausgabe, B XXII)
    TTBB,solo voice,2.2.2.2. 4.3.3.1.
    timp,cym,strings MUSIKWISS.
    ISMN M-50025-033-3                  (B834)

  Mayr-Kantate (from Kritische
    Gesamtausgabe, B XXII)
    TTBB,TTBB soli,0.2.0.2. 3.2.3.0.
    MUSIKWISS. ISMN M-50025-033-3
                                        (B835)

  Vergissmeinnicht (from Kritische
    Gesamtausgabe, B XXII)
    SSAATTBB,SATB soli,pno MUSIKWISS.
    ISMN M-50025-033-3                  (B836)

BRUGK, HANS MELCHIOR (1909-    )
  Musik, Op. 34 No. 6
    men cor,acap BOHM                   (B837)

BRUN, FRITZ (1878-1959)
  Bauernregel
    wom cor,acap MULLES                 (B838)

  Er Ist's
    wom cor,acap MULLES                 (B839)

  Frühlinsruhe
    wom cor,acap MULLES                 (B840)

  Gebet
    wom cor,acap MULLES                 (B841)
    men cor,acap MULLES                 (B842)

**BRUN, FRITZ** (cont'd.)
   In Der Nacht
     wom cor,acap MULLES (B843)

   Lebewohl, Du Fühlest Nicht
     wom cor,acap MULLES (B844)

   Mausefallensprüchlein
     wom cor,acap MULLES (B845)

   Morgen, Der
     wom cor,acap MULLES (B846)

   Nachtlied
     wom cor,acap MULLES (B847)

   Scheiden Und Meiden
     wom cor,acap MULLES (B848)

   Schmied, Der
     wom cor,acap MULLES (B849)

   Verlassene, Die
     wom cor,acap MULLES (B850)

   Vom Himmel Abe Chunt E Stärn
     wom cor,acap MULLES (B851)

**BRUNE AUX YEUX VERTS, LA** see Bron, Patrick

**BRUNEL**
   Hymne Aux Morts Pour La Patrie
     4pt men cor,Bar solo BILLAUDOT (B852)

**BRUNNER**
   O Music
     SATB,pno,vcl BOOSEY-ENG OCTB6800 (B853)
     2pt treb cor,pno,vcl BOOSEY-ENG OCTB6798 (B854)

   Still, Still, Still
     mix cor BOOSEY-ENG OCTB6757 (B855)

   Winter Changes
     unis cor BOOSEY-ENG OCTB6753 (B856)

**BRURAMARSJ FRÅ OSRE**
   (Bøe, Bernt) 3pt mix cor,acap NOTON N-9323 (B857)

**BRYARS, GAVIN**
   Glorious Hill
     men cor SCHOTTS ED 12461 (B858)

**BRYDSON, JOHN**
   Merry Month Of May, The
     SATB BANKS 1406 (B859)

**BUCCHI, VALENTINO** (1916-1976)
   Colloquio Corale
     cor,narrator,solo,0.3.0.3. 0.3.0.0. perc,strings sc RICORDI-IT 132011 (B860)

**BÛCHERON, QUITTE TA HACHE!** see Kaelin, Pierre

**BÛCHERONS, LES** see Doret, Gustave

**BUISSON**
   Amant Discret, L'
     4pt men cor BILLAUDOT (B861)

**BULLET TRAIN** see Ritenour, Lee

**BUNDES-SCHWUR** see Schmid, Walter

**BUNDES-TREUE** see Schmid, Walter

**BUNDESLIED** see Beethoven, Ludwig van

**BUNGART, HEINRICH**
   Am Brünnelein
     men cor,acap MULLES (B862)

**BURGE, JOHN** (1961- )
   That We May Not Lose Loss
     [Eng] SATB,S solo,2(pic).2.2.2. 2.2.3.1. timp,2perc,strings CAN.MUS.CENT. (B863)

**BURGER, DAVID MARK** (1950- )
   Hatikvah
     [Heb] SATB,pno (med) HAZA HZ-031 (B864)

   We Came To Sing In Jerusalem
     [Eng] SATB,solo voice,pno (med) HAZA HZ-032 (B865)

**BURKARD, WILLI**
   Alte Guggisberger Lied, Das
     wom cor,acap MULLES (B866)

   Bärn, Du Edle Schizerstärn
     wom cor,acap MULLES (B867)

   Es Burebüebli Mah-N-I Nid
     wom cor,acap MULLES (B868)

   Mond Ist Aufgegangen, Der
     wom cor,acap MULLES (B869)

**BURKARD, WILLI** (cont'd.)
   Ranz Des Vaches, Le
     wom cor,acap MULLES (B870)

   Vom Himmel Abe Chunt E Stärn
     wom cor,acap MULLES (B871)

**BURKE**
   But Beautiful (composed with Van Heusen; Zegree)
     SATB SHAWNEE A-1991 (B872)

**BURKHART, F.**
   Aus Österreichs Bergen
     wom cor,kbd/orch BOHM (B873)

   Es Taget Vor Dem Walde
     mix cor,opt bass inst BOHM (B874)

**BURNELL, MARK**
   Spring Can Really Hang You Up The Most
     SATB,acap (gr. IV) UNC JP (B875)

   Star Spangled Banner
     (Burnell, Mark) SATB,acap (gr. III) UNC JP (B876)

**BURRELL, DIANA** (1948- )
   Lights And Shadows
     jr cor/SATB,0.0.0.0. 2.3.2.2. rec, 2perc,vla,vcl voc sc UNITED MUS perf mat rent (B877)

   Night Songs
     SATB,S solo,orch UNITED MUS (B878)

**BURRITT, LLOYD** (1940- )
   Two Great Soaring Eagles
     SATB,pno, rain sticks CAN.MUS.CENT. (B879)

**BURROUGHS**
   Consider It Pure Joy
     SATB,fl KJOS GC156 (B880)

**BÜRTHEL, JAKOB** (1926- )
   Neue Quodlibets *CCU
     FIDULA 6015 f.s. from well-known canons, folksongs, and children songs (B881)

**BUSSOTTI, SYLVANO** (1931- )
   Siciliano
     TB BERBEN BERBEN 9937 (B882)

**BUT BEAUTIFUL** see Burke

**BUTLER**
   Sweet Spring
     SSA LESLIE 3053 (B883)

**BUTTON UP YOUR OVERCOAT**
   (Anderson, Milton) SATB WARNER CH9539 (B884)
   (Anderson, Milton) SAB WARNER CH9540 (B885)
   (Anderson, Milton) SSA WARNER CH9541 (B886)

**BUTZ, J.CHR.**
   Furchtsame Jäger, Der
     SAB BUTZ 1313 (B887)

**BUTZ, JOSEF** (1891-1989)
   Wenn Die Bettelleute Tanzen
     mix cor BUTZ 719 (B888)

**BUXTEHUDE, DIETRICH** (ca. 1637-1707)
   Be Joyful With Singing
     (Liebergen) SAB,opt fl WARNER SV9535 (B889)

**BY FIRE** see Lang

**BYE, BYE BABY** see Ray

**BYE, BYE BLACKBIRD**
   (Arabiantini, April) SSAA,acap (gr. III/gr. IV) UNC JP (B890)
   (Mccullough, Jim) SATB,pno,db,perc (gr. III) UNC JP (B891)
   see Henderson

**BYGONE DAYS** see Smart, Henry Thomas

**BYKER HILL** see Three North Country Folk Songs

**BYRD, WILLIAM** (1543-1623)
   Though Amaryllis Dance
     (Swingle, Ward) SATTB (gr. II) voc pt,pts UNC JP SM-5 (B892)

# C

**CABENA, BARRIE** (1933- )
   Music Hath Charms
     SATB,harp/kbd CAN.MUS.CENT. (C1)

**CABLE**
   Sing Sea To Sea
     SSA WARCH 35231 (C2)

**CABLE, HOWARD**
   Anne Of Green Gables
     SSA THOMP.G VG346 (C3)
     SATB THOMP.G VG472 (C4)

   Canadian Errant, Un
     see Pastiche Qubecois

   Dans Tous Les Cantons
     see Pastiche Qubecois

   Pastiche Qubecois
     SATB,brass pts THOMP.G f.s. contains: Canadian Errant, Un; Dans Tous Les Cantons (C5)

   Up On A Rooftop
     SATB THOMP.G VEI1127 (C6)

**CACCINI, GIULIO** (1546-1618)
   Nuove Musiche, Le *cant
     SCELTE (C7)

   Nuove Musiche E Nuova Maniera Di Scriverle *cant
     SCELTE (C8)

**CADET ROUSSELLE** see Naudier

**CADOW, PAUL** (1908- )
   Es War Einmal
     men cor,bass inst BOHM (C9)

   Herbstwind
     mix cor,acap BOHM (C10)

**CAECILIA I** *CC65U
   eq voices,acap HUG 7441 f.s. (C11)

**CAECILIA II** *CC63U
   eq voices,acap HUG 7481 f.s. (C12)

**CAECILIAM CANTATE** see Galante, Carlo

**CALENDAR GIRLS**
   (Funk, Jeff) TTB (medley incl. Pretty Woman, Chantilly Lace, Runaround Sue & Calendar Girl) WARNER C0314C4X (C13)

**CALICE DES BAISERS, LE** see Mermoud, Robert

**CALKIN, J. BAPTISTE** (1827-1905)
   Chivalry Of Labour, The
     (Dicks, E.A.) SATB BANKS 534 (C14)

**CALL, THE** see Vaughan Williams, Ralph

**CALME DU SOIR** see Broquet, Louis see Mayor, Ch.

**CALP YO' HANDS (CLAP YOUR HANDS)** see Gershwin, George

**CALVARY**
   (Shaw) SATB,Bar solo LEONARD-US 50303980 (C15)

**CALVERT**
   Cape Breton Lullaby
     SATB WARCH 34487 (C16)
     SSA WARCH 34403 (C17)

   When I Wake In The Morning
     SATB WARCH 35677 (C18)

**CALVERT, STUART**
   Fare Thee Well Love
     SSA THOMP.G VG350 (C19)
     SATB THOMP.G VG477 (C20)

   Ye Banks And Braes
     SSA THOMP.G VG345 (C21)
     SATB THOMP.G VA4003 (C22)

**CALYPSO CAROL** see Perry

**CALYPSO NOEL** see Spevacek, Linda

**CAMEL, KNEEL SOFTLY** see Schram, Ruth Elaine

**CAMEROON** see Majuka, Dorothy

**CAMILLERI, CHARLES** (1931- )
   Malta Yok!
     SATB,acap ROBERTON 63235 (C23)
     SSAA,acap ROBERTON 75408 (C24)
     TTBB,acap ROBERTON 53155 (C25)

CAMISCIOLI, STEFANN (1948-    )
    Diffugere Nives
        mix cor,acap ZERBONI 8393    (C26)

CAMP,THE see Grainger, Percy Aldridge

CAMPANE DI SERA see Kreis, Otto

CAMPANE NEL VESPERO see Torti, Lorenzo

CAMPANULES, LES see Bovet, J.

CAMPBELL-TOWELL, LEE
    Betsy Ross Rag
        SOUTHERN SC486    (C27)

    Colors Of America, The
        3pt cor oct SOUTHERN SC435    (C28)

    Hats Off! To America
        SA oct SOUTHERN SC444    (C29)

    I Am A Child
        SOUTHERN SC462    (C30)

CAMPSIE
    Christmas Lullaby
        SSA WARCH 35248    (C31)

CAMPTOWN RACES, DE see Poné, Gundaris

CAMPTOWN RACES, THE see Foster, Stephen Collins

CAN SANTA MAKE IT THROUGH TONIGHT? see Althouse, Jay

CANADIAN ERRANT, UN see Cable, Howard

CANCION see Encinar, Jose Ramon

CANCION CON TODOS see Isella, César

CANCIONES DE CUNA see Grau, Alberto

CANCIONES POPULARES DE TODO EL MUNDO VOL.I *CC9L
    (Russo, Antonio) 2-3pt cor (easy) LAGOS f.s.    (C32)

CANCIONES POPULARES DE TODO EL MUNDO VOL.II *CC9L
    (Russo, Antonio) 2-3pt cor (easy/med) LAGOS f.s.    (C33)

CANCONETAS VOOR ANA-CATARINA, OP. 95 see Kersters, Willem

CANNON, DAVID
    Good Life
        SATB/SATBB,acap (gr. III) UNC JP    (C34)

CANON see Bach, Johann Sebastian see Toebosch, Louis see Tuinen, Feike van

CANONI SUI PRINCIPI ELEMENTARI see Sabbatini, Antonio Luigi

CANONS see Mozart, Wolfgang Amadeus

CANONS FOR WOMEN'S VOICES, OP. 113 (G) see Brahms, Johannes

CAN'T YOU HEAR THOSE FREEDOM BELLS RINGING?
    (Mclin) SATB KJOS 8763    (C35)

CANTAR FRIULANO see Anonymous

CANTAR VENETO see Anonymous

CANTATA see Husa, Karel

CANTATA CAMPESTRE see Beethoven, Ludwig van

CANTATA HURBINEK, LA see Arrigo, Girolamo

CANTATE D'ELISABEAU see Planel, Jean

CANTATE DES SAISONS see Sauguet, Henri

CANTE JONDO see Tamas, Janos

CANTELOUBE, JOSEPH
    A L'ombre D'un Ormeau *17th cent
        mix cor BILLAUDOT    (C36)

    Ah! Maudit Soit L'amour!
        see Trois Chansons De France

    Amour De Moi, L'
        mix cor BILLAUDOT    (C37)

    Avril *16th cent
        mix cor BILLAUDOT    (C38)

    Beau Papillon, Vit', Marie-Toi!
        see Trois Chansons De France

    C'est À Paris Dans Un Vert Pré
        see Trois Chansons De France

CANTELOUBE, JOSEPH (cont'd.)
    Dodo, Nanette
        eq voices,solo voice HUG 7047    (C39)

    Du Temps Que J'allais Voir Ma Mie
        3 eq voices HUG 8596    (C40)

    Elle Est La Fill' D'un Laboureur
        see Trois Chansons De France

    Il Était Une Barque
        eq voices HUG 8597    (C41)

    Ino Amphigouri *17th cent
        mix cor BILLAUDOT    (C42)

    J'ai Pris La Fantaisie
        eq voices HUG 8596    (C43)

    Meunier, Meunier
        eq voices HUG 7896    (C44)

    Pauvre Cigale
        eq voices HUG 7046    (C45)

    Péronnelle, La
        eq voices,S solo HUG 7049    (C46)

    Quand La Feuille Était Verte
        eq voices HUG 7049    (C47)

    Quand Le Berger Sort Son Troupeau
        see Trois Chansons De France

    Quarts Du Soir
        4pt wom cor BILLAUDOT    (C48)

    Rossignol Qui Vas En France
        eq voices,S solo HUG 7048    (C49)

    Rossignolet Du Bois
        eq voices HUG 7468    (C50)

    Tous Ceux Qui Veul'
        see Trois Chansons De France

    Trois Chansons De France
        eq voices HUG 7957 f.s.
        contains: Beau Papillon, Vit', Marie-Toi!; C'est À Paris Dans Un Vert Pré; Quand Le Berger Sort Son Troupeau    (C51)

    Trois Chansons De France
        men cor HUG 7045 f.s.
        contains: Ah! Maudit Soit L'amour!; Elle Est La Fill' D'un Laboureur; Tous Ceux Qui Veul'    (C52)

CANTEMUS
    SVERIG SK 800 f.s.    (C53)

CANTICLES OF WINDS see Niimi, Tokuhide

CANTICOS DE AMOR see Prado, José-Antonio (Almeida)

CANTIENI, R.
    Garde Grisonne, La
        men cor HUG 6309    (C54)

CANTILÈNE DE LA PLUIE, LA see Sala, Andre

CANTIONES DE CIRCULO GYRANTE see Huber, Klaus

CANTIQUE see Vuataz, Roger

CANTIQUE SUISSE see Zwissig, A.

CANTO A LAS MADRES DE LOS MILICIANOS MUERTOS see Testi, Flavio

CANTO ALLA MIA TERRA see Bianchi, Italo

CANTO DI EROS see Lombardi, Luca

CANTO DI LODE see Mendelssohn-Bartholdy, Felix, Lobgesang

CANTO MATTUTINO see Dall'albero, Claudio

CANTORIA *CC66U
    men cor,acap HUG 6761 f.s.    (C55)

CANTUS CARINTHICUS *CCU,cant
    (Mittergradnegger, Günther) cor, solo voices&narrator,inst HEYN ISBN 3 85366 611 6    (C56)

CAPE BRETON LULLABY see Calvert

CAPE COD CHANTEY see Julseth-Heinrich, Jeanne

CAPE COD SHANTY
    (Paynes) 2pt mix cor BANKS ECS0189    (C57)

CAPEHART, JERRY
    Turn Around, Look At Me
        (Schram, Ruth) SATB WARNER WBCH93167    (C58)
        (Schram, Ruth) SAB WARNER WBCH93168    (C59)

CAPO,B.
    Piel Canela
        (Olivieri, L.) "Tan Skin" SATB THOMAS 1C0859303    (C60)

    Tan Skin
        see Piel Canela

CAPRICE HONGROIS see Mouchet

CARAVAN see Anderson, Tom see Ellington, Edward Kennedy (Duke)

CARAVANE TURQUE SUR LA MARCHE TURQUE see Mozart, Wolfgang Amadeus

CAREY
    Spring Morning
        unis treb cor BOOSEY-ENG OCTB6734    (C61)
        unis cor BOOSEY-ENG OCTB6734    (C62)

CAREY, HENRY (ca. 1687-1743)
    Chant National
        men cor HUG 2314    (C63)

CARGADO DE TANTOS MALES see Anonymous

CARILLON DES CHANSONS, LE see Delor

CARILLONS DE PÂQUES see Naudier

CARL
    Autumn Song
        2pt treb cor BOOSEY-ENG OCTB6743    (C64)

CARLOS, GLENN
    Blame It On My Youth
        SATB,acap (gr. III) UNC JP    (C65)

    Celebrer
        SATB, solo voices (gr. III) UNC JP    (C66)

CARMICHAEL, HOAGY (1899-1981)
    I Get Along Without You Very Well
        SAB WARCH 35606    (C67)
        SATB WARCH 35607    (C68)

    Lazy River (composed with Rochberg, A. George)
        SATB WARNER 0076LC1X ipa    (C69)
        SAB WARNER 0076LC3X ipa    (C70)

    Skylark
        (Chinn, Teena) SATB,acap WARNER WBCH9313    (C71)

    Star Dust
        (Strommen, Carl) SATB WARNER 8172SC1X    (C72)
        (Strommen, Carl) SAB WARNER 8172SC3X    (C73)

    Up A Lazy River
        (Swingle, Ward) SSAATTBB,acap (gr. IV) voc pt,pts UNC JP SS-3    (C74)

CARNAVAL ENFANTIN see Marechal, Henri-Charles

CAROL FESTIVAL see Strommen, Carl

CAROL OF THE BIRDS
    (Shaw) SATB,S solo,acap LEONARD-US 50304960    (C75)

CAROLING! see Grier, Gene

CAROLS OF FRENCH CANADA see Applebaum

CARR, EDWIN
    Six Choral Pieces
        SATB UNIV.OTAGO    (C76)

CARRIERS OF THE LIGHT see Estes, Jerry

CARROSSE, LE see Mireille

CARROUSEL see Kaelin, Pierre

CARRY THE LIGHT see Pethel, Stanley

CARSON, PHILIPPE
    Mouvement Pour Dix-Huit Voix D'hommes
        men cor BILLAUDOT    (C77)

CARTER, ALLEN
    Dis Be Da Bop
        SSAATTBB,pno,db,drums (gr. IV) UNC JP    (C78)

    Silly Little Song
        SSAATTBB,pno,db,drums (gr. IV) UNC JP    (C79)

CARULLI, GUSTAVO
    Good Night
        SATB BANKS 444    (C80)

## CASEY
Drill Ye Tarriers, Drill (composed with Connelly)
(Rodgers, Thomas) SATB,pno LAWSON 52746 (C81)

## CASKEN, JOHN (1949- )
Three Choral Pieces
mix cor SCHOTTS ED 12421 (C82)

## CASSILS
Firefly
2pt cor LESLIE 2076 (C83)

Life's Too Short To Be Silent
SA LESLIE 2083 (C84)

May I Learn To Be Silent
2pt cor LESLIE 2072 (C85)

Will You Stand By Me
unis cor/2pt cor LESLIE 2087 (C86)

## CASTIGLIONI, NICCOLÒ (1932- )
Favole Di Esopo, Le *ora
SATB,orch sc RICORDI-IT 133003 (C87)

Oltre La Sfera Che Più Larga Gira
6pt cor RICORDI-IT 133241 (C88)

Sonetto In Memoriam Igor Strawinsky
6pt mix cor RICORDI-IT 133438 (C89)

CASTLE ON A CLOUD see Schonberg, Claude-Michel

## CASTRO, JEAN DE (ca. 1540-ca. 1611)
Chansons, Odes, Et Sonetz De Pierre Ronsard (1576) *CCU,Renaissance
(Brooks, Jeanice) 4-8pt cor A-R ED ISBN 0-89579-289-3 (C90)

CATCH A LITTLE SUNBEAM see Simituk

CATHERINE DE FINHAUT see Broquet, Louis

CATHERINE DE FINHAUT, LA see Broquet, Louis

## CATHERWOOD, DAVID
Into Your Loving Care
SATB WARNER BSC00297 (C91)

CATS, FRIENDS AND LOVERS see Paulus, Stephen Harrison

CAUGHT IN THE ACT see Purcell, Henry

CAVALIER À LA FONTAINE see Reichel, Bernard

CE CHANT DE LA TERRE see Kaelin, Pierre

CE JOUR-LÀ see Mermoud, Robert

CE N'EST QU'UNE CHANSON QUI PASSE see Pasquier, Marius

CÉ QU'È LAINO *pop
mix cor HUG 6809 (C92)

CEBOLLITA Y HUEVO see Marziali, Jorge

## CEDERBERG, ANNA
Jordens Sång
mix cor,pno SVERIG SK 744 (C93)
SA,pno SVERIG SK 745 (C94)

Min Finaste Sten
SA,pno SVERIG SK 812 (C95)

Nu Viljusen Tänt
SSA SVERIG SK 746 (C96)

Sommarsången
2 eq voices,pno SVERIG SK793 (C97)

Tärnans Visa
SSAA SVERIG SK 743 (C98)

Två Lussevisor
SA,pno SVERIG SK742 (C99)

Vita Duva
2 eq voices,pno SVERIG SK 794 (C100)

CELA FILE AVEC LE TEMPS see Boller, Carlo

CELEBRATE THE FEAST OF LIGHTS see Albrecht, Sally K.

CELEBRATIO AMERICAE see Prado, José-Antonio (Almeida)

CELEBRATIO AMORIS see Prado, José-Antonio (Almeida)

CÉLÉBRATION DES SAISONS see De Senger, H.

CELEBRATION OF LIFE, THE see Kanno, Yoshihiro

CÉLÈBRE RÊVERIE see Schumann, Robert (Alexander)

CELEBRER see Carlos, Glenn

CELTIC TRIPTYCH,A see Jeffers, Ron

## CERHA, FRIEDRICH (1926- )
An Die Herrscher Der Welt
mix cor DOBLINGER 44 744 (C101)

Drei Dedenkliche Geschichten Für Kammerchor Und Streichquintett
mix cor,string quin DOBLINGER 46 080 (C102)

CERISES, LES see Binet, Jean see Marechal, Henri-Charles

## CERTON, PIERRE (ca. 1510-1572)
I Have Never Been So Carefree see Je Ne Fus Jamais Si Aise

Je Ne Fus Jamais Si Aise
eq voices HUG 7938 (C103)
(Meredith) "I Have Never Been So Carefree" SAB KJOS 5757 (C104)

CES VOISINS QUI LORGNENT see Moniuszko, Stanislaw

C'EST À BOIRE QU'IL NOUS FAUT! see Boller, Carlo

C'EST À PARIS DANS UN VERT PRÉ see Canteloube, Joseph

C'EST DIMANCHE see Sala, Andre

C'EST EN FORGEANT... see Daetwyler, Jean

C'EST LA FÊTE DU HAMEAU see Broquet, Louis

C'EST LA FILLE AU VIGNERON see Doret, Gustave

C'EST LA VIE! see Miche, Paul

C'EST LE BON LEVER see Boller, Carlo

C'EST LE CHEVRIER QUI PASSE see Henchoz, Emile

C'EST LE JOLY MOIS DE MAY see Corboz, Michel

C'EST LE VENT DU PRINTEMPS see Broquet, Louis

C'EST MOI QUI VOUS LE DIS see Martin

C'EST TOI see Bovet, J.

C'EST TOUJOURS UNE EAU NOUVELLE see Sala, Andre

C'EST UN VIGNERON see Kaelin, Pierre

C'EST UN VRAI BATEAU see Vuataz, Roger

CET AMI QUE MON COEUR ESPÈRE see Martin

C'ÉTAIT UN GARÇON BIEN SAGE... see Broquet, Louis

CEUX DES VILLAGES see Mermoud, Robert

## CHABRIER, [ALEXIS-] EMMANUEL (1841-1894)
Cocodette Et Cocorico
cor,solo voice,pno BILLAUDOT (C105)

Monsieur Et Madame Orchestre
cor,solo voice,pno BILLAUDOT (C106)

## CHADWICK, GEORGE WHITEFIELD (1854-1931)
Lovely Rosabelle
SATB,ST soli,pno voc sc RECITAL 448 (C107)

CHAGRIN DE MADELEINE, LE see Bovet, J.

## CHAILLEY, JACQUES (1910- )
Charité Saint Martin, La
mix cor BILLAUDOT (C108)

Oeuvres Originales et Harmonisations
mix cor,acap SALABERT EAS 19109 (C109)

CHAMBERED NAUTILUS OP.66,THE see Beach, [Mrs.] H.H.A. (Amy Marcy Cheney)

CHAMOIS ROUGE, LE see Jaques-Dalcroze, Émile

## CHAN MALI CHAN
(Tan) SATB (malaysian folksong) KJOS 8782 (C110)

## CHANCE, NANCY LAIRD (1931- )
Motet
dbl cor SEESAW (C111)

CHANDELLE, LA see Pasquier, Marius

CHANSO DES QUATRE FOUS DE MAI see Jaques-Dalcroze, Émile

CHANSON see Sutermeister, Heinrich

CHANSON À BOIRE see Doret, Gustave see Haenni, G. see Henchoz, Emile see Schumann, Robert (Alexander) see Vuataz, Roger

CHANSON À BOIRE ET À DANSER see Henchoz, Emile

CHANSON À DANSER see Doret, Gustave

CHANSON À GRAND VENT see Pantillon, François

CHANSON À LA LUNE see Jaques-Dalcroze, Émile

CHANSON À LA VIERGE see Chatton, Pierre

CHANSON À QUATRE VOIX see Ronsard

CHANSON BACHIQUE see Lang, H. see Mozart, Wolfgang Amadeus

CHANSON D'AMOUR see Doret, Gustave

CHANSON DANS LE VENT see Corboz, Michel

CHANSON D'AUTOMNE see Boller, Carlo

CHANSON DE BARBERINE see Cools, Eugène

CHANSON DE BORD see Gaillard, Paul-Andre

CHANSON DE CHARRUE see Martin

CHANSON DE CHASSE see Ithier

CHANSON DE FORTUNIO see Cools, Eugène

CHANSON DE LA BELLE see Delannoy, Marcel

CHANSON DE LA BELLE JULIE see Doret, Gustave

CHANSON DE LA BERGÈRE, LA see Ammann, Benno

CHANSON DE LA CIME, LA see Boller, Carlo

CHANSON DE LA DOUCE see Pantillon, François

CHANSON DE LA GLU see Lang, H.

CHANSON DE LA LISETTE see Lang, H.

CHANSON DE LA MI-ÉTÉ DE TAVEYANNE see Gaillard, Paul-Andre

CHANSON DE LA PETITE TREILLE see Hemmerling, Carlos

CHANSON DE LA REINE BERTHE see Jaques-Dalcroze, Émile

CHANSON DE LA SOURCE see Daetwyler, Jean

CHANSON DE LA VIGNE see Daetwyler, Jean

CHANSON DE LA VIGNERONNE (from Terre Et L'étoile, La)
mix cor HUG 8843 (C112)

CHANSON DE LABOUR see Janáček, Leoš

CHANSON DE L'ALPE see Bovet, J.

CHANSON DE L'ARMAILLI see Boller, Carlo

CHANSON DE L'EAU see Pasquier, Marius

CHANSON DE MAI see Bournel see Dyck, C. see Mendelssohn-Bartholdy, Felix see Moret, Oscar see Robert-Lalouet, M.

CHANSON DE MARIAGE see Boller, Carlo see Lesur, Daniel

CHANSON DE MON AMI, LA see Kaelin, Pierre

CHANSON DE NÖEL see Balissat, J.

CHANSON DE NOS DEUX COEURS, LA see Vuataz, Roger

CHANSON DE TROUPE see Boller, Carlo

CHANSON DES ADIEUX see Doret, Gustave

CHANSON DES ANGES, LA see Doret, Gustave

CHANSON DES BLÉS, LA see Daetwyler, Jean

CHANSON DES BÛCHERONS see Doret, Gustave

CHANSON DES CLOCHES, LA see Doret, Gustave

CHANSON DES COURONNES see Miche, Paul

CHANSON DES EFFEUILLES see Doret, Gustave see Hemmerling, Carlos

CHANSON DES ENFANTS STUDIEUX, LA see Naudier

CHANSON DES ÉTOILES, LA see Plumhof, H.

CHANSON DES FANEUSES see Boller, Carlo

CHANSON DES FAUCHEURS ET FANEUSES see Doret, Gustave

CHANSON DES FAUCHEURS ET FANEUSES see Doret, Gustave

CHANSON DES GLAÇONS see Boller, Carlo

CHANSON DES JARDINIERS ET JARDINIÈRES see De Senger,H. see Doret, Gustave

CHANSON DES LAVANDIÈRES, LA see Miche, Paul

CHANSON DES MAÏENTZETTES see Jaques-Dalcroze, Émile

CHANSON DES MAYENTZETS see Boller, Carlo

CHANSON DES MOISSONS see Hemmerling, Carlos see Henchoz, Emile

CHANSON DES NAINS see Boller, Carlo

CHANSON DES POMMES, LA see Doret, Gustave

CHANSON DES PRÉSENTS, LA see Binet, Jean

CHANSON DES QUATRE TEMPS see Vuataz, Roger

CHANSON DES TEMPS ANCIENS see Rochat, Jean

CHANSON DES VAUDOIS see Lang, H.

CHANSON DES VENDANGEURS see Doret, Gustave

CHANSON DES VIELLES ET DES VIEUX see Doret, Gustave

CHANSON DES VIEUX see Boller, Carlo

CHANSON DES VIEUX ET DES VIELLES see Doret, Gustave

CHANSON DES VIEUX MEÏENTZETS see Jaques-Dalcroze, Émile

CHANSON DES VIGNERONS see Boller, Carlo

CHANSON DES VILLAGES, LA see Chatton, Pierre

CHANSON D'HIVER see Apotheloz, Jean

CHANSON D'ICI, LA see Kaelin, Pierre

CHANSON DU BLÉ see Balissat, J.

CHANSON DU BLÉ, LA see Gaillard, Paul-Andre see Jaques-Dalcroze, Émile

CHANSON DU BLÉ QUI LÈVE see Doret, Gustave

CHANSON DU CHALET, LA see Daetwyler, Jean

CHANSON DU CHEVRIER see Doret, Gustave

CHANSON DU COUCOU see Doret, Gustave

CHANSON DU CROQUANT, LA see Bron, Patrick

CHANSON DU DIMANCHE see Boller, Carlo

CHANSON DU MERLE ET DE LA VIGNE QUI PLEURE see Balissat, J.

CHANSON DU PÊCHEUR see Hemmerling, Carlos

CHANSON DU PRESSIOR, LA see Doret, Gustave

CHANSON DU RAMONEUR, LA see Doret, Gustave

CHANSON DU ROI ET DE LA REINE see Jaques-Dalcroze, Émile

CHANSON DU SOL NATAL, LA see Jaques-Dalcroze, Émile

CHANSON DU SOL VAUDOIS, LA see Boller, Carlo

CHANSON DU TABAC, LA see Mermoud, Robert

CHANSON DU TIR À LA ROSE see Bovet, J.

CHANSON DU VENT see Lagger, Oscar

CHANSON DU VENT CLAIR see Bovet, J.

CHANSON DU VENT DE MER, LA see Sala, Andre

CHANSON DU VIGNERON see Martin

CHANSON DU VIOLONEUX see Gesseney, L.

CHANSON ESPAGNOLE see Boller, Carlo

CHANSON OUBLIÉE see Urfer, Albert

CHANSON POUR ELLE see Pantillon, François

CHANSON POUR LES VENDANGES see Rochat, Jean

CHANSON POUR MA BELLE see Miche, Paul

CHANSON POUR MA MÈRE see Zbinden, Julien-François

CHANSON POUR UN AMI LOINTAIN see Kaelin, Pierre

CHANSON POUR UNE FONTAINE see Mermoud, Robert

CHANSONNIER ROMAND DE LA SOCIÉTÉ FÉDÉRALE DE CHANT *CC70U
men cor,acap HUG 7350 f.s. (C113)

CHANSONS 1-17 see Janequin, Clement

CHANSONS 18-73 see Janequin, Clement

CHANSONS 74-114 see Janequin, Clement

CHANSONS 115- 170 see Janequin, Clement

CHANSONS 171-219 see Janequin, Clement

CHANSONS 220-254 see Janequin, Clement

CHANSONS DE BORD TOME 1 TROIS CHANSONS DU GAILLARD D'AVANT ET TROIS CHANSONS À HISSER see Dutilleux, Henri

CHANSONS DE BORD TOME 2 QUATRE CHANSONS À VIRER see Dutilleux, Henri

CHANSONS DE CLÉMENT MAROT see Lancien, Nöel

CHANSONS DE TROUPE *CCU
eq voices HUG 6735 f.s. (C114)

CHANSONS DES ROSES, LES see Lauridsen, Morten Johannes

CHANSONS, ODES, ET SONETZ DE PIERRE RONSARD (1576) see Castro, Jean de

CHANSONS POPULAIRES CAHIER II see Lesur, Daniel

CHANSONS POUR M'AMIE: see Pantillon, François

CHANT CANADIEN, UN see Halley, Song For Candada

CHANT D'AMOUR see Janácek, Leoš

CHANT D'AUTOMNE ET DE VENDANGE see Bohly

CHANT DE LA BIÈRE, LE see Breard

CHANT DE LA BROYE see Mermoud, Robert

CHANT DE LA FIDÉLITÉ see Boller, Carlo

CHANT DE LA GITANE, LE see Breard

CHANT DE LA LANDSGEMEINDE D' APPENZELL see Tobler, J.H.

CHANT DE LA MÉDITERRANÉE, LE see Breard

CHANT DE LA MINE, LE see Breard

CHANT DE LA NOCE see Doret, Gustave

CHANT DE LA PAIX, LE see Pastor

CHANT DE LA ROSE, LE see Breard

CHANT DE LA TERRE, LE see Breard

CHANT DE L'ALOUETTE, LE see Mendelssohn-Bartholdy, Felix

CHANT DE L'AURORE see Bovet, J.

CHANT DE L'EUROPE, LE see Daetwyler, Jean

CHANT DE MA MÈRE see Bovet, J.

CHANT DE MAI see Bovet, J.

CHANT DE MARIAGE see Jaques-Dalcroze, Émile

CHANT DE NOS COEURS, LE see Miche, Paul

CHANT DE NOURRICE see Indy, Vincent d'

CHANT DES BERGERS GRECS, LE see Breard

CHANT DES BRACONNIERS see Boller, Carlo

CHANT DES CIMES, LE see Breard

CHANT DES LILAS, LE see Breard

CHANT DES LYS, LE see Breard

CHANT DES MARGUERITES, LE see Breard

CHANT DES MATELOTS see Wagner, Richard

CHANT DES MIMOSAS, LE see Breard

CHANT DES MOISSONEURS see Doret, Gustave

CHANT DES MOISSONNEURS see Doret, Gustave

CHANT DES OEILLETS, LE see Breard

CHANT DES ORANGERS, LE see Breard

CHANT DES PÂTRES see Doret, Gustave

CHANT DES PETITS BERGERS & BERGÈRES see Doret, Gustave

CHANT DES PEUPLES, LE see Pons

CHANT DES SAISONS, LE see Lhomme

CHANT DES SUISSES see Doret, Gustave

CHANT DES SUISSES À L'ÉTRANGER see Bovet, J.

CHANT DES TONNELIERS see De Senger,H.

CHANT DES VANNIERS see Doret, Gustave

CHANT DES VIOLETTES, LE see Breard

CHANT D'ÉTÉ see Gluck

CHANT D'ORIENT, LE see Breard

CHANT DU BERGER see Boller, Carlo

CHANT DU CHASSEUR, LE see Schumann, Robert (Alexander), Jägerland

CHANT DU COUCOU, LE see Martin

CHANT DU DÉPART, LE see Méhul, Étienne-Nicolas

CHANT DU DRAPEAU see Boller, Carlo

CHANT DU LAC see Boller, Carlo see Hemmerling, Carlos

CHANT DU MUGUET, LE see Breard

CHANT DU MYOSOTIS, LE see Breard

CHANT DU PAYS see Boller, Carlo

CHANT DU PAYSAN see Boller, Carlo

CHANT DU SOIR see Breard see Kaelin, Pierre

CHANT DU SOIR, LE see Breard

CHANT DU TRAVAIL, LE see Naudier

CHANT DU VOYAGEUR see Schumann, Robert (Alexander), Wanderlied

CHANT GENERAL,LE
4pt wom cor,pno MULLES (C115)

CHANT LUNAIRE see Daetwyler, Jean

CHANT NATIONAL see Carey, Henry

CHANT NORVÉGIEN see Parchet, A.

CHANT NUPTIAL see Miche, Paul

CHANTE see Delmas, Marc-Jean-Baptiste

CHANTE L'ALOUETTE! see Doret, Gustave

CHANTE, MONTAGNARD! see Moudon, E.

CHANTEFLEURS ET CHANTEFABLES DE R. DESNOS see Lancien, Noël

CHANTEZ AU SEIGNEUR UN CHANT NOUVEAU see Corboz, Michel

CHANTEZ FONTAINES CLAIRES see Martin

CHANTONS GAIEMENT see Naudier

CHANTONS JEUNESSE see Inghelbrecht, Germaine

CHANTONS LES VINS FRANÇAIS see Naudier

CHANTONS NOËL SUR LA MUSETTE see Aubanel, Georges

CHANTONS, RIONS, JOUONS... see Lang, H.

CHANTS see Vivier, Claude

CHANTS DE L'AMOUR, LES see Grisey, Gerard

CHANTS D'HIER ET DE DEMAIN see Jolivet, Andre

CHANTS INCANTATOIRES see Bernier, Rene

CHANUKA VARIATIONS see Jacobson, Joshua

CHANZUN DEL GUITADER see Furrer, Walter

CHAPPEL
   Dinosaurs Dance In My Dreams
     unis cor LESLIE 1192    (C116)

CHARIOT CHILDREN, THE see Raminsh, Imant

CHARITÉ SAINT MARTIN, LA see Chailley, Jacques

CHARLATAN, LE see Breard

CHARPENTIER, GUSTAVE (1860-1956)
   Fleurs Du Mal,Les
     [Fr] wom cor, solo voices RECITAL
     326    (C117)

CHARRUE, LA see La Tombelle, Fernand de

CHASSE, LA see Apotheloz, Jean see Gounod, Charles François see La Tombelle, Fernand de see Mendelssohn-Bartholdy, Felix

CHASSE EST OUVERTE, LA see Hemmerling, Carlos

CHASSEUR, REPRENDS TA CARABINE see Martin

CHAT DE LA MÈRE MICHEL, LE see Mozart, Wolfgang Amadeus

CHÂTEAU, TA FORTERESSE... see Boller, Carlo

CHATMAN
   John Kanaka
     SATB WARCH 34492    (C118)

CHATS, LES see Mermoud, Robert

CHATTON, PIERRE
   Chanson À La Vierge
     mix cor HUG 8255    (C119)

   Chanson Des Villages, La
     mix cor HUG 8469    (C120)

CHAYA POR TOCONAS see Leguizamón, Gustavo

CHEERILY see Ouchterlony

CHEKLER, EDOUARD
   Moi J'irai Dans La Lune
     3pt wom cor BILLAUDOT    (C121)
     3 eq voices BILLAUDOT    (C122)

CHEMIN see Martelli, Henri

CHEMINEAU, LE see Mermoud, Robert

CHEMINS DE LA MER, LES see Kaelin, Pierre

CHEN, YI
   Set Of Chinese Folksongs, A
     [Chin] men cor/SATB,acap,opt string
     quar/string orch (med diff)
     PRESSER 312-41682    (C123)

CHÈRE MAISON, LA see Jaques-Dalcroze, Émile

CHERRY TREE, THE see Heard, Brenda

CHERRY TREE CAROL
   (Shaw And Parker) SATB,T solo,acap
   LEONARD-US 50304792    (C124)
   see Applebaum

CHERUBINI, LUIGI (1760-1842)
   Like As A Father
     SSA WARCH 40715    (C125)

CHEVALIER DU GUET see Jouineau, Jacques

CHEVAUCHÉE see Schumann, Robert (Alexander)

CHÈVRE, LA see Lesur, Daniel

CHÈVRES DE GRUYÈRES, LES see Bovet, J.

CHEVRIERS, LES see Boller, Carlo

CHEZ NOUS see Bovet, J.

CHIEN ET CHAT see Pantillon, François

CHIEN ET LE CHAT, LE see Breard

CHIHEISEN NO KANATA see Kinoshita, Makiko

CHIKAI NO KOTOBA see Saito, Takanobu

CHILDREN, GO WHERE I SEND THEE
   (Hayes) SATB ALFRED 11628    (C126)

CHILDREN OF THE EARTH - A LETTER FROM HOME see Takashima, Midori

CHILDREN OF THE FUTURE see Coghlan

CHILDREN SINGING
   (Archer, Violet) [Eng/Fr] 1-2pt jr
   cor,pno CAN.MUS.CENT. f.s.
   contains: Anonymous, I Had Little
   Pony; Belloc, Hilaire, Yak,The;
   Carroll, How Doth The Little
   Crocodile; Rosetti, Who Has Seen
   The Wind; Stevenson, Ronald, Cow,
   The    (C127)

CHILDREN SINGING see Archer, Violet

CHILDREN'S WINTER see O'Reilly, Dermott

CHILD'S GARDEN OF VERSES, A see Mourant, Walter

CHILLEMONT
   Paysage Provençal
     4pt men cor BILLAUDOT    (C128)

CHIMES see Ohana, Maurice

CHINDIA see Pascanu, Alexandru

CHING A RING CHAW AND GREAT GITTIN' UP MORNIN' see Spevacek, Linda

CHINOOK see Walker

CHIVALRY OF LABOUR,THE see Calkin, J. Baptiste

CHLINI CHÜGELI MUESS ME GIESSE see Märki, Ernst

CHNABE VO CHAPPEL,DIE
   (Gand-Kreis-Märki) men cor,acap
   MULLES    (C129)

CHOEUR D'ARMIDE see Gluck, Christoph Willibald, Ritter von

CHOEUR DE LA LUMIÈE see Sutermeister, Heinrich

CHOEUR DES CHASSEURS see Weber, Carl Maria von

CHOEUR DES HÉBREUX see Verdi, Giuseppe

CHOEUR DES JEUNES FILLES see Bovet, J.

CHOEUR DES MOISSONNEURS see Haug

CHOEUR DES PÈLERINS see Wagner, Richard

CHOEUR DES PRÊTRES see Mozart, Wolfgang Amadeus

CHOEUR DES SOLDATS see Gounod, Charles François

CHOEUR DES VENDANGEURS see Mendelssohn-Bartholdy, Felix

CHOEUR FINAL "LE SONGE D'UNE NUIT D'ÉTÉ" see Mendelssohn-Bartholdy, Felix

CHOEURS D'HOMMES A CAPPELLA *CCU
   men cor HUG 8035 f.s.    (C130)

CHOEURS FACILES POUR ENFANTS see Mozart, Wolfgang Amadeus

CHOPIN, FRÉDÉRIC (1810-1849)
   Marche Funèbre
     (Andrieu) 4pt men cor BILLAUDOT
       (C131)
     (Andrieu) 4pt mix cor BILLAUDOT
       (C132)

CHOPLIN, PEPPER
   Once Upon A Tree
     SATB SHAWNEE A-6911    (C133)

CHOR DER FISCHER see Müller, Joseph Ivar

CHORAL À LA MONTAGNE see Gaillard, Paul-Andre

CHORAL DES ADIEUX see Boller, Carlo

CHORAL FANFARE, A see Spevacek, Linda

CHORAL POUR LA PAIX see Uy, Paul

CHORAL SKILLS #1 see Hatcher, W.

CHORAL SKILLS #1 & 2 see Petker, Allan R.

CHORAL SKILLS #2 see Petker, Allan R.

CHORALE PRELUDE see Bach, Johann Sebastian

CHORLIEDERBUCH *CCU,Austrian
   (Mittergradnegger, Günther) HEYN
   ISBN 3 85366482 2 f.s.    (C134)

CHORUS OF THE HEBREW SLAVES FROM "NABUCCO" see Verdi, Giuseppe

CHORUS SUITE see Ideta, Keizo

CHORUSES FROM 'GODSPELL' AND 'CHILDREN OF EDEN' see Schwartz

CHORUSES FROM 'IL TRAVATORE', 'NABUCCO' & 'AIDA' see Verdi, Giuseppe

CHRESTOMATHIE see Martelli, Henri

CHRISTIANSEN, PAUL (1914- )
   West Wind, The
     SATB,acap SUMMA SP 2034    (C135)

CHRISTMAS see Archer

CHRISTMAS BELLS see Gray, Cynthia

CHRISTMAS CAROL, A see Dello Joio, Norman

CHRISTMAS, CHRISTMAS EVERYWHERE see Syme

CHRISTMAS DAY see Minikel

CHRISTMAS FANFARE see Gray, Cynthia

CHRISTMAS GHOST-STORY,A see Dijker, Mathieu

CHRISTMAS IS A FEELING see Schwartz, Dan

CHRISTMAS JOY see Kirkland, Terry

CHRISTMAS LULLABY see Campsie

CHRISTMAS MAGIC IN THE AIR see Loughton, Lynnette

CHRISTMAS MEMORIES (from Sleigh Ride, Chestnuts Roasting, We Need A Little Christmas, Most Wonderful Time)
   (Ancira) ALEX.HSE. oct DTE33262, sc
   DTR33262    (C136)

CHRISTMAS PAST AND CHRISTMAS PRESENT see Mechem, Kirke Lewis

CHRISTMAS REMEMBERED see Strommen, Carl

CHRISTMAS ROCKIN' EVE see Ciancioso, Carole

CHRISTMAS RUSH, THE see Albrecht, Sally K.

CHRISTMAS SONG,THE see Henley, Rod see Torme

CHRISTMAS SWEET, A see Elliott, D.J.

CHRISTMAS TIME! *medley
   (Funk, Jeff) SATB,horn pts WARNER
   CM9543SH CM9543    (C137)
   (Funk, Jeff) 3pt mix cor,horn pts
   WARNER CM9543SH CM9544    (C138)
   (Funk, Jeff) 2pt cor,horn pts WARNER
   CM9543SH CM9545    (C139)

CHRISTMAS TIME IS HERE
  (Pugh, David) 2pt cor WARNER 2621CC5X
    (C140)
  (Pugh, David) SATB WARNER 2621CC1X
    (C141)
  (Pugh, David) 3pt mix cor WARNER
    2621CC3X (C142)

CHRISTMAS TOYS  *medley
  (Kinsale, Hillary) 1-2pt cor WARNER
    C0305C5X (C143)

CHRISTMAS TRADITIONS: A REVUE
  (Schram, Ruth Elaine) 1-2pt cor
    WARNER voc sc CM9594S, pno-cond sc
    CM9594C (C144)

CHRISTMAS WILL BE HERE ANY DAY see
  Schwartz, Dan

CHRISTMAS WISH,A see Strommen, Carl

CHRYSANTHÈME, LE see Hemmerling, Carlos

CHUM ÜBERS MÄTTELI see Stoessel, Albert

CIANCIOSO, CAROLE
  Christmas Rockin' Eve (composed with
    Ciancioso, Ron)
    (Funk, Jeff) SATB,horn pts WARNER
      WBSH93225 WBCH93225 (C145)
    (Funk, Jeff) SAB,horn pts WARNER
      WBSH93225 WBCH93226 (C146)
    (Funk, Jeff) 2pt cor,horn pts
      WARNER WBSH93225 WBCH93227 (C147)

CICONIA, JOHANNES
  Motets And Latin Contrafacta *CCU
    (Bent, Hallmark) OISEAU RE 912 f.s.
      (C148)
  Secular Works  *CCU
    (Bent, Hallmark) OISEAU RE 913 f.s.
      (C149)

CIEL, AIR ET VENT see Jannequin

CIGALE ET LA FOURMI, LA see Gounod,
  Charles François see Sala, Andre

CINQ CANONS see Mozart, Wolfgang
  Amadeus

CINQ CHANSONS FRANÇAISES see Auric,
  Georges

CINQUE CANTI POPOLARI SARDI see Bossi,
  Renzo

CINQUE POESIE DI ALDO PALAZZESCHI see
  Mortari, Virgilio

CIRANDA see Prado, José-Antonio
  (Almeida)

CIRCLE OF FRIENDS see Hamilton, Arthur

CITY SCAPES
  (Schmutte, Pete) SATB,horn (medley
    incl. New York New York, Kansas
    City, & I Left My Heart in San
    Francisco) pts WARNER C0342CH
    C0342C1X (C150)
  (Schmutte, Pete) SAB,horn (medley
    incl. New York New York, Kansas
    City, & I Left My Heart in San
    Francisco) pts WARNER C0342CH
    C0342C3X (C151)

CLAIRE DE LUNE see Debussy, Claude

CLARK, DEREK J.
  I Got A Robe
    TTBB,acap ROBERTON 53099 (C152)
  Piper O' Dundee, The
    TTBB,acap ROBERTON 53100 (C153)

CLARKE (-WHITFIELD), [DR.] JOHN
  (1770-1836)
  Wide O'er The Brim
    (Dicks, E.A.) SATB BANKS 539 (C154)

CLARTÉS see Mozart, Wolfgang Amadeus

CLAUDE IS AN ELEGANT CAT see Shields,
  Valerie

CLAUSEN, ALF
  Legacy, The
    SSAATB,acap (gr. IV) UNC JP (C155)

CLAUSEN, RENE
  Jubilant Song, A
    SATB,acap FOSTER MF 3048 (C156)
  Whispers Of Heavenly Death
    SSAATTBB,orch/opt kbd FOSTER
    MF 3047 f.s., MF 3047R pts rent
    (C157)

CLAVIÉ
  Sur Nos Landes Aimées
    2 eq voices BILLAUDOT (C158)
  Vers Les Sentiers Pleins D'allégresse
    2 eq voices BILLAUDOT (C159)

CLEARFIELD, ANDREA (1958- )
  Nes Gadol Hayah Sham
    SATB,SB soli,pno,vcl HILD 09423A
      (C160)

CLEMENS
  Heitere Weisen Des Lebens  *CC3U
    men cor,acap BOHM f.s. (C161)

CLEMENTI, ALDO (1925- )
  Im Frieden Dein, O Herre Mein  *mot
    8pt cor,acap ZERBONI 8738 (C162)
  Mottetto Su Re, Mi...
    wom cor,acap ZERBONI 10027 (C163)

CLEMENTS, JOHN (1910- )
  I Love All Beauteous Things
    SATB BANKS 1363 (C164)

CLICHÉS (IN PRAISE OF PHRASE) see
  Gallina

CLOCHE DANS LE CIEL, LA see Binet, Jean

CLOCHE DU BONHEUR, LA see Bovet, J.

CLOCHERS, LES see Boller, Carlo

CLOCHERS DE MON PAYS see Miche, Paul

CLOSE EVERY DOOR see Lloyd Webber,
  Andrew

CLOTHES, LES see Haenni, G.

CLOUDS see Moments In Time see Ohana,
  Maurice

COASTS OF HIGH BARBARY, THE see
  Julseth-Heinrich, Jeanne

COCK-A-DOODLE-DOO see Freedman

COCLICÔT see Boller, Carlo

COCODETTE ET COCORICO see Chabrier,
  [Alexis-] Emmanuel

COEUR DE MA MIE, LE see Jaques-
  Dalcroze, Émile

COEURS EN FÊTE see Naudier

COGHLAN
  Children Of The Future
    2pt cor LESLIE 2090 (C165)
  Dream A New Dream
    2pt cor LESLIE 2089 (C166)
  Seasons
    SA LESLIE 2082 (C167)

COGHLAN, MICHAEL
  Look Away
    SSA THOMP.G VG344 (C168)

COGLIEREMO UN RAMO DI FIORI see Bovet,
  J.

COIN DE CIEL BLEU, UN see Mermoud,
  Robert

COIN DU FEU,LE see Furrer, Walter

COIN DU PARADIS, UN see Mermoud, Robert

COL FRATELLO, A SETTIGNANO see
  Prosperi, Carlo

COLE, NAT (KING)
  Straighten Up And Fly Right
    (Ames, Morgan) SSAB/SATB,acap (gr.
      III) UNC JP (C169)

COLEMAN
  Big Spender (from Sweet Charity)
    SATB NOVELLO 090130 (C170)

COLIN see Broquet, Louis

COLIN ET MARIETTE see Kaelin, Pierre

COLLINS
  Mary Had A Little Blues
    2pt treb cor,pno BOOSEY-ENG
    OCTB6758 (C171)

COLLINS, PHIL
  Hero (composed with Crosby, David)
    (Schmutte, Pete) SATB WARNER
      WBCH9346 (C172)
    (Schmutte, Pete) SAB WARNER
      WBCH9347 (C173)

COLLOQUIO CORALE see Bucchi, Valentino

COLONEL'S SOLILOQUI,THE see Dijker,
  Mathieu

COLORADO TRAIL, THE  *folk song,US
  (Erb) SATB,ST soli LAWSON 4-52661
    (C174)

COLORS OF AMERICA, THE see Campbell-
  Towell, Lee

COLTRANE, JOHN
  Giant Steps
    (Meader,) SSATB,perc (gr. V) UNC JP
      (C175)

COLUMBIA, THE GEM OF THE OCEAN see
  Poné, Gundaris

COME AGAIN see Dowland

COME ALL YOU BOLD CANADIANS see
  Henderson, Ruth Watson

COME, ALL YOU FAIR AND TENDER LADIES
  *folk song
  (Zytowski) SSA LAWSON 4-52644 (C176)

COME AWAY, DEATH see Strohbach,
  Siegfried

COME BACK see Zaruba, Robin

COME, FOLLOW ME see Purcell, Henry

COME FOLLOW THE BANDS  *medley
  (Althouse, Jay) SATB,horn pts WARNER
    C0337CH C0337C1X (C177)
  (Althouse, Jay) SAB,horn pts WARNER
    C0337CH C0337C3X (C178)
  (Althouse, Jay) 2pt cor,horn pts
    WARNER C0337CH C0337C5X (C179)

COME LET US GATHER COCKLES see Vaughan
  Williams, Ralph

COME LET US SING see Albrecht, Sally K.

COME, LIFT YOUR VOICE see Grier, Gene

COME LIVE WITH ME see Swingle, Ward

COME, LIVE WITH PLEASURE see Handel,
  George Frideric

COME MY WAY (from Scarborough Fair)
  (Delong, Richard) 3pt mix cor WARNER
    SV9431 (C180)

COME NOW, MY DARLING see Corigliano,
  John

COME RAIN, COME SHINE see Alcivar, Bob

COME SAIL AWAY WITH ME see Schubert

COME SEE ABOUT ME
  (Schmutte, Pete) SSA WARNER CH9513
    (C181)

COME, SING! COME, DANCE! see Spevacek,
  Linda

COME SUNDAY see Ellington, Edward
  Kennedy (Duke)

COME TO ME, MY LOVE see Dello Joio,
  Norman

COME TO YOUR SENSES see Lovelace,
  Austin Cole

COME, WALK WITH ME see Lord, Suzanne

COME YE SONS OF ART see Purcell, Henry

COMME AUTREFOIS see Martin

COMME IL FAIT NOIR see Broquet, Louis

COMME UNE FLÛTE SUE DE L'HERBE see
  Corboz, Michel

COMMENT VOULOIR QU'UNE PERSONNE CHANTE?
  see Suter, L.M.

COMO MOISES ES EL VIEJO see Pablo, Luis
  de

COMPAGNON, HISSE LA VOILE! see Boller,
  Carlo

COMPANY OF HEAVEN, THE see Britten,
  [Sir] Benjamin

COMPLAINTE see Pasquier, Marius

COMPLAINTE DU MERCENAIRE, LA see Binet,
  Jean

COMPLAINTE DU PAYSAN-SOLDAT see Bitsch,
  Marcel

COMPLAINTE PICARDE see Baruchet, Joseph

COMPLETE CHANSONS see Janequin, Clement

COMPLETE SERIES see Janequin, Clement
  see Machaut, Guillaume de

COMPLETE SET see Landini, Francesco

COMPLETE WORKS OF STEVEN JENKS see
  Jenks, Stephen

COMPLETE WORKS see Landini, Francesco

COMPLETE WORKS see Machaut, Guillaume de

COMPLETE WORKS see Vitry, Philippe de

COMPOSITION FOR CHORUS NO. 14 see Mamiya, Michio

COMPOSITION NO. 46 see Koch-Raphael, Erwin

COMPTINE see Zbinden, Julien-François

CON ALAS EN LOS OJOS see Balzanelli

CONCERT PRINTANIER see Wurmser

CONCERTI DI ANDREA, ET DI GIO. GABRIELLI see Gabrieli, Andrea

CONCERTO À SIX see Telemann, Georg Philipp

CONCI, NICOLA
   Musica Dolce *CC30U
     jr cor,pno&gtr&perc ZERBONI 10358
     f.s.                          (C182)

CONFIDENCE see Bitsch, Marcel

CONNAISSEZ-VOUS, LÀ-BAS? see Henchoz, Emile

CONSEILLERS, LES see Martin

CONSIDER IT PURE JOY see Burroughs

CONSIDER YOURSELF
   SATB WARCH 34795         (C183)

CONTAS GADAS
   SATB,acap MULLES           (C184)

CONTETTO see Killmayer, Wilhelm

CONTINO, GIOVANNI
   Madrigali A Cinque Voci - Libro I
     *CCU
     (Vettori, R.) 5pt cor,acap ZERBONI
     9487 f.s.              (C185)

CONTRE QUI, ROSE see Lauridsen, Morten Johannes

CONVIVIO see Zecchi, Adone

COOLS, EUGÈNE (1877-1936)
   Chanson De Barberine
     4pt mix cor BILLAUDOT    (C186)

   Chanson De Fortunio
     4pt mix cor BILLAUDOT    (C187)

   Mimi Pinson
     4pt men cor BILLAUDOT    (C188)

   Vendanges, Les
     4pt men cor BILLAUDOT    (C189)

COOMBES, DOUGLAS
   Do We Listen ?
     1-2pt cor,pno LINDSAY     (C190)

   Dreams Of Africa: A Song For Elephants
     1-2pt cor,pno PRESSER 512-00627
                            (C191)
     1-2pt cor,pno LINDSAY     (C192)

   Whales Swimming Free
     1-2pt cor,pno (easy) PRESSER
     512-00626              (C193)

COOPER, PAUL (1926- )
   Credo
     SATB&SATB,2+pic.2+English horn.2+
     bass clar.2. 4.3.2.1. perc,timp,
     cel,strings SCHIRM.G    (C194)

   Equinox
     cor,fl,vcl,pno SCHIRM.G   (C195)

   Music for a Festive Occasion
     cor,8trp&2trp,horn,trom,tuba
     SCHIRM.G               (C196)
     SATB,4trp,0.0.0.0. 4.3.3.1. strings
     SCHIRM.G               (C197)

   Omnia Tempus Habent
   "To Everything There Is A Season"
     cor,org SCHIRM.G        (C198)

   Refrains
     dbl cor,SBar soli,2.2+English
     horn.2+bass clar.2. 4.3.3.1.
     timp,3perc,cel,strings SCHIRM.G
                            (C199)

   To Everything There Is A Season see Omnia Tempus Habent

   Voyagers
     SATB,2.2+English horn.2+bass
     clar.2. 4.4.3.1. timp,3perc,cel,
     strings SCHIRM.G       (C200)

COOTS, JOHN FREDERICK (1897- )
   For All We Know
     (Bell, Rick) SATB (gr. III/gr. IV)
     UNC JP                 (C201)

COPLAND, AARON (1900-1990)
   That's The Idea Of Freedom
     SATB WARCH 40730       (C202)

COQ ET LE RENARD, LE see Reibel, Guy

COR A LANCÉ SON APPEL, LE see Brahms, Johannes, Ich Schwing Mein Horn

COR MEUM, OP. 35 see Heininen, Paavo

CORBLEU, MARION! see Sala, Andre

CORBOZ, MICHEL
   C'est Le Joly Mois De May
     mix cor,solo HUG 8341    (C203)

   Chanson Dans Le Vent
     mix cor HUG 8342        (C204)
     men cor HUG 8343        (C205)

   Chantez Au Seigneur Un Chant Nouveau
     mix cor HUG 8302        (C206)

   Comme Une Flûte Sue De L'herbe
     men cor HUG 8218        (C207)

   Dame Folie Singe La Sagesse
     men cor HUG 8301        (C208)

   Gentil Coqu'licot
     mix cor HUG 8341        (C209)

   Jour Est Là, Le
     mix cor HUG 8342        (C210)
     men cor HUG 8343        (C211)

   O Ma Joie
     mix cor HUG 8282        (C212)

   Prière Du Loup
     men cor HUG 8369        (C213)

   Prière Du Moineau
     eq voices HUG 8319      (C214)

   Prière Du Petit Écureuil
     eq voices HUG 8319      (C215)

COREA, CHICK
   Sea-Crystal Journey
     (Anderson, Tom) SSATBB,perc (gr.
     III) UNC JP            (C216)

   Spain
     (Crenshaw, Randy) SATTBB,acap (gr.
     III/gr. IV) UNC JP      (C217)

   You're Everything
     (Bell, Rick) SATB,perc (gr. IV) UNC
     JP                       (C218)

CORELLI, ARCANGELO (1653-1713)
   Adagio
     SATB KJOS C8328         (C219)

CORGHI, AZIO (1937- )
   Musiche Di Scena
     8pt cor,trom ZERBONI 9568 (C220)

CORI POPOLARI ITALIANI *CC17U
   cor ZERBONI 6086 f.s. various
   composers & arrangers    (C221)

CORIGLIANO, JOHN (1938- )
   Come Now, My Darling (from Ghosts of Versailles, The)
     SSAB,pno SCHIRM.G 50481812 (C222)

   O God of Love (from Ghosts of Versailles, The)
     SSSATT,pno SCHIRM.G 50481814 (C223)

CORINNA see Sauseng, Wolfgang

CORNYSHE, WILLIAM (CORNISH)
   ( ? -ca. 1523)
   Ah, Robin, Gentle Robin
     (Mckenzie) TBB,acap WARNER OCT02572
                            (C224)

COROS DE NATAL see Nobre, Marlos

CORTÈGE D'ORPHÉE, LE see Michans, Carlos

COSTELEY, GUILLAUME (1531-1606)
   Allon Gay Bergeres
     (Shaw) SATB,acap LEONARD-US
     50305000              (C225)

   Mignonne, Allons Voir Si La Rose
     eq voices HUG 8054      (C226)

COTTON EYE JOE
   (Glick-Herrington) 2pt jr cor PAVAN
   P1049                  (C227)

COTTON FIELDS see Ledbetter

COUCOU see Boller, Carlo

COUCOU, CASSE-COU see Vuataz, Roger

COUNTRY DANCES see Anonymous

COUNTRY JAMBOUREE see Spevacek, Linda

COUPE D'ORPHÉ, LA see Delmas, Marc-Jean-Baptiste

COUPERIN, FRANÇOIS (LE GRAND) (1668-1733)
   Couperin,La
     (Swingle, Ward) SATB,db,drums (gr.
     II) voc pt,pts UNC JP RG-2X
                            (C228)

   Douze "Tenbury" Motets
     see Musique Vocale

   Leçons De Ténèbres; Élévations;
   Motets
     see Musique Vocale

   Musique Vocal Set
     see Musique Vocale

   Musique Vocale Profane; Motets
     see Musique Vocale

   Musique Vocale
     OISEAU f.s.
     contains: Douze "Tenbury" Motets;
     Leçons De Ténèbres; Élévations;
     Motets; Musique Vocal Set;
     Musique Vocale Profane; Motets
                            (C229)

COUPERIN,LA see Couperin, François (le Grand)

COUR DES MIRACLES, LA see Delibes, Léo

COUREZ PAR LA PLAINE see Rameau, Jean-Philippe

COURONNE D'ETOILES, LA see Denereaz, Alexandre

CRAB,THE (from Cats And Bats And Things With Wings)
   (Vogel, R.) TTBB,pno THOMAS 1C0999392
                            (C230)
   see Vogel, Roger Craig

CRADLE SONGS see Grau, Alberto, Canciones De Cuna

CRAWLEY, CLIFFORD (1929- )
   Late At Night
     unis cor/2pt cor LESLIE 2090 (C231)

   Peace
     unis jr cor/SSA,pno CAN.MUS.CENT.
                            (C232)
     3pt cor LESLIE 3052     (C233)

   Trolls
     unis cor,pno CAN.MUS.CENT. (C234)
     unis cor LESLIE 193      (C235)

CRAZY TIMES see Henderson, Ruth Watson
   see Henderson, Ruth Watson

CREDO see Cooper, Paul

CREEPIN' see Morris, Stevland (Stevie Wonder)

CRENSHAW, RANDY
   And You Know That
     SATB,perc (gr. IV) UNC JP (C236)

   Gone
     SATBB,acap (gr. IV) UNC JP (C237)

CRÉPUSCULE D'ARMOR see Le Flem, Paul

CREW OF THE LONG SERPENT,THE see Grainger, Percy Aldridge

CRIEUR PUBLIC, LE see Boller, Carlo

CROCKETT, DONALD (1951- )
   White Night
     SATB MMB S940002       (C238)

CROISIRE see Falquet, Rene

CROIX, LA see Henchoz, Emile

CROQUIS see Falquet, Rene

CROSS, DAVE
   For All We Know
     SSAA,acap (gr. IV) UNC JP (C239)

CROUCH
   Soon And Very Soon
     (Schrader) SATB HOPE GC 952 (C240)

CROUCH, FREDERICK NICHOLLS (1808-1896)
   Kathleen Mavourneen
     (Dicks, E.A.) SATB BANKS 466 (C241)

CROYEZ-VOUS, MADAME..., LE see Mozart, Wolfgang Amadeus

CRÜGER, JOHANN (1598-1662)
   Soir Descend Et Le Soleil Décline, Le
     mix cor HUG 1929         (C242)

CRUISIN' CROWD see Rogers

CRY OUT AND SHOUT see Nystedt

CUANDO EL REY NIMROD
   (Lazar, Matthew) SATB,T/S solo,pno,
   opt tamb,castanets (med, old
   spanish jewish melody, text in
   ladino) HAZA HZ-008      (C243)

CUANDO NACEN LOS VIENTOS see Balzanelli

CUATRO CAMINOS, CANCION see Sanchez, Damian

CUATRO OBRAS PARA CORO MIXTO see Sanchez, Damian

CUCARACHA, LA  *CC4U,Mex/Span
   (Lemmermann, Heinz) 4pt mix cor
     FIDULA 6081 f.s.       (C244)

CUCKOO IS PRETTY BIRD see Kisby-Hicks

CUEILLONS, MA JOLIE! see Miche, Paul

CULTURAL MOSAIC see Telfer, Nancy

CULTURAL MOSAIC, THE see Telfer, Nancy

CUPIDOOTJE see Kersters, Willem

CURRY, CRAIG
   Ezekiel Went Walkin'
     SATB HERITAGE 15-1093   (C245)

CURTI, F.
   Away From The Roll Of The Sea
     SSA WARCH 35227       (C246)

CUTE see Anderson, Tom

CUTTER
   Out Of The Stars
     2pt cor,fl SHAWNEE EA-169  (C247)

CUTTER, WILLIAM (BILL)
   Rainbow, The  *Gen
     TTBB,pno DEAN 15-1210 R  (C248)

   Sun
     SATB,pno/string orch MUSIC SEV. 622
                                (C249)

   Three Herrick Songs
     SATB,acap DEAN 15-1082  (C250)

CWSG see Hugh-Jones, Llifon, Sleep

CYPRESS AND RED POPPIES, A see Hayashi, Hikaru

CZERNOGORSK FUGUE, OP.14 (1956 REV. 1991) see Svoboda, Tomas

# D

DA BIST DU, WINZERSMANN! see Boller, Carlo

DA GUGGU HÄT JA GÖLBE FÜASS  *CCU, Austrian
   (Fuchs, Peter) mix cor HEYN
     ISBN 3 85366 322 3 f.s.  (D1)

DAAR GINGEN TWEE GESPEELKENS GOED see Toebosch, Louis

DAETWYLER, JEAN
   Au Bord De L'eau
     3 eq voices HUG 8412   (D2)

   Ballade Du Lac
     mix cor HUG 8411       (D3)

   C'est En Forgeant...
     men cor HUG 8111       (D4)

   Chanson De La Source
     mix cor HUG 8367       (D5)

   Chanson De La Vigne
     mix cor HUG 8382       (D6)

   Chanson Des Blés, La
     mix cor HUG 8029       (D7)

   Chanson Du Chalet, La
     mix cor HUG 8327       (D8)

   Chant De L'europe, Le
     mix cor HUG 8467       (D9)
     men cor HUG 8468       (D10)

   Chant Lunaire
     men cor HUG 8297       (D11)

   En Se Mirant Dans La Fontaine
     mix cor HUG 8250       (D12)

   Invocation À La Vierge
     mix cor HUG 8322       (D13)

   Pays, Terre Ardente
     mix cor HUG 8451       (D14)
     men cor HUG 8452       (D15)

   Petite Cantate Rhodanienne
     mix cor HUG 8411       (D16)

   Rhône Danse, Le
     mix cor HUG 8560       (D17)

   Suisse À L'étranger, Le
     men cor HUG 8112       (D18)

   Sulfateurs, Les
     men cor HUG 8256       (D19)

   Vive Le Muscat
     men cor HUG 8488       (D20)

   Voici Le Rhône
     mix cor HUG 8411       (D21)

DAHAM IN MEIN HÄUSLAN  *CCU
   (Schmid, Anton) men cor HEYN NR. 50
   f.s.                     (D22)

DALEY, ELEANOR
   Birds
     unis cor THOMP.G VG1011  (D23)

   False Young Man
     SA THOMP.G VG258      (D24)

   I Sing Of A Maiden
     SA THOMP.G VG260      (D25)

   In Flanders Fields
     SATB THOMP.G VEI1141   (D26)

   O My Dear Heart
     SSAA THOMP.G VEI1130   (D27)

DALL'ALBERO, CLAUDIO (1957-   )
   Canto Mattutino
     6pt mix cor,acap BERBEN BERBEN 3014
                               (D28)

DALLAPICCOLA, LUIGI (1904-1975)
   Exhortatio
     see Tempus Destruendi - Tempus Aedificandi

   Ploratus
     see Tempus Destruendi - Tempus Aedificandi

   Tempus Destruendi - Tempus Aedificandi
     mix cor,acap ZERBONI 7112 f.s.
     contains: Exhortatio; Ploratus
                              (D29)

DALLINGER, GERHARD (1929-   )
   Schneepanther
     mix cor DOBLINGER G 827  (D30)

   Winter Auf Dem Lande
     mix cor DOBLINGER G 828  (D31)

DALPOLSKA see Pim-Pim

DAME FOLIE SINGE LA SAGESSE see Corboz, Michel

DANACH "...MIT BEIDN HÄNDEN DEIN GESICHT UMSCHLIESSEN" see Helmschrott, Robert M.

"DANAÉ", LA see Aubanel, Georges

DANCE OF THE WILLOW see Ebel-Sabo, V.

DANCING IN THE STREET see Stevenson, William

DANIDERFF, PIERRE
   J'irai Au Pôle Sud
     3 eq voices,gtr BILLAUDOT  (D32)

DANIELI, IRLANDO (1944-   )
   Pierres Milliaires Et Feux Follets
     4-6pt mix cor,5trom sc RICORDI-IT
     132465                (D33)

DANK A DS CHORNHUUS see Schweizer, Theodor

DANKLIED see Schmid, Walter

DANN see Helmschrott, Robert M.

DANS see Thorarinsson, Leifur

DANS CETTE ÉTABLE see Boller, Carlo

DANS LA FORÊT see Schubert, Franz (Peter)

DANS LA PLAINE see Martin

DANS LA VIGNE, VIGNE, VIGNE... see Doret, Gustave

DANS LE BOIS QUI CHANTE see Doret, Gustave

DANS LE JARDIN DE LA MAIRIE see Boller, Carlo

DANS LE PETIT BOIS PRÈS DU RUISSEAU see Darcieux, F.

DANS LE VALLON QU'ARROSE see Lagger, Oscar

DANS LE VERGER DÉSERT see Boller, Carlo

DANS LE VERGER FLEURI see Miche, Paul

DANS LES BOIS see Broquet, Louis

DANS LES JARDINS DE LOVATENS see Mermoud, Robert

DANS TOUS LES CANTONS see Cable, Howard

DANSE, LA see Jordan

DANSE DES ANIMAUX, LA see Vercken, François

DANSE, MON MOINE, DANSE see Six Canadian Folksongs

DANZA! see Spevacek, Linda

DANZIG, EVELYN
   Scarlett Ribbons (For Her Hair)
     (Schmutte, Pete) SATB WARNER
     0703SC1X             (D34)

DAQUIN, LOUIS-CLAUDE (1694-1772)
   Rondo "Le Coucou"
     (Swingle, Ward) SATB,db,drums (gr.
     IV) voc pt,pts UNC JP RG-7X (D35)

DARCIEUX, F.
   Bourrée Des Sabots
     4pt mix cor BILLAUDOT   (D36)

   Dans Le Petit Bois Près Du Ruisseau
     4pt men cor BILLAUDOT   (D37)

DARDESS
   Merrily We Sing Noel (Celebrate A Happy Hanukkah)
     SATB ALFRED 5787      (D38)
     3pt cor ALFRED 5788    (D39)

DARDESS, BETTY
   Sing A Song Of Nonsense
     unis cor BOOSEY-ENG OCTB6695 (D40)

DARE TO DREAM! see Lightfoot, Mary Lynn

DARIN, BOBBY
  Splish Splash (composed with Murray,
      Jean)
    (Althouse, Jay) 3pt mix cor WARNER
      5056SC3X                          (D41)
    (Althouse, Jay) SATB WARNER
      5056SC1X                          (D42)

DASHING THROUGH THE SNOW see Pierpont,
  James

DAUGHTER, AWAKE WITH THE MOON see
  Hamer, Janice

DAVID
  What The World Needs Now Is Love
      (composed with Bacharach, Burt
      F.)
    (Spevacek, Linda) SATB SHAWNEE
      A-1993                            (D43)
    (Spevacek, Linda) SAB/3pt mix cor
      SHAWNEE D-472                     (D44)
    (Spevacek, Linda) 2pt cor SHAWNEE
      EA-196                            (D45)

DAVIDS, BRENT MICHAEL
  Mohican Friends
    2pt cor,2fl,perc BEAUT BSP-600
                                        (D46)

DAVIDS, LOUIS
  Naar Buiten Met Louis Davids
    (Brand, Hans V.D.) SABar,pno EXC.MH
      19.800.022                        (D47)

DAVIES
  Holly And The Ivy
    SATB WARCH 34490                    (D48)

DAVIES, VICTOR (1939-    )
  Holly And The Ivy
    SATB THOMP.G VEI1112                (D49)

DAVIS
  Little Drummer Boy (composed with
      Honorati; Simeone)
    SATB WARCH 33684                    (D50)
    SSA WARCH 33684                     (D51)
    SA WARCH 33685                      (D52)
    unis cor WARCH 35111                (D53)

DAWN see Terashima, Rikuya

DAWN OF SPRING, THE see Baxter, Francis
  H.

DAWN ON THE HILLS see Vaughan Williams,
  Ralph

DAWSON, WILLIAM LEVI (1898-1990)
  Rugged Yank, The
    TTBB KJOS T132                      (D54)

DAY BY DAY see Martin, Joseph M.

DAYLIGHT AND MOONLIGHT see White

DAYS OF WINE AND ROSES see Mancini,
  Henry

D'BÄRNERTRACHT see Oetiker, August

DE CE CASTEL ENCHANTEUR see Roy,
  Alphonse

DE GRANDIS, RENATO (1927-   )
  Invoccazione Alla Terra
    mix cor,acap ZERBONI 1708           (D55)

  Signore Dal Volto Luminoso All Terra,
      Il
    dbl cor,opt orch ZERBONI 8254       (D56)

DE HAMLANE TÜR (from "Neue Kärntner
    Chorblätter" Edited By Reinhard
    Kühr) CCU
  (Kleewein, Otto) mix cor/men cor HEYN
    ISBN 3 85366 575 6 f.s.             (D57)

DE JOGGELI see Kraehenbuehl, J.G.

DE L'HIVER AU PRINTEMPS see Huguenin,
  Charles

DE LOS MONTES VENGO see Orrego-Salas,
  Juan A.

DE MI ESPERANZA see Morales

DE PROFUNDIS see Pizzetti, Ildebrando

DE PUNTA Y TACO see Anonymous

DE QUOI NOURRIT-ON LES FEMMES? see
  Boller, Carlo

DE RAMIS DADUNT FOLIA see
  Sigurbjornsson, Hrodmar Ingi

DE SENGER,H.
  A La Nature (from Célébration Des
      Saisons)
    mix cor,opt pno/org/orch HUG 2246
                                        (D58)
  Célébration Des Saisons
    mix cor,orch cor pts HUG 6123 (D59)

DE SENGER,H. (cont'd.)
  Chanson Des Jardiniers Et Jardinières
      (from Célébration Des Saisons)
    mix cor,opt pno/org/orch HUG 2077
                                        (D60)
  Chant Des Tonneliers
    men cor HUG 2081                    (D61)

DE TON REVE TROP PLEINE see Lauridsen,
  Morten Johannes

DE TROIS COULEURS, GRIS, TANNÉ ET NOIR
  see Arrieu, Claude

DE TROIS ROSES see Vuataz, Roger

DE TRUMMLER see Niggli, Friedrich

DE ZOETE TIJD KOMT AAN see Toebosch,
  Louis

DEÁK, CSABA (1932-   )
  Momento Mare
    mix cor,band STIM                   (D62)

DEALING WITH THE REINDEER see Albrecht,
  Sally K.

DEBUSSY, CLAUDE (1862-1918)
  Claire De Lune
    (Swingle, Ward) SSAATTBB,acap (gr.
      IV) voc pt,pts UNC JP SC-2X (D63)

  Trois Chansons
    [Fr/Ger] CARUS 70.070 f.s.
      contains: Trois Chansons, Nr.1
      (SATB); Trois Chansons, Nr.2
      (ATTB,A solo); Trois Chansons,
      Nr.3 (cor,SATB soli)              (D64)

  Trois Chansons, Nr.1
    see Trois Chansons

  Trois Chansons, Nr.2
    see Trois Chansons

  Trois Chansons, Nr.3
    see Trois Chansons

DECEMBER see Swerts, Piet

DECEMBER EPITAPHS see Ghezzo, Dinu
  Dumitru

DECENCUENTROS,LOS see Gustavino, Carlos

DÉCIMATIONS see Desjardins, Jacques

DECK THE HALLS
  (Ohrwall, Anders) mix cor,acap SVERIG
    SK 783                              (D65)
  see Aston, Peter G. see Ayer,Pete
  see Holman

DECKER, WILHELM (1860-1938)
  Auf Wiederseh'n
    men cor,acap MULLES                 (D66)

DÉCLIC! see Gesseney, L.

DEDANS LA COUR DU ROI see Boller, Carlo

DEDANS MA CHAUMIÈRE see Bovet, J.

DEDICA see Manzoni, Giacomo

DELANNOY, MARCEL (1898-1962)
  Chanson De La Belle
    3pt wom cor BILLAUDOT               (D67)

  Petite Ville Du Dimanche
    3pt wom cor BILLAUDOT               (D68)

  Tortillard, Le
    3pt wom cor BILLAUDOT               (D69)

DELIBES, LÉO (1836-1891)
  Abeilles, Les
    2 eq voices BILLAUDOT               (D70)
    3 eq voices BILLAUDOT               (D71)

  Au Printemps
    3 eq voices BILLAUDOT               (D72)

  Cour Des Miracles, La
    4pt men cor BILLAUDOT               (D73)

  Dimanche, Le
    2 eq voices BILLAUDOT               (D74)
    3pt jr cor BILLAUDOT                (D75)

  Écheveau De Fil, L'
    3 eq voices BILLAUDOT               (D76)

  Pifferari, Les
    3pt jr cor BILLAUDOT                (D77)

  Pommier, Le
    3pt jr cor BILLAUDOT                (D78)

DELIUS, FREDERICK (1862-1934)
  Sea Drift (G-E)
    mix cor,orch voc sc JERONA JC1001
      perf mat rent                     (D79)

DELLO JOIO, NORMAN (1913-   )
  Christmas Carol, A
    mix cor LEONARD-US 00007523         (D80)

  Come To Me, My Love
    mix cor LEONARD-US 00007541         (D81)

  Dello Joio Choral Sampler, Norman
      *CC9L
    mix cor LEONARD-US 50488568         (D82)

  Hymns Without Words (First Movement)
    mix cor LEONARD-US 50233850         (D83)

  I Dreamed Of A City Invincible
    mix cor LEONARD-US 50480022         (D84)

  Poet's Song, The
    mix cor LEONARD-US 50231770         (D85)

  Psalmist's Meditation, The
    mix cor LEONARD-US 50233860         (D86)

  Sing A Song Universal
    mix cor LEONARD-US 50489995         (D87)

  Tears
    mix cor LEONARD-US 00004344         (D88)

DELLO JOIO CHORAL SAMPLER, NORMAN see
  Dello Joio, Norman

DELMAS, MARC-JEAN-BAPTISTE (1885-1931)
  Adieu
    4pt men cor BILLAUDOT               (D89)

  Auberge De La Vie, L'
    4pt men cor BILLAUDOT               (D90)

  Chante
    4pt men cor BILLAUDOT               (D91)

  Coupe D'orphé, La
    4pt men cor BILLAUDOT               (D92)

  Doux Sommeil
    4pt men cor BILLAUDOT               (D93)

  Embarquement Pour Cythère, L'
    4pt men cor BILLAUDOT               (D94)

  Hymne À La Musique
    2pt wom cor BILLAUDOT               (D95)

  Hymne Au Soleil
    4pt mix cor BILLAUDOT               (D96)

  Ma Petite Maison
    4pt men cor BILLAUDOT               (D97)
    4pt mix cor BILLAUDOT               (D98)

  Maman
    4pt men cor BILLAUDOT               (D99)
    4pt mix cor BILLAUDOT              (D100)

  Musique Florentine
    4pt men cor BILLAUDOT              (D101)

  Retour Des Champs
    4pt men cor BILLAUDOT              (D102)

  Vague Du Soir, La
    4pt men cor BILLAUDOT              (D103)

  Vieux Moulin, Le
    4pt men cor BILLAUDOT              (D104)

  Voix Du Souvenir, La
    4pt men cor BILLAUDOT              (D105)

  Wallonie
    3 eq voices BILLAUDOT              (D106)

DELOR
  Au Vert Bocage
    see Petite Suite Genevoise

  Carillon Des Chansons, Le *CCU
    eq voices HUG 7900 f.s.            (D107)

  Furet, Le
    see Petite Suite Genevoise

  Nous N'irons Plus Au Bois
    see Petite Suite Genevoise

  Petite Suite Genevoise
    eq voices HUG 7911 f.s.
      contains: Au Vert Bocage; Furet,
      Le; Nous N'irons Plus Au Bois;
      Vive La Rose!                    (D108)

  Vive La Rose!
    see Petite Suite Genevoise

DELSON, ERIC
  From Far, From Eve And Morning
    TTBB,acap LAWSON 52546             (D109)

DEM HIMMEL WILL ICH KLAGEN see Silcher,
  Friedrich

DEM KÖNIG FOLG ICH see Weismann, Julius

DEM SCHWEIZERLAND see Krenger, J.R. see Saladin, O.

DEM VATERLAND see Schmid, A. see Wolf, Hugo

DEMAIN see Mermoud, Robert

DEMIEVILLE, ROLAND
   Qui Chante Son Mal...
     men cor HUG 8804 (D110)

DEN FYRSTE SONG
   (Volle, Sverre) 3pt mix cor,acap
     NOTON N-9368 (D111)

DEN NAESVISE FLUE see Volle, Sverre

DENBOW, STEFANIA BJÖRNSON (1916- )
   All Glory
     SATB,org/pno SEESAW (D112)

DENEREAZ, ALEXANDRE (1875-1947)
   Couronne D'etoiles, La
     men cor HUG 6069 (D113)

   Pour Un Seul Mot
     men cor HUG 6393 (D114)

DENGLER
   Things That Never Die
     SATB SHAWNEE A-1961 (D115)

DENY IT AS SHE WILL see Mechem, Kirke Lewis

DÉPART DU PRINTEMPS, LE see Doret, Gustave

DÉPART DU SOLDAT, LE (ADDIO, MIA BELL'ADDIO) see Boller, Carlo

DEPARTURE see Dijker, Mathieu

DERRIÈR' CHEZ MON PÈRE see Lagger, Oscar

DERUNGS, GION GIUS.
   Muntogna,La
     men cor,acap,opt 2trp&2trom MULLES (D116)

   Sta
     men cor,acap MULLES (D117)

DES LIEUX PROFONDS JE CRIE À TOI see Hassler, Hans Leo

DES MATINES JUSQU'AU SOIR see Honegger, Arthur

DES PREZ, JOSQUIN (ca. 1440-1521)
   Mille Regrets De Vous Abandonner
     SATB EXC.MH 19.800.028 (D118)

DES SENNEN ABSCHIED (PIEMONTESISCHE MELODIE) see Masini

DES SENNEN MORGENLIED see Krenger, R.

DESJARDINS, JACQUES (1962- )
   Décimations
     [Fr] mix cor,S solo,org,0.1.1.0. 1.1.1.0. string quar
     CAN.MUS.CENT. (D119)

DESPAIRING LOVER see Halley

DESTITUYO LAS ROSAS, CHAMARRITA see Sanchez, Damian

DET ÄR TID FÖR EN LÅNG RESA see Hallberg, Bengt

DÉTRESSE see Vuataz, Roger

DEUTSCHE LIEDER *CC9L
   (Krings, Alfred) mix cor,acap LAAB AV 101 (D120)

DEUTSCHE VOLKSLIED,DAS 1978 (from Kärntner Chorblätter)
   (Mittergradnegger, Günther) mix cor HEYN (D121)

DEUTSCHE VOLKSLIEDER *CCU,folk song, Ger
   (Anderluh, Anton) men cor HEYN NR. 57 f.s. (D122)

DEUTSCHER MÄNNERCHOR. HEFT I
   (Amft, Georg) men cor RECITAL 466 f.s. various German composers (D123)

DEUTSCHER MÄNNERCHOR. HEFT II
   (Amft, Georg) men cor RECITAL 467 f.s. various German composers (D124)

DEUTSCHER MÄNNERCHOR. HEFT III
   (Amft, Georg) men cor RECITAL 468 f.s. various German composers (D125)

DEUTSCHMANN, GERHARD (1933- )
   Geburtstagsgruss
     SATB BOHM (D126)

DEUX AMANTS PRÈS DU LAC BLEU see Jaques-Dalcroze, Émile

DEUX CHANSONNETTES see Broquet, Louis

DEUX CHANSONS DE BORD see Lesur, Daniel

DEUX CHANSONS DE FRANCE see Boller, Carlo

DEUX CHANSONS DE MARINS see Lesur, Daniel

DEUX CHANSONS VALAISANNES see Broquet, Louis

DEUX CHOEURS SUR UN POÈME DE TH. GAUTHIER see Brenta, Gaston

DEUX MOTETS see Froberger, Johann Jakob

DEUX PÊCHEURS, LES see Henchoz, Emile

DEUX PIÈCES see Liszt, Franz

DEUX POÉSIES D'AGRIPPA D'AUBIGNÉ see Mihalovici, Marcel

DEUX VALSES, LES see Zbinden, Julien-François

DEVANT LA FLAMME see Mermoud, Robert

DEVIL'S NINE QUESTIONS, THE *folk song,Eng
   (Pfautsch) SATB,pno LAWSON 52768 (D127)

DEVIL'S PUNCHBOWL, THE see Bainbridge, Simon

DEWITT
   Fourth Of July
     SATB oct SOUTHERN SC408 (D128)

   Mustang, The
     TTB oct SOUTHERN SC445 (D129)
     TB oct SOUTHERN SC446 (D130)

   My Mountain Home
     SA oct SOUTHERN SC414 (D131)
     SSA oct SOUTHERN SC413 (D132)

   My Neighbor's Roses
     SATB SOUTHERN SC426 (D133)

DI NOTTE see Prosperi, Carlo

DIABLE SUR LA MURAILLE, LE see Martin

DIABLERIE see Toebosch, Louis

DICKS, ERNEST A.
   Little Billee
     SATB BANKS 691 (D134)

   Why So Pale ?
     SATB BANKS 647 (D135)

DICTÉE DE L'ARAIGNÉE, LA see Mermoud, Robert

DIDO AND AENEAS see Purcell, Henry

DIEB UND DER KÖNIG,DER see Schwaen, Kurt

DIEMER, EMMA LOU (1927- )
   Is It A Dream ?
     SATB,kbd SANTA SBMP 42 (D136)

   Reasons Briefly Set Downe
     TTBB,pno SEESAW (D137)

   There Is A Morn Unseen
     SATB,S/T solo,2.2.2.2. 4.3.3.1. 3perc,strings SEESAW (D138)

   Visionary
     SSA,pno SEESAW (D139)

DIENER, THEODOR (1908- )
   Falke,Der
     wom cor,acap MULLES (D140)

   Garten Des Herrn Ming
     wom cor,pno MULLES (D141)

   Lustigen Musikanten,Die
     men cor,acap MULLES (D142)

   Maiwunder
     wom cor,acap MULLES (D143)

   Schneiders Höllenfahrt
     men cor,3sax MULLES (D144)
     dbl cor,3sax MULLES (D145)

   Unter Der Linde
     wom cor,acap MULLES (D146)

   Zuckersüsse Stadt, Eine *CC10L
     men cor,acap MULLES f.s. (D147)

DIENSTAGS-GRUSS (FRIEDENS-GRUSS) see Stockhausen, Karlheinz

DIEU DES VICTOIRES see Handel, George Frideric

DIFFUGERE NIVES see Camiscioli, Stefann

DIJKER, MATHIEU (1927- )
   Christmas Ghost-Story,A
     see War Poems

   Colonel's Soliloqui,The
     see War Poems

   Departure
     see War Poems

   Drummer Hodge
     see War Poems

   Embarcation
     see War Poems

   Sick Battle-God,The
     see War Poems

   War Poems
     4pt mix cor,Bar solo,org sc DONEMUS f.s.
     contains: Christmas Ghost-Story, A; Colonel's Soliloqui,The; Departure; Drummer Hodge; Embarcation; Sick Battle-God, The (D148)

DIMANCHE, LE see Delibes, Léo

DIMANCHE AU SOIR see Bovet, J.

DIMANCHE AUX BORDS DU RHIN see Schumann, Robert (Alexander)

DIMANCHE DU BERGER, LE see Kreutzer, Conrad

DIMANCHE MATIN see Mermoud, Robert

DIME ROZINA
   (Braun, Yehezkel-Jacobson, Joshua) TB,pno (med easy, text in Ladino) HAZA HZ-024 (D149)

DINDIRIN, DINDIRINDAÑA
   (Guentner) SATB,gtr/kbd,tamb (med diff) PRESSER 312-41639 (D150)

DING, DANG, DÅLÅMEINN see Fem Folkeviser Fra Gausdal

DING, DONG
   (Öhrwall, Anders) mix cor,acap SVERIG SK 698 (D151)

DING DONG! MERRILY ON HIGH
   (Helvey) SATB SHAWNEE A-1970 (D152)
   (Shur) SSA LAWSON 4-52627 (D153)
   see Porterfield, Sherrie

DINOSAURS DANCE IN MY DREAMS see Chappel

DION, DENIS (1957- )
   À Propos De Saint-Denis Gameau
     [Fr] SATB,acap CAN.MUS.CENT. (D154)

DIPIAZZA, ORLANDO (1929- )
   Motetti *CCU
     eq voices/mix cor,acap ZERBONI 10827 f.s. (D155)

DIPTYCHON see Schweizer, Alfred

DIR ZU EIGEN see Keller, Wilhelm

DIRAIT-ON see Lauridsen, Morten Johannes

DIS BE DA BOP see Carter, Allen

DIS, COMPAGNON... see Rochat, Jean

DIS-MOI, CHARBONNIER see Jordan

DIS OUI, MA BONNE AMIE see Kaelin, Pierre

DISTANT SHORE, A see Donnelly, Mary

DIVINE IMAGE, THE see Hagen, Daron

DIX CHANSONS POPULAIRES DE FRANCE, EN DEUX CAHIERS see Planel, Jean

DO A LITTLE SOMETHIN' see Fry, Gary D.

DO WAH DIDDY DIDDY see Barry, Jeff

DO WE LISTEN ? see Coombes, Douglas

DOCTOR JAZZ see Shaw, Kirby

DODICI CANTI POPOLARI FRIULANI see Anonymous

DODO, NANETTE see Canteloube, Joseph

DODSWORTH, STEPHEN
  Rapture,The
    SATB BANKS ECS 113         (D156)

DOJOJI ENGI see Suzuki, Teruaki

DOLF, B.
  Sper Il Pass Alpin
    men cor,acap MULLES        (D157)

DOM GJORDE BOD see Fem Folkeviser Fra Gausdal

DOMINIQUE, MONICA
  Tillägnan
    SATB,pno SVERIG SK 807     (D158)

DON AMADI
  (Braun, Yehezkel-Jacobson, Joshua)
    SA,pno (med easy, text in Ladino)
    HAZA HZ-025                (D159)

DON QUICHOTTE ET SANCHO PANÇA see Hemmerling, Carlos

DONAHUE, BERTHA TERRY
  New Year Carol, A
    SATB,acap LAWSON 52515     (D160)

DONATI, BALDASSARE (DONATO)
  (ca. 1530-1603)
  Villanelle
    mix cor HUG 6047           (D161)
    men cor HUG 3652           (D162)

DONATO
  All Ye Who Music Love
    3pt cor ALFRED 11623       (D163)

DONATONI, FRANCO (1927-    )
  In Cauda
    SATB,3.3.3.3. 4.3.3.1. timp,perc,
      strings sc RICORDI-IT 133288
                               (D164)

DONDE see Fischer, Clare

DÓNDE ESTÁS HERMANO? see Nono, Luigi

DONKEY-THE BARN OWL see Henderson

DONNELLY
  Operatunities (composed with Strid)
    2pt cor SHAWNEE EA-187     (D165)

  We Are One (composed with Strid)
    2-3pt cor SHAWNEE EA-178   (D166)

DONNELLY, MARY
  Distant Shore, A (composed with
      Strid, George L.O.)
    SAB ALFRED 11561           (D167)
    2pt cor ALFRED 11562       (D168)

  Dream Lives On!, The (composed with
      Strid, George L.O.)
    2pt cor HERITAGE 15-1106   (D169)

  Sailor's Life For Me, The
    2pt cor ALFRED 11374       (D170)

  'Tis The Season (A Partner Song With
      "The Holly And The Ivy")
      (composed with Strid, George
      L.O.)
    2pt cor ALFRED 11347       (D171)

DONNEZ-LA-MOI see Falquet, Rene

DON'T CRY FOR ME ARGENTINA see Lloyd Webber, Andrew

DON'T GET AROUND MUCH ANYMORE
  (Althouse) 2pt cor/SSA ALFRED 11646
                               (D172)
  (Althouse) SATB ALFRED 11644 (D173)
  (Althouse) SAB ALFRED 11645  (D174)

DON'T STOP see McVie, Christine

DON'T YOU KNOW I CARE see Ellington, Edward Kennedy (Duke)

DORET, GUSTAVE (1866-1943)
  A La Santé De Noé (from Fête Des
      Vignerons 1927 (Unsere Erde))
    mix cor,opt pno/org/orch HUG 6245
                               (D175)
  A Qui Donner La Rose? (from Fête Des
      Vignerons 1927 (Unsere Erde))
    mix cor,opt pno/org/orch HUG 7217
                               (D176)
    eq voices,opt pno/org/orch HUG 6376
                               (D177)
  Absente, L'
    mix cor HUG 3372           (D178)
    men cor HUG 3678           (D179)

  Allez Zu Jardin
    mix cor HUG 6452           (D180)

  Au Jardin De Mon Père
    see Terre Et L'eau

  Automne, L' (from Fête Des Vignerons
      1905)
    mix cor HUG 3084           (D181)

DORET, GUSTAVE (cont'd.)

  men cor HUG 5113             (D182)

  Baptême, Le (from Fête Des Vignerons
      1927 (Unsere Erde))
    mix cor,opt pno/org/orch HUG 6215
                               (D183)
    eq voices,opt pno/org/orch HUG 6377
                               (D184)
  Bergerette, La
    mix cor HUG 3373           (D185)
    men cor HUG 3676           (D186)

  Bûcherons, Les (from Fête Des
      Vignerons 1927 (Unsere Erde))
    men cor,pno/org/orch HUG 6213
                               (D187)
  C'est La Fille Au Vigneron
    mix cor HUG 6668           (D188)

  Chanson À Boire
    men cor HUG 6678           (D189)

  Chanson À Danser
    mix cor HUG 7203           (D190)

  Chanson D'amour
    mix cor HUG 3551           (D191)

  Chanson De La Belle Julie (from Fête
      Des Vignerons 1927 (Unsere Erde))
    mix cor,opt pno/org/orch HUG 6234
                               (D192)
    men cor,opt pno/org/orch HUG 6371
                               (D193)
  Chanson Des Adieux
    mix cor,S solo HUG 3375    (D194)
    men cor HUG 3674           (D195)

  Chanson Des Anges, La
    eq voices HUG 7216         (D196)

  Chanson Des Bûcherons (from Fête Des
      Vignerons 1905)
    eq voices,opt pno/org/orch HUG 6074
                               (D197)
  Chanson Des Cloches, La
    eq voices HUG 7215         (D198)

  Chanson Des Effeuilles (from Fête Des
      Vignerons 1927 (Unsere Erde))
    mix cor HUG 6235           (D199)

  Chanson Des Faucheurs Et Faneuses
      (from Fête Des Vignerons 1927
      (Unsere Erde))
    mix cor,opt pno/org/orch HUG 6211
                               (D200)
    men cor,opt pno/org/orch HUG 6372
                               (D201)
  Chanson Des Faucheurs Et Faneuses
      (from Fête Des Vignerons 1905)
    mix cor,opt pno/org/orch HUG 5604
                               (D202)
  Chanson Des Jardiniers Et Jardinières
      (from Fête Des Vignerons 1905)
    mix cor,opt pno/org/orch HUG 5603
                               (D203)
    mix cor,pno/org/orch HUG 6238
                               (D204)
  Chanson Des Pommes, La
    men cor HUG 6914           (D205)

  Chanson Des Vendangeurs (from Fête
      Des Vignerons 1927 (Unsere Erde))
    mix cor,opt pno/org/orch HUG 6235
                               (D206)
  Chanson Des Vielles Et Des Vieux
      (from Fête Des Vignerons 1905)
    eq voices,opt pno/org/orch HUG 2348
                               (D207)
  Chanson Des Vieux Et Des Vielles
      (from Fête Des Vignerons 1927
      (Unsere Erde))
    mix cor,pno/org/orch HUG 6231
                               (D208)
  Chanson Du Blé Qui Lève (from Fête
      Des Vignerons 1927 (Unsere Erde))
    mix cor,solo voice,pno/org/orch
      HUG 7778                 (D209)
    men cor HUG 6323           (D210)

  Chanson Du Chevrier (from Fête Des
      Vignerons 1927 (Unsere Erde))
    mix cor,solo voice HUG 7777 (D211)
    eq voices,solo voice,opt pno/org/
      orch HUG 6320            (D212)
  Chanson Du Coucou
    mix cor HUG 7781           (D213)

  Chanson Du Pressior, La (from Fête
      Des Vignerons 1927 (Unsere Erde))
    mix cor,T solo,opt pno/org/orch HUG
      6324                     (D214)
  Chanson Du Ramoneur, La
    mix cor HUG 7057           (D215)
    men cor HUG 6712           (D216)
    eq voices HUG 7465         (D217)

  Chant De La Noce (from Servante
      D'evolène, La)
    mix cor,acap HUG 6949      (D218)

DORET, GUSTAVE (cont'd.)

  Chant Des Moissoneurs (from Fête Des
      Vignerons 1927 (Unsere Erde))
    mix cor,opt pno/org/orch HUG 6214
                               (D219)
    men cor,opt pno/org/orch HUG 6373
                               (D220)
  Chant Des Moissonneurs (from Fête Des
      Vignerons 1905)
    mix cor,opt pno/org/orch HUG 6214
                               (D221)
    eq voices,opt pno/org/orch HUG 6074
                               (D222)
  Chant Des Pâtres (from Tell)
    men cor,opt pno/org/orch HUG 2589
                               (D223)
  Chant Des Petits Bergers & Bergères
    eq voices HUG 6239         (D224)

  Chant Des Suisses (from Tell)
    mix cor,opt pno/org/orch HUG 2597
                               (D225)
    eq voices HUG 3367         (D226)
    men cor,opt pno/org/orch HUG 2602
                               (D227)
  Chant Des Vanniers (from Fête Des
      Vignerons 1927 (Unsere Erde))
    mix cor,T solo,opt pno/org/orch HUG
      6325                     (D228)
  Chante L'alouette!
    mix cor HUG 7091           (D229)
    men cor HUG 7105           (D230)
    eq voices HUG 7106         (D231)

  Dans La Vigne, Vigne, Vigne...
    men cor HUG 7062           (D232)
    eq voices HUG 7460         (D233)
    see Terre Et L'eau

  Dans Le Bois Qui Chante
    eq voices HUG 6593         (D234)

  Départ Du Printemps, Le
    mix cor,T solo,pno/org/orch HUG
      6204                     (D235)
  Église, L'
    men cor HUG 3790           (D236)

  Femme Du Guide, La
    mix cor HUG 7206           (D237)

  Fille Reine, La (from Servante
      D'evolène, La)
    mix cor,acap HUG 6947      (D238)

  Filles D'evolène
    mix cor HUG 6785           (D239)
    men cor HUG 6913           (D240)

  Foi-Amour-Espérance (from Tell)
    eq voices HUG 2593         (D241)

  Forgerons, Les (from Fête Des
      Vignerons 1927 (Unsere Erde))
    men cor,opt pno/org/orch HUG 6212
                               (D242)
  Freiburger Kühreihen
    see Ranz Des Vaches, Le

  Gärtnerlied (from Fête Des Vignerons
      1927 (Unsere Erde))
    [Ger] mix cor,opt pno/org/orch HUG
      6508                     (D243)
  Geissbub, Der (from Fête Des
      Vignerons 1927 (Unsere Erde))
    [Ger] mix cor,opt pno/org/orch HUG
      6512                     (D244)
  Glaneuses, Les (from Fête Des
      Vignerons 1905)
    eq voices,opt pno/org/orch HUG 5607
                               (D245)
  Henriette
    mix cor,ST&speaking voice,acap (In
      Four Parts) HUG 6500     (D246)
  Hiver, L' (from Fête Des Vignerons
      1905)
    mix cor,opt pno/org/orch HUG 5597
                               (D247)
  Hochzeit (from Fête Des Vignerons
      1927 (Unsere Erde))
    [Ger] mix cor HUG 6684     (D248)

  Holzfäller, Die (from Fête Des
      Vignerons 1927 (Unsere Erde))
    [Ger] men cor HUG 6683     (D249)

  Hymne À La Terre (from Fête Des
      Vignerons 1927 (Unsere Erde))
    mix cor,STB soli,pno/org/orch HUG
      6202                     (D250)
  Hymne An Die Heimaterde (from Fête
      Des Vignerons 1927 (Unsere Erde))
    [Ger] mix cor,opt pno/org/orch HUG
      6507                     (D251)
  Hymne Au Pays (from Fête Des
      Vignerons 1927 (Unsere Erde))
    mix cor,pno/org/orch HUG 6206
                               (D252)

**DORET, GUSTAVE** (cont'd.)
Hymne Au Travail (from Fête Des Vignerons 1905)
  mix cor,pno/org/orch HUG 5614 (D253)
  men cor,opt pno/org/orch HUG 5114 (D254)
Il Était Une Fille (from Davel, Drame Historique)
  mix cor,acap HUG 3702 (D255)
Im Heu (from Fête Des Vignerons 1927 (Unsere Erde))
  [Ger] mix cor HUG 6687 (D256)
Invocation À L'hiver (from Fête Des Vignerons 1927 (Unsere Erde))
  mix cor,pno/org/orch HUG 6201 (D257)
  men cor,opt pno/org/orch HUG 6374 (D258)
Invocation Au Printemps (from Fête Des Vignerons 1927 (Unsere Erde))
  mix cor,pno/org/orch HUG 6205 (D259)
Jardinière Du Roy, La
  mix cor,T solo HUG 6484 (D260)
  men cor HUG 8504 (D261)
  eq voices HUG 6594 (D262)
Je Ne Veux Pas Du Vieux Mari (from Servante D'evolène, La)
  mix cor,acap HUG 6946 (D263)
Jean P'tit Jean
  mix cor HUG 6528 (D264)
Joli Meunier, Le (from Fête Des Vignerons 1927 (Unsere Erde))
  mix cor,opt pno/org/orch HUG 6237 (D265)
  eq voices,opt pno/org/orch HUG 6378 (D266)
  men cor HUG 6375 (D267)
Lied Der Alten, Das (from Fête Des Vignerons 1927 (Unsere Erde))
  [Ger] mix cor,opt pno/org/orch HUG 6505 (D268)
Lied Vom Reifenden Korn, Das (from Fête Des Vignerons 1927 (Unsere Erde))
  [Ger] mix cor,opt pno/org/orch HUG 6504 (D269)
  [Ger] men cor HUG 6553 (D270)
Maedeli Du Siebethal, S'
  mix cor HUG 6457 (D271)
  eq voices HUG 6595 (D272)
"Mi-Été" De Taveyanne, La
  mix cor HUG 6240 (D273)
Mon Ami Est Monté (from Tell)
  mix cor HUG 2591 (D274)
Müllersknab, Der (from Fête Des Vignerons 1927 (Unsere Erde))
  [Ger] mix cor HUG 6509 (D275)
  [Ger] men cor HUG 6554 (D276)
Neige Fond Sur Les Montagnes,La (from Servante D'evolène, La)
  mix cor,acap HUG 6948 (D277)
  eq voices,acap HUG 7065 (D278)
Noce, La (from Fête Des Vignerons 1905)
  mix cor,opt pno/org/orch HUG 5600 (D279)
  eq voices,opt pno/org/orch HUG 2349 (D280)
  mix cor HUG 6230 (D281)
Nuit De L'alliance, La (from Tell)
  mix cor HUG 2594 (D282)
  men cor HUG 6295 (D283)
Nuit Des Quatre Temps
  mix cor,pno (In Four Parts) HUG 2262 (D284)
O Jour Le Plus Beau De Ma Vie (from Davel, Drama Historique)
  mix cor,acap HUG 3704 (D285)
Pastourelle, La
  eq voices HUG 6596 (D286)
Petit Jardin Plein D'ombre (from Henriette)
  mix cor HUG 6502 (D287)
Petit Jardinier, Le
  eq voices HUG 7457 (D288)
Pressoir, Le
  mix cor HUG 6749 (D289)
Prière Du Rütli (from Tell)
  mix cor HUG 6021 (D290)
  eq voices HUG 4000 (D291)
  men cor HUG 2595 (D292)

**DORET, GUSTAVE** (cont'd.)
Printemps, Le (Invocation Á Palès) (from Fête Des Vignerons 1905)
  mix cor,S solo,pno/org/orch HUG 5601 (D293)
Psaume XVII (from Davel, Drama Historique)
  mix cor,acap HUG 3712 (D294)
Qu'avez-Vous À Soupirer (from Fête Des Vignerons 1927 (Unsere Erde))
  mix cor HUG 7779, 6236 (D295)
Ranz Des Vaches, Le (from Fête Des Vignerons 1927 (Unsere Erde))
  "Freiburger Kühreihen" [Fr/Ger] mix cor,T solo,opt pno/org/orch HUG 6243, 7780 (D296)
  "Freiburger Kühreihen" [Fr/Ger] men cor,T solo,opt pno/org/orch HUG 6299 (D297)
Roeseli
  mix cor HUG 3380 (D298)
Rose Du Rosier Blanc, La
  eq voices HUG 6597 (D299)
Rossignolet Gentil
  mix cor HUG 6469 (D300)
  eq voices HUG 6598 (D301)
Rouchelines, Les
  mix cor,S solo HUG 7205 (D302)
Schmied, Der (from Fête Des Vignerons 1927 (Unsere Erde))
  [Ger] men cor HUG 6682 (D303)
Schnitterlied (from Fête Des Vignerons 1927 (Unsere Erde))
  [Ger] mix cor,opt pno/org/orch HUG 6510 (D304)
  [Ger] men cor HUG 6555 (D305)
Schöne Anneliese, Die (from Fête Des Vignerons 1927 (Unsere Erde))
  [Ger] mix cor HUG 6685 (D306)
Seigneur, Dans Votre Main... (from Servante D'evolène, La)
  mix cor,acap HUG 6590 (D307)
  eq voices,acap HUG 7782 (D308)
  men cor HUG 7060 (D309)
Servante D'evolène, La
  mix cor,acap (In Four Parts) cor pts HUG 6945 (D310)
Si J'etais
  eq voices HUG 3571 (D311)
Soleil De Juin (from Henriette)
  mix cor,T solo HUG 6501 (D312)
Symphorien
  mix cor HUG 7204 (D313)
Tell
  mix cor, solo voices,orch/pno HUG 2493 (D314)
Terre Et L'eau
  mix cor,acap HUG f.s.
  contains: Au Jardin De Mon Père; Dans La Vigne, Vigne, Vigne...; Vendange, La; Vigne En Fleur, La (D315)
Travaux De La Vigne, Les (from Fête Des Vignerons 1927 (Unsere Erde))
  mix cor,pno/org/orch HUG 6210 (D316)
Vendange, La
  see Terre Et L'eau
Vigne En Fleur, La
  see Terre Et L'eau
Vigne Est En Fleur, La
  eq voices HUG 7469 (D317)
Vreneli Du Guggisberg
  men cor HUG 6673 (D318)
  eq voices HUG 6599 (D319)
Warum Seufzest Du So Schwer? (from Fête Des Vignerons 1927 (Unsere Erde))
  [Ger] mix cor HUG 6511 (D320)
Wem Geb Ich Wohl Die Rose? (from Fête Des Vignerons 1927 (Unsere Erde))
  [Ger] mix cor HUG 6686 (D321)

DÖRFCHEN, DAS see Schubert, Franz (Peter)

DÖRFER see Schmid, Walter

DORMI, BEL BAMBIN see Furrer, Walter

DORMI, DORMI, BEL BAMBIN see Boller, Carlo

DORMI, NON PIANGERE see Furrer, Walter

DORMITE, BEGL' OCCHI see Rossi, Luigi

DORS, MON AMOUR... see Tichy, O.A.

D'OÙ VIENS-TU? see Lang, H.

DOUCE ANNIE *US
  (Guibat) mix cor HUG 7672 (D322)

DOUCE NUIT see Bovet, J.

DOUCE NUIT D'ÉTÉ see Naudier

DOUX PÈLERINAGES see Meyland, J.

DOUX SOMMEIL see Delmas, Marc-Jean-Baptiste

DOUZE MOIS,LES see Malec, Ivo

DOUZE "TENBURY" MOTETS see Couperin, François (le Grand)

**DOWLAND**
Come Again
  (Swingle, Ward) SATB,A solo,db, drums,synthesizer (gr. I) voc pt, pts UNC JP SM-6 (D323)

**DOWLAND, JOHN** (1562-1626)
Evelle-Toi
  mix cor HUG 6052 (D324)
Susses Lieb
  mix cor BUTZ 224 (D325)

DOWN AT THE RIVER see Gallina

DOWN BY THE FAIR RIVER (from Milkwhite Steed ,The)
  (Tilley, A.) SATB,acap THOMAS 1C0979501 (D326)

DOWN BY THE RIVERSIDE see Printz, Brad

DOWN BY THE SALLY GARDENS *folk song
  (Shaw-Parker) TTBB LAWSON 4-51019 (D327)

DRAVIDIAN DITHYRAMB see Paranjoti

DREAM, THE see Telfer, Nancy

DREAM A NEW DREAM see Coghlan

DREAM LIVES ON!, THE see Donnelly, Mary

DREAM TREE, THE see Sainte-Marie, Buffy

DREAM WITH ME see Bernstein, Leonard

DREAM WITHIN A DREAM, A see Schudel, Thomas

DREAMKING AND HIS LOVE see Parker, Horatio William

DREAMLOVER see Hall, Dave

DREAMS OF AFRICA: A SONG FOR ELEPHANTS see Coombes, Douglas

DREAMS OF MINE see Itoh, Mikio

DREI ABENDLIEDER see Benninghoff, Ortwin

DREI BERNER NAMENS JOHANN BIERI, OTTO NOTTER, SAMI STREIT see Schweizer, Alfred

DREI CHÖRE, OP. 111B see Reger, Max

DREI CHÖRE, OP. 111B see Reger, Max

DREI CHORLIEDER see Jensen, Adolf

DREI DEDENKLICHE GESCHICHTEN FÜR KAMMERCHOR UND STREICHQUINTETT see Cerha, Friedrich

DREI HUMORESKEN see Hess, Carlheinz

DREI KANONS ZUM SINGEN UND MUSIZIEREN see Egner, Hermann

DREI MÄNNERCHÖRE OP.31 see Weismann, Julius

DREI QUARTETTE see Bozay, Attila

DREI SONGS FÜR KINDER see Schindler, Peter

DREI SPRÜCHE see Vollenweider, Hans

DREIMAL TAUSEND JAHRE see Schoenberg, Arnold

DRESSONS LE MAI see Mermoud, Robert

DRIE LIEDEREN see Toebosch, Louis

DRIE MINIATUREN see Tuinen, Feike van

DRILL YE TARRIERS, DRILL see Casey

DRINK TO ME ONLY WITH THINE EYES
  (Edlund, Lars) mix cor,acap SVERIG
  SK 734 (D328)
  (Parker-Shaw) TTBB LAWSON 4-530
  (D329)

DRINKING SONG FROM THE 14TH CENTURY see
  Schubert, Franz (Peter)

DRISCHNER, MAX (1891-1971)
  Vier Lieder Zur Jahreswende *CC4U
  mix cor SCHUL CLS 169 f.s. (D330)

DRUMMER HODGE see Dijker, Mathieu

DRUNKEN SAILOR, THE
  (Smith, Gregg) mix cor LEONARD-US
  50309490 (D331)

DRUNTEN IM UNTERLAND see Silcher,
  Friedrich

DRYNAN
  Fate Of Gilbert Gim
  unis cor WARCH 35247 (D332)

D'S BURECHÄTZELI see Furrer, Walter

D'S GEISSBUEBLI see Zahler, J.R.

D'S HÜSLI see Höchle, E. see Krenger, R.

DS SILBERGLEGGLI see Huber, Walter Simon

DS VRENELI AB EM GUGGISBÄRG see Ruprecht, Ernst

DU ÄR SKÖN SÅSOM TIRSA see Schönberg, Stig Gustav

DU BIST DIE RUH see Schubert, Franz (Peter)

DU, DU LIEGST MIR IM HERZEN see Fischer, Clare

DU MEI HAMAT GHEARST MEIN *CC64U, Austrian
  (Drewes, Helmut-Mittergradnegger, Günther) 2-3 eq voices HEYN
  ISBN 3 85366 087 8 f.s. (D333)

DU SKA ITTE TRØ I GRASET see Volle, Bjarne

DU STANDEST AM FENSTER see Kreis, Otto

DU TEMPS QUE J'ALLAIS VOIR MA MIE see Canteloube, Joseph

DUALITY see Tuck, Danny

DUBOIS, PIERRE-MAX (1930- )
  Pauvre Aveugle
  4pt mix cor BILLAUDOT (D334)

DUCK, THE see Henderson, Ruth Watson

DUE COMPOSIZIONI A TRE PARTI see Balas, Arpad

DUE MADRIGALI IN STILE DEL 1500 see Muci, Italo Ruggero

DUET OF THE WIND see Morisaki,Takatoshi

DUFTENDEN NELKE, DER see Rodrigo, Joaquín, A La Clavelina

DUKE'S PLACE (C JAM BLUES) see Ellington, Edward Kennedy (Duke)

DUNKLE NACHT IST ÜBER UNS see Gumpeltzhaimer, Adam

DUNN, MARY LOU
  That Holiday Spirit
  2pt cor WARNER SV9406 (D335)

DUO MEDII AEVI CANTICA see Braun, Yeheskiel

DURCH DEN WALD see Müller, Joseph Ivar

DURCH FELD UND BUCHENHALLEN see Märki, Ernst

DURCHN WINTAWALD GEAHN (from Chorblätter)
  (Streiner, Hans) mix cor HEYN (D336)
  (Streiner, Hans) men cor HEYN (D337)

DURME, DURME
  (Braun, Yehezkel-Jacobson, Joshua)
  SAATBB,pno (med easy, old spanish jewish lullaby, text in ladino)
  HAZA HZ-012 (D338)

DUTILLEUX, HENRI (1916- )
  Adieu, Cher Camarade
    see Chansons De Bord Tome 1 Trois Chansons Du Gaillard D'avant Et Trois Chansons À Hisser

  Chansons De Bord Tome 1 Trois Chansons Du Gaillard D'avant Et Trois Chansons À Hisser
    3pt jr cor BILLAUDOT f.s.
    contains: Adieu, Cher Camarade; Marins De Croix,Les; Nous Irons À Valparaiso; Pique La Baleine; Sur Le Pont De Morlaix; Ya Z'un Petit Bois (D339)

  Chansons De Bord Tome 2 Quatre Chansons À Virer
    3pt jr cor BILLAUDOT f.s.
    contains: Filles De La Rochelle, Les; Grand Coureur, Le; Je N'verrons Plus Marion; Margot, La (D340)

  Filles De La Rochelle, Les
    see Chansons De Bord Tome 2 Quatre Chansons À Virer

  Grand Coureur, Le
    see Chansons De Bord Tome 2 Quatre Chansons À Virer

  Je N'verrons Plus Marion (from Chansons De Bord)
    3pt jr cor BILLAUDOT (D341)
    see Chansons De Bord Tome 2 Quatre Chansons À Virer

  Margot, La
    see Chansons De Bord Tome 2 Quatre Chansons À Virer

  Marins De Croix,Les
    see Chansons De Bord Tome 1 Trois Chansons Du Gaillard D'avant Et Trois Chansons À Hisser

  Marins De Groix (from Chansons De Bord)
    3pt jr cor BILLAUDOT (D342)

  Nous Irons À Valparaiso (from Chansons De Bord)
    3pt jr cor BILLAUDOT (D343)
    see Chansons De Bord Tome 1 Trois Chansons Du Gaillard D'avant Et Trois Chansons À Hisser

  Pique La Baleine
    see Chansons De Bord Tome 1 Trois Chansons Du Gaillard D'avant Et Trois Chansons À Hisser

  Sur Le Pont De Morlaix
    see Chansons De Bord Tome 1 Trois Chansons Du Gaillard D'avant Et Trois Chansons À Hisser

  Ya Z'un Petit Bois
    see Chansons De Bord Tome 1 Trois Chansons Du Gaillard D'avant Et Trois Chansons À Hisser

D'VISITESTUBE see Schleidt, Wilhelm

DVORÁK, ANTONÍN (1841-1904)
  Berceuse
    mix cor HUG 8093 (D344)

  Hiver A Fui..., L'
    mix cor HUG 8094 (D345)

  Steal Away
    (Leavitt, John) SATB,pno,opt English horn WARNER SV9412 ipa (D346)

DYCK, C.
  Bourrée D'Auvergne
    4pt men cor BILLAUDOT (D347)

  Chanson De Mai
    4pt men cor BILLAUDOT (D348)

DYLAN
  Ring Them Bells (composed with Gilpin, Greg)
  SATB SHAWNEE A-1975 (D349)

D'ZYT ISCH CHO see Aeschbacher, C.

# E

È L'ÜSELIN DEL BOSCH... ANDREMO A STRAPÀ I SELARI, L' see Anonymous

E-RI-E, THE see Johnson, Neil

E SUBITO RIPRENDE IL VIAGGIO see Lombardi, Luca

EARLY IN THE SPRING see Vaughan Williams, Ralph

EARTH IS TIRED, THE see Grau, Alberto, Kasar Mie La Gahi

EARTH, WIND AND FIRE MEDLEY
  (Lyons, Bill) SATB,acap UNC JP (E1)

EARTH WOMAN see Parker, Alice

EASY WIND, GO SOFTLY see Kreutz, Robert Edward

EAU DU CIEL, L' see Naudier

EBEL-SABO, V.
  Dance Of The Willow
    unis cor BOOSEY-ENG OCTB6745 (E2)

  Who Has Seen The Wind?
    2pt wom cor BOOSEY-ENG OCTB6773 (E3)

  Winter Wind
    2pt treb cor BOOSEY-ENG OCTB6746 (E4)

ECCARD, JOHANNES (1553-1611)
  Je Viens À Vous Du Haut Des Cieux
    mix cor HUG 1872 (E5)

ÉCHEVEAU DE FIL, L' see Delibes, Léo

ECHI see Morricone, Ennio

ECHO see Young, Robert H.

ECHO CAROL see Whitehead

ECHOS PRINTANIERS see Segard

ECOUTEZ, LÁ-BAS... see Broquet, Louis

ECOUTEZ LA NOUVELLE see Praetorius, Michael

ECOUTEZ, LE TEMPS S'ARRÊTE see Martin

EDDLEMAN, DAVID (1936- )
  Fanfare For A Musical Gathering
    SATB KJOS 8761 (E6)

  Hanukkah Dedication
    4 eq voices KJOS 6231 (E7)

EDDYSTONE LIGHT, THE
  (Levi) TTBB,acap LAWSON 52703 (E8)

EDMUNDS, CHRISTOPHER (1899- )
  To Morning
    SATB BANKS 855 (E9)

EDWARDS, A.H.
  Oft In The Stilly Night
    SATB BANKS 95 (E10)

EDWARDS, GEOFFREY
  Au Clair De La Lune
    see Three French Folk Songs

  Frére Jacques
    see Three French Folk Songs

  Nous N'irons Plus Au Bois
    see Three French Folk Songs

  Three French Folk Songs
    [Eng/Fr] 2 eq voices HERITAGE 15-1008 f.s.
    contains: Au Clair De La Lune, "By The Glowing Moonlight"; Frére Jacques, "Brother John"; Nous N'irons Plus Au Bois, "Come In To The Shady Glade" (E11)

EDWARDS, SHERMAN (1919-1981)
  See You In September
    (Chinn, Teena) SATB,acap WARNER WBCH93230 (E12)

EG GJAETTE TULLA see Møller, Svein

EGLANTINE, L' see Bovet, J.

ÉGLISE, L' see Doret, Gustave

EGNER, HERMANN
  Drei Kanons Zum Singen Und Musizieren
    cor,winds RUNDEL ARTIKEL-NR.5033 (E13)

EHRENBORG
   Nu Tändas Tusen Juleljus
      (Swingle, Ward) SATB,acap voc pt,
      pts UNC JP SSC-1                (E14)

EICHENDORFF see Metzler, Friedrich

EIGENÖSSISCHES DANKLIED
   (Gand-Kreis) men cor,acap MULLES
                                      (E15)

EIGHT PARTSONGS see Schumann, Robert
   (Alexander)

EIGHT SHORT SONGS FOR YOUNG SINGERS see
   Archer, Violet

EINEM, GOTTFRIED VON (1918-    )
   Votivlieder Für Frauenchor
      (Busta) wom cor DOBLINGER 64 482
                                      (E16)

EINER VERLASSENEN see Kunz, Ernst

EINES TAGES IN ALLABENDLICHEN WINDEN
   see Niedermann, Gustav

EINKEHR see Schweizer, Alfred

EINSIEDLER, DER see Hilger, Manfred

EL PAISANITO see Anonymous

ELAINE see Fornerod, Aloys

ELANOY
   (Hoffman) SATB LAWSON 4-52668    (E17)

ÉLÉPHANT BLANC, L' see Breard

ELEVEN PALINDROMES see Smith, Gregg

ELFENLIED see Wolf, Hugo

ELGAR, [SIR] EDWARD (WILLIAM)
   (1857-1934)
   As Torrents In Summer
      (Livingston) SATB,acap (med easy)
      PRESSER 392-41784                (E18)
      (Livingston) SSA (med easy) PRESSER
      392-41569                        (E19)
      (Livingston) SAB,opt kbd (med easy)
      PRESSER 392-41783                (E20)

   Fly, Singing Bird *Op.26,No.2
      SSA,orch sc RECITAL 515          (E21)

   Snow,The *Op.26,No.2
      SSA,orch sc RECITAL 514          (E22)

ELKINS
   No Greater Love (composed with Hayes)
      SATB SHAWNEE A-6195 ipa          (E23)

ELL'COURT, ELL'COURT LA MUSIQUE see
   Landowski, Marcel

ELLE EST LA FILL' D'UN LABOUREUR see
   Canteloube, Joseph

ELLINGTON, EDWARD KENNEDY (DUKE)
   (1899-1974)
   Caravan
      (New York Voices) SSATB,perc (gr.
      V) UNC JP                        (E24)

   Come Sunday
      (The Real Group) SSATB,acap (gr.
      IV) UNC JP                       (E25)

   Don't You Know I Care
      (Paquin-Salerno, Chris) SATB, solo
      voices,perc (gr. III) UNC JP
                                       (E26)

   Duke's Place (C Jam Blues)
      (Anderson, Tom) SATB WARNER
      T0027CC1 ipa                     (E27)
      (Anderson, Tom) SAB WARNER T0027CC3
      ipa                              (E28)
      (Anderson, Tom) 2pt cor/SSA WARNER
      T0027CC5 ipa                     (E29)

   It Don't Mean A Thing
      (Edenroth, Anders) SSATB,soli,acap
      (gr. V) UNC JP                   (E30)

ELLIOT, ALONZO
   Hiker's Prayer (There's A Long, Long
      Trail)
      (Sowash, Rick) SA,pno MUSIC SEV.
                                       (E31)

ELLIOTT, D.J.
   Christmas Sweet, A
      SATB,pno BOOSEY-ENG OCTB6731     (E32)

   Kentucky Jazz Jam
      3pt treb cor,pno,elec bass,drums
      BOOSEY-ENG sc OCTB6750, pts
      ENB400                           (E33)

ELLIPSE III see Ferrero, Lorenzo

ELLSTEIN, ABE
   Abi Gezint
      [Yiddish] SATB,A solo,pno&clar
      (med) HAZA voc sc HZ-048, pt
      NZ-048C                          (E34)

ELOQUENCE, L' see Haydn, [Franz] Joseph

EMBARCATION see Dijker, Mathieu

EMBARQUEMENT POUR CYTHÈRE, L' see
   Delmas, Marc-Jean-Baptiste

EMBRACEABLE YOU see Gershwin, George

EMERALD RAINBOW,THE see Rippentrop,
   Denice

ÉMIGRANTS, LES see Martin

EN BATEAU see Gesseney, L.

EN CE DOUX ASILE see Rameau, Jean-
   Philippe

EN CE JOUR NEUF see Rochat, Jean

EN DOFT, ETT STRÅK AV KÅDA see Haapala,
   Tuomo

EN GEDI
   (Wiesenberg, Menachem) [Heb] mix cor,
   acap (text: A.Peretz; melody:
   D.Aharony) ISR.MUS.INST. IMI 6974
                                       (E35)

EN HALVVÄGS VALS see Yancey, Thomas
   Leland

EN KJAERLIGHEDSVISE see Volle, Bjarne

EN LITEN VISE see Volle, Bjarne

EN LITER VISE see Volle, Bjarne

EN MARCHANT AU PAS see Hemmerling,
   Carlos

EN PASSANT PAR LA LORRAINE see Aubanel,
   Georges see Boller, Carlo

EN REVENANT DE LA FOIRE see Lagger,
   Oscar

EN ROULANT
   (Charles Pelletier) TB,B solo,opt
   drums FOSTER MF 1072                (E36)

EN SE MIRANT DANS LA FONTAINE see
   Daetwyler, Jean

EN UN PASTORAL ALBERGUE see Orrego-
   Salas, Juan A.

EN UNE SEULE FLEUR see Lauridsen,
   Morten Johannes

ENCINA, JUAN DEL (1468-1529)
   Mas Vale Trocar
      (Swingle, Ward) SATB,db,drums,
      synthesizer (gr. II) voc pt,pts
      UNC JP SM-4                      (E37)

ENCINAR, JOSE RAMON (1954-    )
   Cancion
      wom cor,fl,2clar,pno,vcl,3vla
      ZERBONI 8894                     (E38)

ENDO, MASAO (1947-    )
   Shapes Of Love, The
      wom cor,pno JAPAN                (E39)

ENFANT, L' see Boller, Carlo

ENGINN GRAETUR ISLENDING see
   Sigurbjornsson, Hrodmar Ingi

ENGLAND see Hatton, John Liptrot

ENGLISCHE MADRIGALE *CC8L
   (Krings, Alfred) mix cor,acap LAAB
   AV 104                              (E40)

ENGLISH, TINA
   Go And Find Your Dream (composed with
      Andrews, Michael)
      SATB HERITAGE 15-1091            (E41)

ENNS, LEONARD
   Logos
      SATB THOMP.G VEI1149             (E42)

ENTENDEZ LA TROMPETTE see Boller, Carlo

ENTERREMENT D'UNE FOURMI, L' see
   Robert-Lalouet, M.

ENTERTAINER,THE see Joplin

ENTOURAGE INTIME, L' see Leroux,
   Philippe

ENTRE LE BOEUF ET L'ÂNE GRIS see
   Boller, Carlo

ENTRE VOUS TOUS, GENS DE LA VILLE see
   Lagger, Oscar

ENTSAGEN see Bruckner, Anton

EPISODES DE LA VIE D'UN ARTISTE (H.
   BERLIOZ, H. SMITHSON, D.K. HOLOMAN)
   see Bank, Jacques

EPITAPHE POUR UN CHAT see Vuataz, Roger

EPITAPHS see Jeffers, Ron

EPITHALAME see Vuataz, Roger

ÉPOUSAILLES,LES see La Tombelle,
   Fernand de

EQUINOX see Cooper, Paul

ER IST'S see Brun, Fritz see Reger, Max

ERB, JAMES
   Shenandoah
      TTBBB,acap LAWSON 52677          (E43)

ERDMANN, GUNTHER
   Sommermädchen-Küssetauschelächel-
      Beichte
      mix cor,acap sc SCHOTTS C 47676
                                       (E44)

ERGEBUNG see Märki, Ernst

ERGO BIBAMUS see Feibel, Norbert

ERIK A SOM see Bardos, Lajos

ERNEST, THE UNBELIEVING REINDEER see
   Weston, Mark

ERNIEDRIGT-GEKNECHTET-VERLASSEN-
   VERZCHTET see Huber, Klaus

ERNTEDANK see Schmid, Walter

EROS I (1990) see Antoniou, Theodore

ERTEVISE see Vea, Ketil

ERUPTION
   (Clapp, Marti) SSAA,perc (gr. IV) UNC
   JP                                  (E45)

ES BUREBÜEBLI MAH-N-I NID see Burkard,
   Willi

ES CHNÖI see Zwöi Bärndütschi Lieder

ES, ES, ES UND ES see Hollfelder,
   Waldram

ES FLIEGT MANCH VÖGLEIN see Silcher,
   Friedrich

ES HÄÄGLI see Amman, Ulrich

ES HAUSDÄCH BRAT ÜBAR (from "Neue
   Kärntner Chorblätter" Edited By
   Reinhard Kühr) CCU,Austrian
   (Kahlhammer, Jelle) mix cor HEYN
   ISBN 3 85366 623 X f.s. neue
   kärntnerlieder                      (E46)

ES IST WOHL A SCHEANE ZEIT see
   Anderluh, Anton

ES LEBE UNSER TEURER FÜRST see
   Beethoven, Ludwig van

ES LÖSCHT DAS MEER DIE SONNE AUS see
   Silcher, Friedrich

ES SASS EIN HÄSLEIN see Silcher,
   Friedrich

ES SIND ES MAL ZWÖI GSPÜSLI GSI see
   Furrer, Walter

ES STEHT EIN LIND IN JENEM TAL see
   Hollfelder, Waldram see Jaeggi,
   Oswald

ES TAGET VOR DEM WALDE see Burkhart, F.
   see Ruprecht, Ernst

ES WAR EINMAL see Cadow, Paul see
   Lincke, Paul

ES WAR EINMAL EIN SEGELSCHIFFCHEN see
   Marx, Karl, Il Etait Un Petit
   Navire

ES WOLLTE SICH EINSCHLEICHEN see Haus,
   Karl

ES WÜNSCH MIR EINER WAS ER WILL see
   Spranger, Jörg

ESCALADA, OSCAR
   Tangueando
      SATB,acap LAWSON 52729           (E47)

ESHI YO see Suzuki, Teruaki

ESKIMO HUNTING SONG see Six Canadian
   Folksongs

ESTA RAKHEL
   (Braun, Yehezkel-Jacobson, Joshua)
   SATB,pno (med easy, text in Ladino)
   HAZA HZ-022                         (E48)

ESTES, JERRY
  All Around The World Tonight
    3pt mix cor HERITAGE 15-1197H (E49)
    2pt cor HERITAGE 15-1200H (E50)

  Carriers Of The Light
    3pt cor ALFRED 11582 (E51)
    2pt cor ALFRED 11583 (E52)

  For America
    SATB ALFRED 11358 (E53)
    3pt cor ALFRED 11359 (E54)
    2pt cor ALFRED 11360 (E55)

  Melody Flow
    SATB ALFRED 11361 (E56)
    3pt cor ALFRED 11362 (E57)
    2pt cor ALFRED 11363 (E58)

  Our Gift For You
    3pt cor ( opt signing) ALFRED 11364 (E59)
    2pt cor ( opt signing) ALFRED 11365 (E60)

  Sing Merrily, Sing For Joy!
    3pt mix cor HERITAGE 15-1033 (E61)
    2pt cor HERITAGE 15-1017 (E62)

  Sing With Jubilation!
    3pt mix cor HERITAGE 15-1198H (E63)
    2pt cor HERITAGE 15-1199H (E64)

  Solitary Snowflake
    3pt cor ALFRED 11618 (E65)
    2pt cor ALFRED 11619 (E66)

  Three Songs Of Nature
    3pt cor ALFRED 11335 (E67)

  Wherever Music Lives (composed with Gibbons, Thomas)
    3pt mix cor HERITAGE 15-1032 (E68)
    2pt cor HERITAGE 15-1002 (E69)

  Wherever You Go
    3pt cor ALFRED 11578 (E70)
    2pt cor ALFRED 11579 (E71)

ESTEVEZ, ANTONIO (1916- )
  Mata Del Anima Sola
    "Tree Of The Lonely Soul" SATB,T solo EARTHSNG ES-38 (E72)

  Tree Of The Lonely Soul
    see Mata Del Anima Sola

ESTREZ, D'
  Légende De Diane, La
    4pt men cor BILLAUDOT (E73)

ESVAN
  Amour De Moi, L'
    4pt men cor BILLAUDOT (E74)

...ET LA JEUNESSE N'EN SAIT RIEN! see Henchoz, Emile

ET VITAM VENTURI SAECULI see Roxburgh, Edwin

ETÉ see Henchoz, Emile

ETOILE DES LANGUES, L' see Pousseur, Henri

ETOILE DU MATIN see Jordan, Leon

ÉTRANGER, L' see Mermoud, Robert

EU VÖGL BAIN A MIA BELLA see Furrer, Walter

EUROPA-LIED see Löffler, Edmund

EUROPA UNITA CANTA, L' see Anonymous

EUROPÄISCHE WEIHNACHTSLIEDER *CCU
  (Mittergradnegger, Günther) mix cor HEYN NR. 125 f.s. (E75)

EVANS, ROBERT
  Light Becomming
    SATB THOMP.G VEI1143 (E76)

  People Look East
    SATB THOMP.G VG475 (E77)

EVELLE-TOI see Dowland, John

EVENING see Taneyev

EVER TRUE see Hatton, John Liptrot

EVERLY, PHIL
  When Will I Be Loved
    (Baker, Andy) SATB WARNER 6937WC1X (E78)
    (Baker, Andy) 3pt mix cor WARNER 6937WC3X (E79)

EVERY NIGHT AND EVERY MORN see Hayes, Mark

EVERYBODY NEEDS SOMEBODY
  (The Real Group) SSATB,acap (gr. III) UNC JP (E80)

EVERYDAY PEOPLE
  (Schmutte, Pete) SATB WARNER CH9514 (E81)
  (Schmutte, Pete) SAB WARNER CH9515 (E82)
  (Schmutte, Pete) 2pt cor WARNER CH9516 (E83)

EVERYONE HAS HIS DAY see Haydn, [Franz] Joseph see Haydn, [Franz] Joseph, Alles Hat Sein Zeit

EVITA see Lloyd Webber, Andrew

EV'RYBODY SHOUT! see Simms, Patsy Ford

EWIG JUNG IST NUR DIE SONNE see Bella, Rudolf

EXCELSIOR! see Balfe, Michael William

EXHORTATIO see Dallapiccola, Luigi

EXPRESS YOURSELF
  (Chinn, Teena) SSA (medley containing Express Yourself, Material Girl & Vogue) WARNER WBCH9315 (E84)

EZEKIEL WENT WALKIN' see Curry, Craig

# F

FABEL see Tamas, Janos

FABULETTE see Schweizer, Alfred

FAGEN, DONALD
  Maxine
    (Henley, Rod) SATB,perc (gr. III/gr. IV) UNC JP (F1)

FÄHNE see Oetiker, August

FAHNENFLUCHT see Balmer, Luc

FAHNENLIED see Boller, Carlo, Chant Du Drapeau

FAHNENSCHWINGERLIED see Meister, Casimir

FAHR WOHL, DU SCHÖNER MAIENTRAUM see Pfeil, H.

FÄHRMANN, DER see Güdel, W.

FAIN WOULD I CHANGE THAT NOTE see Wilan

FAIR AND FAIR see Holman

FAIR IN FACE see Willan, Healey

FAIRE DU BIEN see Bovet, J.

FAIRY QUEEN,THE see Purcell, Henry

FALKE,DER see Diener, Theodor

FALQUET, RENE
  Bateau De Yangtsé, Le
    see Trois Chansons À L'encre De Chine

  Croisìre
    see Traffic

  Croquis
    mix cor HUG f.s.
      contains: Mayens Sous La Neige; Vieux Pommier, Le; Village De Mémoire, Le (F2)

  Donnez-La-Moi
    men cor HUG 8836 (F3)

  Fille De La Rizière, La
    see Trois Chansons À L'encre De Chine

  Kaleidoscope
    mix cor HUG 8860 (F4)

  Long-Courrier
    see Traffic

  Mayens Sous La Neige
    see Croquis

  Pèlerin De La Montagne
    see Trois Chansons À L'encre De Chine

  Petite Suite Romande *CCUL
    mix cor,pno/orch HUG 8820 f.s. (F5)

  Rêvons D'un Enfant
    mix cor HUG 8849 (F6)

  T.G.V.
    see Traffic

  Tant Que Vivrai
    3-4pt mix cor HUG 8819A (F7)

  Traffic
    mix cor HUG f.s.
      contains: Croisìre; Long-Courrier; T.G.V. (F8)

  Trois Chansons À L'encre De Chine
    mix cor HUG f.s.
      contains: Bateau De Yangtsé, Le; Fille De La Rizière, La; Pèlerin De La Montagne (F9)

  Vieux Pommier, Le
    see Croquis

  Village De Mémoire, Le
    see Croquis

FALSE BRIDE see Holman, Derek

FALSE YOUNG MAN see Daley, Eleanor

FALU
  Volvedora, La
    (Gomez, Eduardo) mix cor LAGOS (F10)

FALU (cont'd.)

    Zamba De La Candelaria
      mix cor LAGOS     (F11)

FÅN see Mossenmark, Staffan

FANCIES see Rees-Davies, Ieuan

FANCY see Pfautsch

FANFARE DU PRINTEMPS, LA see Bovet, J.

FANFARE FOR A MUSICAL GATHERING see Eddleman, David

FANTASY OF SHARDS see Fujikake, Hiroyuki

FANTASY ON JEWISH THEMES see Barnes, Milton

FARANDOLE see Broquet, Louis

FARANDOLE DES HEURES see Haenni, G.

FARBENSPIEL
    4pt wom cor MULLES M&S 872     (F12)
    see Furer, Arthur

FARE THEE WELL LOVE see Calvert, Stuart

FAREWELL, DEAR LOVE see Jones

FAREWELL, LAD
    (O'neill) "Adé Donzallet" SSA ALFRED
    5766     (F13)

FAREWELL OVERTURE, THE see Belmont, Jean

FARIES, THE see Hadley, Henry (Kimball)

FARIGOUL, J.
    Muletiers De Tolède, Les
      4pt men cor BILLAUDOT     (F14)

FARKAS, FERENC (1905- )
    Sonetto CCCXXXIII Di Petrarca
      [It] mix cor EMB 14015     (F15)

FARMER'S BOY, THE see Three North Country Folk Songs

FARMER'S CURST WIFE, THE see Adler, Samuel Hans

FARRELL, JIM
    Playrooms
      SSAA, acap UNC JP     (F16)

FARROW, LARRY
    Jamaican Market Place
      SA, pno, perc GENTRY JG2173     (F17)
      SAB, pno, perc GENTRY JG2187     (F18)
      2pt treb cor GENTRY JG2173     (F19)

FASCINATING RHYTHM see Gershwin, George

FÄSSLER, GUIDO
    Ich Versprach Dir Nie
      men cor, acap MULLES     (F20)

    Wenn Du Mich Mit Dem Boot
      wom cor, acap MULLES     (F21)

FAT MAN, THE (1976) see Wright, Maurice

FATE OF GILBERT GIM see Drynan

FAUCHEURS, LES see Planel, Jean

FAUST SCENE see Hensel, Fanny Mendelssohn

FAVOLE DI ESOPO, LE see Castiglioni, Niccolò

FAVORITE SON
    (Althouse, Jay) SATB WARNER 0180FC1X
    ipa     (F22)
    (Althouse, Jay) SAB WARNER 0180FC3X
    ipa     (F23)
    (Althouse, Jay) 2pt cor WARNER
    0180FC5X ipa     (F24)

FEAST, THE see Rasiuk, Moshe

FEBRUARI-MEEUW see Swerts, Piet

FEEL GOOD see Tyson

FEELINGS see Billingsley

FEGIN I FANGI MINU see Sigurbjornsson, Hrodmar Ingi

FEIBEL, NORBERT
    Ergo Bibamus
      mix cor BUTZ 1144     (F25)

    Freunde, Lasst Uns Singen
      mix cor BUTZ 1143     (F26)

FEIBEL, NORBERT (cont'd.)

    Harmonie
      mix cor BUTZ 1140     (F27)

    Lied Und Wein
      mix cor BUTZ 1139     (F28)

    Musik
      mix cor BUTZ 1141     (F29)

    Muskateller-Lied
      mix cor BUTZ 1138     (F30)

    Ständchen
      mix cor BUTZ 1142     (F31)

FELLEGARA, VITTORIO (1927- )
    Shakespearian Sonnet
      mix cor,opt timp ZERBONI 9570 (F32)

FEM FOLKEVISER FRA GAUSDAL *Op.42
    (Karlsen, Kjell Mørk) NOTON N-8919
    f.s.
    contains: Å Gu 'Dagen Du Inga Mi;
    Ding, Dang, Dålåmeinn; Dom Gjorde
    Bod; Meinn, Meinn Mysuraev; So Ro
    Liten Tull     (F33)

FEMALE CHORUS see Tangiwa, Tadihiro

FEMME DU GUIDE, LA see Doret, Gustave

FEMMES DE CHEZ NOUS, LES see Boller, Carlo

FERDALOK see Sigurbjornsson, Hrodmar Ingi

FERDINAND-LA-TORPILLE see Zbinden, Julien-François

FERGUSON, HOWARD (1908- )
    Lovely Armoy
      SATB BANKS ECS 270     (F34)

FERME DE CHEZ NOUS, UNE see Miche, Paul

FERNAND
    Au Pays Basque
      4pt mix cor (ronde carnavalesque)
      BILLAUDOT     (F35)

FERNEN STERNE GLÜHEN see Leuthold, W.

FERRERO, LORENZO (1951- )
    Ellipse III
      4pt cor sc RICORDI-IT 132461 (F36)

    Néant Où L'on Ne Peut Arriver, Le
      2pt mix cor&treb cor, SSATBarB soli,
      7brass, 7perc sc RICORDI-IT 132510
          (F37)

FERRYMAN-WHO'S THAT KNOCKING see Parke

FEST AUF SOLHAUG, DAS see Wolf, Hugo

FEST DER LIEDER see Schmid, Walter

FEST-KANTATA see Bruckner, Anton

FESTGESANG see Bruckner, Anton

FESTGRUSS see Schmid, Walter

FESTIVAL see Stockhausen, Karlheinz

FESTIVAL FOR MEN'S CHOIR see Svoboda, Tomas

FESTIVAL JUBILATE see Beach, [Mrs.] H.H.A. (Amy Marcy Cheney)

FESTLICHER MORGEN see Schmid, Walter

FESTLICHER TAG see Schmid, Walter

FÊTE DES CHANTEURS, LA see Bron, Patrick

FEUERREITER, DER see Wolf, Hugo

FEVRIER, HENRI (1875-1957)
    Hymne À La Nature
      4pt men cor BILLAUDOT     (F38)

    Mirage, Le
      4pt men cor BILLAUDOT     (F39)

    Petit Mitron, Le
      4pt men cor BILLAUDOT     (F40)
      4pt mix cor BILLAUDOT     (F41)

    Ruisseau, Le
      4pt men cor BILLAUDOT     (F42)

FI MI LOVE
    (Lewin) SA (jamaican folksong) KJOS
    6242     (F43)

FICCO, LITO
    Zamba Para Sarmiento
      3pt cor LAGOS     (F44)

FIDÉLITÉ see Bovet, J.

FIE, NAY, PRITHEE, JOHN see Purcell, Henry

FIELD OF DREAMS see Strommen, Carl

FIEVET, PAUL (1892- )
    Hymne Au Soleil
      4pt men cor BILLAUDOT     (F45)

    Rossignolet Au Bois
      4pt mix cor BILLAUDOT     (F46)

FIFTEEN PASSOVER SONGS see Braun, Yeheskiel

FILASTROCHE see Alderighi, Dante

FILE, FILE AU FIL DE L'EAU see Boller, Carlo

FILE TON ROUET see Jaques-Dalcroze, Émile

FILEUSE, LA see Martin

FILLE À COLIN, LA see Boller, Carlo

FILLE À LA FONTAINE, UNE see Mermoud, Robert

FILLE DE LA RIZIÈRE, LA see Falquet, Rene

FILLE DU VIGNERON, LA see Broquet, Louis

FILLE ET LE POULAIN, LA see Mermoud, Robert

FILLE REINE, LA see Doret, Gustave

FILLES, LES see Binet, Jean

FILLES DE LA ROCHELLE, LES see Dutilleux, Henri

FILLES D'EVOLÈNE see Doret, Gustave

FILLES DU JURA, LES see Miche, Paul

FINE
    Beautiful Soup (from Alice In Wonderland)
      SSA BOOSEY-ENG FIN13     (F47)

    Knave's Letter, The (from Alice In Wonderland)
      SSA BOOSEY-ENG FIN11     (F48)

    White Knight's Song, The
      SA, S solo (from alice in wonderland) BOOSEY-ENG FIN12     (F49)

FINNISSY, MICHAEL (1946- )
    Haiyim
      SATB, 2vcl UNITED MUS     (F50)

FIREFLY see Cassils

FIRST BOOK OF MADRIGALS FOR FIVE VOICES (1602) see Pecci, Tomaso

FIRST IMPRESSIONS see Garcia, Antonio

FIRST SIN, THE see Klein, Gideon

FIRST SIN AND TWO MADRIGALS see Klein, Gideon

FISCHER, CLARE
    Donde
      SATBB, perc (gr. V) UNC JP     (F51)

    Du, Du Liegst Mir Im Herzen
      SATB, perc (gr. IV) UNC JP     (F52)

    Freefall
      SATB, gtr, soprano sax, perc (gr. IV) UNC JP     (F53)

    Funquiado
      SATB, soprano sax, perc (gr. IV) UNC JP     (F54)

    Guajira Pa La Jeva
      SATB, perc, soprano sax (gr. IV) UNC JP     (F55)

    Leavin'
      SATB, perc (gr. IV) UNC JP     (F56)

    Legacy
      SATB, perc (gr. IV) UNC JP     (F57)

    Melancolico
      SATB, perc (gr. V) UNC JP     (F58)

    Morning
      SATB, perc (gr. IV) UNC JP     (F59)

    Night We Called It A Day, The
      SATB, acap (gr. IV) UNC JP     (F60)

FISCHER, CLARE (cont'd.)
  Ronda, La
    SATB,perc (gr. IV) UNC JP      (F61)
  Shake Out All Those Blues
    SATBB,perc (gr. V) UNC JP      (F62)
  Thru The Age
    SATB,perc (gr. IV) UNC JP      (F63)

FISCHERWEISE see Schubert, Franz (Peter)

FISHER, MARK
  When Your Smiling (The Whole World Smiles With You) (composed with Goodwin, Joe; Shay, Larry) (Schmutte, Pete) 2pt cor WARNER 6881WC5X      (F64)

FISHERMAN'S GOOD NIGHT,THE see Bishop, [Sir] Henry (Rowley)

FIVE AMERICAN SONGS see Poné, Gundaris

FIVE CENTURIES OF CHORAL MUSIC (VOL.1)
    *CCU
    mix cor SCHIRM.G 50330320      (F65)

FIVE CENTURIES OF CHORAL MUSIC (VOL.2)
    *CCU
    mix cor SCHIRM.G 50488859      (F66)

FIVE CHAPTERS ON MIE see Shibata, Minao

FIVE MINIATURES ON LOVE see Hutchison, (David) Warner

FIVE ONTARIO FOLKSONGS see Henderson, Ruth Watson

FIVE PORTUGUESE VILLANCICOS see Anonymous

FIVE SONGS see Asaoka, Makiko

FIVE UNISON SONGS see Rees-Davies, Ieuan

FLEISCHMAN, PAUL
  Labyrinth Of Love
    SSAA/6pt wom cor SEESAW      (F67)

FLEMING
  Afton Water
    SA WARCH 34389      (F68)

  Great Big Sea
    SA WARCH 34392      (F69)

  King Of Glory
    SA WARCH 35223      (F70)

  Lark In The Clear Air
    SA WARCH 34393      (F71)

FLETCHER, LINDA
  Love This World My Children (composed with Fraser)
    2pt cor LESLIE 2091      (F72)

FLEUR DE LOTUS, LA see Schumann, Robert (Alexander)

FLEUR DU MATIN see Rougnon, Paul

FLEURS DU MAL,LES see Charpentier, Gustave

FLEUVE, LE see Broquet, Louis

FLIEGERLIED,DAS see Logar, Mihovil

FLIGHT OF THE BUMBLE-BEE see Rimsky-Korsakov, Nikolai

FLOH, DER see Hess, Carlheinz see Widmann, Erasmus

FLOR DE LA MEIL,LA see Grau, Alberto

FLORES DEL ROMERO, LAS see Orrego-Salas, Juan A.

FLOS FLORUM, OVVERO LE TRASFORMAZIONI DELLA MATERIA SONORA see Sciarrino, Salvatore

FLOT ET LE VENT, LE see Bovet, J.

FLOWER DRUM SONG see Fung Yang Kuh Lai

FLOWER OF THE HONEY, THE see Grau, Alberto, Flor De La Meil,La

FLOWERS see Rees-Davies, Ieuan

FLUSS,DER see Schmid, Walter

FLÛTIAU, LE see Jaques-Dalcroze, Émile

FLY ME TO THE MOON
  (Shaw, Kirby) SATB/SSATB,perc (gr. III/gr. IV) UNC JP      (F73)
  see Howard

FLY, SINGING BIRD see Elgar, [Sir] Edward (William)

FLY, WHITE BUTTERFLIES see Sapieyewski, Jerzy

FLYING see Lessia

FÖHN see Hägler, Paul

FÖHNNACHT IM MEIJE see Vollenweider, Hans

FOI-AMOUR-ESPÉRANCE see Doret, Gustave

FOL QUI NE CHANTE PAS see Mermoud, Robert

FOLA, FOLA BLAKKEN see Grieg, Edvard Hagerup

FOLLE ABEILLE see Wissmer, Pierre

FOLLOW THE DRINKIN' GOURD see Bray, Julie Gardner

FOLLOW THE DRINKING GOURD
  (Althouse) SATB ALFRED 11599      (F74)
  (Althouse) SAB ALFRED 11600      (F75)
  (Althouse) 2pt cor ALFRED 11601  (F76)

FONSECA, JULIO
  Mananitas De Mi Terra
    (Dusi, M.) SATB THOMAS 1C0859304      (F77)

FONTAINE SOLAIRE see Apotheloz, Jean

FONTAINES see Henchoz, Emile

FONTENAILLES, H. DE
  Legend Of Miana,The
    SSAA,S solo,pno RECITAL 533      (F78)

FOOLS OF CHELM, THE see Terashima, Rikuya

FOOTPRINTS see Kino, Seiichiro

FOR ALL WE KNOW see Coots, John Frederick see Cross, Dave see Murphy, Kevin

FOR AMERICA see Estes, Jerry

FOR FEMALE CHORUS AND PIANO see Yamagishi, Mao

FOR LENA AND LENNIE see Marois, Rejean

FOR THE FALLEN see Sammes, Mike

FORD
  April
    SA WARCH 35654      (F79)

FORÊT see Naudier

FOREVER AND EVER
  (Chinn, Teena) SATB (medley containing Forever's As Far As I'll Go, In This Life & Forever And Ever, Amen) WARNER C0354C1X      (F80)
  (Chinn, Teena) SAB (medley containing Forever's As Far As I'll Go, In This Life & Forever And Ever, Amen) WARNER C0354C3X      (F81)
  (Chinn, Teena) 2pt mix cor (medley containing Forever's As Far As I'll Go, In This Life & Forever And Ever, Amen) WARNER C0354C5X      (F82)

FOREVER'S AS FAR AS I'LL GO
  (Chinn, Teena) SATB WARNER CH9501      (F83)
  (Chinn, Teena) SAB WARNER CH9502      (F84)

FORGE, LA see Naudier

FORGERON, LE see Indy, Vincent d'

FORGERONS, LES see Doret, Gustave

FORGERONS DE L'OMBRE, LES see Mermoud, Robert

FORNEROD, ALOYS (1890-1965)
  Elaine
    men cor,soli,2.2.2.2. 2.2.0.0. timp,strings HENN HL 454      (F85)

FORSCHEN NACH GOTT see Kreutzer, Konradin

FORSYTH, MALCOLM (1936- )
  Three Zulu Songs
    SSA,fl&ob THOMP.G VG333, pts VG333A      (F86)

FORT, P.
  Ronde
    (Defontaine) 2 eq voices BILLAUDOT      (F87)

FORTY-SECOND STREET see Manhattan Melodies

FORTY SONGS FOR CHILDREN see Theodorakis, Mikis

FOSCJER, JOACHIN
  Swing & Latin (composed with Fuhre, Uli; Rizzi, Werner) *CC27UL, canon
    FIDULA      (F88)

FOSTER
  St. Elmo's Fire-Love Theme
    SATB WARCH 34198      (F89)
    SAB WARCH 33861      (F90)

FOSTER, STEPHEN COLLINS (1826-1864)
  Beautiful Dreamer
    (Düsing, David) SSA,kbd LAWSON 52767      (F91)

  Camptown Races, The
    (Düsing, David) 3pt treb cor,pno LAWSON      (F92)

  Ma Vieille Maison
    (Guibat) mix cor HUG 7673      (F93)
    (Guibat) "Ma Vieille Maison" men cor HUG 7674      (F94)
    see Ma Vieille Maison

  Nelly Bly
    (Halloran, Jack) SSAATTBB,acap GENTRY JG2169      (F95)

  Oh! Susanna!
    (Düsing, David) SSA,acap LAWSON 52755      (F96)
    (Printz, Brad) 2pt cor,opt perc HERITAGE 15-1194H      (F97)

FOUQUÉ, MARTIN
  Meine Freund' Ist Die...
    SATB,pno (each vocal part separately available) APOLLO sc AV 5728, cor pts AV 5728-01      (F98)
    TTBB,pno (each vocal part available separately) sc APOLLO AV 5811      (F99)

FOUR ANCIENT CHINESE PAINTINGS see Baxter, Francis H.

FOUR CHINESE CHILDREN'S SONGS
  (Baxter, Francis H.) SA,pno LAWSON 52722      (F100)

FOUR CHORAL MINIATURES see Pitfield, Thomas Baron

FOUR CHORUSES see Ohana, Maurice

FOUR FOLKSONGS FOR WOMEN'S CHOIR see Schumann, Robert (Alexander)

FOUR JAZZ SPIRITUALS *CC4U
  (Arch) jr cor FABER 51523 1      (F101)

FOUR LITTLE FOXES see Henderson, Ruth Watson

FOUR MADRIGALS ON OLD PORTUGUESE TEXTS see Hartke, Stephen Paul

FOUR PIECES, OP. 27 see Schoenberg, Arnold

FOUR POEMS OF WILLIAM BLAKE see Hagen, Daron see Hagen, Daron

FOUR SHAKESPEARIAN PART-SONGS see Lehmann, Liza

FOUR SONGS FOR WOMEN'S CHORUS see Brown, Rayner

FOUR SONGS WITHOUT WORDS see Hajdu, Andre

FOUR TRANQUIL POEMS AFTER D.H. LAWRENCE see Blumenfeld, Harold

FOUR-VOICE CANZONETTAS WITH ORIGINAL TEXTS AND CONTRAFACTA BY VALENTIN HAUSSMANN AND OTHERS, THE see Vecchi, Orazio (Horatio)

FOURTH OF JULY see Dewitt

FRAGMENTS D'UNE ODE À LA FAIM see Ballif, Claude

FRAMMENTI DA "AU GRAND SOLEIL D'AMOUR CHARGÉ" see Nono, Luigi

FRAMMENTI DA 'CHIARA' see Knussen, Oliver

FRANCE AIMÉE see Bohly

FRANKENFAHRT see Schnepper, Othmar

FRANZ
  Wonne Der Wehmut
    4pt mix cor,pno CRON      (F102)

FRANZ UND VRENELI see Kaelin, Pierre

FRANZÖSISCHE CHANSONS *CC8L
  (Krings, Alfred) mix cor,acap LAAB
    AV 105                           (F103)

FREE PEN see Silverman, Faye-Ellen

FREEDMAN
  Betty Botter
    SSA WARCH 34411                  (F104)

  Cock-A-Doodle-Doo
    SSA WARCH 34407                  (F105)

  Keewaydin
    SSA WARCH 35234                  (F106)

  Ride A Cock Horse
    SSA WARCH 34408                  (F107)

  Simple Simon
    SSA WARCH 34409                  (F108)

FREEDMAN, HARRY (1922-    )
  Rock Around The Clock
    SATB NOVELLO 090830              (F109)

FREEDOM COME see Allaway, Ben

FREEDOM'S SONG see Perry, Dave

FREEFALL see Fischer, Clare

FREI, FRIEDRICH
  In Den Bergen
    men cor,acap MULLES              (F110)

FREIBURGER KÜHREIHEN see Doret, Gustave, Ranz Des Vaches, Le

FREIE HEIMAT see Schmid, A.

FREIES LIED,EIN see Schmid, Walter

FREMDE WEISEN AUS ALLER WELT see Märki, Ernst

FRENCH SECULAR MUSIC *CCU
  cor ZEN-ON 732122 f.s.             (F111)

FRÈRE JACQUES see Edwards, Geoffrey

FRESCOBALDI, GIROLAMO (1583-1643)
  Primo Libro Dei Madrigali, Il *CCU
    (Bianconi, L.) 5pt cor,acap ZERBONI
      9269 f.s.                      (F112)

FREUDIG SCHALLEN UNSERE LIEDER see Schmid, Walter

FREUNDE, LASST UNS SINGEN see Feibel, Norbert

FREUNDESKREIS,DER see Zentner, Johannes

FREY, CARL
  Hab Sonne Im Herzen
    SATB BOHM                        (F113)

FRIEDE see Schmid, Walter

FRIEND TO FRIEND, HEART TO HEART see McPheeters

FRIEND WHO WILL UNDERSTAND, A see Riley

FRIENDS HOLD IN THEIR ARMS LIGHT see Okada, Shodai

FRISCH, ALBERT T. (1916-1976)
  Two Different Worlds (composed with Wayne, Sid)
    (Snyder, Audrey) SATB WARNER
      WBCH9340                       (F114)
    (Snyder, Audrey) SAB WARNER
      WBCH9341                       (F115)

FRISCH FRÖHLICH WEND WIR SINGEN (RÖSELIGARTEN) see Kreis, Otto

FRISCH GESUNGEN (I. TEIL) *CCU
  (Anderluh, Anton) 2-3 eq voices HEYN
    f.s.                             (F116)

FRISCH GESUNGEN (II. TEIL) *CCU
  (Anderluh, Anton) 2-3 eq voices HEYN
    f.s.                             (F117)

FRISCH GEWAGT see Meister, Casimir

FRISCHE FAHRT see Märki, Ernst

FRIVOLE LIEDJES, OP. 91, NO. 1 see Kersters, Willem

FRIVOLE LIEDJES, OP. 91, NO. 2 see Kersters, Willem

FRIVOLE LIEDJES, OP. 91, NO. 3 see Kersters, Willem

FROBERGER, JOHANN JAKOB (1616-1667)
  Deux Motets *CCU
    (Ruggeri) SST,2vln&cont OISEAU
      OL 251 f.s.                    (F118)

FROGS see Skog, Ylva

FROHE WANDERSCHAFT see Schmid, Walter

FROHE WEISE see Güdel, W.

FRÖHLICH LIED ZUR RECHTEN ZEIT, EIN (HEFT 2) see Anderluh, Anton

FRÖHLICH WIR NUN ALL FANGEN AN see Zipp, Friedrich

FRÖHLICHE WANDERUNG see Zahler, J.R.

FRÖHLICHES WIEN see Tamas, Janos

FROM A RAILWAY CARRIAGE see Lightfoot, Mary Lynn

FROM FAR, FROM EVE AND MORNING see Delson, Eric

FROSCH UND DER OCHSE, DER see Asriel, André

FRUEHLING,DER see Bach, Wilhelm Friedemann

FRÜHLING see Märki, Ernst see Schmid, A.

FRÜHLING,DER see Tobler, J.H.

FRÜHLING, DER HELLE FRÜHLING see Schmid, Walter

FRÜHLING, DU BIST DA see Aeschbacher, C.

FRÜHLING KOMMT,DER see Zahler, J.R.

FRÜHLING, O GOLDENE ZEIT see Bella, Rudolf

FRÜHLING UND LIEDER see Mahr, Curt

FRÜHLING, WACH AUF see Hägler, Paul

FRÜHLINGSABEND see Schmid, Walter

FRÜHLINGSAHNUNG see Weber, Carl Maria von

FRÜHLINGSBOTEN see Bieri, Albrecht

FRÜHLINGSCHOR AUS "MANUEL VENEGAS" see Wolf, Hugo

FRÜHLINGSFAHRT see Schmid, Walter

FRÜHLINGSJUBEL see Munzinger, Carl

FRÜHLINGSLIED see Luengen, Ramona see Märki, Ernst

FRÜHLINGSMARSCH see Bovet, J.

FRÜHLINGSMORGEN see Meister, Casimir

FRÜHLINGSTAG see Schmid, Walter

FRÜHLINSRUHE see Brun, Fritz

FRÜHLINSTAG see Schmid, Walter

FRÜHLINSWUNSCH see Schmid, Walter

FRUITS SONT MÛRS, LES see Boller, Carlo

FRÜLINGSGLAUBE see Biebl, Franz

FRY
  Help Of My Friends, The
    SATB SHAWNEE A-1998              (F119)

FRY, GARY D. (1955-    )
  Do A Little Somethin'
    3pt cor HOPE K 315               (F120)
    SATB HOPE K 314, pno-cond sc
      K 314S, pts K 314P             (F121)

FUCHS UND DIE TRAUBEN, DER see Asriel, André see Brand, Theo

FUGE see Mozart, Wolfgang Amadeus see Vivaldi, Antonio

FUGUE IN C MINOR see Bach, Johann Sebastian

FUGUE IN D MAJOR see Bach, Johann Sebastian

FUGUE IN D MINOR see Bach, Johann Sebastian see Muffat, Georg

FUHRE, ULI
  Jazz-Kanons (composed with Rizzi, Werner) *CC19U
    FIDULA 341 ostinati & patterns, introduction and explanatios
                                     (F122)

FUJIEDA, MAMORU (1955-    )
  Night Chant No. 2
    mix cor JAPAN                    (F123)

FUJII, TAKASHI (1959-    )
  Gingatetsudo No Yoru
    jr cor JAPAN                     (F124)

  Song Of Meandering Stars
    mix cor,orch&prepared pno JAPAN
                                     (F125)

FUJIIE, KEIKO (1963-    )
  Ju-Gyu Zu
    men cor JAPAN                    (F126)

FUJIKAKE, HIROYUKI (1949-    )
  Fantasy Of Shards
    mix cor,pno,2perc,synthesizer JAPAN
                                     (F127)

FUKUSHI, NORIO (1945-    )
  Ai No Grammatology *Suite
    "Grammatology Of Love" mix cor
      ONGAKU 545240                  (F128)

  Grammatology Of Love
    see Ai No Grammatology

FUKUSHIMA, YUJIRO (1932-    )
  Michi No Shimauta
    wom cor JAPAN                    (F129)

  Uo Niou Machi
    wom cor,pno JAPAN                (F130)

FÜLLEKRUSS, E.
  O Schöne Zeit
    men cor,acap MULLES              (F131)

FUM FUM FUM
  (Ames, Morgan) SSAA,acap UNC JP
                                     (F132)
  (Shaw And Averre) SA,pno LEONARD-US
    50480260                         (F133)
  (Shaw And Averre) SSA,opt acap/pno
    LEONARD-US 50317390              (F134)

FUMÉE see Pantillon, François

FÜNF HEITERE ALPENLÄNDISCHE VOLKSLIEDER
  *CC5U,folk song
  (Mittergradnegger, Günther) mix cor
    HEYN NR. 133 f.s.                (F135)

FÜNF HEITERE ALPENLÄNDISCHE VOLKSLIEDER UND JODLER *CCU
  (Mittergradnegger, Günther) mix cor
    HEYN NR. 134 f.s.                (F136)

FÜNF KÄRTNER VOLKS LIEDER see Anderluh, Anton

FÜNF KLEINE ELEGIEN see Misteli, Werner

FÜNF VOLKSLIEDSÄTZE (ZUCCALMAGLIO) (1968) see Lück, Rudolf

FUNG YANG KUH LAI *folk song,Chin
  (Marvin, Jameson) "Flower Drum Song"
    TTBB,acap LAWSON 52701           (F137)

FUNK, JEFF
  I Swing The Eighth Notes, Therefore I Am
    SATB HOPE K 319, pts K 319P      (F138)

  Let's Turn On The Night
    SATB HOPE K 318                  (F139)

FUNKEN LEBENSFREUDE, EINEN (from Chorblätter)
  (Streiner, Hans) mix cor HEYN      (F140)
  (Streiner, Hans) men cor HEYN      (F141)

FUNQUIADO see Fischer, Clare

FÜR EIN GESANGFEST see Schmid, Walter

FURCHTSAME JÄGER, DER see Butz, J.Chr.

FURER, ARTHUR (1924-    )
  Blumenlieder, Op. 15
    wom cor,acap MULLES              (F142)

  Farbenspiel
    wom cor,acap MULLES              (F143)

  Kleines Lied,Ein
    wom cor,acap MULLES              (F144)

  Krokus & Steinbrech
    wom cor,acap MULLES              (F145)

  Noli Me Tangere
    wom cor,acap MULLES              (F146)

  Sonnenblume
    wom cor,acap MULLES              (F147)

  Stengelloser Enzian
    wom cor,acap MULLES              (F148)

  Taubnessel
    wom cor,acap MULLES              (F149)

FURER, ARTHUR (cont'd.)
   Tausendguldenkraut
     wom cor,acap MULLES      (F150)

FURER, SAMUEL
   Bärn, Du Edle Schwizerstärn
     men cor,acap MULLES      (F151)

FURET, LE see Delor see La Tombelle, Fernand de

FURRER, WALTER
   Bionda, Bella Bionda
     wom cor,acap MULLES      (F152)

   Bonheur N'est Qu'un Rêve,Le
     wom cor,acap MULLES      (F153)

   Chanzun Del Guitader
     wom cor,acap MULLES      (F154)

   Coin Du Feu,Le
     wom cor,acap MULLES      (F155)

   Dormi, Bel Bambin *Xmas
     wom cor,acap MULLES      (F156)

   Dormi, Non Piangere *Xmas
     wom cor,acap MULLES      (F157)

   D's Burechätzeli
     wom cor,acap MULLES      (F158)

   Es Sind Es Mal Zwöi Gspüsli Gsi
     wom cor,acap MULLES      (F159)

   Eu Vögl Bain A Mia Bella
     wom cor,acap MULLES      (F160)

   Giat E La Mür,Il
     wom cor,acap MULLES      (F161)

   Hopsa, Annelisi
     wom cor,acap MULLES      (F162)

   Jäger,Der
     wom cor,acap MULLES      (F163)

   Katze Und Maus
     wom cor,acap MULLES      (F164)

   Mariä Wiegenlied
     wom cor,acap MULLES      (F165)

   Meitschi, Putz Di
     wom cor,acap MULLES      (F166)

   Nachtwächterlied
     wom cor,acap MULLES      (F167)

   Oiseau Bleu
     wom cor,acap MULLES      (F168)

   S'marliseli Ischt Es Fyns
     wom cor,acap MULLES      (F169)

   Spunta Il Sol
     wom cor,acap MULLES      (F170)

FURUSATO NO SUSABI see Oguri, Katsuhiro

# G

GÅ INTE SÅ HÅRT I GRÄSET see Volle, Bjarne

GABRIELI, ANDREA (1510-1586)
   Concerti Di Andrea, Et Di Gio. Gabrielli (composed with Gabrieli, Giovanni)
     6-16pt cor (contains instrumental music and madrigals in two volumes) RICORDI-IT 134666 (G1)

   Libro Primo De Madrigali A Tre
     3pt cor RICORDI-IT 6 1575  (G2)

   Madrigali Et Ricercari
     4pt cor RICORDI-IT 14 1589  (G3)

   Primo Libro De Madrigali A Sei Voci, Il
     6pt cor RICORDI-IT 5 1574  (G4)

   Primo Libro Di Madrigali A Cinque Voci, Il
     5pt cor RICORDI-IT 2 1566  (G5)

   Secondo Libro De Madrigali A Sei Voci, Il
     6pt cor RICORDI-IT 8 1580  (G6)

   Secondo Libro Di Madrigali A Cinque Voci, Insieme Doi A Sei Et Uno Dialogo A Otto, Il
     5-8pt cor RICORDI-IT 135337  (G7)

   Terzo Libro De Madrigali A Cinque Voci, Il
     5pt cor RICORDI-IT 13 1589  (G8)

GAGNEBIN, HENRI (1886-1977)
   Mystères de la Foi, Les
     cor,2.2.2.2. 3.2.0.0. timp,harp, cimbalom,strings HENN HL 830 (G9)

   Vanités du Monde, Les
     cor,3(pic).2.2.2. 4.3.3.1. timp, harp,perc,org,strings HENN HL 160 (G10)

GAI LABOUREUR, LE see Schumann, Robert (Alexander)

GAILLARD, PAUL-ANDRE
   Au Seuil De L'infini
     men cor HUG 8187      (G11)

   Chanson De Bord
     men cor HUG 8030      (G12)

   Chanson De La Mi-Été De Taveyanne
     men cor HUG 8204      (G13)

   Chanson Du Blé, La
     men cor HUG 8186      (G14)

   Choral À La Montagne
     men cor HUG 8185      (G15)

   Herr Der Stunden, Herr Der Tage
     [Ger] men cor HUG 8199  (G16)

   Il Faut Tant De Choses...
     eq voices HUG 7783    (G17)

   J'ai Rêvé D'une Maison
     mix cor,TS soli HUG 7836  (G18)

   Là-Haut
     men cor HUG 8185      (G19)

   Levez Les Yeux
     men cor HUG 8204      (G20)

   Maître De Nos Heures
     men cor HUG 8198      (G21)

   Rémouleur, Le
     men cor HUG 8186      (G22)

   Seemannslied
     [Ger] men cor HUG 8422  (G23)

GAIS COMPAGNONS see Schubert, Franz (Peter)

GAL, HANS (1890-1987)
   Malgré Tout
     men cor HUG 8530      (G24)

GALANTE, CARLO
   Caeciliam Cantate
     men cor,2trom ZERBONI 9582  (G25)

GALÉ CHUDÂ see Boller, Carlo

GALÉ GRINGO see Bovet, J.

GALINNE, RACHEL
   And We Shall Sing My Songs Of Praise
     [Heb] 16pt mix cor,acap (text: Isaiah 38:10-18) ISR.MUS.INST. IMI 7012 (G26)

GALLANT WEAVER,THE *folk song,Scot
   (Torrance, W.P.) SATB BANKS 1461 (G27)

GALLINA
   Clichés (In Praise Of Phrase)
     SATB SHAWNEE A-1980  (G28)
     3pt mix cor SHAWNEE D-463  (G29)
     2pt cor SHAWNEE EA-185  (G30)

   Down At The River
     SATB SHAWNEE A-1976  (G31)

   Guardians Of The Earth
     2pt cor SHAWNEE EA-0205  (G32)

   Hands 'Cross The Ocean
     2pt cor SHAWNEE EA-191  (G33)

   Home Within Our Heart, A
     SATB SHAWNEE A-1981  (G34)
     3pt mix cor SHAWNEE D-464  (G35)
     2pt cor SHAWNEE EA-186  (G36)

   Ode To Peace
     2pt cor SHAWNEE EA-188  (G37)

   On A Starlit Night
     2pt cor SHAWNEE EA-193  (G38)

   Round 'Bout Winter, A
     2pt cor SHAWNEE EA-174  (G39)

   Sing A Song Of Joy
     2pt cor SHAWNEE EA-0203  (G40)

   Some Folks Do
     2pt cor SHAWNEE EA-0198  (G41)

   Three Robert Louis Stevenson Settings
     3pt mix cor SHAWNEE D-0477  (G42)
     2pt cor SHAWNEE EA-0210  (G43)

GAMBERINI, LEOPOLDO (1922- )
   Anna Franck
     cor,S solo,2.2.2.2. 4.4.4.0. timp, bells,electronic tape,strings RICORDI-IT (G44)

GAMLE MAN see Alldahl, Per-Gunnar

GÅNGLÅT
   (Janunger, Kjell) 4pt mix cor,acap NOTON N-8933 (G45)

GARCIA, ANTONIO
   First Impressions
     SATB,perc (gr. III) UNC JP  (G46)

   Metanola
     SSATB,acap (gr. III) UNC JP  (G47)

GARÇONS D'YVERDON, LES see Jaques-Dalcroze, Émile

GARDE GRISONNE, LA see Cantieni, R.

GARDE LE SOLEIL... see Rochat, Jean

GARDE PASSE, LA see Grétry, André Ernest Modeste

GARDEN GATE, THE
   (Fliarkovsky, A.) "Kalitka" [Russ] SATB,S solo RUSSICA FS 005 (G48)

GARDEN SONGS see Hensel, Fanny Mendelssohn, Gartenlieder

GARDEN SONGS,THE see Hensel, Fanny Mendelssohn

GARDEWEG, FRANZ, X.
   Kleines Lied, Ein
     mix cor BUTZ 934      (G49)

GARE AU ZAZOU see Bezencon, Gilbert

GARNER, ERROLL (1923-1977)
   Misty
     SSATB WARCH 33869   (G50)
     (Strommen, Carl) SATB WARNER 2928MC1X (G51)
     (Strommen, Carl) SAB WARNER 2928MC3X (G52)

GARTEN DES HERRN MING see Diener, Theodor

GARTENLIEDER see Hensel, Fanny Mendelssohn

GÄRTNERLIED see Doret, Gustave

GARWOOD, MARGARET (1927- )
   Haikuzoo
     SATB,acap (six songs) HILD study sc 09421A, cor pts 09421B (G53)

GARWOOD, MARGARET (cont'd.)

   Rainsongs
     SATB,boy solo,orch HILD study sc
     09420A, sc,pts 09420B      (G54)

   Tombsongs
     SATB,orch HILD study sc 09419A, sc,
     pts 09419B      (G55)

GASCONGNE, MATHIEU
   Je Ne Saurais Chanter Ni Rire
     (Swingle, Ward) SATB,db,drums,
     synthesizer (gr. I) voc pt,pts
     UNC JP SM-14X      (G56)

GASSER, ULRICH (1950-    )
   Aus Den Sprüchen Das Lieder Weisheit
     STB [10'] RICORDI-IT SY. 2418 (G57)

   Zur Kalten Zeit
     SATB,acap [15'] RICORDI-IT SY. 2417
     (G58)

GASTIBELZA see Brassens, Georges

GASTOLDI, GIOVANNI GIACOMO
   (ca. 1556-1622)
   Amour Passager, L'
     mix cor HUG 6037      (G59)

   Hark To The Fanfare Sounding
     (Guentner, Francis) SSATB,acap
     WARNER OCT02571      (G60)

   J'ouvre Doucement La Porte
     mix cor HUG 8011      (G61)

   Mettons-Nous En Route!
     4 eq voices HUG 8525      (G62)

   Where Do You Go So Hasty?
     SSATB,acap (ed. by f. guentner)
     WARNER OCT02588      (G63)

GATES, CRAWFORD (1921-    )
   Ring Out Wild Bells
     SATB oct THOMAS 1C0137913 (G64)

GAUDEAMUS IGITUR
   (F.W.Wilson) 2 or 4 choirs, each of 4
   voices, acap ALLAIR      (G65)

GAVE, LE see Kunc, P.

GAVOTTE DES PRISEURS, LA see Bovet, J.

GAWTHROP, DANIEL E.
   Bright Journeys; Songs Of Love And
   Light
     SATB,acap DUN DH9402      (G66)

GEBET see Brun, Fritz see Weber, Carl
   Maria von

GEBET ZUM ALTAÏ see Mermoud, Robert

GEBHARD, HANS (1929-    )
   Lieder Der Minne
     men cor,2vln/fl,gtr/kbd BOHM (G67)

GEBT MIR ZU TRINKEN see Schumann,
   Robert (Alexander)

GEBURTSTAGSGRUSS see Deutschmann,
   Gerhard

GEDANKEN SIND FREI,DIE see Müller-
   Zürich, Paul

GEGENWART see Zentner, Johannes

GEISSBUB, DER see Doret, Gustave

GELBART, M.
   I Have A Little Dreydel
     [Eng] SATB,T solo,pno (med easy)
     HAZA HZ-002      (G68)

GELBKE, JOHANNES
   Heimkehr
     men cor,acap MULLES      (G69)

GELD, GARY (1935-    )
   Sealed With A Kiss
     (Cederberg, Anna) mix cor,acap
     SVERIG SK 723      (G70)

GEMS AUF DEM STEIN,EIN see Spranger,
   Jörg

GENKI NO ENGINE MAWASOYO see Kino,
   Seiichiro

GENTIL COQU'LICOT see Bovet, J. see
   Broquet, Louis see Corboz, Michel

GENTILUCCI, ARMANDO (1939-    )
   Angelo Del Povero, L'
     see Strofe Di Ungaretti

   Non Gridate Piu
     see Strofe Di Ungaretti

   Secrete Vie,Le
     SMezATBar,3.3.3.3. 4.2.3.1. timp,
     perc,harp,strings [30'] RICORDI-

GENTILUCCI, ARMANDO (cont'd.)

     IT 133233      (G71)

   Silenzio Stellato
     see Strofe Di Ungaretti

   Strofe Di Ungaretti
     6pt cor RICORDI-IT 131530 f.s.
     contains: Angelo Del Povero, L';
     Non Gridate Piu; Silenzio
     Stellato      (G72)

GENTLE BIRD see Gray, Cynthia

GENTLE NIGHT see Lully, Jean-Baptiste
   (Lulli)

GENZMER
   Sechs Lieder (from G. Mistral)
     mix cor,acap PETERS 8669 (G73)

GEOFFRAY, CESAR (1901-1972)
   Printemps N'a Point Tant De Fleurs,
   Le
     men cor HUG 8373      (G74)

GERMAN LULLABY see Perry

GERMANENZUG see Bruckner, Anton

GERSBACH, FRITZ
   Im Frühlingswind
     wom cor,acap MULLES      (G75)

   Nun Geht Der Mond Durch Wolkennacht
     wom cor,acap MULLES      (G76)

   Singende Welt
     wom cor,acap MULLES      (G77)
     men cor,acap MULLES      (G78)

GERSHWIN, GEORGE (1898-1937)
   Calp Yo' Hands (Clap Your Hands)
   (composed with Gershwin, Ira)
     (Gilpin, Greg) 3pt mix cor WARNER
     CH9526      (G79)
     (Gilpin, Greg) 2pt cor WARNER
     CH9527      (G80)
     (Gilpin, Greg) SATB WARNER CH9525
     (G81)

   Embraceable You (composed with
   Gershwin, Ira)
     (Strommen, Carl) SATB WARNER
     WBCH93169      (G82)
     (Strommen, Carl) SAB WARNER
     WBCH93170      (G83)

   Fascinating Rhythm
     (Saunders) SATB,acap CAMDEN CM088
     (G84)

   I Got Rhythm
     (Saunders) SATB,pno CAMDEN CM087
     (G85)

   Love Walked Right In
     (Saunders) SATB,acap CAMDEN CM089
     (G86)

   Man I Love, The (composed with
   Gershwin, Ira)
     (Leavitt, John) SSA/SSAA WARNER
     SV9514      (G87)

   Oh, Lady Be Good! (composed with
   Gershwin, Ira)
     (Strommen, Carl) SATB WARNER
     WBCH93174      (G88)
     (Strommen, Carl) SAB WARNER
     WBCH93175      (G89)

   Someone To Watch Over Me (composed
   with Gershwin, Ira)
     (Schmutte, Pete) SATB WARNER CH9536
     (G90)

GERSHWIN FOR GIRLS
   (Chinn, Teena) SSA (medley containing
   Someone To Watch Over Me, The Man I
   Love And I've Got A Crush On You)
   WARNER WBCH9410      (G91)

GESANG DER SELIGEN see Kreis, Otto

GESEGN DICH LAUB, GESEGN DICH GRAS see
   Ziegler, Josef W.

GESELLIG GESUNGEN see Miller, Franz R.

GESPENST GEHT UM IN DER WELT, EIN see
   Nono, Luigi

GESSENEY, ANDRE
   P'tit's Fill's, Les
     eq voices HUG 7845      (G92)

GESSENEY, L.
   Aube Claire
     mix cor HUG 8173      (G93)
     men cor HUG 7734      (G94)

   Avare, L'
     men cor HUG 7479      (G95)

   Brouillard
     mix cor HUG 7190      (G96)

GESSENEY, L. (cont'd.)

   Chanson Du Violoneux
     eq voices HUG 7838      (G97)

   Déclic!
     men cor, solo voices HUG 7474 (G98)

   En Bateau
     mix cor HUG 8585      (G99)
     men cor HUG 8586      (G100)

   Grisants Vertiges
     mix cor HUG 8720      (G101)
     men cor HUG 8721      (G102)

   Hiver Sur Mon Jardin, L'
     mix cor HUG 7728      (G103)
     men cor HUG 7839      (G104)
     eq voices HUG 7727      (G105)

   Maison Du Bonheur, La
     mix cor HUG 7607      (G106)
     men cor HUG 7184      (G107)
     eq voices HUG 7604      (G108)

   Manège
     men cor HUG 7677      (G109)

   On Dance Là-Haut
     mix cor HUG 7186      (G110)

   Rémouleur, Le
     men cor HUG 7480      (G111)

   Renouveau
     mix cor HUG 8584      (G112)

   Verger Au Soleil
     mix cor HUG 7584      (G113)
     men cor HUG 7583      (G114)

   Verger Du Souvenir
     men cor HUG 7770      (G115)

GESTÖRTE STÄNDCHEN, DAS see Mozart,
   Wolfgang Amadeus

GET HAPPY
   (Kinsale, Hillary) 2pt cor (medley
   containing Great Day, Get Happy &
   Happy Days Are Here Again) WARNER
   C0317C5X      (G116)

GET ON BOARD THIS TRAIN see Besig

GET ON YOUR FEET
   SATB (medley containing Your Mama
   Don't Dance, Dancing In The Street
   & Get On Your Feet) WARNER CM9561
   ipa      (G117)
   SAB (medley containing Your Mama
   Don't Dance, Dancing In The Street
   & Get On Your Feet) WARNER CM9562
   ipa      (G118)
   2pt cor (medley containing Your Mama
   Don't Dance, Dancing In The Street
   & Get On Your Feet) WARNER CM9563
   ipa      (G119)

GET READY
   (Gilpin, Greg) SATB WARNER CH9503
     (G120)
   (Gilpin, Greg) SAB WARNER CH9504
     (G121)
   (Gilpin, Greg) 2pt cor WARNER CH9505
     (G122)

GET TO BED see Six Canadian Folksongs

GETTIN' READY FOR CHRISTMAS see
   Albrecht, Sally K.

GEÜBTES HERZ see Kubli, M.

GHEZZO, DINU DUMITRU (1941-    )
   December Epitaphs
     cor,instrumental ensemble SEESAW
     (G123)

GIANT STEPS see Coltrane,John

GIAT E LA MÜR, IL see Furrer, Walter

GIBBONS
   Silver Swan,The
     (Swingle, Ward) SAATB,S solo (gr.
     I) voc pt,pts UNC JP SM-3 (G124)

GIBBONS, ORLANDO (1583-1625)
   Silver Swan, The
     (Smith, Gregg) mix cor LEONARD-US
     50502150      (G125)

GIBE NID AB see Oetiker, August

GIFTS OF LOVE
   (Leavitt) SATB SHAWNEE A-1978 (G126)
   (Leavitt) SAB SHAWNEE D-460 (G127)

GIGUE see Bach, Johann Sebastian

GILBERT
   Autumn Tints
     SA WARCH 35216      (G128)

GILLESPIE, S.
　Shropshire Lad,A
　　SATB PAVAN P1030　　　　　　　(G129)
GILPIN, GREG
　Best Of Times
　　SATB SHAWNEE A-1983　　　　　(G130)

　I Hear Liberty Singing
　　2pt jr cor GILPIN HT9407　　(G131)
　　SAB GILPIN HT9406　　　　　　(G132)

　I Know A Silly Song
　　2pt cor SHAWNEE EA-0211　　　(G133)

　Reaching Higher And Higher
　　SATB SHAWNEE A-2001　　　　　(G134)

　Swinging On A Star
　　2pt cor SHAWNEE EA-0202　　　(G135)

GINDRON-JANEQUIN
　Qui Trouvera La Femme Vertueuse
　　mix cor HUG 8119　　　　　　　(G136)

GINER, BRUNO
　Pour Le Rire D'un Enfant
　　jr cor,2 narrators,acap TRANSAT.
　　TR001886　　　　　　　　　　　(G137)

GINGATETSUDO NO YORU see Fujii, Takashi

GINSBURG, NED
　Time To Give
　　3pt mix cor WARNER SV9346　　(G138)
　　2pt cor WARNER SV9437　　　　(G139)

GINTHER, A.
　Heiwehbänkli, 'S
　　wom cor,acap MULLES　　　　　(G140)

GIPSIES' LAUGHING TRIO,THE see Glover, Stephen

GIRAFFES *N OC12435 see Jennings, Carolyn

GIRL'S GARDEN, A see Wagner, Douglas Edward

GIRLS, GIRLS, GIRLS!
　TTBB/TBB (medley containing California Girls, My Girl & Calendar Girl) WARNER C0334C4X
　　　　　　　　　　　　　　　　　(G141)

GIROFLE GIROFLE see Jouineau, Jacques

GIVE UP THE WORLD see McLin

GIVE YOUR HEART AT CHRISTMAS see Grier, Gene

GJENTELEIK see Volle, Bjarne

GLÄDJENS BLOMSTER see Hultin, Lennart

GLANEUSES, LES see Doret, Gustave

GLEICHWIE AUF DUNKLEM GRUNDE see Spranger, Jörg

GLICK, SRUL IRVING (1934- )
　In Memoriam Leonard Bernstein
　　SATB THOMP.G VEI1148　　　　(G142)

GLICKMAN, SYLVIA (1932- )
　Seven Deadly Sins
　　SATB,SATB soli,pno/chamber orch
　　HILD study sc 09425A, cor pts 09425B　　　　　　　　　　　(G143)

GLOIRE À LA FRANCE see Bazin, François-Emanuel-Joseph

GLOIRE AU SEIGNEUR see Broquet, Louis

GLORIOUS DAY see Martin

GLORIOUS HILL see Bryars, Gavin

GLORIOUS MORNING see Barrett

GLORY TRAIN, THE see Grier, Gene

GLOVER, STEPHEN
　Gipsies' Laughing Trio,The
　　(Dicks, E.A.) SATB BANKS 372　(G144)

GLUCK
　Chant D'été
　　men cor HUG 8531　　　　　　　(G145)

GLUCK, CHRISTOPH WILLIBALD, RITTER VON (1714-1787)
　Air D'Armide
　　4pt mix cor BILLAUDOT　　　　(G146)
　　3 eq voices BILLAUDOT　　　　(G147)

　Choeur D'Armide
　　(Brochart) 3 eq voices BILLAUDOT
　　　　　　　　　　　　　　　　　(G148)
　Hymne (from Iphigénie En Tauride)
　　men cor HUG 6482　　　　　　　(G149)

GLUCK, CHRISTOPH WILLIBALD, RITTER VON (cont'd.)
　Hymne À L'auteur De Toute Grâce
　　mix cor HUG 4805　　　　　　　(G150)

　Pâques
　　mix cor HUG 5810　　　　　　　(G151)

　Prière, La
　　mix cor HUG 2617　　　　　　　(G152)

GLÜCK AUF *CCU
　(Anderluh, Anton) mix cor HEYN
　　mountain dwellers' songs　　(G153)

GLÜCK AUF (HEFT 1) see Anderluh, Anton

GLÜCK DER HEIMAT see Schmid, Walter

GLÜCK UND SCHMÄRZ see Märki, Ernst

GLÜCK ZUM NEUEN JAHR see Biebl, Franz

GLÜCKAUF, DER SONN ENTGEGEN see Schmid, Walter

GLÜCKWUNSCH see Kupp, Albert

GLÜHWÜRMCHEN IDYLL see Lincke, Paul

GO AND FIND YOUR DREAM see English, Tina

GO, LOVELY ROSE see Henderson, Mark see Whitacre, Eric

GO PHOENIX! see Yuyama, Akira

GOD see Hutcheson, Jere T.

GOD BLESS THE CHILD see Herzog

GOD BLESS THE MASTER see Vaughan Williams, Ralph

GOD'S GRANDEUR see Barber, Samuel

GOELANDS, LES see Breard

GOEMANNE
　Lead Us Safely Home
　　SA/SATB KJOS 8755　　　　　　(G154)

GOETZ, ADOLF
　Lieder Der Berge
　　men cor, accordion orchestra (each instrumental part available separately) APOLLO sc AV 2428-10, cor pts AV 2428-18　(G155)

GOETZE, M.
　Sing As The Prairie
　　2pt treb cor,pno BOOSEY-ENG OCTB6733　　　　　　　　　　(G156)

　Under My Command
　　unis cor BOOSEY-ENG OCTB6765　(G157)

　When Children Sing
　　treb cor BOOSEY-ENG OCTB6764　(G158)

GOGO NO REMON-SUI see Naka, Yukichi

GOIN' TO THE AUCTION see Stroope, Z. Randall

GOLD AND ROSE see Schudel, Thomas

GOLDEN SLUMBERS KISS YOUR EYES
　(Dicks, E.A.) SATB BANKS 560　(G159)

GOLDNE ABENDSONNE see Lehrndorfer, F.

GOLSON, BENNY
　I Remember Clifford
　　(Sheehan, Ray) SSAA,acap (gr. III) UNC JP　　　　　　　(G160)

GOMBERT, NICOLAS (ca. 1490-1550)
　Triste Depart
　　SATTB [2'10"] JOED G01　　　(G161)

GONE see Crenshaw, Randy

GONNA BUILD A MOUNTAIN see Bricusse

GOOD-BYE see Lyons,Bill

GOOD-BYE, FARE YE WELL
　(Shaw-Parker) TTBB LAWSON 4-51050
　　　　　　　　　　　　　　　　　(G162)

GOOD KING WENCESLAS
　(Shaw And Parker) SATB,SB soli LEONARD-US 50305060　　　(G163)

GOOD LIFE see Cannon, David

GOOD NIGHT see Barnby, [Sir] Joseph see Carulli, Gustavo

GOOD NIGHT, THOU GLORIOUS SUN see Smart, Henry Thomas

GOODBYE, GOODBYE TO EVERYTHING see Reed, Everett

GOSPEL CHRISTMAS, A
　(Runswick) mix cor FABER 51514 2
　　　　　　　　　　　　　　　　　(G164)

GOTISCHE FENSTER see Kathedrale

GOTTA BE THIS OR THAT see Skylar, Sunny (Selig Sidney Shaftel)

GOTTA GET MYSELF TOGETHER see Schwartz, Dan

GOUD IN HAAR EIGEN AFGLANS STAAT DE MAAN see Voorn, Joop

GOULD
　Springtime Is Calling You
　　unis cor/SA LESLIE 2079　　　(G165)

GOULD, RAYMOND
　Mid-Winter Blues
　　SA LESLIE 2067　　　　　　　　(G166)

　More Homework
　　unis cor/2pt cor LESLIE 2088　(G167)

　Raggedy Ann "N" Andy
　　2pt cor LESLIE 2077　　　　　(G168)

　We Wish You A Very Happy Holiday
　　2pt cor LESLIE 2075　　　　　(G169)

GOUNOD, CHARLES FRANÇOIS (1818-1893)
　Chasse,La
　　TTBB,pno EXC.MH 19.800.021　(G170)

　Choeur Des Soldats (from Faust)
　　men cor HUG 8420　　　　　　　(G171)

　Cigale Et La Fourmi, La
　　mix cor HUG 7377　　　　　　　(G172)
　　eq voices HUG 7766　　　　　　(G173)

GOVEDAS
　Snow
　　2pt cor LESLIE 2086　　　　　(G174)

　Where Go The Boats
　　2pt cor LESLIE 2099　　　　　(G175)

GRABGESANG see Hofer-Schneeberger, Emma

GRACE FOR 10 DOWNING STREET, A see Howells

GRACEY, WILLIAM A.
　Mother Goose Medley
　　SATB BANKS 767　　　　　　　　(G176)

GRAF, ALBERT
　O Wüsst Ich Doch Den Weg
　　men cor,acap MULLES　　　　　(G177)

　Weine Nicht, Mütterlein
　　men cor,acap MULLES　　　　　(G178)

GRAHAM
　Animal Cracker Animals
　　unis cor LESLIE 1194　　　　　(G179)

GRAHAM, R.
　Bonhomme
　　unis cor THOMP.G VG1018　　　(G180)

　Pleasant Simmer Over
　　SA THOMP.G VG262　　　　　　　(G181)

GRAINGER, PERCY ALDRIDGE (1882-1961)
　Camp,The
　　men cor/mix cor BARDIC BD 0351
　　　　　　　　　　　　　　　　　(G182)
　Crew Of The Long Serpent,The
　　SATBarB,acap BARDIC BD 0357　(G183)

　March Of The Men Of Harlech
　　SSAATTBB,drums BARDIC BD 0350
　　　　　　　　　　　　　　　　　(G184)
　My Loves In Germanie
　　SATB,SATB soli,acap BARDIC BD 0353
　　　　　　　　　　　　　　　　　(G185)
　O Gin I Were Where Gadie Rins
　　SATB,acap BARDIC BD 0352　　(G186)

GRAMMATOLOGY OF LOVE see Fukushi, Norio, Ai No Grammatology

GRANA see Albéniz, Isaac

GRANADA
　(Baker, Andy) SAB WARNER CH9580
　　　　　　　　　　　　　　　　　(G187)
　(Baker, Andy) SATB WARNER CH9579
　　　　　　　　　　　　　　　　　(G188)

GRANADOS, ENRIQUE (1867-1916)
　Andaluza
　　(Swingle, Ward) STTBB,S solo,db, drums (gr. II) voc pt,pts UNC JP SOS-9X　　　　　　　　　　(G189)

　Rondalla Aragonesa
　　(Swingle, Ward) SSAATTBB,db,drums (gr. IV) voc pt,pts UNC JP SOS-3X
　　　　　　　　　　　　　　　　　(G190)

GRAND BOEUFS AU LABOUR, LES see Bovet, J.

GRAND COUREUR, LE see Dutilleux, Henri

GRAND-GUILLAUME see Apotheloz, Jean

GRAND KNOWING YOU see Bock, Jerry

GRANDMA'S ADVICE (from Milkwhite Steed ,The)
  (Tilley, A.) SATB,acap THOMAS
  1C0979502 (G191)
  (Tilley, A.) SATB THOMAS 1C979502 (G192)

GRASS see Takemitsu, Toru

GRAST, F.
  Scènes Du Printemps
    mix cor HUG 2247 (G193)

GRAU, ALBERTO
  Canciones De Cuna
    "Cradle Songs" SATB EARTHSNG ES-39 (G194)
  Cradle Songs
    see Canciones De Cuna
  Earth Is Tired, The
    see Kasar Mie La Gahi
  Flor De La Meil,La
    "Flower Of The Honey, The" [Span]
    SSAA,S solo EARTHSNG ES-47 (G195)
  Flower Of The Honey, The
    see Flor De La Meil,La
  Kasar Mie La Gahi
    "Earth Is Tired, The" SATB EARTHSNG ES-43 (G196)

GRAVE POSTS IN THE SEA, THE see Ikebe, Shin-Ichiro

GRAY, CYNTHIA
  Christmas Bells
    2 eq voices,opt handbells/glock HERITAGE 15-1178H (G197)
  Christmas Fanfare
    3pt mix cor,opt trp HERITAGE 15-1120 (G198)
  Gentle Bird
    SATB HERITAGE 15-1201H (G199)
  In The Stillness
    SSA,pno HERITAGE 15-1170 (G200)
  We'll Find A Way
    SATB HERITAGE 15-1172H (G201)
    3pt mix cor HERITAGE 15-1097 (G202)
  Where Earth Meets The Sky
    SATB HERITAGE 15-1037 (G203)

GREAT BIG SEA see Fleming

GREATEST LOVE OF ALL see Masser

GREEN see Blumenfeld, Harold

GREEN HILLS OF ENGLAND see Longmire, John

GREEN PASTURES see Barrett, Richard

GREENLAND WHALE see Holman, Derek

GREENLEE
  Lift Your Hearts (composed with Thompson, Gwen)
    unis cor THOMP.G VA1000 (G204)

GREENSLEEVES see Henchoz, Emile

GREIFT ZUM BECHER see Studer, Hans

GRENOUILLE ET BOEUF, LA see Broquet, Louis

GRETCHEN FEIN see Bovet, J., Barcarolle

GRÉTRY, ANDRÉ ERNEST MODESTE (1741-1813)
  Garde Passe, La
    men cor HUG 6613 (G205)
  Rossignol, Le
    men cor HUG 8531 (G206)

GRIEBLING, MARY ANN
  Return From Town, The
    SSA,pno/harp WILLIS 11608 (G207)

GRIEBLING, S.T.
  Hurry Up!
    SATB WILLIS 11596 (G208)

GRIEG, EDVARD HAGERUP (1843-1907)
  Fola, Fola Blakken
    (Volle, Sverre) 3pt mix cor,acap NOTON (G209)

GRIEG, EDVARD HAGERUP (cont'd.)
  Humoresque
    (Harris) 2pt treb cor HOPE K 311 (G210)
  J'allais Sur La Grand'route
    men cor,opt B solo HUG 8015 (G211)
  Jean-Gaspard
    men cor HUG 8025 (G212)
  Sieben Kinderlieder *Op.61
    3pt wom cor/3pt jr cor PETERS 8797 (G213)

GRIER, GENE (1942- )
  Adrift! A Little Boat Adrift!
    (composed with Everson, Lowell)
    2pt cor,opt fl HERITAGE 15-1149 (G214)
  Caroling! (composed with Everson, Lowell)
    SATB HERITAGE 15-1034 (G215)
  Come, Lift Your Voice (composed with Everson, Lowell)
    SATB WARNER SV9442 (G216)
    SAB WARNER SV9443 (G217)
    2pt cor WARNER SV9444 (G218)
  Give Your Heart At Christmas (composed with Everson, Lowell)
    2pt cor WARNER SV9344 (G219)
    SATB WARNER SV9343 (G220)
  Glory Train, The (composed with Everson, Lowell)
    2pt cor&opt speaking cor HERITAGE 15-1125 (G221)
  'Tis The Season To Be Jolly (composed with Everson, Lowell)
    WARNER (G222)
  Where Have All The Forests Gone? (composed with Everson, Lowell)
    3pt mix cor,fl HERITAGE 15-1104 (G223)
    2pt cor HERITAGE H5896 (G224)

GRILLON, LE see Niverd, Raymond

GRIMANI, MARIA MARGHERITA
  Ogni Colle
    SAB,hpsd,strings ARS FEM EAF 35-09 (G225)

GRISANTS VERTIGES see Gesseney, L.

GRISEY, GERARD (1946- )
  Chants De L'amour, Les
    12pt mix cor,synthesizer RICORDI-IT R. 2363 (G226)

GRISHMA see Bhatia, Vanraj A.

GROTENHUIS, DALE
  Arise, Your Light Has Come
    SATB KJOS 8775 (G227)

GROUND OF SKY see Takashima, Midori

GRUBER
  Swingle Bells VII *Xmas,carol
    (Swingle, Ward) SSAATTBB,db,drums, synthesizer (gr. III) voc pt,pts UNC JP SBS-7 (G228)

GRÜN WAR DEIN SOMMER-KLEID (from Greensleeves) folk song,Ir
  (Welker) SATTBB sc APOLLO AV 6064 (G229)

GRUNDAHL, NANCY
  Native American Spring Songs
    SSAA,fl FOSTER MF 963 (G230)

GRUNDER, KARL
  Möcht Wüsse, Wie-N-Es Chäm
    men cor,acap MULLES (G231)

GRÜNES BLATT see Aeschbacher, Walther

GRUSS AN DAS SCHWEIZERLAND see Hofer-Schneeberger, Emma

GUAJIRA PA LA JEVA see Fischer, Clare

GUANTANAMERA (GUAJIRA GUANTANAMERA)
  (Baker, Andy) [Eng/Span] 2pt cor WARNER 6717GC5X ipa (G232)
  (Baker, Andy) [Eng/Span] SATB WARNER 6717GC1X ipa (G233)
  (Baker, Andy) [Eng/Span] SAB WARNER 6717GC3X ipa (G234)

GUARDIANS OF THE EARTH see Gallina

GÜDEL, W.
  Fährmann,Der
    men cor,acap MULLES (G235)
  Frohe Weise
    men cor,acap MULLES (G236)
  Heilige Flamme,Die
    men cor,acap MULLES (G237)

GÜDEL, W. (cont'd.)
  Heimatrosen
    men cor,Bar solo,acap MULLES (G238)
  Heut Ist Heut
    men cor,acap MULLES (G239)
  Himmel,Der
    wom cor,acap MULLES (G240)
  Morgenwanderung
    men cor,acap MULLES (G241)
  Singe Mein Herz
    men cor,acap MULLES (G242)
  Sommer Gib Acht
    men cor,acap MULLES (G243)
  Spielmann,Der
    men cor,acap MULLES (G244)
  Wanderlied
    men cor,acap MULLES (G245)
  Wein Und Rosen
    men cor,acap MULLES (G246)

GUÉRINEL
  Quatre Poèmes D'Eugenio Montale *CC4U
    12pt mix cor BILLAUDOT f.s. (G247)
  Sept Fragments D'Archiloque
    12pt mix cor BILLAUDOT (G248)

GUERRE DES BALEINIERS, LA see Apotheloz, Jean

GUERRERO, FRANCISCO (1951- )
  Anemos B
    12pt mix cor,acap pts ZERBONI 8871 (G249)

GUESS WHO I SAW TODAY see Argersinger, Charles

GUGUE see Telemann, Georg Philipp

GUILLEDOU, LE see Rochat, Jean

GÜLDENE SCHELLE, DIE see Balmer, Luc

GÜLDNE SONNE,DIE see Zipp, Friedrich

GUMMOE, JOE
  Rhythm Of The Rain
    (Chinn, Teena) SATB,acap WARNER WBCH9314 (G250)

GUMPELTZHAIMER, ADAM (ca. 1559-1625)
  Dunkle Nacht Ist Über Uns
    wom cor,acap MULLES (G251)
  Wacht Auf, Ihr Lieben Vögelein
    wom cor,acap MULLES (G252)

GUNSENHEIMER, GUSTAV (1934- )
  Auf, Ihr Brüder, Seid Bereit
    mix cor,opt instrumental ensemble BOHM (G253)

GURRELIEDER see Schoenberg, Arnold

GURTE-LIEDLI see Keller, Hugo

GUSTAVINO, CARLOS
  Decencuentros,Los
    4pt mix cor LAGOS (G254)
  Lejos De Santa Fe
    4pt mix cor LAGOS (G255)
  Miedo (Allegretto)
    see Tres Canciones De Cuna
  Noche, La (Allegretto)
    see Tres Canciones De Cuna
  Noches De Santa Fe
    4pt mix cor LAGOS (G256)
  Ojos De Tempo
    4pt mix cor LAGOS (G257)
  Pampamapa
    4pt mix cor LAGOS (G258)
  Sampedrino,El
    4pt mix cor LAGOS (G259)
    3pt mix cor LAGOS (G260)
  Tempra,Lanera
    4pt mix cor LAGOS (G261)
  Tres Canciones De Cuna
    4pt mix cor LAGOS f.s.
    contains: Miedo (Allegretto); Noche, La (Allegretto); Yo No Tengo Soledad (Adagio) (G262)
  Yo, Maestra
    4pt mix cor LAGOS (G263)

# SECULAR CHORAL MUSIC

GUSTAVINO, CARLOS (cont'd.)
  Yo No Tengo Soledad (Adagio)
    see Tres Canciones De Cuna

GUTE ZIEL,DAS see Jenny, Albert

GUTES WOLLEN see Jessler, Fritz

GUTHRIE
  So Long It's Been Good To Know Yuh
    SA/TB WARCH 34809 (G264)

  This Land Is Your Land
    SA/TB WARCH 34803 (G265)
    SSA WARCH 34814 (G266)
    SATB WARCH 34816 (G267)

GUTIÉRREZ, PEDRO
  Alma Llanera
    "Soul Of The Plains" SATB EARTHSNG
    ES-37 (G268)

  Soul Of The Plains
    see Alma Llanera

GWYNNE, UNA
  Pioneers,The
    unis cor BANKS 1485 (G269)

GYGECHASCHTE see Zwöi Bärndütschi Lieder

GYGECHASCHTE, DER
  3pt wom cor MULLES MKKB (G270)

GYMEL E CORALE see Benvenuti, Arrigo

GYPSY ROVER, THE
  (Loughton, Lynnette-Steed, Gordon)
  3pt mix cor WARNER SV9312 (G271)

GYPSY SONG NO. 5 see Brahms, Johannes, Zigeunerlieder

## H

HA AN EM ORT ES BLÜEMLI GSEH see Wehrli, Werner

HAAPALA, TUOMO (1945- )
  En Doft, Ett Stråk Av Kåda
    mix cor STIM (H1)

HAASE-ALTENDORF, HELMUT (1912-1990)
  Intermezzo Festivo
    mix cor,winds RUNDEL cor pts
    ARTIKEL-NR.1022C, sc
    ARTIKEL-NR.1022 (H2)

HAB OFT IM KREIS DER LIEBEN see Silcher, Friedrich

HAB SONNE IM HERZEN see Frey, Carl

HACIA BELEN VA UN BORRICO
  (Shaw) SATB,Bar solo LEONARD-US
  50305070 (H3)

HADAKA see Suzuki, Teruaki

HADLEY, HENRY (KIMBALL) (1871-1937)
  Faries,The *Op.3
    SATB,solo voice,orch voc sc RECITAL
    516 (H4)

HAENNI, CH.
  Aprikosental, Das
    [Ger] mix cor HUG 7961 (H5)
    [Ger] eq voices HUG 7963 (H6)

  Sous Les Tilleuls En Fleurs
    mix cor,solo voice HUG 7828 (H7)
    eq voices,solo voice HUG 7829 (H8)

HAENNI, G.
  Alouette, L'
    mix cor HUG 7774 (H9)

  Aprikosental, Das
    [Ger] men cor HUG 7962 (H10)

  Baiser, Le
    mix cor HUG 7773 (H11)

  Berger, Le
    mix cor,solo voice HUG 7835 (H12)

  Chanson À Boire
    men cor HUG 6932 (H13)

  Clothes, Les
    mix cor HUG 8162 (H14)

  Farandole Des Heures
    mix cor HUG 7964 (H15)
    men cor HUG 7965 (H16)

  Huit Motets Dans Le Style Simple
    men cor HUG 7968 (H17)

  Jusqu'à Demain
    mix cor HUG 8164 (H18)

  Ma Mie
    men cor HUG 8234 (H19)

  Marchand De Bonheur, Le
    mix cor HUG 7966 (H20)
    men cor HUG 7967 (H21)

  Mariez-Vous, La Belle
    mix cor HUG 8305 (H22)

  Mon Flacon
    men cor HUG 8413 (H23)

  O Vieux Clocher!
    eq voices HUG 8161 (H24)

  O Vieux Valais!
    mix cor HUG 8306 (H25)

  On Est Fait Pour Aimer
    mix cor HUG 8163 (H26)

  Papillon Bleu, Le
    mix cor HUG 7969 (H27)

  Pourquoi Je Chante
    eq voices HUG 8303 (H28)

  Sentiers Valaisans, Les
    mix cor HUG 7730 (H29)
    eq voices HUG 7819 (H30)
    men cor HUG 7752 (H31)

  Si J'étais Une Fleur Jolie
    mix cor HUG 8304 (H32)

  Sous Les Tilleuls En Fleurs
    mix cor HUG 7828 (H33)

  Sur Le Faîte De La Tour
    eq voices HUG 8419 (H34)

HAENNI, G. (cont'd.)
  Timidité
    men cor HUG 8414 (H35)

  Trois Pensées
    mix cor HUG 8416 (H36)

  Venez Voir S'envoler
    mix cor HUG 8418 (H37)

  Vin Radieux
    men cor HUG 8415 (H38)

  Vous Me Plaisez!
    mix cor HUG 8417 (H39)

HAGEN, DARON
  Auguries Of Innocence
    see Four Poems Of William Blake

  Divine Image, The
    see Four Poems Of William Blake

  Four Poems Of William Blake
    SATB,kbd DEAN 15-1208R f.s.
    contains: Auguries Of Innocence;
    Divine Image, The; Lamb, The;
    Night (H40)

  Four Poems Of William Blake *Gen
    SATB DEAN 15-1208 R (H41)

  Joyful Music! *Xmas/Gen
    SATB,Mez solo,2pno/orch [15'] DEAN
    voc sc 65-1025, sc 30-1073, pts
    30-1074 (H42)

  Lamb, The
    see Four Poems Of William Blake

  Night
    see Four Poems Of William Blake

  Voice Within, The
    SATB DEAN 15-1129 (H43)

HAGI, KYOKO (1956- )
  Letters From An Emigrant
    mix cor,pno&perc JAPAN (H44)

HAGIWARA, HIDEHICO (1933- )
  Mystère De La Vie
    men cor,S solo,pno JAPAN (H45)

  Petit Arc-En-Ciel, Le
    wom cor,pno JAPAN (H46)

  Trois Images
    mix cor JAPAN (H47)

HÄGLER, PAUL
  Föhn
    men cor,acap MULLES (H48)

  Frühling, Wach Auf
    men cor,acap MULLES (H49)

  In Der Nacht
    wom cor,acap MULLES (H50)

  Kleines Liebeslied
    wom cor,acap MULLES (H51)

  Nacht,Die
    wom cor,acap MULLES (H52)

  Nachtgruss
    wom cor,acap MULLES (H53)

  Was Liebe Ist
    wom cor,acap MULLES (H54)

  Winternacht
    wom cor,acap MULLES (H55)

  Wundersames Wolkenspiel
    men cor,acap MULLES (H56)

HAIKUZOO see Garwood, Margaret

HAIL, BRIGHT CECILIA! see Purcell, Henry

HAIYIM see Finnissy, Michael

HAJDU, ANDRE (1937- )
  Four Songs Without Words *CC4U
    6pt jr cor,pno ISR.MUS.INST.
    IMI 6961 f.s. (H57)

HAKUCHO see Takashima, Midori

HAKURYU LAKE, THE see Adachi, Hiromi

HALDID TIL HALLARINNAR see Asgeirsson, Jon

HALL, DAVE
  Dreamlover (composed with Carey, Mariah)
    (Chinn, Teena) SSA WARNER WBCH93161 (H58)
    (Chinn, Teena) SATB WARNER WBCH93159 (H59)
    (Chinn, Teena) SSAB WARNER

HALL, DAVE (cont'd.)
    WBCH93160 (H60)

HALLBERG, BENGT (1932- )
  Det År Tid För En Lång Resa
    mix cor,acap SVERIG SK 243 (H61)

  Music And Sweet Poetry
    mix cor,pno STIM (H62)

HALLEY
  Bailiff's Daughter
    SATB WARCH 34495 (H63)

  Chant Canadien, Un
    see Song For Candada

  Despairing Lover
    SATB WARCH 34497 (H64)

  Lover's Arithmetic
    SATB WARCH 34498 (H65)

  Maypole
    SATB WARCH 34499 (H66)

  Seeds Of Love
    SATB WARCH 34500 (H67)

  Soldier, Won't You Marry Me?
    SATB WARCH 34501 (H68)

  Song For Candada
    "Chant Canadien, Un" [Eng/Fr] SATB/
    unis cor&desc,kbd PRESSER
    392-02512 (H69)

HAM, TAE KYUM
  Are You Going Away?
    see Kashiri

  Kashiri
    "Are You Going Away?" [Kor] SATB,
    pno EARTHSNG ES-44 (H70)
    "Are You Going Away?" SSAA,S solo,
    pno EARTHSNG EW-14 (H71)

HAMARSANGEN see Waaler, Fredrikke

HAMAT, HAMAT
  men cor HEYN NR. 47 (H72)

HAMBE, ALF
  Kajsas Udde
    (Volle, Bjarne) men cor,acap NOTON
    N-8950 (H73)

  Månbubblor
    men cor,acap NOTON N-8949 (H74)

HAMBRAEUS, BENGT (1928- )
  Songs Of The Mountain, The Moon And
  Television
    SATB,2(pic).2.2.2. 2.2.1.0. timp,
    perc,strings (includes The Power
    Of The Mountain, The Winter Moon
    And The Song Of Television)
    CAN.MUS.CENT. (H75)

HAMEL, KEITH (1956- )
  Salem, 1692
    wom cor,acap CAN.MUS.CENT. (H76)

HAMER, JANICE (1947- )
  Daughter, Awake With The Moon
    wom cor,acap (4 mvts.) HILD study
    sc 09426A, cor pts 09426B (H77)

HAMILTON, ARTHUR
  Circle Of Friends (composed with
  Goodrum, Randy)
    1-2pt cor WARNER WBC1008 (H78)
    SATB WARNER WBC1006 (H79)
    SAB WARNER WBC1007 (H80)

HAMLISCH, MARVIN F. (1944- )
  Ice Castles (Eyes Of Love)
    SATB WARCH 33880 (H81)
    SAB WARCH 33881 (H82)

  Throught The Eyes Of Love
    SSA WARCH 35271 (H83)

HAMMARSTRÖM, HUGO (1891-1974)
  Lucia Och Staffan
    (Stureborg, Helene) mix cor,acap
    SVERIG SK 775 (H84)

  Sankta Lucia *CC2U
    (Stureborg, Helene) SSA SVERIG
    SK 776 f.s. (H85)

HÅN JÅ LEI DIH *CCU,Austrian
  (Inzko, Josef) HEYN f.s. mix cor
    ISBN 3 85366 596 9; men cor
    ISBN 3 85366 595 0; wom cor
    ISBN 3 85366 597 7 (H86)

HANA-GATAMI see Kurokami, Yoshimitsu

HANAKO NO HANAICHI-MON-ME see Kawasaki, Etsuo

HAND MIRROR IN SPRING see Nakajima, Haru

HANDEL, GEORGE FRIDERIC (1685-1759)
  Air (from The Harmonious Blacksmith)
    (Swingle, Ward) SATB,db,drums (gr.
    IV) UNC JP GB-1 (H87)

  Allegro
    (Swingle, Ward) SSAATTBB,db,drums
    (gr. III) UNC JP GB-9X (H88)

  Belshazzar
    SATB NOVELLO 705333 (H89)

  Come, Live With Pleasure
    SAB,kbd,opt fl WARNER SV9422 (H90)

  Dieu Des Victoires
    mix cor HUG 7944 (H91)

  Largo
    mix cor,winds RUNDEL sc
    ARTIKEL-NR.0251, cor pts
    ARTIKEL-NR.0251C (H92)
    (Mouchet) 4pt men cor BILLAUDOT (H93)

  My Song Shall Be Alway
    SATB NOVELLO 724533 (H94)

  Oh Lovely Peace (from Judas Maccabaeus)
    wom cor,pno JERONA JC2003 (H95)

  Qu'il Est Admirable
    mix cor HUG 6127 (H96)

  See The Conqu'ring Hero Comes
    mix cor,pno JERONA JC2001 (H97)

  Where'er You Walk
    unis cor WARCH 34386 (H98)

HANDMADE PROVERBS see Takemitsu, Toru

HANDS 'CROSS THE OCEAN see Gallina

HANDWERKSBURSCHEN ABSCHIED see Andreae, Volkmar

HANDY
  St. Louis Blues
    (Spevacek, Linda) 3pt mix cor
    SHAWNEE D-0479 (H99)

HANSEN
  Tous Les Yeux
    4pt mix cor BILLAUDOT (H100)

HANSEN, VIDAR
  Blåveisskogen
    SSA,fl,pno NOTON N-9314 (H101)

HANUKAH TARANTELLA see Polansky, David

HANUKKAH DEDICATION see Eddleman, David

HAP-HAP-HAPPIEST SEASON, THE see Lawrence

HAPPYING see Broadley, Sharon

HARK TO THE FANFARE SOUNDING see Gastoldi, Giovanni Giacomo

HARMON, JOHN
  Harvest (from The Third Movement Of "Harvest")
    (Snapp, Doug) SATBB (gr. V) UNC JP (H102)

HARMONIE see Feibel, Norbert

HARMONIE DU SOIR see Aliprandi, Paul

HAROLD HARFAGER see Parker, Horatio William

HARP THAT ONCE THRO' TARA'S HALL
  SATB WARCH 34489 (H103)

HARRIS, JERRY WESELEY (1933- )
  All Through The Day
    SSA,acap BOSTON 14295 (H104)

  There Is A Ladye
    TB,pno BOSTON 14268 (H105)

  To The Shady Woods
    SSATB BOSTON 14227 (H106)

HART, LORENZ
  Isn't It Romantic (composed with Rodgers, Richard)
    (Chinn, Teena) SATB,acap WARNER
    6054IC1X (H107)

HARTKE, STEPHEN PAUL (1952- )
  Four Madrigals On Old Portuguese Texts
    [Port] SATB,SSATB soli,acap,
    optional chamber choir MMB
    S850001 (H108)

"HARU" "NATSU" "AKI" "FUYU" see Kobashi, Minoru

HARU NO TEKAGAMI see Nakajima, Hal

HARVEST see Bhatia, Vanraj A., Shishir
  see Harmon, John

HASEGAWA, TSUTOMU (1949- )
  Three Songs By Kenji Miyazawa
    wom cor,pno JAPAN (H109)

  Zwei Lieder Aus Man-Yo
    jr cor,S solo,pno JAPAN (H110)

HASHKIVENU see Zucker, Yosef

HÄSLER, HANS
  Was Hülfe Es Dir?
    wom cor,acap MÜLLES (H111)

HASQUENOPH, PIERRE (1922-1982)
  Six Chansons (from Tour Du Pin,La) CC6U
    mix cor BILLAUDOT f.s. (H112)

HASSLER, HANS LEO (1564-1612)
  Des Lieux Profonds Je Crie À Toi
    mix cor HUG 1839 (H113)

  Love Betrayed (from Lustgarten Neuer Teutscher Gestang)
    [Eng] SSATB,acap LAWSON 52632 (H114)

  Mein Lieb Will Mit Mir Kriegen
    (Swingle, Ward) SSAATTBB (gr. II)
    voc pt,pts UNC JP SM-11X (H115)

HASTA QUE CAIGAN LAS PUERTAS DEL ODIO see Lombardi, Luca

HATCHER, W.
  Choral Skills #1
    SATB BOCK BG0276 (H116)

HATFIELD, S.
  African Celebration
    4pt treb cor,3 solo voices BOOSEY-
    ENG OCTB6706 (H117)

  Amarillas, Las
    3pt treb cor,acap BOOSEY-ENG
    OCTB6784 (H118)

  Apple-Tree Wassail
    3pt treb cor BOOSEY-ENG OCTB6759 (H119)

  Nukapianguaq
    4pt treb cor BOOSEY-ENG OCTB6700 (H120)

  Ya Faraoule
    4pt treb cor,perc,opt fl&ob BOOSEY-
    ENG OCTB6760 (H121)

HATIKVAH see Burger, David Mark

HATO YO see Asakawa, Haruo

HATS OFF! TO AMERICA see Campbell-Towell, Lee

HÄTT I DI NIT BA MIR (from Chorblätter)
  (Streiner, Hans) mix cor HEYN
  (Streiner, Hans) men cor HEYN (H122)
(H123)

HATTON, JOHN LIPTROT (1809-1886)
  England
    SATB BANKS 119 (H124)

  Ever True
    SATB BANKS 324 (H125)

  Of A' The Airts The Wind Can Blaw
    SATB BANKS 190 (H126)

  Softly Fall The Shades
    SATB BANKS 69 (H127)

HAUG
  Choeur Des Moissonneurs
    men cor HUG 8168 (H128)

HAUGER, KRISTIAN
  So Ro, Perlemor
    (Volle, Sverre) SSA,acap NOTON
    N-9019 (H129)

HAUGLAND, A. OSCAR (1922- )
  Rondel For September
    SATB HOA (H130)

  Simplicity
    SSAA HOA (H131)

  Sweet Betsy From Pike
    SATB HOA (H132)

HAUS, KARL (1928- )
  Es Wollte Sich Einschleichen
    3pt mix cor BOHM (H133)

  Mass Und Unmass
    men cor,acap BOHM (H134)

  Neue Haus Ist Aufgericht, Das
    2-3pt jr cor,strings/kbd,perc BOHM (H135)

HAUS, KARL (cont'd.)
   Schaut Nur An Den Schönen Morgen
     3pt mix cor BOHM     (H136)

HAUSAMMANN, R.
   Soleil Et La Lune, Le
     mix cor HUG 8850     (H137)

HAVA NASHIRA see Julseth-Heinrich, Jeanne

HAVE YOU HEARD? (A CHRISTMAS SPIRITUAL) see Althouse, Jay

HAVE YOURSELF A MERRY LITTLE CHRISTMAS
   (Snyder, Audrey) 3pt mix cor WARNER
    SV9342     (H138)

HAVSMÄSSA see Lundin, Dag

HAYASHI, HIKARU (1931- )
   Cypress And Red Poppies, A *Fantasy
    14pt cor,pno JAPAN     (H139)

   Threni
    6pt men cor JAPAN     (H140)

   Your Passion
    2pt mix cor,clar&vln&pno&org JAPAN     (H141)

HAYDN, [FRANZ] JOSEPH (1732-1809)
   Alles Hat Sein Zeit (composed with Herman, Sally)
    "Everyone Has His Day" SATB DEAN 15-1209R     (H142)
    see Everyone Has His Day

   Eloquence, L'
    mix cor HUG 8013     (H143)
    men cor HUG 6427     (H144)

   Everyone Has His Day *Gen
    (Herman) "Alles Hat Sein Zeit" SATB
    (med) DEAN 15-1209 R     (H145)
    see Alles Hat Sein Zeit

   Vieillard, Le
    mix cor HUG 7850     (H146)

   Viens, Doux Printemps
    mix cor HUG 3915     (H147)

HAYDN, [JOHANN] MICHAEL (1737-1806)
   Accueillez-Moi, Forêts Tranquilles see An Den Wald

   An Den Wald
    men cor,acap MULLES     (H148)
    "Accueillez-Moi, Forêts Tranquilles" [Fr/Ger] men cor HUG 8097     (H149)

   Or Il Se Fit Soudain
    men cor HUG 8532     (H150)

HAYES, ISAAC (1942- )
   Soul Man (composed with Porter, David)
    (Schmutte, Pete) SATB WARNER WBCH9318 ipa     (H151)
    (Schmutte, Pete) SAB WARNER WBCH9319 ipa     (H152)

HAYES, MARK
   Every Night And Every Morn (from William Blake's Auguries Of Innocence)
    SATB HERITAGE 15-1144     (H153)

HAYFORD, JACK W.
   Majesty
    SATB WARCH 11792     (H154)

HAZAMIR see Low, Leo

HE AIN'T HEAVY, HE'S MY BROTHER
   (Althouse) SATB ALFRED 11649     (H155)
   (Althouse) SAB ALFRED 11650     (H156)
   (Althouse) 2pt cor/SSA ALFRED 11651     (H157)

HE CAME ALL SO STILL see Bialosky, Marshall H.

HE, KARNTNA, GEH LEICH MA DEI LIAD (from Chorblätter)
   (Streiner, Hans) mix cor HEYN     (H158)
   (Streiner, Hans) men cor HEYN     (H159)

HEAL THE WORLD see Jackson, Michael

HEARD, BRENDA
   Cherry Tree, The
    SATB,opt kbd FOSTER MF 3053     (H160)

HEARING THE COSMOS see Niimi, Tokuhide

HEART OF A HERO
   (Pugh, David) SATB WARNER 1831HC1X ipa     (H161)
   (Pugh, David) SAB WARNER 1831HC3X ipa     (H162)

HEART TO CLIMB THE MOUNTAIN, THE
   (Ginsburg, Ned) SATB WARNER 1829HC1X     (H163)
   (Ginsburg, Ned) SAB WARNER 1829HC3X     (H164)

   (Ginsburg, Ned) 2pt cor WARNER 1829HCSX     (H165)

HEART'S MUSIC see Vaughan Williams, Ralph

HEDELIN, FREDRIK (1965- )
   Soa-Soe
    mix cor STIM     (H166)

HEFT 1 see Neue Kärntnerlieder Für Gemischten Chor see Neue Kärntnerlieder Für Männerchor

HEFT 1 - AUSGABE FÜR GEMISCHTEN CHOR see Liada Aus'n Liesertal

HEFT 1 - AUSGABE FÜR MÄNNERCHOR see Liada Aus'n Liesertal

HEFT 2 see Neue Kärntnerlieder Für Gemischten Chor see Neue Kärntnerlieder Für Männerchor

HEFT 2 - AUSGABE FÜR GEMISCHTEN CHOR see Liada Aus'n Liesertal

HEFT 2 - AUSGABE FÜR MÄNNERCHOR see Liada Aus'n Liesertal

HEFT 3 see Neue Kärntnerlieder Für Gemischten Chor see Neue Kärntnerlieder Für Männerchor

HEFT 4 see Neue Kärntnerlieder Für Gemischten Chor see Neue Kärntnerlieder Für Männerchor

HEFT 5 see Neue Kärntnerlieder Für Gemischten Chor see Neue Kärntnerlieder Für Männerchor

HEI TSUKI BUSHI *folk song,Jap
   (Baxter, Francis) SATB,pno SANTA SBMP 59     (H167)

HEIDENRÖSLEIN see Schubert, Franz (Peter)

HEILIGE FLAMME,DIE see Güdel, W.

HEILIGSTE NACHT see Schmid, Walter

HEIM, IGNATZ
   O Beau Pays
    men cor HUG 7176     (H168)

   Vinéta
    men cor HUG 6310     (H169)

HEIMAT see Krenger, R. see Oetiker, August

HEIMAT, DEINE GLOCKEN KLINGEN see Schmid, Walter

HEIMATGEBET see Schmid, A.

HEIMATGEDENKEN see Märki, Ernst

HEIMATLIED: ICH BIN STILLER ... see Schmid, Walter

HEIMATLIED: WOHL DEM, DER SOLCHE ... see Schmid, Walter

HEIMATROSEN see Güdel, W.

HEIMET see Schmid, Walter

HEIMETDÖRFLI, 'S see Schmid, Walter

HEIMETGLÜCK see Schmid, Walter

HEIMKEHR see Gelbke, Johannes

HEIMLIGI LIEBI see Ruprecht, Ernst

HEIMWEH see Boller, Carlo see Pesson, Ch.

HEIMWEHLIEDLI see Müller, Joseph Ivar

HEININEN, PAAVO (1938- )
   Autumns, Op. 22, The
    mix cor,acap FAZER     (H170)

   Cor Meum, Op. 35
    mix cor,acap FAZER     (H171)

HEINRICHS, WILHELM (1914- )
   Jascha Joue
    men cor HUG 8374     (H172)

HEITERE WEISEN DES LEBENS see Clemens

HEITERES HERBARIUM see Keller, Wilhelm

HEIWEHBÄNKLI, 'S see Ginther, A.

HELGOLAND see Bruckner, Anton

HELIOTROPE BOUQUET see Joplin

HELLE GRÜHLING,DER see Schmid, A.

HELLE WEG,DER see Schmid, Walter

HELLO, BEATLES see Mori, Konate

HELMSCHROTT, ROBERT M. (1938- )
   Äusserste, Das
    see Begegnung

   Begegnung
    mix cor,acap SCHOTTS f.s.
    contains: Äusserste, Das; Begegnung; Dann; Nachts; Schweigen; Unsere Zeit; Wir     (H173)

   Begegnung
    see Begegnung

   Danach "...Mit Beidn Händen Dein Gesicht Umschliessen"
    see Menschenzeit

   Dann
    see Begegnung

   Höchste Zeit "Wenn Du Liebst"
    see Menschenzeit

   Inhalt: Lebenslauf "Warten Auf Den Augenblick"
    see Menschenzeit

   Menschenzeit
    mix cor,acap sc SCHOTTS C 48235 f.s.
    contains: Danach "...Mit Beidn Händen Dein Gesicht Umschliessen"; Höchste Zeit "Wenn Du Liebst"; Inhalt: Lebenslauf "Warten Auf Den Augenblick"; Schlaflos "Gegen Drei Hätten Die Lippen Genügt"; Vigilie "Ob Die Zärtlichkeiten Endlich Angekommen"     (H174)

   Nachts
    see Begegnung

   Schlaflos "Gegen Drei Hätten Die Lippen Genügt"
    see Menschenzeit

   Schweigen
    see Begegnung

   Unsere Zeit
    see Begegnung

   Vigilie "Ob Die Zärtlichkeiten Endlich Angekommen"
    see Menschenzeit

   Wir
    see Begegnung

HELP OF MY FRIENDS, THE see Fry

HELVÉTIE, MA PATRIE see Bovet, J.

HEMANT see Bhatia, Vanraj A.

HEMBERG, ESKIL (1938- )
   Tre Citat Av Ulla Isaksson *Op.85
    mix cor STIM     (H175)

HEMMERLING, CARLOS
   Arbre Bruyant Comme Une Ville
    men cor HUG 7817     (H176)

   Arbre Immense
    men cor HUG 7816     (H177)

   Au Petit Jardin (from Rives Bleues)
    mix cor,opt pno/org/orch HUG 7434     (H178)

   Berceuse De Grand'maman, La
    eq voices HUG 7388     (H179)

   Bon Syndic, Le
    men cor HUG 7482     (H180)

   Bonne Grand'mère, La
    mix cor HUG 7530     (H181)

   Chanson De La Petite Treille
    men cor HUG 7437     (H182)

   Chanson Des Effeuilles (from Rives Bleues)
    mix cor,opt pno/org/orch HUG 7431     (H183)

   Chanson Des Moissons (from Rives Bleues)
    mix cor HUG 7433     (H184)

   Chanson Du Pêcheur (from Rives Bleues)
    mix cor,opt pno/org/orch HUG 7432     (H185)
    eq voices HUG 7798     (H186)

   Chant Du Lac (from Rives Bleues)
    mix cor,opt pno/org/orch HUG 7430     (H187)
    eq voices HUG 7958     (H188)

HEMMERLING, CARLOS (cont'd.)
   Chasse Est Ouverte, La
     men cor HUG 7483   (H189)

   Chrysanthème, Le
     mix cor HUG 7925   (H190)

   Don Quichotte Et Sancho Pança
     mix cor HUG 7537   (H191)

   En Marchant Au Pas
     men cor HUG 7159   (H192)

   Heureux Ceux Qui Sont Morts
     men cor HUG 7380   (H193)

   Je Te L'avais Bien Dit...
     eq voices HUG 7220   (H194)

   Là-Haut (from Rives Bleues)
     mix cor HUG 8796   (H195)

   Léman
     men cor HUG 7450   (H196)

   Maison, Une
     men cor HUG 7451   (H197)

   Marivaudage
     men cor HUG 7561   (H198)

   Nous N'avons Chez Nous
     mix cor HUG 8727   (H199)

   Novembre
     men cor HUG 7219   (H200)

   Quatre Roses
     4 eq voices HUG 8381   (H201)

   Qu'il Fait Bon Sur Terre
     men cor,SBar soli HUG 8046   (H202)

   Reine Des Prés, La
     eq voices HUG 7907   (H203)

   Ritournelle De Février (from Rives
    Bleues)
     mix cor HUG 7508   (H204)
     eq voices HUG 7797   (H205)

   Ritournelle Du Vin Nouveau
     mix cor HUG 7443   (H206)

   Rives Bleues
     mix cor, solo voices,orch HUG voc
      pt 7435, cor pts 7436   (H207)

   Saison S'échappe, La (from Rives
    Bleues)
     mix cor HUG 8797   (H208)

   Vieux Bûcheron
     men cor HUG 7815   (H209)

   Vigne Fleurit, La (from Rives Bleues)
     mix cor HUG 7187   (H210)
     eq voices HUG 7799   (H211)

HENCHOZ, EMILE
   A La Rencontre
     mix cor HUG 8028   (H212)

   Allons, Mes Compagnons!
    see Trois Chansons De Route

   Au Bout Du Monde
     3pt mix cor HUG 8750   (H213)
     men cor HUG 8521   (H214)

   Au Fond Des Yeux
     mix cor HUG 8741   (H215)

   Beau Berger, Le
     mix cor HUG 7398   (H216)

   Berger Du Ciel
     mix cor/eq voices HUG 8799   (H217)

   Bonnes Gens, Applaudissez!
     mix cor HUG 7794   (H218)
     men cor HUG 7795   (H219)

   Bricoleur, Le
     men cor HUG 8102   (H220)

   C'est Le Chevrier Qui Passe
     men cor HUG 8022   (H221)

   Chanson À Boire
     men cor HUG 8291   (H222)

   Chanson À Boire Et Á Danser
     mix cor HUG 8517   (H223)
     3pt mix cor HUG 8517A   (H224)
     men cor HUG 8520   (H225)

   Chanson Des Moissons
     men cor HUG 7611   (H226)

   Connaissez-Vous, Là-Bas?
     men cor HUG 8738   (H227)

HENCHOZ, EMILE (cont'd.)
   Croix, La
     men cor HUG 8573   (H228)

   Deux Pêcheurs, Les
     mix cor HUG 7723   (H229)

   ...Et La Jeunesse N'en Sait Rien!
     mix cor HUG 8587   (H230)

   Eté
     eq voices HUG 7725   (H231)

   Fontaines
     mix cor HUG 7613   (H232)

   Greensleeves
     "Mon Trésor Ou Ma Peine" 3-4pt mix
      cor HUG 8762   (H233)
     "Mon Trésor Ou Ma Peine" eq voices
      HUG 8763   (H234)
     "Mon Trésor Ou Ma Peine" men cor
      HUG 8763   (H235)

   Jardin
     mix cor HUG 8572   (H236)

   Jardins Se Sont Tus, Les
     mix cor HUG 8505   (H237)

   Je N'irai Pas...
     mix cor HUG 8614   (H238)

   Laisse Tes Peines...
    see Trois Chansons De Route

   Laitière, La
     mix cor HUG 8653   (H239)
     men cor HUG 8207   (H240)

   Lavandières
     mix cor HUG 7614   (H241)

   Mon Lac
     mix cor HUG 8206   (H242)

   Mon Trésor Ou Ma Peine
    see Greensleeves

   Où Cours-Tu, La Belle?
     mix cor HUG 8178   (H243)
     men cor HUG 7902   (H244)

   Pari, Le
     men cor HUG 8779   (H245)

   Pas Plus Haut Que Trois Pommes
     mix cor HUG 8740   (H246)

   Petit Chalutier Du Ciel, Le
     2 eq voices,opt pno/org/orch HUG
      8351   (H247)

   Petit Savoir-Vivre
     mix cor HUG 8800   (H248)
     eq voices,pno/org/orch HUG 8807
        (H249)
     men cor HUG 8801   (H250)

   Pour Un Mariage
     mix cor HUG 8325   (H251)
     eq voices HUG 8326   (H252)

   Quand Tu Vois À Ton Réveil
    see Trois Chansons De Route

   Robe De Saison, La
     mix cor HUG 8176   (H253)

   Seigneur Dieu
     men cor HUG 8290   (H254)

   Seigneur, La Joie
     mix cor HUG 8193   (H255)
     men cor HUG 8194   (H256)

   Si Malbrough L'avait Voulu...
     mix cor HUG 8175   (H257)
     3pt mix cor HUG 8175A   (H258)
     men cor HUG 8027   (H259)

   Sonneur, Qui Te Penches...
     mix cor HUG 7615   (H260)
     eq voices,opt pno/org/orch HUG 7616
        (H261)

   Source Abondante De Joie
     mix cor HUG 8210   (H262)
     eq voices HUG 8209   (H263)

   Sous L'étoile Du Nord
     men cor HUG 8574   (H264)

   Sous Une Pluie...
     mix cor HUG 8688   (H265)

   Sur Ce Petit Pont De Pierre
     mix cor HUG 8179   (H266)
     men cor,solo voice HUG 7936   (H267)

   Sur Le Bord Du Torrent
     mix cor HUG 8742   (H268)

   Tant De Fleurs
     mix cor HUG 8579   (H269)

HENCHOZ, EMILE (cont'd.)
   Temps Vole, Le
     men cor HUG 8739   (H270)

   Terre Meurtrie
     men cor HUG 8613   (H271)

   Toast Valaisan
     men cor HUG 8779   (H272)

   Trois Chansons De Route
     mix cor HUG 8640 f.s.
      contains: Allons, Mes
      Compagnons!; Laisse Tes
      Peines...; Quand Tu Vois À Ton
      Réveil   (H273)

   Trois Commères, Les
     mix cor HUG 8038   (H274)
     3pt mix cor HUG 8038A   (H275)
     eq voices HUG 8039   (H276)
     men cor HUG 7724   (H277)

   Trois Grappes...
     mix cor HUG 7935   (H278)

   Un P'tit Train
     2 eq voices,opt pno/org/orch HUG
      8351   (H279)

   Violoneux, Le
     mix cor,T/Bar solo HUG 8208   (H280)

   Votre Pays Est Toujours Là
     mix cor HUG 7705   (H281)
     eq voices HUG 7704   (H282)

HENDERSON
   Boar And The Dromedar, Don't Ever
    Squeeze
     unis cor WARCH 34340   (H283)

   Bye Bye Blackbird (composed with
    Djambazian, Awedio)
     (Althouse) 2pt cor ALFRED 5838
        (H284)
     (Althouse) SATB ALFRED 5836   (H285)
     (Althouse) 3pt cor ALFRED 5837
        (H286)

   Donkey-The Barn Owl
     unis cor WARCH 35657   (H287)

   Slave Of The Moon
     3 eq voices WARCH 35232   (H288)

   Storm
     SA WARCH 35236   (H289)

   Tree Toad And Lone Dog
     unis cor WARCH 34384   (H290)

   Twelve Days Of Christmas
     (Strommen, Carl) SATB SSA WARCH
      35233   (H291)
     (Strommen, Carl) SATB unis cor
      WARCH 35663   (H292)

   Yak And The Train Dogs
     SA WARCH 35226   (H293)

HENDERSON, MARK
   Go, Lovely Rose
     SATB,opt kbd FOSTER MF 3052   (H294)

HENDERSON, RUTH WATSON (1932-   )
   Banks Of The Don
    see Five Ontario Folksongs

   Come All You Bold Canadians
    see Five Ontario Folksongs

   Crazy Times
     SATB THOMP.G f.s.
      contains: Crazy Times;
      Horoscopes; Laughter; Lullaby;
      When The Shoe Is On The Other
      Foot For A Change   (H295)

   Crazy Times
    see Crazy Times

   Duck, The
     unis cor WARCH 34345   (H296)

   Five Ontario Folksongs
     SATB THOMP.G f.s.
      contains: Banks Of The Don; Come
      All You Bold Canadians; Maggie
      Hunter; Poor Little Girls Of
      Ontario; Scarborogh Settler's
      Lament   (H297)

   Four Little Foxes
     SSA WARCH 34404   (H298)

   Horoscopes
    see Crazy Times

   In Flanders Field
     SSA THOMP.G VG352   (H299)

   Last Straw
     SSA THOMP.G VG347   (H300)

HENDERSON, RUTH WATSON (cont'd.)
   Laughter
     see Crazy Times

   Lullaby
     see Crazy Times

   Maggie Hunter
     see Five Ontario Folksongs

   Mary Ann
     SATB WARCH 34502     (H301)

   O Canada
     unis cor THOMP.G VG198     (H302)

   Poor Little Girls Of Ontario
     see Five Ontario Folksongs

   Popcorn
     SSA WARCH 34396     (H303)

   Promptement Levez-Vous
     SSA THOMP.G VG342     (H304)

   Raftsmen, Les
     SATB WARCH 34493     (H305)

   Robin, The
     unis cor WARCH 34382     (H306)

   Scarborogh Settler's Lament
     see Five Ontario Folksongs

   Song My Paddle Sings
     SATB THOMP.G VG473     (H307)

   Travelling Musicians, The (from
     Musicians Of Bremen)
     4pt jr cor,fl,clar,vcl,pno
     CAN.MUS.CENT.     (H308)

   Voices Of Earth
     SATB&SATB&jr cor THOMP.G VEI1125
            (H309)

   When The Shoe Is On The Other Foot
     For A Change
     see Crazy Times

   Winter Store (from Voices Of Earth)
     THOMP.G VG246     (H310)

HENLEY, ROD
   Christmas Song,The
     TTBB,soli,perc (gr. III) UNC JP
            (H311)

HENRIETTE see Doret, Gustave

HENRY VIII, KING OF ENGLAND (1491-1547)
   Agincourt Song,The
     (Swingle, Ward) SSAATTBB,acap (gr.
     III) voc pt,pts UNC JP SR-2
            (H312)

   Pastime With Good Company
     (Swingle, Ward) SSAATTBB,acap (gr.
     II) voc pt,pts UNC JP SR-1 (H313)

HENSEL, FANNY MENDELSSOHN (1805-1847)
   Faust Scene
     SSAA,S solo,pno HILD study sc
     09429A, sc,pts 09429B     (H314)

   Garden Songs
     see Gartenlieder

   Garden Songs,The
     SATB,opt acap HILD 09535A     (H315)

   Gartenlieder
     "Garden Songs" [Ger] SATB EARTHSNG
     ER-6     (H316)

   Nachtreigen
     SSAATTBB CARUS voc sc 40.219-05, sc
     40.219-01     (H317)

   Three Duets
     SA,pno HILD 09405A     (H318)

   Two Duets
     SA,acap HILD 09406A     (H319)

HERBST see Benninghoff, Ortwin see
   Schmid, S.W. see Zentner, Johannes

HERBSTGEFÜHL see Bella, Rudolf

HERBSTLIED see Hofer-Schneeberger, Emma
   see Schmid, Walter see Stocker,
   Karl

HERBSTWIND see Cadow, Paul

HERE WE ARE see McPheeters

HERE WE COME A-CAROLING
   (Adams, Brant) SATB,pno SANTA SBMP 90
            (H320)

HÉRITAGE, L' see Broquet, Louis

HERO see Afanasieff, Walter see
   Collins, Phil

HERR DER STUNDEN, HERR DER TAGE see
   Gaillard, Paul-Andre

HERR, DU WEISST, WIE ARM WIR WANDERN
   see Schmid, Ernst

HERRLICHE NACHT see Sauseng, Wolfgang

HERZLICHEN GLÜCKWUNSCH see Lincke, Paul

HERZOG
   God Bless The Child (composed with
     Holiday, Billie)
     (Marois, Rejean) SSATBB,perc (gr.
     III) UNC JP     (H321)

HERZOG, EMIL
   Bänkli, 'S
     men cor,T solo,acap MULLES     (H322)

HE'S GONE AWAY *folk song
   (Terri) SATB,female solo&male solo
     LAWSON 4-633     (H323)

HESS, CARLHEINZ (1934- )
   Drei Humoresken
     SATB,acap BUTZ 1234 f.s.
       contains: Floh, Der; Mann Und Der
       Teufel, Der; Schneider Und Die
       Spatzen, Der     (H324)

   Floh, Der
     see Drei Humoresken

   Mann Und Der Teufel, Der
     see Drei Humoresken

   Schneider Und Die Spatzen, Der
     see Drei Humoresken

HET WAS STIL... see Kersters, Willem

HEUKEN, HANS JAKOB (1904- )
   Im Dorfkurg
     men cor,acap BOHM     (H325)

HEURES, LES see Mermoud, Robert

HEUREUX CEUX QUI SONT MORTS see
   Hemmerling, Carlos

HEUT IST HEUT see Güdel, W.

HEY GIRL!, HEY GIRL! see Anderson

HEY, ROBIN, JOLLY ROBIN see Strohbach,
   Siegfried

HI NO KURURU see Kino, Seiichiro

HIDING IN THE FOGGY DEW *folk song,Ir
   (Rice, Martin R.) TBB,pno MUSIC SEV.
   738     (H326)

HIER IM REICH DER FREUDE see Rameau,
   Jean-Philippe, Courez Par La Plaine

HIGH BARBARY see Smith, Gregg

HIGHER AND HIGHER
   (medley containing I Want To Take You
   Higher, Ain't No Mountain High
   Enough) WARNER     (H327)

HIGHLIGHTS FROM BLOOD BROTHERS
   (Billingsley) SATB SHAWNEE A-1986 ipa
            (H328)
   (Billingsley) SAB SHAWNEE D-467 ipa
            (H329)

HIKARI NO TAMAGO O MIGOMORU-TAME NI see
   Abe, Ryotaro

HIKER'S PRAYER (THERE'S A LONG, LONG
   TRAIL) see Elliot, Alonzo

HILGER, MANFRED (1941- )
   Einsiedler, Der
     mix cor BUTZ 1294     (H330)

   Immer Wieder Lasst Uns Singen
     mix cor BUTZ 1295     (H331)

HILLER
   Sonntag
     (Schmid) men cor,acap MULLES (H332)

HILLS OF ENGLAND see Penrose, P.

HILLS OF GLENSHEE *folk song,Scot
   (Printz, Brad) SATB,pno SANTA SBMP 65
            (H333)

HIMES, WILLIAM
   All That I Am
     SATB HOPE GC 963     (H334)

HIMMEL,DER see Güdel, W.

HIMMEL LACHT, DER see Silcher,
   Friedrich

HIMMEL OHNE SONN',EIN see Lampart,
   Reinhold

HIN-NUN see Pagh-Paan, Younghi

HINE MA TOV see Naplan, A.

HINES, ROBERT S.
   Love Song
     SATB,pno LAWSON 52696     (H335)

HIRAYOSHI, KUNITAKE
   Sea In My Country, The
     see Umi-Furusato No

   Umi-Furusato No *Suite
     "Sea In My Country, The" mix cor
     ONGAKU 545130     (H336)

HIRONDELLE MESSAGERE DES AMOURS, L' see
   Anonymous

HIROSE, RYOHEI (1930- )
   In The Forest Of Kamui
     mix cor,pno&3perc JAPAN     (H337)

   Shushogi
     mix cor JAPAN     (H338)

   Tancho
     mix cor JAPAN     (H339)

HISATOME, TOMOYUKI (1955- )
   Stone's Voice
     jr cor,SBarB soli,pno&cel&2perc
     JAPAN     (H340)

HIVER, L' see Doret, Gustave

HIVER A FUI..., L' see Dvorák, Antonín

HIVER SUR MON JARDIN, L' see Gesseney,
   L.

HOCH, FRANCESCO (1943- )
   Arcano
     cor,acap ZERBONI 8190     (H341)

   Postludio Degli Spettatori
     treb cor/eq voices/mix cor ZERBONI
     10616     (H342)

HOCH AUF DEM GELBEN WAGEN see Märki,
   Ernst

HÖCHI ZYT see Märki, Ernst

HÖCHLE, E.
   D's Hüsli
     men cor,acap MULLES     (H343)

HOCHSOMMERNACHT see Bella, Rudolf

HÖCHSTE ZEIT "WENN DU LIEBST" see
   Helmschrott, Robert M.

HOCHZEIT see Doret, Gustave

HOCHZEITSFREUDE see Olpen, Friedrich W.

HOCHZEITSLIED see Müller, Joseph Ivar

HOCHZEITSLIEDER see Anderluh, Anton

HOCHZEITSMADRIGAL see Josef

HOCKEY see Broughton, Marilyn

HODGE, STEPHEN
   Tenderly, My Love, I'll Come To Thee
     TTBB, opt kbd FOSTER MF 1070 (H344)

HOFER-SCHNEEBERGER, EMMA
   Alpufzug
     wom cor,acap MULLES     (H345)

   Am Mühlbach
     wom cor,acap MULLES     (H346)
     men cor,acap MULLES     (H347)

   Grabgesang
     wom cor,acap MULLES     (H348)

   Gruss An Das Schweizerland
     wom cor,acap MULLES     (H349)

   Herbstlied
     wom cor,acap MULLES     (H350)

   I Ne Alphütte Bin-I Gange
     wom cor,acap MULLES     (H351)

   Mein Heim
     wom cor,acap MULLES     (H352)

   Schweizers Abschied Von Der Heimat
     wom cor,acap MULLES     (H353)

   Sehnsucht Nach Den Bergen
     wom cor,acap MULLES     (H354)

   Weinachtslied
     wom cor,acap MULLES     (H355)

   Wenn D'schneeballe Blüeit
     wom cor,acap MULLES     (H356)

   Wenn D'schneeballe Blüejt
     men cor,acap MULLES     (H357)

HOFFMANN
  Select Unison Anthems
    unis cor SHAWNEE GF-5001    (H358)

HÖHENSEHNSUCHT see Schmid, A.

HOL-DI-RI-DI see Lesur, Daniel

HOLIDAY BLUES see Treece, Roger

HOLIDAY MADRIGAL see Spevacek, Linda

HOLIDAY SONGS FOR LITTLE FOLKS see Thomas

HOLIDAY TANGO see Spevacek, Linda

HOLIDAY WISH, A see Althouse, Jay

HOLLAND, BRIAN
  Stop! In The Name Of Love
    (Althouse, Jay) SSA WARNER 6456SC2X
                                    (H359)
    (Althouse, Jay) 2pt cor WARNER
      6456SC5X                      (H360)

HOLLERING SUN see Parker, Alice

HOLLFELDER, WALDRAM (1924- )
  Es, Es, Es Und Es
    3pt mix cor BOHM               (H361)

  Es Steht Ein Lind In Jenem Tal
    3pt mix cor BOHM               (H362)

  Horch, Was Kommt Von Draussen Rein
    3pt mix cor BOHM               (H363)

  Im Krug Zum Grünen Kranze
    3pt mix cor BOHM               (H364)

HOLLMANN, MARK
  Hope Is The Thing With Feathers
    SAB,pno FOSTER MF 3051         (H365)

HOLLY AND THE IVY
  (Shaw And Parker) SATB,acap LEONARD-
    US 50305090                    (H366)
  see Davies see Davies, Victor

HOLMAN
  Deck The Halls
    SATB WARCH 34472               (H367)

  Fair And Fair
    SATB WARCH 34508               (H368)

  Love Unfeigned
    SATB WARCH 34507               (H369)

  Lullaby
    SATB WARCH 35669               (H370)

  Madrigal
    SATB WARCH 34505               (H371)

  Song
    SATB WARCH 34506               (H372)

  What Hath Night To Do With Sleep
    SATB WARCH 35670               (H373)

  Witches Charm
    SATB WARCH 35671               (H374)

HOLMAN, DEREK
  Bluebird
    see Three Canadian Folk Songs

  False Bride
    see Three Canadian Folk Songs

  Greenland Whale
    see Three Canadian Folk Songs

  Hye Nonny, Nonny Noe
    see Present Time

  It Was A Lover And His Lass
    see Present Time

  Love And Time
    see Present Time

  O Mistress Mine
    see Present Time

  Present Time
    SATB THOMP.G f.s.
      contains: Hye Nonny, Nonny Noe;
        It Was A Lover And His Lass;
        Love And Time; O Mistress Mine;
        Weep You No More Sad Fountains
                                    (H375)
  Three Canadian Folk Songs
    SATB THOMP.G f.s.
      contains: Bluebird; False Bride;
        Greenland Whale              (H376)

  Weep You No More Sad Fountains
    see Present Time

HOLMBERG, LEIF (1951- )
  Två Träd
    4pt mix cor,pno NOTON S-8909-12
                                    (H377)
HOLMBERG, PAT
  Sing About Love
    SATB,acap VOICE HOPAC06        (H378)

HOLZFÄLLER, DIE see Doret, Gustave

HOMA see Kokaji, Kunitaka

HOMAGE TO DUSK see Nakajima, Haru

HOMBRE QUE NO COME CARAMELOS, UN see Balzanelli

HOME, SWEET HOME see Bishop see Bishop, [Sir] Henry (Rowley)

HOME WITHIN OUR HEART, A see Gallina

HOMEWARD BOUND see Simon, Eric

HOMMAGE see Smetana, Bedrich

HONEGGER, ARTHUR (1892-1955)
  Des Matines Jusqu'au Soir
    eq voices,opt pno/org/orch HUG 8431
                                    (H379)
  Mort De David, La (from Roi David, Le)
    mix cor,S solo HUG 3776        (H380)

  Nicolas De Flüe
    [Fr] mix cor&jr cor,narrator,orch
      HUG voc sc 7050, cor pts
      7051, 7051A                   (H381)

  Niklaus von Flüe
    [Ger] mix cor&jr cor,narrator,orch
      HUG kbd pt 7221, cor pts
      7222, 7222A                   (H382)

  Roi David, Le
    [Fr/Ger] mix cor,narrator,orch HUG
      voc sc 5990, cor pts 2205    (H383)

HONOKANI HITOTSU see Yasugi, Tadatoshi

HOPE IS THE THING WITH FEATHERS see Hollmann, Mark

HOPKINS
  Swingle Bells IX  *Xmas,carol/medley
    (Swingle, Ward) SSAATTBB,db,drums
      (gr. III) voc pt,pts UNC JP SBS-9
                                    (H384)
HOPSA, ANNELISI see Furrer, Walter

HORCH, WAS KOMMT VON DRAUSSEN REIN see Hollfelder, Waldram

HORIKOSHI, RYUICHI (1949- )
  Nazotoki Tanteidan
    jr cor,pno JAPAN               (H385)

HORLOGE, L' see Breard

HORLOGER, L' see Mermoud, Robert

HORN, THE see Pearson, William Dean

HOROSCOPES see Henderson, Ruth Watson

HORSE-WATCHER'S SONGS, THE see Lassek, Eugene E.

HORTICULTURAL WIFE, THE see Smith, Gregg

HOS MIN DOKTOR see Sjöberg, Birger

HOSHIZORA NO MUKO KARA see Kurachi, Tatsuya

HOSOKAWA, TOSHIO (1955- )
  Tenebrae
    jr cor JAPAN                   (H386)

HOTLOGERS, LES see Pantillon, François

HOTSHOT see Joplin

HOUSES IN HEAVEN see Beckwith, John

HOW DO I LOVE THEE? see Swingle, Ward

HOW LOVELY THY PLACE see Kubik

HOW SWEET THE MOONLIGHT SLEEPS see Leslie, Henry David

HOWARD
  Fly Me To The Moon
    SATB WARCH 34820               (H387)

HOWELLS
  Grace For 10 Downing Street, A
    SATB,acap NOVELLO 086530       (H388)

HØYBYE, JOHN
  Paraplyboken
    (children's chorus method) sc
      SVERIG SK 740                 (H389)
    (children's chorus method) voc sc
HØYBYE, JOHN (cont'd.)
      SVERIG SK 741                (H390)

HUBER, KLAUS (1924- )
  Beati Pauperes II
    cor,7 soli,3.1.2.1. 3.1.0.0. perc,
      pno,gtr,strings sc RICORDI-IT
      SY. 2345                      (H391)

  Cantiones De Circulo Gyrante
    cor,soli,14inst RICORDI-IT     (H392)

  Erniedrigt-Geknechtet-Verlassen-
    Verzchtet
    cor,5 soli,4.2.4.2. 3.4.4.1. timp,
      3perc,gtr,mand,pno,hpsd,
      2electronic tape,strings sc
      RICORDI-IT SY. 2350            (H393)

  ...Nudo Que Ansi Juntáis...
    SATB sc RICORDI-IT SY. 2460    (H394)

HUBER, PAUL (1918- )
  Leben, Das
    men cor,acap MULLES            (H395)

  Stradun
    men cor,acap MULLES            (H396)

  Uebergang
    men cor,acap MULLES            (H397)

HUBER, WALTER SIMON (1898-1978)
  Abendlied (Lueged, Vo Bärge Und Tal)
    (Burkard) wom cor,acap MULLES
                                    (H398)
  Augenblicke Werden Stunden
    men cor,acap MULLES            (H399)

  Ds Silbergleggli
    wom cor,acap MULLES            (H400)

  Lueget, Vo Bärge Und Tal
    (Oetiker) wom cor,acap MULLES
                                    (H401)
  Morgen
    men cor,acap MULLES            (H402)

  Morgenlied
    wom cor,acap MULLES            (H403)

  Phantasie, Du Jugendschöne
    men cor,acap MULLES            (H404)

  Sängerfahrt
    men cor,acap MULLES            (H405)

  Trinklied
    men cor,acap MULLES            (H406)

HÜBSCH UND FEURIG see Kamp, Richard

HUG, FRITZ
  Blätterfall
    wom cor,acap MULLES            (H407)

HUGH
  Raggle Taggle Gypsies, The
    2pt treb cor,pno BOOSEY-ENG
      OCTB6747                      (H408)

HUGH, R.I.
  Kenya Melodies
    treb cor BOOSEY-ENG OCTB6751   (H409)

HUGH-JONES, LLIFON (1918- )
  Cwsg
    see Sleep

  Sleep
    "Cwsg" SATB,pno ROBERTON 63234
                                    (H410)
HUGUENIN, CHARLES (1870-1939)
  De L'Hiver Au Printemps
    mix cor,acap HUGUENIN CH 2108
                                    (H411)
  Nous Etions Trois Filles
    mix cor,acap HUGUENIN CH 2109
                                    (H412)
HUHN UND KARPFEN see Zwei Tierlieder

HUIT MOTETS DANS LE STYLE SIMPLE see Haenni, G.

HULDEGEDICHT AAN SINGER, OP. 89 see Kersters, Willem

HULTIN, LENNART (1927- )
  Glädjens Blomster
    SSAB NOTERIA 2761              (H413)

  Jag Vet En Dejlig Rosa
    SAB NOTERIA 2763               (H414)

HUMBLOT
  Petite Violette
    2 eq voices BILLAUDOT          (H415)

HUMORESKE see Vea, Ketil

HUMORESQUE see Grieg, Edvard Hagerup

HUNTING SONG see Martin, Robert

HUPFELD, HERMAN (1894-1951)
   When Yuba Plays The Rumba On The Tuba
     (Strommen, Carl) 2pt cor WARNER
      WBCH9357 (H416)
     (Strommen, Carl) SATB WARNER
      WBCH9354 (H417)
     (Strommen, Carl) SAB WARNER
      WBCH9355 (H418)
     (Strommen, Carl) TBB WARNER
      WBCH9356 (H419)

HURNI, JAKOB
   Liebeslied
     wom cor,acap MULLES (H420)

HURRY UP! see Griebling, S.T.

HUSA, KAREL (1921- )
   Cantata
     men cor,brass quin/pno AMP 50488707 (H421)

HUSTAGELIEDLI see Juker, A.

HÜT DU DICH see Brahms, Johannes

HUTCHESON, JERE T. (1938- )
   God
     SATB,English horn/clar SEESAW (H422)

HUTCHISON, (DAVID) WARNER (1930- )
   Five Miniatures On Love
     SATB,pno SEESAW (H423)

HVER TAR SIN see Volle, Bjarne

HYE NONNY, NONNY NOE see Holman, Derek

HYLIN, BIRGITTA
   Sommarn Och Jag
     (Eriksson, Gunnar) mix cor,acap
      SVERIG SK 732 (H424)

HYMME À LA GRUYÈRE see Bovet, J.

HYMME NUPTIAL see Bovet, J.

HYMN À LA NUIT see Rameau, Jean-Philippe

HYMNE see Gluck, Christoph Willibald, Ritter von

HYMNE À LA BANNIÈRE see Vuataz, Roger

HYMNE À LA CHARITÉ see Broquet, Louis

HYMNE À LA MUSIQUE see Delmas, Marc-Jean-Baptiste

HYMNE À LA NATURE see Fevrier, Henri

HYMNE À LA NUIT see Rameau, Jean-Philippe

HYMNE À LA PATRIE see Barblan, Otto see Boller, Carlo see Jaques-Dalcroze, Émile

HYMNE À LA SAGESSE see Broquet, Louis

HYMNE À LA TERRE see Doret, Gustave

HYMNE À L'AUTEUR DE TOUTE GRÂCE see Gluck, Christoph Willibald, Ritter von

HYMNE AN DAS SCHWEIZERLAND see Saladin, O.

HYMNE AN DAS VATERLAND see Boller, Carlo

HYMNE AN DIE HEIMATERDE see Doret, Gustave

HYMNE AN DIE MUSIK see Lachner, V.

HYMNE AU BLÉ see Naudier

HYMNE AU PAYS see Doret, Gustave

HYMNE AU PRINTEMPS see Jaques-Dalcroze, Émile

HYMNE AU SOLEIL see Arnoud, J. see Boulanger, Lili see Delmas, Marc-Jean-Baptiste see Fievet, Paul see Mozart, Wolfgang Amadeus see Rameau, Jean-Philippe

HYMNE AU TRAVAIL see Doret, Gustave

HYMNE AU VIN see Breard

HYMNE AUX MORTS POUR LA PATRIE see Brunel

HYMNE AUX NATIONS LATINES see Breard

HYMNE DU MATIN see Broquet, Louis

HYMNE NEUCHÂTELOIS see North

HYMNE VAUDOIS *pop
     mix cor HUG 6809 (H425)

HYMNS WITHOUT WORDS (FIRST MOVEMENT) see Dello Joio, Norman


# I

I AM A CHILD see Campbell-Towell, Lee

I AM A POET see Volk

I BI SOLDAT UND DU BISCH SOLDAT see Rolli

I D' FRÖNDI see Kölliker, G.

I DENNA LJUVA SOMMARTID see Öhrwall, Anders

I DENNE JORD see Nyhus, Rolf

I DER FRÖMDI see Boesch, Balthasar

I DO LIKE TO BE BESIDE THE SEASIDE see Kind, Glover

I DON'T KNOW WHY I LOVE YOU LIKE I DO
   (Ames, Morgan) SSAA,acap (gr. I) UNC
     JP (I1)
   see Ames, Morgan

I DR FRÖMDI see Boesch, Balthasar

I DREAMED A DREAM see Schonberg, Claude-Michel

I DREAMED OF A CITY INVINCIBLE see Dello Joio, Norman

I GAN NID HEI BIS WÄLLELED see Märki, Ernst

I GET ALONG WITHOUT YOU VERY WELL see Carmichael, Hoagy

I GLEDINNI see Asgeirsson, Jon

I GOT A ROBE see Clark, Derek J.

I GOT RHYTHM see Gershwin, George

I HÄB DI TREU G'LIABT see Anderluh, Anton

I HALLINGTONE see Nyhus, Rolf

I HAN ESMOL ES SCHÄTZELI GHA see Ruprecht, Ernst

I HAVE A LITTLE DREYDEL see Gelbart, M.

I HAVE NEVER BEEN SO CAREFREE see Certon, Pierre, Je Ne Fus Jamais Si Aise

I HEAR AMERICA SINGING see Thomas, Andre

I HEAR LIBERTY SINGING see Gilpin, Greg

I HIDE MYSELF see Whitacre, Eric

I HOLL GODMUNDAR see Asgeirsson, Jon

I JUST CALLED TO SAY I LOVE YOU see Morris, Stevland (Stevie Wonder)

I KNOW A SILLY SONG see Gilpin, Greg

I KNOW HIM SO WELL see Andersson

I LOVE A PIANO see Berlin

I LOVE ALL BEAUTEOUS THINGS see Clements, John

I LOVE MUSIC see McPheeters, T.

I LOVE MY LOVE  *folk song
   (Marvin, Jameson) TTBB,acap (cornish)
     LAWSON 52712 (I2)

I MADRIGALI DI CLAUDIO MONTEVERDI see Schiavo, Gianpaolo

I MÖCHT, I MÖCHT SINGE see Märki, Ernst

I NE ALPHÜTTE BIN-I GANGE see Hofer-Schneeberger, Emma

I-NO-RI see Takenaka, Atsuhiko

I REMEMBER CLIFFOR see Golson, Benny

I SAW THREE SHIPS
   (Shaw And Parker) SATB,acap LEONARD-
     US 50305100 (I3)

I SING OF A MAIDEN see Daley, Eleanor

I SKOVENS DYBE, STILLE RO
   (Nyhus, Rolf) 4pt mix cor,acap NOTON
     N-9208 (I4)

I SWEAR
  (Strommen, Carl) SATB WARNER WBCH9421
                                              (I5)
  (Strommen, Carl) SAB WARNER WBCH9422
                                              (I6)
  (Strommen, Carl) TTB WARNER WBCH9423
                                              (I7)
I SWING THE EIGHTH NOTES, THEREFORE I
  AM see Funk, Jeff

I THOUGHT ABOUT YOU
  (Cross, Dave) SSAA,perc (gr. III) UNC
  JP                                          (I8)
  (Cross, Dave) SATB,perc (gr. III) UNC
  JP                                          (I9)

I TICINESI *pop
  mix cor HUG 6809                            (I10)

I VAGHI FIOR see Muci, Italo Ruggero

I VÅRDTRÄDETS see Lindström, Lars

I VERINU see Asgeirsson, Jon

I WANT TO BE THERE see Schwartz, Dan

I WHISTLE A HAPPY TUNE see Rodgers,
  Richard

I WILL ALWAYS LOVE YOU
  (Schmutte, Pete) SATB WARNER 7426IC1X
                                              (I11)
  (Schmutte, Pete) SAB WARNER 7426IC3X
                                              (I12)

I WILL BRING YOU BROOCHES see Boshkoff,
  Ruth

I WILL LIE DOWN see Kernis, Aaron Jay

I WISH I WAS SINGLE AGAIN see Spevacek,
  Linda

I WONDER WHAT I'LL BE see Simpson

I WOULDA, COULDA, SHOULDA BEEN SO GOOD
  THIS YEAR! see Lawrence, Stephen L.

I WRITE THE SONGS see Johnston

ICE CASTLES (EYES OF LOVE) see
  Hamlisch, Marvin F.

ICH ARMES KÄUZLEIN KLEINE see Senfl,
  Ludwig

ICH GING EINMAL SPAZIEREN see Silcher,
  Friedrich

ICH HAB DIE HEIMAT LIEB see Keller,
  Hugo

ICH KANN UND MAG NICHT see Silcher,
  Friedrich

ICH LIED DURCH DEINE GASSEN see Schmid,
  A.

ICH SCHEIDE NUN see Studer, Hans

ICH SCHELL MEIN HORN see Weismann,
  Julius

ICH SCHWING MEIN HORN see Brahms,
  Johannes

ICH VERSPRACH DIR NIE see Fässler,
  Guido

ICH WEISS NICHT, WAS SOLL ES BEDEUTEN
  see Silcher, Friedrich

ICHIYANAGI, TOSHI (1933-    )
  Shi No Naka No Fukei
    mix cor JAPAN                             (I13)

  Shiroi Uma
    men cor JAPAN                             (I14)

I'D DO ANYTHING see Bart

I'D RATHER BE EATING ICE CREAM see
  Lyons,Bill

IDEM IN DIALEKT see Leicht

IDETA, KEIZO (1955-    )
  Chorus Suite
    mix cor,pno JAPAN                         (I15)

  Your Hand, My Heart
    jr cor&men cor,chamber group JAPAN
                                              (I16)
    mix cor,orch JAPAN                        (I17)

IDIOTE DU VILLAGE, L' see Vuataz, Roger

IDYLLE see Parker, Horatio William

IDYLLE PRINTANIÈRE see Moudon, E.

IF A MAN DOES NOT KEEP PACE see
  Armstrong, Matthew

IF ALL BE TRUE see Purcell, Henry

IF I COULD see Sharron, Marti

IF I GOT MY TICKET, CAN I RIDE?
  (Shaw) SATB,T solo,acap LEONARD-US
  50303900                                    (I18)

IF I HAD A HAMMER see Seeger, Pete

IF I ONLY HAD A BRAIN
  (Sturm, Fred) SSATBB,acap (gr. III)
  UNC JP                                      (I19)

IF LOVE WERE THE ROSES see Sapieyevski,
  Jerzy

IF MUSIC BE THE FOOD OF LOVE see
  Belmont

IF SHE BE MADE OF WHITE AND RED see
  Strohbach, Siegfried

IF WE LOVE see Beebe, Hank

IGARASHI, TADASHI (1918-    )
  Listen Intently
    wom cor JAPAN                             (I20)

  Season Of Children *Suite
    wom cor JAPAN                             (I21)

IGEL UND AGEL, OP. 130A see Kratochwil,
  Heinz

IGNORANT, L' see Mermoud, Robert

IHR FALTERMÄDCHEN, WOHIN? see Kreis,
  Otto

IKARI MAKU see Kino, Seiichiro

IKARUS see Klein, Richard Rudolf

IKEBE, SHIN-ICHIRO (1943-    )
  Airmails Toward A Hope, The
    mix cor,pno JAPAN                         (I22)

  Grave Posts In The Sea, The
    wom cor,pno JAPAN                         (I23)

  Letter Without Address, A
    mix cor,pno JAPAN                         (I24)

  Search For Songs, The
    mix cor,pno JAPAN                         (I25)

  Shin, Zen, Bi - Cantata In
    Celebration
    mix cor,orch JAPAN                        (I26)

  Sky, Sea And Mountains Of Yawatahama,
    The
    jr cor,pno JAPAN                          (I27)

  Taro No Ki
    "Taro's Tree" (chorus opera) ONGAKU
    543170                                    (I28)

Taro's Tree
  see Taro No Ki

IKIKATOU see Mermoud, Robert

IL AVAIT L'ÂME BIEN NOIRE see Lagger,
  Oscar

IL CIEL CHE RADO see Arcadelt, Jacob

IL EN FAUT DU TEMPS see Boller, Carlo

IL EST BEAU DE LOUER... see Staden,
  Johann

IL EST BEL ET BON see Passereau

IL EST JOUL, DIT L'ALOUETTE see Jaques-
  Dalcroze, Émile

IL EST NÉ, LE DIVIN ENFANT see Mermoud,
  Robert

IL EST UN RAISIN DORÉ see Miche, Paul

IL EST UN VIEUX POMMIER see Bovet, J.

IL EST UNE MAISON see Aeschbacher,
  Walther

IL ETAIT UN PETIT NAVIRE see Marx, Karl

IL ÉTAIT UNE BARQUE see Canteloube,
  Joseph

IL ÉTAIT UNE FILLE see Doret, Gustave

IL FAUT AVOIR UNE ÂME CLAIRE see
  Reichel, Bernard

IL FAUT PEU DE CHOSE see Bovet, J.

IL FAUT TANT DE CHOSES... see Gaillard,
  Paul-Andre

IL N'EST AMOUR QUE LE PRINTEMPS see
  Mouchet

IL N'EST PLUS LE TEMPS see Martin

IL PAESAGGIO DELLE ANALOGIE see
  Tristano, Gerardo

IL PASSA see Bovet, J.

IL PLEURE DANS MON COUER see
  Benninghoff, Ortwin

IL S'EN EST ALLÉ see Mermoud, Robert

IL SUFFIT DE CHANTER see Urfer, Albert

I'LL ALWAYS REMEMBER YOU see Simms,
  Patsy Ford

I'LL BE THERE
  (Chinn, Teena) SATB WARNER 3737C1X
                                              (I29)
  (Chinn, Teena) 3pt mix cor WARNER
  3737IC3X                                    (I30)
  (Chinn, Teena) 2pt mix cor WARNER
  3737IC5X                                    (I31)

I'LL BE YOUR FRIEND UNTIL FOREVER see
  McPheeters

I'LL CARRY YOU IN MY HEART see
  Broughton, Bobby

I'LL GIVE MY LOVE AND APPLE see
  Raminsh, Imant

I'LL NEVER SMILE AGAIN see Ames, Morgan

I'LL TAKE YOU THERE
  (Baker, Andy) SATB WARNER CH9517 ipa
                                              (I32)
  (Baker, Andy) SAB WARNER CH9518 ipa
                                              (I33)

IM ALTE LANDGRICHT STÄRNEBÄRG see
  Kreis, Otto

I'M BEGINNING TO SEE THE LIGHT see
  James

I'M BOUND AWAY
  (Moore, Donald) TTB WARNER SV9313
                                              (I34)

IM DORFKURG see Heuken, Hans Jakob

I'M EVERY WOMAN
  (Chinn, Teena) SSA WARNER 4284IC2X
                                              (I35)

I'M FREE see Secada, Jon

IM FRIEDEN DEIN, O HERRE MEIN see
  Clementi, Aldo

IM FRÜHLING see Zahler, J.R.

IM FRÜHLINGSWIND see Gersbach, Fritz

IM FRÜHLINGSWIND (GIB MIR DIE HAND) see
  Jaeggi, Oswald

IM FRÜLING ("UNSRE WIESEN GRÜNEN
  WIEDER"), KV ANH.262 see Mozart,
  Wolfgang Amadeus

IM GEGENWÄRTIGEN VERGANGENES see
  Schubert, Franz (Peter)

IM HEU see Doret, Gustave

IM HIMMELREICH EIN HAUS STEHT see
  Reger, Max

I'M IN A HURRY (AND I DON'T KNOW WHY)
  see Warmer, Randy

IM KRUG ZUM GRÜNEN KRANZE see
  Hollfelder, Waldram

IM PARK, OP. 130B see Kratochwil, Heinz

IM SCHATTE see Vollenweider, Hans

IM SUNNELAND see Märki, Ernst

I'M TRAMPIN' see Johnson, Neil

IM VOLKSTON see Kaufmann, Fred

IM WALD, IM HELLEN SONNENSCHEIN see
  Jensen, Adolf

IM WÄRDE see Märki, Ernst

IM WÄTTERSTURM see Schmid, Walter

I'M WITH YOU
  (The Real Group) SSATB,female solo,
  acap (gr. IV/gr. V) UNC JP                  (I36)

IMA IKIRU KODOMO MARCH see Yuyama,
  Akira

IMAGES DE MON PAYS see Boller, Carlo

IMAGES DE SOLEIL see Bron, Patrick

IMMAGINE DI ARPOCRATE, UN' see Sciarrino, Salvatore

IMMER WIEDER LASST UNS SINGEN see Hilger, Manfred

IMMORTELLE DE JEAN, L' see Bovet, J.

IMPRISONED ONCE AT NANTES
  (Charles Pelletier) SSA,opt triangle
  FOSTER MF 962 (I37)

IMPROMPTU see Mechem, Kirke Lewis

IN A MIST see Beiderbecke

IN A SENTIMENTAL MOOD
  (Moore, Donald) SATB WARNER 4791IC1X
  ipa (I38)

IN ALASKA IN A MAJOR see Beattie, Donald

IN CAUDA see Donatoni, Franco

IN DAR LERCHARLEITN *CCU,Austrian
  (Inzko, Josef) HEYN f.s. mix cor
  ISBN 3 85366 723 6; men cor
  ISBN 3 85366 724 4 (I39)

IN DEN BERGEN see Frei, Friedrich see Schmid, Walter

IN DEN GRÜNEN TAG HINEIN see Schmid, Walter

IN DER FRÜHE see Stocker, Karl

IN DER NACHT see Brun, Fritz see Hägler, Paul

IN DER SPERLINGSGASSE see Lincke, Paul

IN EINEM KÜHLEN GRUNDE see Silcher, Friedrich

IN FLANDERS FIELD see Henderson, Ruth Watson

IN FLANDERS FIELDS see Daley, Eleanor

IN GOLDENER FÜLLE see Müller, Joseph Ivar

IN GUILTY NIGHT see Purcell, Henry

IN MEMORIAM LEONARD BERNSTEIN see Glick, Srul Irving

IN PARADISE see Beattie, Donald

IN PARAISE OF A VIRTUOUS WOMAN see Talma, Louise

IN TERRA PAX see Ogikubo, Kazuaki

IN THE FOREST OF KAMUI see Hirose, Ryohei

IN THE STILLNESS see Gray, Cynthia

IN THE SWING
  (Billingsley) SATB SHAWNEE A-1973 ipa
  (I40)

IN THESE DELIGHTFUL PLEASANT GROVES see Purcell, Henry

IN THIS LIFE
  (Chinn, Teena) SATB WARNER 4871IC1X
  (I41)
  (Chinn, Teena) SAB WARNER 4871IC3X
  (I42)

IN TIME FOR CHRISTMAS see Schwartz, Dan

INCANTATION see Bernier, Rene see Vuataz, Roger

INCANTATIONS see Bernier, Rene

INCH WORM
  (Rosander, Christine) SATB,acap (gr. III) UNC JP (I43)

INDIAN QUEEN,THE see Purcell, Henry

INDORATORIUM I see Wullur, Sinta

INDY, VINCENT D' (1851-1931)
  Chant De Nourrice
    3 eq voices BILLAUDOT (I44)

  Forgeron, Le
    3pt mix cor,string quar BILLAUDOT
    (I45)

  Trois Fileuses, Les
    3 eq voices BILLAUDOT (I46)

INFERNALISCHE ABENDMAHL,DAS see Tamas, Janos

INFERNO see Vlijmen, Jan van

INGHELBRECHT, GERMAINE
  Chantons Jeunesse *CC10U
    3 eq voices BILLAUDOT f.s. (I47)

INGRID DARDELS POLSKA see Taube, Evert

INHALT: LEBENSLAUF "WARTEN AUF DEN AUGENBLICK" see Helmschrott, Robert M.

INNORIA see Patriquin, Donald

INO AMPHIGOURI see Canteloube, Joseph

INOCHI NO HOHOEMI see Konkoh, Iwao

INSCRIPTION OF HOPE see Stroope, Z. Randall

INSTANT DU BONHEUR, L' see Bovet, J.

INTERLUDIO see Bosco, Gilberto

INTERMEZZO FESTIVO see Haase-Altendorf, Helmut

INTERMINABLE ENNUI, L' see Jordan

INTERNATIONAL CAROLS, SET 1
  (Spevacek, Linda) SATB HERITAGE
  15-1146 f.s.
    contains: Ballou Lammy; Let Carols Ring; Masters In This Hall (I48)

INTERNATIONAL CAROLS, SET 2 see Spevacek, Linda

INTERNATIONAL FOLK see Anonymous

INTERPERSONAL RELATIONSHIPS see Togawa, Yohichi

INTO YOUR LOVING CARE see Catherwood, David

INVENTION IN C MAJOR see Bach, Johann Sebastian

INVITATIONS see Belmont, Jean

INVOCATION see Smetana, Bedrich

INVOCATION À LA VIERGE see Daetwyler, Jean

INVOCATION À L'HIVER see Doret, Gustave

INVOCATION AU PRINTEMPS see Doret, Gustave

INVOCCAZIONE ALLA TERRA see De Grandis, Renato

IO DICO CHE FRA VOI see Arcadelt, Jacob

IO NON AMO... see Zecchi, Adone

IRELAND, JOHN (1879-1962)
  See How The Morning Smiles
    2pt cor BANKS ECS 147 (I49)

IRISH AIRMAN, AN see Adams, Byron

IRISH BLESSING, AN see Moore, Donald

IROQUOIS, L' see Pantillon, François

IS IT A DREAM ? see Diemer, Emma Lou

IS SCHON STILL UMAN SEE *CCU,Austrian
  (Mittergradnegger, Günther-Glawischnig, Gerhard) mix cor HEYN
  ISBN 3 85366 426 1 f.s. (I50)

ISAAC, HEINRICH (ca. 1450-1517)
  Adieu, L'
    mix cor HUG 7886 (I51)

I'SE THE D'Y (from When The Outports Sing)
  (Telfer) SSA KJOS 6224 (I52)

ISELLA, CÉSAR
  Cancion Con Todos
    (Balzanelli, Alberto) 3pt wom cor/
    3pt jr cor LAGOS (I53)
    (Balzanelli, Alberto) 4pt mix cor
    LAGOS (I54)

ISHI NI KIKU see Shibata, Minao

ISLENSKIR SONGDANSAR see Asgeirsson, Jon

ISN'T IT ROMANTIC see Hart, Lorenz

IT COULDN'T BE DONE see Lieuwen, Peter

IT DON'T MEAN A THING see Ellington, Edward Kennedy (Duke)

IT WAS A LOVER AND HIS LASS see Holman, Derek see Larkin, Michael see Strohbach, Siegfried see Swingle, Ward

ITALIENISCHE MADRIGALE *CC7L
  (Krings, Alfred) mix cor,acap LAAB
  AV 103 (I55)

ITHIER
  Berceuse Des Tout Petits
    2 eq voices BILLAUDOT (I56)

  Chanson De Chasse
    2 eq voices BILLAUDOT (I57)

  Joyeux Printemps
    3 eq voices BILLAUDOT (I58)

  Source Enchantée, La
    2 eq voices BILLAUDOT (I59)

  Vendangeurs, Les
    2 eq voices BILLAUDOT (I60)

ITOH, MIKIO (1942-  )
  Alone In Woods
    mix cor,pno JAPAN (I61)

  Dreams Of Mine
    mix cor,pno JAPAN (I62)

IT'S ALL RIGHT WITH ME see Porter, Cole

(IT'S JUST) TALK see Metheny,Pat

IT'S MY TURN see Masser, Michael

IT'S ONLY A PAPER MOON see Arlen, Harold

IT'S THE MOST WONDERFUL TIME OF THE YEAR see Winter's Wonderland

IT'S THE TALK OF THE TOWN see Kern

ITSUKI NO KOMORI UTA *folk song,Jap
  (Baxter, Francis H.) SATB,pno,opt fl
  LAWSON 52733 (I63)

I'VE NEVER BEEN IN LOVE BEFORE see Loesser, Frank

IZUMISHIKIBU see Nakajima, Hal see Nakajima, Haru

# J

JABERWOCKY see Pierce, (Anne) Alexandra

JABOULI BOULETTE see Apotheloz, Jean

JACK THE SAILOR see Vaughan Williams, Ralph

JACKSON
   Let There Be Peace On Earth (composed with Miller)
     SA WARCH 35692          (J1)
     SATB WARCH 35693        (J2)
     SSA WARCH 35694         (J3)

JACKSON, MICHAEL
   Heal The World
     (Strommen, Carl) 2pt cor WARNER
      WBCH9330              (J4)
     (Strommen, Carl) SATB WARNER
      WBCH9328              (J5)
     (Strommen, Carl) SAB WARNER
      WBCH9329              (J6)
   Will You Be There
     (Schmutte, Pete) SATB WARNER
      WBCH9352              (J7)
     (Schmutte, Pete) SAB WARNER
      WBCH9353              (J8)
     (Schmutte, Pete) 1-2pt cor WARNER
      WBCH9367              (J9)

JACOBSON, JOSHUA
   Chanuka Variations *folk song,Jew [Heb] SATB,S&T soli (med) HAZA HZ-003              (J10)

JAEGGI, OSWALD (1913- )
   Es Steht Ein Lind In Jenem Tal
     4pt mix cor CRON        (J11)
   Im Frühlingswind (Gib Mir Die Hand)
     4pt men cor CRON       (J12)
   Mein Schätzlein Hör Ich Singen
     4pt mix cor CRON        (J13)
   Stärne
     4pt men cor CRON       (J14)
   Wandern
     4pt men cor CRON       (J15)

JAG ÄR EN MÄNNISKA I VÄRLDEN see Wieh, Michael

JAG VET EN DEJLIG ROSA see Hultin, Lennart

JÄGER,DER see Furrer, Walter

JÄGERLAND see Schumann, Robert (Alexander)

JÄGERLIED see Vollenweider, Hans

JAGODA, FLORY
   Ocho Kandelikas
     (Jacobson, Joshua) SATB,S solo,gtr, opt perc (med easy, text in ladino) HAZA HZ-015   (J16)

JAHR HEBT AN, DAS see Rothschuh, Fritz

JÅHR IS LEI A WIND,DÅS *CCU,Austrian
   (Drewes, Helmut-Hopfgartner, Josef) HEYN f.s. mix cor
     ISBN 3 85366 341 9; men cor
     ISBN 3 85366 326 5     (J17)

JAHRESZEITENLIEDER *CC8L
   3pt wom cor, solo voices,opt 3vln MULLES M&S 1197 f.s.   (J18)

J'AI DESCENDU AU VERGER see Jaques-Dalcroze, Émile

J'AI PRIS LA FANTAISIE see Canteloube, Joseph

J'AI QUITTÉ MA MAISON see Boller, Carlo

J'AI RÊVÉ D'UNE MAISON see Gaillard, Paul-Andre

J'AI UN LONG VOYAGE À FAIRE see Lesur, Daniel

J'AI VU LE LOUP see Sala, Andre

JAKKÔ-AIKA see Nishimura, Akira

JAKOBITENLIED see Weismann, Julius

J'ALLAIS SUR LA GRAND'ROUTE see Grieg, Edvard Hagerup

JAM UP!
   (Schmutte, Pete) SATB (medley of Uptight (Everything's Alright), Jam Up & Jelly Tight) WARNER C0313C1X ipa               (J19)
   (Schmutte, Pete) SAB (medley of Uptight (Everything's Alright), Jam Up & Jelly Tight) WARNER C0313C3X ipa              (J20)

JAMAICAN MARKET PLACE see Farrow, Larry

JAMAIS JE N'OUBLIERAI see Lagger, Oscar

JAMAIS, PLUS JAMAIS LA GUERRE see Kaelin, Pierre

JAMBE ME FAIT MAL, LA see Aubanel, Georges

JAMES
   Australian Christmas Carol Medley
     SATB WARCH 36058       (J21)
   I'm Beginning To See The Light
     SATB NOVELLO 890530    (J22)

JANÁCEK, LEOŠ (1854-1928)
   Bouleau Qui Murmure
     men cor HUG 8114       (J23)
   Chanson De Labour
     men cor HUG 8113       (J24)
   Chant D'amour
     men cor HUG 8694       (J25)

JANEQUIN, CLEMENT (ca. 1485-ca. 1560)
   Chansons 1-17
     see Complete Chansons
   Chansons 18-73
     see Complete Chansons
   Chansons 74-114
     see Complete Chansons
   Chansons 115- 170
     see Complete Chansons
   Chansons 171-219
     see Complete Chansons
   Chansons 220-254
     see Complete Chansons
   Complete Chansons
     (Merritt, Lesure) OISEAU f.s. contains: Chansons 1-17; Chansons 18-73; Chansons 74-114; Chansons 115- 170; Chansons 171-219; Chansons 220-254; Complete Series     (J26)
   Complete Series
     see Complete Chansons

JANNEQUIN
   Ciel, Air Et Vent
     mix cor BILLAUDOT      (J27)

JANSSON, GUNNAR (1944- )
   Tystnad
     men cor (lamento) STIM  (J28)

JANUNGER, KJELL
   Brittsommarmålaren
     4pt mix cor,acap NOTON S-8909-6                 (J29)
   Sommarskogmelodi
     4pt mix cor,acap NOTON S-8909-9                 (J30)
   Vänta Inte Med Att Sjunga
     4pt mix cor,acap NOTON S-8909-7                 (J31)
   Vårfantasi
     unis cor,fl NOTON N-8923  (J32)

JAQUES-DALCROZE, ÉMILE (1865-1950)
   A Travers Bois
     mix cor,opt pno/org/orch HUG 1014                   (J33)
     eq voices,opt pno/org/orch HUG 1438                  (J34)
     men cor HUG 481        (J35)
   Adieu, Petite Rose
     eq voices HUG 517       (J36)
     mix cor,opt pno/org/orch HUG 1015                   (J37)
     men cor HUG 478        (J38)
   Alouette, L'
     mix cor HUG 7044        (J39)
   Armaillis, Les
     mix cor HUG 7240        (J40)
   Bel Étranger
     mix cor,opt pno/org/orch HUG 927                    (J41)
     men cor HUG 8822       (J42)
   Bonnes Dames De St-Gervais, Les
     mix cor HUG 7803        (J43)
   Chamois Rouge, Le
     mix cor,opt pno/org/orch HUG 930                    (J44)

JAQUES-DALCROZE, ÉMILE (cont'd.)
     men cor HUG 482        (J45)
   Chanso Des Quatre Fous De Mai
     see Trois Chansons Du "Jeu Du Feuillu"
   Chanson À La Lune
     mix cor,Bar solo,opt pno/org/orch HUG 1602                (J46)
   Chanson De La Reine Berthe
     mix cor HUG 7801        (J47)
   Chanson Des Maïentzettes (from Jeu Du Feuillu)
     mix cor,opt pno/org/orch HUG 1007                   (J48)
     see Trois Chansons Du "Jeu Du Feuillu"
   Chanson Des Vieux Meïentzets (from Jeu Du Feuillu)
     mix cor,opt pno/org/orch HUG 1008                   (J49)
   Chanson Du Blé, La
     mix cor HUG 7233        (J50)
   Chanson Du Roi Et De La Reine
     see Trois Chansons Du "Jeu Du Feuillu"
   Chanson Du Sol Natal, La
     mix cor,opt pno/org/orch HUG 935                    (J51)
     eq voices,opt pno/org/orch HUG 1440                  (J52)
     men cor HUG 466        (J53)
   Chant De Mariage
     mix cor,opt pno/org/orch HUG 399                    (J54)
   Chère Maison, La
     mix cor HUG 1597        (J55)
     men cor HUG 1577       (J56)
   Coeur De Ma Mie, Le
     mix cor HUG 7973        (J57)
     eq voices HUG 1619     (J58)
     men cor HUG 1579       (J59)
   Deux Amants Près Du Lac Bleu
     mix cor HUG 1592        (J60)
     men cor HUG 1572       (J61)
   File Ton Rouet
     mix cor HUG 8764        (J62)
   Flûtiau, Le
     mix cor,opt pno/org/orch HUG 6734                   (J63)
     eq voices HUG 7466     (J64)
   Garçons D'yverdon, Les
     eq voices HUG 1629     (J65)
   Hymne À La Patrie
     mix cor,opt pno/org/orch HUG 1287                   (J66)
   Hymne Au Printemps
     mix cor,pno/org/orch HUG 1006  (J67)
     eq voices HUG 1653     (J68)
   Il Est Joul, Dit L'alouette
     mix cor HUG 7802        (J69)
   J'ai Descendu Au Verger
     mix cor HUG 1608        (J70)
   J'voudrais Bien Me Marier
     mix cor HUG 1594A       (J71)
   Marche Vaudoise
     SA/TB,opt pno/org/orch HUG 1005A-B                  (J72)
     men cor,opt pno/org/orch HUG 1657                   (J73)
   Marinette
     mix cor HUG 1641        (J74)
     eq voices HUG 1640     (J75)
   Mon Hameau
     mix cor HUG 1598        (J76)
     eq voices HUG 1618     (J77)
     men cor HUG 1578       (J78)
   Mon Lac Est Pur
     mix cor HUG 1592        (J79)
     men cor HUG 1572       (J80)
   Mousse, La
     mix cor HUG 7234        (J81)
     eq voices HUG 7462     (J82)
   Notre Terre À Nous
     mix cor HUG 934         (J83)
   Oiselet, L'
     mix cor HUG 1605        (J84)
     eq voices HUG 1625     (J85)
   Petit Village, Le
     mix cor HUG 932         (J86)
     eq voices,opt pno/org/orch HUG 1439

JAQUES-DALCROZE, ÉMILE (cont'd.)
  (J87)
 men cor HUG 476 (J88)

 Plantons La Vigne
  mix cor HUG 1593 (J89)
  men cor HUG 1573 (J90)

 Prière Patriotique
  mix cor HUG 400 (J91)
  men cor HUG 390 (J92)

 Quand Le Mai Va V'nir
  mix cor HUG 1595 (J93)
  eq voices HUG 1615 (J94)
  men cor HUG 1575 (J95)

 Quand Même
  mix cor HUG 7079 (J96)

 Sur L'alpe Voisine
  mix cor HUG 1684 (J97)
  men cor HUG 6894, 8244 (J98)

 Tout Simplement
  mix cor HUG 926 (J99)
  eq voices HUG 408 (J100)
  mix cor,acap HUG 926A (J101)
  men cor HUG 389 (J102)

 Trois Chansons Du "Jeu Du Feuillu"
  HUG 7928 f.s.
   contains: Chanso Des Quatre Fous
   De Mai; Chanson Des
   Maïentzettes; Chanson Du Roi Et
   De La Reine (J103)

 Trois Oiseaux Chantants, Les
  mix cor HUG 7237 (J104)

 Vielle Ville, La
  men cor HUG 477 (J105)

 Vieux, Les
  men cor HUG 1560 (J106)

 Vivons En Chantant
  mix cor HUG 1601 (J107)

 Voix Du Lac, La
  mix cor HUG 7152 (J108)
  men cor HUG 7151 (J109)

JARDIN see Henchoz, Emile

JARDIN D'AMOUR see Mayor, Ch.

JARDIN PUBLIC see Sala, Andre

JARDINIÈRE DU ROI, LA see Aubanel, Georges

JARDINIÈRE DU ROY, LA see Doret, Gustave see Ruprecht, Ernst

JARDINIERS, LES see Boller, Carlo

JARDINS SE SONT TUS, LES see Henchoz, Emile

JARDINS SECRETS see Boller, Carlo

JARREAU, AL
 We're In This Love Together
  (Henley, Rod) TTBB,perc (gr. II)
  UNC JP (J110)

JASCHA JOUE see Heinrichs, Wilhelm

JAUCHZENDES LEBEN see Schmid, Walter

JAVELOT
 Tayau, Tayau
  3 eq voices BILLAUDOT (J111)

JAZZ FANTASIA see Alexander, Josef

JAZZ! JAZZ! AMERICAN JAZZ! see Mourant, Walter

JAZZ-KANONS see Fuhre, Uli

JAZZY JINGLE BELLS (from Jingle Bells)
 (Chinn, Teena) SATB WARNER 6883JC1X (J112)
 (Chinn, Teena) SAB WARNER 6883JC3X (J113)
 (Chinn, Teena) 2pt cor WARNER 6883JC5X (J114)

JAZZY OLD SAINT NICHOLAS (from Jolly Old Saint Nicholas)
 (Anderson, Tom) SATB WARNER CH95109 (J115)
 (Anderson, Tom) 3pt mix cor WARNER CH95110 (J116)
 (Anderson, Tom) 2pt mix cor WARNER CH95111 (J117)

JAZZY RHYTHM OF LIFE see Bell

JE DOIS PARTIR see Brahms, Johannes

JE L'ATTENDAIS *pop
 mix cor HUG 8242 (J118)

JE NE CHERCHE PAS... see Rochat, Jean

JE NE FUS JAMAIS SI AISE see Certon, Pierre

JE NE SAURAIS CHANTER NI RIRE see Gascongne, Mathieu

JE NE VEUX PAS DU VIEUX MARI see Doret, Gustave

JE N'IRAI PAS... see Henchoz, Emile

JE N'VERRONS PLUS MARION see Dutilleux, Henri

JE SUIS SEUL, TOUJOURS SEUL... see Tichy, O.A.

JE T'ATTENDRAI see Mermoud, Robert

JE TE L'AVAIS BIEN DIT... see Hemmerling, Carlos

JE VIENS À VOUS DU HAUT DES CIEUX see Eccard, Johannes see Praetorius, Michael

JE VOUS CHOISIS see Mermoud, Robert

JEAN DE LA "BOILLETTE" see Bovet, J.

JEAN-GASPARD see Grieg, Edvard Hagerup

JEAN L'ÉCLOPÉ see Bovet, J.

JEAN P'TIT JEAN see Doret, Gustave

JEANNETTE AU JARDINET see Bovet, J.

JEEP, JOHANN (1581-1644)
 Ach Schatz, Ich Muss Mich Scheiden
  see Zwei Liebes Lieder

 Ach Schätzlein, Zart Schöns Jungfräulein
  see Zwei Liebes Lieder

 Zwei Liebes Lieder (from "Studentengärtlein" Nbg. 1614 Bonitz, Eberhard)
  mix cor SCHUL CLS 348 f.s.
   contains: Ach Schatz, Ich Muss Mich Scheiden; Ach Schätzlein, Zart Schöns Jungfräulein (J119)

JEFFERS, RON
 Celtic Triptych,A
  TTBB EARTHSNG EM-18 (J120)

 Epitaphs
  SSA EARTHSNG EW-15 (J121)

 Serpent, The
  SATB EARTHSNG ES-5 (J122)
  SSA EARTHSNG EW-8 (J123)
  TBB EARTHSNG EM-6 (J124)

JEG TAENK TE, JEG BLEV see Volle, Sverre

JEHRLANDER, K-F.
 Lull-Lull *CCU,folk song
  SATB NOTERIA 2785 f.s. (J125)

JENKS, STEPHEN (1772-1856)
 Complete Works Of Steven Jenks *CCU, US
  (Steel, David Warren) A-R ED (J126)

JENNEFELT, THOMAS (1954- )
 Triumf Ätt Finnas Till
  SSAAB,2pno SVERIG sc SK 788, voc sc SK789 (J127)

JENNINGS, CAROLYN
 Bandicoot, The (from Menagerie Of Songs By Carolyn Jennings, A)
  jr cor,pno LEONARD-US OC12434 (J128)

 Giraffes *N Oc12435 (from Menagerie Of Songs By Carolyn Jennings, A)
  jr cor,pno LEONARD-US (J129)

 Panda (from Menagerie Of Songs By Carolyn Jennings, A)
  3pt cor LEONARD-US OC12439 (J130)

 Penguin (from Menagerie Of Songs By Carolyn Jennings, A)
  jr cor,pno LEONARD-US OC12436 (J131)

 Rhinoceros
  see Sloth

 Sloth (from Menagerie Of Songs By Carolyn Jennings, A)
  jr cor,pno LEONARD-US OC12437
   contains also: Rhinoceros (J132)

 Whale (Aqua Blues) (from Menagerie Of Songs By Carolyn Jennings, A)
  2pt cor LEONARD-US OC12438 (J133)

JENNINGS, WILL
 Best Years Of My Life, The (composed with Davis, Stephen)
  (Funk, Jeff) SATB WARNER 8072BC1X (J134)
  (Funk, Jeff) SAB WARNER 8072BC3X (J135)

JENNY, ALBERT (1912- )
 Gute Ziel,Das
  wom cor,acap MULLES (J136)
  3pt wom cor,winds/strings/org/pno MULLES pno red f.s., cor pts f.s., pts ipa (J137)

 Mailied
  4pt mix cor CRON (J138)

JENSEN, ADOLF (1837-1879)
 Drei Chorlieder *Op.28
  SATB CARUS 40.264 f.s.
   contains: Im Wald, Im Hellen Sonnenschein; Nachtlied; Wenn Die Reb' Im Safte Schwillt (J139)

 Im Wald, Im Hellen Sonnenschein
  see Drei Chorlieder

 Nachtlied
  see Drei Chorlieder

 Wenn Die Reb' Im Safte Schwillt
  see Drei Chorlieder

J'ENTENDS LE MOULIN
 (Patriquin, Donald) [Fr] SS,pno,opt perc EARTHSNG EW-10 (J140)
 see Patriquin, Donald

JERGENSON, DALE
 Big Fat Hairy Vision Of Evil
  cor,7 solo voices LAURN CH-1011 (J141)

JERUSALEM see Parry, [Sir] Charles Hubert Hastings

JERUSALEM OF GOLD
 (Braun, Yehezkel) [Heb] SSA (text & melody: Shemer, Naomi) ISR.MUS.INST. IMI 6957 (J142)

JESSEL, LEON (1871-1942)
 Parade Of The Wooden Soldiers
  (Vaccaro,J.) SAB GENTRY JG2057 (J143)

JESSLER, FRITZ
 Gutes Wollen
  SATB,acap BOHM (J144)

 Laub Fällt
  SATB,acap BOHM (J145)

 Man Müsste
  men cor,SA soli BOHM (J146)

JEUNE, CLAUDE LE (1528-1600)
 Reveci Venir Du Printemps
  SSATB EXC.MH 19.800.024 (J147)

JEUNE MÉNÉTRIER, LE see Loucheur, Raymond

JEUNES FILLES DE VAL D'ILLIEZ, LES see Boller, Carlo

JINGLE ALL THE WAY see Albrecht, Sally K.

JINGLE BELLS
 (Althouse) SATB ALFRED 11371 (J148)
 (Althouse) SAB ALFRED 11372 (J149)
 (Althouse) 2pt cor ALFRED 11373 (J150)
 see Pierpont, James

JINGLE BELLS FESTIVO (from Jingle Bells)
 (Porterfield, Sherri) SATB WARNER SV933 (J151)

J'IRAI AU PÔLE SUD see Daniderff, Pierre

JO-KEI see Sato, Toshinao

JOHANNISNACHT see Olpen, Friedrich W.

JOHN BARLEYCORN see Vaughan Williams, Ralph

JOHN HENRY *folk song,US
 (Shur, Laura) SATB,pno LAWSON 52700 (J152)

JOHN KANAKA see Chatman

JOHNNY APPLESEED see Sowash, Rick

JOHNNY AROO'
 (Jeffers, Ron) SSA EARTHSNG EW-11 (J153)

JOHNNY TODD see Walters, Edmund

JOHNSON, NEIL
 Americans West
  2pt cor,opt vln solo HERITAGE 15-1065 (J154)

JOHNSON, NEIL (cont'd.)
E-Ri-E, The
2pt cor HERITAGE 15-1118 (J155)

I'm Trampin'
3pt mix cor,pno HERITAGE 15-1195H (J156)

JOHNSON, SHEILA HILTON
My Magic World
SA THOMP.G VG256 (J157)

JOHNSON, VICTOR COHEN
Lovers Love The Spring (from Shakespeare's As You Like It)
SATB HERITAGE 15-1214H (J158)

JOHNSTON
I Write The Songs
SATB WARCH 34778 (J159)

JOLI GRINGOT see Boller, Carlo see Bovet, J., Galé Gringo

JOLI LAPIN BLANC, LE see Berthomieu, Marc

JOLI MEUNIER, LE see Doret, Gustave

JOLIVET, ANDRE (1905-1974)
Chants D'hier Et De Demain
men cor,male solo,pno BILLAUDOT (J160)

Sonnet De Ronsard
3pt wom cor BILLAUDOT (J161)

"JOMON-A I" see Ogikubo, Kazuaki

JONES
Farewell, Dear Love
(Swingle, Ward) SATB,solo voice,db& drums&synthesizer (gr. I) voc pt, pts UNC JP SM-10 (J162)

Sing Us
(Swingle, Ward) cor,pno,db,drums, gtr (gr. V) voc pt,pts UNC JP SK-8X (J163)

JONES, QUINCY
Love Is In Control
(Crenshaw, Randy) SATBB,acap (gr. III) UNC JP (J164)

JOPLIN
Entertainer,The
(Swingle, Ward) SSAATTBB,pno,db, drums (gr. III) voc pt,pts UNC JP RTJ-9X (J165)

Heliotrope Bouquet
(Swingle, Ward) SSAATTBB,A solo, pno,db,drums (gr. II) voc pt,pts UNC JP RTJ-6X (J166)

Hotshot
(Swingle, Ward) SSAATTBB,pno,db, drums (gr. II) voc pt,pts UNC JP RTJ-1X (J167)

Mr. Superman (from "Elite Syncopations")
(Swingle, Ward) SSAATTBB,pno,db, drums (gr. II) voc pt,pts UNC JP RTJ-5X (J168)

Satchmo (from Twelfth Street Rag)
(Swingle, Ward) SSAATTBB,pno,db, drums (gr. III) voc pt,pts UNC JP RTJ-10X (J169)

Wanderer,The
(Swingle, Ward) SSAATTBB,S solo, pno&db&drums (gr. II) voc pt,pts UNC JP RTJ-2X (J170)

Weeping Willow
(Swingle, Ward) TTBB,pno,db,drums (gr. II) voc pt,pts UNC JP RTJ-8X (J171)

JORDAN
Danse, La
mix cor HUG 8789 (J172)

Dis-Moi, Charbonnier
mix cor HUG 8856 (J173)

Interminable Ennui, L'
mix cor HUG 8853 (J174)
eq voices HUG 8854 (J175)
men cor HUG 8841 (J176)

Lune Blanche, La
mix cor HUG 8851 (J177)
eq voices HUG 8852 (J178)
men cor HUG 8840 (J179)

Maître Charbonnier
mix cor HUG 8856 (J180)

Que Tu Es Beau, Mon Village
mix cor HUG 8783 (J181)
3-4 eq voices HUG 8785 (J182)
men cor HUG 8784 (J183)

JORDAN (cont'd.)
Ritournelle
mix cor HUG 8786 (J184)
eq voices HUG 8787 (J185)

JORDAN, LEON
Etoile Du Matin
men cor,acap HUGUENIN CH 2105 (J186)

JORDENS SÅNG see Cederberg, Anna

JOSEF
Hochzeitsmadrigal
(Butz) SAB BUTZ 1314 (J187)

JOSEPH AND THE AMAZING TECHNICOLOR DREAMCOAT see Lloyd Webber, Andrew

JOSEPH LIEBER, JOSEPH MEIN see Walter, Samuel

JOUINEAU, JACQUES
Chevalier Du Guet
3pt jr cor,solo voice BILLAUDOT (J188)

Girofle Girofle
3pt jr cor,solo voice BILLAUDOT (J189)

Mistanlaire, La
3pt jr cor,solo voice BILLAUDOT (J190)

Petit Pierrot, Le
3pt jr cor,solo voice BILLAUDOT (J191)
4pt wom cor BILLAUDOT (J192)

Petit Roi D'angleterre, Le
3pt jr cor,solo voice BILLAUDOT (J193)

Poule Blanche, Une
3pt jr cor,solo voice BILLAUDOT (J194)

Ronde Des Fleurs, La
3pt jr cor,solo voice BILLAUDOT (J195)

Tour Prends Garde, La
3pt jr cor,solo voice BILLAUDOT (J196)

JOUR, LE see Broquet, Louis

JOUR A PASSÉ, LE see Rochat, Jean

JOUR DE GRÂCE see Brahms, Johannes

JOUR DE MAI see Brahms, Johannes

JOUR EST LÀ, LE see Corboz, Michel

JOUR EST PRÈS D'ÉCLORE, LE see Broquet, Louis

JOUR SE LÈVE, LE see Lavater, H.

JOUR S'EN VA..., UN see Vuataz, Roger

JOURNEY see Telfer, Nancy

JOURNEY, THE see Telfer

JOURNEY TO IXTLAN see Mackey, Steven

JOURNEYS & SECRETS see Levi, Paul Alan

JOURS S'EN VONT, LES see Miche, Paul

J'OUVRE DOUCEMENT LA PORTE see Gastoldi, Giovanni Giacomo

JOVIAL YOUNG SAILOR see Six Canadian Folksongs

JOY IN THE MORNING see Spevacek, Linda

JOY OF ALL THE EARTH see Lantz

JOY OF HANUKKAH, THE see Spevacek, Linda

JOY OVERFLOWING see Berry

JOYEUSE DIANE see Bovet, J.

JOYEUX NOEL, FELIZ NAVIDAD see Albrecht, Sally K.

JOYEUX PRINTEMPS see Ithier

JOYFUL MUSIC! see Hagen, Daron

JOYFUL NOISE see Le Siege, Annette

JOYFUL SONG see Archer, Violet

JU-GYU ZU see Fujiie, Keiko

JUBILANT SONG, A see Clausen, Rene

JUBILATE, SING JOYFULLY see Perry

JUGABA LA NIÑA AQUELLA see Balzanelli

JUGEND SINGT II
(Katt, Leopold) eq voices SCHUL CLS 125 f.s.
contains: Abschied Und Herzeleid;
Von Liebe Und Treue (J197)

JUGEND SINGT III *CCU
(Katt, Leopold) 2-3 eq voices SCHUL f.s. (J198)

JUKER, A.
Alte Liebi Sunne,Die
wom cor,acap MULLES (J199)

Hustageliedli
wom cor,acap MULLES (J200)

JULI-VEER see Swerts, Piet

JULSETH-HEINRICH, JEANNE
All Things Are Connected
3pt mix cor,pno HERITAGE 15-1218H (J201)
2pt cor HERITAGE 15-1219H (J202)

Cape Cod Chantey
2pt cor HERITAGE 15-1011 (J203)

Coasts Of High Barbary, The
3pt mix cor HERITAGE 15-1022 (J204)
2pt cor HERITAGE H5899 (J205)

Hava Nashira
3 eq voices,opt mel inst HERITAGE 15-1013 (J206)

JUMMY DOWN see Singh, Vijay

JUMPING JACKS, SIX HUMOROUS SONGS, OP.29 see Kenessey, Stefania Maria de

JUNGI LIEBI see Ruprecht, Ernst

JUSQU'À DEMAIN see Haenni, G.

JUST LIKE ME-THE TELEPHONE WIRES see Broughton

JUST ONE VOICE see Mortifee, Ann

JUSTE MILIEU, LE see Vuataz, Roger

J'VOUDRAIS BIEN ME MARIER see Jaques-Dalcroze, Émile

# K

KAELIN, PIERRE
   Adyu Mon Bi Payi
      mix cor,T solo HUG 8855    (K1)

   Aimer La Terre
      mix cor HUG 8649    (K2)
      men cor HUG 8794    (K3)

   Alleluia
      men cor HUG 7712    (K4)

   Aquèlos Mountagnos
      men cor,T solo HUG 7610    (K5)

   Au Soleil De L'Amitié
      mix cor,opt pno/org/orch HUG 8619    (K6)
      men cor HUG 8718    (K7)

   Au Temps De Neige
      mix cor HUG 8712    (K8)
      men cor HUG 8713    (K9)

   Bûcheron, Quitte Ta Hache!
      men cor HUG 7181    (K10)

   Carrousel
      mix cor,opt pno/gtr HUG 8386    (K11)
      eq voices,opt pno/gtr HUG 8385    (K12)
      men cor,opt pno/org/orch HUG 8387    (K13)

   Ce Chant De La Terre
      men cor HUG 7161    (K14)

   C'est Un Vigneron
      mix cor HUG 8714    (K15)
      men cor HUG 8715    (K16)

   Chanson De Mon Ami, La
      mix cor HUG 7325    (K17)

   Chanson D'Ici, La
      mix cor HUG 8624    (K18)
      eq voices HUG 8626    (K19)
      men cor HUG 8625    (K20)

   Chanson Pour Un Ami Lointain
      mix cor HUG 8236    (K21)
      eq voices HUG 8283    (K22)
      men cor HUG 8237    (K23)

   Chant Du Soir
      mix cor HUG 7324    (K24)

   Chemins De La Mer, Les
      mix cor,opt acord HUG 8620    (K25)
      eq voices,opt acord HUG 8798    (K26)
      men cor,opt acord HUG 8621    (K27)

   Colin Et Mariette
      mix cor HUG 7326    (K28)

   Dis Oui, Ma Bonne Amie
      mix cor HUG 7170    (K29)
      men cor HUG 7171    (K30)

   Franz Und Vreneli
      [Ger] mix cor HUG 7834    (K31)

   Jamais, Plus Jamais La Guerre
      mix cor,opt pno/org/orch HUG 8627    (K32)
      eq voices,opt pno/org/orch HUG 8629    (K33)
      men cor,opt pno/org/orch HUG 8628    (K34)

   Notre Vie Est Un Voyage
      mix cor HUG 7702    (K35)
      men cor HUG 7703    (K36)

   Nuit Foraine, La
      mix cor HUG 8616    (K37)
      eq voices HUG 8618    (K38)
      men cor,opt pno/org/orch HUG 8617    (K39)

   Ode Au Saint-Gothard
      men cor HUG 7323    (K40)

   Oeillet, L'
      mix cor,solo HUG 8726    (K41)

   Pour Bâtir Une Maison
      mix cor HUG 8716    (K42)
      men cor HUG 8717    (K43)

   Rondeau Du Contentement
      mix cor HUG 7786    (K44)

   Rosier Blanc, Le
      mix cor, solo voices HUG 7818    (K45)

   Sag' Ja, Mein Mägdelein
      [Ger] mix cor HUG 7833    (K46)

   Soldat De Fribourg
      men cor HUG 7160    (K47)

KAELIN, PIERRE (cont'd.)
   Sur La Rout'd'estavayer
      men cor HUG 7701    (K48)

   Terre Sois Douce
      men cor HUG 8487    (K49)

   Village Vous Dit: Bonjour!, Un
      mix cor HUG 7720    (K50)

   Zähringerlied
      men cor,acap MULLES    (K51)

KÄGI, WALTER
   Wanderlied
      wom cor,acap MULLES    (K52)

KAITENMOKUBA YO MAWARE see Saito, Takanobu

KAJSAS UDDE see Hambe, Alf

KALEIDOSCOPE see Falquet, Rene

KALITKA see Garden Gate,The

KALITZKE, JOHANNES
   Nachtschleife *madrigal
      SSATBarB GRAV    (K53)

KAMINFEGERLIED see Leuthold, W.

KAMMERER, IMANUEL JOHANNES (1896-1964)
   Weite Flur
      men cor,acap MULLES    (K54)

KAMMERKANTATE, EINE see Nielsen, Riccardo

KAMP, RICHARD (1913- )
   Hübsch Und Feurig
      men cor,acap BÖHM    (K55)

KAN Y'ÉTHÉ DZOUVENÈTA see Bovet, J.

KANDER, JOHN (1927)
   New York New York, Theme From
      SATB WARCH 33882    (K56)
      SAB WARCH 33884    (K57)

KANEKO, SHIN-ICHI (1937- )
   Kokoro
      mix cor,pno JAPAN    (K58)

K'ANG-TING LOVE SONG *folk song,Chin
   (Marvin, Jameson) TTB,acap LAWSON 52702    (K59)

KANGOUROU BOXEUR, LE see Berthomieu, Marc

KANNO, YOSHIHIRO (1953- )
   Celebration Of Life, The
      mix cor,orch JAPAN    (K60)

KANPO NO MATO NI NARITARU see Kino, Seiichiro

KANTI-KANTATE see Tamas, Janos

KAPELLE,DIE see Vollenweider, Hans

KARAKURI ZOSHI see Minami, Satoshi

KARKOFF, MAURICE (1927- )
   Nu Är Det Sommar
      SATB NOTERIA 2798    (K61)

   Två Fågelkörer
      mix cor NOTERIA 2813    (K62)

KARLSEN, KJELL MØRK (1947- )
   Norsk Suite
      4pt mix cor,acap NOTON N-9434-B    (K63)

KÄRNTENS LIEDERSCHATZ *CCU,folk song, Austrian
   (Anderluh, Anton -Mittergradnegger, Günther) wom cor HEYN NR. 154 f.s.    (K64)

KÄRNTENS LIEDERSCHATZ (HEFT 3) *CCU, folk song,Austrian
   mix cor HEYN NR. 109 f.s.    (K65)

KÄRNTNERLIEDER *CCU
   (Mittergradnegger, Günther) 4pt mix cor HEYN NR. 112 f.s.    (K66)

KASA-JIZO see Kato, Yumiko

KASAR MIE LA GAHI see Grau, Alberto

KÄSEBANDE, DIE see Schindler, Peter

KASHIRI see Ham, Tae Kyum

KATÁBRIO see Sagvik, Stellan

KATHEDRALE
   6pt wom cor MULLES f.s.
   contains: Gotische Fenster; Münster,Das; Wasserspeier    (K67)

KATHLEEN MAVOURNEEN see Crouch, Frederick Nicholls

KATJUSCHA *folk song,Russ
   (Welker) TTBB sc APOLLO AV 5875    (K68)

KATO, YUMIKO (1958- )
   Kasa-Jizo
      wom cor,SSSMezMez soli,pno,fl JAPAN    (K69)

KATZ, PAUL
   Zwei Lieder *CC2U
      mix cor SCHUL CLS 45    (K70)

KATZE UND MAUS see Furrer, Walter

KATZER, GEORG (1935- )
   Vom Fischer Un Sin Fru
      cor, solo voices,acap NEUE NM 1507    (K71)

KAUFMANN, FRED
   Ackersonntag
      wom cor,acap MULLES    (K72)

   Im Volkston
      men cor,acap MULLES    (K73)

   Sommerwiese,Die
      wom cor,acap MULLES    (K74)

KAWASAKI, ETSUO (1959- )
   Ame No Oto
      jr cor,pno JAPAN    (K75)

   Hanako No Hanaichi-Mon-Me
      jr cor,pno JAPAN    (K76)

   Kaze-Yo
      jr cor,pno JAPAN    (K77)

   Sayo-Nara
      jr cor,pno JAPAN    (K78)

   Singer
      mix cor,synthesizer JAPAN    (K79)

   Umi O Mi-Ni Yuko
      jr cor,pno JAPAN    (K80)

KAZE NI NARU FUE see Takashima, Midori

KAZE NO KOE see Suzuki, Teruaki

KAZE NO SUKITOTTA UTA see Terashima, Rikuya

KAZE-YO see Kawasaki, Etsuo

KAZOKU see Suzuki, Yukikazu

KEEFER, EUPHROSYNE (1919- )
   Siren Songs
      SSAA,acap CAN.MUS.CENT.    (K81)

KEEP ON SMILIN' see Steffy

KEEPER, THE *folk song,Eng
   (Coombes, Douglas) SSA,acap LINDSAY    (K82)

KEEWAYDIN see Freedman

KEIHALÁ see Robinovitch, Sid

KELLER, HUGO
   Bärner Buebe
      wom cor,acap MULLES    (K83)

   Gurte-Liedli
      wom cor,acap MULLES    (K84)

   Ich Hab Die Heimat Lieb
      wom cor,acap MULLES    (K85)

   Tschulimung-Liedli
      wom cor,acap MULLES    (K86)

KELLER, JOHN
   Love Is (composed with K., Tonio)
      SAB WARNER WBCH 9338 ipa    (K87)
      SATB WARNER WBCH9337 ipa    (K88)

KELLER, WILHELM (1920- )
   Auftakteule, Die *CC14U
      mix cor FIDULA 6021 f.s.    (K89)

   Dir Zu Eigen (composed with Klein, Richard Rudolf; Marx, Karl; Weber, Horst) *CC11U
      2pt mix cor FIDULA 6053 f.s.
      european love songs    (K90)

   Heiteres Herbarium (composed with Klein, Richard Rudolf; Poser, Hans; Weber, Horst) *CCU
      1-3 eq voices FIDULA 6051 f.s.
      canons and songs    (K91)

   Nigunim *CCU
      4pt mix cor,opt inst FIDULA 6023 f.s. dance songs    (K92)

KELLY, BRYAN (1934- )
   Africa
      SATB&jr cor,T solo,pno,opt timp/perc/orch [16'] (med) PRESSER 492-00022    (K93)

KEMPFER, LOTHAR
   Sängergruss
      men cor,S solo,acap MULLES   (K94)

KENESSEY, STEFANIA MARIA DE (1956-   )
   Jumping Jacks, Six Humorous Songs,
     Op.29
      SATB,acap HILD study sc 09432A, cor
      pts 09432B   (K95)

   Two Elizabethan Lyrics, Op.24
      SSA HILD study sc 09431A, cor pts
      09431B   (K96)

KENT
   Tide Rises , The Tide Falls (composed
     with Longfellow)
      SATB LAWSON 4-52045   (K97)

KENTUCKY JAZZ JAM see Elliott, D.J.

KENYA MELODIES see Hugh, R.I.

KEREDOMO DAICHI WA see Takashima,
   Midori

KERN
   All The Things You Are
      SATB WARCH 30015   (K98)
      SAB WARCH 30016   (K99)
      SSA WARCH 30017   (K100)

   Bright Lights
      2pt cor SHAWNEE EA-184   (K101)

   It's The Talk Of The Town
      SATB SHAWNEE A-1968 ipa   (K102)

KERN, JEROME (1885-1945)
   All The Things You Are
     (Swingle, Ward) SSAATTBB,acap (gr.
     V) voc pt,pts UNC JP SS-1   (K103)

   Ol' Man River
      SATB NOVELLO 090230   (K104)

   Song Is You,The
     (Carter, Allen) SSATB,acap (gr. IV)
     UNC JP   (K105)

KERN, PHILIP
   Sing, Sing, Sing
     (Anderson, Tom) SSATBB,perc (gr.
     IV) UNC JP   (K106)

KERNIS, AARON JAY (1960-   )
   I Will Lie Down
      SATB,pno SCHIRM.G   (K107)

   Praise Ye The Lord
      mix cor,acap SCHIRM.G   (K108)

   Stein Times Seven
      SSATB,pno SCHIRM.G 50481533   (K109)

   Teach Me Thy Way, O Lord
      SATB,org SCHIRM.G   (K110)

KERSTENS, HUUB (1947-   )
   Als Ghy Van De Doodt Sult Zijn
     Verbeten, Op. 38 (from Visscher)
      5pt mix cor [4'] sc DONEMUS   (K111)

   Apocalypse, Op. 40 (from Hopkins)
      8pt mix cor [13'] sc DONEMUS   (K112)

   Tiefe Lied, Op. 36, Das (from Trakl)
      6pt mix cor,3trp,3trom [19'] sc
      DONEMUS   (K113)

KERSTERS, WILLEM (1929-   )
   Canconetas Voor Ana-Catarina, Op. 95
      wom cor,fl,ob,harp [14'] CBDM   (K114)

   Cupidootje
     see Frivole Liedjes, Op. 91, No. 1

   Frivole Liedjes, Op. 91, No. 1 (from
     Van Scheltema)
      men cor,acap CBDM f.s.
        contains: Cupidootje; Meisje
        (K115)

   Frivole Liedjes, Op. 91, No. 2
      men cor,acap CBDM f.s.
        contains: Het Was Stil... (from
        Gorter); Laat Van Je Lippen...
        (from Perk)   (K116)

   Frivole Liedjes, Op. 91, No. 3
      men cor,acap CBDM f.s.
        contains: Liedje (from Van
        Ostayen); Zij Schoof Den
        Linteldoek Opzij... (from
        Leopold)   (K117)

   Het Was Stil...
     see Frivole Liedjes, Op. 91, No. 2

   Huldegedicht Aan Singer, Op. 89
      girl cor,pno [6'] CBDM   (K118)

   Laat Van Je Lippen...
     see Frivole Liedjes, Op. 91, No. 2

KERSTERS, WILLEM (cont'd.)
   L'énamorat Li Deia-Wat De Geliefde
     Haar Zegde, Op. 92
      mix cor,acap [8'15"] CBDM   (K119)

   Liedje
     see Frivole Liedjes, Op. 91, No. 3

   Meisje
     see Frivole Liedjes, Op. 91, No. 1

   Zij Schoof Den Linteldoek Opzij...
     see Frivole Liedjes, Op. 91, No. 3

KI REI see Yamamoto, Junnosuke

KIBI-JI, SYMPHONIC POEM see Kushida,
   Tetsunosuke

KIESLICH, L.
   Pinson Du Bois, Le
      mix cor HUG 7732   (K120)

KIKUCHI, MASAHARU (1938-   )
   Mittsu No Yuki No Uta *Suite
      wom cor,elec org JAPAN   (K121)

KILARNEY see Balfe, Michael William

KILLMAYER, WILHELM (1927-   )
   Contetto
     see Vier Chorstücke

   Licht Auf Dem Scheffel, Das
      mix cor sc SCHOTTS C 47474   (K122)

   Lu Labbru
     see Vier Chorstücke

   Still In Luft
     see Vier Chorstücke

   Vier Chorstücke
      mix cor,soli,acap sc SCHOTTS 20029
      f.s.
        contains: Contetto; Lu Labbru;
        Still In Luft; Villanella
        (K123)

   Villanella
     see Vier Chorstücke

KIM, EARL (1920-   )
   Some Thoughts On Keats And Coleridge
      SATB,acap (med diff) PRESSER
      342-40162   (K124)

KIMES, JANICE
   Set Your Heart A Singin'
      2pt cor,opt inst BEAUT BSP-506
      (K125)

   Soundings
      2pt cor,pno BEAUT BSP-502   (K126)

KIMURA, MASANOBU (1941-   )
   Song Of Yomitan
      wom cor JAPAN   (K127)

KIND, GLOVER
   I Do Like To Be Beside The Seaside
     (Canning, Andrew) SSAA,pno NOTERIA
     2800   (K128)

KINDLING OF WINTER see Okasaka, Keiki

KING, CAROLE
   You've Got A Friend
     (Farrell, Jim) SAB, solo voices
     (gr. II) UNC JP   (K129)

KING ARTHUR AND HIS SONS *folk song,
   Eng
   (Coombes, Douglas) SSA,acap LINDSAY
     (K130)

KING GORM THE GRIM see Parker, Horatio
   William

KING OF GLORY see Fleming

KING SOLOMON'S PROVERBS see Braun,
   Yeheskiel

KINGS AND QUEENS see Beattie, Donald

KING'S CONTEST, THE see Mechem, Kirke
   Lewis

KINO, SEIICHIRO (1946-   )
   Footprints
      mix cor,pno JAPAN   (K131)

   Genki No Engine Mawasoyo
      jr cor,gtr JAPAN   (K132)

   Hi No Kururu
      mix cor,pno JAPAN   (K133)

   Ikari Maku
      mix cor,pno JAPAN   (K134)

   Kanpo No Mato Ni Naritaru
      mix cor,pno JAPAN   (K135)

   Koi No Nai Hi
      men cor JAPAN   (K136)

KINO, SEIICHIRO (cont'd.)
   Ondine
      wom cor,pno JAPAN   (K137)

   Three Strange Stories
      mix cor,pno JAPAN   (K138)

   Yumemita Mono Wa
      mix cor,pno JAPAN   (K139)

KINOSHITA, MAKIKO (1956-   )
   Beyond The Horizon
     see Chiheisen No Kanata

   Chiheisen No Kanata
      "Beyond The Horizon" mix cor ONGAKU
      543950   (K140)

KIRI NI NAI FUTATSU NO SENRITSU see
   Abe, Ryotaro

KIRK
   About Love
      SATB KJOS 8759   (K141)

   Year's At The Spring, The
      SA KJOS 6239   (K142)

KIRKLAND, TERRY
   Christmas Joy
      3pt mix cor,opt handbells, or opt
      handchimes HERITAGE 15-1031
      (K143)

   We Wish You A Merry Christmas
      2pt cor,opt perc HERITAGE 15-1018
      (K144)

KISBY-HICKS
   Cuckoo Is Pretty Bird
      unis cor WARCH 34342   (K145)

KISO BUSHI *folk song,Jap
   (Baxter, Francis) SATB,pno SANTA
     SBMP 58   (K146)

KISS, A see Suben, Joel Eric

KISSED BY SUN see Stefansson, Finnur
   Torfi

KITES see Kreutz, Robert Edward

KITTE see Oguri, Katsuhiro

KLÄNGE #1 see Brahms, Johannes

KLÄNGE #2 see Brahms, Johannes

KLÁRISOK see Kurtag, György

KLEIN, GIDEON (1919-1945)
   First Sin, The
     see First Sin And Two Madrigals

   First Sin And Two Madrigals
      (diff) PRESSER 512-00608 f.s.
        contains: First Sin, The (TTBB);
        Two Madrigals (SSATB)   (K147)

   Sündenfall
      men cor BOTE   (K148)

   Two Madrigals
     see First Sin And Two Madrigals

   Zwei Madrigale *CC2U
      SSATB BOTE f.s.   (K149)

KLEIN, RICHARD RUDOLF (1921-   )
   Ikarus
      4pt mix cor,narrator,pno,perc
      FIDULA   (K150)

   Löwen-Ländler *CCU
      unis cor FIDULA 6034 f.s.   (K151)

   Pony-Polonaise
      3pt cor,inst (dance suite) FIDULA
      6035   (K152)

   Tanzbär-Blues *CCU
      FIDULA 6033 f.s.   (K153)

   Weggefährten (Heft 4) *CCU
      FIDULA 6044 f.s. cheerful and
      contemplative canons   (K154)

   Weggefährten (Heft 5) *CCU
      FIDULA 6045 f.s. songs and canons
      throughout the year   (K155)

   Weggefärten (Heft 1) *CCU
      FIDULA 6041 f.s. songs and canons
      (K156)

   Weggefährten (Heft 3) *CCU
      FIDULA 6043 f.s. comic sons and
      canons   (K157)

   Zwischen Traum Und Wachen *CCU
      3pt wom cor FIDULA f.s.   (K158)

KLEINE CHÖRE U. AUSLÄNDISCHE
   VOLKSLIEDER 1980 (from Kärntner
   Chorblätter) CCU
   (Mittergradnegger, Günther) mix cor
     HEYN f.s.   (K159)

KLEINE CHORSCHULE see Aichele, Karl

KLEINE HEX,DIE
  MULLES M&S 1155 (K160)

KLEINE SOLOTHURNER - SUITE see Märki, Ernst

KLEINE SPUFMUSIK, EINE see Spevacek, Linda

KLEINES HUHN FLIEGT UM DIE WELT,EIN see Schindler, Peter

KLEINES LAND, EIN SCHÖNES LAND,EIN
  (from Chorblätter)
  (Streiner, Hans) mix cor HEYN (K161)
  (Streiner, Hans) men cor HEYN (K162)

KLEINES LIEBESLIED see Hägler, Paul

KLEINES LIED,EIN
  3pt wom cor MULLES M&S 756 (K163)
  see Furer, Arthur see Gardeweg, Franz, X.

KLEINES WANDERLIED see Schmid, Walter

KLEVBERG
  Aladdin Song Kit #31
    unis cor THOMP.G K7990101 (K164)

KLING, GLOCKCHEN see Spevacek, Linda

KLUCHT VN PIERLALA, DE see Maessen, Antoon

KNAVE'S LETTER, THE see Fine

KNEPHAS see Xenakis, Yannis (Iannis)

KNOTS (JACK AND JILL FOR GROWN-UPS) see Beeson, Jack Hamilton

KNUSSEN, OLIVER (1952- )
  Frammenti Da 'Chiara'
    jr cor&wom cor FABER 51109 0 (K165)

KOBASHI, MINORU (1928- )
  "Haru" "Natsu" "Aki" "Fuyu"
    jr cor JAPAN (K166)

  Kyoryu Zetsumetsu
    jr cor JAPAN (K167)

  Pika Don
    jr cor JAPAN (K168)

KOBAYASHI, ARATA (1929- )
  Plastic Arts Of Clay, The *Suite
    mix cor, tsuzumi JAPAN (K169)

  Safran, Le *Suite
    mix cor,pno ONGAKU 543660 (K170)

KOBOLDS,THE see Parker, Horatio William

KOCH
  Am Wellenspiel Der Aare
    (Keller) wom cor,acap MULLES (K171)

KOCH-RAPHAEL, ERWIN (1949- )
  Composition No. 46
    10pt mix cor,solo voice,fl fac ed
    BOTE (K172)

KODÁLY, ZOLTÁN (1882-1967)
  Bohémien, Le
    mix cor HUG 8376 (K173)

  Ne Crains Point
    men cor HUG 7539 (K174)

  Peuple, Sois Fort!
    men cor HUG 7684 (K175)

  Prière Du Gueux, La
    mix cor HUG 8578 (K176)
    men cor HUG 7524 (K177)

KODOMO NO MAINICHI see Ueda, Akira

KOEHLER
  Stormy Weather (composed with Arlen, Harold)
    (Althouse) SAB ALFRED 5832 (K178)
    (Althouse) SSA ALFRED 5833 (K179)
    (Althouse) SATB ALFRED 5831 (K180)

KOEPKE, ALLEN
  One More Mountain To Climb
    SATB WARNER SV9440 ipa (K181)
    SAB/3pt mix cor WARNER SV9441 ipa (K182)

  Speak To The Child Of Love
    SSA,pno SANTA SBMP 96 (K183)

KOI NO NAI HI see Kino, Seiichiro

KOKAJI, KUNITAKA (1955- )
  Homa
    mix cor,orch JAPAN (K184)

  Madrigali II, O Allegoria D'amore
    wom cor,pno JAPAN (K185)

KOKORO see Kaneko, Shin-Ichi

KÖLLIKER, G.
  I D' Fröndi
    wom cor,acap MULLES (K186)

  Kommt All' Herein, Ihr Engelein
    wom cor,acap MULLES (K187)

  Müeti Rüeft, 'S
    wom cor,acap MULLES (K188)

  Müetis Tisch, 'S
    wom cor,acap MULLES (K189)

  Mys Briefli
    wom cor,acap MULLES (K190)

KOLYADA
  Al Die Willen Te Kap'ren Varen
    SATB EXC.MH 19.001.002 (K191)

KOM, SKAL VI KLIPPE SAUEN see Møller, Svein

KOMMT ALL' HEREIN, IHR ENGELEIN see Kölliker, G.

KOMMT, SINGT EIN LIED see Schmid, Walter

KOMMT ZUM SINGEN see Mittergradnegger, Günter

KOMMT ZUM SINGEN (HEFT 1) *CCU
  (Mittergradnegger, Günther) mix cor
  HEYN NR. 129 f.s. (K192)

KOMMT ZUM SINGEN (HEFT 2) *CCU
  (Mittergradnegger, Günther) mix cor
  HEYN NR. 130 f.s. (K193)

KOMORIUTA, KOMORIUTA YO see Tsuchida, Eisuke

KONDOH, HARUE (1957- )
  Song Of The Heroes Of Traditional Japanese Children's Stories
    jr cor HUG (K194)

KONKOH, IWAO (1933- )
  Inochi No Hohoemi *Suite
    "Smile Of Life" mix cor ONGAKU
    543690 (K195)

  Smile Of Life
    see Inochi No Hohoemi

KOSMOS see Mellnäs, Arne

KOTOBA WA IRANAI see Saito, Takanobu

KRAEHENBUEHL, J.G.
  De Joggeli
    men cor,acap MULLES (K196)

  Lob Des Chüjerstandes
    men cor,acap MULLES (K197)

  Soldatenabschied
    men cor,acap MULLES (K198)

  Zapfenstreich
    men cor,acap MULLES (K199)

KRATOCHWIL, HEINZ (1932- )
  Abschiedslied (Heinrich Issak Um 1490)
    mix cor BERBEN G 787 (K200)
    mix cor DOBLINGER G 787 (K201)

  Igel Und Agel, Op. 130a
    mix cor BERBEN G 810 (K202)
    mix cor DOBLINGER G 810 (K203)

  Im Park, Op. 130b (from Ringelnatz)
    3pt mix cor,acap BERBEN G 811 (K204)
    3pt mix cor,acap DOBLINGER G 811 (K205)

  Tanz, Op. 166d, Der
    mix cor BERBEN G 812 (K206)
    mix cor DOBLINGER G 812 (K207)

KRAUER, A
  Bonjour Au Nouveau-Né
    mix cor HUG 8453 (K208)

  Pour Un Nouvel Élu
    mix cor HUG 8453 (K209)

KRAYENBÜHL, F.
  Unterm Ahornbaum
    men cor,acap MULLES (K210)

KREIS, OTTO
  Abend Im Tessin
    men cor,acap MULLES (K211)

  Bekehrte,Der
    wom cor,acap MULLES (K212)

  Campane Di Sera
    wom cor,acap MULLES (K213)

KREIS, OTTO (cont'd.)
  Du Standest Am Fenster
    wom cor,acap MULLES (K214)

  Frisch Fröhlich Wend Wir Singen (Röseligarten)
    men cor,acap MULLES (K215)

  Gesang Der Seligen
    wom cor,acap MULLES (K216)

  Ihr Faltermädchen, Wohin?
    wom cor,acap MULLES (K217)

  Im Alte Landgricht Stärnebärg
    men cor,acap MULLES (K218)

  Madonna Del Sasso
    wom cor,acap MULLES (K219)

  Morgenlied
    wom cor,acap MULLES (K220)

  Nachtmusik
    men cor,acap MULLES (K221)

  Nachtstille
    wom cor,acap MULLES (K222)

  O Du Liebs Aengeli, Rosmarinstängeli
    men cor,acap MULLES (K223)

  Primavera
    wom cor,acap MULLES (K224)

  Requiem
    wom cor,acap MULLES (K225)

  Rosenfenster
    wom cor,acap MULLES (K226)

  Rosenläuten
    wom cor,acap MULLES (K227)

  Schweizerspruch
    men cor,acap MULLES (K228)

  Serenata
    wom cor,acap MULLES (K229)

  Silberne Nacht, Dein Weisses Boot
    wom cor,acap MULLES (K230)

  Spruch
    men cor,acap MULLES (K231)

  Tag Im Herbst
    wom cor,acap MULLES (K232)

  Tagesneige
    wom cor,acap MULLES (K233)

  Vom Balkone
    men cor,acap MULLES (K234)

  Wappenspruch
    men cor,acap MULLES (K235)

  Was Sind Die Jahre?
    men cor,acap MULLES (K236)

  Weisser Flieder
    wom cor,acap MULLES (K237)

  Wetterweibchen
    wom cor,acap MULLES (K238)

  Wille
    men cor,acap MULLES (K239)

  Wo Sind Die Quellen?
    wom cor,acap MULLES (K240)

KRENGER, J.R.
  Dem Schweizerland
    men cor,acap MULLES (K241)

KRENGER, R.
  Alpsegen
    wom cor,acap MULLES (K242)

  Auf Die Höhen
    wom cor,acap MULLES (K243)

  Des Sennen Morgenlied
    wom cor,acap MULLES (K244)

  D's Hüsli
    wom cor,acap MULLES (K245)

  Heimat
    wom cor,acap MULLES (K246)

  Schönste Zeit,Die
    wom cor,acap MULLES (K247)

  Unser Leben Gleicht Der Reise
    wom cor,acap MULLES (K248)

KRESNIK see Nieder, Fabio

KRETZSCHMAR, GÜNTHER (1929-    )
    Brückenbogen B,Der  *CC14U
      3 eq voices FIDULA            (K249)

    Quintentraum,Der  *CC11U
      unis cor,pno FIDULA 6061 f.s.
      lively interval study         (K250)

KREUTZ
    Afternoon On A Hill
      SA KJOS 6232                  (K251)

KREUTZ, ROBERT EDWARD (1922-    )
    Easy Wind, Go Softly
      SATB,acap MUSIC SEV. 735      (K252)

    Kites
      SATB,acap MUSIC SEV. 736      (K253)

KREUTZER, CONRAD
    Dimanche Du Berger, Le
      men cor HUG 2370              (K254)

KREUTZER, KONRADIN (1780-1849)
    Forschen Nach Gott
      mix cor BUTZ 290              (K255)

KRIEGER, FRITZ (1902-1963)
    Zwei Trinksprüche Und Glückwunsch
      SATB BOHM                     (K256)

KROKUS & STEINBRECH see Furer, Arthur

KRONE
    Rondo Gotlandica
      mix cor,fl,2vln,2vla,vcl,db STIM
                                    (K257)

KRUG MIT OLIVEN,EIN see Schwaen, Kurt

KU-KU  *folk song,Polish
    (Cormier, Robert De) 2pt jr cor,pno
    LAWSON 52795                     (K258)

KUBIK
    How Lovely Thy Place
      SATB LAWSON 4-52274           (K259)

KUBLI, M.
    Geübtes Herz
      men cor,acap MULLES           (K260)

KUHLAU, FRIEDRICH (1786-1832)
    Soir, Le
      mix cor HUG 3912              (K261)

KUHN, E.
    Morgenlied (Kein Stimmlein Noch
      Schallt)
      wom cor,acap MULLES           (K262)

KUMBAYAH
    (Simms) 2pt cor ALFRED 11321  (K263)
    (Simms) 2-3pt cor ALFRED 11322 (K264)

KUNC, P.
    Gave, Le
      4pt mix cor BILLAUDOT         (K265)

KUNIEDA, HARUE (1958-    )
    Aki No Michi
      wom cor HUG                   (K266)

KUNTERBUNT see Lampart, Reinhold see
    Lampart, Reinhold

KUNZ, ERNST (1891-    )
    Einer Verlassenen
      wom cor,acap MULLES           (K267)

KUPP, ALBERT
    Auf, Zum Tanz (from Haydn's Symphony
      No. 97)
      SATB,orch&pno/pno BUTZ 1239 (K268)

    Glückwunsch
      mix cor BUTZ 1352             (K269)

    Sah Ein Knab Ein Röslein Stehn
      mix cor BUTZ 1305             (K270)

    Sinnsprüche  *CC32U,canon
      mix cor BUTZ 1285 f.s.        (K271)

    Ständchen
      mix cor BUTZ 916              (K272)

    Wandern Ist Des Müllers Lust, Das
      mix cor BUTZ 1287             (K273)

    Wenn In Stiller Stunde
      mix cor BUTZ 1335             (K274)

KURACHI, TATSUYA (1962-    )
    Hoshizora No Muko Kara
      wom cor,pno HUG               (K275)

    Nightmare
      wom cor/jr cor HUG            (K276)

    Sentei Minage (from Tale Of The
      Heike, The)
      men cor HUG                   (K277)

KUROKAMI, YOSHIMITSU (1933-    )
    Hana-Gatami
      mix cor HUG                   (K278)

KURTAG, GYÖRGY (1926-    )
    Beads
      see Klárisok

    Klárisok
      "Beads" [Hung] mix cor EMB Z 13955
                                    (K279)

KUSHIDA, TETSUNOSUKE (1935-    )
    Kibi-Ji, Symphonic Poem
      mix cor&jr cor,brass, and japanese
      inst HUG                      (K280)

    Man-Yo
      wom cor, harp ens HUG         (K281)

KY CHORORO see Sampayo, Anibal

KYORYU ZETSUMETSU see Kobashi, Minoru

KYOTO 1200, TRADITION & CREATION see
    Mayuzumi, Toshiro

# L

LÀ-BAS, DANS LE HAMEAU see Bovet, J.

LÀ-BAS, SUR LA MER see Pantillon,
    François

LÂ-BAS, VERS LA FONTAINE see Lagger,
    Oscar

LA FONTANA see Zecca, Giannino

LÀ-HAUT see Broquet, Louis see
    Gaillard, Paul-André see
    Hemmerling, Carlos see Moudon, E.

LÀ-HAUT, SUR LA MONTAGNE see Bovet, J.

LÀ-HAUT, TOUT EN HAUT see Bovet, J.

LA TOMBELLE, FERNAND DE (1854-1928)
    Charrue, La
      4pt men cor BILLAUDOT         (L1)

    Chasse, La
      4pt mix cor BILLAUDOT         (L2)

    Épousailles,Les
      5pt mix cor BILLAUDOT         (L3)

    Furet, Le
      4pt men cor BILLAUDOT         (L4)

    Soleil De Minuit, Le
      4pt mix cor BILLAUDOT         (L5)

    Vers La Lumière
      4pt mix cor BILLAUDOT         (L6)

LAAT VAN JE LIPPEN... see Kersters,
    Willem

LABES, JEF
    Shir Ahavah
      [Heb] SATB,solo voice,pno,fl&drums&
      db (med, each instrumental part
      separately available) HAZA HZ-050
                                    (L7)

LABYRINTH OF LOVE see Fleischman, Paul

LAC ET LA VIGNE, LE see Pasquier,
    Marius

LAC PROFOND, LE see Schumann, Robert
    (Alexander)

LACHNER, V.
    Hymne An Die Musik
      men cor,acap MULLES           (L8)

LACRIMOSA see Oguri, Katsuhiro

LACROIX
    Quand La Belle S'en Fut Au Bois
      4pt mix cor BILLAUDOT         (L9)

LAGANA, RUGGERO (1956-    )
    Tre Canti
      mix cor,acap ZERBONI 8822     (L10)

LAGGER, OSCAR
    Autre Jour, L'
      see Trois Chanson De France:

    Autre Jour En Voulant Danser, L'
      mix cor HUG 8537              (L11)

    Belle Attendait, La
      mix cor HUG 8536              (L12)

    Belle Jeannetoon, La
      men cor HUG 8639              (L13)

    Belle Rose, La
      mix cor HUG 8655              (L14)
      men cor HUG 8656              (L15)

    Chanson Du Vent
      mix cor HUG 8515              (L16)

    Dans Le Vallon Qu'arrose
      3 eq voices HUG 8539          (L17)

    Derrièr' Chez Mon Père
      3 eq voices HUG 8539          (L18)

    En Revenant De La Foire
      see Trois Chanson De France:

    Entre Vous Tous, Gens De La Ville
      mix cor HUG 8590              (L19)

    Il Avait L'âme Bien Noire
      mix cor HUG 8535              (L20)

    Jamais Je N'oublierai
      mix cor HUG 8537              (L21)

    Lâ-Bas, Vers La Fontaine
      mix cor HUG 8655              (L22)
      men cor HUG 8656              (L23)

LAGGER, OSCAR (cont'd.)
  Margoton
    mix cor HUG 8472 (L24)

  Mariage En Auvergne
    mix cor HUG 8589 (L25)
    men cor HUG 8482 (L26)

  Nicolas Si Tu Es Sage
    see Trois Chanson De France:

  Quand La Marie
    men cor HUG 8639 (L27)

  Ronde
    mix cor HUG 8538 (L28)

  Rossignolet Gentil
    mix cor HUG 8795 (L29)

  Tout Respire...
    [Fr/Lat] mix cor HUG 8791 (L30)
    [Fr/Lat] men cor HUG 8788 (L31)

  Trois Chanson De France:
    mix cor HUG 8508 f.s.
    contains: Autre Jour, L'; En
      Revenant De La Foire; Nicolas
      Si Tu Es Sage (L32)

  Trois Jeun's Fill's Ont Tant Dansé
    mix cor HUG 8471 (L33)

  Ubi Caritas Et Amor
    mix cor HUG 8288 (L34)

  Violette Double, La
    mix cor HUG 8536 (L35)

  Y Avait Dix Filles Dans Un Pré
    mix cor HUG 8591 (L36)

LAGSTUFUR UR "ATOMSTÖDINN" see
  Sigurbjörnsson, Thorkell

LAISSE CHANTER LE VENT see Mozart,
  Wolfgang Amadeus

LAISSE TES PEINES... see Henchoz, Emile

LAITIÈRE, LA see Henchoz, Emile

LAMB, THE see Hagen, Daron

LAMPART, REINHOLD
  Bändeltanz,Der
    see Kunterbunt

  Himmel Ohne Sonn',Ein
    see Kunterbunt

  Kunterbunt
    1-2pt jr cor,kbd BOHM f.s.
    contains: Bändeltanz,Der; Himmel
      Ohne Sonn',Ein; Kunterbunt;
      Storch Schnibelschnabel;
      Wiegele, Wagele (L37)

  Kunterbunt
    see Kunterbunt

  Storch Schnibelschnabel
    see Kunterbunt

  Wiegele, Wagele
    see Kunterbunt

LAMPE D'ARGILE see Marescotti, André
  François

LANCIEN, NOËL
  Chansons De Clément Marot *CCU
    mix cor BILLAUDOT f.s. (L38)

  Chantefleurs Et Chantefables De R.
    Desnos
    4pt jr cor BILLAUDOT (L39)

  Recueil Complet
    4pt jr cor BILLAUDOT (L40)

  Renoncule, La
    4pt wom cor BILLAUDOT (L41)

  Souci, Le (from Recueil)
    3pt wom cor BILLAUDOT (L42)
    4pt jr cor BILLAUDOT (L43)

LAND-HO! see Leslie, Henry David

LAND UND FREIHEIT see Schule, Bernard
  see Schule, Bernard, Terre Libre

LAND UND LEUT IM LIED *CCU
  (Wulz, Helmut) men cor HEYN
  ISBN 3 85366 504 7 f.s. (L44)

LANDESLIED see Schmid, Walter

LANDINI, FRANCESCO (1325-1397)
  Complete Set
    see Complete Works

LANDINI, FRANCESCO (cont'd.)
  Complete Works
    (Schrade) OISEAU f.s.
    contains: Complete Set; Three
      Part Ballate, Madrigals,
      Caccia; Two-Part Ballate (L45)

  Three Part Ballate, Madrigals, Caccia
    see Complete Works

  Two-Part Ballate
    see Complete Works

LÄNDLICHER TANZ see Löffler, Edmund

LANDOWSKI, MARCEL (1915- )
  Ell'court, Ell'court La Musique
    cor,orch SALABERT EAS 19151 (L46)

  Leçons de Ténèbres
    cor,soli,org,vcl,instrumental
    ensemble/orch SALABERT EAS 19005
    (L47)

  Quatre Chants D'innocence *CC4U
    wom cor,female solo BILLAUDOT f.s.
    (L48)

  Quatre Chants D'innocence *CC4U
    jr cor&wom cor BILLAUDOT (L49)

LANDUZZI, CRISTINA (1961- )
  Quel Giorno...Infine...
    wom cor,fl,harp,vcl ZERBONI 10146
    (L50)

LANG
  By Fire
    SATB,SB soli NOVELLO 350333 (L51)

LANG, H.
  A Mon Pays
    mix cor HUG 8158 (L52)
    men cor HUG 8157 (L53)

  Bal Des Insects, Le
    4 eq voices HUG 8352 (L54)

  Beaux Souvenirs D'antan
    men cor HUG 7975 (L55)

  Chanson Bachique
    men cor HUG 8571 (L56)

  Chanson De La Glu
    men cor HUG 8529 (L57)

  Chanson De La Lisette
    mix cor HUG 8345 (L58)

  Chanson Des Vaudois
    men cor HUG 8230 (L59)

  Chantons, Rions, Jouons...
    eq voices HUG 7974 (L60)

  D'où Viens-Tu?
    eq voices HUG 7948 (L61)

  Madrigal
    mix cor HUG 8421 (L62)
    men cor HUG 8426 (L63)

  Mai
    eq voices HUG 6892 (L64)

  Maison, La
    men cor HUG 7947 (L65)

  Malchanceux, Le
    men cor HUG 8355 (L66)

  Marche Du Printemps
    men cor HUG 7981 (L67)

  Mon Pays, Rustique Séjour
    mix cor HUG 7519 (L68)
    men cor HUG 7347 (L69)

  Musique, Doux Mystère
    mix cor HUG 7979 (L70)

  Petite Marche Du Printemps
    men cor HUG 7921 (L71)

  Quand Vous Serez Bien Vielle
    mix cor HUG 8258 (L72)

  Que J'aime, Ô Cher Pays...
    men cor HUG 7976 (L73)

  Rosa, La Rose
    eq voices HUG 8159 (L74)

  Valse Tendre
    mix cor HUG 8344 (L75)

  Vaudoises, Les
    men cor HUG 8512 (L76)

  Viens, Nuit Sereine
    mix cor HUG 7978 (L77)

LANGER, RICHARD (1907- )
  Nachtgesang
    men cor,acap MULLES (L78)

LANGUIR ME FAIS see Sermisy, Claude de
  (Claudin)

LANTZ
  Joy Of All The Earth
    SATB,fl SHAWNEE A-6498 (L79)

  Like A River
    SATB ALFRED 11567 (L80)
    SAB ALFRED 11568 (L81)
    SSA ALFRED 11569 (L82)

LARGO see Bach, Johann Sebastian see
  Handel, George Frideric see
  Telemann, Georg Philipp

LARK IN THE CLEAR AIR see Fleming

LARK IN THE CLEAR AIR,THE
  (Deale, Edgar M.) SATB BANKS ECS 12
  (L83)

LARKIN, MICHAEL
  It Was A Lover And His Lass
    SATB WARNER OCT02594 (L84)

  Morning
    SSA WARNER OCT02573 (L85)

  O Mistress Mine
    SATB WARNER OCT02566 (L86)

  Shall I Compare Thee?
    SATB,pno LAWSON 52682 (L87)

  Take, O Take Those Lips Away
    SATB WARNER OCT02595 (L88)

LARSON, MARTIN (1967- )
  Alchemist:, The
    mix cor,SATB soli,4perc (a rite)
    STIM (L89)

LASS, HERR, DEIN LICHT ERSCHEINEN see
  Schmid, Walter

LASS OF RICHMOND HILL,THE
  (Leslie, Henry) SATB BANKS 74 (L90)

LASSEK, EUGENE E.
  Horse-Watcher's Songs,The *CCU
    cor,narrator,acap EGAN f.s. (L91)

LASSET UNS SINGEN *CC31U
  (Stern, Hermann) 2-4 eq voices pap
  SCHUL CLS 153 f.s. (L92)

LASST LAUTENSPIEL UND BECHERKLANG see
  Schumann, Robert (Alexander)

LASSUS, ROLAND DE (ORLANDUS)
  (1532-1594)
  Bon Jour, Mon Coeur
    (Swingle, Ward) SATB,db,drums,
    synthesizer (gr. II) voc pt,pts
    UNC JP SM-8 (L93)

  Matona, Mia Cara
    mix cor HUG 6035 (L94)
    men cor HUG 3625 (L95)

  Sçais-Tu Dir' L'ave?
    mix cor HUG 6056 (L96)

LAST NIGHT OF THE WORLD, THE see
  Schonberg, Claude-Michel

LAST NIGHT OF THE YEAR,THE see
  Sullivan, [Sir] Arthur Seymour

LAST STRAW see Henderson, Ruth Watson

LASTER, JAMES
  Madrigal For Spring, A (from "Welcome
    Lovely Spring")
    4pt wom cor,acap BOOSEY-ENG
    OCTB6697 (L97)

  O Lovely Dove (from "Welcome Lovely
    Spring")
    4pt wom cor,acap BOOSEY-ENG
    OCTB6696 (L98)

  Welcome, Sweet Pleasure (from
    "Welcome Lovely Spring")
    4pt wom cor,acap BOOSEY-ENG
    OCTB6698 (L99)

LATE AT NIGHT see Crawley, Clifford

LATELY see Morris, Stevland (Stevie
  Wonder)

LATTICE FENCE see Mechem, Kirke Lewis

LAU
  Winds Through The Olive Trees
    SATB SHAWNEE A-6862 (L100)

LAUB FÄLLT see Jessler, Fritz

LAUGHTER see Moments In Time see
  Henderson, Ruth Watson

LAURIDSEN, MORTEN JOHANNES (1943- )
　　Chansons Des Roses, Les (from Rilke)
　　　mix cor,pno PEER f.s.
　　　contains: Contre Qui, Rose; De
　　　Ton Reve Trop Pleine; Dirait-
　　　On; En Une Seule Fleur; Rose
　　　Complete, La　　　　　　　(L101)

　　Contre Qui, Rose
　　　see Chansons Des Roses, Les

　　De Ton Reve Trop Pleine
　　　see Chansons Des Roses, Les

　　Dirait-On
　　　see Chansons Des Roses, Les

　　En Une Seule Fleur
　　　see Chansons Des Roses, Les

　　Rose Complete, La
　　　see Chansons Des Roses, Les

LAVANDIÈRES see Henchoz, Emile

LAVANDIÈRES, LES see Mermoud, Robert

LAVATER, H. (1885- )
　　Jour Se Lève, Le
　　　men cor HUG 7923　　　　　(L102)

　　Réveille-Toi!
　　　men cor HUG 9722　　　　　(L103)

LAVENDER'S BLUE
　　SSA WARCH 34410　　　　　　(L104)

LAWRENCE
　　Hap-Hap-Happiest Season, The
　　　SATB ALFRED 5792　　　　　(L105)
　　　3pt cor ALFRED 5793　　　(L106)
　　　2pt cor ALFRED 5794　　　(L107)

　　One Great Nation
　　　SATB ALFRED 5805　　　　　(L108)
　　　3pt cor ALFRED 5806　　　(L109)
　　　2pt cor ALFRED 5807　　　(L110)

LAWRENCE, STEPHEN L.
　　Book Bag Boogie
　　　3-4pt mix cor WARNER SV9511 (L111)

　　I Woulda, Coulda, Shoulda Been So
　　　Good This Year!
　　　3pt mix cor HERITAGE 15-1020 (L112)

　　No Elephant
　　　1-2pt cor WARNER SV9524　　(L113)

　　Popcorn
　　　2-3pt cor HERITAGE 15-1186H (L114)

　　Reindeer Twist,The
　　　2pt cor&opt audience WARNER SV9405
　　　　　　　　　　　　　　　　(L115)
　　Song For Mother Earth
　　　(Walter, Lana) 2-3pt cor (native
　　　american chants) WARNER SV9523
　　　　　　　　　　　　　　　　(L116)
　　Stop, Look, And Listen (An Ecology
　　　Song)
　　　2-3 eq voices HERITAGE 15-1117
　　　　　　　　　　　　　　　　(L117)
　　Study Hall Blues
　　　SATB WARNER SV9304　　　　(L118)
　　　3pt mix cor WARNER SV9305　(L119)

　　Tennis Shoe-Be-Doos
　　　3pt mix cor/SATB WARNER SV9404
　　　　　　　　　　　　　　　　(L120)
　　Three Little Pigs: A "Howling"
　　　Success Story, The
　　　unis cor HERITAGE 15-1101　(L121)
　　　SATB HERITAGE 15-1100　　　(L122)

　　Twelve Dogs Of Christmas, The
　　　1-2pt cor HERITAGE 15-1187H (L123)

LAWSON, PHILIP
　　Legend
　　　2pt cor BANKS ECS 226　　　(L124)

LAY DOWN YOUR STAFFS
　　(Shaw And Parker) SATB,acap LEONARD-
　　　US 50305110　　　　　　　　(L125)

LAYS, LES see Machaut, Guillaume de

LAZY RIVER see Carmichael, Hoagy see
　　Marois, Rejean

LE BLANC, DIDIER (fl. ca. 1580)
　　O Doux Baisers Colombin
　　　(Raugel) mix cor BILLAUDOT　(L126)

　　On Peut Feindre Par Le Cizeau
　　　(Raugel) mix cor BILLAUDOT　(L127)

　　Pour Avoir Ma Fin Assurée
　　　(Raugel) mix cor BILLAUDOT　(L128)

　　Quand J'esprouve En Aimant La Rigueur
　　　D'une Dame
　　　(Raugel) mix cor BILLAUDOT　(L129)

LE BLANC, DIDIER (cont'd.)
　　Si Tost Que Vostre Oeil M'eut Blessé
　　　(Raugel) mix cor BILLAUDOT　(L130)

LE FLEM, PAUL (1881-1984)
　　Crépuscule D'armor
　　　[Fr] wom cor,pno RECITAL 460 (L131)

LE SIEGE, ANNETTE
　　Joyful Noise　*CC4UL
　　　SATB,pno SEESAW　　　　　　(L132)

LEAD US SAFELY HOME see Goemanne

LEAP OF ROUSHAN BEG,THE see Parker,
　　Horatio William

LEAVE ALL MY DREAMS TO ME see Schwartz,
　　Dan

LEAVIN' see Fischer, Clare

LEAVITT, JOHN
　　Song Of The Open Road
　　　SAB WARNER SV9317　　　　　(L133)
　　　SATB WARNER SV9315　　　　(L134)
　　　SSA WARNER SV9316　　　　　(L135)

　　Ubi Caritas
　　　SATB,inst WARNER SV9113　　(L136)
　　　SSA,inst WARNER SV9114　　 (L137)
　　　SAB,inst WARNER SV9115　　 (L138)

LEBEN,DAS see Huber, Paul

LEBENSART see Uhlmann, Otto

LEBENSFREUDE see Schmid, Walter

LEBEWOHL, DU FÜHLEST NICHT see Brun,
　　Fritz

LEBN ZOL COLUMBUS see Perlmutter, Aaron

LEÇONS DE TÉNÈBRES see Landowski,
　　Marcel

LEÇONS DE TÉNÈBRES; ÉLÉVATIONS; MOTETS
　　see Couperin, François (le Grand)

LEDBETTER
　　Cotton Fields
　　　SATB WARCH 34798　　　　　　(L139)

LEFEVRE, JACQUES
　　A La Musique
　　　4pt mix cor BILLAUDOT　　　(L140)

LEGACY see Fischer, Clare

LEGACY, THE see Clausen, Alf

LEGEND see Lawson, Philip

LEGEND OF MIANA,THE see Fontenailles,
　　H. de

LÉGENDE DE DIANE, LA see Estrez, D'

LEGUIZAMÓN, GUSTAVO
　　Chaya Por Toconas
　　　4pt mix cor LAGOS　　　　　(L141)

LEHMANN, LIZA (1862-1918)
　　Four Shakespearian Part-Songs
　　　SATB,acap RECITAL 473　　　(L142)

LEHRNDORFER, F.
　　Goldne Abendsonne
　　　SATB,acap BOHM　　　　　　 (L143)

LEI LIABM, LEI LIABM, WIA A WIND
　　UMAFLIEAGN ... (from Chorblätter)
　　　(Streiner, Hans) mix cor HEYN (L144)
　　　(Streiner, Hans) men cor HEYN (L145)

LEICHT
　　Idem In Dialekt
　　　4pt men cor CRON　　　　　 (L146)

　　Ring Hab Ich Von Dir, Einen
　　　3pt wom cor/4pt men cor CRON (L147)

　　Tod Von Basel,Der
　　　4pt men cor CRON　　　　　 (L148)

LEININGER, W.
　　Since First I Saw Your Face
　　　SATB oct SOUTHERN SC424　　(L149)
　　　SAB oct SOUTHERN SC425　　 (L150)

　　There Is A Ladye
　　　TBB oct SOUTHERN SC416　　 (L151)

LEISY, JAMES FRANKLIN (1927- )
　　Scrooge (composed with Lambert)
　　　SSATBB SHAWNEE rent　　　　(L152)

LEJEUNE
　　Revecy Venir Du Printemps
　　　(Swingle, Ward) SSAATB (gr. III)
　　　voc pt,pts UNC JP SM-13X 3X
　　　　　　　　　　　　　　　　(L153)

LEJOS DE SANTA FE see Gustavino, Carlos

LEKBERG
　　Weep, O Willow
　　　SSAATTBB,S solo WARCH 40733 (L154)

LÉMAN see Hemmerling, Carlos

LEMMERMANN, HEINZ (1930- )
　　Servus, Tante Annegret　*CCU
　　　1-3pt jr cor FIDULA 383 songs and
　　　speech songs　　　　　　　(L155)

　　Tiritomba
　　　3 eq voices/mix cor FIDULA 6084
　　　　　　　　　　　　　　　　(L156)

L'ÉNAMORAT LI DEIA-WAT DE GELIEFDE HAAR
　　ZEGDE, OP. 92 see Kersters, Willem

LÉNELI DU SIMMELIBERG see Bovet, J.

LENGGANG KANGKONG
　　(Tan) SATB (malaysian folksong) KJOS
　　　8784　　　　　　　　　　　(L157)

LENNON, JOHN (1940-1980)
　　When I'm 64 (composed with McCartney,
　　[John] Paul)
　　　(Swingle, Ward) SSAATTBB,acap (gr.
　　　IV) voc pt,pts UNC JP SS-4 (L158)

LENZLIED see Schmid, Walter

LEONCAVALLO, RUGGIERO (1858-1919)
　　Bell Chorus From "Il Pagliacci"
　　　(Pliska-Dik) 3pt treb cor BOOSEY-
　　　ENG MET0004　　　　　　　　(L159)

LEONTOVICH, M.
　　Bell Carol
　　　(Thompson, Dick) SA,pno,opt
　　　handbells SANTA SBMP 72　　(L160)

LERNER
　　Almost Like Being In Love (composed
　　　with Loewe)
　　　SATB WARNER CH9555　　　　(L161)
　　　SAB WARNER CH9556　　　　 (L162)
　　　SSA WARNER CH9557　　　　 (L163)

LEROUX, PHILIPPE (1959- )
　　Entourage Intime, L'
　　　3 quartets of satb BILLAUDOT (L164)

LESLIE, HENRY DAVID (1882-1896)
　　Arise, Sweet Love
　　　SATB BANKS 600　　　　　　 (L165)

　　Awake! Awake! The Flow'rs Unfold
　　　SATB BANKS 154　　　　　　 (L166)

　　How Sweet The Moonlight Sleeps
　　　SATB BANKS 182　　　　　　 (L167)

　　Land-Ho!
　　　SATB BANKS 198　　　　　　 (L168)

　　Song Of The Flax Spinner
　　　SATB BANKS 215　　　　　　 (L169)

LESSIA
　　Flying
　　　SATB,pno SANTA SBMP 89　　 (L170)

　　Listen To Me Pharaoh
　　　SATB,pno SANTA SBMP 84　　 (L171)

　　Shine
　　　SA,pno SANTA SBMP 80　　　(L172)
　　　SATB,pno SANTA SBMP 81　　(L173)

　　Unicorn,The
　　　SSA,pno SANTA SBMP 86　　　(L174)

LESUR, DANIEL (1908- )
　　Ah! Dis-Moi Donc Bergère
　　　3 eq voices BILLAUDOT　　　(L175)
　　　3pt wom cor BILLAUDOT　　　(L176)

　　Ann Hini Goz
　　　3pt wom cor BILLAUDOT　　　(L177)
　　　3 eq voices,solo voice BILLAUDOT
　　　　　　　　　　　　　　　　(L178)
　　Au Bord De La Rivière
　　　3 eq voices BILLAUDOT　　　(L179)

　　Chanson De Mariage
　　　3-4pt wom cor BILLAUDOT　　(L180)

　　Chansons Populaires Cahier II　*CCU
　　　3 eq voices BILLAUDOT f.s.　(L181)

　　Chèvre, La
　　　3pt wom cor BILLAUDOT　　　(L182)
　　　3 eq voices BILLAUDOT　　　(L183)

　　Deux Chansons De Bord　*CC2U
　　　mix cor BILLAUDOT f.s.　　 (L184)

　　Deux Chansons De Marins　*CC2U
　　　3pt men cor BILLAUDOT f.s.　(L185)

　　Hol-Di-Ri-Di
　　　3 eq voices BILLAUDOT　　　(L186)
　　　3pt wom cor BILLAUDOT　　　(L187)

LESUR, DANIEL (cont'd.)

   J'ai Un Long Voyage À Faire
     3 eq voices BILLAUDOT   (L188)

   Lou Farandoulaine
     6 eq voices BILLAUDOT   (L189)

   Toutouik
     3 eq voices BILLAUDOT   (L190)
     3pt wom cor BILLAUDOT   (L191)

   Vielle, La
     3 eq voices BILLAUDOT   (L192)

LET BEAUTY AWAKE! see Lightfoot, Mary Lynn

LET CAROLS RING see International Carols, Set 1

LET FREEDOM RING see Althouse, Jay

LET FREEDOM SING! see Lightfoot, Mary Lynn

LET IT SHINE! see Price

LET IT SNOW! see Winter's Wonderland

LET IT SNOW! LET IT SNOW! LET IT SNOW! see Styne, Jule (Jules Stein)

LET THE MUSIC ROLL ON see Schmutte, Pete

LET THE SUN SHINE DOWN ON ME see Ritchie, Jean

LET THERE BE MUSIC see Williams

LET THERE BE PEACE ON EARTH see Jackson

LET US JOIN IN CELEBRATION FROM "THE BARTERED BRIDE" see Smetana, Bedrich

LET US WALK IN PEACE see Simms, Patsy Ford

LETANIA DE NUESTRO SEÑOR DON QUIJOTE see Brown, Rayner

LET'S BUILD A CITY see Winfrey, Robert

LET'S FLY see Schwartz, Dan

LET'S TURN ON THE NIGHT see Funk, Jeff

LETTER FROM PATMOS see Prado, José-Antonio (Almeida)

LETTER WITHOUT ADDRESS, A see Ikebe, Shin-Ichiro

LETTERS FROM AN EMIGRANT see Hagi, Kyoko

LEUTHOLD, W.
   Fernen Sterne Glühen
     men cor,acap MULLES   (L193)

   Kaminfegerlied
     men cor,acap MULLES   (L194)

   Uebermut
     men cor,acap MULLES   (L195)

LÈVE TON REGARD... see Mendelssohn-Bartholdy, Felix

LEVEZ LES YEUX see Gaillard, Paul-Andre

LEVI, PAUL ALAN (1941- )
   Journeys & Secrets
     mix cor,chamber orch JERONA perf mat rent sc JBPL503, voc sc   (L196)

LHOMME
   Chant Des Saisons, Le
     4pt mix cor BILLAUDOT   (L197)

LIADA AUS'N LIESERTAL
   (Pleschberger, Hans) HEYN f.s.
   contains: Heft 1 - Ausgabe Für Gemischten Chor (mix cor); Heft 1 - Ausgabe Für Männerchor (men cor); Heft 2 - Ausgabe Für Gemischten Chor (mix cor); Heft 2 - Ausgabe Für Männerchor (men cor)   (L198)

LIANDLAN SING MA ÜBERÀLL *CC10L
   (Streiner, Hans) HEYN f.s. mix cor 3 85366 487 3; men cor 3 85366 486 5   (L199)

LIBONATI, DANA
   Pass De Deux
     SATB,acap (gr. II) UNC JP   (L200)

LIBRO PRIMO DE MADRIGALI A TRE see Gabrieli, Andrea

LICHT AUF DEM SCHEFFEL, DAS see Killmayer, Wilhelm

LIDDELL, CLAIRE
   Song Remembered
     men cor BARDIC BD 0318   (L201)

LIDSTRÖM, JOHN (1957- )
   Wenn Wir In Höchsten Nöten Sein
     mix cor,pno STIM   (L202)

LIE UND LEBEN see Schmid, Walter

LIEBE ALTE LIEDER see Anderluh, Anton

LIEBE RAUSCHT DES SILBERBACH see Schubert, Franz (Peter)

LIEBE UND WEIN, OP. 50, NR. 5 see Mendelssohn-Bartholdy, Felix

LIEBEN BRINGT GROSS' FREUND, DAS see Silcher, Friedrich

LIEBEN RINGT GROSS FREUD, DAS
   (Smith, Gregg) "Oh, Love Can Bring Great Joy" [Ger/Eng] mix cor LEONARD-US 50309550   (L203)

LIEBESLIED see Hurni, Jakob

LIEBESLIEDER - WALZER, OP. 52 see Brahms, Johannes

LIEBESSCHMERZ see Olpen, Friedrich W.

LIED,DAS see Schmid, Walter

LIED DER ALTEN, DAS see Doret, Gustave

LIED DER HEIMAT see Amman, Ulrich see Schmid, Walter

LIED DES AUSLANDSCHWEIZER see Bovet, J. see Bovet, J., Chant Des Suisses À L'étranger

LIED IN DIE HAUSHALTUNG, EIN see Schweizer, Alfred

LIED UND WEIN see Feibel, Norbert

LIED VOM HIRTENMÄDCHEN, DAS see Ammann, Benno

LIED VOM KREUZ, DAS see Vuataz, Roger, Hymne À La Bannière

LIED VOM MÜETI, 'S see Märki, Ernst

LIED VOM REIFENDEN KORN, DAS see Doret, Gustave

LIED VOM SCHWEIZERSTERN,,DAS see Schmid, Walter

LIEDER AUS ALLER WELT *CCU,folk song/spir
   (Mittergradnegger, Günther) mix cor/men cor/wom cor HEYN ISBN 3 85366 701 5 f.s.   (L204)

LIEDER DER BERGE see Goetz, Adolf

LIEDER DER MINNE see Gebhard, Hans

LIEDER FÜR FESTE, FEIERN UND FROHES SINGEN *CCU
   (Mittergradnegger, Günther) mix cor HEYN NR. 210 f.s.   (L205)

LIEDER FÜR GEMISCHTEN CHOR see Waht Da Wind Uban See

LIEDER FÜR MÄNNERCHOR see Waht Da Wind Uban See

LIEDERHEFT FÜR MÄNNERCHOR (from "Neue Kärntner Chorblätter" Edited By Reinhard Kühr) CCU
   men cor HEYN ISBN 3 85366 358 3 f.s.   (L206)

LIEDERMORGEN see Schmid, Walter

LIEDJE see Kersters, Willem

LIERRE ET LE THYM, LE see Breard

LIEUWEN, PETER (1953- )
   It Couldn't Be Done
     TTBB sc MMB X094006   (L207)

LIFE HAS LOVELINESS TO SELL see McCray, James

LIFE HAS MANY RHYTHMS see Pfautsch, Lloyd Alvin

LIFE'S TOO SHORT TO BE SILENT see Cassils

LIFT YOUR HEARTS see Greenlee

LIGHT BECOMING see Evans, Robert

LIGHT COLORED SONGS see Bekku, Sadao, Tansai-Syo

LIGHT COMES FORTH see Rippentrop, Denice

LIGHT OF THE MORNING see Pennington, Chester

LIGHT ONE LITTLE CANDLE
   (Thomas) SATB SHAWNEE A-1982   (L208)

LIGHT THE LIGHT see Strommen, Carl

LIGHTFOOT, MARY LYNN
   Arrow And The Song, The
     2pt cor HERITAGE 15-1162   (L209)

   Dare To Dream! (from The Musical "Chris Crossed")
     2 eq voices,pno HERITAGE 15-1006   (L210)
     3pt mix cor HERITAGE 15-1027   (L211)

   From A Railway Carriage
     2 eq voices,opt narrator,perc HERITAGE 15-1019   (L212)

   Let Beauty Awake!
     SSA,pno HOFFMAN,R H5014   (L213)
     wom cor HOFFMAN,R H5014   (L214)

   Let Freedom Sing!
     3pt mix cor HERITAGE 15-1030   (L215)
     2pt cor HERITAGE H5516   (L216)

   O Wind! (from Robert Louis Stevenson's "The Wind")
     SSA HERITAGE 15-1038   (L217)
     2pt cor HERITAGE H5888   (L218)

   Sing Out The Season!
     3pt mix cor (title song from the musical) HERITAGE 15-1112   (L219)
     2pt cor (title song from the musical) HERITAGE H5793   (L220)

   Swing, The
     2pt cor HERITAGE 15-1174H   (L221)

LIGHTHEARTED LOVERS, THE see Mechem, Kirke Lewis

LIGHTS AND SHADOWS see Burrell, Diana

LIGHTS OF HANUKKAH see Solomon, Joan

LIKE A RIVER see Lantz

LIKE A SHEPHERD see Weston, Mark

LIKE AN EAGLE see Strommen, Carl

LIKE AS A FATHER see Cherubini, Luigi

LIKE MT. FUJI see Sugino, Yasuhiko

LIKE SOMEONE IN LOVE
   (Arabian-Tini) SATB SHAWNEE A-1972 ipa   (L222)

LILY OF ERABU ISLE *Jap
   (Jergenson, D) [Jap] SATB,pno,opt perc LAURN CH-1096   (L223)

LINBERG, PER
   When The Stars Begin To Fall
     SATB NOTERIA 2772   (L224)

LINCKE, PAUL (1866-1946)
   Abend Bei Paul Lincke,Ein *CC19L
     SSATTBB,pno sc APOLLO AV 5831 f.s. each vocal part available separately   (L225)

   Abend Bei Paul Lincke,Ein *CCU
     TTBB,pno sc APOLLO AV 5871 f.s. each vocal part separately available   (L226)

   Berliner Luft
     TTBB,pno APOLLO sc AV 5807, cor pts AV 5807-01   (L227)
     (Rische, Quirin) SATB,pno (each vocal part available separately) APOLLO sc AV 5002-70, cor pts AV 5002-71   (L228)

   Es War Einmal
     TTBB,pno (each vocal part separately available) APOLLO sc AV 5802, cor pts AV 5802-01   (L229)
     (Fouque, Martin) SATB,pno APOLLO sc AV 5142-70, cor pts AV 5142-71   (L230)

   Glühwürmchen Idyll
     TTBB,pno APOLLO sc AV 5800, cor pts AV 5800-01   (L231)
     (Fouque, Martin) SATB,pno APOLLO sc AV 5108-70, cor pts AV 5108-71   (L232)

   Herzlichen Glückwunsch
     SATBB sc APOLLO AV 5881   (L233)
     TTBB sc APOLLO AV 5873   (L234)

LINCKE, PAUL (cont'd.)
  In Der Sperlingsgasse
    men cor,pno sc APOLLO AV 5805
      (L235)
    SATB APOLLO sc AV 5098, cor pts
      AV 5098-01 (L236)

  O Frühling, Wie Bist Du So Schön
    TTBB,pno (each vocal part available
      separately) sc APOLLO 5872 (L237)
    SSATTBB,pno (each vocal part
      separately available) sc APOLLO
      AV 5834 (L238)

  Schenk Mir Doch Ein Kleines Bisschen
    Liebe
    men cor,pno sc APOLLO AV 5806
      (L239)
    (Rische, Quirin) SATB,pno (each
      vocal part separately available)
      APOLLO sc AV 5023-70, cor pts
      AV 5023-71 (L240)

LINDEN TREE, THE see Porterfield,
  Sherrie

LINDENBAUM, DIE see Schubert, Franz
  (Peter)

LINDROTH, PETER (1950- )
  Achtung Spitfeuer
    men cor STIM (L241)

  Prepared Statement; With Regard To,
    The
    mix cor,soli STIM (L242)

LINDSTRÖM, LARS
  I Vårdträdets
    SAB NOTERIA 2829 (L243)

LION IN HITTITE, THE see Adachi, Hiromi

LION SLEEPS TONIGHT, THE
  SATB WARCH 34802 (L244)
  (Funk, Jeff) SATB WARNER WBCH9424
    (L245)
  (Funk, Jeff) 3pt mix cor WARNER
    WBCH9425 (L246)
  (Funk, Jeff) 2pt cor WARNER WBCH9426
    (L247)

LIONCOURT, GUY DE (1885-1961)
  Mystère de l'Emmanuel
    SATB,fl&strings HENN HL 543 (L248)

LIQUEUR DES MOTS, LA see Bron, Patrick

LISA S'EN VA JOYEUSE see Bovet, J.

LISCHKA, RAINER (1942- )
  Uhrmacherladen, Der
    DEUTSCHER DV 7950 (L249)

LISELI DU MUHLETAL see Bovet, J.

LISTEN INTENTLY see Igarashi, Tadashi

LISTEN TO ME PHARAOH see Lessia

LISTEN TO THE MOCKING BIRD see Smith,
  Gregg

LISTEN TO THE MUSIC see Althouse, Jay

LISTEN TO THE STARS see Martin

LISZT, FRANZ (1811-1886)
  A La Musique
    men cor HUG 3734 (L250)

  Deux Pièces *CC2U
    3-5pt wom cor BILLAUDOT f.s. (L251)

  Printemps
    men cor HUG 3620 (L252)

LITENEI AND NACHT UND TRAUME see
  Schubert, Franz (Peter)

LITTLE BILLEE see Dicks, Ernest A.

LITTLE BOY BLUE see Ahrold, Frank A.

LITTLE DRUMMER BOY
  (Buffa, Todd) SSAA,acap (gr. III) UNC
    JP (L253)
  see Davis

LITTLE ONES see Zorman, Moshe

LITTLE "SPOOF" MUSIC, A see Spevacek,
  Linda, Kleine Spufmusik, Eine

LITTLE THINGS see Tan

LITTLE TIME, A see Sapieyevski, Jerzy

LIUBA see Bovet, J.

LLOYD WEBBER, ANDREW (1949- )
  All I Ask Of You (from Phantom Of The
    Opera, The)
    SATB NOVELLO 091030 (L254)

LLOYD WEBBER, ANDREW (cont'd.)
  Any Dream Will Do (from Joseph And
    The Amazing Technicolor
    Dreamcoat)
    SATB NOVELLO 091230 (L255)

  Aspects Of Love
    SATB (choral suite) NOVELLO 092333
      (L256)

  Close Every Door (from Joseph And The
    Amazing Technicolor Dreamcoat)
    SATB NOVELLO 091530 (L257)

  Don't Cry For Me Argentina (from
    Evita)
    SATB NOVELLO 091630 (L258)

  Evita
    SATB (choral suite) NOVELLO 092433
      (L259)

  Joseph And The Amazing Technicolor
    Dreamcoat
    SATB (choral suite) NOVELLO 092533
      (L260)

  Love Changes Everything (from Aspects
    Of Love)
    SATB NOVELLO 091930 (L261)

  Memory
    SSA WARCH 11742 (L262)
    SATB WARCH 22486 (L263)
    SAB WARCH 30108 (L264)

  Memory And Other Choruses From Cats
    *CC4L
    (Gritton) FABER mix cor 51339 5;
    SSA,pno 51318 2 contains The Old
    Gumbie Cat, Bustopher Jones,
    Memory, Skimbleshanks the Railway
    Cat (L265)

  Mr. Mistoffelees And Other Choruses
    From Cats *CC5L
    (Arch G) SSA,pno FABER 51341 7
    contains Macavity, Old
    Deuteronomy, Grizabella,
    Mungojerrie & Rumpleteazer, Mr.
    Mistoffelees (L266)

  Mr. Mistoffelees And Other Choruses
    From Cats *CC5L
    (Gritton) mix cor FABER 51461 8
    contains Macavity, Old
    Deuteronomy, Grizabella,
    Mungojerrie & Rumpleteazer, Mr.
    Mistoffelees (L267)

  On This Night Of A Thousand Stars
    (from Evita)
    SATB NOVELLO 092030 (L268)

  Phantom Of The Opera, The
    SATB (choral suite) NOVELLO 092833
      (L269)

  Seeing Is Believing (from Aspects Of
    Love)
    SATB NOVELLO 092130 (L270)

  Wishing You Were Somehow Here Again
    (from Phantom Of The Opera, The)
    SATB NOVELLO 092230 (L271)

LO, FRAMMENTO DAL "PROMETEO" see Nono,
  Luigi

LOB DER FREUNDSCHAFT see Albert,
  Heinrich

LOB DER RAST see Schmid, Walter

LOB DES CHÜJERSTANDES see Kraehenbuehl,
  J.G.

LOB DES GESANGES see Müller, Joseph
  Ivar see Schmid, Walter

LOB DES SINGENS see Saladin, O.

LOBGESANG see Mendelssohn-Bartholdy,
  Felix

LOCH LOMOND *folk song,Scot
  (Shaw-Parker) TTBB LAWSON 4-51023
    (L272)

LOCK, W.
  Oliver Cromwell
    SATB WOODL A050208 (L273)

LOESSER, FRANK (1910-1969)
  I've Never Been In Love Before
    (Read, Paul) SATB,acap (gr. IV) UNC
      JP (L274)

LOEWE, CARL GOTTFRIED (1796-1869)
  Zahn, Der
    3pt jr cor,kbd BOHM (L275)

LÖFFLER, EDMUND
  Europa-Lied
    unis cor/men cor/mix cor,winds
    RUNDEL sc ARTIKEL-NR.0218, cor
    pts ARTIKEL-NR.0218C, voc pt
    ARTIKEL-NR.0218S (L276)

LÖFFLER, EDMUND (cont'd.)
  Ländlicher Tanz
    mix cor,winds RUNDEL sc
    ARTIKEL-NR.5050, cor pts
    ARTIKEL-NR.5050C (L277)

LOGAR, MIHOVIL (1902- )
  Fliegerlied,Das *madrigal
    mix cor,acap GRAV (L278)

LOGOS see Enns, Leonard

LOMBARDI, LUCA (1945- )
  Alle Fronde Dei Salici
    12pt cor,acap ZERBONI 8691 (L279)

  Canto Di Eros
    SMezTB,countertenor RICORDI-IT
      (L280)

  E Subito Riprende Il Viaggio
    5pt cor,acap ZERBONI 8666 (L281)

  Hasta Que Caigan Las Puertas Del Odio
    SATB,acap ZERBONI 8313 (L282)

LONDON, EDWIN (1929- )
  Polonius Platitudes,The
    men cor JERONA J3132 (L283)

LONE DOG see Britten, [Sir] Benjamin

LONE JACK see Metheny,Pat

LONESOME ROAD see Schwartz, Dan

LONG AGO ON A FINE SPRING DAY see
  Sowash, Rick

LONG-COURRIER see Falquet, Rene

LONGMIRE, JOHN
  Green Hills Of England
    unis cor BANKS 1217 (L284)

LOOK AWAY see Coghlan, Michael

LOOK! MOUNT FUJI IN THE WEST WIND see
  Saegusa, Shigeaki

LOOK TO THE ROSE see Martin

LOPING ALONG see Walker

LORD, SUZANNE
  Come, Walk With Me
    2pt cor HERITAGE 15-001 (L285)

LORD RANDALL
  (Vea, Ketil) 4pt mix cor,acap NOTON
    -9106 (L286)

LORSQU'AVRIL APPARAÎTRA see Parchet, A.

LORSQUE L'AMOUR PART POUR LA CHASSE see
  Boller, Carlo

LOST AND FOUND
  (Chinn, Teena) SATB (medley incl.
    Little Boy Lost, Corner Of The Sky,
    The Colors Of My Life & This Is The
    Moment) WARNER C0298C1X (L287)
  (Chinn, Teena) SAB (medley incl.
    Little Boy Lost, Corner Of The Sky,
    The Colors Of My Life & This Is The
    Moment) WARNER C0298C3X (L288)

LOTTI, ANTONIO (1667-1740)
  Vere Languores Nostros
    [Fr/Lat] men cor HUG 7889 (L289)

  Vois Sourire La Rose
    mix cor HUG 8678 (L290)
    eq voices HUG 8782 (L291)

LOU FARANDOULAINE see Lesur, Daniel

LOU PAÏSAN see Robert-Lalouet, M.

LOU SALOMÉ, SUITE see Sinopoli,
  Giuseppe

LOUANGE À TOI, PAYS! see Boller, Carlo

LOUCHEUR, RAYMOND (1899-1979)
  Jeune Ménétrier, Le
    3 eq voices BILLAUDOT (L292)

  Renard Et Chantecler
    3 eq voices BILLAUDOT (L293)

LOUDOVA, IVANA (1941- )
  Sonetto
    treb cor,acap ZERBONI 8488 (L294)

LOUGHTON, LYNNETTE
  Christmas Magic In The Air (composed
    with Steed, Gordon)
    2pt cor,pno 4-hands HERITAGE
      15-1005 (L295)
    3pt mix cor HERITAGE 15-1024 (L296)

LOVE see Ogikubo, Kazuaki, "Jomon-A I"

LOVE AND TIME see Holman, Derek

LOVE BETRAYED see Hassler, Hans Leo

LOVE CHANGES EVERYTHING see Lloyd Webber, Andrew

LOVE IS see Keller, John

LOVE IS A SICKNESS see Vaughan Williams, Ralph

LOVE IS COME AGAIN see Shaw, Kirby

LOVE IS ENOUGH see Lyell, Margaret

LOVE IS HERE TO STAY see Pelz, Walter L.

LOVE IS IN CONTROL see Jones, Quincy

LOVE SONG see Hines, Robert S.

LOVE THE SENTINELL see Williamson, Malcolm

LOVE THIS WORLD MY CHILDREN see Fletcher, Linda

LOVE UNFEIGNED see Holman

LOVE WALKED RIGHT IN see Gershwin, George

LOVE WILL FIND A WAY see Zaruba, Robin

LOVE, YOU SPOKE A WORD see Medema

LOVELACE, AUSTIN COLE (1919- )
   Apple Tree Carol
     unis cor KERBY 50481043 (L297)
     SATB KERBY 50481072 (L298)

   Come To Your Senses
     SATB KERBY 50480958 (L299)

LOVELY ARMOY see Ferguson, Howard

LOVELY ROSABELLE see Chadwick, George Whitefield

LOVER'S ARITHMETIC see Halley

LOVERS LOVE THE SPRING see Johnson, Victor Cohen

LOVE'S ANTIPHON see Pfautsch, Lloyd Alvin

LOVING FATHER, A see Bacon, Boyd

LOW, LEO
   Hazamir
     [Heb] SATB,opt pno (med) HAZA voc
     sc HZ-033, study sc HZ-033-OSS,
     sc HZ-033-OSL, pts HZ-033-OP
                                       (L300)
   Mir Trogen A Gezang
     [Yiddish] SATB,opt pno, full
     orchestration available (med)
     HAZA HZ-034 (L301)

LÖWEN-LÄNDLER see Klein, Richard Rudolf

LU LABBRU see Killmayer, Wilhelm

LUCAS, THEODORE D. (1941- )
   Together
     SATB,acap SANTA SBMP 48 (L302)

LUCIA OCH STAFFAN see Hammarström, Hugo

LUCIFER'S FAREWELL see Stockhausen, Karlheinz, Luzifers Abschied

LÜCK, RUDOLF (1927- )
   Fünf Volksliedsätze (Zuccalmaglio) (1968)
     SAB GRAV EG 709 (L303)

LUEGET, VO BÄRGE UND TAL see Huber, Walter Simon

LUENGEN, RAMONA (1960- )
   Frühlingslied
     [Ger] SATB,acap CAN.MUS.CENT.
                                          (L304)
     SATB THOMP.G VG471 (L305)

   O Lacrimosa
     [Ger] SATB,acap CAN.MUS.CENT.
                                          (L306)

LUITENANT JANEDOME see Maessen, Antoon

LULL-LULL see Jehrlander, K-F.

LULLABY see Henderson, Ruth Watson see Holman

LULLABY OF BIRDLAND see Shearing, George Albert

LULLABY OF BROADWAY see Manhattan Melodies

LULLABY OF THE LITTLE ANGELS see Anderson see Anderson, William H.

LULLAY MY BABY see Winn, Julie

LULLY, JEAN-BAPTISTE (LULLI) (1632-1687)
   Gentle Night (from Bois Epais')
     (Challinor, F.A.) SATB BANKS 972
                                          (L307)
   Revenez, Amours, Revenez
     mix cor HUG 7736 (L308)

   Revenez, Revenez...
     mix cor HUG 7940 (L309)

LULULU see Moulinie, E.

LUNA see Barnby, [Sir] Joseph

LUNDBERG
   My Love Has Departed
     3pt treb cor BOOSEY-ENG OCTB6707
                                          (L310)

LUNDIN, DAG (1943- )
   Havsmässa
     mix cor,S&narrator,pno STIM (L311)

LUNE BLANCHE, LA see Jordan

LUNE JAUNE, LA see Apotheloz, Jean

LUNE, LUNE, TRISTE LUNE see Pasquier, Marius

LURIANA, LURALEE see Telfer, Nancy

LUSTIGEN MUSIKANTEN, DIE see Diener, Theodor

LUSTIN' TO ROAM see Rogers

LUTIN, LE see Martin

LUZIFERS ABSCHIED see Stockhausen, Karlheinz

LYELL, MARGARET (1910- )
   Love Is Enough
     SATB,acap BARDIC BD 0355 (L312)

   Three Aesop Fables
     TTBB,acap BARDIC BD 0356 (L313)

LYONS, BILL
   Beep-Bop
     SATBB,acap (gr. III) UNC JP (L314)

   Good-Bye
     SATB,acap (gr. III) UNC JP (L315)

   I'd Rather Be Eating Ice Cream
     SATBB,acap (gr. III) UNC JP (L316)

   Prelude 2
     SATB,acap (gr. III) UNC JP (L317)

   Wi Shi Kood
     SATB,acap (gr. III) UNC JP (L318)

LYS ROUGE, LE see Sala, Andre

LYSE GLAUBE see Märki, Ernst

# M

MA BELLE SI TU VOULAIS see Anonymous

MA BONNE TERRE see Mermoud, Robert

MA DOUCE ANNETTE see Mirouze

MA DOUCE ENFANT see Brahms, Johannes

MA FEMME EST MORTE see Martin

MA FORÊT see Mendelssohn-Bartholdy, Felix

MA MIE see Haenni, G.

MA PETITE MAISON see Delmas, Marc-Jean-Baptiste

MA PIPE see Rochat, Jean

MA SARINE see Bovet, J.

MA VIEILLE MAISON see Foster, Stephen Collins see Foster, Stephen Collins, Ma Vieille Maison

MAART see Swerts, Piet

MCCARTHY
   You Made Me Love You (composed with Monaco)
     (Althouse) SATB ALFRED 11332 (M1)
     (Althouse) 3pt mix cor ALFRED 11333 (M2)
     (Althouse) SSA ALFRED 11334 (M3)

MACCHI, EGISTO (1928-1992)
   Voci
     mix cor BERBEN BERBEN 9963 (M4)

MCCRAY, JAMES
   Life Has Loveliness To Sell
     SATB,opt kbd FOSTER MF 3055 (M5)

MACDOWELL, EDWARD ALEXANDER (1861-1908)
   To A Wild Rose
     SATB,acap BARDIC BD 0343 (M6)

MACFARREN, WALTER [CECIL] (1826-1905)
   You Stole My Love
     4pt mix cor,acap ALLAIR (M7)

MACGILLIVRAY, ALLISTER
   Away From The Roll Of The Sea
     SATB THOMP.G VEI1110 (M8)
     SSA THOMP.G VG340 (M9)

   Song For Peace
     (Loomer,A) SAB CYPRS CP1018 (M10)
     (Loomer,A) SA CYPRS CP1017 (M11)
     (Loomer,A) TTB CYPRS CP1019 (M12)

   Song For The Mira
     SSA WARCH 35102 (M13)

MACHAUT, GUILLAUME DE (ca. 1300-1377)
   Ballades, Les
     see Complete Works

   Complete Series
     see Complete Works

   Complete Works
     (Schrade) OISEAU f.s.
     contains: Ballades, Les; Complete Series; Lays, Les; Messe De Nostre Dame, Double Hoquet, Remede De Fortune; Motets, Les; Virelais, Les (M14)

   Lays, Les
     see Complete Works

   Messe De Nostre Dame, Double Hoquet, Remede De Fortune
     see Complete Works

   Motets, Les
     see Complete Works

   Virelais, Les
     see Complete Works

MACHIBITOGOKKO see Takashima, Midori

MACKEY, STEVEN (1956- )
   Journey To Ixtlan
     SATB,winds [19'] MARGUN MP5034 (M15)

MCLEAN
   Song For Bedtime
     unis cor WARCH 35659 (M16)

MCLIN
   Give Up The World
     unis cor KJOS 6236 (M17)

MACMILLAN, JAMES (1959- )
  So Deep
    SSAATTBB BOOSEY-ENG OCTB7020  (M18)

MCPHEETERS
  All People Are Created Equal
    SATB SHAWNEE A-2011  (M19)

  Friend To Friend, Heart To Heart
    SATB SHAWNEE A-1960  (M20)

  Here We Are
    3pt mix cor SHAWNEE D-468  (M21)
    2pt cor SHAWNEE EA-189  (M22)
    SATB SHAWNEE A-1957  (M23)

  I'll Be Your Friend Until Forever
    SATB SHAWNEE A-1979  (M24)

  Through The Middle Of It All
    SATB SHAWNEE A-2010  (M25)

  You're My Best Friend
    2pt cor SHAWNEE EA-181  (M26)

MCPHEETERS, T.
  I Love Music
    2pt treb cor GILPIN HT9403  (M27)

  On The Whispering Wind
    SATB GILPIN HT9405  (M28)

MCTELL, RALPH
  Streets Of London
    SA/TB WARCH 34782  (M29)
    SATB,solo voice WARCH 34794  (M30)

MCVIE, CHRISTINE
  Don't Stop
    (Funk, Jeff) 3pt mix cor,opt tenor
      sax solo WARNER WBCH9343  (M31)
    (Funk, Jeff) SATB,opt tenor sax
      solo WARNER WBCH9342  (M32)

MADAME LA JOIE see Martin

MÄDCHEN TANZE, SING UND SPRINGE see
  Marx, Karl, Su Salte, Bale, Putele

MÄDCHENLIED see Balmer, Luc

MADELEINE see Mermoud, Robert

MADELEINE EST D'HUMEUR CHAGRINE see
  Martin

MADERNA, BRUNO (1920-1973)
  All The World's A Stage
    mix cor,acap sc RICORDI-IT 132826
      (M33)

MADONNA DEL SASSO see Kreis, Otto

MADONNA LAURA see Andriessen, Jurriaan

MADRIGAL see Brahms, Johannes see
  Holman see Lang, H. see Mefano,
  Paul see Monteverdi, Claudio

MADRIGAL FOR SPRING, A see Laster,
  James

MADRIGALE-VILANELLEN *CCU,Ger/It
  (Lenders, Hans-Günter) 4-5pt mix cor
    FIDULA 6058 f.s.  (M34)

MADRIGALI A CINQUE VOCI - LIBRO I see
  Contino, Giovanni

MADRIGALI DI DIVERSI AUTORI *CCU,
  madrigal
  (Rasi, F.) SCELTE f.s.  (M35)

MADRIGALI ET RICERCARI see Gabrieli,
  Andrea

MADRIGALI II, O ALLEGORIA D'AMORE see
  Kokaji, Kunitaka

MADRIGALS 1, 2 AND 3 see Straesser,
  Joep

MADRIGALS ON THE RIVER see Pearce,
  Malcolm

MAEDELI DU SIEBETHAL, S' see Doret,
  Gustave

MAESSEN, ANTOON (1919- )
  Klucht Vn Pierlala, De
    4pt mix cor,4bsn [18'] DONEMUS sc
      f.s., pts f.s.  (M36)

  Luitenant Janedome
    SATB,acap BANK 11.900.042  (M37)

  To You
    SATB,acap BANK 11.900.018  (M38)

MAGGIE HUNTER see Henderson, Ruth
  Watson

MAGIC TO DO
  (Leavitt, John) SATB WARNER SV9335
    (M39)
  (Leavitt, John) SAB WARNER SV9336
    (M40)

MAGNETIC NORTH see Wearmouth, Graham

MAGNOLIA PETALS see Bach, Johann
  Sebastian

MÄHDERLIED see Amman, Ulrich

MAHR, CURT
  Frühling Und Lieder
    TTBB, accordion orchestra (each
      instrumental part available
      separately) APOLLO sc AV 1962-10,
      cor pts AV 1962-20  (M41)

  Von Der Waterkant Bis Zum Alpenland
    *folk song
    men cor, accordion orchestra (each
      instrumental part available
      separately) APOLLO sc AV 2380-10,
      cor pts AV 2380-18  (M42)

MAI see Lang, H.

MAI TRITT EIN MIT FREUDEN, DER see
  Silcher, Friedrich

MAIABEND see Zentner, Johannes

MAIDEN'S FAREWELL, THE see Spevacek,
  Linda

MAÏENTZETS, LES see Bovet, J.

MAILIED see Jenny, Albert see Schumann,
  Robert (Alexander)

MAILIED: GRÜNER WIRD DIE AU see
  Schubert, Franz (Peter)

MAILLARD, RENÉ
  Amours Perdit Les Traict Qu'il Me
    Tira
    (Raugel) mix cor BILLAUDOT  (M43)

MAISON, LA see Binet, Jean see Lang, H.

MAISON, UNE see Hemmerling, Carlos

MAISON DES ANCÊTRES, LA see Bovet, J.

MAISON DU BONHEUR, LA see Gesseney, L.

MAÎTRE CHARBONNIER see Jordan

MAÎTRE DE NOS HEURES see Gaillard,
  Paul-Andre

MAIWUNDER see Diener, Theodor

MAJESTY see Hayford, Jack W.

MAJUKA, DOROTHY
  Cameroon
    2pt cor WARNER SV9533  (M44)

MAKE A DIFFERENCE see Snyder, Audrey

MAKE A RAINBOW see Nelson, Portia

MAKE YOUR OWN KIND OF MUSIC see
  Spevacek, Linda

MAKHELORA see Avni, Tzvi

MAL DU PAYS see Binet, Jean see Tichy,
  O.A.

MAL WAS ANDRES see Schweizer, Alfred

MALBROUK see Broquet, Louis

MALCHANCEUX, LE see Lang, H.

MALEC, IVO (1925- )
  Douze Mois,Les
    2pt men cor BILLAUDOT  (M45)

  Roses Du Midi
    2pt men cor BILLAUDOT  (M46)

MALGRÉ TOUT see Gal, Hans

MALLOW, MONTI
  You've Got What It Takes (composed
    with Steffaro, Julius)
    SAB,kbd (med) PRESSER 392-41854
      (M47)

MALMLÖF-FORSSLING, CARIN (1916- )
  Albero
    mix cor,acap STIM  (M48)

MALTA YOK! see Camilleri, Charles

MAMAN see Delmas, Marc-Jean-Baptiste

MAMII FUSAKO GENBAKU TAIKENKI YORI
  "NIJI YO EIEN NI" see Nakamura,
  Yukitake

MAMIYA, MICHIO (1929- )
  Composition For Chorus No. 14
    HUG  (M49)

  White Shell Woman, Composition For
    Chorus No. 13
    men cor,perc HUG  (M50)

MAN FROM OKERBOKER see Whicher, James

MAN I LOVE, THE see Gershwin, George

MAN IN THE MOON, THE see Stultz, Marie

MAN MÜSSTE see Jessler, Fritz

MAN NEHME see Barthelme, Georg

MAN-YO see Kushida, Tetsunosuke

MANANITAS DE MI TERRA see Fonseca,
  Julio

MANANITAS DE MI TIERRA
  (Belan, W.) SATB THOMAS 1C0859304
    (M51)

MÅNBUBBLOR see Hambe, Alf

MANCHAI PUITO
  (Escalada) "Two Little Doves" SATB
    KJOS 8758  (M52)

MANCINI, HENRY (1924-1994)
  Days Of Wine And Roses
    (Robinson, Russ) SATB,acap WARNER
      WBCH9433  (M53)

  Moon River
    SATB WARCH 33870  (M54)

MANDEL, JOHNNY ALFRED (1925- )
  Unless It's You
    SSAA,acap (gr. IV) UNC JP  (M55)
    (Ames, Morgan) SSAB,acap (gr. V)
      UNC JP  (M56)

MANÈGE see Gesseney, L.

MANGWANI MPULELE
  (Cor, Robert Demier) 3pt wom cor,pno&
    opt perc (Zulu) LAWSON 52716  (M57)
  (Walter, Lana) 2-3pt cor (zulu
    folksong) WARNER SV9521  (M58)

MANHATTAN MELODIES
  (Schmutte, Pete) WARNER ipa SATB
    C0316C1X; SAB C0316C3X
    contains: Forty-Second Street;
    Lullaby Of Broadway; Theme From
    New York, New York  (M59)

MANN UND DER TEUFEL, DER see Hess,
  Carlheinz

MÄNNERCHÖRE IM KÄRNTNER VOLKSTON (HEFT
  1) *CCU
  (Koschat, Thomas) men cor HEYN
    NR. 207 f.s.  (M60)

MÄNNERCHÖRE IM KÄRNTNER VOLKSTON (HEFT
  2) *CCU
  (Koschat, Thomas) men cor HEYN
    NR. 208 f.s.  (M61)

MANNERS, RICHARD
  Across The Great Divide
    SSATBB,perc (gr. III) UNC JP  (M62)

MANNINO, FRANCO (1924- )
  Sinfonia N. 6 *Op.262
    mix cor,4.3.3.0. 4.3.3.1. timp,
      perc,harp,pno,cel,strings sc
      RICORDI-IT 134208  (M63)

  Supreme Love *Op.174, cant
    cor,soli,3.3.3.3. 4.3.2.0. timp,
      perc,cel,harp,strings sc RICORDI-
      IT 132783  (M64)

MANTRA OF THE LIGHT see Nishimura,
  Akira

MANZONI, GIACOMO (1932- )
  Dedica
    mix cor,B solo,fl&orch sc RICORDI-
      IT 134112  (M65)

  Parole Da Beckett
    dbl cor,inst&electronic tape sc
      RICORDI-IT 130802  (M66)

  Scene Sinfoniche Per Il Doktor
    Faustus
    cor,orch sc RICORDI-IT 133790  (M67)

  Studio Per Il Finale Del Doktor
    Faustus
    mix cor,3.3.4.3. 4.4.3.1. perc,cel,
      timp,harp,strings, ondes martenot
      sc RICORDI-IT 133935  (M68)

  Suite "Robespierre"
    cor,SSMezBarB&2 narrators,2.1.3.2.
      4.3.3.1. timp,perc,strings sc
      RICORDI-IT 132501  (M69)

MARCEL, J.M.
  Porteur De Journaux, Le
    mix cor HUG 8069  (M70)
    men cor HUG 8067  (M71)

  Vieux Bohémien
    mix cor HUG 8570  (M72)

MARCELLO, BENEDETTO (1686-1739)
  Presto
    (Swingle, Ward) SATB,B solo,db,
      drums (gr. III) voc pt,pts UNC JP
      RG-8X                          (M73)

MARCH DES PAYSANS see Boller, Carlo

MARCH DES PETITS OIGNONS, LA see Bovet, J.

MARCH OF THE CHRISTMAS CHILDREN see Sebesky, Gerald John

MARCH OF THE KINGS
    (Shaw And Parker) [Fr] TTBB,acap
      LEONARD-US 50305120            (M74)

MARCH OF THE MEN OF HARLECH see Grainger, Percy Aldridge

MARCHAND DE BONHEUR, LE see Haenni, G.

MARCHANDE DE FLEURS, LA see Mermoud, Robert

MARCHE DE LIMOGES, LE see Mouton, Charles

MARCHE DES TONNEAUX see Robert-Lalouet, M.

MARCHE DU PRINTEMPS see Lang, H.

MARCHE FUNÈBRE see Chopin, Frédéric

MARCHE FUNÈBRE SUR LA MORT D'UN PAPAGALLO see Alkan, Charles-Henri Valentin

MARCHE VAUDOISE see Jaques-Dalcroze, Émile

MARCIA E CORO see Wagner, Richard

MARCIA NUZIALE see Wagner, Richard

MARCUS
  One More Mountain To Climb (composed with Feldman; Leavitt)
    SAB SHAWNEE D-0469               (M75)
    SATB SHAWNEE A-1987              (M76)
    SSA SHAWNEE B-0564               (M77)

MARDI GRAS IN RIO see Schwartz, Dan

MARECHAL, HENRI-CHARLES (1842-1924)
  Carnaval Enfantin
    3pt jr cor BILLAUDOT             (M78)

  Cerises, Les
    3pt jr cor BILLAUDOT             (M79)

MARENZIO, LUCA (1553-1599)
  Aimez-Moi Bien, M'amie
    eq voices HUG 7949               (M80)

  O Grands Yeux
    eq voices HUG 7949               (M81)

  Ton Âme Et Ton Visage
    5pt mix cor HUG 8012             (M82)

MARESCOTTI, ANDRÉ FRANÇOIS (1902-    )
  Lampe d'Argile *ora
    SATB,S&male solo,2.2.2.2. 4.2.2.0.
      perc,pno,strings HENN HL 436-A
                                     (M83)

MARGOT, LA see Dutilleux, Henri

MARGOT, LABOURÉS LES VIGNES see Arcadelt, Jacob

MARGOTON see Lagger, Oscar

MARIA see Bernstein, Leonard

MARIÄ WIEGENLIED see Furrer, Walter

MARIAGE, LE see Boller, Carlo

MARIAGE EN AUVERGNE see Lagger, Oscar

MARIANNE (from Three North Country Folk Songs)
    (Wilby, Philip) SATB BANKS ECS 225
                                     (M84)
    see Three North Country Folk Songs

MARIANNES KUMMER see Bovet, J.

MARIE, JEAN ÉTIENNE (1917-    )
  Pièce Vocale Sur Des Textes Du 3e Dimanche De Carême
    4 eq voices,solo voice BILLAUDOT
                                     (M85)
  Poésies
    mix cor, solo voices BILLAUDOT
                                     (M86)
    wom cor,6 female soli BILLAUDOT
                                     (M87)

MARIE-MADELON see Boller, Carlo

MARIE-MARION see Bron, Patrick

MARIE MIEUX-AIMÉE see Bron, Patrick

MARIENLIED see Vollenweider, Hans

MARIETTE see Bovet, J.

MARIEZ-VOUS, LA BELLE see Haenni, G.

MARIN see Morillo, Roberto García

MARINETTE see Jaques-Dalcroze, Émile

MARINS DE CROIX,LES see Dutilleux, Henri

MARINS DE GROIX see Dutilleux, Henri

MARINS D'EAU DOUCE, LES see Zbinden, Julien-François

MARIVAUDAGE see Hemmerling, Carlos

MARJOLAINE see Pantillon, François

MÄRKI, ERNST
  Abend In Sils-Maria
    men cor,acap MULLES              (M88)
  Agnes
    see Zwei Einfache Weisen
  Alpenglühen
    men cor,acap MULLES              (M89)
  Alte Lied, 'S
    men cor,acap MULLES              (M90)
  Alte Linde,Die
    men cor,acap MULLES              (M91)
  Alte Tisch,Der
    men cor,acap MULLES              (M92)
  An Das Herz
    men cor,acap MULLES              (M93)
  An Die Tulpe
    men cor,acap MULLES              (M94)
  Chlini Chügeli Muess Me Giesse
    wom cor,acap MULLES              (M95)
  Durch Feld Und Buchenhallen
    men cor,acap MULLES              (M96)
  Ergebung
    wom cor,acap MULLES              (M97)
  Fremde Weisen Aus Aller Welt  *CC11L
    men cor,acap MULLES f.s.         (M98)
  Frische Fahrt
    wom cor,acap MULLES              (M99)
  Frühling
    wom cor,acap MULLES              (M100)
  Frühlingslied
    men cor,acap MULLES              (M101)
  Glück Und Schmärz
    wom cor,acap MULLES              (M102)
  Heimatgedenken
    men cor,Bar solo,acap MULLES     (M103)
  Hoch Auf Dem Gelben Wagen
    men cor,acap MULLES              (M104)
  Höchi Zyt
    wom cor,acap MULLES              (M105)
  I Gan Nid Hei Bis Wälleled
    wom cor,acap MULLES              (M106)
  I Möcht, I Möcht Singe
    see Kleine Solothurner - Suite
  Im Sunneland
    men cor,acap MULLES              (M107)
  Im Wärde
    men cor,acap MULLES              (M108)
  Kleine Solothurner - Suite
    wom cor,acap MULLES f.s.
      contains: I Möcht, I Möcht Singe;
      O Mueter, I Möcht Der Säge; S'
      Sternli; Uf Em Bärgli          (M109)
  Lied Vom Müeti, 'S
    men cor,acap MULLES              (M110)
  Lyse Glaube
    wom cor,acap MULLES              (M111)
  Nachtmusik
    see Zwei Einfache Weisen
  Neus Läbe
    men cor,acap MULLES              (M112)
  Niemand Kennt Das Leid
    wom cor,acap MULLES              (M113)

MÄRKI, ERNST (cont'd.)
  O Mueter, I Möcht Der Säge
    see Kleine Solothurner - Suite
  Petite Gilberte De Courgenay,La
    men cor,acap MULLES              (M114)
  Reiselied
    men cor,acap MULLES              (M115)
  Reiter,Der
    men cor,acap MULLES              (M116)
  Riesenrad Der Sterne,Das
    wom cor,acap MULLES              (M117)
  S' Sternli
    see Kleine Solothurner - Suite
  Sänger,Der
    men cor,acap MULLES              (M118)
  Sängerfahrt Nach Dem Süden  *CC8L
    men cor,acap MULLES f.s.         (M119)
  Schneeglöggli
    wom cor,acap MULLES              (M120)
  Schöni Heimet
    men cor,acap MULLES              (M121)
  Schwedisches Seemannlied (Es Weht...)
    men cor,acap MULLES              (M122)
  Seeland
    men cor,Bar solo,acap MULLES     (M123)
  S'urewig Gsetz
    men cor,acap MULLES              (M124)
  Trutzlied
    men cor,acap MULLES              (M125)
  Ueber Die Heide
    men cor,acap MULLES              (M126)
  Ueberbautes Land
    men cor,acap MULLES              (M127)
  Uf Em Bärgli
    see Kleine Solothurner - Suite
  Vaterlandsliebe
    wom cor,acap MULLES              (M128)
  Vergässe Chönne
    wom cor,acap MULLES              (M129)
  Vom Ewige Brunne
    wom cor,acap MULLES              (M130)
  Waldessehnen
    men cor,acap MULLES              (M131)
  Wanderlied
    men cor,acap MULLES              (M132)
  Weckruf
    men cor,acap MULLES              (M133)
  Zwei Einfache Weisen
    wom cor,acap MULLES f.s.
      contains: Agnes; Nachtmusik
                                     (M134)

MARKS, JOHNNY D. (1909-1985)
  Rudolph The Red Nosed Reindeer
    SATB WARCH 33687                 (M135)

MAROIS, REJEAN
  For Lena And Lennie
    SSATBB,perc (gr. IV) UNC JP      (M136)
  Lazy River
    SATB,perc (gr. V) UNC JP         (M137)
  Tangerine
    SATB,brass,perc UNC JP           (M138)

MARRYOTT, RALPH E. (1908- ? )
  Season Of Dreams (composed with Angerman, David)
    SATB SHAWNEE A-2013              (M139)

MARSCHLIED DES INF RG 45
    (Gand-Kreis) men cor,acap MULLES
                                     (M140)

MARSEILLAISE, LA see Rouget de l'Isle, Claude Joseph

MARSHALL, JANE M. (MRS. ELBERT H.) (1924-    )
  All Praise To Those Who Make Music
    SATB,acap LAWSON 52662           (M141)

  Seen And Unseen
    SATB,acap LAWSON 52684           (M142)

MARTELLI, HENRI (1895-1980)
  Chemin  *Op.14
    mix cor,SAT soli BILLAUDOT       (M143)

  Chrestomathie  *Op.72
    3pt wom cor BILLAUDOT            (M144)

MARTIN
  A La Fontaine Bellerie
    mix cor HUG 7807 (M145)
  Ah! Que Le Vin Est Bon!
    men cor HUG 8224 (M146)
  Allons Au Bois
    men cor HUG 7997 (M147)
  And It Was Night
    SATB SHAWNEE A-6916 (M148)
  Attente
    men cor,solo voice HUG 7814 (M149)
  Beau Petit Coeur
    men cor HUG 8055 (M150)
  Bel Astre Que J'adore
    mix cor HUG 8191 (M151)
  Bergère Aux Champs, La
    mix cor HUG 8060 (M152)
  Blow Out The Trumpet
    SATB SHAWNEE A-6884 ipa (M153)
  Bohémiens, Les
    men cor HUG 8088 (M154)
  Bonsoir
    mix cor HUG 7901 (M155)
  C'est Moi Qui Vous Le Dis
    men cor HUG 8031 (M156)
  Cet Ami Que Mon Coeur Espère
    mix cor HUG 8008 (M157)
  Chanson De Charrue
    mix cor HUG 8057 (M158)
  Chanson Du Vigneron
    men cor HUG 7946 (M159)
  Chant Du Coucou, Le
    eq voices HUG 7909 (M160)
  Chantez Fontaines Claires
    mix cor,opt pno/org/orch HUG 8253 (M161)
    eq voices,opt pno/org/orch HUG 8254 (M162)
    men cor,opt pno/org/orch HUG 8252 (M163)
  Chasseur, Reprends Ta Carabine
    men cor HUG 8130 (M164)
  Comme Autrefois
    mix cor HUG 8292 (M165)
  Conseillers, Les
    men cor HUG 8311 (M166)
  Dans La Plaine
    men cor HUG 8050 (M167)
  Diable Sur La Muraille, Le
    men cor HUG 8182 (M168)
  Ecoutez, Le Temps S'arrête
    eq voices HUG 8203 (M169)
  Émigrants, Les
    men cor HUG 7910 (M170)
  Fileuse, La
    eq voices HUG 8310 (M171)
  Glorious Day (composed with Angerman, David)
    SATB SHAWNEE A-6933 ipa (M172)
  Il N'est Plus Le Temps
    mix cor HUG 8100 (M173)
  Listen To The Stars
    SATB SHAWNEE A-6952 (M174)
  Look To The Rose
    SATB SHAWNEE A-6923 (M175)
  Lutin, Le
    mix cor HUG 8241 (M176)
  Ma Femme Est Morte
    mix cor HUG 7960 (M177)
  Madame La Joie
    mix cor HUG 7934 (M178)
  Madeleine Est D'humeur Chagrine
    mix cor HUG 8056 (M179)
  Mère, Mariez-Moi!
    mix cor HUG 8059 (M180)
  Mon Vieux Village
    mix cor HUG 8265 (M181)
    men cor HUG 8264 (M182)
  Motets
    [Lat] men cor HUG 8092 (M183)

MARTIN (cont'd.)
  Music Will Always Be There
    2pt cor SHAWNEE EA-0200 (M184)
  N'avez-Vous Rien À Déclarer?
    mix cor HUG 7951 (M185)
  Noce Du Cantonnier, La
    mix cor HUG 7950 (M186)
    men cor HUG 7945 (M187)
  O Merveilleuse Nuit!
    mix cor HUG 8201 (M188)
  O Petet Bourg De Palestine
    men cor HUG 8202 (M189)
  Paysage
    men cor HUG 7808 (M190)
  Petete Rue, La
    mix cor HUG 8181 (M191)
  Petit Bossu, Le
    mix cor HUG 7960 (M192)
  Petite Vallée
    mix cor HUG 7998 (M193)
  Porteur De Journaux, Le
    mix cor HUG 8069 (M194)
    men cor HUG 8067 (M195)
  Pour Chanter Le Pays
    mix cor HUG 8115 (M196)
    men cor HUG 8121 (M197)
  Première Fleur, La
    mix cor HUG 8241 (M198)
  Quand Vous Serez Bien Vielle
    mix cor HUG 7789 (M199)
  Que Faites-Vous?
    mix cor HUG 8058 (M200)
  Que Viens-Tu Quérir?
    mix cor HUG 7953 (M201)
  Qui N'a Pas Son Programme?
    men cor HUG 8183 (M202)
  Rhône Valaisan, Le
    mix cor HUG 8251 (M203)
  Rigodon
    mix cor HUG 7952 (M204)
  Rossignol Chante
    men cor HUG 8224 (M205)
  Rossignolet D'amour
    mix cor,solo HUG 8026 (M206)
  Santé!
    eq voices HUG 8266 (M207)
  Sapeurs-Pompiers, Les
    mix cor HUG 8069 (M208)
    men cor HUG 8007 (M209)
  Séguedille
    men cor HUG 7996 (M210)
  Sentier, Le
    eq voices HUG 8286 (M211)
  S'il Vous Faut
    mix cor HUG 8087 (M212)
  Soir D'été
    mix cor HUG 7790 (M213)
  Tout Renaîtra
    mix cor HUG 8293 (M214)
  Trois Petits Oiseaux Dans Les Blés
    men cor HUG 7522 (M215)
  Tu Es Mon Berger
    mix cor HUG 8051 (M216)
  Vieux Garçon, Le
    mix cor HUG 8009 (M217)
    men cor HUG 8067 (M218)
  Violoneux, Le
    mix cor HUG 8010 (M219)

MARTIN, GILBERT M. (1941- )
  Annie Laurie
    SATB,opt solo HERITAGE 15-1147 (M220)
  Aura Lee
    SATB,opt solo,pno HERITAGE 15-1040 (M221)

MARTIN, JOSEPH M.
  Day By Day (from Godspell)
    (Poorman, Sonja) 2pt cor WARNER CH9535 (M222)
    (Poorman, Sonja) SATB WARNER CH9533 (M223)
    (Poorman, Sonja) SAB WARNER CH9534 (M224)
    (Poorman, Sonja) SATB,pno WARNER BSC00287 (M225)
  One Who Stands Alone, The
    SATB WARNER OCT02579 (M226)

MARTIN, ROBERT
  Hunting Song
    SATB BANKS 851 (M227)

MARTIN DE FÊTE (from Terre Et L'étoile, La)
  mix cor HUG 8842 (M228)

MARTYRS AUX ARÈNES, LES see Rille, L. de

MARX, KARL (1897-1985)
  Es War Einmal Ein Segelschiffchen
    see Il Etait Un Petit Navire
  Il Etait Un Petit Navire *cant
    "Es War Einmal Ein Segelschiffchen"
    3 eq voices,2rec,2vln,perc FIDULA sc 6110, cor pts 6111 (M229)
  Mädchen Tanze, Sing Und Springe
    see Su Salte, Bale, Putele
  Su Salte, Bale, Putele
    "Mädchen Tanze, Sing Und Springe"
    4pt mix cor,rec/winds,strings FIDULA sc 6120, cor pts 6121 (M230)
  Tailor And The Mouse,The
    1-2 eq voices,inst FIDULA sc 6130, cor pts 6131 (M231)

MARY ANN see Bissell see Henderson, Ruth Watson

MARY HAD A LITTLE BLUES see Collins

MARY WONDERED WHAT IT MEANT see Telfer, Nancy

MARYLISE see Miche, Paul

MARY'S SONG see Telfer, Nancy

MARZIALI, JORGE
  Cebollita Y Huevo
    (Pace, Daniel Di) 2-3pt cor LAGOS (M232)

MAS VALE TROCAR see Encina, Juan del

MASCAGNI, PIETRO (1863-1945)
  Regina Coeli From "Cavalleria Rusticana"
    SATB,pno BOOSEY-ENG MET0003 (M233)

MASINI
  Des Sennen Abschied (Piemontesische Melodie)
    wom cor,acap MULLES (M234)

MASON
  Sing With Joy (composed with Moore)
    2pt cor ALFRED 11370 (M235)

MASS UND UNMASS see Haus, Karl

MASSENET, JULES (1842-1912)
  Poème Des Fleurs,Le
    [Fr] SSA,A solo,pno RECITAL 465 (M236)

MASSER
  Greatest Love Of All
    SAB WARCH 33865 (M237)
    SSA WARCH 23292 (M238)

MASSER, MICHAEL (1941- )
  It's My Turn
    (Funk, Jeff) SSA/SSAA WARNER WBCH9408 (M239)

MASSIAS, GERARD (1933- )
  Aveux, Les
    4 eq voices BILLAUDOT (M240)

MASTERS IN THIS HALL
  (Shur) SA LAWSON 4-52623 (M241)
  see International Carols, Set 1

MATA DEL ANIMA SOLA see Estevez, Antonio

MATHAUSEN see Theodorakis, Mikis

MATIN, LE see Reichel, Bernard

MATIN DE MAI see Boller, Carlo

MATIN JOYEUX see Miche, Paul

MATONA, MIA CARA see Lassus, Roland de (Orlandus)

MATSUOKA, YUMIKO
  Water Is Wide,The
    SATBB,acap (gr. III) UNC JP (M242)

MATSUSHITA, ISAO (1951-    )
    October Nocturne  *Suite
        wom cor HUG                          (M243)

MATTSUOKA, TOSHIKATSU (1952-    )
    Otona No Marchen
        wom cor,pno HUG                      (M244)

MAUSEFALLENSPRÜCHLEIN see Brun, Fritz

MAW
    One Foot In Eden
        SATB, solo voices,acap FABER
            51406 5                          (M245)

MAXINE see Fagen,Donald

MAY I LEARN TO BE SILENT see Cassils

MAY OUR PATHS MEET AGAIN see Althouse, Jay

MAY SONG see Schumann, Robert
    (Alexander) see Schumann, Robert
    (Alexander), Mailied

MAY SUNSHINE LIGHT YOUR WAY see
    Althouse, Jay

MAY THERE ALWAYS BE SUNSHINE  *Russ
    (Cor, Robert Demier) 3pt wom cor,pno
        LAWSON 52717                         (M246)

MAYENS SOUS LA NEIGE see Falquet, Rene

MAYER, WILLIAM ROBERT (1925-    )
    Ae Fond Kiss
        SATB,fl&vcl&pno LAWSON 52686 (M247)

MAYOMBÉ see Ohana, Maurice

MAYOR, CH.
    Calme Du Soir
        men cor HUG 6228                     (M248)

    Jardin D'amour
        eq voices HUG 7806                   (M249)

    Oh! Que La Vie Est Douce Chose...
        3pt mix cor HUG 7506A                (M250)
        mix cor HUG 7506                     (M251)
        eq voices HUG 7618                   (M252)

MAYPOLE see Halley

MAYR-KANTATA see Bruckner, Anton

MAYUZUMI, TOSHIRO (1929-    )
    Kyoto 1200, Tradition & Creation
        *ora
        mix cor,narrator,orch, and Japanese
            inst HUG                         (M253)

MAZURKA see Skaarset, Ivar

ME PLAÎT LA GRÂCE see Apotheloz, Jean

MEADER, DARMON
    Baroque Samba
        (New York Voices) SSATB,perc (gr.
            III) UNC JP                      (M254)

    National Amnesia
        (New York Voices) SSATB,
            synthesizer,perc (gr. III/gr. IV)
            UNC JP                           (M255)

MEASURE ME, SKY see Porterfield, Sherrie

MECHEM, KIRKE LEWIS (1925-    )
    Barter
        SA,trp,pno 4-hands SCHIRM.G          (M256)

    Christmas Past And Christmas Present
        mix cor LEONARD-US 50488839          (M257)

    Deny It As She Will
        mix cor LEONARD-US 5029120           (M258)

    Impromptu
        mix cor LEONARD-US 50229110          (M259)

    King's Contest, The
        mix cor LEONARD-US 50480274          (M260)
        mix cor,MezTBarB soli,pno/chamber
            orch&pno/orch pno-cond sc
            SCHIRM.G 50480274                (M261)

    Lattice Fence
        mix cor LEONARD-US 50230390          (M262)

    Lighthearted Lovers, The
        mix cor LEONARD-US 50323010          (M263)

    Mechem Choral Sampler, Kirke  *CC10L
        mix cor LEONARD-US 50488570 score
            and cassette recording           (M264)

    Moral Precept
        mix cor LEONARD-US 5050360           (M265)

    Odor-Organ, The
        mix cor LEONARD-US 50230380          (M266)

MECHEM, KIRKE LEWIS (cont'd.)
    Questionnaire
        mix cor LEONARD-US 50230370  (M267)

    Shadows Of The Moon
        TBB,pno FISCHER.C CM8403     (M268)

    Shepherd And His Love, The
        SATB,vla,pic,pno SCHIRM.G 50481781
                                     (M269)
    Songs of the Slave (from John Brown)
        SATB,B solo,orch SCHIRM.G 50482274
                                     (M270)
    Wedding Gift
        mix cor LEONARD-US 50323020  (M271)

    Winged Joy , The  *CC7L
        wom cor,pno SCHIRM.G f.s.    (M272)

MECHEM CHORAL SAMPLER, KIRKE see
    Mechem, Kirke Lewis

MEDEMA
    Love, You Spoke A Word (composed with
        Kelley)
        SATB SHAWNEE A-6031 ipa      (M273)

MEFANO, PAUL (1937-    )
    Madrigal
        2-3pt wom cor,countertenor,
            instrumental ensemble SALABERT
            EAS 17020                (M274)

MEHRSTIMMIGE GESÄNG see Beethoven,
    Ludwig van

MÉHUL, ÉTIENNE-NICOLAS (1763-1817)
    Chant Du Départ, Le
        (Brun) 3 eq voices BILLAUDOT (M275)

MEIER, M.
    Bringe Grüsse, Kleines Vögelein  *CCU
        mix cor BOHM f.s.            (M276)

MEIN HEIM see Hofer-Schneeberger, Emma

MEIN LIEB WILL MIT MIR KRIEGEN see
    Hassler, Hans Leo

MEIN LIEBES SCHWEIZERLAND see Zahler,
    J.R.

MEIN SCHÄTZLE IST FEIN see Silcher,
    Friedrich

MEIN SCHÄTZLEIN HÖR ICH SINGEN see
    Jaeggi, Oswald

MEINE ALP see Boller, Carlo

MEINE FREUND' IST DIE... see Fouqué,
    Martin

MEINE HEIMAT see Boesch, Balthasar

MEINE ZELLE see Zentner, Johannes

MEINES KINDES ABENDGEBET see Niggli,
    Friedrich

MEINN, MEINN MYSURAEV see Fem
    Folkeviser Fra Gausdal

MEISJE see Kersters, Willem

MEISTER, CASIMIR (1869-1941)
    Begegnung
        men cor,acap MULLES          (M277)

    Fahnenschwingerlied
        men cor,acap MULLES          (M278)

    Frisch Gewagt
        men cor,acap MULLES          (M279)

    Frühlingsmorgen
        men cor,acap MULLES          (M280)

    Soldatenlied
        men cor,acap MULLES          (M281)

    Was Brucht E Rechte Schwyzerma?
        men cor,acap MULLES          (M282)

MEITSCHI, PUTZ DI see Furrer, Walter

MELANCOLICO see Fischer, Clare

MÉLI-MÉLO see Bovet, J.

MELLNÄS, ARNE (1933-    )
    Kosmos  *CC11U
        SATB,acap SVERIG SK 737 f.s. (M283)

MELODIE see Tuinen, Feike van

MELODIE NATALIZIE. ELABORAZIONI CORALI
    DI MELODIE TRADIZIONALI PER CORO DI
    VOCI PARI E DISPARI
    (Da Ros) BERBEN BERBEN 3353 f.s.
        includes works by Gauntlett, Ros,
        Spinadin, Gruber and anonymous
                                     (M284)

MELODY FLOW see Estes, Jerry

MEMORY see Lloyd Webber, Andrew

MEMORY AND OTHER CHORUSES FROM CATS see
    Lloyd Webber, Andrew

MEM'RIES see Price

MEN OF HARLECH
    (Barnby, J.) SATB BANKS 468      (M285)

MENDELSSOHN-BARTHOLDY, FELIX
    (1809-1847)
    A La Forêt
        mix cor HUG 2273             (M286)

    Amour Est Un Enfant Moqueur, L'
        men cor HUG 6906             (M287)

    Andante (from String Quartet Op. 44
        No. 7)
        (Swingle, Ward) SATB,db,drums (gr.
            IV) voc pt,pts UNC JP GR-5X
                                     (M288)
    Au Léman
        mix cor HUG 2360             (M289)

    Beati Mortui
        [Fr/Lat] men cor HUG 8261    (M290)

    Canto Di Lode
        see Lobgesang

    Chanson De Mai
        mix cor HUG 7232             (M291)

    Chant De L'alouette, Le
        mix cor HUG 2242             (M292)
        (Arnoud) 3 eq voices BILLAUDOT
                                     (M293)
    Chasse, La
        mix cor HUG 3777             (M294)

    Choeur Des Vendangeurs
        men cor HUG 7333             (M295)

    Choeur Final "Le Songe D'une Nuit
        D'été"
        eq voices,opt pno/org/orch HUG 5817
                                     (M296)
    Lève Ton Regard...
        eq voices HUG 7776           (M297)

    Liebe Und Wein, Op. 50, Nr. 5
        TTBB,Bar solo,acap BANK 11.900.064
                                     (M298)
    Lobgesang (from Symphony No. 2, Op.
        52)
        "Canto Di Lode" cor,SST soli,
        2.2.2.2. 4.2.3.0. timp,org,
        strings RICORDI-IT           (M299)

    Ma Forêt
        (Arnoud) 3 eq voices BILLAUDOT
                                     (M300)
    Nachtgesang
        men cor,acap MULLES          (M301)

    Oiseau Des Bois
        mix cor HUG 2243             (M302)

    Pendant L'absence
        men cor HUG 6165             (M303)

    Premier Printemps
        mix cor HUG 7942             (M304)

    Présage Du Printemps
        mix cor HUG 3912             (M305)

    Printemps, Le
        mix cor HUG 2599             (M306)

    Sechs Lieder  *Op.50, CC6U
        DEUTSCHER DV 7705 f.s.       (M307)

    Spinner,The (from "Songs Without
        Words")
        (Swingle, Ward) SATB,db,drums (gr.
            IV) voc pt,pts UNC JP GR-3X
                                     (M308)
    There Shall A Star
        (Fleet) SATB KJOS 8773       (M309)

    Tout L'univers Est Plein De Sa
        Magnificence
        mix cor,opt pno/org/orch HUG 5181
                                     (M310)
    Two Mendelssohn Part Songs
        (Guenter) SATB DEAN 15-1084  (M311)

    Vier Lieder  *Op.100,No.1-4
        mix cor PETERS 8844          (M312)

    Winzerchor
        (Krenger) wom cor,acap MULLES
                                     (M313)

MÉNÉTRIERS DE VILLAGE see Bovet, J.

MENICHETTI, DINO
    Saluto All'italia
        [8'] sc BONGIOVANI 2659      (M314)

MENSCHENZEIT see Helmschrott, Robert M.

MENUET see Rameau, Jean-Philippe

MENUETTO see Mozart, Wolfgang Amadeus

MÈRE, MARIEZ-MOI! see Martin

MERMAID, THE
  (Levi, Michael) TTBB WARNER SV9504
    (M315)

MERMOUD, ROBERT
  A Châtillens, Au Point Du Jour
    see Chant De La Broye

  A Dakar, Au Sénégal
    men cor HUG 8485 (M316)

  Aiguilleur, L'
    men cor,opt pno/org/orch HUG 7428 (M317)

  Alouette
    see Très Riches Heures, Les

  Arbre Comme Un Oiseau
    see Très Riches Heures, Les

  Armurier, L'
    mix cor,Bar solo HUG 7636 (M318)

  Au Mois De Mai, La Feuille Est Neuve
    mix cor HUG 8478 (M319)
    3 eq voices HUG 8477 (M320)

  Aveugle, L' (from Trèfle À Quatre Personnages)
    mix cor,opt pno/org/orch HUG 8693 (M321)
    men cor,opt pno/org/orch HUG 8673 (M322)
    3 eq voices,opt pno/org/orch HUG 8698 (M323)

  Bagueur D'oiseaux, Le (from Trèfle À Quatre Personnages)
    mix cor,opt pno/org/orch HUG 8694 (M324)
    men cor,opt pno/org/orch HUG 8674 (M325)
    3 eq voices,opt pno/org/orch HUG 8699 (M326)

  Beaux Danseurs (from Ce Jour-La)
    mix cor,acap/pno HUG 7695 (M327)

  Calice Des Baisers, Le
    eq voices HUG 7680 (M328)

  Ce Jour-Là *Suite
    mix cor,soli,pno/orch cor pts HUG 7823 (M329)

  Ceux Des Villages
    mix cor HUG 8608 (M330)

  Chanson Du Tabac, La
    mix cor&opt jr cor HUG 8330 (M331)
    eq voices&men cor&jr cor HUG 8329 (M332)

  Chanson Pour Une Fontaine
    mix cor HUG 8331 (M333)
    men cor HUG 8328 (M334)

  Chant De La Broye
    mix cor HUG f.s.
      contains: A Châtillens, Au Point Du Jour; Coin Du Paradis, Un; Dans Les Jardins De Lovatens; Petit Ville, La; Rassemblés Sur La Montagne; Rebuse Du Coucou, La (M335)

  Chats, Les (from Ce Jour-La)
    mix cor,acap/pno HUG 7692 (M336)

  Chemineau, Le
    men cor HUG 7486 (M337)

  Coin De Ciel Bleu, Un (from Silence De La Terre, La)
    mix cor HUG 8019 (M338)

  Coin Du Paradis, Un
    see Chant De La Broye

  Dans Les Jardins De Lovatens
    see Chant De La Broye

  Demain (from Ce Jour-La)
    mix cor,SBar soli,acap/pno HUG 7754 (M339)

  Devant La Flamme
    men cor HUG 8442 (M340)
    see Très Riches Heures, Les

  Dictée De L'araignée, La
    3pt jr cor HUG 8622 (M341)

  Dimanche Matin
    mix cor HUG 8605 (M342)

  Dressons Le Mai *canon
    3-8 eq voices HUG 8444 (M343)
    see Très Riches Heures, Les

MERMOUD, ROBERT (cont'd.)
  Étranger, L' (from Trèfle À Quatre Personnages)
    mix cor,opt pno/org/orch HUG 8692 (M344)
    men cor,opt pno/org/orch HUG 8672 (M345)
    3 eq voices,opt pno/org/orch HUG 8697 (M346)

  Fille À La Fontaine, Une (from Ce Jour-La)
    mix cor,acap/pno HUG 7693 (M347)

  Fille Et Le Poulain, La
    unis jr cor,inst HUG 8514 (M348)

  Fol Qui Ne Chante Pas
    see Très Riches Heures, Les

  Forgerons De L'ombre, Les
    men cor HUG 8392 (M349)

  Gebet Zum Altaï
    [Ger] men cor HUG 8480 (M350)

  Heures, Les (from Silence De La Terre, La)
    mix cor HUG 8018 (M351)

  Horloger, L'
    mix cor HUG 7805 (M352)

  Ignorant, L' (from Trèfle À Quatre Personnages)
    4 eq voices,opt pno/org/orch HUG 8700 (M353)
    mix cor,opt pno/org/orch HUG 8695 (M354)
    men cor,opt pno/org/orch HUG 8675 (M355)

  Ikikatou
    eq voices HUG 8492 (M356)

  Il Est Né, Le Divin Enfant
    eq voices HUG 8048 (M357)

  Il S'en Est Allé
    mix cor HUG 8390 (M358)

  Je T'attendrai
    4 eq voices HUG 8443 (M359)
    see Très Riches Heures, Les

  Je Vous Choisis
    mix cor HUG 8645 (M360)

  Lavandières, Les (from Ce Jour-La)
    mix cor,acap/pno HUG 7694 (M361)

  Ma Bonne Terre
    mix cor HUG 8647 (M362)

  Madeleine (from Ce Jour-La)
    mix cor,acap/pno HUG 7743 (M363)

  Marchande De Fleurs, La
    eq voices HUG 7804 (M364)

  Mon Père A Planté D'la Vigne *Russ
    mix cor HUG 8396 (M365)

  Morgengruss An Die Heimat
    [Ger] mix cor HUG 7856 (M366)
    [Ger] men cor HUG 7857 (M367)

  Mouettes, Les
    eq voices HUG 7688 (M368)

  Musicien Des Rues, Le
    mix cor,solo voice HUG 7894 (M369)

  O Doux Bocage
    jr cor HUG 8606 (M370)

  O Force Des Saisons
    men cor HUG 8447 (M371)
    see Très Riches Heures, Les

  Oiseleur, L'
    mix cor,pno/org/orch HUG 7429 (M372)

  Ouverture
    see Très Riches Heures, Les

  Pays, Un (from Trèfle À Quatre Personnages)
    4 eq voices,opt pno/org/orch HUG 8696 (M373)
    mix cor,opt pno/org/orch HUG 8691 (M374)
    men cor,opt pno/org/orch HUG 8671 (M375)

  Petit D'homme, Les Yeux Vifs
    unis cor,inst HUG 8448 (M376)
    see Très Riches Heures, Les

  Petit Train, Le (from Ce Jour-La)
    mix cor,acap/pno HUG 7697 (M377)

  Petit Village, Le (from Silence De L A Terre, La)
    mix cor HUG 8017 (M378)

MERMOUD, ROBERT (cont'd.)
  Petit Ville, La
    see Chant De La Broye

  Petite Danseuse De Ballet, La
    eq voices HUG 7635 (M379)

  Port, Le (from Ce Jour-La)
    mix cor,acap/pno HUG 7696 (M380)
    men cor HUG 7796 (M381)

  Pour Toi, Pays
    mix cor HUG 7812 (M382)
    men cor HUG 7813 (M383)

  Prière À L'altaï
    men cor HUG 8393 (M384)

  Quand?
    mix cor,pno/org/orch HUG 8648 (M385)

  Quel Mazzolin Di Fiori
    men cor HUG 8490 (M386)
    eq voices HUG 8733 (M387)

  Rassemblés Sur La Montagne
    see Chant De La Broye

  Rebuse Du Coucou, La
    see Chant De La Broye

  Rois De L'abbaye, Les
    men cor HUG 8020 (M388)

  Schattenschmiede, Die
    [Ger] men cor HUG 8506 (M389)

  Si La Vigne Était Une Fille
    men cor HUG 8476 (M390)

  Si Les Petits Jardins (from Ce Jour-La)
    mix cor,acap/pno HUG 7687 (M391)

  Silence De La Terre, La
    mix cor,acap (Drama) cor pts HUG 8016 (M392)

  Sonneur Du Prieuré, Le (from Ce Jour-La)
    mix cor,Bar solo,acap/pno HUG 7691 (M393)

  Tant Vous Aime
    mix cor HUG 8646 (M394)

  Tarasque De Tarascon, La
    mix cor HUG 8231 (M395)

  Tir De Jean P'tit Jean, Le
    eq voices HUG 8332 (M396)

  Très Riches Heures, Les
    HUG f.s.
      contains: Alouette (mix cor,acap/pno/org); Arbre Comme Un Oiseau (mix cor,acap/pno/orch); Devant La Flamme (men cor,acap/pno/orch); Dressons Le Mai (3pt cor,inst); Fol Qui Ne Chante Pas (wom cor&mix cor&men cor, pno/org/orch); Je T'attendrai (wom cor,acap/pno/orch); O Force Des Saisons (men cor, acap/pno/orch); Ouverture (mix cor,acap/pno/orch); Ouverture (men cor,acap/pno/orch); Ouverture (wom cor,acap/pno/orch); Petit D'homme, Les Yeux Vifs (jr cor,acap/pno/orch) (M397)

  Tricoteuses, Les (from Ce Jour-La)
    mix cor,acap/pno HUG 7690 (M398)
    eq voices HUG 7716 (M399)
    eq voices HUG 7716 (M400)

  Vent D'automne, Le
    men cor,opt pno/org/orch HUG 7686 (M401)

  Vie Est Un Ruisseau, La
    mix cor,opt pno/org/orch HUG 7594 (M402)

  Vieilles Gens, Les (from Ce Jour-La)
    mix cor,acap/pno HUG 7689 (M403)

  Vielle, La
    mix cor HUG 8607 (M404)

  Vieux Tilleul, Le (from Ce Jour-La)
    mix cor,acap/pno HUG 7698 (M405)

  Vitrier, Le
    men cor,opt pno/org/orch HUG 7427 (M406)

MERRILY WE SING NOEL (CELEBRATE A HAPPY HANUKKAH) see Dardess

MERRY CHRISTMAS, A
  (Warrell, Arthur) SATB,acap EXC.MH 19.800.019 (M407)

MERRY CHRISTMAS, DARLING
  (Chinn, Teena) SATB WARNER CH9549 (M408)
  (Chinn, Teena) 3pt mix cor WARNER CH9550 (M409)

(Chinn, Teena) SSA WARNER CH9551 (M410)

MERRY MONTH OF MAY,THE see Brydson, John

MESSE DE NOSTRE DAME, DOUBLE HOQUET, REMEDE DE FORTUNE see Machaut, Guillaume de

METAMORPHOSIS I see Yamamoto, Hiroyuki

METANOLA see Garcia, Antonio

METHENY, PAT
   (It's Just) Talk
     (Kamp, Tommy) unis cor,inst (gr. IV) UNC JP (M411)

   Lone Jack (composed with Mays,Lyle)
     (Gailey, Dan) SATBB,perc (gr. III) UNC JP (M412)

METTONS-NOUS EN ROUTE! see Gastoldi, Giovanni Giacomo

METZLER, FRIEDRICH (1910-1979)
   Eichendorff
     3pt mix cor RIES 65027 (M413)

MEUNIER, MEUNIER see Canteloube, Joseph

MEYLAND, J.
   Doux Pèlerinages
     men cor HUG 3644 (M414)

MI CANTO A LA NOCHEBUENA see Valdez, Peluza

"MI-ÉTÉ" DE TAVEYANNE, LA see Doret, Gustave

MICAH'S WORDS see Broege, Timothy

MICHAELS HEIMKEHR (ACT III) see Stockhausen, Karlheinz

MICHAEL'S HOME-COMING see Stockhausen, Karlheinz, Michaels Heimkehr (Act Iii)

MICHANS, CARLOS (1950- )
   Cortège D'orphée, Le (from Apollinaire) CC9L
     4pt mix cor,acord/orch sc DONEMUS f.s. (M415)

   Six Épigrammes (from Martialis) CC6U
     4pt mix cor,harp,2vln,vla,vcl,db sc DONEMUS f.s. (M416)

MICHE, PAUL
   Accordéon
     mix cor HUG 8036 (M417)

   Amour Trahi
     men cor HUG 6658 (M418)

   Au Jardin De La Vie
     men cor HUG 7972 (M419)

   Au Temps Des Cerisettes
     eq voices HUG 6790 (M420)

   Bergerette
     men cor HUG 6644 (M421)

   Bienvenue
     mix cor HUG 7419 (M422)
     men cor HUG 7514 (M423)

   Boîte À Musique
     mix cor HUG 7706 (M424)

   Bonheur Au Village, Le
     mix cor HUG 7825 (M425)
     men cor HUG 7870 (M426)

   Bouquets De Romandie
     men cor HUG 7869 (M427)

   C'est La Vie!
     mix cor HUG 7707 (M428)

   Chanson Des Couronnes
     men cor HUG 7768 (M429)

   Chanson Des Lavandières, La
     mix cor HUG 7328 (M430)

   Chanson Pour Ma Belle
     mix cor HUG 8120 (M431)

   Chant De Nos Coeurs, Le
     men cor HUG 7903 (M432)

   Chant Nuptial
     mix cor HUG 7330 (M433)

   Clochers De Mon Pays
     men cor HUG 7329 (M434)

   Cueillons, Ma Jolie!
     eq voices HUG 7634 (M435)

MICHE, PAUL (cont'd.)

   Dans Le Verger Fleuri
     mix cor HUG 7874 (M436)

   Ferme De Chez Nous, Une
     mix cor HUG 7513 (M437)
     men cor HUG 7376 (M438)

   Filles Du Jura, Les
     mix cor HUG 7769 (M439)
     men cor HUG 7418 (M440)

   Il Est Un Raisin Doré
     mix cor HUG 7188 (M441)

   Jours S'en Vont, Les
     men cor HUG 7185 (M442)

   Marylise
     mix cor HUG 7824 (M443)

   Matin Joyeux
     men cor HUG 7871 (M444)

   Partir N'est Pas Mourir Un Peu
     mix cor HUG 6621 (M445)

   Paysan, Prépare Ta Terre!
     men cor HUG 7494 (M446)

   Pour Parler À Nos Coeurs
     men cor HUG 8109 (M447)

   Presqu'une Chanson
     men cor HUG 6007 (M448)

   Prière À La Fenêtre, La
     mix cor HUG 6889 (M449)

   Prière D'automne
     mix cor HUG 8037 (M450)

   P'tit Soldat D'ci, P'tit Soldat D'là!
     eq voices HUG 6790 (M451)

   Qu'as-Tu Vu Dans Les Vignes?
     mix cor HUG 7178 (M452)
     men cor HUG 8005 (M453)

   Si J'avais Une Humble Maison
     mix cor HUG 7873 (M454)
     men cor HUG 7872 (M455)

   Sur La Route Du Matin
     men cor HUG 7531 (M456)

   Terre De Calme Et De Douce Plaisance
     mix cor HUG 7002 (M457)
     men cor HUG 6078 (M458)

   Terre Jurassienne
     mix cor HUG 7245 (M459)
     men cor HUG 7246 (M460)

   Un Village Selon Mon Coeur
     mix cor HUG 7512 (M461)

   Vieux Pont Du Village, Le
     mix cor HUG 6623 (M462)

   Vigneron Dit À Sa Vigne..., Le
     mix cor HUG 7632 (M463)
     men cor HUG 7633 (M464)

   Village, Le
     mix cor HUG 6768 (M465)

   Village Selon Mon Coeur, Un
     men cor HUG 7375 (M466)

   Villanelle Printanière
     mix cor HUG 7785 (M467)

MICHI NO SHIMAUTA see Fukushima, Yujiro

MICROMÉGAS see Apotheloz, Jean

MID-WINTER BLUES see Gould, Raymond

MIDARE-GAMI see Suzuki, Teruaki

MIEDO (ALLEGRETTO) see Gustavino, Carlos

MIGNON SUISSE see Bovet, J.

MIGNONNE, ALLONS VOIR SI LA ROSE see Costeley, Guillaume

MIHALOVICI, MARCEL (1898- )
   Deux Poésies D'Agrippa D'Aubigné *CC2U
     mix cor BILLAUDOT f.s. (M468)

MIKAMI, JIRO (1961- )
   Poem In Praise Of Nagasaki, A
     mix cor,winds HUG (M469)

MILDE, FRIEDRICH
   Unser Schönes Land
     men cor,opt narrator,kbd BOHM (M470)

MILLE REGRETS DE VOUS ABANDONNER see Des Prez, Josquin

MILLER, FRANZ R. (1926- )
   Gesellig Gesungen *CCU
     men cor FIDULA 6056 f.s. new speech songs (M471)

MIMI PINSON see Cools, Eugène see Niverd, Raymond

MIMKOMCHA see Bitkin, Ze'ev

MIN FINASTE STEN see Cederberg, Anna

MIN GODE, FAGRE BARNEHEIM see Nyhus, Rolf

MINAMI, SATOSHI (1955- )
   Karakuri Zoshi *Op.27
     mix cor HUG (M472)

MINEURS, LES see Naudier

MINIKEL
   All I Want For Christmas (Is You)
     see Two Christmas Songs

   Christmas Day
     see Two Christmas Songs

   Two Christmas Songs
     jr cor LEONARD-US OC 12426 f.s. contains: All I Want For Christmas (Is You); Christmas Day (M473)

MINNELIED see Adam de la Hale see Neuhaus, Gérard

MINUIT SONNE ALLÈGREMENT see Allain, E.J.

MIR IST EIN FEINS BRAUNS MAIDELEIN see Othmayr, Kaspar

MIR IST'S ZU WOHL ERGANGEN see Silcher, Friedrich

MIR TRÄUMTE VON EINEM MYRTENBAUM see Müller, Joseph Ivar

MIR TROGEN A GEZANG see Low, Leo

MIRACLE, LE see Naudier

MIRAGE, LE see Fevrier, Henri

MIREILLE
   Carrosse, Le
     [Fr] 3pt mix cor,acap A COEUR JOIE 1054 (M474)

MIROUZE
   Ma Douce Annette
     4pt mix cor BILLAUDOT (M475)

MISCH-MASCH see Bovet, J.

MISERABLES, LES see Schonberg, Claude-Michel

MISHA, THE FELINE QUEEN see Shields, Valerie

MISHIMBA MISHAMBA see Tawe-Jones, D.

MISRAKI, P.
   Qu'est C'qu'on Attend Pour Être Heureux
     [Fr] SATB,pno A COEUR JOIE 24009 (M476)

   Tiens! Tiens! Tiens!
     [Fr] SATB,pno A COEUR JOIE 24010 (M477)

MISS SAIGON see Schonberg, Claude-Michel

MISSA, EDMOND JEAN LOUIS (1861-1910)
   Sur Mer
     2 eq voices BILLAUDOT (M478)

MISTANLAIRE, LA see Jouineau, Jacques

MISTELI, WERNER
   Fünf Kleine Elegien *CC5U
     wom cor,acap MULLES f.s. (M479)

MISTERO, IL see Bettinelli, Bruno

MISTRESS
   (Novikov, A.) "Barïnia" [Russ] SATB RUSSICA FS 004 (M480)

MISTY see Garner, Erroll

MITTERGRADNEGGER, GÜNTER (1923- )
   Amål I, Amål Du
     mix cor HEYN NR. 120 (M481)

   Kommt Zum Singen
     mix cor HEYN NR. 118 (M482)

   Und Da Wind Verwaht's Lab
     mix cor HEYN NR. 124 (M483)

MITTSU NO YUKI NO UTA see Kikuchi, Masaharu

MIYAMA IYAYAMA see Shibata, Minao

MOÇA TAN FERMOSA see Orrego-Salas, Juan A.

MÖCHT WÜSSE, WIE-N-ES CHÄM see Grunder, Karl

MÖCHT'N VIEL ZACHARLAN  *CCU,Austrian
   (Kühr, Reinhard -Fuchs, Monika) men
   cor&mix cor HEYN ISBN 3 85366 468 7
   f.s.   (M484)

MÖCKL, FRANZ (1925-  )
   Abschiedslied Und Liebeslied
     men cor,acap BOHM   (M485)

MOHICAN FRIENDS see Davids, Brent Michael

MOI J'IRAI DANS LA LUNE see Chekler, Edouard

MOISSON, LA see Broquet, Louis

MOISSONNEURS see Broquet, Louis

MØLLER, SVEIN (1958-  )
   Barnerim
     SSA,acap NOTON N-9212   (M486)

   Eg Gjaette Tulla
     SSA,acap NOTON N-9213   (M487)

   Kom, Skal Vi Klippe Sauen
     SSA,fl,pno NOTON N-9214   (M488)

MOMENT TO MOMENT
   (Schram, Ruth) SATB WARNER CH9506   (M489)
   (Schram, Ruth) SAB WARNER CH9507   (M490)
   (Schram, Ruth) SSA WARNER CH9508   (M491)

MOMENTO MARE see Deák, Csaba

MOMENTS IN TIME
   SA THOMP.G f.s.
     contains: Clouds; Laughter; Orders;
     Spider Danced A Cozy Gigue; Time
        (M492)

MON AMI EST MONTÉ see Doret, Gustave

MON COEUR EST LAS see Bovet, J.

MON DOUX PAYS DE VAUD see Moudon, E.

MON ÉCOLE EST TOUTE EN VERRE see Pasquier, Marius

MON FAIBLE C'EST LE VIN see Mozart, Wolfgang Amadeus

MON FLACON see Haenni, G.

MON HAMEAU see Jaques-Dalcroze, Émile

MON LAC see Henchoz, Emile

MON LAC EST PUR see Jaques-Dalcroze, Émile

MON PAYS see Piaget, Ada May

MON PAYS, RUSTIQUE SÉJOUR see Lang, H.

MON PAYS, SOIS SATISFAIT DE TA BEAUTÉ see Broquet, Louis

MON PÈR' N'VEUT PAS... see Pidoux, E.

MON PÈRE A PLANTÉ D'LA VIGNE see Mermoud, Robert

MON PÈRE AVAIT CINQ CENT MOUTONS see Planel, Jean

MON PÈRE AVAIT CINQ CENTS MOUTONS see Broquet, Louis

MON PETIT "CHEZ NOUS" see Bovet, J.

MON TRÉSOR OU MA PEINE see Henchoz, Emile, Greensleeves

MON VIEUX VILLAGE see Martin

MON VILLAGE see Bovet, J.

MOND IST AUFGEGANGEN,DER see Burkard, Willi

MONIUSZKO, STANISLAW (1819-1872)
   Ces Voisins Qui Lorgnent (from Vivante Pologne)
     mix cor,opt pno/org/orch HUG 8775   (M493)
     men cor HUG 8778   (M494)

   Rebelle, La (from Vivante Pologne)
     men cor HUG 8777   (M495)
     mix cor,opt pno/org/orch HUG 8774   (M496)

   Si Tu M'aimes... (from Vivante Pologne)
     men cor HUG 8776   (M497)

MONIUSZKO, STANISLAW (cont'd.)
     mix cor,opt pno/org/orch HUG 8773   (M498)

MONK,THELONIUS
   You Need Love
     (Rogalski) SSATBB, solo voices (gr. III) UNC JP   (M499)

MONOLOGUE DE LA NUIT see Nodaira, Ichiro

MONSIEUR ET MADAME ORCHESTRE see Chabrier, [Alexis-] Emmanuel

MONSOON see Bhatia, Vanraj A., Varsha

MONTAGNARDS FORÉZIENS, LES see Naudier

MONTAGNE, LA see Bovet, J.

MONTAGUE, STEPHEN (1943-  )
   Tigida Pipa
     SATB,perc&electronic tape UNITED MUS   (M500)

MONTÉE À L'ALPAGE, LA see Bovet, J.

MONTEVERDI, CLAUDIO (ca. 1567-1643)
   A Quest'olmo (from Libro VII Dei Madrigali)
     cor,2.2.2.1. 1.0.0.0. harp,strings
     sc RICORDI-IT 129046   (M501)

   Madrigal
     men cor HUG 8527   (M502)

   Quatre Canzonette A Tre Voci
     3 eq voices HUG 8454   (M503)

MOON MAGIC
   (Strommen, Carl) SATB (medley incl. Blue Moon & Moonlight Serenade) WARNER CO332C1X   (M504)
   (Strommen, Carl) SAB (medley incl. Blue Moon & Moonlight Serenade) WARNER CO332C3X   (M505)

MOON RIVER see Mancini, Henry

MOONDANCE see Morrison,Van

MOORE
   Music Alone Shall Live
     2pt cor ALFRED 11555   (M506)

MOORE, DONALD
   Irish Blessing, An
     TTB WARNER SV9421   (M507)

MORAL PRECEPT see Mechem, Kirke Lewis

MORALES
   De Mi Esperanza
     (Vincent, Carlos) 4pt mix cor LAGOS   (M508)

MORE HOMEWORK see Gould, Raymond

MORE LOVE see Argersinger, Charles

MORENICA
   (Braun, Yehezkel-Jacobson, Joshua) SATB,opt S solo,pno (med easy, text: old spanish jewish love story in ladino) HAZA HZ-013   (M509)

MORET, OSCAR
   Chanson De Mai
     mix cor HUG 8350   (M510)

   Pantins, Les
     mix cor HUG 8457   (M511)

   Tracteur À Zéphirin
     mix cor,opt pno/org/orch HUG 8466   (M512)

MORGAN, J.
   Three Justin Morgan Choruses
     (Smith, Gregg) (contains: despair, amanda, montgomery) LEONARD-US 50322160   (M513)

MORGEN see Huber, Walter Simon see Studer, Hans

MORGEN,DER see Brun, Fritz

MORGEN MUSS ICH FORT VON HIER see Silcher, Friedrich

MORGENGRUSS see Zentner, Johannes

MORGENGRUSS AN DIE HEIMAT see Mermoud, Robert

MORGENHYMNUS see Wolf, Hugo

MORGENLIED
   jr cor&3pt wom cor MULLES   (M514)
   jr cor MULLES   (M515)
   see Huber, Walter Simon see Kreis, Otto see Öser, Hans

MORGENLIED (KEIN STIMMLEIN NOCH SCHALLT) see Kuhn, E.

MORGENSEGEN see Studer, Hans

MORGENWANDERUNG see Güdel, W.

MORI, KONATE (1950-  )
   Hello, Beatles
     wom cor/jr cor HUG   (M516)

   Play With Children's Play
     jr cor HUG   (M517)

MORIANA see Morillo, Roberto García

MORILLO, ROBERTO GARCÍA (1911-  )
   Marin  *Op.18, cant
     cor,T solo,3.3.3.1. 2.2.0.0. timp,perc,pno,strings RICORDI-IT   (M518)

   Moriana  *cant
     cor,STBar soli,2.3.2.1. 2.2.0.0. timp,perc,hpsd,strings RICORDI-IT   (M519)

MORISAKI,TAKATOSHI (1951-  )
   Beyond The Blue Sky
     mix cor HUG   (M520)

   Duet Of The Wind
     mix cor HUG   (M521)

   Shout Over The Ocean
     mix cor HUG   (M522)

MORLEY, THOMAS (1557-1602)
   Sing We And Chant It
     (Robinson) 3pt cor,acap ALFRED 5809   (M523)

MORNING see Fischer, Clare see Larkin, Michael

MORNING DEW, THE  *folk song,Nor Am
   (Anderson, Jean) SSA,pno LAWSON 52649   (M524)

MORNING TRUMPET, THE see Barnes, Edward

MORRICONE, ENNIO (1928-  )
   Echi
     wom cor/men cor,opt vcl ZERBONI 9911   (M525)

MORRIS, HAYDN
   Saucepans
     see Sosban Fach

   Sosban Fach
     "Saucepans" [Welsh/Eng] SATB BANKS 1404   (M526)

MORRIS, STEVLAND (STEVIE WONDER) (1950-  )
   Creepin'
     (Lyons, Bill) SATBB,acap (gr. III) UNC JP   (M527)

   I Just Called To Say I Love You
     SATB WARCH 12105   (M528)

   Lately
     SATB WARNER 0116LC1X   (M529)
     SAB WARNER 0116LC3X   (M530)

MORRISON,VAN
   Moondance
     SSAA,perc (gr. III) UNC JP   (M531)
     (Burnell, Mark) SATB,solo voice, perc (gr. III) UNC JP   (M532)
     (Cross, Dave) SATB,pno,db,drums (gr. III) UNC JP   (M533)

MORSE
   Oysters And Clams
     (Düsing) SATB,kbd (med diff) PRESSER 392-02514   (M534)

MORT DE DAVID, LA see Honegger, Arthur

MORT DU CHÊNE, LA see Boller, Carlo

MORTARI, VIRGILIO (1902-1994)
   Cinque Poesie Di Aldo Palazzeschi
     treb cor,harp RICORDI-IT 134313   (M535)

MORTE DI DIDONE, LA see Rossini, Gioacchino

MORTIFEE, ANN
   Just One Voice
     SATB WARCH 35666   (M536)

MOSER-SCHWEIZER, ERNST
   Rüste Des Tages
     men cor,acap MULLES   (M537)

MOSES, LEONARD
   Airborne, The
     TB oct SOUTHERN SC420   (M538)
     TTB oct SOUTHERN SC419   (M539)

MOSSENMARK, STAFFAN
   Fån
     cor, with mobile telephones STIM   (M540)

MOST BEAUTIFUL GIRL IN THE WORLD, THE
   (Schmutte, Pete) SATB WARNER CH9592   (M541)
   (Schmutte, Pete) TTB WARNER CH9593   (M542)

MOTET see Chance, Nancy Laird see
    Naegeli, Hans Georg

MOTETS see Martin

MOTETS, LES see Machaut, Guillaume de

MOTETS AND LATIN CONTRAFACTA see
    Ciconia, Johannes

MOTETTE, IMMER WIEDER WERDEN GÄRTEN
    SEIN see Schweizer, Alfred

MOTETTI see Dipiazza, Orlando

MOTHER GOOSE MEDLEY see Gracey, William
    A.

MOTHER'S LOVE see Siltman

MOTOWN, THE BEST OF  *CCU
    SAB WARCH 36275           (M543)

MOTTETTI PER LA PASSIONE see Petrassi,
    Goffredo

MOTTETTO SU RE, MI... see Clementi,
    Aldo

MOTTO see Schweizer, Alfred

MOUCHET
    Caprice Hongrois
        4pt men cor BILLAUDOT  (M544)

    Il N'est Amour Que Le Printemps
        4pt mix cor BILLAUDOT  (M545)

MOUDON, E.
    Chante, Montagnard!
        mix cor,S/T solo HUG 6572  (M546)
        men cor,T solo HUG 6569    (M547)

    Idylle Printanière
        mix cor HUG 6580       (M548)

    Là-Haut
        men cor HUG 6217       (M549)

    Mon Doux Pays De Vaud
        men cor HUG 6217       (M550)

    Pâtre Du Jura, Le
        men cor HUG 6349       (M551)

    Souvenirs D'Enfance
        men cor HUG 6647       (M552)

MOUETTES, LES see Mermoud, Robert

MOULIN, LE see Bovet, J.

MOULINIE, E.
    Lululu (from Chopin's Funeral March)
        mix cor/men cor,pno HUG  (M553)

MOUNTAIN SONG see Brings, Allen Stephen

MOURANT, WALTER (1910-    )
    Child's Garden Of Verses, A
        unis cor,pno (book i) LAURN CH-1120
                               (M554)

    Jazz! Jazz! American Jazz!
        1-3pt cor,pno,opt alto sax LAURN
        CH-1108                (M555)

MOUSSE, LA see Jaques-Dalcroze, Émile

MOUTON, CHARLES
    Marche De Limoges, Le (from "Pictures
        At An Exhibition")
        (Swingle, Ward) SATB,db,drums (gr.
        IV) voc pt,pts UNC JP GR-4X
                               (M556)

MOUVEMENT POUR DIX-HUIT VOIX D'HOMMES
    see Carson, Philippe

MOVIE CLASSICS: GOLDEN LOVE SONGS OF
    THE '70S
    (Ginsburg, Ned) SATB (medley incl. A
        Time For Us, Love Story & You Light
        Up My Life) WARNER CO296C1X (M557)
    (Ginsburg, Ned) SAB (medley incl. A
        Time For Us, Love Story & You Light
        Up My Life) WARNER CO296C3X (M558)
    (Ginsburg, Ned) 2pt cor/SSA (medley
        incl. A Time For Us, Love Story &
        You Light Up My Life) WARNER
        CO296C5X               (M559)

MOVIE MAGIC
    (Schram, Ruth) SATB (medley incl.
        This Used To Be My Playground, The
        Crying Game & End Of The Road)
        WARNER CO328C1X        (M560)
    (Schram, Ruth) SAB (medley incl. This
        Used To Be My Playground, The
        Crying Game & End Of The Road)
        WARNER CO328C3X        (M561)

MOZART, WOLFGANG AMADEUS (1756-1791)
    Allegretto (from Piano Sonata In C
        Major)
        (Swingle, Ward) SATB,db,drums (gr.
        III) voc pt,pts UNC JP AFM-3
                               (M562)

MOZART, WOLFGANG AMADEUS (cont'd.)
    Allegro (from C Major Sonata)
        (Swingle, Ward) SATB,db,drums (gr.
        IV) voc pt,pts UNC JP AFM-1
                               (M563)
    Allegro (from Eine Kleine Nachtmusik)
        (Swingle, Ward) SATB,db,drums (gr.
        III) voc pt,pts UNC JP AFM-4
                               (M564)
    Allegro (from Sonata No. 14)
        (Swingle, Ward) SATB,db,drums (gr.
        III) voc pt,pts UNC JP AFM-8X
                               (M565)
    Alphabet, The
        (Martin) SSA,acap (very easy)
        PRESSER 392-41780      (M566)

    Andante (from Piano Sonata In C
        Major)
        (Swingle, Ward) STB,db,drums (gr.
        II) voc pt,pts UNC JP  (M567)

    Bald Prangt, Den Morgen Zu Verkünden
        Aus "Die Zauberflöte"
        (Weber) wom cor DOBLINGER 65 908
                               (M568)

    Bäurin Hat D'katz Verlorn, D'
        see Chat De La Mère Michel, Le

    Canons
        [It/Fr] mix cor/eq voices HUG 7899
                               (M569)

    Caravane Turque Sur La Marche Turque
        (Mouchet) 4pt men cor BILLAUDOT
                               (M570)

    Chanson Bachique  *canon
        men cor HUG 3255       (M571)

    Chat De La Mère Michel, Le
        "Bäurin Hat D'katz Verlorn, D'" mix
        cor HUG 7849           (M572)

    Choeur Des Prêtres (from Magic Flute,
        The)
        men cor HUG 3260       (M573)

    Choeurs Faciles pour Enfants
        (composed with Schumann, Robert
        (Alexander))
        eq voices SALABERT EAS 19111 (M574)

    Cinq Canons
        men cor HUG 7853       (M575)
        eq voices HUG 7853     (M576)

    Clartés (from Magic Flute, The)
        men cor HUG 6227       (M577)

    Croyez-Vous, Madame..., Le
        [It/Fr] 3pt mix cor HUG 7851 (M578)

    Fugue (from Sonata For Violin And
        Piano Kv 402)
        (Swingle, Ward) SATB,db,drums (gr.
        III) voc pt,pts UNC JP AFM-9X
                               (M579)

    Gestörte Ständchen, Das
        "Sérénade Brouillée, La" 3pt men
        cor HUG 7848           (M580)

    Hymne Au Soleil
        3pt men cor,pno/org/orch HUG 6560
                               (M581)

    Im Früling ("Unsre Wiesen Grünen
        Wieder"), Kv Anh.262
        (Weber) wom cor DOBLINGER 64 306
                               (M582)

    Laisse Chanter Le Vent
        eq voices HUG 7852     (M583)

    Menuetto (from Eine Kleine
        Nachtmusik)
        (Swingle, Ward) SATB,db,drums (gr.
        I) voc pt,pts UNC JP   (M584)

    Mon Faible C'est Le Vin
        (Ducasse) 3 eq voices BILLAUDOT
                               (M585)

    Nos Chants
        mix cor HUG 6126       (M586)
        men cor HUG 6165       (M587)

    Nuit D'été
        mix cor HUG 6126       (M588)

    Overture To The Marriage Of Figaro
        (Swingle, Ward) SSAATTBB,acap (gr.
        V) voc pt,pts UNC JP SC-3X (M589)

    Quelques Canons
        3-4pt men cor HUG 7899 (M590)

    Romance (from Eine Kleine Nachtmusik)
        (Swingle, Ward) SATB,db,drums (gr.
        II) voc pt,pts UNC JP AFM-5
                               (M591)

    Rondo (from Eine Kleine Nachtmusik)
        (Swingle, Ward) SATB,db,drums (gr.
        IV) voc pt,pts UNC JP AFM-7
                               (M592)

    Sérénade Brouillée, La
        see Gestörte Ständchen, Das

MOZART, WOLFGANG AMADEUS (cont'd.)
    Sing, Come Sing A Song Of Gladness
        (from Exsultate Jubilate)
        (Larson, Lloyd) SA,pno GENTRY
        JG2185                 (M593)
        (Larson, Lloyd) SAB,pno GENTRY
        JG2184                 (M594)

    Variations On "Ah! Vous Dirai-Je,
        Maman"
        (Swingle, Ward) SSAATTBB, solo
        voices,db,drums (gr. IV) voc pt,
        pts UNC JP AFM-10X     (M595)

    Venerabilis Barba Capucinorum
        men cor HUG 6428       (M596)

MR. FROGGIE WENT A-COURTIN'
    (Frank Clark) SATB,pno,opt db FOSTER
    MF 3056                    (M597)

MR. MISTOFFELEES AND OTHER CHORUSES
    FROM CATS see Lloyd Webber, Andrew

MR. SUPERMAN see Joplin

MUCI, ITALO RUGGERO
    Due Madrigali In Stile Del 1500
        3-4pt cor BERBEN BERBEN 2693 f.s.
        contains: I Vaghi Fior; Non Al
        Suo Amante             (M598)

    I Vaghi Fior
        see Due Madrigali In Stile Del 1500

    Non Al Suo Amante
        see Due Madrigali In Stile Del 1500

MÜETI RÜEFT, 'S see Kölliker, G.

MÜETIS TISCH, 'S see Kölliker, G.

MUFFAT, GEORG (ca. 1645-1704)
    Fugue In D Minor
        (Swingle, Ward) SATB,db,drums (gr.
        II) voc pt,pts UNC JP RG-4X
                               (M599)

MULETIERS DE TOLÈDE, LES see Farigoul,
    J.

MÜLLER, JOSEPH IVAR (1892-    )
    Chor Der Fischer
        men cor,acap MULLES    (M600)

    Durch Den Wald
        men cor,acap MULLES    (M601)

    Heimwehliedli
        men cor,acap MULLES    (M602)

    Hochzeitslied
        men cor,acap MULLES    (M603)

    In Goldener Fülle
        men cor,acap MULLES    (M604)

    Lob Des Gesanges
        men cor,acap MULLES    (M605)

    Mir Träumte Von Einem Myrtenbaum
        wom cor,acap MULLES    (M606)

    Reiterlied
        men cor,acap MULLES    (M607)

    Sommermadrigal
        wom cor,acap MULLES    (M608)
        3pt men cor,acap MULLES (M609)

    Vaterland, Ruh In Gotteshand
        men cor,acap MULLES    (M610)

    Vreneli Vom Thunersee, 'S
        (Krähenbühl) men cor,acap MULLES
                               (M611)

    Zwei Kurze Wahlsprüche  *CC2U
        wom cor,acap MULLES f.s. (M612)

MÜLLER, P.
    Ronde, La
        mix cor HUG 8380       (M613)

    Tu N'es Pas Un Grain De Sable
        men cor HUG 8470       (M614)

    Vacances
        men cor HUG 8379       (M615)

MÜLLER-ZÜRICH, PAUL (1898-    )
    Gedanken Sind Frei, Die
        men cor,acap MULLES    (M616)

    Nun Will Der Lenz Uns Grüssen
        wom cor,acap MULLES    (M617)

    Wenn Alle Brünnlein Fliessen
        wom cor,acap MULLES    (M618)

MÜLLERSKNAB, DER see Doret, Gustave

MULTIPLE ECHOES (from Echo Song by
    Orlando di Lasso)
    (Smith Singers, Gregg) SATB,acap
    LAURN CH-1071              (M619)

MÜNSTER,DAS see Kathedrale

MUNTOGNA,LA see Derungs, Gion Gius.

MUNZINGER, CARL
   Am Volkstage
     men cor,acap MULLES      (M620)

   Frühlingsjubel
     (Krenger) wom cor,acap MULLES
                                   (M621)

   Vreneli Ab Em Guggisberg (Dur), 'S
     men cor,acap MULLES      (M622)

MURPHY, KEVIN
   For All We Know
     SSATB,pno (gr. III/gr. IV) UNC JP
                                   (M623)

   Summer Heat
     SSATB,S solo,pno,db,drums (gr. III)
     UNC JP                (M624)

MUSENSOHN, DER see Schubert, Franz (Peter)

MUSIC ALONE SHALL LIVE
   (Roff, J.) SAB oct THOMAS 1C0108215
                                   (M625)
   see Moore

MUSIC AND SWEET POETRY see Hallberg, Bengt

MUSIC FOR A FESTIVE OCCASION see Cooper, Paul

MUSIC FROM "HANSEL AND GRETEL"
   (Gallina) 2pt cor SHAWNEE EA-172
                                   (M626)

MUSIC HATH CHARMS see Cabena, Barrie

MUSIC HISTORY 101 see Anonymous

MUSIC WILL ALWAYS BE THERE see Martin

MUSICA see Zentner, Johannes

MUSICA DOLCE see Conci, Nicola

MUSICA POPULAR ARGENTINA (VOLUMEN I)
   (Zadoff, Nestor) mix cor LAGOS f.s.
   contains: Piazzolla, Astor, Jacinto
     Chiclana; Ramirez, Ariel, Allá
     Lejos Y Hace Tiempo; Walsh,
     Serenata Para La Tierra De Uno
                                   (M627)

MUSICA POPULAR ARGENTINA (VOLUMEN II)
   (Zadoff, Nestor) mix cor LAGOS f.s.
   contains: Ocampo,Oscar Cardozo,
     Zamba Del Nuevo Dia; Piazzolla,
     Astor, Muerte Del Angel, La;
     Sanchez, Damian, Erbol Ya Fue
     Plantado, El        (M628)

MUSICHE DI SCENA see Corghi, Azio

MUSICHE PER "I BEI COLLOQUI" DI AURELIO PES see Sciarrino, Salvatore

MUSICHE PER "LA NAVE" DI G. D'ANNUNZIO see Pizzetti, Ildebrando

MUSICHE PER LE "TRACHINIE" DI SOFOCLE see Sciarrino, Salvatore

MUSICIANS OF BREMEN, THE see Williamson, Malcolm

MUSICIEN DES RUES, LE see Mermoud, Robert

MUSICORUM COLLEGIO: SIX FOURTEENTH CENTURY MUSICIANS' MOTETS *CC6U
   (Harrison) OISEAU RE 910 f.s. (M629)

MUSIK see Feibel, Norbert

MUSIK, DU BIST DIE TIEFSTE LABE see Päppert, Walter

MUSIK, DU MÄCHTIGE! see Schmid, Walter

MUSIK IST EINE GOTTESGAB see Schmid, Walter

MUSIK, OP. 34 NO. 6 see Brugk, Hans Melchior

MUSIK UND WEIN *CC9L
   (Krings, Alfred) mix cor,acap LAAB
   AV 102                (M630)

MUSIKALISCHE KURZWEIL,DIE see Widmann, Erasmus

MUSIQUE see Pasquier, Marius

MUSIQUE, LA see Sutermeister, Heinrich

MUSIQUE, DOUX MYSTÈRE see Lang, H.

MUSIQUE FLORENTINE see Delmas, Marc-Jean-Baptiste

MUSIQUE VOCAL SET see Couperin, François (le Grand)

MUSIQUE VOCALE PROFANE; MOTETS see Couperin, François (le Grand)

MUSIQUE VOCALE see Couperin, François (le Grand)

MUSKATELLER-LIED see Feibel, Norbert

MUSTANG, THE see Dewitt

MUTTER WIR GRÜSSEN DICH! *CCU
   (Anderluh, Anton) mix cor HEYN
   NR. 104 f.s. mother's day songs
                                   (M631)

MY BALLOON see Bell

MY BELOVED SPAKE see Purcell, Henry

MY CATERPILLAR see Broughton

MY DRIVER'S TEST see Beebe, Hank

MY FUNNY VALENTINE see Rodgers, Richard

MY GUY
   (Schmutte, Pete) SAA WARNER 8055MC2X
   ipa                   (M632)

MY HEART see Pfautsch, Lloyd Alvin

MY HEART'S IN THE HIGHLAND see Strommen, Carl

MY LADYBUG FRIEND see Rippentrop, Denice

MY LOVE HAS DEPARTED see Lundberg

MY LOVES IN GERMANIE see Grainger, Percy Aldridge

MY MAGIC WORLD see Johnson, Sheila Hilton

MY MOTHER'S LOVE see Siltman

MY MOUNTAIN HOME see Dewitt

MY NATIVE LAND see Pfautsch, Lloyd Alvin

MY NEIGHBOR'S ROSES see Dewitt

MY PLANE see Rees-Davies, Ieuan

MY SECRET GARDEN see Rippentrop, Denice

MY SONG SHALL BE ALWAY see Handel, George Frideric

MY UNKNOWN SOMEONE
   (Snyder, Audrey) SATB WARNER 8256MC1X
                                     (M633)
   (Snyder, Audrey) SSA WARNER 8256MC2X
                                     (M634)
   (Snyder, Audrey) SAB WARNER 8256MC3X
                                     (M635)

MY YOUNGER YEARS see Pfautsch, Lloyd Alvin

MYGGEN see Volle, Bjarne

MYS BÄRN see Balmer, Luc

MYS BRIEFLI see Kölliker, G.

MYSTÈRE DE LA VIE see Hagiwara, Hidehico

MYSTÈRE DE L'EMMANUEL see Lioncourt, Guy de

MYSTÈRES DE LA FOI, LES see Gagnebin, Henri

MYSTICAL GARDEN see Shaw, Marshall L.

# N

NAAR BUITEN MET LOUIS DAVIDS see Davids, Louis

NACHT,DIE see Hägler, Paul see Schubert, Franz (Peter)

NACHTGESANG see Langer, Richard see Mendelssohn-Bartholdy, Felix

NACHTGRUSS see Hägler, Paul

NACHTLIED see Brun, Fritz see Jensen, Adolf

NACHTMUSIK see Kreis, Otto see Märki, Ernst

NACHTREIGEN see Hensel, Fanny Mendelssohn

NACHTREISE see Aeschbacher, Walther

NACHTS see Helmschrott, Robert M.

NACHTSCHLEIFE see Kalitzke, Johannes

NACHTSTILLE see Kreis, Otto

NACHTWÄCHTERLIED see Furrer, Walter

NAEGELI, HANS GEORG (1773-1836)
   Motet
     men cor HUG 6285       (N1)

NAKA, YUKICHI (1903-   )
   Gogo No Remon-Sui
     mix cor HUG           (N2)

NAKAJIMA, HAL (1942-   )
   Haru No Tekagami
     wom cor,solo voice ZEN-ON 71908
                                   (N3)

   Izumishikibu
     wom cor ZEN-ON 719078   (N4)

NAKAJIMA, HARU (1942-   )
   Hand Mirror In Spring
     wom cor,Mez solo,pno HUG  (N5)

   Homage To Dusk
     mix cor,timp, and japanese inst HUG
                                   (N6)

   Izumishikibu
     wom cor HUG           (N7)

NAKAJIMA, YOSHIFUMI (1944-   )
   Rennyo-Shonin *cant
     mix cor,boy solo,narrator,orch HUG
                                   (N8)

NAKAMURA, SHIGENOBU (1950-   )
   Saioh Fantasy *Suite
     mix cor,pno HUG       (N9)

NAKAMURA, YUKITAKE (1944-   )
   Mamii Fusako Genbaku Taikenki Yori
     "Niji Yo Eien Ni"
     jr cor,Mez solo,pno HUG  (N10)

NAKANE, YUKO (1954-   )
   Rakan Ondo
     wom cor,pno HUG      (N11)

NAKANISHI, SATORU (1934-   )
   Three Japanese Worksongs
     wom cor,pno HUG      (N12)

   Three Man-Yo Song
     wom cor,pno HUG      (N13)

N'ALLEZ PLUS AU BOIS see Urfer, Albert

NANI, NANI
   (Braun, Yehezkel-Jacobson, Joshua)
   SATB,S solo,pno (med easy, text in
   Ladino) HAZA HZ-023   (N14)

NAPLAN, A.
   Hine Ma Tov
     unis cor BOOSEY-ENG OCTB6782 (N15)

NÄR LJUVT NATUREN GRÖNSKAR see Bengtsson, Bernt

NARRENKANON see Schweizer, Alfred

NATIONAL AMNESIA see Meader, Darmon

NATIVE AMERICAN SPRING SONGS see Grundahl, Nancy

NATURE ET L'AMOUR,LA see Tchaikovsky, Piotr Ilyich

NAUDIER
   Avril
     4pt mix cor BILLAUDOT  (N16)

NAUDIER (cont'd.)
   Badinerie
      4pt mix cor BILLAUDOT     (N17)

   Banquet De Sainte Ccile
      4pt mix cor BILLAUDOT     (N18)

   Cadet Rousselle
      4pt mix cor BILLAUDOT     (N19)

   Carillons De Pâques
      4pt mix cor BILLAUDOT     (N20)

   Chanson Des Enfants Studieux, La
      3 eq voices BILLAUDOT    (N21)

   Chant Du Travail, Le
      3 eq voices BILLAUDOT    (N22)

   Chantons Gaiement
      4pt men cor BILLAUDOT    (N23)

   Chantons Les Vins Français
      4pt men cor BILLAUDOT    (N24)

   Coeurs En Fête
      4pt mix cor BILLAUDOT     (N25)

   Douce Nuit D'été
      4pt mix cor BILLAUDOT     (N26)

   Eau Du Ciel, L'
      4pt men cor BILLAUDOT    (N27)

   Forêt
      4pt men cor BILLAUDOT    (N28)

   Forge, La
      4pt men cor BILLAUDOT    (N29)

   Hymne Au Blé
      4pt men cor BILLAUDOT    (N30)

   Mineurs, Les
      4pt men cor BILLAUDOT    (N31)

   Miracle, Le
      4pt men cor BILLAUDOT    (N32)

   Montagnards Foréziens, Les
      4pt men cor BILLAUDOT    (N33)

   Océan Fauve, L'
      4pt men cor BILLAUDOT    (N34)

   Ode À La Jeunesse
      4pt mix cor BILLAUDOT     (N35)

   Ode À La Lumière
      4pt men cor BILLAUDOT    (N36)

   Orage Sur La Mer, L'
      4pt men cor BILLAUDOT    (N37)

   Pharamond
      4pt men cor BILLAUDOT    (N38)

   Prométhée
      4pt men cor BILLAUDOT    (N39)

   Recueillement
      4pt mix cor BILLAUDOT     (N40)

   Rive Enchanteresse
      4pt men cor BILLAUDOT    (N41)

   Ronde Du Mugnet, La
      4pt men cor BILLAUDOT    (N42)

   Ronde Du Muguet, La
      4pt mix cor BILLAUDOT     (N43)

   Rondeau Printanier
      4pt mix cor BILLAUDOT     (N44)

   Sous Les Pommiers En Fleurs
      3pt wom cor BILLAUDOT    (N45)

   Splendeur Du Jour
      4pt men cor BILLAUDOT    (N46)

   Terre Natale
      4pt men cor BILLAUDOT    (N47)

   Torrent, Le
      4pt men cor BILLAUDOT    (N48)

NAUGHTY BUT NICE
  (Chinn, Teena) SSA (medley incl. Big Spender, Steam Heat & Blues In The Night) WARNER CO307C2X ipa   (N49)

N'AVEZ-VOUS RIEN À DÉCLARER? see Martin

NAZOTOKI TANTEIDAN see Horikoshi, Ryuichi

NE CRAINS POINT see Kodály, Zoltán

NE T'ARRÊTE PAS... see Tichy, O.A.

NÉANT OÙ L'ON NE PEUT ARRIVER, LE see Ferrero, Lorenzo

NEBEL IM WATTENMEER see Tamas, Janos

NEIGE FOND SUR LES MONTAGNES,LA see Doret, Gustave

NEIN ZUR LEBENSANGST see Bergman, Erik

NELL'ORTO see Prosperi, Carlo

NELLY BLY see Foster, Stephen Collins

NELSON
   Bavarian Yodelling Song
      SA WARCH 34390          (N50)

   Stay Little Blackbird
      unis cor WARCH 34383     (N51)

NELSON, PORTIA
   Make A Rainbow
      WARNER WBCH9332         (N52)
      unis cor/2pt cor WARNER WBCH9331  (N53)

NES GADOL HAYAH SHAM see Clearfield, Andrea

NEUE HAUS IST AUFGERICHT, DAS see Haus, Karl

NEUE KÄRNTNER LIED,DAS 1979 (from Kärntner Chorblätter) (Mittergradnegger, Günther) mix cor HEYN   (N54)

NEUE KÄRNTNERLIEDER FÜR GEMISCHTEN CHOR *Austrian
  (Schmid, Anton) mix cor HEYN f.s. contains: Heft 1; Heft 2; Heft 3; Heft 4; Heft 5   (N55)

NEUE KÄRNTNERLIEDER FÜR MÄNNERCHOR
  (Schmid, Anton) men cor HEYN f.s. contains: Heft 1; Heft 2; Heft 3; Heft 4; Heft 5   (N56)

NEUE QUODLIBETS see Bürthel, Jakob

NEUER FRÜHLING see Schmid, Walter

NEUHAUS, GÉRARD
   Abendlied
      wom cor,acap MULLES     (N57)

   Minnelied
      men cor,acap MULLES     (N58)

   Schweizerland
      men cor,acap MULLES     (N59)

NEUS LÄBE see Märki, Ernst

NEVER MET A MAN I DIDN'T LIKE
  (O'neill, Jackie) SATB WARNER 1564NC1X   (N60)
  (O'neill, Jackie) SAB WARNER 1564NC3X   (N61)

NEW COMMONWEALTH, THE see Vaughan Williams, Ralph

NEW ENGLAND IMAGES see Sarmanto, Heikki

NEW SONG, A see Pote

NEW YEAR CAROL see Wishart, Peter

NEW YEAR CAROL, A see Donahue, Bertha Terry

NEW YORK NEW YORK, THEME FROM see Kander, John

NICOLAS DE FLÜE see Honegger, Arthur

NICOLAS SI TU ES SAGE see Lagger, Oscar

NIEDER, FABIO (1957- )
   Kresnik
      cor,2 high soli,pno,4perc, or actor-musician sc RICORDI-IT 134262   (N62)

NIEDERMANN, GUSTAV (1881- )
   Blümlein Blüht Am Wege,Ein
      men cor,acap MULLES     (N63)

   Eines Tages In Allabendlichen Winden
      men cor,acap MULLES     (N64)

NIELSEN, RICCARDO (1908- )
   Kammerkantate, Eine
      wom cor,S solo,fl,xylo/vibra,pno, timp,perc sc RICORDI-IT 131732   (N65)

NIEMAND KENNT DAS LEID see Märki, Ernst

NIGGLI, FRIEDRICH
   De Trummler
      men cor,acap MULLES     (N66)

   Meines Kindes Abendgebet
      wom cor,acap MULLES     (N67)

   Sennelied
      men cor,acap MULLES     (N68)

NIGGUN
  (Heller) SATB (hasidic folksong) KJOS 8779   (N69)

NIGHT see Hagen, Daron see Schubert, Franz (Peter)

NIGHT AND DAY see Porter, Cole

NIGHT CHANT NO. 2 see Fujieda, Mamoru

NIGHT MUSIC see Pitfield, Thomas Baron

NIGHT SONGS see Burrell, Diana see Wilson, Thomas

NIGHT WE CALLED IT A DAY, THE see Fischer, Clare

NIGHTMARE see Kurachi, Tatsuya

NIGHT'S MYSTERIES, THE see Rippentrop, Denice

NIGUNIM see Keller, Wilhelm

NIIKURA, KEN (1951- )
   Ballet Fantasie Suikazura
      mix cor,orch HUG      (N70)

   Three Chansons
      wom cor,pno HUG      (N71)

   Village De Japon
      mix cor,string quar&pno HUG  (N72)

NIIMI, TOKUHIDE (1947- )
   Canticles Of Winds
      mix cor HUG      (N73)

   Hearing The Cosmos
      mix cor,pno 4-hands&perc HUG  (N74)

   Ou-No-Kuni
      mix cor,pno,perc ZEN-ON 719078  (N75)

   Silver Moonlight...
      wom cor HUG      (N76)

   Sound Of Tides
      wom cor,org HUG      (N77)

   Tree Of Life
      mix cor,pno 4-hands HUG  (N78)

   Wall Has Disappeared, The
      men cor HUG      (N79)

   Wind In Light Blue
      wom cor HUG      (N80)

NIJI NO WA see Suzuki, Yukikazu

NIKLAUS VON FLÜE see Honegger, Arthur

NILES, JOHN JACOB (1892-1980)
   What Is Beauty
     (Leavitt, John) SATB WARNER SV9328   (N81)

NILSSON, STEFAN
   Som Luft Och Vatten
      mix cor,acap SVERIG SK 767  (N82)

NISHIDA, YUMIKO (1951- )
   Tada Soredake No Hanashi Desu
      mix cor,pno HUG      (N83)

   Wasurenagusa Mo Koishiteru
      mix cor,pno HUG      (N84)

NISHIMURA, AKIRA (1953- )
   Aqua Invocation
      mix cor,pno HUG      (N85)

   Jakkô-Aika
      wom cor ZEN-ON 719075    (N86)

   Mantra Of The Light
      wom cor,orch HUG     (N87)

   Seven Poems Of Princess Shikishi
      mix cor,acap ONGAKU 544710  (N88)

NIVERD, RAYMOND (1922- )
   Grillon, Le
      4pt men cor BILLAUDOT    (N89)

   Mimi Pinson
      4pt men cor BILLAUDOT    (N90)

NO ELEPHANT see Lawrence, Stephen L.

NO GREATER LOVE see Elkins

NO MOUTH see Broughton

NOBODY KNOWS THE TROUBLE I'VE SEEN
  (Althouse) SATB ALFRED 11552  (N91)
  (Althouse) SAB ALFRED 11553  (N92)
  see Anonymous see Barron, John

NOBRE, MARLOS (1939- )
   Coros de Natal
      SATB SEESAW          (N93)

NOCE, LA see Apotheloz, Jean see Doret, Gustave

NOCE DE VILLAGE, LA see Rille, L. de

NOCE DU CANTONNIER, LA see Martin

NOCES, LES see Bovet, J.

NOCHE, LA (ALLEGRETTO) see Gustavino, Carlos

NOCHES DE SANTA FE see Gustavino, Carlos

NOCTURNE see Schubert, Franz (Peter) see Vuataz, Roger

NODAIRA, ICHIRO (1953- )
   Monologue De La Nuit
     mix cor,fl HUG   (N94)

NODLE KANGBYON
   (Harnady, Wallace) "Beside The Nodle River" [Kor] 2pt treb cor,pno EARTHSNG EW-12   (N95)

NOÉ see Rochat, Jean

NOLA, G. DOMENICO DA
   On This Delightful Day
     (Liebergen, Patrick) 3pt mix cor, acap WARNER SV9309   (N96)

NOLI ME TANGERE see Furer, Arthur

NON AL SUO AMANTE see Muci, Italo Ruggero

NON GRIDATE PIU see Gentilucci, Armando

NONO, LUIGI (1924-1990)
   Atmende Klarsein, Das
     jr cor,bass fl,electronic equipment sc RICORDI-IT 133476   (N97)

   Dónde Estás Hermano?
     SSMezA RICORDI-IT 133477   (N98)

   Frammenti Da "Au Grand Soleil D'amour Chargé"
     cor,soli,4.4.4.4. 4.4.4.0. 2timp, perc,marimba,strings,electronic tape sc RICORDI-IT 134420   (N99)

   Gespenst Geht Um In Der Welt, Ein
     cor,S solo,4.4.4.4. 4.4.4.0. perc, strings sc RICORDI-IT 131806   (N100)

   Lo, Frammento Dal "Prometeo"
     jr cor,3S,bass fl,contrabass clar, electronic equipment sc RICORDI-IT 133368   (N101)

   Y Entonces Comprendió
     cor,6 female soli,electronic tape sc RICORDI-IT 131647   (N102)

NONSENSE see Petrassi, Goffredo

NORA-DOKEI see Takenaka, Atsuhiko

NORMAND, CLAUDE
   Violoncelliste
     [Fr] SATB,acap A COEUR JOIE 823   (N103)

NORSK SUITE see Karlsen, Kjell Mørk

NORTH
   Hymne Neuchâtelois
     mix cor HUG 6809   (N104)
     men cor HUG 4412   (N105)

NOS CHANTS see Mozart, Wolfgang Amadeus

NOSTALGIE see Boller, Carlo

NOTHING ELSE TO DO see Ward, William Reed

NOTHING IS HERE FOR TEARS see Vaughan Williams, Ralph

NOTRE CHALET, LÀ-HAUT see Boller, Carlo

NOTRE SUISSE see Bovet, J.

NOTRE TERRE À NOUS see Jaques-Dalcroze, Émile

NOTRE VIE EST UN VOYAGE see Kaelin, Pierre

NOUS ÉTIONS TROIS FILLES see Boller, Carlo see Huguenin, Charles

NOUS IRONS À VALPARAISO see Dutilleux, Henri

NOUS N'AVONS CHEZ NOUS see Hemmerling, Carlos

NOUS N'IRONS PLUS AU BOIS see Delor see Edwards, Geoffrey

NOUVELLE ANTHOLOGIE CHORALE I *CCU
   eq voices,acap HUG 6656 f.s.   (N106)

NOUVELLE ANTHOLOGIE CHORALE, VOL. IV *CCU
   eq voices,acap HUG 7916 f.s.   (N107)

NOVEMBERBLAREN see Swerts, Piet

NOVEMBRE see Hemmerling, Carlos

NOW AND FOREVER
   (Chinn, Teena) SATB WARNER 6740NC1X   (N108)
   (Chinn, Teena) SAB WARNER 6740NC3X   (N109)
   (Chinn, Teena) 2pt mix cor WARNER 6740NC5X   (N110)

NOW DOES THE GLORIOUS DAY APPEAR see Purcell, Henry

NOW I WALK IN BEAUTY
   (Smith, Gregg) mix cor (navajo prayer) LEONARD-US 50322060   (N111)

NOW OR NEVER
   (New York Voices) SSATB,S solo,perc (diff) UNC JP   (N112)

NOW THAT LOVE IS OVER
   (Meader, Darmon) SSATB,Mez solo,pno, db,drums,synthesizer (gr. III/gr. IV) UNC JP   (N113)

NU ÄR DET SOMMAR see Karkoff, Maurice

NU ÄR VÅREN HÄR see Riedel, Georg

NU TÄNDAS TUSEN JULELJUS see Ehrenborg

NU VILJUSEN TÄNT see Cederberg, Anna

...NUDO QUE ANSI JUNTÁIS... see Huber, Klaus

NUIT, LA see Schubert, Franz (Peter) see Schubert, Franz (Peter), Nacht, Die

NUIT DE L'ALLIANCE, LA see Doret, Gustave

NUIT DES QUATRE TEMPS see Doret, Gustave

NUIT D'ÉTÉ see Mozart, Wolfgang Amadeus

NUIT FORAINE, LA see Kaelin, Pierre

NUITS D'ÉTÉ see Broquet, Louis

NUKAPIANGUAQ see Hatfield, S.

NUN GEHT DER MOND DURCH WOLKENNACHT see Gersbach, Fritz

NUN LEB WOHL, DU KLEINE GASSE see Silcher, Friedrich

NUN RUHEN ALLE WÄLDER see Bach, Johann Sebastian

NUN WILL DER LENZ UNS GRÜSSEN see Müller-Zürich, Paul

NUNES, EMMANUEL (1941- )
   Vislumbre
     mix cor,acap sc RICORDI-IT SY. 3023   (N114)

NUNEZ, CAROLD
   Three Dominican Folksongs *CC3U
     treb cor BOOSEY-ENG OCTB6737 f.s.   (N115)

NUNNI, NUNNI, CHINDLI see Vollenweider, Hans

NUOVE MUSICHE, LE see Caccini, Giulio

NUOVE MUSICHE E NUOVA MANIERA DI SCRIVERLE see Caccini, Giulio

NURSERY RHYME NONSENSE see Broughton

NUTCRACKER JINGLES
   (Bridwell) cor ALEX.HSE. oct CK253112. sc CK673112   (N116)

NYHUS, ROLF (1938- )
   I Denne Jord
     4pt mix cor,acap,S solo NOTON N-9421   (N117)

   I Hallingtone
     men cor,acap NOTON N-9127   (N118)

   Min Gode, Fagre Barneheim
     4pt mix cor,acap NOTON N-9129   (N119)

   Song Til Rørosvidda
     4pt mix cor,acap NOTON N-9210   (N120)

   Vårmorgen
     4pt mix cor,acap NOTON N-9128   (N121)

NYHUS, ROLF (cont'd.)
   Ved Nyingen
     men cor,acap NOTON N-N9126   (N122)

NYNA, BUSCHELI, SCHLOF see Steiger, F.

NYSTEDT
   Cry Out And Shout
     SSATTB WARCH 40705   (N123)

NYSTROM, HAMPUS HULDT
   As The Deer
     (Wilson) SATB HOPE A 677   (N124)

# O

O BE JOYFUL see Willan, Healey

O BEAU PAYS see Heim, Ignatz

O BERGE, HOHE HEIMAT see Schmid, Walter

O CANADA see Henderson, Ruth Watson see Ridout, Godfrey

O-CHI-BA see Takenaka, Atsuhiko

O DOUX BAISERS COLOMBIN see Le Blanc, Didier

O DOUX BOCAGE see Mermoud, Robert

O DU LIEBS AENGELI, ROSMARINSTÄNGELI see Kreis, Otto

O DU WUNDERLICHE WELT see Aeschbacher, C.

O FORCE DES SAISONS see Mermoud, Robert

O FRÜHLING, WIE BIST DU SO SCHÖN see Lincke, Paul

O GIN I WERE WHERE GADIE RINS see Grainger, Percy Aldridge

O GOD OF LOVE see Corigliano, John

O GRANDS YEUX see Marenzio, Luca

O HOW AMIABLE see Vaughan Williams, Ralph

O JEANIE, THERE'S NAETHING TO FEAR YE
   (Smith, Gregg) mix cor (scottish folk song) LEONARD-US 50502130   (01)

O JOUR LE PLUS BEAU DE MA VIE see Doret, Gustave

O LACRIMOSA see Luengen, Ramona

O LET ME LIVE FOR TRUE LOVE see Tomkins, T.

O LOVELY DOVE see Laster, James

O MA GRUYÈRE see Boller, Carlo

O MA JOIE see Corboz, Michel

O MARIETTE, JOLIETTE see Bovet, J.

O MERVEILLEUSE NUIT! see Martin

O MISTRESS MINE see Holman, Derek see Larkin, Michael see Strohbach, Siegfried see Williams, Arnold

O MOISSON DE MON ENFANCE see Balissat, J.

O MON PAYS see Vuataz, Roger

O MONS PAYS see Vuataz, Roger

O MUETER, I MÖCHT DER SÄGE see Märki, Ernst

O MUSIC see Brunner

O MY DEAR HEART see Daley, Eleanor

O PETET BOURG DE PALESTINE see Martin

O SAISONS, Ô CHÂTEAUX see Surtel, Maarten

O SCHÖNE ZEIT see Füllekruss, E.

O SEI GEGRÜSST MEIN VATERLAND see Boesch, Balthasar

O SONS AND DAUGHTERS
   (Shaw And Parker) SATB,acap LEONARD-US 50304000   (02)

O TANNEBAUM
   (Smith, Gregg) SATB LEONARD-US 50481499   (03)

O TANNENBAUM
   (Shaw) TTBB,T solo,acap LEONARD-US 50305170   (04)
   (Smith, Gregg) mix cor LEONARD-US 5048   (05)

O VIEUX CLOCHER! see Haenni, G.

O VIEUX VALAIS! see Haenni, G.

O VOUS QUI REPOSEZ see Boller, Carlo

O WIE FREUN WIR UNS see Zahler, J.R.

O WIND! see Lightfoot, Mary Lynn

O WÜSST ICH DOCH DEN WEG see Graf, Albert

OBOE SOMMERSO see Pierucci, Armando

OCÉAN FAUVE, L' see Naudier

OCEAN WAS BLUE, THE see Shur, Laura

OCEAN'S SKY,THE see Rippentrop, Denice

OCHO KANDELIKAS see Jagoda, Flory

OCTOBER NOCTURNE see Matsushita, Isao

OCTOBRE see Pantillon, François see Sala, Andre

ODE À DIANE ET APOLLON see Binet, Jean

ODE À LA JEUNESSE see Naudier

ODE À LA LUMIÈRE see Naudier

ODE AU SAINT-GOTHARD see Kaelin, Pierre

ODE TO FREEDOM see Washburn, Robert Brooks

ODE TO JOY (R) see Tchaikovsky, Piotr Ilyich

ODE TO MUSIC see Williamson, Malcolm

ODE TO PEACE see Gallina

ODOR-ORGAN, THE see Mechem, Kirke Lewis

OEILLET, L' see Kaelin, Pierre

OETIKER, AUGUST (1874- )
   Aufschwung
      wom cor,acap MULLES   (06)
      men cor,acap MULLES   (07)

   D'bärnertracht
      men cor,acap MULLES   (08)

   Fähne
      men cor,acap MULLES   (09)

   Gibe Nid Ab
      wom cor,acap MULLES   (010)

   Heimat
      3-4pt wom cor MULLES   (011)
      men cor,acap MULLES   (012)

   Stets In Trure Muess I Läbe
      wom cor,acap MULLES   (013)

   Stets In Truure Muess I Läbe
      men cor,acap MULLES   (014)

   Wach Auf, Mein's Herzens Schöne
      wom cor,acap MULLES   (015)
      men cor,acap MULLES   (016)

   Wenn Alle Brünnlein Fliessen
      wom cor,acap MULLES   (017)

OEUVRES ORIGINALES ET HARMONISATIONS see Chailley, Jacques

OF A' THE AIRTS THE WIND CAN BLAW see Hatton, John Liptrot

OF LIBERTY (1976) see Wright, Maurice

OFT IN THE STILLY NIGHT see Edwards, A.H.

OGIKUBO, KAZUAKI (1953- )
   In Terra Pax *Suite
      wom cor ONGAKU 553470   (018)

   "Jomon-A I" *Suite
      "Love" men cor ONGAKU 548810   (019)

   Love
      see "Jomon-A I"

OGNI COLLE see Grimani, Maria Margherita

OGURI, KATSUHIRO (1962- )
   Furusato No Susabi
      mix cor HUG   (020)

   Kitte
      mix cor HUG   (021)

   Lacrimosa
      mix cor HUG   (022)

   Sora-Wa
      mix cor HUG   (023)

OH, DOVE! see Asakawa, Haruo, Hato Yo

OH HAPPY DAY
   (Schmutte, Pete) 2pt cor (medley containing Oh Happy Day, Dancing In The Street & Ode To Joy) WARNER C0359C5X   (024)
   (Schmutte, Pete) SATB (medley containing Oh Happy Day, Dancing In The Street & Ode To Joy) WARNER C0359C1X   (025)
   (Schmutte, Pete) SAB (medley containing Oh Happy Day, Dancing In The Street & Ode To Joy) WARNER C0359C3X   (026)

OH! IF MY MONK WOULD LIKE TO DANCE see Patriquin, Donald, Ah! Si Mon Moine Voulait Danser

OH, JOHNNY, OH! see Olman

OH, LADY BE GOOD! see Gershwin, George

OH, LOVE CAN BRING GREAT JOY see Lieben Ringt Gross Freud, Das

OH LOVELY PEACE see Handel, George Frideric

OH! QUE LA VIE EST DOUCE CHOSE... see Mayor, Ch.

OH! SUSANNA! see Foster, Stephen Collins

OHANA, MAURICE (1914-1992)
   Chimes
      see Four Choruses

   Clouds
      see Four Choruses

   Four Choruses
      treb cor (diff) PRESSER 362-03399 f.s.
      contains: Chimes; Clouds; Mayombé; Snow On The Orange Groves   (027)

   Mayombé
      see Four Choruses

   Snow On The Orange Groves
      see Four Choruses

   Tombeau De Louise Labbé, Le
      12pt mix cor,perc (O doux yeux bruns) BILLAUDOT   (028)

OHÉ HO! *CCU
   eq voices HUG 6688 f.s.   (029)

OHÉ, LE MARIÉ! see Boller, Carlo

OHNE DICH WIE LANGE see Silcher, Friedrich

ÖHRWALL, ANDERS (1932- )
   I Denna Ljuva Sommartid
      SSA SVERIG SK 699   (030)

OISEAU BLEU see Furrer, Walter

OISEAU DES BOIS see Mendelssohn-Bartholdy, Felix

OISEAU DU PRINTEMPS, L' see Boller, Carlo

OISELET, L' see Jaques-Dalcroze, Émile

OISELEUR, L' see Mermoud, Robert

OJOS DE TEMPO see Gustavino, Carlos

OKADA, SHODAI (1929- )
   Friends Hold In Their Arms Light
      mix cor HUG   (031)

OKASAKA, KEIKI (1940- )
   Kindling Of Winter
      wom cor,orch HUG   (032)

   Time-Echo In The North
      wom cor,pno HUG   (033)

OKTOBERLUCHT see Swerts, Piet

OKUMA, TAKAKO (1961- )
   Tomodachi To
      jr cor HUG   (034)

OL' MAN RIVER see Kern, Jerome

OL' TEXAS *CCU,folk song
   (Lemmermann, Heinz) 4pt mix cor FIDULA 6082 f.s.   (035)

OLD BLACK JOE see Poné, Gundaris

OLD FASHIONEED LOVE SONG, AN see Williams

OLD FOLKS AT HOME, THE see Boller, Carlo

OLD MAN VARIATIONS, THE see Bertaux

OLD MAN'S BACK IN TOWN, THE
  (Pugh, David) SATB WARNER 37940C1X
    ipa (036)
  (Pugh, David) SAB WARNER 37940C3X ipa
    (037)

OLD WEST MEDLEY
  (Hayes) SATB SHAWNEE A-1996 ipa (038)

OLIVER see Bart

OLIVER CROMWELL see Lock, W.

OLMAN
  Oh, Johnny, Oh!
    (Swingle, Ward) SSAATTBB, solo
    voices,acap (gr. III) voc pt,pts
    UNC JP SS-2X (039)

OLPEN, FRIEDRICH W.
  Hochzeitsfreude *folk song,Eur
    3pt mix cor BOHM (040)

  Johannisnacht *folk song,Eur
    3pt mix cor BOHM (041)

  Liebesschmerz *folk song,Eur
    3pt mix cor BOHM (042)

  Schöne Adler *folk song,Eur
    3pt mix cor BOHM (043)

  Sehnsucht *folk song,Eur
    3pt mix cor BOHM (044)

  Zur Hochzeit *folk song,Eur
    BOHM (045)
    SATB BOHM (046)

OLTRE LA SFERA CHE PIÙ LARGA GIRA see Castiglioni, Niccolò

OM SLARAFFENLAND see Schumann, Robert (Alexander)

OMNIA TEMPUS HABENT see Cooper, Paul

ON A STARLIT NIGHT see Gallina

ON BENDED KNEE
  (Chinn, Teena) SATB WARNER CH9581 (047)
  (Chinn, Teena) TTBB WARNER CH9582 (048)

ON DANCE LÀ-HAUT see Gesseney, L.

ON EST FAIT POUR AIMER see Haenni, G.

ON PEUT FEINDRE PAR LE CIZEAU see Le Blanc, Didier

ON THE BANKS OF ALLAN WATER
  (Dicks, E.A.) SATB BANKS 631 (049)

ON THE BEACH AT NIGHT see Smith, Gregg

ON THE WHISPERING WIND see McPheeters, T.

ON THIS DELIGHTFUL DAY see Nola, G. Domenico da

ON THIS NIGHT OF A THOUSAND STARS see Lloyd Webber, Andrew

ON WITH THE SHOW
  (Chinn, Teena) SATB (medley
    containing Cabaret, Applause & This
    Is It) WARNER CM9558 ipa (050)
  (Chinn, Teena) SAB (medley containing
    Cabaret, Applause & This Is It)
    WARNER CM9559 ipa (051)
  (Chinn, Teena) 2pt cor (medley
    containing Cabaret, Applause & This
    Is It) WARNER CM9560 ipa (052)

ONCE IN OUR LIVES see Purcell, Henry

ONCE UPON A CHRISTMAS see Strommen, Carl

ONCE UPON A CHRISTMAS TIME (from What Child)
  (Ames, Morgan) SATB,acap (gr. III)
    UNC JP (053)

ONCE UPON A DREAM see Shaw, Kirby

ONCE UPON A TIME *folk song,Jew
  (Snyder, Audrey) SATB WARNER T54610C1 (054)
  (Snyder, Audrey) SAB WARNER T54610C3 (055)
  (Wiesenberg, Menachem) 3pt wom cor/
    3pt jr cor,acap ISR.MUS.INST.
    IMI 6973 (056)

ONCE UPON A TREE see Choplin, Pepper

ONDINE see Kino, Seiichiro

ONE CANDLE LIGHTS THE WAY see Althouse, Jay

ONE DAY AT A TIME see Wilkin

ONE FOOT IN EDEN see Maw

ONE GREAT NATION see Lawrence

ONE HUNDRED WAYS see Tini, April Arabian

ONE MAN SHALL MOW MY MEADOW
  (Emlen) SATB,rec,vcl,contrabsn (med
    easy) PRESSER 392-03031 (057)

ONE MORE MOUNTAIN TO CLIMB see Koepke, Allen see Marcus

ONE MORE SONG see Strommen, Carl

ONE O'CLOCK JUMP see Basie, William (Count)

ONE SINGLE LIGHT see Perry

ONE SONG
  (Gilpin, Greg) SATB WARNER CH9570 (058)
  (Gilpin, Greg) 3pt mix cor WARNER CH9571 (059)
  (Gilpin, Greg) 2pt cor WARNER CH9572 (060)

ONE WHO STANDS ALONE, THE see Martin, Joseph M.

ONI NO KOROKU see Suzuki, Norio

ONLY YOU
  (Taylor, Peter) TTBB,T solo,perc (gr.
    II) UNC JP (061)

ONOE, KAZUHIKO (1942- )
  Song Of The Bird *ora
    jr cor&2pt mix cor,MezBar soli,orch
    HUG (062)

ONZE NOVEMBRE see Breard

OOGST-ZEE see Swerts, Piet

OPERATUNITIES see Donnelly

OPFERLIED see Beethoven, Ludwig van

OPTIMISTISCH LIED see Strategier, Herman

OR IL SE FIT SOUDAIN see Haydn, [Johann] Michael

ORAGE SUR LA MER, L' see Naudier

ORDERS see Moments In Time

O'REILLY, DERMOTT
  Children's Winter (composed with Cable)
    SA WARCH 35222 (063)

ORGAN FUGUE BWV 578 see Bach, Johann Sebastian

ORGANUM JERONIMUS see Arrigo, Girolamo

ORREGO-SALAS, JUAN A. (1919- )
  Amarilis
    see Three Madrigals

  De Los Montes Vengo
    see Romances Pastorales

  En Un Pastoral Albergue
    see Romances Pastorales

  Flores Del Romero, Las
    see Romances Pastorales

  Moça Tan Fermosa
    see Three Madrigals

  Pidiole A Narciso
    see Three Madrigals

  Romance A Lo Divino *Op.7
    [Span] SATB sc MMB X094007 (064)

  Romances Pastorales *Op.10
    [Span] SATB sc MMB X094008 f.s.
    contains: De Los Montes Vengo; En
    Un Pastoral Albergue; Flores
    Del Romero, Las (065)

  Three Madrigals *Op.62
    [Span/Eng] SATB sc MMB 094009 f.s.
    contains: Amarilis; Moça Tan
    Fermosa; Pidiole A Narciso (066)

ORTEGA
  Pues Que Me Tienes, Miguel
    (Swingle, Ward) SSAA (gr. III) voc
    pt,pts UNC JP SM-9 (067)

OS JUSTI see Takenaka, Atsuhiko

OSER, HANS (1895-1951)
  Morgenlied
    men cor,acap MULLES (068)

  Schweizergeist
    men cor,acap MULLES (069)

  Waldeinsamkeit
    men cor,acap MULLES (070)

ÖSTERREICHISCHE VOLKSLIEDER (HEFT 1)
  *CCU,folk song,Austrian
  (Anderluh, Anton) wom cor HEYN
    NR. 151 f.s. (071)

ÖSTERREICHISCHE VOLKSLIEDER (HEFT 2)
  *CCU,folk song,Austrian
  (Anderluh, Anton) wom cor HEYN
    NR. 152 f.s. (072)

OSTINAAT see Tuinen, Feike van

OTA, SAKURAKO (1958- )
  Blooming In Spring
    mix cor HUG (073)

  Breathing Earth, The
    mix cor HUG (074)

  Wish For An Everlasting Earth, A
    mix cor HUG (075)

OTHMAYR, KASPAR (1515-1553)
  Au Bord D'un Grand Verger
    mix cor HUG 7888 (076)

  Mir Ist Ein Feins Brauns Maidelein
    (Swingle, Ward) SATB,db,drums,
    synthesizer (gr. I) voc pt,pts
    UNC JP SM-7 (077)

OTONA NO MARCHEN see Mattsuoka, Toshikatsu

OÙ COURS-TU, LA BELLE? see Henchoz, Emile

OU-NO-KUNI see Niimi, Tokuhide

OU T'EN VAS-TU PETITE SOURIS ? see Severin, Marc

OUCHTERLONY
  Cheerily
    unis cor WARCH 35220 (078)

  Peter On De Sea Sea Sea
    SSA WARCH 34406 (079)
    SATB WARCH 34503 (080)

OUR GIFT FOR YOU see Estes, Jerry

OUR LIFE IS HID see Parker

OUR LOVE WHERE DID IT GO? see Schwartz, Dan

OUT OF NIGHT see Sapieyevski, Jerzy

OUT OF THE STARS see Cutter

OUVERTURE see Mermoud, Robert

OVER THE RAIONBOW
  (Snyder, Audrey) SATB WARNER T87880C1 (081)
  (Snyder, Audrey) SAB WARNER T87880C3 (082)
  (Snyder, Audrey) 2pt cor WARNER T87870C5 (083)

OVER THE RIVER AND THROUGH THE WOOD see Porterfield, Sherrie

OVERTURE TO THE MARRIAGE OF FIGARO see Mozart, Wolfgang Amadeus

OWL,THE (from Cats And Bats And Things With Wings)
  (Vogel, R.) SSAA,pno THOMAS 1C0999391 (084)

OYAMA, JUNKO (1954- )
  Bappuku-Don
    men cor,pno HUG (085)

OYSTERS AND CLAMS see Morse

OZI VEZIMRAT YAH
  (Epstein, Eleanor) [Heb] SATB,tamb,
    tofs (easy, traditional yemenite
    melody) HAZA HZ-006 (086)

## P

PABLO, LUIS DE (1930- )
  Como Moises Es El Viejo
    12pt mix cor pts ZERBONI 9496  (P1)

PAGE
  She Shall Have Music
    2pt treb cor,pno BOOSEY-ENG
      OCTB6761  (P2)

PAGE NEUVE see Reichel, Bernard

PAGH-PAAN, YOUNGHI (1945- )
  Hin-Nun
    SSMezMezAA,perc sc RICORDI-IT
      SY. 3007  (P3)

PAIN, LE see Parchet, A.

PAIX DU SOIR, LA see Reichel, Bernard

PAMPA VERDE, LA see Alem, Oscar

PAMPAMAPA see Gustavino, Carlos

PANDA see Jennings, Carolyn

PANDORE see Pantillon, François

PANTHER,DER see Zwei Tierlieder

PANTILLON, FRANÇOIS (1928- )
  Bacchanale
    men cor HUG 8489  (P4)
  Chanson À Grand Vent
    men cor HUG 8188  (P5)
  Chanson De La Douce
    mix cor HUG 8397  (P6)
  Chanson Pour Elle
    mix cor HUG 8402  (P7)
  Chansons Pour m'Amie:
    men cor HUG f.s.
      contains: Marjolaine; Rose Des
        Sables; Transjuran, J'ai Chanté
          (P8)
  Chien Et Chat
    men cor HUG 8324  (P9)
  Fumée
    men cor HUG 8233  (P10)
  Hotlogers, Les
    mix cor HUG 8232  (P11)
  Iroquois, L'
    men cor HUG 8544  (P12)
  Là-Bas, Sur La Mer
    men cor HUG 8481  (P13)
  Marjolaine
    see Chansons Pour m'Amie:
  Octobre
    men cor HUG 8394  (P14)
  Pandore
    men cor HUG 8542  (P15)
  Petit Cordonnier, Le
    men cor HUG 8215  (P16)
  Petit Vin Doux
    men cor,acap MULLES  (P17)
  Printemps Sévère
    men cor HUG 8216  (P18)
  Roi d'Yvetot, Le
    men cor HUG 8391  (P19)
  Rondo (Ich Will Singen Froh)
    men cor,acap MULLES  (P20)
  Rose Des Sables
    see Chansons Pour m'Amie:
  Transjuran, J'ai Chanté
    see Chansons Pour m'Amie:

PANTINS, LES see Moret, Oscar

PAPILLON BLEU, LE see Haenni, G.

PAPIR IZ DOCH VAIS
  (Jacobson, Joshua) TTBB&opt SSA,T
    solo (med easy, russian yiddish
    love song) HAZA HZ-014  (P21)

PAPPERT, WALTER (1936- )
  Musik, Du Bist Die Tiefste Labe
    men cor sc SCHOTTS C47687  (P22)

PÂQUERETTE see Robert-Lalouet, M.

PÂQUES see Gluck, Christoph Willibald, Ritter von

PAR CE BLEU MATIN D'ÉTÉ see Boller, Carlo

PAR-DESSUS LA CLÔTURE see Boller, Carlo

PAR JEU! see Bovet, J.

PAR UN BEAU JOUR DE MAI... see Boller, Carlo

PARADE OF THE WOODEN SOLDIERS see Jessel, Leon

PARADISO see Aracil, Alfredo

PARANA EN UNA ZAMBA,EL see Ramirez, Ariel

PARANJOTI
  Dravidian Dithyramb
    SATB (phonetic text) EARTHSNG ES-42
      (P23)

PARAPLYBOKEN see Høybye, John

PARCHET, A.
  Chant Norvégien
    men cor HUG 6432  (P24)
  Lorsqu'avril Apparaîtra
    mix cor HUG 8249  (P25)
  Pain, Le
    men cor HUG 8248  (P26)
  Valais, Mon Beau Valais
    men cor HUG 7918  (P27)
  Vent Du Nord, Le
    men cor HUG 7913  (P28)

PARDON DE MADELEINE, LE see Bovet, J.

PARDONNEZ-MOI see Sala, Andre

PARI, LE see Henchoz, Emile

PARIAS, LES see Breard

PARKE
  Ferryman-Who's That Knocking
    unis cor WARCH 34346  (P29)

PARKER
  Our Life Is Hid
    SATB LAWSON 4-52624  (P30)

PARKER, ALICE (1925- )
  Earth Woman
    see Hollering Sun
  Hollering Sun
    SATB,acap LAWSON f.s.
      contains: Earth Woman; Prayer;
        Quiet; Sky Family; Together
          (P31)
  Prayer
    see Hollering Sun
  Quiet
    see Hollering Sun
  Sky Family
    see Hollering Sun
  Together
    see Hollering Sun

PARKER, HORATIO WILLIAM (1863-1919)
  Alice Brand *Op.76
    SSA, solo voices,pno RECITAL 447
      (P32)
  Ballad Of A Knight And His Daughter, The *Op.6
    SATB, solo quartet voc sc RECITAL 436  (P33)
  Dreamking And His Love *Op.31
    [Ger/Eng] SATB,T solo,orch voc sc
      RECITAL 440  (P34)
  Harold Harfager *Op.26
    SATB,A solo,pno RECITAL 439  (P35)
  Idylle *Op.15
    [Ger/Eng] SATB,TB soli voc sc
      RECITAL 437  (P36)
  King Gorm The Grim *Op.64
    SATB,orch voc sc RECITAL 444  (P37)
  Kobolds,The *Op.21
    SATB,orch voc sc RECITAL 438  (P38)
  Leap Of Roushan Beg,The *Op.75
    men cor,T solo voc sc RECITAL 446
      (P39)
  Seven Greek Pastoral Scenes *Op.74
    SSAA,SA soli,ob, harp & strings or
      piano voc sc RECITAL 435  (P40)
  Song Of Times,A *Op.73
    SATB,S solo voc sc RECITAL 445
      (P41)

PARKER, HORATIO WILLIAM (cont'd.)
  Spirit Of Beauty *Op.61
    TTBB,orch/band voc sc RECITAL 443
      (P42)
  Star Song,A *Op.54
    cor, solo quartet, orch. voc sc
      RECITAL 442  (P43)

PARODI,TENESA
  Pedro Canoero
    (Pace, Daniel Di) 2-3pt cor LAGOS
      (P44)

PAROLE DA BECKETT see Manzoni, Giacomo

PARRY
  Seven Partsongs *CC7L
    mix cor FABER 51380 8  (P45)

PARRY, [SIR] CHARLES HUBERT HASTINGS (1848-1918)
  Jerusalem
    (Smith, Gregg) SATB LEONARD-US
      50481500  (P46)

PARTING KISS,THE see Pinsuti, Ciro

PARTIR N'EST PAS MOURIR UN PEU see Miche, Paul

PAS PLUS HAUT QUE TROIS POMMES see Henchoz, Emile

PASCANU, ALEXANDRU
  Chindia
    SATB,acap SANTA SBMP 44  (P47)

PASQUIER, MARIUS
  Ce N'est Qu'une Chanson Qui Passe
    mix cor HUG 8395  (P48)
  Chandelle, La
    3 eq voices HUG 8398  (P49)
  Chanson De L'eau
    3 eq voices HUG 8383  (P50)
  Complainte
    mix cor HUG 8771  (P51)
  Lac Et La Vigne, Le
    3 eq voices HUG 8399  (P52)
  Lune, Lune, Triste Lune
    3 eq voices HUG 8548  (P53)
  Mon École Est Toute En Verre
    3 eq voices HUG 8559  (P54)
  Musique
    3 eq voices HUG 8549  (P55)
  Perplexité
    eq voices HUG 7971  (P56)
  Va-T-En Guerre, Le
    men cor HUG 8558  (P57)
  Vallée, La
    men cor HUG 8484  (P58)

PASS DE DEUX see Libonati, Dana

PASSANI, EMILE (1905-1974)
  Bestiaire Et L'herbier, Le (from
    Chantefables Et Chantefleurs) CCU
    4 eq voices BILLAUDOT f.s.  (P59)

PASSERBY,A see Adams, Byron

PASSEREAU
  Il Est Bel Et Bon
    (Swingle, Ward) SATB,db,drums,
      synthesizer (gr. III) voc pt,pts
      UNC JP SM-1  (P60)

PASSION, THE see Yanai, Kazumi

PASTICHE QUBECOIS see Cable, Howard

PASTIME WITH GOOD COMPANY see Henry VIII, King of England

PASTOR
  Chant De La Paix, Le
    4pt men cor BILLAUDOT  (P61)

PASTORALE GRUÉRIENNE see Boller, Carlo

PASTOURELLE, LA see Doret, Gustave

PAT-A-PAN-FUM, FUM
  (Kern) SATB,opt fl&perc ALFRED 11307
    (P62)

PÂTRE DU JURA, LE see Moudon, E.

PATRIOTIC FESTIVAL, A
  (Williams) 2pt cor ALFRED 4349  (P63)
  (Williams) 3pt mix cor ALFRED 4348
    (P64)

PATRIQUIN, DONALD
  Ah! Si Mon Moine Voulait Danser (from
    Songs Of Early Canada)
    "Oh! If My Monk Would Like To
    Dance" [Fr] SATB,pno EARTHSNG
    ES-46  (P65)

PATRIQUIN, DONALD (cont'd.)
  Innoria (from Songs Of Early Canada)
    SATB,pno EARTHSNG ES-46   (P66)

  J'entends Le Moulin
    [Fr] SATB,pno EARTHSNG ES-6  (P67)

  Oh! If My Monk Would Like To Dance
    see Ah! Si Mon Moine Voulait Danser

  Savory, Sage, Rosemary And Thyme
    (from Songs Of Early Canada)
    SATB,pno EARTHSNG ES-46   (P68)

PATTERSON
  Spare Parts
    SATB WARCH 30529   (P69)

PAULUS, STEPHEN HARRISON (1949-   )
  Cats, Friends And Lovers
    wom cor EUR.AM.MUS. EA00744  (P70)

PAUVRE AVEUGLE see DuBois, Pierre-Max

PAUVRE CIGALE see Canteloube, Joseph

PAUVRE HOMME REVENANT DU BOIS, UN see Boller, Carlo

PAVANE see Anonymous

PAVANE DES PINGOUINS, LA see Bovet, J.

PAYS, UN see Mermoud, Robert

PAYS DU LAC see Boller, Carlo

PAYS ÉCOUTE! see Boller, Carlo

PAYS, TERRE ARDENTE see Daetwyler, Jean

PAYS, TU ES COMME UNE COUPE CLAIRE see Boller, Carlo

PAYSAGE see Martin

PAYSAGE PROVENÇAL see Chillemont

PAYSAN, PRÉPARE TA TERRE! see Miche, Paul

PAYSAN, QUE TON CHANT S'ÉLÈVE see Bovet, J.

PEACE see Crawley, Clifford see Silver, Horace

PEACE ON EARTH see Schoenberg, Arnold

PEARCE, MALCOLM
  Always It's Spring (from E.E. Cummings) cant
    SATB,brass quin/org CAMDEN  (P71)

  Madrigals On The River
    SATB,acap CAMDEN CM045  (P72)

PEARSON, WILLIAM DEAN (1905-   )
  Horn,The
    unis cor BANKS 1255  (P73)

PECCI, TOMASO (1576-ca. 1606)
  First Book Of Madrigals For Five Voices (1602) *CC21U
    (Foxe, Wilfred) 5pt cor ANTICO AE34 f.s.  (P74)

PÊCHEURS, LES see Boller, Carlo

PÊCHEURS DE GROIX, LES see Aubanel, Georges

PEDRO CANOERO see Parodi,Tenesa

PÈLERIN DE LA MONTAGNE see Falquet, Rene

PELZ, WALTER L. (1926-   )
  Love Is Here To Stay
    TTBB,kbd MORN.ST. MSM-50-9753  (P75)

PENDANT L'ABSENCE see Mendelssohn-Bartholdy, Felix

PENGUIN see Jennings, Carolyn

PENNINGTON, CHESTER
  Light Of The Morning
    SATB KJOS 8767  (P76)

PENROSE, P.
  Hills Of England
    unis cor BANKS 1200  (P77)

PEOPLE LOOK EAST see Evans, Robert

PERCE-NEIGE, LES see Bovet, J.

PERDER, KJELL (1954-   )
  Wings As Eagles
    mix cor,3perc STIM  (P78)

PERLMUTTER, AARON
  Lebn Zol Columbus
    [Yiddish] SATB,A solo,pno (med easy) HAZA HZ-049  (P79)

PÉRONNELLE, LA see Canteloube, Joseph

PERPLEXITÉ see Pasquier, Marius

PERRY
  Beggar's Song, The
    TTB SHAWNEE C-0285  (P80)

  Calypso Carol (composed with Pote)
    SAB/SA/TB,opt fl&perc HOPE AD 2052  (P81)

  German Lullaby
    2pt cor SHAWNEE EA-0201  (P82)

  Jubilate, Sing Joyfully
    SAB SHAWNEE D-457  (P83)

  One Single Light
    2pt cor ALFRED 5830  (P84)

  Two Latin Choruses From Amadeus
    2pt cor SHAWNEE EA-183 ipa  (P85)

  Your SSA Choir
    SSA SHAWNEE GB-5003  (P86)

PERRY, DAVE
  Freedom's Song (composed with Perry, Jean)
    3pt mix cor,opt solo HERITAGE 15-1098  (P87)

PERSIANI, I see Respighi, Ottorino

PESSON, CH.
  Heimweh
    mix cor HUG 2806  (P88)
    men cor HUG 2989  (P89)

PETER ON DE SEA SEA SEA see Ouchterlony

PETETE RUE, LA see Martin

PETHEL, STANLEY (1950-   )
  Carry The Light
    SATB HOPE GC 955  (P90)

PETIT ARC-EN-CIEL, LE see Hagiwara, Hidehico

PETIT BOSSU, LE see Martin

PETIT CHALUTIER DU CIEL, LE see Henchoz, Emile

PETIT COEUR see Bovet, J.

PETIT CORDONNIER, LE see Pantillon, François

PETIT D'HOMME, LES YEUX VIFS see Mermoud, Robert

PETIT GAS, LE see Boller, Carlo

PETIT JARDIN PLEIN D'OMBRE see Doret, Gustave

PETIT JARDINIER, LE see Doret, Gustave

PETIT MITRON, LE see Fevrier, Henri

PETIT PIERROT, LE see Jouineau, Jacques

PETIT PORT BRETON,LE see Body

PETIT ROI D'ANGLETERRE, LE see Jouineau, Jacques

PETIT SAVOIR-VIVRE see Henchoz, Emile

PETIT SOLDAT see Boller, Carlo, Galé Chudâ

PETIT TRAIN, LE see Mermoud, Robert

PETIT VILLAGE, LE see Jaques-Dalcroze, Émile see Mermoud, Robert

PETIT VILLE, LA see Mermoud, Robert

PETIT VIN DOUX see Pantillon, François

PETITE CANTATE RHODANIENNE see Daetwyler, Jean

PETITE CHANSON see Boller, Carlo

PETITE DANSEUSE DE BALLET, LA see Mermoud, Robert

PETITE ÉGLISE DE CHEZ NOUS see Boller, Carlo

PETITE GILBERTE DE COURGENAY,LA
  (Gand-Kreis-Märki) men cor,acap MULLES  (P91)
  see Märki, Ernst

PETITE MARCHE DU PRINTEMPS see Lang, H.

PETITE MARJOLAINE see Bovet, J.

PETITE SOEUR EN FLEURS see Bron, Patrick

PETITE SUITE GENEVOISE see Delor

PETITE SUITE ROMANDE see Falquet, Rene

PETITE VALLÉE see Martin

PETITE VILLE DU DIMANCHE see Delannoy, Marcel

PETITE VIOLETTE see Humblot

PETITS AIRS, LES see Boller, Carlo

PETITS CHEVRIERS, LES see Bovet, J.

PETITS GLANEURS, LES see Binet, Jean

PETKER, ALLAN R.
  Choral Skills #1 & 2
    2pt mix cor BOCK BG0511  (P92)

  Choral Skills #2
    SATB BOCK BG0510  (P93)

PETRARCA SUITE see Bergman, Erik

PETRASSI, GOFFREDO (1904-   )
  Mottetti Per La Passione
    mix cor,acap ZERBONI 6533  (P94)

  Nonsense
    [It/Eng] mix cor,acap ZERBONI 4924  (P95)
    [Eng] mix cor,opt pno ZERBONI 6707  (P96)

  Sesto Non-Senso
    mix cor,acap ZERBONI 6531  (P97)

PETTI
  A La Claire Fontaine
    SATB WARCH 34485  (P98)

PETTI, ANTHONY
  A La Claire Fontaine
    SATB THOMP.G VG421  (P99)

PETTY HARBOUR BAIT SKIFF, THE (from When The Outports Sing)
  (Telfer) SSA KJOS 6226  (P100)

PEUPLE, SOIS FORT! see Kodály, Zoltán

PFAUTSCH
  Fancy
    SSA LAWSON 4-52640  (P101)

PFAUTSCH, LLOYD ALVIN (1921-   )
  Life Has Many Rhythms
    SATB,org/pno LAWSON 52676  (P102)

  Love's Antiphon
    SSAATTBB DEAN 15-1047  (P103)

  My Heart
    see Three Songs

  My Native Land
    see Three Songs

  My Younger Years
    see Three Songs

  Three Songs
    LAWSON f.s.
    contains: My Heart (TTBB,pno); My Native Land (TTBB,pno); My Younger Years (TTBB,acap)  (P104)

PFEIL, H.
  Fahr Wohl, Du Schöner Maientraum
    men cor,acap MULLES  (P105)

PHANTASIE, DU JUGENDSCHÖNE see Huber, Walter Simon

PHANTOM OF THE OPERA, THE see Lloyd Webber, Andrew

PHARAMOND see Naudier

PHAUDRIG CROHOORE see Stanford, Charles Villiers

PHILIDOR
  A Chanter, Rire Et Boire...
    men cor HUG 6429  (P106)

PHILLIPS, HENRY
  To Our Next Merry Meeting
    (Dicks, E.A.) SATB BANKS 624  (P107)

PIAGET, ADA MAY
  Allons Pêcher Le Poisson
    mix cor HUG 8340  (P108)

  Boîte À Musique
    men cor,opt pno/org/orch HUG 8339  (P109)

PIAGET, ADA MAY (cont'd.)
   Mon Pays
     men cor HUG 7937          (P110)

PIANTO see Roxburgh, Edwin

PIANTO DELLA TERRA, IL see Pratali, Marino

PICK A BALE OF COTTON
   (Childs) 2pt cor SHAWNEE EA-165
                          (P111)

PICK UP THE EARTH see Schudel, Thomas

PIDIOLE A NARCISO see Orrego-Salas, Juan A.

PIDOUX, E.
   Mon Pèr' N'veut Pas...
     mix cor HUG 8615         (P112)

PIÈCE VOCALE SUR DES TEXTES DU 3E DIMANCHE DE CARÊME see Marie, Jean Étienne

PIEL CANELA
   (Belan, W.) SATB THOMAS 1C0859303
                          (P113)
   see Capo,B.

PIERCE, (ANNE) ALEXANDRA (1934- )
   Jaberwocky
     SATB,pno HILD study sc 09504A, cor pts 09504B       (P114)

   Report To God
     SATB,pno SEESAW          (P115)

PIERPONT, JAMES (1822-1893)
   Dashing Through The Snow
     (Leavitt, John) 2pt cor WARNER SV9507              (P116)

   Jingle Bells
     (Ohrwall, Anders) mix cor,acap SVERIG SK 782         (P117)

PIERRES MILLIAIRES ET FEUX FOLLETS see Danieli, Irlando

PIERSON, HENRY HUGO (1815-1873)
   Ye Mariners Of England
     SATB BANKS 665           (P118)

PIERUCCI, ARMANDO (1935- )
   Ancora Dell'inferno
     see Tre Cori

   Oboe Sommerso
     see Tre Cori

   Preghiera Alla Pioggia
     see Tre Cori

   Tre Cori
     SATB BERBEN BERBEN 1829 f.s. text by Quasimodo
     contains: Ancora Dell'inferno; Oboe Sommerso; Preghiera Alla Pioggia     (P119)

PIFFERARI, LES see Delibes, Léo

PIGEON VOLE! see Bron, Patrick

PIKA DON see Kobashi, Minoru

PILEUR, G.
   Aubade
     mix cor HUG 6794         (P120)
     men cor HUG 6793         (P121)

PILLON
   A Nous Le Bel Âge
     2 eq voices BILLAUDOT   (P122)

PIM-PIM
   Dalpolska
     (Sund, Robert) mix cor,acap SVERIG SK 772          (P123)

PINSON DU BOIS, LE see Kieslich, L.

PINSUTI, CIRO (1829-1888)
   Parting Kiss,The
     SATB BANKS 280           (P124)

   Spring Song,A
     SATB BANKS 463           (P125)

PINTIER, LE see Zbinden, Julien-François

PIONEERS,THE see Gwynne, Una

PIPER AND THE CHIMING PEAS see Anderson, William H.

PIPER O' DUNDEE, THE see Clark, Derek J.

PIPPA'S SONG see Borishansky, Elliot

PIQUE LA BALEINE see Boller, Carlo see Dutilleux, Henri

PITFIELD, THOMAS BARON (1903- )
   Four Choral Miniatures
     SATB,pno BARDIC BD 0417 (P126)

   Night Music
     4-6pt mix cor,acap BARDIC BD 0422                  (P127)

PIZZETTI, ILDEBRANDO (1880-1968)
   De Profundis
     7pt mix cor sc RICORDI-IT 124102                   (P128)

   Musiche Per "La Nave" Di G. D'annunzio
     cor,3.3.0.1. 4.4.0.0. timp,perc, org,3harp sc RICORDI-IT 131326                   (P129)

PLANEL, JEAN
   Aviron, L'
     4 eq voices BILLAUDOT   (P130)

   Belle Françoise, La (from Dix Chansons Populaires De France)
     3pt jr cor BILLAUDOT    (P131)

   Cantate D'Elisabeau
     4 eq voices BILLAUDOT   (P132)

   Dix Chansons Populaires De France, En Deux Cahiers *CC10U
     3pt jr cor BILLAUDOT f.s. (P133)

   Faucheurs, Les
     3pt jr cor BILLAUDOT    (P134)

   Mon Père Avait Cinq Cent Moutons
     3pt jr cor BILLAUDOT    (P135)

   Sur Le Pont D'avignon (from Dix Chansons Populaires De France)
     3pt jr cor BILLAUDOT    (P136)

   Voici La Saint-Jean (from Dix Chansons Populaires De France)
     3pt jr cor BILLAUDOT    (P137)

PLANTING OF THE APPLE TREE, THE see Sowash, Rick

PLANTONS LA VIGNE see Jaques-Dalcroze, Émile

PLASTIC ARTS OF CLAY, THE see Kobayashi, Arata

PLAY WITH CHILDREN'S PLAY see Mori, Konate

PLAYROOMS see Farrell, Jim

PLEASANT SIMMER OVER see Graham, R.

PLORATUS see Dallapiccola, Luigi

PLOT AGAINST THE GIANT,THE (CANATATA I) see Westergaard, Peter

PLUMHOF, H.
   Chanson Des Étoiles, La
     men cor HUG 4316         (P138)

PODBERTSKY, TH.
   Tief Ist Die Mühle Verschneit
     men cor,acap MULLES     (P139)

POEM IN PRAISE OF NAGASAKI, A see Mikami, Jiro

POÈME DES FLEURS,LE see Massenet, Jules

POESIA DI NATALE, UNA see Rossellini, Renzo

POESIE DI TIZIANA see Bettinelli, Bruno

POÉSIES see Marie, Jean Étienne

POÈTE, LE see Apotheloz, Jean

POÈTE EST PASSÉ PAR LÀ, LE (from Terre Et L'étoile, La)
   mix cor HUG 8848           (P140)

POET'S SONG, THE see Dello Joio, Norman

POLANSKY, DAVID
   Hanukah Tarantella
     [Eng] SATB,pno (med) HAZA HZ-035                   (P141)

POLITTICO see Bellucci, Giacomo

POLKA see Sutermeister, Heinrich

POLONIUS PLATITUDES,THE see London, Edwin

POLYPHONIC MUSIC OF THE FOURTEENTH CENTURY
   (Schrade, Harrison, Von Fischer, Bent) OISEAU CS1 f.s. in 25 vols                         (P142)

POMMIER, LE see Delibes, Léo

PONCHIELLI, AMILCARE (1834-1886)
   Ballabile (from Figliuol Prodigo, Il)
     cor,orch RICORDI-IT      (P143)

PONÉ, GUNDARIS (1932-1994)
   Battle Cry Of Freedom, The
     see Five American Songs

   Camptown Races, De
     see Five American Songs

   Columbia, The Gem Of The Ocean
     see Five American Songs

   Five American Songs
     SATB,pno sc MMB X094010 f.s. also available on rental for medium voice or chorus and chamber orchestra
     contains: Battle Cry Of Freedom, The; Camptown Races, De; Columbia, The Gem Of The Ocean; Old Black Joe; Tenting Tonight       (P144)

   Old Black Joe
     see Five American Songs

   Tenting Tonight
     see Five American Songs

PONS
   Chant Des Peuples, Le
     4pt mix cor BILLAUDOT    (P145)

   Printemps Fleuri
     4pt men cor BILLAUDOT    (P146)

PONY OF STAR, A see Yanagida, Takayoshi

PONY-POLONAISE see Klein, Richard Rudolf

POOR LITTLE GIRLS OF ONTARIO see Henderson, Ruth Watson

POPCORN see Henderson, Ruth Watson see Lawrence, Stephen L.

POR QUE LLORAX
   (Braun, Yehezkel-Jacobson, Joshua) SATB,pno (med easy, text in Ladino) HAZA HZ-021            (P147)

PORT, LE see Mermoud, Robert

PORTER, COLE (1892-1964)
   It's All Right With Me
     (Swingle, Ward) SSAATTBB,solo voice,acap (gr. IV) voc pt,pts UNC JP SS-6             (P148)

   Night And Day
     (Schmutte, Pete) SAB WARNER WBCH9415               (P149)
     (Schmutte, Pete) SATB WARNER WBCH9414               (P150)

PORTERFIELD, SHERRIE
   Blow, Blow, Thou Winter Wind
     TTB/TBB WARNER SV9430   (P151)

   Ding Dong! Merrily On High
     3pt mix cor,pno HERITAGE 15-1184H                 (P152)

   Linden Tree, The
     SSA HERITAGE 15-1039    (P153)

   Measure Me, Sky
     SSA WARNER SV9515      (P154)

   Over The River And Through The Wood
     2pt cor HERITAGE 15-1015 (P155)

   Power Of Music,The
     SATB WARNER SV9306     (P156)

   Something Told The Wild Geese
     2pt cor HERITAGE H5890   (P157)
     SATB,pno HERITAGE 15-1202H (P158)
     TTB HERITAGE 15-1203H   (P159)
     3pt mix cor HERITAGE 15-1025 (P160)

   Stars
     3pt mix cor,pno HERITAGE 15-1090                 (P161)

   Swing Low, Sweet Chariot
     3pt mix cor,pno HERITAGE 15-1179H                (P162)

   Thoughts In The Night
     2pt cor, optional toy piano HERITAGE 15-1169H             (P163)

   White Moon, The
     SATB WARNER SV9526     (P164)

   Who Has Seen The Wind?
     2pt cor,pno HERITAGE 15-1014 (P165)

   Winter Carol
     SATB ALFRED 5767         (P166)
     SSA,opt inst ALFRED 5768 (P167)

   Ye Shall Have A Song
     SATB ALFRED 11604        (P168)
     3pt cor ALFRED 11605    (P169)

PORTERFIELD, SHERRIE (cont'd.)
Your Friend Shall Be The Tall Wind
3pt mix cor,pno HERITAGE 15-1166H
(P170)
2pt cor HERITAGE H5871 (P171)

PORTEUR DE JOURNAUX, LE see Marcel, J.M. see Martin

PORTEUR D'EAU, LE see Apotheloz, Jean

POSTLUDIO DEGLI SPETTATORI see Hoch, Francesco

POTE
New Song, A
SATB HOPE A 685 (P172)

POULE BLANCHE, UNE see Jouineau, Jacques

POUR AVOIR MA FIN ASSURÉE see Le Blanc, Didier

POUR BÂTIR UNE MAISON see Kaelin, Pierre

POUR CHANTER LE PAYS see Martin

POUR ÊTRE HEUREUX see Binet, Jean

POUR LA PAIX see Xenakis, Yannis (Iannis)

POUR LE RIRE D'UN ENFANT see Giner, Bruno

POUR PARLER À NOS COEURS see Miche, Paul

POUR TOI MA BONNE MÈRE see Boieldieu, François-Adrien

POUR TOI, PAYS see Mermoud, Robert

POUR TROUVER UN COEUR PUR see Reichel, Bernard

POUR UN MARIAGE see Henchoz, Emile

POUR UN NOUVEL ÉLU see Krauer, A

POUR UN SEUL MOT see Denereaz, Alexandre

POURQUOI JE CHANTE see Haenni, G.

POURQUOI ME QUITTER? see Rochat, Jean

POURQUOI N'ÊTRE PAS GAI? see Bovet, J.

POUSSEUR, HENRI (1929- )
Etoile Des Langues, L'
mix cor,narrator,acap ZERBONI 9385
(P173)

POWER OF MUSIC,THE see Porterfield, Sherrie

POYA, LA (LA MONTÉE À L'ALPAGE see Bovet, J.

PRADO, JOSÉ-ANTONIO (ALMEIDA) (1943- )
Alegoria Buffa
SATB,inst SEESAW (P174)

Canticos de Amor
SATB SEESAW (P175)

Celebratio Americae
SATB SEESAW (P176)

Celebratio Amoris
SATB,gtr SEESAW (P177)

Ciranda
SA SEESAW (P178)

Letter from Patmos
SATB,S solo,org,3trp,2horn,2trom, perc SEESAW (P179)

Therese, L'amour de Dieu
SATB,2 solo voices,1.1.1.1. 2.2.1.0. perc,strings SEESAW
(P180)

Villegagnon
SATB,SB&2 narrators,2.2.2.2. 3.4.3.0. strings SEESAW (P181)

PRAETORIUS, MICHAEL (1571-1621)
A Toi Mon Coeur
mix cor HUG 1852 (P182)

Aubade Sur Le Fleuve
mix cor HUG 6048 (P183)
men cor HUG 3655 (P184)

Ecoutez La Nouvelle
mix cor HUG 1926 (P185)

Je Viens À Vous Du Haut Des Cieux
mix cor HUG 1903 (P186)

PRAISE YE THE LORD see Kernis, Aaron Jay

PRARIE, THE see Raum, Elizabeth

PRATALI, MARINO
Pianto Della Terra, Il
men cor sc RICORDI-IT 131589 (P187)

PRAYER see Parker, Alice

PREAMBULE see Bach, Johann Sebastian

PREGHIERA ALLA PIOGGIA see Pierucci, Armando

PRÉLUDE see Bovet, J.

PRELUDE 2 see Lyons,Bill

PRELUDE IN C MAJOR see Bach, Johann Sebastian

PRELUDE IN F MINOR see Bach, Johann Sebastian

PRELUDE NO. 9 see Bach, Johann Sebastian

PRELUDE NO. 19 see Bach, Johann Sebastian

PRELUDE NO. 22 see Bach, Johann Sebastian

PRELUDE NO. 24 see Bach, Johann Sebastian

PREMIER PRINTEMPS see Mendelssohn-Bartholdy, Felix

PREMIÈRE FLEUR, LA see Martin

PRENONS-LE, C'EST LE BLANC CHEMIN see Boller, Carlo

PREPARED STATEMENT; WITH REGARD TO, THE see Lindroth, Peter

PRÈS DE LA FORÊT see Boller, Carlo

PRÉSAGE DU PRINTEMPS see Mendelssohn-Bartholdy, Felix

PRESENT TIME see Holman, Derek

PRESQU'UNE CHANSON see Miche, Paul

PRESSOIR, LE see Doret, Gustave

PRESTO see Marcello, Benedetto see Telemann, Georg Philipp

PRETTY SARO
(Gill, Randall) SATB,pno (appalachian folk song) SANTA SBMP 91 (P188)

PRICE
Let It Shine! (composed with Besig)
2pt cor SHAWNEE EA-173 (P189)

Mem'ries (composed with Besig)
SATB SHAWNEE A-1995 (P190)

Say It With A Song! (composed with Besig)
SATB SHAWNEE A-1989 (P191)

We Will Sing! (composed with Besig)
2pt cor SHAWNEE EA-0195 (P192)

PRIÈRE, LA see Gluck, Christoph Willibald, Ritter von

PRIÈRE À LA FENÊTRE, LA see Miche, Paul

PRIÈRE À L'ALTAÏ see Mermoud, Robert

PRIÈRE D'AUTOMNE see Miche, Paul

PRIÈRE DES MAYENTZETS see Boller, Carlo

PRIÈRE DU GUEUX, LA see Kodály, Zoltán

PRIÈRE DU LOUP see Corboz, Michel

PRIÈRE DU MOINEAU see Corboz, Michel

PRIÈRE DU PÂTRE, LA see Bovet, J.

PRIÈRE DU PETIT ÉCUREUIL see Corboz, Michel

PRIÈRE DU RÜTLI see Doret, Gustave

PRIÈRE PATRIOTIQUE see Jaques-Dalcroze, Émile

PRIÈRE POUR DEMANDER UNE ÉTOILE see Veretti, Antonio

PRIÈRE POUR LES MORTS see Boller, Carlo

PRIMAVERA see Kreis, Otto

PRIMO LIBRO DE MADRIGALI A SEI VOCI, IL see Gabrieli, Andrea

PRIMO LIBRO DEI MADRIGALI, IL see Frescobaldi, Girolamo

PRIMO LIBRO DELLE *CCU
(Materassi, M. Giustiniane, Il) 3pt cor,acap ZERBONI 8911 f.s. by various composers (P193)

PRIMO LIBRO DI MADRIGALI A CINQUE VOCI, IL see Gabrieli, Andrea

PRINTEMPS see Liszt, Franz see Schubert, Franz (Peter) see Weber, Carl Maria von

PRINTEMPS, LE see Mendelssohn-Bartholdy, Felix

PRINTEMPS, LE (INVOCATION Á PALÈS) see Doret, Gustave

PRINTEMPS FLEURI see Pons

PRINTEMPS N'A POINT TANT DE FLEURS, LE see Geoffray, Cesar

PRINTEMPS SÉVÈRE see Pantillon, François

PRINTZ, BRAD
Down By The Riverside
2pt cor HERITAGE 15-012 (P194)
3pt mix cor HERITAGE 15-1023 (P195)

Shenandoah
3pt mix cor,pno HERITAGE 15-1021
(P196)

PRO PHUNDO BASSO see Bliss, P. Paul

PROLOGUE FROM "MEFISTOFELE" (I-E) see Boito, Arrigo

PROMÉTHÉE see Naudier

PROMETHEUS (1983) see Antoniou, Theodore

PROMPTEMENT LEVEZ-VOUS see Henderson, Ruth Watson

PROPHECY OF PEACE, A see Adler, Samuel Hans

PROSPERI, CARLO (1921- )
Col Fratello, A Settignano
see Tre Canti Di Betocchi

Di Notte
see Tre Canti Di Betocchi

Nell'orto
see Tre Canti Di Betocchi

Tre Canti Di Betocchi
cor,3fl sc RICORDI-IT 131627 f.s.
contains: Col Fratello, A Settignano; Di Notte; Nell'orto
(P197)

PROVERBS see Braun, Yeheskiel

PSALMIST'S MEDITATION, THE see Dello Joio, Norman

PSAUME XVII see Doret, Gustave

P'TIT SOLDAT D'CI, P'TIT SOLDAT D'LÀ! see Miche, Paul

P'TIT'S FILL'S, LES see Gesseney, Andre

PU WIJNUEJ WE FYP see Xenakis, Yannis (Iannis)

PUES QUE ME TIENES, MIGUEL see Ortega

PUFF (THE MAGIC DRAGON) see Yarrow, Peter

PURCELL, HENRY (1658 or 59-1695)
Caught In The Act
(Hagemann, P) 3-4pt men cor,acap LAURN CH-1084 f.s. four catches contains: Fie, Nay, Prithee, John; If All Be True; Once In Our Lives; 'Tis Woman Makes Us Love (P198)

Come, Follow Me (from Purcell's King Arthur)
SSATB KJOS 8764 (P199)

Come Ye Sons Of Art
mix cor,vln I,vln II,vla,vcl,2ob, 2trp,timp (birthday song for Queen Mary (1694)) KING'S sc, pts
(P200)

Dido And Aeneas
mix cor, solo voices,vln I,vln II, vla,db sc KING'S (P201)

Fairy Queen,The
cor,vln I,vln II,vla,db,2rec,2ob, 2trp,timp, (ten.ob, bsn. ad lib)

PURCELL, HENRY (cont'd.)
   KING'S sc, cor pts, pts    (P202)
  Fie, Nay, Prithee, John
    see Caught In The Act
  Hail, Bright Cecilia!
    cor,vln I,vln II,vla,db,2rec,2ob,
    2trp,timp (song for St. Cecilia's
    Day, 1692) KING'S sc, cor pts,
    pts    (P203)
  If All Be True
    see Caught In The Act
  In Guilty Night (from Saul And The
    Witch Of Endor)
    SAB/STB,cont KING'S    (P204)
  In These Delightful Pleasant Groves
    (Robinson) 3pt cor ALFRED 11342    (P205)
    (Thompson) SATB,acap (med easy)
    PRESSER 392-41777    (P206)
  Indian Queen,The
    cor, solo voices,vln I,vln II,vla,
    db,2rec, 2ob (ten.ob), bsn, trp,
    timp KING'S sc, cor pts, pts    (P207)
  My Beloved Spake
    SATBB,ATBB/TTBB soli,vln I,vln II,
    vla,db,cont KING'S sc, pts (P208)
  Now Does The Glorious Day Appear
    cor,vln I,vln II,vln III/vla I,vla
    II,db (ode for Queen Mary's
    birthday (1689)) KING'S sc, pts    (P209)
  Once In Our Lives
    see Caught In The Act
  Shepherd, Shepherd (from King Arthur)
    (Meredith) SA KJOS 6233    (P210)
  They That Go Down To The Sea In Ships
    SAB/TB,ATB soli,vln I,vln II,db,
    cont KING'S sc, cor pts, pts    (P211)
  'Tis Woman Makes Us Love
    see Caught In The Act
  Welcome To All Pleasures
    cor,vln I,vln II,vla,db (ode for
    St. Cecelia's day (1683)) KING'S
    sc, cor pts, pts    (P212)
  When On My Sick Bed I Languish
    TTB/TBarB,cont KING'S sc, pts    (P213)
PURVIS
  What Strangers Are These?
    SSAA/TTBB WARCH 40734    (P214)

# Q

QUAND? see Mermoud, Robert

QUAND J'ESPROUVE EN AIMANT LA RIGUEUR D'UNE DAME see Le Blanc, Didier

QUAND LA BELLE S'EN FUT AU BOIS see Lacroix

QUAND LA FEUILLE ÉTAIT VERTE see Canteloube, Joseph

QUAND LA MARIE see Lagger, Oscar

QUAND LE BERGER SORT SON TROUPEAU see Canteloube, Joseph

QUAND LE MAI VA V'NIR see Jaques-Dalcroze, Émile

QUAND MA MÈRE CHANTAIT see Bovet, J.

QUAND MÊME see Jaques-Dalcroze, Émile

QUAND PASSENT LES OISEAUX see Vuataz, Roger

QUAND TU VOIS À TON RÉVEIL see Henchoz, Emile

QUAND VIENDRA L'HEURE DE LA MORT see Bach, Johann Sebastian

QUAND VOUS SEREZ BIEN VIELLE see Lang, H. see Martin

QUARTS DU SOIR see Canteloube, Joseph

QU'AS-TU VU DANS LES VIGNES? see Miche, Paul

QUATRE CANZONETTE A TRE VOCI see Monteverdi, Claudio

QUATRE CHANTS D'INNOCENCE see Landowski, Marcel

QUATRE CHANTS D'INNOCENCE see Landowski, Marcel

QUATRE CONTES MUSICAUX see Aboulker

QUATRE POÈMES D'EUGENIO MONTALE see Guérinel

QUATRE ROSES see Hemmerling, Carlos

QUATTORDICI CANTI POPOLARI
  (Casagrande, Ramous) TTBB BERBEN
  BERBEN 652    (Q1)

QUATTORDICI CANTI POPOLARI FRIULANI see Anonymous

QUATTRO ELABORAZIONI CORALI see Anonymous

QU'AVEZ-VOUS À SOUPIRER see Doret, Gustave

QU'AVEZ-VOUS TROUVÉ? see Robert-Lalouet, M.

QUE DIEU PROTÈGE TON VOYAGE see Boller, Carlo

QUE FAITES-VOUS? see Martin

QUE J'AIME, Ô CHER PAYS... see Lang, H.

QUE L'ON CHANTE, QUE L'ON S'EMPRESSE see Rameau, Jean-Philippe

QUE TU ES BEAU, MON VILLAGE see Jordan

QUE VIENS-TU QUÉRIR? see Martin

QUEEN OF SOUL *medley
  (Funk, Jeff) SATB WARNER CM9589 ipa    (Q2)
  (Funk, Jeff) SAB WARNER CM9590 ipa    (Q3)
  (Funk, Jeff) SSA WARNER CM9591 ipa    (Q4)

QUEL GIORNO...INFINE... see Landuzzi, Cristina

QUEL MAZZOLIN DI FIORI see Mermoud, Robert

QUELQUES CANONS see Mozart, Wolfgang Amadeus

QU'EST C'QU'ON ATTEND POUR ÊTRE HEUREUX see Misraki, P.

QUESTIONNAIRE see Mechem, Kirke Lewis

QUI CHANTE SON MAL... see Demieville, Roland

QUI L'EÛT CRU? see Vuataz, Roger

QUI N'A PAS SON PROGRAMME? see Martin

QUI TROUVERA LA FEMME VERTUEUSE see Gindron-Janequin

QUIET see Parker, Alice

QUIET PLACE, A
  (Crenshaw, Randy) TTBB,acap (gr. III)
  UNC JP    (Q5)

QU'IL EST ADMIRABLE see Handel, George Frideric

QU'IL FAIT BON SUR TERRE see Hemmerling, Carlos

QUIMEY NEUQUEN see Berbel, Marcelo

QUINTENTRAUM,DER see Kretzschmar, Günther

QU'ON ME RENDE À CETTE TERRE see Alexandrov, Alexander Vasilievich

# R

RACHMANINOFF, SERGEY VASSILIEVICH (1873-1943)
   Three Russian Songs, Op. 41 *CC3U
    (Brower F) AB,2pno sc DONEMUS f.s. (R1)
   Six Choruses For Treble Voices, Op.15 *CC6U
    [Russ] SA,pno RUSSICA RA-6 CH f.s. (R2)

RACINE, FERNAND
   Si Je Trouvais...
    mix cor HUG 8518 (R3)

RACLETTE VALAISANNE, LA see Bovet, J.

RAFTSMEN, LES see Henderson, Ruth Watson

RAGGED LEEVY
   (Morrow) TTBB LAWSON 4-52638 (R4)

RAGGEDY ANN "N" ANDY see Gould, Raymond

RAGGLE TAGGLE GYPSIES, THE see Hugh

RAGNARSSON, HJALMAR H. (1952- )
   Afangar
    mix cor,2(pic).2.2.2. 2.2.2.1.
    timp,perc,strings ICELAND 030-041 (R5)

RAIN STORM
   (Braun, Yehezkel) [Heb] mix cor,pno (text: O.Hille; melody: Argov, Alexander) ISR.MUS.INST. IMI 6988 (R6)

RAINBOW, THE see Cutter, William (Bill)

RAINDROPS KEEP FALLIN' ON MY HEAD see Bacharach, Burt F.

RAINSONGS see Garwood, Margaret

RAINWATER, ERIC
   Yellow
    2pt cor,pno HOFFMAN,R H5015 (R7)

RAINY DAY,THE see Sullivan, [Sir] Arthur Seymour

RAIZ see Sanchez, Damian

RAKAN ONDO see Nakane, Yuko

RÄKNEEXEMPLET LIVET see Ahlin, Sven

RAMAGE OPPORTUN see Bovet, J.

RAMEAU, JEAN-PHILIPPE (1683-1764)
   Au Son Du Tambourin
    (Février) 4pt mix cor BILLAUDOT (R8)
   Courez Par La Plaine
    "Hier Im Reich Der Freude" mix cor HUG 6693 (R9)
   En Ce Doux Asile
    (Poisot) 4pt mix cor BILLAUDOT (R10)
   Hier Im Reich Der Freude
    see Courez Par La Plaine
   Hymn À La Nuit
    (Arnoud) 4pt men cor BILLAUDOT (R11)
   Hymne À La Nuit
    mix cor HUG 7231 (R12)
    men cor HUG 3565 (R13)
    2 eq voices BILLAUDOT (R14)
    (Mouchet) 4pt men cor BILLAUDOT (R15)
    (Mouchet) 4pt mix cor BILLAUDOT (R16)
    (Rillé, De) 3 eq voices BILLAUDOT (R17)
   Hymne Au Soleil
    men cor HUG 6642 (R18)
   Menuet
    3pt mix cor HUG 8751 (R19)
   Que L'on Chante, Que L'on S'empresse
    mix cor,opt pno/org/orch HUG 7648 (R20)
    eq voices,opt pno/org/orch HUG 7775 (R21)
    men cor HUG 6294 (R22)

RAMINSH, IMANT (1943- )
   Chariot Children, The
    3pt treb cor,pno BOOSEY-ENG OCTB6728 (R23)
   I'll Give My Love And Apple
    2pt treb cor,ob,pno BOOSEY-ENG OCTB6694 (R24)
   Sing Hey! It's Christmas Day!
    SATB,acap JAYMAR (R25)

RAMINSH, IMANT (cont'd.)
   Vestigia
    3pt treb cor,vln,vla,pno BOOSEY-ENG OCTB6717 (R26)

RAMIREZ, ARIEL
   Parana En Una Zamba,El
    (Gomez, Eduardo) mix cor LAGOS (R27)
   Zamba De Usted
    mix cor LAGOS (R28)

RAMSETH, BETTY ANN
   Slumbertown
    (Ramseth Hoiland, Melinda) unis jr cor,Orff inst AUG-FOR 11-10315 (R29)

RANSIGNOLETS DU BOIS JOLI see Bovet, J.

RANZ DES VACHES, LE see Bovet, J. see Burkard, Willi see Doret, Gustave

RAOUL WALLENBERG PORTRAIT:, A see Björlin, Ulf

RAPPAPORT, MOSHE
   Yerushalayim
    (Jacobson, Joshua) [Heb] SSA,S solo,pno (easy) HAZA HZ-018 (R30)

RAPPEL DU FOYER, LE see Bovet, J.

RAPTURE,THE see Dodsworth, Stephen

RASIUK, MOSHE (1954- )
   Feast,The
    [Heb] 4pt girl cor,acap (text: Alterman, Nathn) ISR.MUS.INST. IMI 6967 (R31)

RASKIN
   Those Were The Days
    SSA WARCH 34808 (R32)
    SATB WARCH 34810 (R33)

RASSEMBLÉS SUR LA MONTAGNE see Mermoud, Robert

RAT see Vollenweider, Hans

RATHGEBER, VALENTIN (1682-1750)
   Augsburger Tafelconfect,Das (composed with Seyfert, Johann Caspar)
    (Poser, Hans) 3pt mix cor,3inst FIDULA voc sc 6141, pts 6142 (R34)
   Wir Haben Drei Katzen
    mix cor SCHUL CLS 190 (R35)

RAUCH, ANDREAS
   Aller Augen Warten Auf Dich
    wom cor,acap MULLES (R36)

RAUM, ELIZABETH (1945- )
   Ballad To Saskatchewan
    see Prarie, The
   Prarie, The
    satb swing choir with orchestra sc, pno red,pts CAN.MUS.CENT.
    contains also: Ballad To Saskatchewan (R37)
   Shadows Of Dusk (from Symphony Of Youth)
    4pt jr cor,orch CAN.MUS.CENT. sc, cor pts (R38)
   Song Of Life (from Symphony Of Youth)
    youth choir and swing choir, stage band and youth orchestra CAN.MUS.CENT. sc, cor pts (R39)
   This Is Where It's At (from Symphony Of Youth)
    jr cor,band CAN.MUS.CENT. sc, cor pts (R40)

RAUSCH AUF, O LIED see Schmid, Walter

RAY
   Bye, Bye Baby
    SSA SHAWNEE D-452 (R41)

RAZZLE, JAZZLE see Stanton

REACH OUT, I'LL BE THERE
   (Billingsley, Alan) SATB WARNER 1416RC1X (R42)
   (Billingsley, Alan) SAB WARNER 1416RC3X (R43)

REACHING HIGHER AND HIGHER see Gilpin, Greg

REACHING TO THE FUTURE see Telfer, Nancy

REASONS BRIEFLY SET DOWNE see Diemer, Emma Lou

REBBE,DER
   (Sperber, Stanley) SATB,opt pno (med easy, text in yiddish) HAZA voc sc HZ-017, sc HZ-017-PV (R44)

REBELLE, LA see Moniuszko, Stanislaw

REBUSE DU COUCOU, LA see Mermoud, Robert

RECIT OUBILE,D' UN see Alsina, Carlos Roqué

RECUEIL COMPLET see Lancien, Noël

RECUEIL DES TROIS CHANSONS see Arrieu, Claude

RECUEILLEMENT see Naudier

RED HOT COUNTRY BOOGIE *medley
   (Chinn, Teena) SATB WARNER C0355C1X (R45)
   (Chinn, Teena) SAB WARNER C0355C3X (R46)
   (Chinn, Teena) 2pt mix cor WARNER C0355C5X (R47)

RED HOT COUNTRY SHOWDOWN REVUE
   (Chinn, Teena) SATB,pno voc sc WARNER C0341C1XS (R48)
   (Chinn, Teena) pno-cond sc WARNER C0341C1X (R49)
   (Chinn, Teena) SAB,pno voc sc WARNER C0341C3XS (R50)
   (Chinn, Teena) pno-cond sc WARNER C0341C3X (R51)
   (Chinn, Teena) 2pt mix cor,pno voc sc WARNER C0341C5XS (R52)
   (Chinn, Teena) pno-cond sc WARNER C0341C5X (R53)

RED, RED ROSE, A see Adams, Jonathan

REED, EVERETT
   Goodbye, Goodbye To Everything
    SATB,pno ASPEN 2011 (R54)

REEDS OF INNOCENCE see Swingle, Ward

REES-DAVIES, IEUAN
   Birthday Song,A
    see Five Unison Songs
   Fancies
    see Five Unison Songs
   Five Unison Songs
    unis cor BANKS 1335 f.s.
    contains: Birthday Song,A; Fancies; Flowers; My Plane; Sunset In Town (R55)
   Flowers
    see Five Unison Songs
   My Plane
    see Five Unison Songs
   Sunset In Town
    see Five Unison Songs

REFRAIN DE L'OISEAU, LE see Bovet, J.

REFRAINS see Cooper, Paul

REGARDS TO BROADWAY! see Besig

REGENLIED see Stocker, Karl

REGER, MAX (1873-1916)
   Abendgesang Im Lenz
    see Drei Chöre, Op. 111b
    see Drei Chöre, Op. 111b
   Drei Chöre, Op. 111b
    mix cor BERBEN f.s.
    contains: Abendgesang Im Lenz; Er Ist's; Im Himmelreich Ein Haus Steht (R56)
   Drei Chöre, Op. 111b
    mix cor DOBLINGER f.s.
    contains: Abendgesang Im Lenz; Er Ist's; Im Himmelreich Ein Haus Steht (R57)
   Er Ist's
    see Drei Chöre, Op. 111b
    see Drei Chöre, Op. 111b
   Im Himmelreich Ein Haus Steht
    see Drei Chöre, Op. 111b
    see Drei Chöre, Op. 111b

REGINA COELI FROM "CAVALLERIA RUSTICANA" see Mascagni, Pietro

REGNART, JACOB (ca. 1540-1599)
   Tu Tu Tu...
    men cor HUG 6061 (R58)

REIBEL, GUY (1936- )
   Coq Et Le Renard, Le
    3pt cor,fl BILLAUDOT (R59)

REICHEL, BERNARD (1901-1992)
   Avril
    mix cor HUG 8298 (R60)

REICHEL, BERNARD (cont'd.)
   Cavalier À La Fontaine
     mix cor HUG 8546 (R61)

   Il Faut Avoir Une Âme Claire
     eq voices HUG 8336 (R62)

   Matin, Le
     eq voices HUG 8299 (R63)

   Page Neuve
     4 eq voices HUG 8493 (R64)

   Paix Du Soir, La
     mix cor HUG 8545 (R65)

   Pour Trouver Un Coeur Pur
     mix cor HUG 8496 (R66)

   Temps A Laissè Son Manteau, Le
     mix cor HUG 8547 (R67)

REID
   Whiter Shade Of Pale, A (composed with Brooker)
     SATB NOVELLO 090930 (R68)

REINDEER TWIST,THE see Lawrence, Stephen L.

REINE DES PRÉS, LA see Hemmerling, Carlos

REINHARDT, BRUNO (1929-    )
   Twelve Months, The
     jr cor OR-TAV (R69)

REISELIED see Märki, Ernst

REITER,DER see Märki, Ernst

REITERLIED see Müller, Joseph Ivar

REJECTED LOVER, THE  *folk song,US
   (Mechell, Harry) SATB,SBar soli,acap MUSIC SEV. (R70)

REMARKABLE TALE OF QUENTIN B. QUAIL see Whicher, James

RÉMINISCENCE see Zbinden, Julien-François

RÉMOULEUR, LE see Gaillard, Paul-Andre
   see Gesseney, L.

RENARD ET CHANTECLER see Loucheur, Raymond

RENCONTRE DE FÊTE see Breard

RENDEZ-VOUS DEMAIN MATIN see Boller, Carlo

RENGAINE see Vuataz, Roger

RENNYO-SHONIN see Nakajima, Yoshifumi

RENONCULE, LA see Lancien, Noël

RENOUVEAU see Broquet, Louis see Gesseney, L.

REPORT TO GOD see Pierce, (Anne) Alexandra

REQUIEM see Kreis, Otto

RESPIGHI, OTTORINO (1879-1936)
   Persiani, I *cant
     men cor,MezT soli,3.3.4.3. 6.3.3.1. timp,harp,cel,strings sc RICORDI-IT 134223 (R71)

RETOUR, LE *pop
   mix cor HUG 2360 (R72)

RETOUR DES CHAMPS see Delmas, Marc-Jean-Baptiste

RETOUR DES FRONTIÈRES see Bovet, J.

RETURN FROM TOWN, THE see Griebling, Mary Ann

REUCHSEL
   Trois Chants Grec *CC3U
     4pt mix cor,harp BILLAUDOT f.s. (R73)

REVECI VENIR DU PRINTEMPS see Jeune, Claude Le

RECECY VENIR DU PRINTEMPS see Lejeune

RÉVEILLE-TOI! see Lavater, H.

REVENEZ, AMOURS, REVENEZ see Lully, Jean-Baptiste (Lulli)

REVENEZ, REVENEZ... see Lully, Jean-Baptiste (Lulli)

RÊVER see Bovet, J.

REVIL, H.
   Winter Light (composed with Ronstadt, Linda; Kaz, Eric)
     (O'neill, Jackie) SATB WARNER 5911WC1X (R74)
     (O'neill, Jackie) SAB WARNER 5911WC3X (R75)

RÊVONS D'UN ENFANT see Falquet, Rene

RHEINBERGER, JOSEF (1839-1901)
   Vom Goldenen Horn  *Op.182
     SATB,4 soli,pno (Türkisches Liederspiel) CARUS sc 50.182-01, voc sc 50.182-05 (R76)

RHINOCEROS see Jennings, Carolyn

RHÔNE DANSE, LE see Daetwyler, Jean

RHÔNE VALAISAN, LE see Martin

RHYTHM ESCAPADES  *medley
   (Schmutte, Pete) SATB WARNER C0318C1X ipa (R77)
   (Schmutte, Pete) SAB WARNER C0318C3X ipa (R78)

RHYTHM OF THE RAIN see Gummoe, Joe

RHYTHMISCHE SPRECHCHÖRE see Werdin, Eberhard

RICERCARE FESTIVO see Rossum, Van

RICHARDS, [HENRY] BRINLEY (1817-1885)
   Up! Quit Thy Bower
     (Dicks, E.A.) SATB BANKS 533 (R79)

RIDE A COCK HORSE see Freedman

RIDOUT
   When Age And Youth Unite
     SATB WARCH 35676 (R80)

RIDOUT, GODFREY (1918-    )
   O Canada
     SSA THOMP.G VG308 (R81)
     SATB THOMP.G VG415 (R82)

RIEDEL, GEORG (1934-    )
   Nu Är Våren Här
     SSA,pno SVERIG SK 766 (R83)

RIES, HUBERT (1802-1886)
   Sonnenwende
     (Steffen) men cor RIES 63013 (R84)

   Volksweise
     (Steffen) men cor RIES 63014 (R85)

RIESENRAD DER STERNE,DAS see Märki, Ernst

RIGODON see Martin

RILEY
   Friend Who Will Understand, A (composed with Wilson)
     3pt mix cor SHAWNEE D-462 (R86)
     SATB SHAWNEE A-1984 (R87)

   Welcome Sweet Spring
     SSA oct SOUTHERN SC434 (R88)

RILLE, L. DE
   Martyrs Aux Arènes, Les
     4pt men cor BILLAUDOT (R89)

   Noce De Village, La
     2 eq voices BILLAUDOT (R90)

RIMSKY-KORSAKOV, NIKOLAI (1844-1908)
   Flight Of The Bumble-Bee
     (Swingle, Ward) SSAATTBB,acap (gr. V) voc pt,pts UNC JP SC-1 (R91)

RING HAB ICH VON DIR, EINEN see Leicht

RING OUT THE BELLS! see Vance, Margaret

RING OUT WILD BELLS see Gates, Crawford

RING THEM BELLS see Dylan

RINGWALD, ROY (1910-1995)
   Bleak Midwinter, The
     SATB SHAWNEE A-1969 (R92)

RIO GRANDE
   (Lewin) TTBB (jamaican folksong) KJOS 5567 (R93)

RIPPENTROP, DENICE
   As The Moon Rose
     SSA,pno,2fl BEAUT BSP-146 (R94)

   Blue Sky,The
     SATB,acap BEAUT BSP-102 (R95)

   Emerald Rainbow,The
     2pt cor,pno,glock BEAUT BSP-131 (R96)

   Light Comes Forth
     BEAUT BSP-120 f.s.
       contains: Night's Mysteries, The

RIPPENTROP, DENICE (cont'd.)
     (SSA,pno); White Land (SSA, pno); Wisdom Of Wind, The (SSA, pno, wind chimes) (R97)

   My Ladybug Friend
     unis jr cor BEAUT BSP-135 (R98)

   My Secret Garden
     SSA,pno,fl BEAUT BSP-137 (R99)

   Night's Mysteries, The
     see Light Comes Forth

   Ocean's Sky,The
     SATB,pno 4-hands, and wind chimes BEAUT BSP-141 (R100)

   Singing Free
     2pt cor,pno BEAUT BSP-128 (R101)

   Stars And Moonbeams
     2pt cor,pno, wind chimes BEAUT BSP-142 (R102)

   Sunflower,The
     2pt cor BEAUT BSP-129 (R103)

   White Land
     see Light Comes Forth

   Wisdom Of Wind, The
     see Light Comes Forth

RIQUI, RIQUI , RIQUIRRÁN
   (Smith, Gregg) mix cor (venezuelan folksong) LEONARD-US 50312360 (R104)

RISE UP MY LOVE see Snyder, Timothy

RITCHIE, JEAN (1922-    )
   Let The Sun Shine Down On Me
     (Ralph) SATB,Mez solo,tamb,acap (med easy) PRESSER (R105)

RITENOUR,LEE
   Bullet Train (composed with Watts, Ernie)
     (Paquin-Salerno, Chris) SATB, solo voices,perc (gr. IV) UNC JP (R106)

RITOURNELLE see Jordan

RITOURNELLE DE FÉVRIER see Hemmerling, Carlos

RITOURNELLE DU VIN NOUVEAU see Hemmerling, Carlos

RIVE ENCHANTERESSE see Naudier

RIVER,THE see Brooks, Garth

RIVER RUN see Strommen, Carl

RIVES BLEUES see Hemmerling, Carlos

ROAD LESS TRAVELED, THE see Strommen, Carl

ROAD NOT TAKEN, THE see Wagner, Douglas Edward

ROADSIDE FIRE, THE see Belmont

ROARING '20S  *medley
   (Funk, Jeff) SATB WARNER CM9519 (R107)
   (Funk, Jeff) SAB WARNER CM9520 (R108)
   (Funk, Jeff) 2pt cor WARNER CM9521 (R109)

ROBBINS, MARTY
   White Sport Coat (And A Pink Carnation), A
     (Funk, Jeff) TTB WARNER 7418AC4X (R110)

ROBE DE SAISON, LA see Henchoz, Emile

ROBERT-LALOUET, M.
   Armor
     mix cor HUG 8118 (R111)

   Berceuse Pour Negrito
     eq voices HUG 8314 (R112)

   Bergerette Au Bois Joly
     mix cor HUG 8651 (R113)
     eq voices HUG 8652 (R114)

   Bonheur Est Dans Le Pré, Le
     mix cor HUG 8118 (R115)
     eq voices HUG 8116 (R116)

   Chanson De Mai
     eq voices HUG 8117 (R117)

   Enterrement D'une Fourmi, L'
     eq voices HUG 8116 (R118)

   Lou Païsan
     mix cor HUG 8651 (R119)
     eq voices HUG 8652 (R120)

ROBERT-LALOUET, M. (cont'd.)
　Marche Des Tonneaux
　　mix cor HUG 8346　　　　　　(R121)
　　men cor HUG 8347　　　　　　(R122)

　Pâquerette
　　mix cor HUG 8312　　　　　　(R123)
　　eq voices HUG 8313　　　　　(R124)

　Qu'avez-Vous Trouvé?
　　eq voices HUG 8117　　　　　(R125)

　Rondel Printanier
　　mix cor HUG 8312　　　　　　(R126)
　　eq voices HUG 8313　　　　　(R127)

ROBIN, THE see Henderson, Ruth Watson

ROBINOVITCH, SID (1942- )
　Keihalá
　　see Soundchants

　Shireem
　　SATB THOMP.G VEI1150　　　　(R128)

　Soundchants
　　SATB,acap/bass drum&maracas
　　CAN.MUS.CENT. MV 6000 S656SO f.s.
　　contains: Keihalá; Ta tikee tei;
　　Zayadana　　　　　　　　　　(R129)

　Ta tikee tei
　　see Soundchants

　Two Inuit Songs
　　SATB THOMP.G VEI1142　　　　(R130)

　Zayadana
　　see Soundchants

ROCHAT, JEAN
　Allons Danser La Saint-Jean
　　3pt mix cor HUG 8749　　　　(R131)
　　men cor HUG 8551　　　　　　(R132)

　Au Bois De La Rosière
　　mix cor HUG 8806　　　　　　(R133)

　Bistro, Le
　　men cor HUG 8827　　　　　　(R134)

　Chanson Des Temps Anciens
　　men cor HUG 8755　　　　　　(R135)

　Chanson Pour Les Vendanges
　　3pt mix cor HUG 8748　　　　(R136)
　　men cor HUG 8550　　　　　　(R137)

　Dis, Compagnon...
　　mix cor HUG 8772　　　　　　(R138)
　　men cor HUG 8756　　　　　　(R139)

　En Ce Jour Neuf
　　mix cor HUG 8829　　　　　　(R140)
　　men cor HUG 8825　　　　　　(R141)

　Garde Le Soleil...
　　mix cor HUG 8802　　　　　　(R142)
　　men cor HUG 8805　　　　　　(R143)

　Guilledou, Le
　　men cor HUG 8753　　　　　　(R144)

　Je Ne Cherche Pas...
　　men cor HUG 8803　　　　　　(R145)

　Jour A Passé, Le
　　mix cor HUG 8812　　　　　　(R146)

　Ma Pipe
　　men cor HUG 8754　　　　　　(R147)

　Noé
　　mix cor HUG 8830　　　　　　(R148)
　　men cor HUG 8826　　　　　　(R149)

　Pourquoi Me Quitter?
　　eq voices HUG 8752　　　　　(R150)

　Temps Pour Tout, Un
　　mix cor HUG 8577　　　　　　(R151)
　　men cor HUG 8540　　　　　　(R152)

　Tiens Bon!
　　3pt mix cor HUG 8747　　　　(R153)

ROCK AROUND THE CLOCK see Freedman, Harry

ROCK ME EASY see Ruddell, Bruce

ROCKIN' AROUND THE CHRISTMAS TREE
　(Schmutte, Pete) SATB WARNER 4711RC1X
　　　　　　　　　　　　　　　　(R154)
　(Schmutte, Pete) SAB WARNER 4711RC3X
　　　　　　　　　　　　　　　　(R155)
　(Schmutte, Pete) 2pt cor WARNER
　　4711RC5X　　　　　　　　　　(R156)

ROCKIN' AT THE HOP
　(Althouse, Jay) SATB (medley
　containing Rocking Pneumonia And
　The Boogie Woogie Flu, Let The Good
　Times Roll, When Will I Be Loved &
　(We're Gonna) Rock Around The
　Clock) WARNER C0309C1X　　　(R157)
　(Althouse, Jay) SAB (medley
　containing Rocking Pneumonia And
　The Boogie Woogie Flu, Let The Good
　Times Roll, When Will I Be Loved &
　(We're Gonna) Rock Around The
　Clock) WARNER C0309C3X　　　(R158)
　(Althouse, Jay) 2pt cor (medley
　containing Rocking Pneumonia And
　The Boogie Woogie Flu, Let The Good
　Times Roll, When Will I Be Loved &
　(We're Gonna) Rock Around The
　Clock) WARNER C0309C5X　　　(R159)

ROCKIN' CHRISTMAS CELEBRATION!
　(Althouse, Jay) SATB (medley
　containing Santa Claus Is Comin' To
　Town, Little Saint Nick & Rockin'
　Around The Christmas Tree) WARNER
　C0297C1X ipa　　　　　　　　(R160)
　(Althouse, Jay) SAB (medley
　containing Santa Claus Is Comin' To
　Town, Little Saint Nick & Rockin'
　Around The Christmas Tree) WARNER
　C0297C3X ipa　　　　　　　　(R161)
　(Althouse, Jay) 2pt cor (medley
　containing Santa Claus Is Comin' To
　Town, Little Saint Nick & Rockin'
　Around The Christmas Tree) WARNER
　C0297C5X ipa　　　　　　　　(R162)

ROCKIN' DOWN THE CHIMNEY TONIGHT! see Albrecht, Sally K.

ROCKIN' JERUSALEM
　(Moore, Donald) SATB WARNER SV9321
　　　　　　　　　　　　　　　　(R163)

ROCKIN' THE BABY see Albrecht, Sally K.

RODBY, WALTER (1917- )
　When Good Men Sing Together  *CC17UL
　　1-4pt men cor HOPE 416 f.s.　(R164)

RODEO (from Western Tunes)
　(Hoffman) SATB LAWSON 4-52669　(R165)

RODGERS, RICHARD (1902-1979)
　Bewitched
　　(Snyder, Audrey) SATB WARNER
　　　WBCH9323　　　　　　　　　(R166)
　　(Snyder, Audrey) SAB WARNER
　　　WBCH9324　　　　　　　　　(R167)

　I Whistle A Happy Tune (composed with
　　Hammerstein, Oscar)
　　SAB WARCH 30083　　　　　　(R168)

　My Funny Valentine
　　(Althouse, Jay) SAB WARNER WBCH9305
　　　　　　　　　　　　　　　　(R169)
　　(Althouse, Jay) SATB WARNER
　　　WBCH9304　　　　　　　　　(R170)

RODRIGO, JOAQUÍN (1902- )
　A La Clavelina
　　[Span/Ger] jr cor,solo,gtr (song
　　sheet) SCHOTTS C047842　　(R171)
　　"Duftenden Nelke, Der" jr cor,solo,
　　opt gtr sc SCHOTTS C 47842 (R172)

　Duftenden Nelke, Der
　　see A La Clavelina

ROESELI see Doret, Gustave

ROGERS
　Cruisin' Crowd (composed with
　　Holmberg, Pat)
　　SAB,pno VOICE ROHOC16　　　(R173)

　Lustin' To Roam (composed with
　　Holmberg, Pat)
　　SAB VOICE ROHOC05　　　　　(R174)

　Unchained Snowbirds (composed with
　　Holmberg, Pat)
　　SAB VOICE ROHOC14　　　　　(R175)

　We're Free (composed with Holmberg, Pat)
　　SAB VOICE ROHOC01　　　　　(R176)

ROI BOIT, LE see Anonymous

ROI DAVID, LE see Honegger, Arthur

ROI DE PERSE, LE see Breard

ROI D'YVETOT, LE see Pantillon, François

ROIS DE L'ABBAYE, LES see Mermoud, Robert

ROLAND-MANUEL, ALEXIS (1891-1966)
　Trois Chansons Populaires Françaises
　　*CC3U
　　3pt mix cor BILLAUDOT f.s.　(R177)

　Trois Chansons Populaires Françaises
　　3pt jr cor BILLAUDOT　　　(R178)

ROLLI
　I Bi Soldat Und Du Bisch Soldat
　　(Ehrismann) men cor,acap MULLES
　　　　　　　　　　　　　　　　(R179)

ROMAN DE FAUVEL, LE  *CCU
　(Schrade) OISEAU RE 908 f.s.　(R180)

ROMANCE see Mozart, Wolfgang Amadeus
　see Schubert, Franz (Peter) see
　Swingle, Ward

ROMANCE A LO DIVINO see Orrego-Salas, Juan A.

ROMANCES PASTORALES see Orrego-Salas, Juan A.

ROMANZA ANDALUZA see Sarasate, Pablo de

ROMANZA ESPANOLA see Anonymous

RONDA,LA see Fischer, Clare

RONDALLA ARAGONESA see Granados, Enrique

RONDE see Fort, P. see Lagger, Oscar

RONDE, LA see Müller, P.

RONDE DES ANNÉES, LA see Boller, Carlo

RONDE DES CHANSONS, LA see Boller, Carlo

RONDE DES ESCARGOTS see Berthomieu, Marc

RONDE DES FLEURS, LA see Boller, Carlo
　see Jouineau, Jacques

RONDE DES MOUETTES, LA see Bovet, J.

RONDE DU MUGNET, LA see Naudier

RONDE DU MUGUET, LA see Naudier

RONDE DU PRINTEMPS see Boller, Carlo

RONDE FANTASQUE see Broquet, Louis

RONDE SUR LA FALAISE, LA see Apotheloz, Jean

RONDEAU DU CONTENTEMENT see Kaelin, Pierre

RONDEAU DU GUAY see Arrieu, Claude

RONDEAU PRINTANIER see Naudier

RONDEAUX DE CLÉMENT MAROT see Arrieu, Claude

RONDEL see Sbordoni, Alessandro

RONDEL FOR SEPTEMBER see Haugland, A. Oscar

RONDEL PRINTANIER see Robert-Lalouet, M.

RONDO see Mozart, Wolfgang Amadeus

RONDO GOTLANDICA see Krone

RONDO (ICH WILL SINGEN FROH) see Pantillon, François

RONDO "LE COUCOU" see Daquin, Louis-Claude

RONSARD
　Chanson À Quatre Voix
　　(Kunc) 4pt mix cor BILLAUDOT (R181)

ROSA, LA ROSE see Lang, H.

ROSE, LA see Broquet, Louis

ROSE, THE
　(Chinn, Teena) SATB WARNER CH95107
　　　　　　　　　　　　　　　　(R182)
　(Chinn, Teena) 3pt mix cor WARNER
　　CH95115　　　　　　　　　　(R183)

ROSE COMPLETE, LA see Lauridsen, Morten Johannes

ROSE DE L'AURORE, LA see Schumann, Robert (Alexander)

ROSE DES SABLES see Pantillon, François

ROSE DU ROSIER BLANC, LA see Doret, Gustave

ROSE ET LE ROSSIGNOL, LA see Vuataz, Roger

ROSEN see Ruprecht, Ernst

ROSENFENSTER see Kreis, Otto

ROSENLÄUTEN see Kreis, Otto

ROSES, LES see Bovet, J.

ROSES DU MIDI see Malec, Ivo

ROSESTOCK HOLDERBLÜT see Silcher, Friedrich

ROSETTI
   What Do The Stars Do? (composed with Porterfield, Sherrie)
     SSA ALFRED 11602 (R184)

ROSEWALL, RICHARD B.
   Year's At The Spring, The
     SATB,pno LAWSON 52595 (R185)

ROSIER BLANC, LE see Kaelin, Pierre

ROSSELLINI, RENZO (1908-1982)
   Poesia Di Natale, Una
     cor,0.0.0.0. 4.3.0.0. timp,tam-tam, strings sc RICORDI-IT 131970 (R186)

ROSSI, LUIGI (1597-1653)
   Dormite, Begl' Occhi (from Orfeo) (Meredith) SSA KJOS 6237 (R187)

ROSSIGNOL, LE see Grétry, André Ernest Modeste

ROSSIGNOL CHANTE see Martin

ROSSIGNOL ET LE PRINCE, LE see Breard

ROSSIGNOL QUI VAS EN FRANCE see Canteloube, Joseph

ROSSIGNOLET AU BOIS see Fievet, Paul

ROSSIGNOLET D'AMOUR see Martin

ROSSIGNOLET DU BOIS see Canteloube, Joseph

ROSSIGNOLET GENTIL see Doret, Gustave see Lagger, Oscar

ROSSIGNOLETSAUVAGE see Anonymous

ROSSINI, GIOACCHINO (1792-1868)
   Morte Di Didone, La
     men cor,S solo,2.3.2.2. 2.2.0.0. timp,strings RICORDI-IT (R188)

   Sinfonia Con Cori (from Ermione)
     cor,2.2.2.2. 4.2.3.0. timp,perc, strings RICORDI-IT (R189)

ROSSUM, VAN
   Ricercare Festivo *Op.52
     mix cor BILLAUDOT (R190)

ROT SCHWYZER,DER see Ruprecht, Ernst

ROTHSCHUH, FRITZ (1921-1978)
   Jahr Hebt An, Das
     SATB,acap BOHM (R191)

   Zwei Lieder Zum Geburtstag Oder Zu Neujahr *CC2U
     wom cor BOHM f.s. (R192)

ROUCHELINES, LES see Doret, Gustave

ROUGET DE L'ISLE, CLAUDE JOSEPH (1760-1836)
   Marseillaise, La
     4pt men cor BILLAUDOT (R193)
     2 eq voices BILLAUDOT (R194)
     mix cor BILLAUDOT (R195)
     2pt wom cor BILLAUDOT (R196)
     (Bréard) 4pt men cor BILLAUDOT (R197)
     (Bréard) 2 eq voices BILLAUDOT (R198)
     (Brun) 3 eq voices BILLAUDOT (R199)

ROUGNON, PAUL
   Fleur Du Matin
     4pt men cor BILLAUDOT (R200)

   Voix De La Foule, Les
     4pt men cor BILLAUDOT (R201)

"ROUND" AND A "ROUND" WE GO! *CC28U
   (Martin) any combination of voices (very easy) PRESSER (R202)

ROUND 'BOUT WINTER, A see Gallina

'ROUND MIDNIGHT
   (Crenshaw, Randy-Terra Nova) SSAA, female solo,acap UNC JP (R203)
   (New York Voices) SSATB,solo voice, perc (gr. V) UNC JP (R204)

'ROUND'EZVOUS see Spevacek, Linda

ROWLEY
   Sleep My Baby
     treb cor BOOSEY-ENG OCTB5449 (R205)

ROXBURGH, EDWIN (1937- )
   Et Vitam Venturi Saeculi
     mix cor,acap UNITED MUS (R206)

   Pianto
     mix cor,acap UNITED MUS (R207)

ROY, ALPHONSE (1906- )
   De Ce Castel Enchanteur
     4 eq voices HUG 8370 (R208)

RUDDELL, BRUCE
   Rock Me Easy
     SATB,T solo,pno LAWSON 52576 (R209)

RUDERN, GESPRÄCHE see Sauseng, Wolfgang

RUDOLPH THE RED NOSED REINDEER see Marks, Johnny D.

RUGGED YANK, THE see Dawson, William Levi

RUINS OF A TOWER, THE see Taneyev

RUISSEAU, LE see Bovet, J. see Fevrier, Henri

RUMSHINSKY, JOSEPH M. (1881-1956)
   Sheyn Vi Di Levoneh
     [Yiddish] SATB,SSA soli,pno (easy) HAZA HZ-047 (R210)

RUNARSDOTTIR, HILDIGUNNUR (1964- )
   Summer Rain
     mix cor,acap,S solo ICELAND 074-014 (R211)

RUPRECHT, ERNST
   Abstimmungs-Sunntig
     men cor,acap MULLES (R212)

   Ds Vreneli Ab Em Guggisbärg
     wom cor,acap MULLES (R213)

   Es Taget Vor Dem Walde
     wom cor,acap MULLES (R214)

   Heimligi Liebi
     wom cor,acap MULLES (R215)

   I Han Esmol Es Schätzeli Gha
     wom cor,acap MULLES (R216)

   Jardiniere Du Roy,La
     wom cor,acap MULLES (R217)

   Jungi Liebi
     wom cor,acap MULLES (R218)

   Rosen
     wom cor,acap MULLES (R219)

   Rot Schwyzer,Der
     wom cor,acap MULLES (R220)

   Schifflein Sah Ich Fahren, Ein
     men cor,acap MULLES (R221)

   Stets In Trure Muess I Läbe
     wom cor,acap MULLES (R222)

   Verlorni Heimat
     wom cor,acap MULLES (R223)

RUSCH, PETER
   Abendlied
     wom cor,acap MULLES (R224)

RUSCIANO, C.D.
   Song For You, A
     (Schmutte, Pete) SATB WARNER 6186SC1X (R225)
     (Schmutte, Pete) SAB WARNER 6186SC3X (R226)

RÜSTE DES TAGES see Moser-Schweizer, Ernst

RYSER, OTTO
   Vier Stämme
     men cor,acap MULLES (R227)

# S

S' STERNLI see Märki, Ernst

SABBATINI, ANTONIO LUIGI (1739-1809)
   Canoni Sui Principi Elementari *CCU (Acciai, G.) cor,acap ZERBONI 10461 f.s. (S1)

SACCO, P.
   Twilight Hours, The
     SATB oct SOUTHERN SC423 (S2)

SAEGUSA, SHIGEAKI (1942- )
   Look! Mount Fuji In The West Wind
     mix cor,orch&pno (piano concerto with chorus) HUG (S3)

   Yamato Takeru *ora
     mix cor&jr cor,SATTBarBarB soli, orch, and japanese inst HUG (S4)

SAFRAN, LE see Kobayashi, Arata

SAG' JA, MEIN MÄGDELEIN see Kaelin, Pierre

SAGESSE see Vuataz, Roger

SAGVIK, STELLAN (1952- )
   Katábrio *Op.183
     boy cor/girl cor/mix cor STIM (S5)

SAH EIN KNAB EIN RÖSLEIN STEHN see Kupp, Albert

SAILOR BY MY RIGHT, A see Bremer, Jetse

SAILOR'S LIFE FOR ME, THE see Donnelly, Mary

ST. ELMO'S FIRE-LOVE THEME see Foster

SAINT-KOPP
   Allobroges, Les
     4pt mix cor BILLAUDOT (S6)

ST. LOUIS BLUES see Handy

ST. NICK AT NIGHT (JOLLY OLD ST. NICHOLAS)
   (Albrecht) 2pt cor ALFRED 5821 (S7)

SAINT RAPHAËL see Aliprandi, Paul

SAINTE-MARIE, BUFFY (1941- )
   Dream Tree, The
     (Allaway, Ben) SSA,kbd,opt ob, tubular bell WARNER SV9410 (S8)

   Up Where We Belong (composed with Nitzsche)
     SA WARCH 22031 (S9)
     (Strommen) SATB WARCH 33885 (S10)

SAINTS FUGUE see Anonymous

SAIOH FANTASY see Nakamura, Shigenobu

SAISON S'ÉCHAPPE, LA see Hemmerling, Carlos

SAISONNIERS, LE see Zbinden, Julien-François

SAISONS see Wissmer, Pierre

SAISONS À LA SAGNE, LES see Boller, Carlo

SAITO, TAKANOBU (1924- )
   Chikai No Kotoba
     cor HUG (S11)

   Kaitenmokuba Yo Maware
     mix cor HUG (S12)

   Kotoba Wa Iranai
     mix cor HUG (S13)

SALA, ANDRE
   Alouette, L'
     mix cor HUG 7626 (S14)

   Bergère
     mix cor HUG 7991 (S15)

   Cantilène De La Pluie, La
     men cor HUG 7994 (S16)

   C'est Dimanche
     mix cor HUG 7993 (S17)

   C'est Toujours Une Eau Nouvelle
     men cor HUG 7534 (S18)

   Chanson Du Vent De Mer, La
     men cor HUG 7719 (S19)

SALA, ANDRE (cont'd.)
  Cigale Et La Fourmi, La
    eq voices HUG 7627             (S20)
  Corbleu, Marion!
    mix cor HUG 8156               (S21)
  J'ai Vu Le Loup
    mix cor HUG 8180               (S22)
  Jardin Public
    men cor HUG 7791               (S23)
  Lys Rouge, Le
    eq voices,S solo HUG 7932      (S24)
  Octobre
    mix cor HUG 7425               (S25)
  Pardonnez-Moi
    men cor HUG 7675               (S26)
  Si Vous Saviez!...
    mix cor HUG 7424               (S27)
    men cor HUG 7423               (S28)
  Sonneur, Le
    men cor HUG 7493               (S29)
  Violette, La
    eq voices HUG 7809             (S30)
  Voici La Saint-Jean
    mix cor HUG 8180               (S31)
  Voici Le Mois De Mai
    mix cor HUG 7421               (S32)

SALADE À LA "DOUCETTE", LA see Bovet, J.

SALADIN, O.
  Dem Schweizerland
    men cor,acap MULLES            (S33)
  Hymne An Das Schweizerland
    men cor,acap MULLES            (S34)
  Lob Des Singens
    men cor,acap MULLES            (S35)
  Wohl In Den Holden Maienschein *folk song
    men cor,acap MULLES            (S36)

SALEM, 1692 see Hamel, Keith

SALIERI, ANTONIO (1750-1825)
  Scherzi Armonici *CCU
    (Acciai, G.) eq voices/mix cor,acap
    ZERBONI 8502 f.s.              (S37)

SALISH SONG see Six Canadian Folksongs

SALLUSTIO, E.
  Scala Di Cristallo, La
    mix cor (text by Hughes) BERBEN
    BERBEN 3022                    (S38)

SALLY GARDENS, THE
  (Larkin, Michael) SATB WARNER SV9545
                                   (S39)

SALUTO ALL'ITALIA see Menichetti, Dino

SAMMES, MIKE
  For The Fallen
    men cor BANKS ECS0214          (S40)

SAMPAYO, ANIBAL
  Ky Chororo
    (Gomez, Eduardo) mix cor LAGOS
                                   (S41)

SAMPEDRINO, EL see Gustavino, Carlos

SANCHEZ, DAMIAN
  Agua Y Viento, Cancion
    see Cuatro Obras Para Coro Mixto
  Cuatro Caminos, Cancion
    see Cuatro Obras Para Coro Mixto
  Cuatro Obras Para Coro Mixto
    4pt mix cor LAGOS f.s.
    contains: Agua Y Viento, Cancion;
    Cuatro Caminos, Cancion;
    Destituyo Las Rosas,
    Chamarrita; Tonada Del Adios,
    Cancion                        (S42)
  Destituyo Las Rosas, Chamarrita
    see Cuatro Obras Para Coro Mixto
  Raiz
    5pt mix cor LAGOS              (S43)
  Tonada Del Adios, Cancion
    see Cuatro Obras Para Coro Mixto

SANDMAN, THE see Brahms, Johannes

SANG SCULE
  (Easson, J. - Torrance, W.P.) unis
    cor,solo voice (song book contains:
    folk songs, chorales, ayres, arias,
    and classical songs) BANKS     (S44)

SÄNGER, DER see Märki, Ernst

SÄNGER WILL ICH BLEIBEN, EIN see Schmid, Walter

SÄNGERFAHRT see Huber, Walter Simon

SÄNGERFAHRT NACH DEM SÜDEN see Märki, Ernst

SÄNGERFREUNDSCHAFT see Schubert, Franz (Peter)

SÄNGERGRUSS see Kempfer, Lothar

SANGERMARSJ see Waaler, Fredrikke

SÄNGERS LETZTER GRUSS see Silcher, Friedrich

SÄNGERTAG see Schmid, Walter

SANKT STAFFAN
  (Oscarsson, Kjell) mix cor,acap
  SVERIG SK 785                    (S45)

SANKTA LUCIA see Hammarström, Hugo

SANTA CLAUS IS COMIN' TO TOWN
  (Besig, Don) SATB WARNER SV8329 (S46)

SANTA CLAUS IS COMING TO TOWN
  (Paquin-Salerno, Chris) SATB/SAB,perc
    (gr. II) UNC JP                (S47)

SANTA WANTS A BRAND NEW BAG see Albrecht, Sally K.

SANTA, WHAT YOU GONNA GET FROM ME? see Weston, Mark

SANTA'S A-COMIN'
  (Schmutte, Pete) SATB (medley
    containing Here Comes Santa Claus,
    Rudolph The Red Nosed Reindeer &
    Santa Claus Is Comin' To Town)
    WARNER C0349C1X ipa            (S48)
  (Schmutte, Pete) SAB (medley
    containing Here Comes Santa Claus,
    Rudolph The Red Nosed Reindeer &
    Santa Claus Is Comin' To Town)
    WARNER C0349C3X ipa            (S49)
  (Schmutte, Pete) 2pt cor (medley
    containing Here Comes Santa Claus,
    Rudolph The Red Nosed Reindeer &
    Santa Claus Is Comin' To Town)
    WARNER C0349C5X ipa            (S50)

SANTA'S WATCHING
  (Ames, Morgan) SATB,T solo,acap (gr.
    III) UNC JP                    (S51)

SANTÉ! see Martin

SAPEURS-POMPIERS, LES see Martin

SAPIEYEVSKI, JERZY (1945-    )
  Fly, White Butterflies
    see Six Choruses
  If Love Were The Roses
    see Six Choruses
  Little Time, A
    see Six Choruses
  Out Of Night
    see Six Choruses
  Six Choruses (from Songs Of The Rose)
    SATB,acap (med) PRESSER f.s.
    contains: Fly, White Butterflies;
    If Love Were The Roses; Little
    Time, A; Out Of Night; What
    Shall Be Done For Sorrow; You
    Hid Your Heart                 (S52)
  What Shall Be Done For Sorrow
    see Six Choruses
  You Hid Your Heart
    see Six Choruses

SARASATE, PABLO DE (1844-1908)
  Romanza Andaluza
    (Swingle, Ward) SSAATTBB,S&T soli
    (gr. III) voc pt,pts UNC JP
    SOS-1X                         (S53)

SARMANTO, HEIKKI
  New England Images
    SATB, jazz ensemble (diff. contains
    the ancient apple tree,
    butterfly, tree frogs, november
    morning frost, birches on the
    hill and red wings) PRESSER
    512-00636                      (S54)

SARTORIUS, THOMAS
  Wohlauf, Ihr Lieben Gäste
    SATB,acap (ed. hannaford) SANTA
    SBMP 49                        (S55)

SASSY SAMBA
  (New York Voices) SSATB,S solo,perc
    (gr. IV) UNC JP                (S56)

SATCHMO see Joplin

SATO, TOSHINAO (1936-    )
  Jo-Kei
    wom cor,pno HUG                (S57)

SAUCEPANS see Morris, Haydn, Sosban Fach

SAUCY SAILOR see Specht, Judy

SAUGUET, HENRI (1901-1989)
  Cantate Des Saisons
    jr cor/wom cor BILLAUDOT       (S58)
    4pt wom cor BILLAUDOT          (S59)

SAUSENG, WOLFGANG
  Corinna
    wom cor DOBLINGER O 392        (S60)
  Herrliche Nacht
    mix cor BERBEN G 816           (S61)
    mix cor DOBLINGER G 816        (S62)
  Rudern, Gespräche
    (Brecht) wom cor DOBLINGER O 391
                                   (S63)
  Tod, Der
    mix cor BERBEN G 815           (S64)
    mix cor DOBLINGER G 815        (S65)

SAUTE LA BRUME see Urfer, Albert

SAVORY, SAGE, ROSEMARY AND THYME see Patriquin, Donald

SAXOPHONE JOE
  (Cross, Dave) SATB,pno,db,db (gr. I)
    UNC JP                         (S66)

SAY IT WITH A SONG! see Price

SAYO-NARA see Kawasaki, Etsuo

SBORDONI, ALESSANDRO (1948-    )
  Rondel
    6pt men cor RICORDI-IT 132628  (S67)

SÇAIS-TU DIR' L'AVE? see Lassus, Roland de (Orlandus)

SCALA DI CRISTALLO, LA see Sallustio, E.

SCARBOROGH SETTLER'S LAMENT see Henderson, Ruth Watson

SCARBOROUGH FAIR
  (Althouse) SATB ALFRED 11308     (S68)
  (Althouse) SAB ALFRED 11309      (S69)
  (Althouse) SSA ALFRED 11310      (S70)
  (Schmutte, Pete) 2pt cor WARNER
    0705SC5X                       (S71)
  (Schmutte, Pete) SATB WARNER 0705SC1X
                                   (S72)
  (Schmutte, Pete) SAB WARNER 0705SC3X
                                   (S73)

SCARLATTI, DOMENICO (1685-1757)
  Serenata (from Quattro Stagioni, Le)
    cor,SSAT soli,chamber group
    RICORDI-IT                     (S74)

SCARLETT RIBBONS (FOR HER HAIR) see Danzig, Evelyn

SCELSI, GIACINTO (1905-1988)
  Yliam
    wom cor,acap SALABERT EAS 18292
                                   (S75)

SCENE SINFONICHE PER IL DOKTOR FAUSTUS see Manzoni, Giacomo

SCÈNES DU PRINTEMPS see Grast, F.

SCHALLEHN, HILGER (1936-    )
  Singen Ist Das Atmen Der Seele
    mix cor&men cor,acap sc SCHOTTS
    C 48052                        (S76)

SCHATTENSCHMIEDE, DIE see Mermoud, Robert

SCHAU, WIA GLIACHT IS DA TÄG *CC14U, Austrian
  (Berger, Erwin) mix cor HEYN
    ISBN 3 85366 474 1 f.s.        (S77)

SCHAUT NUR AN DEN SCHÖNEN MORGEN see Haus, Karl

SCHEIDEN UND MEIDEN see Brun, Fritz

SCHENK MIR DOCH EIN KLEINES BISSCHEN LIEBE see Lincke, Paul

SCHERZI ARMONICI see Salieri, Antonio

SCHERZO see Beethoven, Ludwig van

SCHIAVO, GIANPAOLO (1960-    )
  Avidamente Allargo La Mia Mano
    4pt mix cor,acap (text by
    Quasimodo) BERBEN BERBEN 3081
                                   (S78)

SCHIAVO, GIANPAOLO (cont'd.)

   I Madrigali Di Claudio Monteverdi
      mix cor BERBEN BERBEN 2400 (S79)

SCHIFFLEIN SAH ICH FAHREN, EIN see
   Ruprecht, Ernst

SCHINDLER, PETER (1960- )
   Drei Songs Für Kinder
      1-3pt jr cor,kbd,gtr,db,drums CARUS
      f.s.
         contains: Käsebande, Die; Kleines
         Huhn Fliegt Um Die Welt,Ein;
         Urwaldsong (S80)

   Käsebande, Die
     see Drei Songs Für Kinder

   Kleines Huhn Fliegt Um Die Welt,Ein
     see Drei Songs Für Kinder

   Urwaldsong
     see Drei Songs Für Kinder

SCHINELLI, ACHILLE (1882-1969)
   Trentacinque Canti Popolari Italiani
    *CC35U
      cor,pno ZERBONI 4745 f.s. (S81)

SCHLAFLOS "GEGEN DREI HÄTTEN DIE LIPPEN
   GENÜGT" see Helmschrott, Robert M.

SCHLANGE UND DER KREBS, DIE see Asriel,
   André

SCHLEIDT, WILHELM
   D'visitestube
     wom cor,acap MULLES (S82)
     men cor,acap MULLES (S83)

SCHLERF, L.
   Bauernkantate
     mix cor,kbd BOHM (S84)

SCHLUSSGESANG AUS DER "DEUTSCHEN MESSE"
   see Schubert, Franz (Peter)

SCHMID, A.
   Alte Herz,Das
     men cor,acap MULLES (S85)

   Dem Vaterland
     men cor,acap MULLES (S86)

   Freie Heimat
     men cor,acap MULLES (S87)

   Frühling
     men cor,acap MULLES (S88)

   Heimatgebet
     men cor,acap MULLES (S89)

   Helle Grühling,Der
     (Schmid, W.) wom cor,acap MULLES
     (S90)

   Höhensehnsucht
     men cor,acap MULLES (S91)

   Ich Lied Durch Deine Gassen
     men cor,acap MULLES (S92)

   Schweizerland
     men cor,acap MULLES (S93)

   Stiller Hügel
     wom cor,acap MULLES (S94)

SCHMID, ERNST
   Herr, Du Weisst, Wie Arm Wir Wandern
     wom cor,acap MULLES (S95)

SCHMID, S.W.
   Herbst
     men cor,acap MULLES (S96)

   Sommersegen
     wom cor,acap MULLES (S97)

SCHMID, WALTER (1906- )
   Abschiedslied
     men cor,acap MULLES (S98)

   Alpen
     men cor,acap MULLES (S99)

   Altes Städtchen
     men cor,acap MULLES (S100)

   Am Höhenfeuer
     men cor,acap MULLES (S101)

   An Die Heimat
     wom cor,acap MULLES (S102)
     men cor,acap MULLES (S103)

   Aufbruch
     men cor,acap MULLES (S104)

   Bergsommer
     men cor,acap MULLES (S105)

   Bundes-Schwur
     men cor,acap MULLES (S106)

SCHMID, WALTER (cont'd.)

   Bundes-Treue
     men cor,acap MULLES (S107)

   Danklied
     men cor,acap MULLES (S108)

   Dörfer
     men cor,acap MULLES (S109)

   Erntedank
     men cor,acap MULLES (S110)

   Fest Der Lieder
     men cor,acap MULLES (S111)

   Festgruss
     wom cor,acap MULLES (S112)

   Festlicher Morgen
     wom cor,acap MULLES (S113)
     men cor,acap MULLES (S114)

   Festlicher Tag
     wom cor,acap MULLES (S115)

   Fluss,Der
     men cor,acap MULLES (S116)

   Freies Lied,Ein
     men cor,acap MULLES (S117)

   Freudig Schallen Unsere Lieder
     men cor,acap MULLES (S118)

   Friede
     wom cor,acap MULLES (S119)

   Frohe Wanderschaft
     men cor,acap MULLES (S120)

   Frühling, Der Helle Frühling
     men cor,acap MULLES (S121)

   Frühlingsabend
     wom cor,acap MULLES (S122)

   Frühlingsfahrt
     men cor,acap MULLES (S123)

   Frühlingstag
     men cor,acap MULLES (S124)

   Frühlinstag
     wom cor,acap MULLES (S125)

   Frühlinswunsch
     men cor,acap MULLES (S126)

   Für Ein Gesangfest
     men cor,acap MULLES (S127)

   Glück Der Heimat
     men cor,acap MULLES (S128)

   Glückauf, Der Sonn Entgegen
     wom cor,acap MULLES (S129)

   Heiligste Nacht
     men cor,acap MULLES (S130)

   Heimat, Deine Glocken Klingen
     wom cor,acap MULLES (S131)

   Heimatlied: Ich Bin Stiller ...
     men cor,acap MULLES (S132)

   Heimatlied: Wohl Dem, Der Solche ...
     men cor,acap MULLES (S133)

   Heimet
     men cor,acap MULLES (S134)

   Heimetdörfli, 'S
     men cor,acap MULLES (S135)

   Heimetglück
     wom cor,acap MULLES (S136)

   Helle Weg,Der
     wom cor,acap MULLES (S137)

   Herbstlied
     men cor,acap MULLES (S138)

   Im Wättersturm
     wom cor,acap MULLES (S139)

   In Den Bergen
     wom cor,acap MULLES (S140)
     men cor,acap MULLES (S141)

   In Den Grünen Tag Hinein
     men cor,acap MULLES (S142)

   Jauchzendes Leben
     wom cor,acap MULLES (S143)

   Kleines Wanderlied
     men cor,acap MULLES (S144)

   Kommt, Singt Ein Lied
     wom cor,acap MULLES (S145)
     men cor,acap MULLES (S146)

SCHMID, WALTER (cont'd.)

   Landeslied
     men cor,acap MULLES (S147)

   Lass, Herr, Dein Licht Erscheinen
     wom cor,acap MULLES (S148)

   Lebensfreude
     wom cor,acap MULLES (S149)
     men cor,acap MULLES (S150)

   Lenzlied
     men cor,acap MULLES (S151)

   Lie Und Leben
     men cor,acap MULLES (S152)

   Lied,Das
     men cor,acap MULLES (S153)

   Lied Der Heimat
     wom cor,acap MULLES (S154)
     men cor,acap MULLES (S155)

   Lied Vom Schweizerstern,,Das
     men cor,acap MULLES (S156)

   Liedermorgen
     men cor,acap MULLES (S157)

   Lob Der Rast
     men cor,acap MULLES (S158)

   Lob Des Gesanges
     wom cor,acap MULLES (S159)
     men cor,acap MULLES (S160)

   Musik, Du Mächtige!
     men cor,acap MULLES (S161)

   Musik Ist Eine Gottesgab *cant
     wom cor,pno kbd pt,cor pts MULLES
     (S162)

   Neuer Frühling
     wom cor,acap MULLES (S163)
     men cor,acap MULLES (S164)

   O Berge, Hohe Heimat
     men cor,acap MULLES (S165)

   Rausch Auf, O Lied
     men cor,acap MULLES (S166)
     men cor&jr cor,2trp MULLES (S167)

   Sänger Will Ich Bleiben,Ein
     men cor,acap MULLES (S168)

   Sängertag
     men cor,acap MULLES (S169)

   Schön Ist Der Herbst
     men cor,acap MULLES (S170)

   Schöni Heimet
     wom cor,acap MULLES (S171)
     men cor,acap MULLES (S172)

   Schwizerlied
     wom cor,acap MULLES (S173)

   Singe, Seele, Sing Dich Jung
     wom cor,acap MULLES (S174)

   Singen
     men cor,acap MULLES (S175)

   Sommerblumen
     wom cor,acap MULLES (S176)

   Sommerwanderung
     men cor,acap MULLES (S177)

   Sonntag
     wom cor,acap MULLES (S178)
     men cor,acap MULLES (S179)

   Sonntagslied
     men cor,acap MULLES (S180)

   Spruch
     men cor,acap MULLES (S181)

   Stille Der Felder
     men cor,acap MULLES (S182)

   Trinklied
     men cor,acap MULLES (S183)

   Vaterlandslied
     men cor,acap MULLES (S184)

   Vermahlied An Die Eidgenossenschaft
     unis men cor MULLES (S185)

   Vermahnlied
     men cor,acap MULLES (S186)

   Wanderglück
     wom cor,acap MULLES (S187)
     men cor,acap MULLES (S188)

   Wanderlied
     wom cor,acap MULLES (S189)

SCHMID, WALTER (cont'd.)

    Wanderlust
      men cor,acap MULLES      (S190)

    Wandern
      men cor,acap MULLES      (S191)

    Weihnachtsbotschaft
      men cor,acap MULLES      (S192)

    Wein Und Sang
      men cor,acap MULLES      (S193)

    Wunderliche Hast Des Lebens
      men cor,acap MULLES      (S194)

    Zuversicht
      wom cor,acap MULLES      (S195)
      men cor,acap MULLES      (S196)

SCHMIED,DER see Brun, Fritz see Doret, Gustave

SCHMIEDE-LIED: "I ISCH NÜMME DIE ZYT" see Zingg

SCHMITT, FLORENT (1870-1958)
    Sous Bois
      4pt men cor BILLAUDOT    (S197)

SCHMUTTE, PETE
    Let The Music Roll On
      SATB WARNER 1683LC1X ipa (S198)
      SAB WARNER 1683LC3X ipa  (S199)

SCHNEEGLÖGGLI see Märki, Ernst

SCHNEEPANTHER see Dallinger, Gerhard

SCHNEIDER UND DIE SPATZEN, DER see Hess, Carlheinz

SCHNEIDERS HÖLLENFAHRT see Diener, Theodor

SCHNEPPER, OTHMAR
    Frankenfahrt
      mix cor BUTZ 1167        (S200)

    Trinkspruch
      mix cor BUTZ 1168        (S201)

SCHNITTERLIED see Doret, Gustave

SCHOENBERG, ARNOLD (1874-1951)
    Dreimal Tausend Jahre *Op.50a
      mix cor sc BELMONT BEL-1025 (S202)

    Four Pieces, Op. 27
      mix cor,instrumental ensemble sc
      BELMONT UE-8549 pts rent (S203)

    Gurrelieder
      mix cor,SATTB&speaking voice,8+
      4pic.5+2English horn.1+3clar in
      A+2bass clar+soprano clar in E
      flat.2+contrabsn. 4.3.3.1. timp,
      3perc,2harp,pno,harmonium,strings
      BELMONT study sc UE-18412, pno
      red UE-3696            (S204)

    Peace on Earth *Op.13
      mix cor,acap/chamber orch sc
      BELMONT BEL-1013       (S205)

    Survivor From Warsaw, A *Op.46
      men cor,narrator,2+2pic.2.2.2.
      4.3.3.1. timp,5perc,harp,strings
      BELMONT sc BEL-1030, pno red
      BEL-1046              (S206)

    Three Satires, Op. 28
      mix cor,instrumental ensemble sc
      BELMONT UE-8586 pts rent (S207)

SCHÖN BLUMELEIN see Schumann, Robert (Alexander)

SCHÖN IST DER HERBST see Schmid, Walter

SCHÖN IST DIE JUGEND see Anderluh, Anton

SCHONBERG, CLAUDE-MICHEL
    American Dream, The (from Miss Saigon)
      SATB NOVELLO 091130    (S208)

    Bring Him Home (from Miserables, Les)
      SATB NOVELLO 091330    (S209)

    Castle On A Cloud (from Miserables, Les)
      SATB NOVELLO 091430    (S210)

    I Dreamed A Dream (from Miserables, Les)
      SATB NOVELLO 091730    (S211)

    Last Night Of The World, The (from Miss Saigon)
      SATB NOVELLO 091830    (S212)

SCHONBERG, CLAUDE-MICHEL (cont'd.)

    Miserables, Les
      SATB (choral suite) NOVELLO 092633                      (S213)

    Miss Saigon
      SATB (choral suite) NOVELLO 092733                      (S214)

SCHÖNBERG, STIG GUSTAV (1933- )
    Du Är Skön Såsom Tirsa
      TTBB SVERIG SK 730     (S215)

SCHÖNE ADLER see Olpen, Friedrich W.

SCHÖNE ANNELIESE, DIE see Doret, Gustave

SCHÖNI HEIMET see Märki, Ernst see Schmid, Walter

SCHÖNSTE ZEIT,DIE see Krenger, R.

SCHONTHAL-SECKEL, RUTH (1924- )
    Young Dead Soldiers, The
      SATB,chamber orch/orch HILD study
      sc 09430A, sc,pts 09430B (S216)

SCHRAM, RUTH ELAINE
    Camel, Kneel Softly
      2pt cor WARNER BSC00294  (S217)

    Snow Is Falling
      SSA ALFRED 11356       (S218)
      2pt cor ALFRED 11357   (S219)

    Wind, The
      2pt cor ALFRED 11603   (S220)

SCHUBERT
    Come Sail Away With Me (composed with Williams; Larson)
      3pt mix cor SHAWNEE D-0481 (S221)

SCHUBERT, FRANZ (1808-1878)
    Serenade
      (Pearson, A.) SATB BANKS 989 (S222)

    Who Is Sylvia ?
      SATB BANKS 42         (S223)

SCHUBERT, FRANZ (PETER) (1797-1828)
    A L'absente
      men cor HUG 7891       (S224)

    A Qui Conter Sa Peine?
      see Wohin Soll Ich Mich Wenden?

    Abendlied
      men cor,acap MULLES      (S225)

    An Den Frühling
      men cor,acap MULLES      (S226)

    An Die Musik
      see Vier Gesänge

    Aubade
      men cor HUG 7174       (S227)

    Dans La Forêt
      men cor HUG 8169       (S228)

    Dörfchen, Das
      "Village, Le" [Ger/Fr] eq voices HUG 7840                            (S229)

    Drinking Song From The 14th Century *Op.155
      (Rice, Martin) TBB,pno MUSIC SEV. 693                                (S230)

    Du Bist Die Ruh
      unis cor WARCH 34344    (S231)

    Fischerweise
      unis cor WARCH 34347    (S232)

    Gais Compagnons
      (Mouchet) 4pt men cor BILLAUDOT                                        (S233)

    Heidenröslein
      "Vole Autour Du Monde" [Ger/Fr] mix cor HUG 8356     (S234)
      "Vole Autour Du Monde" men cor HUG 8423                           (S235)

    Im Gegenwärtigen Vergangenes
      (Oetiker, August) wom cor,soli,pno MULLES                              (S236)

    Liebe Rauscht Des Silberbach
      see Vier Gesänge

    Lindenbaum, Die
      "Tilleul, Le" [Ger/Fr] eq voices HUG 7596                           (S237)

    Litenei And Nacht Und Traume
      unis cor WARCH 34376    (S238)

    Mailied: Grüner Wird Die Au
      see Vier Gesänge

    Musensohn, Der
      unis cor WARCH 34341    (S239)

SCHUBERT, FRANZ (PETER) (cont'd.)

    Nacht, Die
      "Nuit, La" [Ger/Fr] eq voices HUG 7597                                (S240)

    Night
      (Hoare, Krummacher) TTBB,acap PRESSER 312-41659     (S241)

    Nocturne *Op.156
      eq voices HUG 7842      (S242)

    Nuit, La
      men cor HUG 6082       (S243)
      see Nacht, Die

    Printemps
      men cor HUG 7891       (S244)
      eq voices HUG 7841      (S245)

    Romance
      men cor HUG 8223       (S246)

    Sängerfreundschaft
      men cor,acap MULLES      (S247)

    Schlussgesang Aus Der "Deutschen Messe"
      see Vier Gesänge

    Sing Forever
      (Liebergen, Patrick) 3pt mix cor WARNER SV9339       (S248)

    Tilleul, Le
      men cor,opt pno/org/orch HUG 4136                               (S249)
      see Lindenbaum, Die

    Vier Gesänge
      wom cor,acap MULLES f.s.
      contains: An Die Musik; Liebe Rauscht Des Silberbach; Mailied: Grüner Wird Die Au; Schlussgesang Aus Der "Deutschen Messe"       (S250)

    Village, Le
      see Dörfchen, Das

    Vole Autour Du Monde
      see Heidenröslein

    Wohin Soll Ich Mich Wenden?
      "A Qui Conter Sa Peine?" [Ger/Fr] eq voices HUG 7525     (S251)

SCHUDEL, THOMAS (1937- )
    Ale
      SATB,acap MUSIC SEV. 664 (S252)

    Another Love Poem
      SATB,acap CAN.MUS.CENT. MV 6000 S384AN         (S253)

    Dream Within A Dream, A
      SATB,acap MUSIC SEV. 663 (S254)

    Gold and Rose
      SATB,acap CAN.MUS.CENT. MV 6000 S384GOL        (S255)

    Pick Up the Earth
      SATB,acap CAN.MUS.CENT. MV 6000 S384PIC        (S256)

SCHULE, BERNARD (1909- )
    Land Und Freiheit
      "Terre Libre" men cor HUG 8078                              (S257)
      see Terre Libre

    Terre Libre
      "Land Und Freiheit" [Fr/Ger] mix cor HUG 8077       (S258)
      see Land Und Freiheit

SCHUMANN, ROBERT (ALEXANDER) (1810-1856)
    Célèbre Rêverie
      (Février) 4pt mix cor BILLAUDOT                            (S259)

    Chanson À Boire
      men cor HUG 8151       (S260)

    Chant Du Chasseur, Le
      see Jägerland

    Chant Du Voyageur
      see Wanderlied

    Chevauchée
      men cor HUG 8148       (S261)

    Dimanche Aux Bords Du Rhin
      men cor HUG 3516       (S262)

    Eight Partsongs *CC8U
      treb cor FABER 51470 7   (S263)

    Fleur De Lotus, La
      eq voices HUG 8152      (S264)

## SCHUMANN, ROBERT (ALEXANDER) (cont'd.)

Four Folksongs For Women's Choir
  SA,pno GENTRY JG2151 f.s.
  contains: May Song; Spring Song;
  To The Evening Star; To The
  Nightingale            (S265)

Gai Laboureur, Le
  (Février) 4pt mix cor BILLAUDOT
                                      (S266)

Gebt Mir Zu Trinken *canon
  men cor,acap MULLES     (S267)

Jägerland
  "Chant Du Chasseur, Le" [Ger/Fr]
  mix cor HUG 8095        (S268)

Lac Profond, Le
  men cor HUG 8014        (S269)

Lasst Lautenspiel Und Becherklang
  *canon
  men cor,acap MULLES     (S270)

Mailied
  (Fleet) "May Song" SA KJOS 6235
                                      (S271)

May Song
  see Four Folksongs For Women's
    Choir
  see Mailied

Om Slaraffenland
  (Sköld) SATB NOTERIA 2827  (S272)

Rose De L'aurore, La
  men cor HUG 8014        (S273)

Schön Blumelein
  (Fleet) SA/TB KJOS 6234   (S274)

Seigneur Des Eaux, Le
  see Wasserman, Der

Spring Song
  see Four Folksongs For Women's
    Choir

To The Evening Star
  see Four Folksongs For Women's
    Choir

To The Nightingale
  see Four Folksongs For Women's
    Choir

Vous Fuyez Bien Loin D'ici
  mix cor HUG 8242        (S275)

Wanderlied
  "Chant Du Voyageur" men cor HUG
  8257                         (S276)

Wasserman, Der
  "Seigneur Des Eaux, Le" [Ger/Fr] eq
  voices HUG 8098        (S277)

Ziegeunerleben
  SATB,pno BUTZ 1233      (S278)

## SCHWAEN, KURT (1909-    )
Brücke Zu Allen Kindern,Eine
  jr cor,kbd (12 kinderlieder) NEUE
  NM 331                (S279)

Dieb Und Der König,Der
  jr cor,kbd NEUE NM307    (S280)

Krug Mit Oliven,Ein
  jr cor, solo voices&speaking voice,
  pno NEUE NM 343        (S281)

## SCHWARTZ
Choruses From 'Godspell' And
  'Children Of Eden' *CCU
  (Parry) mix cor FABER 51491 X
                                      (S282)

Choruses From 'Godspell' And
  'Children Of Eden' *CCU
  (Arch G) SSA,pno FABER 51462 6
                                      (S283)

## SCHWARTZ, DAN
All About Christmas Carols
  SAB/SB/2pt cor,pno (gr. II) UNC JP
                                      (S284)

All I Want To Do Is Dance
  SATB,opt perc (gr. III) UNC JP
                                      (S285)

Are You Aware Of My Love?
  SATB,pno (gr. II) UNC JP  (S286)

Christmas Is A Feeling
  SATB/2pt cor,pno (gr. II) UNC JP
                                      (S287)

Christmas Will Be Here Any Day
  SATB,pno,db,drums (gr. II) UNC JP
                                      (S288)

Gotta Get Myself Together (from Ab,
  Perc, Opt Gt+ Trb+Trp+Saxa+Saxt)
  (gr. II) UNC JP         (S289)

I Want To Be There
  SATB WARNER SV9451     (S290)
  3pt mix cor WARNER SV9452 (S291)
  2pt cor WARNER SV9453   (S292)

## SCHWARTZ, DAN (cont'd.)

In Time For Christmas
  SATB,pno,opt fl&drums (gr. II) UNC
  JP                         (S293)

Leave All My Dreams To Me (from Atb,
  Acap)
  (gr. II/gr. III) UNC JP   (S294)

Let's Fly
  2pt cor (gr. I/gr. II) UNC JP
                                      (S295)

Lonesome Road
  SAB,solo,perc (gr. II) UNC JP
                                      (S296)

Mardi Gras In Rio
  SATB,perc (gr. III) UNC JP (S297)

Our Love Where Did It Go?
  SATB,pno (gr. II) UNC JP  (S298)

Sounds Of The City
  SATB,solo,perc (gr. III) UNC JP
                                      (S299)

Spirit Of Christmas Is Here, The
  SATB,pno FISCHER,C CM8430 (S300)

This Will Be Our Time
  SATB,pno (gr. III) UNC JP (S301)

You Gotta Take Me As Am
  SATB,pno,db,drums,horn (gr. II) UNC
  JP                         (S302)

SCHWEDISCHES SEEMANNLIED (ES WEHT...)
  see Märki, Ernst

SCHWEIGEN see Helmschrott, Robert M.

## SCHWEITZER, BRURIA
Summer Is Here
  SATB (Israel Memorial Day) OR-TAV
                                      (S303)

## SCHWEIZER, ALFRED
Aufbruch
  see Diptychon

Aus Zeit Und Leid, Ein Rückblick?
  dbl cor,Bar solo,2.2.2.2.3sax.
  4.2.3.0. perc,strings [12'15"]
  MULLES cor pts f.s., pts rent
                                      (S304)

Diptychon
  SATB,acap MULLES f.s.
  contains: Aufbruch; Einkehr
                                      (S305)

Drei Berner Namens Johann Bieri, Otto
  Notter, Sami Streit
  SATB,acap [4'] MULLES    (S306)

Einkehr
  see Diptychon

Fabulette
  2pt cor,pno MULLES      (S307)

Lied In Die Haushaltung, Ein
  cor,A solo,pno,vln MULLES (S308)

Mal Was Andres
  SATB,acap [8'] (diff) MULLES (S309)

Motette, Immer Wieder Werden Gärten
  Sein
  SATB,acap MULLES       (S310)

Motto
  SATB,acap MULLES       (S311)

Narrenkanon (from Mal Was Andres)
  SATB,acap MULLES       (S312)

Solfeggio
  3pt wom cor,synthesizer MULLES
                                      (S313)

## SCHWEIZER, THEODOR (1916-    )
Dank A Ds Chornhuus
  men cor,acap MULLES     (S314)

SCHWEIZERGEIST see Oser, Hans

SCHWEIZERLAND see Neuhaus, Gérard see
  Schmid, A.

SCHWEIZERLIED see Tobler, J.H.

SCHWEIZERPSALM: TRITTS IM MORGENROT see
  Zwyssig, Alberich

SCHWEIZERS ABSCHIED VON DER HEIMAT see
  Hofer-Schneeberger, Emma

SCHWEIZERSPRUCH see Kreis, Otto

SCHWIZERLIED see Schmid, Walter

## SCIARRINO, SALVATORE (1947-    )
Flos Florum, Ovvero Le Trasformazioni
  Della Materia Sonora
  SS/MezATT/BarB,4.3.3.3. 6.4.4.1.
  timp,perc,cel,strings sc RICORDI-
  IT 133230            (S315)

## SCIARRINO, SALVATORE (cont'd.)

Immagine Di Arpocrate, Un'
  SS/MezATT/BarB,3.3.3.3. 6.4.4.1.
  cel,2harp,perc,strings sc
  RICORDI-IT 132980      (S316)

Musiche Per "I Bei Colloqui" Di
  Aurelio Pes
  cor RICORDI-IT 131962   (S317)

Musiche Per Le "Trachinie" Di Sofocle
  cor,electronic tape RICORDI-IT
  133111                (S318)

## SCOTT, [LADY] JOHN (ALICIA ANN)
(1810-1900)
Annie Laurie
  (Gates, C.) SATB oct THOMAS
  1C0137726           (S319)

SCROOGE see Leisy, James Franklin

SE AMOR MAI DA VU SE VEDE
  4pt wom cor MULLES M&S 1200 (S320)

SEA-CRYSTAL JOURNEY see Corea,Chick

SEA DRIFT (G-E) see Delius, Frederick

SEA IN MY COUNTRY, THE see Hirayoshi,
  Kunitake, Umi-Furusato No

SEA NYMPHS see Xenakis, Yannis (Iannis)

SEALED WITH A KISS see Geld, Gary

SEARCH FOR SONGS, THE see Ikebe, Shin-
  Ichiro

SEASON OF CHILDREN see Igarashi,
  Tadashi

SEASON OF DREAMS see Marryott, Ralph E.

SEASONS see Coghlan

## SEBESKY, GERALD JOHN (1941-    )
March Of The Christmas Children
  2pt cor ALFRED 11320    (S321)
  SATB ALFRED 11318      (S322)
  3pt cor ALFRED 11319    (S323)

## SECADA, JON
I'm Free (composed with Morejon,
  Miguel A.)
  (Funk, Jeff) [Eng/Span] SATB WARNER
  4277IC1X             (S324)
  (Funk, Jeff) [Eng/Span] SAB WARNER
  4277IC3X             (S325)

SECHS HEITERE ALPENLÄNDISCHE
  VOLKSLIEDER UND JODLER *CC6U
  (Mittergradnegger, Günther) mix cor
  HEYN NR. 132 f.s.      (S326)

SECHS LIEDER see Genzmer see
  Mendelssohn-Bartholdy, Felix

SECHS ÖSTERREICHISCHE VOLKSLIEDER
  *CC6U,folk song,Austrian
  (Anderluh, Anton) men cor HEYN NR. 58
  f.s.                       (S327)

SECHS SPRÜCHE (BERNER LIEDERSPENDE) see
  Studer, Hans

SECHSTE SIEGEL see Terzakis, Dimitri

SECONDO LA PROMESSA see Zanolini, Bruno

SECONDO LIBRO DE MADRIGALI A SEI VOCI,
  IL see Gabrieli, Andrea

SECONDO LIBRO DI MADRIGALI A CINQUE
  VOCI, INSIEME DOI A SEI ET UNO
  DIALOGO A OTTO, IL see Gabrieli,
  Andrea

SECRET DU RUISSEAU, LE see Bovet, J.

SECRETE VIE,LE see Gentilucci, Armando

SECULAR WORKS see Ciconia, Johannes

SEE HOW THE MORNING SMILES see Ireland,
  John

SEE OUR OARS WITH FEATHER'D SPRAY see
  Stevenson, John A.

SEE THE CONQU'RING HERO COMES see
  Handel, George Frideric

SEE YOU IN SEPTEMBER see Edwards,
  Sherman

SEEDS OF LOVE see Halley

## SEEGER, PETE (1919-    )
If I Had A Hammer
  SATB (rock version) WARCH 34780
                                      (S328)
  SSA WARCH 34811        (S329)

SEEGER, PETE (cont'd.)
  Turn Turn Turn
    SATB WARCH 34804                    (S330)

SEEING IS BELIEVING see Lloyd Webber, Andrew

SEELAND see Märki, Ernst

SEEMANNSLIED see Gaillard, Paul-Andre

SEEN AND UNSEEN see Marshall, Jane M. (Mrs. Elbert H.)

SEGARD
  A Cache-Cache
    2 eq voices BILLAUDOT               (S331)

  Echos Printaniers
    2 eq voices BILLAUDOT               (S332)

SEGRETO, IL see Bettinelli, Bruno

SÉGUEDILLE see Martin

SEHNSUCHT see Olpen, Friedrich W.

SEHNSUCHT NACH DEN BERGEN see Hofer-Schneeberger, Emma

SEIGNEUR, DANS VOTRE MAIN... see Doret, Gustave

SEIGNEUR DES EAUX, LE see Schumann, Robert (Alexander), Wasserman, Der

SEIGNEUR DIEU see Henchoz, Emile

SEIGNEUR, LA JOIE see Henchoz, Emile

SEIZE CANTIQUES see Boller, Carlo

SELECT UNISON ANTHEMS see Hoffmann

SEND IN THE CLOWNS see Sondheim, Stephen Joshua

SENFL, LUDWIG (ca. 1490-1543)
  Ich Armes Käuzlein Kleine
    mix cor BUTZ 222                    (S333)

SENNELIED see Niggli, Friedrich

SENSHU, JIRO (1934-    )
  Toast To The Wind  *Suite
    mix cor,pno HUG                     (S334)

SENTEI MINAGE see Kurachi, Tatsuya

SENTIER, LE see Martin

SENTIERS VALAISANS, LES see Haenni, G.

SÉPARATION
  (Charlet) men cor HUG 8604            (S335)

SEPT FRAGMENTS D'ARCHILOQUE see Guérinel

SEPTEMBER see Swerts, Piet

SERAIN, CRAIG
  Water Is Wide,The (from The Gift Of Love)
    SATB,T/female solo,pno,fl,db,drums
    (gr. II/gr. III) UNC JP             (S336)

SERENADE see Schubert, Franz

SÉRÉNADE BROUILLÉE, LA see Mozart, Wolfgang Amadeus, Gestörte Ständchen, Das

SÉRÉNADE SANS GUITARE (from Terre Et L'étoile, La)
  men cor HUG 8847                      (S337)
  see Bron, Patrick

SERENATA see Kreis, Otto see Scarlatti, Domenico

THREE RUSSIAN SONGS, OP. 41 see Rachmaninoff, Sergey Vassilievich

SERMISY, CLAUDE DE (CLAUDIN) (ca. 1490-1562)
  Languir Me Fais
    mix cor HUG 7939                    (S338)
    men cor HUG 8526                    (S339)

  Tant Que Vivrai
    mix cor HUG 1875                    (S340)

SERPENT, THE see Jeffers, Ron

SERVANTE D'EVOLÈNE, LA see Doret, Gustave

SERVUS, TANTE ANNEGRET see Lemmermann, Heinz

SESTO NON-SENSO see Petrassi, Goffredo

SET OF CHINESE FOLKSONGS, A see Chen, Yi

SET YOUR HEART A SINGIN' see Kimes, Janice

SETER VISE FRÅ SUNNDALEN see Bøe, Bernt

SETTE QUARTINE D'OMAR KHAYYÂM see Brero, Cesare

SETZ' AUF MEI GRÜANS HÜATLE  *CCU,folk song,Austrian
  (Anderluh, Anton- Asenbauer, Andreas)
    men cor HEYN NR. 60 f.s.            (S341)

SEULETTE SUIS, SANS MON BERGER see Bovet, J.

SEVEN COURTLY LOVE SONGS see Anonymous

SEVEN DEADLY SINS see Glickman, Sylvia

SEVEN GREEK PASTORAL SCENES see Parker, Horatio William

SEVEN PARTSONGS see Parry

SEVEN POEMS OF PRINCESS SHIKISHI see Nishimura, Akira

SEVEN SONGS FROM SHAKESPEARE'S COMODIES see Strohbach, Siegfried

SEVERIN, MARC
  Ou T'en Vas-Tu Petite Souris ?
    3 eq voices BILLAUDOT               (S342)

SEVILLA see Albéniz, Isaac

SHADOWS OF DUSK see Raum, Elizabeth

SHADOWS OF THE MOON see Mechem, Kirke Lewis

SHAIMAN, MARC
  Wink And A Smile, A (composed with McLean, Ramsey)
    (Leavitt, John) SSA WARNER SV9457   (S343)
    (Leavitt, John) SAB WARNER SV9458   (S344)
    (Leavitt, John) SATB WARNER SV9456  (S345)

SHAKE OUT ALL THOSE BLUES see Fischer, Clare

SHAKESPEARIAN SONNET see Fellegara, Vittorio

SHALL I COMPARE THEE? see Larkin, Michael

SHALOM  *CCU,Isr
  (Lemmermann, Heinz) 3 eq voices/mix cor FIDULA 6083 f.s.  (S346)

SHALOM, MY FRIENDS see Wagner, Douglas Edward

SHALOM YERUSHALAYIM see Shur, Laura

SHAPES OF LOVE, THE see Endo, Masao

SHARAD see Bhatia, Vanraj A.

SHARRON, MARTI
  If I Could (composed with Miller, Ron; Hirsch, Kenny)
    (Chinn, Teena) SATB WARNER WBCH9344 (S347)
    (Chinn, Teena) SAB WARNER WBCH9345  (S348)

SHAW
  Back Bay Shuffle
    (Swingle, Ward) cor,pno,db,drums
    (gr. IV) voc pt,pts UNC JP SK-5X    (S349)

SHAW, KIRBY
  Blues Down To My Shoes
    SATB,perc (gr. I) UNC JP            (S350)

  Doctor Jazz
    SATB/SSATB,perc (gr. III) UNC JP    (S351)

  Love Is Come Again
    SATB,acap LEONARD-US 50304080       (S352)

  Once Upon A Dream
    SSATB,acap (gr. II) UNC JP          (S353)

  Warm-Ups For The Jazz-Show Choir
    SATBB,perc (gr. II) UNC JP          (S354)

SHAW, MARSHALL L.
  Mystical Garden
    unis cor LESLIE 1187                (S355)

SHE NEVER TOLD HER LOVE
  (Hines) SSA KJOS 6222                 (S356)

SHE SHALL HAVE MUSIC see Page

SHEARING, GEORGE ALBERT (1919-    )
  Lullaby Of Birdland
    (Strommen, Carl) SATB WARNER WBCH9358  (S357)
    (Strommen, Carl) SAB WARNER WBCH9359   (S358)

SHENANDOAH see Erb, James see Printz, Brad

SHEPHERD AND HIS LOVE, THE see Mechem, Kirke Lewis

SHEPHERD, SHEPHERD see Purcell, Henry

SHEPHERDESS OF SADNESS  *folk song,Chin
  (Baxter, F) [Chin] SATB,pno,opt fl
    LAURN sc CH-1068, pts CH-1068P      (S359)

SHE'S LIKE THE SWALLOW
  (Specht) 3pt cor WARCH 34398          (S360)
  see Somers

SHEYN VI DI LEVONEH see Rumshinsky, Joseph M.

SHI NO NAKA NO FUKEI see Ichiyanagi, Toshi

SHIBATA, MINAO (1916-    )
  Along The Milky Way
    jr cor/wom cor HUG                  (S361)

  Five Chapters On Mie
    mix cor HUG                         (S362)

  Ishi Ni Kiku
    mix cor HUG                         (S363)

  Miyama Iyayama
    mix cor HUG                         (S364)

  Winter Song
    wom cor HUG                         (S365)

SHIELD, W.
  Song For Winter, A
    unis cor THOMP.G OBH72260           (S366)

SHIELDS, VALERIE
  Basil The Cat
    SSA,acap FOSTER YS 600              (S367)

  Claude Is An Elegant Cat
    SA,kbd FOSTER YS 400                (S368)

  Misha, The Feline Queen
    SA,kbd FOSTER YS 401                (S369)

SHIN, ZEN, BI - CANTATA IN CELEBRATION see Ikebe, Shin-Ichiro

SHINE see Lessia

SHINING RIVER, THE see Young, Ovid

SHIR AHAVAH see Labes, Jef

SHIREEM see Robinovitch, Sid

SHIROI UMA see Ichiyanagi, Toshi

SHISHIR see Bhatia, Vanraj A.

SHORTNIN' BREAD
  (Cross, Dave) SATB,pno,db (gr. I) UNC JP  (S370)

SHOUT OVER THE OCEAN see Morisaki, Takatoshi

SHROPSHIRE LAD,A see Gillespie, S.

SHUR, LAURA
  Ocean Was Blue, The
    SA,pno LAWSON 52651                 (S371)

  Shalom Yerushalayim
    SA,pno LAWSON 52652                 (S372)

  When I Am Dead, My Dearest
    SSA,pno LAWSON 52764                (S373)

SHUSHOGI see Hirose, Ryohei

SI J'AVAIS UNE HUMBLE MAISON see Miche, Paul

SI JE TROUVAIS... see Racine, Fernand

SI J'ETAIS, , , see Doret, Gustave

SI J'ÉTAIS UNE FLEUR JOLIE see Haenni, G.

SI LA VIGNE ÉTAIT UNE FILLE see Mermoud, Robert

SI LES PETITS JARDINS see Mermoud, Robert

SI MALBROUGH L'AVAIT VOULU... see Henchoz, Emile

# SECULAR CHORAL MUSIC

SI TOST QUE VOSTRE OEIL M'EUT BLESSÉ
see Le Blanc, Didier

SI TU M'AIMES... see Moniuszko,
Stanislaw

SI VOUS AVEZ UNE FILLE see Bitsch,
Marcel

SI VOUS SAVIEZ!... see Sala, Andre

SIBELIUS, JEAN (1865-1957)
  Belle Lune Au Doux Visage *Op.18,
    No.8
    men cor HUG 7679     (S374)

  Ursprung Des Feuers,Der
    [Ger/Eng/Finn] TTBB,B solo,pno
    RECITAL 391     (S375)

SICILIANO see Bussotti, Sylvano

SICK BATTLE-GOD,THE see Dijker, Mathieu

SIE KOMMEN see Aeschbacher, C.

SIEBEN KINDERLIEDER see Grieg, Edvard
Hagerup

SIGISMOND LE JARDINIER see Boller,
Carlo

SIGN OF SPRING
  (New York Voices) SSATB, solo voices,
  perc (gr. V) UNC JP     (S376)

SIGNORE DAL VOLTO LUMINOSO ALL TERRA,IL
see De Grandis, Renato

SIGURBJORNSSON, HRODMAR INGI
(1958- )
  Ad Vadi Liggur Leidin
    wom cor ICELAND 052-032     (S377)
    men cor ICELAND 052-033     (S378)

  De Ramis Dadunt Folia
    men cor ICELAND 052-019     (S379)

  Enginn Graetur Islending
    mix cor ICELAND 052-030     (S380)

  Fegin I Fangi Minu
    mix cor ICELAND 052-029     (S381)

  Ferdalok
    mix cor ICELAND 052-028     (S382)

  Tarin Ad Onytu
    mix cor ICELAND 052-031     (S383)

SIGURBJÖRNSSON, THORKELL (1938- )
  Lagstufur Ur "Atomstödinn"
    mix cor ICELAND 022-165     (S384)

  Um Kvold
    jr cor ICELAND 022-202     (S385)

S'IL VOUS FAUT see Martin

SILBERNE NACHT, DEIN WEISSES BOOT see
Kreis, Otto

SILCHER, FRIEDRICH (1789-1860)
  Ach Gott, Wie Weh Tut Scheiden
    (Gardeweg) mix cor BUTZ 1021 (S386)

  Ach, Wie Ist's Möglich Dann
    (Lammerz) mix cor BUTZ 1019 (S387)

  Am Brunnen Vor Dem Tore
    (Butz) SAB BUTZ 1315     (S388)

  Ännchen Von Tharau
    (Lammerz) mix cor BUTZ 1020 (S389)

  Dem Himmel Will Ich Klagen
    (Gardeweg) mix cor BUTZ 1023 (S390)

  Drunten Im Unterland
    (Gardeweg) mix cor BUTZ 1025 (S391)

  Es Fliegt Manch Vöglein
    (Gardeweg) mix cor BUTZ 1027 (S392)

  Es Löscht Das Meer Die Sonne Aus
    (Butz) SAB BUTZ 1316     (S393)

  Es Sass Ein Häslein
    (Gardeweg) mix cor BUTZ 1028 (S394)

  Hab Oft Im Kreis Der Lieben
    (Butz) SAB BUTZ 1317     (S395)

  Himmel Lacht, Der
    (Gardeweg) mix cor BUTZ 1026 (S396)

  Ich Ging Einmal Spazieren
    (Gardeweg) mix cor BUTZ 1029 (S397)

  Ich Kann Und Mag Nicht
    (Gardeweg) mix cor BUTZ 1031 (S398)

  Ich Weiss Nicht, Was Soll Es Bedeuten
    (Lammerz) mix cor BUTZ 1030 (S399)

SILCHER, FRIEDRICH (cont'd.)
  In Einem Kühlen Grunde
    (Butz) SAB BUTZ 1318     (S400)

  Lieben Bringt Gross' Freund, Das
    (Gardeweg) mix cor BUTZ 1022 (S401)

  Mai Tritt Ein Mit Freuden, Der
    (Gardeweg) mix cor BUTZ 1024 (S402)

  Mein Schätzle Ist Fein
    (Gardeweg) mix cor BUTZ 1033 (S403)

  Mir Ist's Zu Wohl Ergangen
    (Lammerz) mix cor BUTZ 1032 (S404)

  Morgen Muss Ich Fort Von Hier
    (Butz) SAB BUTZ 1320     (S405)

  Nun Leb Wohl, Du Kleine Gasse
    (Butz) SAB BUTZ 1319     (S406)

  Ohne Dich Wie Lange
    (Lammerz) mix cor BUTZ 1034 (S407)

  Rosestock Holderblüt
    (Butz) SAB BUTZ 1321     (S408)

  Sängers Letzter Gruss
    men cor,acap MULLES     (S409)

  Stumm Schläft Der Sänger
    men cor,acap MULLES     (S410)

  Von Allen Den Mädchen
    (Gardeweg) mix cor BUTZ 1035 (S411)

  Was Hab Ich Denn Meinem Feinsliebchen
  Getan
    (Lammerz) mix cor BUTZ 1036 (S412)

  Wenn Frühlingstage Neu Beleben
    (Gardeweg) mix cor BUTZ 1038 (S413)

  Wenn Ich Ein Vöglein Wär
    (Butz) SAB BUTZ 1322     (S414)
    (Lammerz) mix cor BUTZ 1037 (S415)

SILENCE see Blumenfeld, Harold

SILENCE DE LA TERRE, LA see Mermoud,
Robert

SILENZIO STELLATO see Gentilucci,
Armando

SILLEHOFER LIEDERBUCH *CC101U,Austrian
(Stöllinger, Heide) 4pt mix cor HEYN
f.s.     (S416)

SILLY LITTLE SONG see Carter, Allen

SILTMAN
  Mother's Love
    SAB oct SOUTHERN SC409     (S417)

  My Mother's Love
    SSA oct SOUTHERN SC438     (S418)
    SA oct SOUTHERN SC439     (S419)

SILVER,HORACE
  Peace
    (Paquin-Salerno, Chris) SATB,perc
    (gr. IV) UNC JP     (S420)

SILVER MOONLIGHT... see Niimi, Tokuhide

SILVER SWAN,THE see Gibbons see
Gibbons, Orlando see Tilley,
Alexander

SILVERMAN, FAYE-ELLEN (1947- )
  Free Pen
    cor, solo voices&narrator,1.1.1.1.
    2.1.1.0. perc,harp,strings SEESAW
      (S421)

SILVERSTEIN
  Unicorn, The
    SSA WARCH 34806     (S422)
    SA WARCH 34819     (S423)

SIMITUK
  Catch A Little Sunbeam
    unis cor LESLIE 1188     (S424)

SIMMENTALER SENNENLIED see Zahler, J.R.

SIMMS, PATSY FORD
  All Night, All Day
    2pt cor ALFRED 5789     (S425)

  Boogie Woogie Rhythm
    2pt jr cor GILPIN HT9505     (S426)

  Ev'rybody Shout!
    3pt cor ALFRED 11338     (S427)
    2pt cor ALFRED 11339     (S428)

  I'll Always Remember You
    SAB (easy) PRESSER 392-41643 (S429)
    2pt cor,kbd (easy) PRESSER
    392-41867     (S430)

SIMMS, PATSY FORD (cont'd.)
  Let Us Walk In Peace
    SAB ALFRED 11574     (S431)
    2pt cor ALFRED 11575     (S432)
    SATB ALFRED 11573     (S433)

  This Is Not Goodbye
    SAB,pno GENTRY JG2158     (S434)

  We're The Future Of Tomorrow
    3pt cor ALFRED 5790     (S435)
    2pt cor ALFRED 5791     (S436)

SIMON, ERIC
  Homeward Bound (composed with
    Spevacek)
    3pt mix cor SHAWNEE D-0478 (S437)

SIMON, PAUL
  You Can Call Me Al
    (Farrell, Jim) SATB,perc (gr. III)
    UNC JP     (S438)

SIMPLE GIFTS
  (Marie Stultz) unis cor/SA,kbd,ob/fl/
  rec MORN.ST.     (S439)

SIMPLE HISTOIRE see Bovet, J.

SIMPLE SIMON see Freedman

SIMPLICITY see Haugland, A. Oscar

SIMPSON
  I Wonder What I'll Be
    unis cor SHAWNEE GF-0060     (S440)

SINCE FIRST I SAW YOUR FACE see
Leininger, W.

SINFONIA see Bach, Johann Sebastian

SINFONIA CON CORI see Rossini,
Gioacchino

SINFONIA N. 6 see Mannino, Franco

SING A SONG OF JOY see Gallina

SING A SONG OF NONSENSE see Dardess,
Betty

SING A SONG UNIVERSAL see Dello Joio,
Norman

SING ABOUT LOVE see Holmberg, Pat

SING AS THE PRAIRIE see Goetze, M.

SING, COME SING A SONG OF GLADNESS see
Mozart, Wolfgang Amadeus

SING FOREVER see Schubert, Franz
(Peter)

SING FREEDOM *CCU
  SATB NOVELLO 350733 f.s.     (S441)

SING HEY! IT'S CHRISTMAS DAY! see
Raminsh, Imant

SING MERRILY, SING FOR JOY! see Estes,
Jerry

SING MIT! *CCU
  (Anderluh, Anton) 2-3 eq voices HEYN
  f.s.     (S442)

SING MIT UNS see Strauss-König, Richard

SING OUT THE SEASON! see Lightfoot,
Mary Lynn

SING OUT WITH JOY see Arcadelt, Jacob

SING SEA TO SEA see Cable

SING, SING, SING see Kern, Philip

SING US see Jones

SING WE AND CHANT IT see Morley, Thomas

SING WE, DANCE WE ON THE GREEN
  (William Bausano) SSATB,acap FOSTER
  MF 3054     (S443)

SING WITH JOY see Mason

SING WITH JOY TODAY!
  (Liebergen, Patrick) 2pt cor,opt fl
  WARNER SV9519     (S444)

SING WITH JUBILATION! see Estes, Jerry

SINGE MEIN HERZ see Güdel, W.

SINGE, SEELE, SING DICH JUNG see
Schmid, Walter

SINGEN see Schmid, Walter

SINGEN IST DAS ATMEN DER SEELE see
Schallehn, Hilger

SINGENDE WELT see Gersbach, Fritz

SINGER see Kawasaki, Etsuo

SINGET LEISE see Bella, Rudolf

SINGH, VIJAY
  Jummy Down
    SATB WARNER SV9527 (S445)
    SAB WARNER SV9528 (S446)

SINGIN' IN THE RAIN see Brown, Nacio Herb

SINGING FREE see Rippentrop, Denice

SINGLE FLOWER GROWS, A see Wagner, Douglas Edward

SINGLE GIRL
  (Stocker, D.) SSA,pno THOMAS
    1C0369316 (S447)
    see Stocker, David

SINNSPRÜCHE see Kupp, Albert

SINOPOLI, GIUSEPPE (1946-    )
  Lou Salomé, Suite
    cor,soli,3.3.4.4. 4.3.3.1. 5perc,
    harp,cel,hpsd,pno,harmonium,
    strings sc RICORDI-IT 134422
    (S448)

SIREN SONGS see Keefer, Euphrosyne

SIX CANADIAN FOLKSONGS
  SATB THOMP.G f.s.
    contains: Banks Of Loch Erin;
    Danse, Mon Moine, Danse; Eskimo
    Hunting Song; Get To Bed; Jovial
    Young Sailor; Salish Song (S449)

SIX CHANSONS see Hasquenoph, Pierre

SIX CHORAL PIECES see Carr, Edwin

SIX CHORUSES see Sapieyevski, Jerzy

SIX CHORUSES FOR TREBLE VOICES, OP.15 see Rachmaninoff, Sergey Vassilievich

SIX ENGLISH LYRICS see Williamson, Malcolm

SIX ÉPIGRAMMES see Michans, Carlos

SIXTY MILLION SNOWFLAKES see Wolfe, Phyllis Aleta

SIYAHAMBA *folk song,So Am
  (Moore, Donald) 2pt cor WARNER SV0532
    (S450)
  (Moore, Donald) SATB WARNER SV9530
    (S451)
  (Moore, Donald) 3pt mix cor WARNER
    SV9531 (S452)

SJÖBERG, BIRGER (1885-1929)
  Aftontankar Vid Fridas Ruta
    (Sund, Robert) TTBB SVERIG SK 754
    (S453)
    (Sund, Robert) TTB SVERIG SK 754
    (S454)

  Hos Min Doktor
    (Hård Af Segerstad, B.) mix cor,
    acap SVERIG SK 777 (S455)

SKAARSET, IVAR
  Mazurka
    (Volle, Bjarne) men cor,acap NOTON
    N-8922 (S456)

SKOG, YLVA (1963-    )
  Frogs
    mix cor STIM (S457)

SKÖLD, BENGT-GÖRAN (1936-    )
  Värmlandsvisan
    SATB NOTERIA 2828 (S458)

  Ye Banks And Braes O'bonnie Doon
    SATB NOTERIA 2759 (S459)

SKY FAMILY see Parker, Alice

SKY, SEA AND MOUNTAINS OF YAWATAHAMA, THE see Ikebe, Shin-Ichiro

SKYE BOAT SONG *folk song,Scot
  (Thompson, Millard) SA,pno SANTA
    SBMP 74 (S460)

SKYLAR, SUNNY (SELIG SIDNEY SHAFTEL) (1913-    )
  Gotta Be This Or That (composed with Gilpin, Greg)
    SATB SHAWNEE A-2008 (S461)

SKYLARK see Carmichael, Hoagy

SLAVE OF THE MOON see Henderson

SLBERDISTELN see Bertogg, Conrad

SLEEP see Hugh-Jones, Llifon

SLEEP MY BABY see Rowley

SLEETH
  Baby What You Goin To Be
    unis cor THOMP.G OCM7791 (S462)

SLEIGH BELLS!
  (Schmutte, Pete) SATB (medley
    containing Sleigh Ride, Button Up
    Your Overcoat & Winter Wonderland)
    WARNER CM9597 ipa (S463)
  (Schmutte, Pete) SAB (medley
    containing Sleigh Ride, Button Up
    Your Overcoat & Winter Wonderland)
    WARNER CM9598 ipa (S464)
  (Schmutte, Pete) 2pt cor (medley
    containing Sleigh Ride, Button Up
    Your Overcoat & Winter Wonderland)
    WARNER CM9599 ipa (S465)

SLEIGH RIDE see Anderson, Leroy

SLEIGH SONG
  (Hatch) 2pt cor ALFRED 11355 (S466)

SLOTH see Jennings, Carolyn

SLOW DANCING IN THE SNOW see Althouse, Jay

SLUMBERTOWN see Ramseth, Betty Ann

SMALING, COR
  Zeventien Dappere Houten Soldaatjes
    (Hoogakker, Will) SATB,perc BANK
    11.900.016 (S467)

SMALL CHILD see Anderson, Leroy

S'MARLISELI ISCHT ES FYNS see Furrer, Walter

SMART, HENRY THOMAS (1813-1879)
  Bygone Days
    SATB BANKS 481 (S468)

  Good Night, Thou Glorious Sun
    SATB BANKS 73 (S469)

  Wake To The Hunting
    SATB BANKS 531 (S470)

SMEDEBY, SUNE (1934-    )
  Strandsvall
    men cor STIM (S471)

SMETANA, BEDRICH (1824-1884)
  Hommage
    men cor HUG 3622 (S472)

  Invocation
    men cor HUG 3117 (S473)

  Let Us Join In Celebration From "The Bartered Bride"
    (Pliska-Dik) 3pt treb cor BOOSEY-ENG MET0006 (S474)

SMILE IS NEVER OUT OF STYLE, A see Steffy, Thurlow

SMILE OF LIFE see Konkoh, Iwao, Inochi No Hohoemi

SMITH, GREGG (1931-    )
  Aesop's Fables No. 1: Introduction
    mix cor LEONARD-US 50319800 (S475)

  Blow The Candles Out
    mix cor LEONARD-US 50312900 (S476)

  Eleven Palindromes
    unis cor,clar/pno,opt clar&pno
    LEONARD-US OC12408 (S477)

  High Barbary
    mix cor LEONARD-US 50311420 (S478)

  Horticultural Wife, The (from Bicentennial Songs From The Great Sentimental Age)
    mix cor,T/Bar solo LEONARD-US 50318810 (S479)

  Listen To The Mocking Bird (from Bicentennial Songs From The Great Sentimental Age)
    mix cor,opt TB soli,opt fl/vln,pno LEONARD-US 50318830 (S480)

  On The Beach At Night
    SATB,pno 4-hands LAURN CH-1116 (S481)

SNOW!
  (Chinn, Teena) SATB (medley
    containing Let It Snow!..., A
    Marshmallow World, Winter
    Wonderland, Jingle Bells & Sleigh
    Ride) WARNER C038C1X (S482)
  (Chinn, Teena) SAB (medley containing
    Let It Snow!..., A Marshmallow
    World, Winter Wonderland, Jingle
    Bells & Sleigh Ride) WARNER C038C3X
    (S483)
  (Chinn, Teena) SSA (medley containing
    Let It Snow!..., A Marshmallow
    World, Winter Wonderland, Jingle
    Bells & Sleigh Ride) WARNER C038C2X
    (S484)
  see Govedas

SNOW,THE see Elgar, [Sir] Edward (William)

SNOW IS FALLING see Schram, Ruth Elaine

SNOW ON THE ORANGE GROVES see Ohana, Maurice

SNOW ON THE RIVER see Baxter, Francis H.

SNOW-WHITE MESSENGER, THE *folk song, Dutch
  (Pfautsch, Lloyd) SATB,pno LAWSON
    52641 (S485)

SNOWMAN see Strommen, Carl

SNYDER, AUDREY
  At Dawn
    SATB WARNER SV9326 (S486)

  Autumn Vesper
    3pt mix cor WARNER SV9411 (S487)
    2pt cor/SSA WARNER SV9401 (S488)

  Make A Difference
    2pt cor WARNER SV9348 (S489)

  Song Of Spring
    2pt treb cor/SSA WARNER SV9505 (S490)

  Wintersong
    2pt treb cor/SSA WARNER SV9332 (S491)

SNYDER, TIMOTHY
  As Imperceptibly As Grief
    SATB,opt S solo,opt kbd FOSTER
    MF 3049 (S492)

  Rise Up My Love
    SSA,pno SANTA SBMP 93 (S493)

SO DEEP see Macmillan, James

SO LONG IT'S BEEN GOOD TO KNOW YUH see Guthrie

SO RO LITEN TULL see Fem Folkeviser Fra Gausdal

SO RO, PERLEMOR see Hauger, Kristian

SOA-SOE see Hedelin, Fredrik

SOFTLY FALL THE SHADES see Hatton, John Liptrot

SOIR, LE (from Terre Et L'étoile, La)
  men cor HUG 8845 (S494)
  see Bron, Patrick see Broquet, Louis see Kuhlau, Friedrich

SOIR DESCEND ET LE SOLEIL DÉCLINE, LE see Crüger, Johann

SOIR D'ÉTÉ see Martin

SOIR SUR LA PLAINE see Boulanger, Lili

SOIR SUR LELAC see Broquet, Louis

SOLBIATI, ALESSANDRO
  Aube
    wom cor,pno ZERBONI 9750 (S495)
    wom cor,harp ZERBONI 10117 (S496)

SOLDAT DE FRIBOURG see Kaelin, Pierre

SOLDAT DE GUERRE see Boller, Carlo

SOLDAT QUI PARS see Boller, Carlo

SOLDAT QUI REVIENS DE LA GUERRE... see Weynandt

SOLDATENABSCHIED see Kraehenbuehl, J.G.

SOLDATENLIED see Boller, Carlo, Au Doux Pays see Meister, Casimir

SOLDIER, WON'T YOU MARRY ME? see Halley

SOLEIL DE JUIN see Doret, Gustave

SOLEIL DE MINUIT, LE see La Tombelle, Fernand de

SOLEIL ET LA LUNE, LE see Hausammann, R. see Trenet, Charles

SOLER, [PADRE] ANTONIO (1729-1783)
  Sonata In D Major
    (Swingle, Ward) SATB (gr. II) voc
    pt,pts UNC JP SOS-8X (S497)

SOLFEGGIETTO see Bach, Carl Philipp Emanuel

SOLFEGGIO see Schweizer, Alfred

SOLITARY SNOWFLAKE see Estes, Jerry

SOLOMON, JOAN
   Lights Of Hanukkah
     2 eq voices,opt tamb HERITAGE
     15-1003 (S498)

SOM LUFT OCH VATTEN see Nilsson, Stefan

SOME FOLKS DO see Gallina

SOME KIND OF WONDERFUL, (SHE'S)
   (Baker, Andy) SATB WARNER CH9528 ipa
     (S499)
   (Baker, Andy) SAB WARNER CH9529 ipa
     (S500)
   (Baker, Andy) 2pt cor WARNER CH9530
     ipa (S501)

SOME THOUGHTS ON KEATS AND COLERIDGE
   see Kim, Earl

SOMEONE TO WATCH OVER ME see Gershwin,
   George

SOMERS
   She's Like The Swallow
     SATB WARCH 35665 (S502)
   Tambour, Le
     SATB WARCH 35667 (S503)
   We Wish You A Merry Christmas
     SATB WARCH 34509 (S504)

SOMETHING TO SING ABOUT see Tapscott,
   Carl

SOMETHING TOLD THE WILD GEESE see
   Porterfield, Sherrie

SOMETIMES I FEEL LIKE A MOTHERLESS
   CHILD *spir
   (Linberg, Per) SATB NOTERIA 2773
     (S505)

SOMMARMINNEN see Yancey, Thomas Leland

SOMMARN OCH JAG see Hylin, Birgitta

SOMMARSÅNGEN see Cederberg, Anna

SOMMARSOLSKOGMELODI see Janunger, Kjell

SOMMER GIB ACHT see Güdel, W.

SOMMERBLUMEN see Schmid, Walter

SOMMERMÄDCHEN-KÜSSETAUSCHELÄCHEL-
   BEICHTE see Erdmann, Gunther

SOMMERMADRIGAL see Müller, Joseph Ivar

SOMMERSEGEN see Schmid, S.W.

SOMMERWANDERUNG see Schmid, Walter

SOMMERWIESE,DIE see Kaufmann, Fred

SONATA IN D MAJOR see Soler, [Padre]
   Antonio

SONDHEIM, STEPHEN JOSHUA (1930- )
   Send In The Clowns (from A Little
     Night Music)
     (Sheehan, Ray) SSAA,acap (gr. IV)
     UNC JP (S506)

SONETTO see Loudova, Ivana

SONETTO CCCXXXIII DI PETRARCA see
   Farkas, Ferenc

SONETTO IN MEMORIAM IGOR STRAWINSKY see
   Castiglioni, Niccolò

SONG see Holman

SONG FOR BEDTIME see McLean

SONG FOR CANDADA see Halley

SONG FOR MOTHER EARTH see Lawrence,
   Stephen L.

SONG FOR PEACE see MacGillivray,
   Allister

SONG FOR THE MIRA see MacGillivray,
   Allister

SONG FOR WINTER, A see Shield, W.

SONG FOR YOU, A see Rusciano, C.D.

SONG IS YOU,THE see Kern, Jerome

SONG MY PADDLE SINGS see Henderson,
   Ruth Watson

SONG OF JOY see Althouse, Jay

SONG OF LIFE see Raum, Elizabeth

SONG OF LONGING
   (Bissell) SATB WARCH 35674 (S507)

SONG OF MEANDERING STARS see Fujii,
   Takashi

SONG OF SPRING see Snyder, Audrey

SONG OF THE BIRD see Onoe, Kazuhiko

SONG OF THE FLAX SPINNER see Leslie,
   Henry David

SONG OF THE HEROES OF TRADITIONAL
   JAPANESE CHILDREN'S STORIES see
   Kondoh, Harue

SONG OF THE LITTLEST ANGEL see Artman,
   Ruth Eleanor

SONG OF THE OPEN ROAD see Leavitt, John

SONG OF THE SEASON see Veress, Sandor

SONG OF TIME, THE see Telfer, Nancy

SONG OF TIMES,A see Parker, Horatio
   William

SONG OF YOMITAN see Kimura, Masanobu

SONG REMEMBERED see Liddell, Claire

SONG TIL RØROSVIDDA see Nyhus, Rolf

SONGEN ER EIT BAND SOM BIND see Volle,
   Martin

SONGES FOR THREE VOYCES see Wythorne,
   T.

SONGS I see Takemitsu, Toru

SONGS II see Takemitsu, Toru

SONGS MY FATHER SANG WITH FRIENDS
   (Prentice, Fred) TTBB,acap GENTRY
     JG2161 (S508)

SONGS OF INNOCENCE see Tipton, Clyde

SONGS OF THE MOUNTAIN, THE MOON AND
   TELEVISION see Hambraeus, Bengt

SONGS OF THE SLAVE see Mechem, Kirke
   Lewis

SONGS OF TIME see Telfer, Nancy

SONGS OF TIME, THE see Telfer, Nancy

SONGS OF WALT WHITMAN see Broege,
   Timothy

SONNENBLUME see Furer, Arthur

SONNENWENDE see Ries, Hubert

SONNET see Baird, John see Williamson,
   Malcolm

SONNET DE RONSARD see Jolivet, Andre

SONNEUR, LE see Sala, Andre

SONNEUR DU PRIEURÉ, LE see Mermoud,
   Robert

SONNEUR, QUI TE PENCHES... see Henchoz,
   Emile

SONNTAG see Hiller see Schmid, Walter
   see Zahler, J.R.

SONNTAGSLIED see Schmid, Walter

SONOHITO GA UTAUTOKI see Terashima,
   Rikuya

SONT LES FILLES DE LA ROCHELLE see
   Boller, Carlo

SOON AND VERY SOON see Crouch

SOON ONE DAY
   (New York Voices) SSATB,solo voice,
     perc (gr. IV/gr. V) UNC JP (S509)

SORA-WA see Oguri, Katsuhiro

SORAN BUSHI  *folk song,Jap
   (Baxter, Francis) SATB,pno SANTA
     SBMP 60 (S510)

SORCIÈRE, LA see Vuataz, Roger

SOSBAN FACH see Morris, Haydn

SOT PETIT JEUNE HOMME see Aubanel,
   Georges

SOUCI, LE see Lancien, Noël

SOUL MAN see Hayes, Isaac

SOUL OF THE PLAINS see Gutiérrez,
   Pedro, Alma Llanera

SOUND OF TIDES see Niimi, Tokuhide

SOUNDCHANTS see Robinovitch, Sid

SOUNDINGS see Kimes, Janice

SOUNDS OF THE CITY see Schwartz, Dan

SOURCE ABONDANTE DE JOIE see Henchoz,
   Emile

SOURCE ENCHANTÉE, LA see Ithier

SOUS BOIS see Schmitt, Florent

SOUS LES NOYERS see Zbinden, Julien-
   François

SOUS LES PLATANES DU PRÉAU see Boller,
   Carlo

SOUS LES POMMIERS EN FLEURS see Naudier

SOUS LES TILLEULS EN FLEURS see Haenni,
   Ch. see Haenni, G.

SOUS L'ÉTOILE DU NORD see Henchoz,
   Emile

SOUS UNE PLUIE... see Henchoz, Emile

SOUVENIRS D' ENFANCE see Moudon, E.

SOUVENIRS DU TEMPS PASSÉ, LES see
   Bovet, J.

SOWASH, RICK
   Bright Cap And Streamers
     SA,acap MUSIC SEV. 742 (S511)
   Johnny Appleseed
     see Three Applesongs
   Long Ago On A Fine Spring Day
     see Three Applesongs
   Planting Of The Apple Tree, The
     see Three Applesongs
   Three Applesongs
     SATB,pno MUSIC SEV. f.s.
       contains: Johnny Appleseed; Long
       Ago On A Fine Spring Day;
       Planting Of The Apple Tree, The
       (S512)

SPAIN see Corea,Chick

SPARE PARTS see Patterson

SPEAK TO THE CHILD OF LOVE see Koepke,
   Allen

SPECHT
   Tree In The Wood
     SA WARCH 34399 (S513)

SPECHT, JUDY
   Saucy Sailor
     SA WARCH 34397 (S514)

SPEDDING, ALAN
   All And Some
     treb cor BANKS ECS 213 (S515)

SPER IL PASS ALPIN see Dolf, B.

SPEVACEK, LINDA
   American Folk Rhapsody
     SATB (medley incorporating Cindy,
     Simple Gifts and Pick A Bale Of
     Cotton) HERITAGE 15-1205H (S516)
     3pt mix cor (medley incorporating
     Cindy, Simple Gifts and Pick A
     Bale Of Cotton) HERITAGE 15-1212H
     (S517)
     2pt cor (medley incorporating
     Cindy, Simple Gifts and Pick A
     Bale Of Cotton) HERITAGE 15-1213H
     (S518)
   Calypso Noel
     2pt cor,opt perc HERITAGE 15-1124
     (S519)
   Ching A Ring Chaw And Great Gittin'
     Up Mornin'
     3pt mix cor,pno HERITAGE 15-1173H
     (S520)
     SATB HERITAGE 15-1123 (S521)
   Choral Fanfare, A
     SAB/3pt mix cor SHAWNEE D-470 ipa
     (S522)
   Come, Sing! Come, Dance!
     SATB,acap HERITAGE 15-1109 (S523)
   Country Jambouree
     2pt cor SHAWNEE EA-182 (S524)
   Danza!
     SATB,opt tamb&castanets HERITAGE
     15-1181H (S525)

SPEVACEK, LINDA (cont'd.)

  Holiday Madrigal
    3pt mix cor HERITAGE 15-1110 (S526)
    2pt cor HERITAGE 15-1108 (S527)

  Holiday Tango
    SATB HERITAGE 15-1204H (S528)

  I Wish I Was Single Again
    TBB SHAWNEE C-283 (S529)

  International Carols, Set 2
    SATB,opt bells (medley incorporating March Of The Three Kings (French), Dormi, Dormi (Italian) and Personent Hodie (German)) HERITAGE 15-1190H (S530)

  Joy In The Morning
    SSA SHAWNEE B-0565 (S531)

  Joy Of Hanukkah, The
    2 eq voices HERITAGE 15-1220H (S532)

  Kleine Spufmusik, Eine
    "Little "Spoof" Music, A" 3pt mix cor,opt acap HERITAGE 15-1075 (S533)
    "Little "Spoof" Music, A" SATB HERITAGE 15-1069 (S534)

  Kling, Glockchen
    2pt cor,opt bells (english verses with german refrain) HERITAGE 15-1193 (S535)

  Little "Spoof" Music, A
    see Kleine Spufmusik, Eine

  Maiden's Farewell, The
    SSA SHAWNEE B-562 (S536)

  Make Your Own Kind Of Music
    2 eq voices HERITAGE 15-1196H (S537)

  'Round'ezvous
    2-4pt cor HOPE K 310 (S538)

  Tiger Rag
    3pt mix cor HERITAGE 15-1126 (S539)

  To Music
    3pt mix cor (opt signing) HERITAGE 15-1076 (S540)

  Toccata For Voices
    3pt mix cor HERITAGE 15-1191H (S541)

  Travelin' Man
    2 eq voices,opt fl&Orff inst HERITAGE 15-1107 (S542)

  Ukrainian Bell Carol
    3pt mix cor,handbells HERITAGE 15-1114 (S543)
    SATB HERITAGE 15-1121 (S544)
    SSA HERITAGE 15-1122 (S545)

  When In Dreamland
    1-2pt cor,opt Orff inst HERITAGE 15-1217H (S546)

SPIDER DANCED A COZY GIGUE see Moments In Time

SPIELMANN,DER see Güdel, W.

SPINNER,THE see Mendelssohn-Bartholdy, Felix

SPIRIT OF BEAUTY see Parker, Horatio William

SPIRIT OF CHRISTMAS IS HERE, THE see Schwartz, Dan

SPLENDEUR DU JOUR see Naudier

SPLISH SPLASH see Darin, Bobby

SPOHR, LUDWIG (LOUIS) (1784-1859)
  Adoration
    mix cor HUG 2617 (S547)

SPRANGER, JÖRG (1911- )
  Es Wünsch Mir Einer Was Er Will
    SAB BUTZ 866 (S548)

  Gems Auf Dem Stein,Ein
    mix cor BUTZ 868 (S549)

  Gleichwie Auf Dunklem Grunde
    mix cor BUTZ 867 (S550)

SPRING see Bhatia, Vanraj A., Basant see Steed, Brad

SPRING CAN REALLY HANG YOU UP THE MOST see Burnell, Mark

SPRING MORNING see Carey

SPRING SONG see Schumann, Robert (Alexander)

SPRING SONG,A see Pinsuti, Ciro

SPRINGTIME IS CALLING YOU see Gould

SPRUCH see Kreis, Otto see Schmid, Walter see Vollenweider, Hans

SPUNTA IL SOL see Furrer, Walter

STA see Derungs, Gion Gius.

STADEN, JOHANN (1581-1634)
  Il Est Beau De Louer...
    men cor HUG 1816 (S551)
    eq voices HUG 1816 (S552)

STAND AS ONE see Strommen, Carl

STANDARD ON THE BRAES O' MAR,THE
  (Martin, Robert) SATB BANKS 852 (S553)

STÄNDCHEN see Feibel, Norbert see Kupp, Albert

STANFORD, CHARLES VILLIERS (1852-1924)
  Phaudrig Crohoore *Op.62
    SATB,orch voc sc RECITAL 509 (S554)

STANTON
  Razzle, Jazzle
    SATB SHAWNEE A-1974 ipa (S555)

STAR DUST see Carmichael, Hoagy

STAR SONG,A see Parker, Horatio William

STAR SPANGLED BANNER
  (Pickard, Wayland) SSAATTBB,acap (gr. III) UNC JP (S556)
  see Burnell, Mark

STAR SPANGLED BANNER, THE
  (Lyons, Bill) SSATBB,acap (gr. III) UNC JP (S557)

STÄRNE see Jaeggi, Oswald

STÄRNEBÄRGLIED see Zahler, J.R.

STARS see Porterfield, Sherrie see Walker, George Theophilus

STARS AND MOONBEAMS see Rippentrop, Denice

STATON, J.F.
  As The Moon's Soft Splendour
    SATB BANKS 1191 (S558)

STAY LITTLE BLACKBIRD see Nelson

STEAL AWAY see Dvořák, Antonín see Walker

STEED, BRAD
  Spring! (from Spring Suite)
    SATB oct THOMAS 1C0909309 (S559)
    SATB THOMAS 1C0909309 (S560)

  Sweet Spring (from Spring Suite)
    SATB oct THOMAS 1C0909307 (S561)
    SATB THOMAS 1C0909307 (S562)

  Though Love (from Spring Suite)
    SATB oct THOMAS 1C0909308 (S563)
    SATB THOMAS 1C0909308 (S564)

STEFANSSON, FINNUR TORFI (1947- )
  Kissed By Sun
    STB,solo voice,pno ICELAND 057-031 (S565)

  Thorrablot
    mix cor ICELAND 057-040 (S566)

  Til Songsins
    mix cor ICELAND 057-034 (S567)

STEFANSSON, FJÖLNIR (1930- )
  Stille Nacht
    jr cor/wom cor ICELAND 004-012 (S568)

STEFFY
  Keep On Smilin' (composed with Mccary)
    SAB,kbd (med) PRESSER 392-41796 (S569)

STEFFY, THURLOW
  Smile Is Never Out Of Style, A
    2pt cor,kbd (med easy) PRESSER 392-41762 (S570)

STEGREIFSÄTZE 1 *CCU,folk_song,Eur/Ger
  (Klein, Richard Rudolf) 3 eq voices/ mix cor FIDULA (S571)

STEGREIFSÄTZE 2 *CCU,spir
  (Klein, Richard Rudolf) 3 eq voices/ mix cor FIDULA folksongs from all the world (S572)

STEIGER, F.
  Bi-N-I Nid E Ryche Möntsch?
    wom cor,acap MULLES (S573)

STEIGER, F. (cont'd.)

  Nyna, Buscheli, Schlof
    wom cor,acap MULLES (S574)

  Was Han I Gseh Im Garte
    wom cor,acap MULLES (S575)

STEIN TIMES SEVEN see Kernis, Aaron Jay

STEINER, LUIS
  Willkommen, Die Gehen Ein Und Aus
    4pt mix cor,inst FIDULA cor pts 6155, pts 6156 (S576)

STENGELLOSER ENZIAN see Furer, Arthur

STEPPIN' OUT-PUTTIN' ON THE RITZ see Broadley, Sharon

STETS IN TRURE MUESS I LÄBE see Oetiker, August see Ruprecht, Ernst

STETS IN TRUURE MUESS I LÄBE see Oetiker, August see Vollenweider, Hans

STEVENSON, JOHN A.
  See Our Oars With Feather'd Spray
    SATB BANKS 365 (S577)

STEVENSON, WILLIAM
  Dancing In The Street (composed with Gay, Mavin; Hunter, Ivy)
    (Chinn, Teena) SAB WARNER 0033DC3X ipa (S578)
    (Chinn, Teena) 2pt cor WARNER 0033DC5X ipa (S579)
    (Chinn, Teena) SATB WARNER 0033DC1X ipa (S580)

STILL A BACH CHRISTMAS (BACH'S "AIR"- "STILL, STILL STILL")
  (Althouse) SAB ALFRED 11616 (S581)
  (Althouse) 2pt cor ALFRED 11617 (S582)
  (Althouse) SATB ALFRED 11615 (S583)

STILL IN LUFT see Killmayer, Wilhelm

STILL, STILL, STILL see Brunner

STILLE DER FELDER see Schmid, Walter

STILLE HOF,DER see Tamas, Janos

STILLE NACHT see Stefansson, Fjölnir

STILLER ALS EINE WOLKE *CC8L
  (Mittergradnegger, Günther) mix cor, acap HEYN ISBN 3 85366 565 9 f.s. (S584)

STILLER HÜGEL see Schmid, A.

STIRLING, ELIZABETH
  All Amoung The Barley
    SATB BANKS 76 (S585)

STOCKER, DAVID (1939- )
  Single Girl
    wom cor THOMAS 1C0369316 (S586)

STOCKER, KARL
  Abendlied
    wom cor,acap MULLES (S587)

  Herbstlied
    wom cor,acap MULLES (S588)

  In Der Frühe
    wom cor,acap MULLES (S589)

  Regenlied
    wom cor,acap MULLES (S590)

  Trost Der Nacht
    wom cor,acap MULLES (S591)

  Weit, Weit
    wom cor,acap MULLES (S592)

  Winter
    wom cor,acap MULLES (S593)

STOCKHAUSEN, KARLHEINZ (1928- )
  Dienstags-Gruss (Friedens-Gruss) (from Dienstag from Licht) "Tuesday Greeting (Peace Greetings)" cor,S solo,9trp, 9trom,2synthesizer, conductor, co-conductor, sound projectionist [21'] STOCKHAUS (S594)

  Festival (from Michael's Home-Coming)
    cor,STB soli,trp,trom,basset horn, 2soprano sax,orch,electronic tape [50'] STOCKHAUS (S595)

  Lucifer's Farewell
    see Luzifers Abschied

  Luzifers Abschied (from Samstag from Licht)
    "Lucifer's Farewell" men cor,org, 7 trombones(live or on tape) [62'] STOCKHAUS (S596)

STOCKHAUSEN, KARLHEINZ (cont'd.)
   Michaels Heimkehr (Act Iii) (from
     Donnerstag from Licht)
     "Michael's Home-Coming" cor,STB
     soli,trp,trom,basset horn,
     2soprano sax,elec org,orch,
     electronic tape [30'] STOCKHAUS
                                 (S597)
   Michael's Home-Coming
     see Michaels Heimkehr (Act Iii)

   Tuesday Greeting (Peace Greetings)
     see Dienstags-Gruss (Friedens-
     Gruss)

STOESSEL, ALBERT (1894-1943)
   Chum Übers Mätteli
     (Niggli) wom cor,acap MULLES (S598)

STOLOFF, BOB
   Wakin' (composed with Broadley,
     Sharon)
     SATB,female solo,perc (gr. II) UNC
     JP                       (S599)

STONE'S VOICE see Hisatome, Tomoyuki

STOP! IN THE NAME OF LOVE see Holland,
   Brian

STOP, LOOK, AND LISTEN (AN ECOLOGY
   SONG) see Lawrence, Stephen L.

STORCH SCHNIBELSCHNABEL see Lampart,
   Reinhold

STORM see Henderson

STORMY WEATHER see Koehler

STRADUN see Huber, Paul

STRAESSER, JOEP (1934- )
   Madrigals 1, 2 And 3 (from
     Hammarskjöld) CC3U
     6pt mix cor sc DONEMUS f.s.  (S600)

STRAIGHTEN UP AND FLY RIGHT see Cole,
   Nat (King)

STRANDSVALL see Smedeby, Sune

STRATEGIER, HERMAN (1912-1988)
   Optimistisch Lied
     SATB,acap BANK 11.900.038   (S601)

STRAUSS, J.
   Wiener-Walzer (from Zigeunerbaron)
     (Schmid, W.) wom cor,acap MULLES
                                 (S602)
     (Schmid, W.) 3pt wom cor,pno kbd
     pt,cor pts MULLES        (S603)

STRAUSS, RICHARD (1864-1949)
   Three Men's Choruses *CC3U
     men cor BOOSEY-ENG OCTB6735 f.s.
                                 (S604)

STRAUSS-KÖNIG, RICHARD (1930- )
   Sing Mit Uns *CCU
     1-2pt jr cor,kbd BOHM f.s.  (S605)

   Wir Tanzen, Wie Es Uns Gefällt
     jr cor,perc FIDULA 5901    (S606)

STRAUSSIADE see Tamas, Janos

STRAYHORN
   Take The A Train
     (Zegree) SATB SHAWNEE A-2009 (S607)

STREET OF LAREDO, THE
   (Cormier, Robert De) SATB,pno LAWSON
   52773                     (S608)

STREET PARTY
   (New York Voices) SATB,male solo,
   perc,synthesizer (gr. III) UNC JP
                                 (S609)

STREET SMARTS
   (Cadwallader, Rex) SSATBB,10brass,
   inst (gr. IV) UNC JP       (S610)

STREETS OF LAREDO *folk song,Nor Am
   (Webb, Merrilee) TBB,pno SANTA
   SBMP 77                 (S611)

STREETS OF LONDON see McTell, Ralph

STRID, GEORGE L.O.
   America, Of Thee I Sing!
     2pt cor ALFRED 5808       (S612)

STROFE DI UNGARETTI see Gentilucci,
   Armando

STROHBACH, SIEGFRIED (1929- )
   All That Glitters Is Not Gold
     see Seven Songs From Shakespeare's
     Comodies

   Come Away, Death
     see Seven Songs From Shakespeare's
     Comodies

STROHBACH, SIEGFRIED (cont'd.)
   Hey, Robin, Jolly Robin
     see Seven Songs From Shakespeare's
     Comodies

   If She Be Made Of White And Red
     see Seven Songs From Shakespeare's
     Comodies

   It Was A Lover And His Lass
     see Seven Songs From Shakespeare's
     Comodies

   O Mistress Mine
     see Seven Songs From Shakespeare's
     Comodies

   Seven Songs From Shakespeare's
     Comodies
     [Eng/Ger] mix cor,acap SCHOTTS f.s.
     contains: All That Glitters Is
     Not Gold; Come Away, Death;
     Hey, Robin, Jolly Robin; If She
     Be Made Of White And Red; It
     Was A Lover And His Lass; O
     Mistress Mine; Take, O Take
     Those Lips Away          (S613)

   Take, O Take Those Lips Away
     see Seven Songs From Shakespeare's
     Comodies

STROMMEN, CARL
   Carol Festival
     3pt cor ALFRED 5782       (S614)
     2pt cor ALFRED 5783       (S615)
     SATB ALFRED 5781          (S616)

   Christmas Remembered
     3pt cor ALFRED 5780       (S617)
     SATB ALFRED 5779          (S618)

   Christmas Wish,A
     SATB WARNER SV9337        (S619)
     3pt mix cor WARNER SV9338  (S620)

   Field Of Dreams
     SATB ALFRED 11592        (S621)
     SSA ALFRED 11593         (S622)

   Light The Light
     SATB ALFRED 11596        (S623)
     3pt cor ALFRED 11597      (S624)
     SSA ALFRED 11598         (S625)

   Like An Eagle
     2pt cor ALFRED 11304      (S626)

   My Heart's In The Highland
     SATB ALFRED 11326        (S627)
     SAB ALFRED 11327         (S628)
     2-3pt treb cor ALFRED 11328 (S629)

   Once Upon A Christmas
     SAB WARNER CH9547        (S630)
     2pt cor WARNER CH9548    (S631)
     SATB WARNER CH9546      (S632)

   One More Song
     2pt cor WARNER CH95105   (S633)
     SATB WARNER CH95103     (S634)
     SAB WARNER CH95104      (S635)

   River Run
     SATB ALFRED 11329        (S636)
     SAB ALFRED 11330         (S637)

   Road Less Traveled, The
     SAB ALFRED 11345        (S638)
     2pt cor ALFRED 11346     (S639)
     SATB ALFRED 11344       (S640)

   Snowman
     2pt cor WARNER SV9426    (S641)

   Stand As One
     SATB ALFRED 11558       (S642)
     SAB ALFRED 11559        (S643)
     SSA ALFRED 11560        (S644)

   That Grace May Abound
     SATB WARNER SV9427      (S645)
     SAB WARNER SV9428       (S646)

   Twist Of The Tongue, A
     3pt cor ALFRED 5773      (S647)
     2pt cor ALFRED 5774      (S648)

   Walk On
     SATB ALFRED 5775        (S649)
     3pt cor ALFRED 5776      (S650)
     SSA ALFRED 5777         (S651)

   We Are The Music
     SATB ALFRED 11563       (S652)
     SAB ALFRED 11564        (S653)
     2pt cor ALFRED 11640     (S654)

   We Sing Feliz Navidad
     SATB ALFRED 11366       (S655)
     3pt cor ALFRED 11367     (S656)
     2pt cor ALFRED 11368     (S657)

STROOPE, Z. RANDALL
   Goin' To The Auction
     SATB,T solo,acap FOSTER MF 3046
                                 (S658)

   Inscription Of Hope
     2pt cor,narrator HERITAGE 15-1081
                                 (S659)
     SATB HERITAGE 15-1085    (S660)

STUDER, HANS (1911- )
   Abendsegen
     wom cor,acap MULLES      (S661)

   Betrachtung Der Zeit
     men cor,acap MULLES      (S662)

   Greift Zum Becher
     men cor,acap MULLES      (S663)

   Ich Scheide Nun
     wom cor,acap MULLES      (S664)

   Morgen
     men cor,acap MULLES      (S665)

   Morgensegen
     wom cor,acap MULLES      (S666)

   Sechs Sprüche (Berner Liederspende)
     *CC6U
     wom cor,acap MULLES f.s.  (S667)

STUDIO PER IL FINALE DEL DOKTOR FAUSTUS
   see Manzoni, Giacomo

STUDY HALL BLUES see Lawrence, Stephen
   L.

STULTZ, MARIE
   Man In The Moon, The
     unis treb cor,kbd MORN.ST.
     MSM-50-9909             (S668)

   Zumba, Zumba
     unis treb cor,kbd,opt finger cym
     MORN.ST. MSM-50-9904    (S669)

STUMM SCHLÄFT DER SÄNGER see Silcher,
   Friedrich

STURM, WILHELM
   Unterm Lindenbaum
     wom cor,acap MULLES      (S670)

   Wanderburschen's Abschied
     men cor,acap MULLES      (S671)

STYNE, JULE (JULES STEIN) (1905-1994)
   Let It Snow! Let It Snow! Let It
     Snow!
     3pt mix cor WARNER SC9513 (S672)

SU SALTE, BALE, PUTELE see Marx, Karl

SUBEN, JOEL ERIC (1946- )
   As Through Earth's Garden Once I
     Strayed
     SSAA,acap LAWSON 52629   (S673)

   Kiss, A
     SSAA,acap LAWSON 52609   (S674)

SUGINO, YASUHIKO (1939- )
   Like Mt. Fuji
     men cor,pno HUG          (S675)

   Weeds *Suite
     mix cor,pno HUG          (S676)

SUGITA HIBI NI YOSETE see Abiko,
   Yoshiro

SUISSE À L'ÉTRANGER, LE see Daetwyler,
   Jean

SUITE CHORALE see Sutermeister,
   Heinrich

SUITE EN LANGUES D'OC
   (Vioque-Lorenzo) 4 eq voices,pno 4-
   hands A COEUR JOIE CA 63   (S677)

SUITE FLEURIE see Bovet, J.

SUITE QUÉBECOISE see Anonymous

SUITE "ROBESPIERRE" see Manzoni,
   Giacomo

SULFATEURS, LES see Daetwyler, Jean

SULIKO *folk song,Eur
   TTBB sc APOLLO AV 5876    (S678)

SULLIVAN, [SIR] ARTHUR SEYMOUR
   (1842-1900)
   Last Night Of The Year,The
     SATB BANKS YS0251        (S679)

   Rainy Day,The
     4pt mix cor,opt pno ALLAIR (S680)

   When The Buds Are Blossoming
     (Lane, Philip) SSA BANKS ECS 218
                                 (S681)

SUMMER see Bhatia, Vanraj A., Grishma

SUMMER DAY IN THE GARDEN see Baxter, Francis H.

SUMMER EVENING, A see Bissel

SUMMER HEAT see Murphy, Kevin

SUMMER IS HERE see Schweitzer, Bruria

SUMMER RAIN see Runarsdottir, Hildigunnur

SUMMERLÅNG *CCU
   mix cor HEYN ISBN 3 85366 6531 f.s. (S682)

SUMMERTIME BLUES
   (Chinn, Teena) SATB WARNER WBCH9427 (S683)
   (Chinn, Teena) SAB WARNER WBCH9428 (S684)
   (Chinn, Teena) 2pt mix cor WARNER WBCH9429 (S685)

SUN see Cutter, William (Bill)

SUN HEART see Broege, Timothy

SUN, MOON, STARS, AND MAN see Vaughan Williams, Ralph

SÜNDENFALL see Klein, Gideon

SUNFLOWER,THE see Rippentrop, Denice

SUNSET IN TOWN see Rees-Davies, Ieuan

SUPREME LOVE see Mannino, Franco

SUR CE PETIT PONT DE PIERRE see Henchoz, Emile

SUR LA LUNE see Zbinden, Julien-François

SUR LA ROUT'D'ESTAVAYER see Kaelin, Pierre

SUR LA ROUTE DU MATIN see Miche, Paul

SUR L'ALPE VOISINE see Jaques-Dalcroze, Émile

SUR LE BORD DU TORRENT see Henchoz, Emile

SUR LE FAÎTE DE LA TOUR see Haenni, G.

SUR LE PONT D'AVIGNON see Planel, Jean

SUR LE PONT DE MORLAIX see Dutilleux, Henri

SUR LES FLANCS DU MOLÉSON see Bovet, J.

SUR LES ROUTES DU MONDE see Boller, Carlo

SUR MER see Missa, Edmond Jean Louis

SUR NOS LANDES AIMÉES see Clavié

S'UREWIG GSETZ see Märki, Ernst

SURIRAM
   (Tan) SATB (malaysian folksong) KJOS 8783 (S686)

SURTEL, MAARTEN
   O Saisons, Ô Châteaux (from Rimbaud)
   8pt mix cor [10'] sc DONEMUS (S687)

SURVIVOR FROM WARSAW, A see Schoenberg, Arnold

SUSANNI
   (Shaw And Parker) SATB,acap LEONARD-US 50304930 (S688)

SUSSES LIEB see Dowland, John

SUTER, L.M.
   A La Claire Fontaine
    men cor HUG (S689)

   Comment Vouloir Qu'une Personne Chante?
    men cor HUG (S690)

   Trois P'tits Tours Et Puis S'en Vont
    men cor HUG 8510 (S691)

SUTERMEISTER, HEINRICH (1910-1995)
   Berceuse De La Vierge
    see Suite Chorale

   Chanson
    see Suite Chorale

   Choeur De La Lumièe
    see Suite Chorale

   Musique, La
    see Suite Chorale

SUTERMEISTER, HEINRICH (cont'd.)
   Polka
    see Suite Chorale

   Suite Chorale
    mix cor HUG f.s.
     contains: Berceuse De La Vierge; Chanson; Choeur De La Lumièe; Musique, La; Polka; Vieux Jardin, Le (S692)

   Vieux Jardin, Le
    see Suite Chorale

SUZUKI, NORIO (1953- )
   Oni No Koroku
    jr cor,narrator,pno HUG (S693)

SUZUKI, TERUAKI (1958- )
   Akigawa No Uta
    mix cor/wom cor HUG (S694)

   Anthologia Graeca
    mix cor HUG (S695)

   Ars Antiqua
    2pt wom cor HUG (S696)

   Dojoji Engi
    mix cor HUG (S697)

   Eshi Yo
    wom cor,pno HUG (S698)

   Hadaka
    mix cor,pno HUG (S699)

   Kaze No Koe (from Toki)
    wom cor,pno HUG (S700)

   Midare-Gami
    wom cor,pno HUG (S701)

SUZUKI, YUKIKAZU (1954- )
   About Beauty
    see Utsukushii Mono Ni Tsuite

   Kazoku
    mix cor&wom cor,pno HUG (S702)

   Niji No Wa
    mix cor,pno HUG (S703)

   Utsukushii Mono Ni Tsuite *Suite
    "About Beauty" wom cor ONGAKU 553920 (S704)

SVETIT SVETEL MESIATS see Brightly Shines The Moon

SVOBODA, TOMAS (1939- )
   Czernogorsk Fugue, Op.14 (1956 Rev. 1991)
    [Czech] SSATTBB,acap oct STANGLAND TCS-37 (S705)

   Festival For Men's Choir
    [Eng] TTBB,TTTTBB soli,acap STANGLAND TCS-36 (S706)

SWEDISH CAROL MEDLEY *carol/medley
   (Swingle, Ward) SSAATTBB,db,drums, synthesizer voc pt,pts UNC JP SSC-3 SC-3 (S707)

SWEELINCK, JAN PIETERSZOON (1562-1621)
   Tout Aussitôt Que J'eus Ouï
    mix cor HUG 1904 (S708)

SWEET AND LOW see Barnby, [Sir] Joseph
   see Williamson, Malcolm

SWEET ARE THE CHARMS OF HER I LOVE
   SATB WARCH 35675 (S709)

SWEET BETSY FROM PIKE
   (Childs) 2pt cor SHAWNEE E-0335 (S710)
   see Haugland, A. Oscar

SWEET SPRING see Butler see Steed, Brad

SWEETEST DAYS, THE
   (Funk, Jeff) SATB WARNER CH9575 (S711)
   (Funk, Jeff) SAB WARNER CH9576 (S712)
   (Funk, Jeff) 2pt mix cor WARNER CH9577 (S713)

SWERTS, PIET
   Apriise Gril (from 10 Kwatrijnen)
    mix cor,acap [1'30"] CBDM (S714)

   December (from 10 Kwatrijnen)
    mix cor,acap [2'] CBDM (S715)

   Februari-Meeuw (from 10 Kwatrijnen)
    mix cor,acap [1'] CBDM (S716)

   Juli-Veer (from 10 Kwatrijnen)
    mix cor,acap [2'] CBDM (S717)

   Maart (from 10 Kwatrijnen)
    mix cor,acap [1'30"] CBDM (S718)

SWERTS, PIET (cont'd.)
   Novemberblaren (from 10 Kwatrijnen)
    mix cor,acap [1'30"] CBDM (S719)

   Oktoberlucht (from 10 Kwatrijnen)
    mix cor,acap [1'40"] CBDM (S720)

   Oogst-Zee (from 10 Kwatrijnen)
    mix cor,acap [2'] CBDM (S721)

   September (from 10 Kwatrijnen)
    mix cor,acap [2'] CBDM (S722)

   Zondag Van Januari (from 10 Kwatrijnen)
    mix cor,acap [1'20"] CBDM (S723)

SWING, THE see Lightfoot, Mary Lynn

SWING & LATIN see Foscjer, Joachin

SWING LOW!
   (Snyder, Audrey) TBB WARNER SV9516 (S724)
   (Snyder, Audrey) 3pt mix cor WARNER SV9518 (S725)
   (Snyder, Audrey) SSA WARNER SV9517 (S726)

SWING LOW, SWEET CHARIOT see Porterfield, Sherrie

SWINGING ON A STAR see Gilpin, Greg

SWINGLE, WARD
   Come Live With Me
    SSAATTBB,acap (gr. IV) UNC JP SO-5X (S727)

   How Do I Love Thee?
    SATB,acap (gr. I) UNC JP SO-3 (S728)

   It Was A Lover And His Lass
    SSAATTBB,acap UNC JP SO-1 (S729)

   Reeds Of Innocence
    SSAA,acap (gr. II) UNC JP SO-6X (S730)

   Romance
    SSAATTBB,Bar solo,acap (gr. II) UNC JP SO-2 (S731)

   Tre Kärleksdikter
    [Swed] SATB,acap (gr. II) UNC JP SO-4 (S732)

SWINGLE BELLS I *Xmas,carol/medley
   (Swingle, Ward) SSAATTBB,db,drums, synthesizer (gr. III) voc pt,pts UNC JP SBS-1 (S733)

SWINGLE BELLS II *Xmas,carol/medley
   (Swingle, Ward) SSAATTBB,db,drums, synthesizer (gr. III) voc pt,pts UNC JP SBS-2 (S734)

SWINGLE BELLS III *Xmas,carol/medley
   (Swingle, Ward) SSAATTBB,db,drums, synthesizer (gr. III) voc pt,pts UNC JP SBS-3 (S735)

SWINGLE BELLS IV *Xmas,carol/medley
   (Swingle, Ward) SSAATTBB,db,drums, synthesizer (gr. III) voc pt,pts UNC JP SBS-4 (S736)

SWINGLE BELLS IX see Hopkins

SWINGLE BELLS V *Xmas,carol/medley
   (Swingle, Ward) SSAATTBB,db,drums, synthesizer (gr. III) voc pt,pts UNC JP SBS-5 (S737)

SWINGLE BELLS VI *Xmas,carol/medley
   (Swingle, Ward) SSAATTBB,db,drums, synthesizer (gr. III) voc pt,pts UNC JP SBS-6 (S738)

SWINGLE BELLS VII see Gruber

SWINGLE BELLS VIII *Xmas,carol/medley
   (Swingle, Ward) SSAATTBB,db,drums, synthesizer (gr. III) voc pt,pts UNC JP SBS-8 (S739)

SWINGLE BELLS X *Xmas,carol/medley
   (Swingle, Ward) SSAATTBB,db,drums, (gr. II) voc pt,pts UNC JP SBS-13X (S740)

SYLVIE see Boller, Carlo

SYME
   Christmas, Christmas Everywhere
    SA WARCH 34391 (S741)

SYMPHONIC SPACE see Tsubonoh, Katsuhiro

SYMPHONY FOR VOICES see Williamson, Malcolm

SYMPHORIEN see Doret, Gustave

SYNCOPATED CLOCK, THE see Anderson, Leroy

# T

T.G.V. see Falquet, Rene

TA TIKEE TEI see Robinovitch, Sid

TADA SOREDAKE NO HANASHI DESU see Nishida, Yumiko

TAG IM HERBST see Kreis, Otto

TAGESNEIGE see Kreis, Otto

TAILOR AND THE MOUSE,THE see Marx, Karl

TAKASHIMA, MIDORI (1954- )
  Children Of The Earth - A Letter From Home
    mix cor,pno HUG (T1)

  Ground Of Sky
    mix cor,pno HUG (T2)

  Hakucho
    mix cor HUG (T3)

  Kaze Ni Naru Fue
    men cor,pno HUG (T4)

  Keredomo Daichi Wa
    mix cor,pno HUG (T5)

  Machibitogokko
    wom cor HUG (T6)

TAKE ME UNDER YOUR WING *folk song
  (Wiesenberg, Menachem) [Heb] mix cor, acap (text: H.N.Bialik)
    ISR.MUS.INST. IMI 6973 (T7)

TAKE, O-TAKE THOSE LIPS AWAY see Larkin, Michael see Strohbach, Siegfried

TAKE THE A TRAIN see Strayhorn

TAKEMITSU, TORU (1930-1996)
  Grass
    men cor SCHOTT,J SJ 1009 (T8)

  Handmade Proverbs *CC4UL
    6pt men cor SCHOTT,J SJ 1041 f.s. (T9)

  Songs I *CC6UL
    mix cor SCHOTT,J SJ 1070 f.s. (T10)

  Songs II *CC6UL
    mix cor SCHOTT,J SJ 1081 f.s. (T11)

  Wind Horse
    mix cor SCHOTT,J SJ 1082 (T12)

TAKENAKA, ATSUHIKO (1962- )
  I-No-Ri
    men cor,T solo,pno HUG (T13)

  Nora-Dokei
    wom cor,pno HUG (T14)

  O-Chi-Ba
    wom cor,pno HUG (T15)

  Os Justi
    [Lat] mix cor,org HUG (T16)

TALKIN' 'BOUT MY BABY
  (Farrell, Jim) SSATBB,acap (gr. II/gr. III) UNC JP (T17)

TALMA, LOUISE (1906- )
  In Paraise Of A Virtuous Woman
    SA,pno LAWSON 52604 (T18)

TAMAS, JANOS
  Ballnacht
    mix cor,pno [16'] MULLES DE 1241 (T19)
    men cor,pno [16'] MULLES DE 1181 (T20)

  Cante Jondo
    wom cor,pno [4'] MULLES (T21)

  Fabel
    speaking cor [9'] MULLES (T22)

  Fröhliches Wien
    mix cor,pno [15'] MULLES DE 1240 (T23)
    men cor,pno [15'] MULLES DE 1180 (T24)

  Infernalische Abendmahl,Das *ora
    SATB,solo voice,orch [20'] MULLES (T25)

  Kanti-Kantate *cant
    speaking cor [7'] MULLES (T26)

  Nebel Im Wattenmeer
    mix cor,A solo MULLES DE 1243 (T27)

TAMAS, JANOS (cont'd.)
  Stille Hof,Der
    mix cor MULLES DE 1242 (T28)

  Straussiade
    mix cor,pno [16'] MULLES DE 1239 (T29)
    men cor,pno [16'] MULLES DE 1179 (T30)

  Traumwald
    mix cor MULLES DE 1246 (T31)

  Über Die Felder
    [3'] MULLES (T32)

TAMBO
  (Lewin) SATB (jamaican folksong) KJOS 8785 (T33)

TAMBOUR, LE see Somers

TAMBOUR, BATS PAS SI FORT! see Boller, Carlo

TAN
  Little Things
    SA KJOS 6230 (T34)

TAN SKIN see Capo,B., Piel Canela

TANCHO see Hirose, Ryohei

TANEYEV
  Ah, Behold-The Dark Of Night *Op.27, No.4 (from Twelve Choruses)
    (Kaiser) [Eng] SATB,acap (med) PRESSER 312-41616 (T35)

  Evening *Op.27,No.2 (from Twelve Choruses)
    (Kaiser) SATB,acap (med diff) PRESSER 312-41614 (T36)

  Ruins Of A Tower, The *Op.27,No.3
    (Kaiser) SATB,acap (med diff) PRESSER 312-41615 (T37)

TANGERINE see Marois, Rejean

TANGIWA, TADIHIRO (1935- )
  Female Chorus (from Toyama Folksong)
    wom cor,pno HUG (T38)

TANGO IN D MAJOR see Albéniz, Isaac

TANGUEANDO see Escalada, Oscar

TANSAI-SYO see Bekku, Sadao

TANT DE FLEURS see Henchoz, Emile

TANT QUE VIVRAI see Falquet, Rene see Sermisy, Claude de (Claudin)

TANT VOUS AIME see Mermoud, Robert

TANZ, OP. 166D, DER see Kratochwil, Heinz

TANZBÄR-BLUES see Klein, Richard Rudolf

TANZLIEDER AUS ÖSTERREICH *CCU
  (Anderluh, Anton) mix cor HEYN NR. 123 f.s. (T39)

TAPSCOTT, CARL
  Something To Sing About
    SATB WARCH 35673 (T40)

TARASQUE DE TARASCON, LA see Mermoud, Robert

TARIN AD ONYTU see Sigurbjornsson, Hrodmar Ingi

TÄRNANS VISA see Cederberg, Anna

TARO NO KI see Ikebe, Shin-Ichiro

TARO'S TREE see Ikebe, Shin-Ichiro, Taro No Ki

TARTARIN DE TARASCON see Bron, Patrick

TAUBE, EVERT (1890-1976)
  Ingrid Dardels Polska
    (Svenson, Anita) mix cor,acap SVERIG SK 768 (T41)

TAUBNESSEL see Furer, Arthur

TAUSENDGULDENKRAUT see Furer, Arthur

TAWE-JONES, D.
  Mishimba Mishamba
    unis cor BANKS YS1394 (T42)

TAYAU, TAYAU see Javelot

TCHAIKOVSKY, PIOTR ILYICH (1840-1893)
  Blommornas Vals
    (Jullander) SAB,pno NOTERIA 2780 (T43)

TCHAIKOVSKY, PIOTR ILYICH (cont'd.)
  Nature Et L'amour,La
    cor,solo voice,pno BILLAUDOT (T44)

  Ode To Joy (R)
    mix cor, solo voices,orch voc sc JERONA JC1010 (T45)

TE VOICI, VIGNERON! see Boller, Carlo

TEACH ME THY WAY, O LORD see Kernis, Aaron Jay

TEARS see Dello Joio, Norman

TEBAKO see Urata, Kenjiro

TELEMANN, GEORG PHILIPP (1681-1767)
  Concerto A Six
    (Swingle, Ward) SSAATTBB,db,drums (gr. IV) voc pt,pts UNC JP RG-1X (T46)

  Gugue (from String Suite "La Lyra")
    (Swingle, Ward) SSAATTBB,S solo,db, drums (gr. III) voc pt,pts UNC JP RG-3X (T47)

  Largo
    (Swingle, Ward) AATTB,A solo,db, drums (gr. II) voc pt,pts UNC JP RG-6X (T48)

  Presto (from Trio Sonata In E Major)
    (Swingle, Ward) SSAATTBB, solo voices,db,drums (gr. III) voc pt, pts UNC JP (T49)

TELFER
  Journey, The
    SATB sc WARCH 34473 (T50)

  Wedding Day
    SA WARCH 34400 (T51)

TELFER, NANCY (1950- )
  Cultural Mosaic
    SATB LESLIE 5032 (T52)

  Cultural Mosaic, The
    see To Sing Of Hopes And Dreams
    see To Sing Of Hopes And Dreams
    see To Sing Of Hopes And Dreams

  Dream, The
    unis cor LESLIE 1190 (T53)

  Journey
    SATB THOMP.G VG430 (T54)

  Luriana, Luralee
    1-2pt cor,pno CAN.MUS.CENT. MV 6101 T271LUR (T55)
    SA LESLIE 2080 (T56)

  Mary Wondered What It Meant
    unis cor THOMP.G VG181 (T57)

  Mary's Song
    SSA KJOS 6223 (T58)

  Reaching To The Future
    SATB LESLIE 5033 (T59)
    see To Sing Of Hopes And Dreams
    see To Sing Of Hopes And Dreams

  Song Of Time, The
    see To Sing Of Hopes And Dreams

  Songs Of Time
    SATB LESLIE 5031 (T60)

  Songs Of Time, The
    see To Sing Of Hopes And Dreams
    see To Sing Of Hopes And Dreams

  There Is A Tall Fir Tree
    1-2pt cor,pno CAN.MUS.CENT. MV 6101 T27THER (T61)
    SA LESLIE 2084 (T62)

  To Sing Of Hopes And Dreams
    SATB,pno CAN.MUS.CENT. f.s.
    contains: Cultural Mosaic, The; Songs Of Time, The (T63)

  To Sing Of Hopes And Dreams
    SATB,band CAN.MUS.CENT. MV 1370 T271TO f.s.
    contains: Cultural Mosaic, The; Reaching To The Future; Song Of Time,The (T64)

  To Sing Of Hopes And Dreams
    jr cor,band CAN.MUS.CENT. MV 6370 T271TO f.s.
    contains: Cultural Mosaic, The; Reaching To The Future; Songs Of Time,The (T65)

  What Then, My Love?
    TTBB KJOS 5566 (T66)

TELL see Doret, Gustave

TELL ME IT'S NOT TRUE
  (Leavitt) SAB SHAWNEE D-466 ipa (T67)
  (Leavitt) SATB SHAWNEE A-1985 ipa
    (T68)
  (Leavitt) SSA SHAWNEE B-563 ipa (T69)

TEMPI I, III, V see Togni, Camillo

TEMPO II see Togni, Camillo

TEMPO IV see Togni, Camillo

TEMPRA,LANERA see Gustavino, Carlos

TEMPS A LAISSÈ SON MANTEAU, LE see Reichel, Bernard

TEMPS DES AMOURS, LE see Vuataz, Roger

TEMPS POUR TOUT, UN see Rochat, Jean

TEMPS VOLE, LE see Henchoz, Emile

TEMPUS DESTRUENDI - TEMPUS AEDIFICANDI see Dallapiccola, Luigi

TEN-NYO GA TONDA see Arashino, Hideo

TEN PICTURES see Adachi, Hiromi

TENDER SHEPHERD (COUNT YOUR SHEEP)
  (Kinsale, Hillary) 2pt cor WARNER
    1537TC5X (T70)

TENDERLY see Alcivar, Bob

TENDERLY, MY LOVE, I'LL COME TO THEE see Hodge, Stephen

TENEBRAE see Hosokawa, Toshio

TENNIS SHOE-BE-DOOS see Lawrence, Stephen L.

TENTING TONIGHT see Poné, Gundaris

TERAHARA, NOBUO (1928- )
  Kanashiki Mujun
    wom cor,S solo,pno HUG (T71)

TERASHIMA, RIKUYA (1964- )
  Bajo La Luna Gitana
    mix cor,pno HUG (T72)

  Dawn
    mix cor,pno HUG (T73)

  Fools Of Chelm, The
    mix cor,pno HUG (T74)

  Kaze No Sukitotta Uta
    mix cor,pno HUG (T75)

  Sonohito Ga Utautoki
    wom cor,pno HUG (T76)

TERRE A REVERDI, LA see Binet, Jean

TERRE DE CALME ET DE DOUCE PLAISANCE see Miche, Paul

TERRE DE MON ENFANCE see Boller, Carlo

TERRE ET L'EAU see Doret, Gustave

TERRE ET L'ÉTOILE, LA see Bron, Patrick

TERRE JURASSIENNE see Miche, Paul

TERRE LIBRE see Schule, Bernard see Schule, Bernard, Land Und Freiheit

TERRE MEURTRIE see Henchoz, Emile

TERRE NATALE see Naudier

TERRE OÙ J'AI VU LE JOUR see Bovet, J.

TERRE SOIS DOUCE see Kaelin, Pierre

TERRE VAUDOISE see Boller, Carlo

TERZAKIS, DIMITRI (1938- )
  Sechste Siegel
    mix cor,kbd,fl&clar&horn&perc&vln& vcl GRAV EG 150 (T77)

TERZO LIBRO DE MADRIGALI A CINQUE VOCI, IL see Gabrieli, Andrea

TES YEUX see Anonymous

TESTI, FLAVIO (1923- )
  Canto A Las Madres De Los Milicianos Muertos *Op.17
    cor,S solo,3.2.2.3. 4.4.4.0. timp, tam-tam,xylo,pno,harp,strings sc RICORDI-IT 131253 (T78)

THAR SEM HAFJOLLIN HEILOG RISA see Baldvinsson, Tryggvi

THAT GRACE MAY ABOUND see Strommen, Carl

THAT HOLIDAY SPIRIT see Dunn, Mary Lou

THAT WE MAY NOT LOSE LOSS see Burge, John

THAT YONGE CHILD
  (Read) SATB BANKS ECS0223 (T79)

THAT'S THE IDEA OF FREEDOM see Copland, Aaron

THAYER, FRED
  There Is Some Luck
    SATB,acap LAWSON 52680 (T80)

THEME FROM "NEW YORK, NEW YORK"
  (Chinn, Teena) 1-2pt cor WARNER
    CH95106 (T81)
    see Manhattan Melodies

THEODORAKIS, MIKIS (1925- )
  Amour Et La Mort,L'
    cor NAKAS (T82)

  Forty Songs For Children
    cor NAKAS EPN 776 (T83)

  Mathausen
    cor NAKAS (T84)

THERE IS A LADYE see Harris, Jerry Weseley see Leininger, W.

THERE IS A MORN UNSEEN see Diemer, Emma Lou

THERE IS A TALL FIR TREE see Telfer, Nancy

THERE IS NO ROSE see Wilson, Thomas

THERE IS SOME LUCK see Thayer, Fred

THERE, I'VE SAID IT AGAIN
  (Gilpin) SATB SHAWNEE A-A963 (T85)

THERE SHALL A STAR see Mendelssohn-Bartholdy, Felix

THERESE, L'AMOUR DE DIEU see Prado, José-Antonio (Almeida)

THEY SAY THAT FALLING IN LOVE IS WONDERFUL see Berlin, Irving

THEY THAT GO DOWN TO THE SEA IN SHIPS see Purcell, Henry

THINGS ARE GETTIN' BETTER
  (Cross, Dave) SSAA,perc (gr. III) UNC JP (T86)

THINGS THAT NEVER DIE see Dengler

THIRIET, MAURICE (1906-1972)
  Trois Fables De La Fontaine
    4pt jr cor BILLAUDOT (T87)

THIS IS IT!
  (Schmutte, Pete) SATB WARNER CH9522
    (T88)
  (Schmutte, Pete) SAB WARNER CH9523
    (T89)
  (Schmutte, Pete) 2pt cor WARNER
    CH9524 (T90)

THIS IS NOT GOODBYE see Simms, Patsy Ford

THIS IS THE MOMENT
  (Chinn, Teena) SATB WARNER CL1039 ipa
    (T91)
  (Chinn, Teena) SAB WARNER CL1040 ipa
    (T92)

THIS IS WHERE IT'S AT see Raum, Elizabeth

THIS LAND IS YOUR LAND see Guthrie

THIS WILL BE OUR TIME see Schwartz, Dan

THOMAS
  Holiday Songs For Little Folks
    (composed with Waring)
    unis cor SHAWNEE GF-0083 (T93)

THOMAS, ANDRE
  I Hear America Singing (from Walk Together Children)
    SATB HERITAGE 15-1067 (T94)

THORARINSSON, LEIFUR (1934- )
  Dans (from Bakkynjum E. Evripides)
    mix cor ICELAND 017-069 (T95)

THORRABLOT see Stefansson, Finnur Torfi

THOSE WERE THE DAYS see Raskin

THOUGH AMARYLLIS DANCE see Byrd, William

THOUGH LOVE see Steed, Brad

THOUGHTS IN THE NIGHT see Porterfield, Sherrie

THREE AESOP FABLES see Lyell, Margaret

THREE AMERICAN CLASSICS *CCU
  (Ringwald) SATB SHAWNEE GA-0103 (T96)

THREE APPLESONGS see Sowash, Rick

THREE BRAHMS SONGS FOR WOMEN'S CHOIR see Brahms, Johannes

THREE BRAHMS SONGS FOR WOMENS CHORUS see Brahms, Johannes

THREE CANADIAN FOLK SONGS see Holman, Derek

THREE CARRIBEAN CALYPSOS *CC3U
  (Gritton) jr cor FABER 51527 4 (T97)

THREE CHANSONS see Niikura, Ken

THREE CHINESE LYRICS see Broege, Timothy

THREE CHORAL PIECES see Casken, John

THREE CHORIC HYMNS see Williamson, Malcolm

THREE DOMINICAN FOLKSONGS see Nunez, Carold

THREE DUETS see Hensel, Fanny Mendelssohn

THREE FRENCH FOLK SONGS see Edwards, Geoffrey

THREE GAELIC SONGS see Vaughan Williams, Ralph

THREE HERRICK SONGS see Cutter, William (Bill)

THREE JAPANESE WORKSONGS see Nakanishi, Satoru

THREE JUSTIN MORGAN CHORUSES see Morgan, J.

THREE LITTLE PIGS: A "HOWLING" SUCCESS STORY, THE see Lawrence, Stephen L.

THREE MADRIGALS BY JACQUES ARCADELT see Arcadelt, Jacob

THREE MADRIGALS see Orrego-Salas, Juan A.

THREE MAN-YO SONG see Nakanishi, Satoru

THREE MEN'S CHORUSES see Strauss, Richard

THREE MYSTICAL SONGS see Benjamin

THREE NORTH COUNTRY FOLK SONGS
  (Wilby, Philip) SATB BANKS ECS 114
    f.s.
    contains: Byker Hill; Farmer's Boy, The; Marianne (T98)

THREE PARISIAN CHANSONS *CC3U
  (Thomas, Bernard) SATB ANTICO AE1
    f.s. various composers (T99)

THREE PART BALLATE, MADRIGALS, CACCIA see Landini, Francesco

THREE RHYMES see Bouman

THREE ROBERT LOUIS STEVENSON SETTINGS see Gallina

THREE SATIRES, OP. 28 see Schoenberg, Arnold

THREE SCOTTISH POEMS see Blumenfeld, Harold

THREE SONGS see Pfautsch, Lloyd Alvin

THREE SONGS BY KENJI MIYAZAWA see Hasegawa, Tsutomu

THREE SONGS OF NATURE see Estes, Jerry

THREE STRANGE STORIES see Kino, Seiichiro

THREE ZULU SONGS see Forsyth, Malcolm

THREE ZULU SONGS *CCU
  (Forsyth) SSA WARCH 35103 (T100)

THRENI see Hayashi, Hikaru

THROUGH THE MIDDLE OF IT ALL see McPheeters

THROUGHT THE EYES OF LOVE see Hamlisch, Marvin F.

THRU THE AGE see Fischer, Clare

THY MORNINGS I SHALL SEEK see Zehavi, Oded

TI INNAMORASTI DEL FIUME see Bettinelli, Bruno

TIBETAN LIGHT see Tsubonoh, Katsuhiro

TICHY, O.A.
  Adieu
    see Trois Chansons De Soldats Tchécoslovaques

  Appel, L'
    see Trois Chansons De Soldats Tchécoslovaques

  Dors, Mon Amour...
    see Trois Chansons Populaires Tchécoslovaques

  Je Suis Seul, Toujours Seul...
    see Trois Chansons Populaires Tchécoslovaques

  Mal Du Pays
    see Trois Chansons De Soldats Tchécoslovaques

  Ne T'arrête Pas...
    see Trois Chansons Populaires Tchécoslovaques

  Trois Chansons De Soldats Tchécoslovaques
    mix cor HUG 8528 f.s.
      contains: Adieu; Appel, L'; Mal Du Pays (T101)

  Trois Chansons Populaires Tchécoslovaques
    mix cor HUG 8513 f.s.
      contains: Dors, Mon Amour...; Je Suis Seul, Toujours Seul...; Ne T'arrête Pas... (T102)

TIDE RISES, THE TIDE FALLS see Kent

TIEF IST DIE MÜHLE VERSCHNEIT see Podbertsky, Th.

TIEFE LIED, OP. 36, DAS see Kerstens, Huub

TIENS BON! see Rochat, Jean

TIENS! TIENS! TIENS! see Misraki, P.

TIGER RAG see Spevacek, Linda

TIGIDA PIPA see Montague, Stephen

TIL SONGSINS see Stefansson, Finnur Torfi

TILLÄGNAN see Dominique, Monica

TILLEUL, LE see Schubert, Franz (Peter)
  see Schubert, Franz (Peter), Lindenbaum, Die

TILLEY, ALEXANDER
  Silver Swan, The
    SSAB,pno BOOSEY-ENG OCTB6721 (T103)

TIME see Moments In Time

TIME AFTER TIME
  (Cross, Dave) SSATB,perc (gr. II/gr. III) UNC JP (T104)

TIME-ECHO IN THE NORTH see Okasaka, Keiki

TIME TO GIVE see Ginsburg, Ned

TIMIDITÉ see Haenni, G.

TINI, APRIL ARABIAN
  One Hundred Ways
    SATB,T solo,kbd,alto sax,elec bass, drums (gr. III) UNC JP (T105)

TIPTON, CLYDE (1934-  )
  Songs Of Innocence
    SSA EARTHSNG EW-9 (T106)

TIR DE JEAN P'TIT JEAN, LE see Mermoud, Robert

TIRA MA LYRE see Zbinden, Julien-François

TIREZ VOS RIDEAUX, DEMOISELLES see Boller, Carlo

TIRITOMBA see Lemmermann, Heinz

'TIS FINISHED
  (Shaw And Parker) SATB LEONARD-US 50303940 (T107)

'TIS THE SEASON (A PARTNER SONG WITH "THE HOLLY AND THE IVY") see Donnelly, Mary

'TIS THE SEASON TO BE JOLLY see Grier, Gene

'TIS WOMAN MAKES US LOVE see Purcell, Henry

TO A THOUSAND MURDERED GIRLS see Ansink, Caroline

TO A WILD ROSE see MacDowell, Edward Alexander

TO DARE THE MOON
  (New York Voices) SSATB,solo,perc (gr. III/gr. IV) UNC JP (T108)

TO EVERYTHING THERE IS A SEASON see Cooper, Paul, Omnia Tempus Habent

TO LADIES' EYES *folk song,Ir
  (Parker) TTBB LAWSON 4-51458 (T109)

TO MORNING see Edmunds, Christopher

TO MUSIC see Spevacek, Linda

TO-MYO-RAI-GO see Tsubonoh, Katsuhiro

TO OUR NEXT MERRY MEETING see Phillips, Henry

TO SING OF HOPES AND DREAMS see Telfer, Nancy

TO SING OF HOPES AND DREAMS see Telfer, Nancy

TO SING OF HOPES AND DREAMS see Telfer, Nancy

TO THE EVENING STAR see Schumann, Robert (Alexander)

TO THE NIGHTINGALE see Schumann, Robert (Alexander)

TO THE PLOUGHBOY see Vaughan Williams, Ralph

TO THE SHADY WOODS see Harris, Jerry Weseley

TO YOU see Maessen, Antoon

TOAST TO THE WIND see Senshu, Jiro

TOAST VALAISAN see Henchoz, Emile

TOBLER, J.H.
  Chant De La Landsgemeinde D'Appenzell
    men cor HUG 8153 (T110)

  Frühling,Der
    men cor,acap MULLES (T111)

  Schweizerlied
    men cor,acap MULLES (T112)

TOCCATA AND FUGUE IN D MINOR see Bach, Johann Sebastian

TOCCATA FOR VOICES see Spevacek, Linda

TOD, DER see Sauseng, Wolfgang

TOD VON BASEL,DER see Leicht

TOEBOSCH, LOUIS (1916-  )
  Boer En Snijder
    see Drie Liederen

  Canon *Op.143b
    4 eq voices EXC.MH 19.007.007 (T113)

  Daar Gingen Twee Gespeelkens Goed
    see Drie Liederen

  De Zoete Tijd Komt Aan
    see Drie Liederen

  Diablerie *Op.82a
    SATB EXC.MH 19.008.001 (T114)

  Drie Liederen *Op.63a
    SATB EXC.MH 19.007.001 f.s.
      contains: Boer En Snijder; Daar Gingen Twee Gespeelkens Goed; De Zoete Tijd Komt Aan (T115)

TOGAWA, YOHICHI (1959-  )
  Interpersonal Relationships
    mix cor HUG (T116)

TOGETHER see Lucas, Theodore D. see Parker, Alice

TOGETHER AS ONE see Althouse, Jay

TOGETHER LET US RANGE THE FIELDS see Boyce, William

TOGNI, CAMILLO (1922-1993)
  Barrabas
    SSMezATTBarB,T solo,4.5.5.5. 6.4.3.1. timp,perc,harp,cel,pno, strings RICORDI-IT f.s.
      contains: Tempi I, Iii, V; Tempo Ii; Tempo Iv (T117)

  Tempi I, Iii, V
    see Barrabas

  Tempo Ii
    see Barrabas

  Tempo Iv
    see Barrabas

TOGNI, PETER
  When The Dawn Appears
    SSA THOMP.G VG349 (T118)

TOI TOMO E see Urata, Kenjiro

TOKIMEKI YOKOHAMA see Yamamoto, Naozumi

TOMBEAU DE LOUISE LABBÉ, LE see Ohana, Maurice

TOMBSONGS see Garwood, Margaret

TOMKINS, T.
  O Let Me Live For True Love
    (Swingle, Ward) SATB,db,drums, synthesizer (gr. II) voc pt,pts UNC JP SM-2 (T119)

TOMODACHI TO see Okuma, Takako

TOM'S GONE TO HILO
  (Shaw-Parker) TTBB LAWSON 4-51064 (T120)

TON ÂME ET TON VISAGE see Marenzio, Luca

TONADA DEL ADIOS, CANCION see Sanchez, Damian

TOOI KAGAMI see Abiko, Yoshiro

TOP SECRET
  (New York Voices) SATB,kbd,tenor sax, drums,db,gtr,synthesizer (gr. IV) UNC JP (T121)

TOPSY-TURVEY LAND see Williams, Arnold

TOREADOR'S SONG, THE see Bizet, Georges

TORME
  Christmas Song,The
    (Swingle, Ward) SSAATTBB,acap (gr. II) voc pt,pts UNC JP SBS-10 (T122)

TORRENT, LE see Naudier

TORTI, LORENZO (1937-  )
  Campane Nel Vespero
    SATB (text by Rizzola) BERBEN BERBEN 3467 (T123)

TORTILLARD, LE see Delannoy, Marcel

TOUR PRENDS GARDE, LA see Jouineau, Jacques

TOUS CEUX QUI VEUL' see Canteloube, Joseph

TOUS LES YEUX see Hansen

TOUT AUSSITÔT QUE J'EUS OUÏ see Sweelinck, Jan Pieterszoon

TOUT CE PAYS AIMÉ see Boller, Carlo

TOUT GARÇON QUI SERT see Anonymous

TOUT LÀ-BAS PRÈS DES ROCHERS see Boller, Carlo

TOUT LÀ-HAUT see Bovet, J.

TOUT L'UNIVERS EST PLEIN DE SA MAGNIFICENCE see Mendelssohn-Bartholdy, Felix

TOUT RENAÎTRA see Martin

TOUT RESPIRE... see Lagger, Oscar

TOUT SIMPLEMENT see Jaques-Dalcroze, Émile

TOUTOUIK see Lesur, Daniel

TOWARD TOMORROW see Tsuchida, Eisuke

TRACTEUR À ZÉPHIRIN see Moret, Oscar

TRÄD FRAM DU NATTENS GUD see Bellman, Carl Michael

TRAFFIC see Falquet, Rene

TRANCE'S CEREMONY see Tsubonoh, Katsuhiro

TRANSJURAN, J'AI CHANTÉ see Pantillon, François

TRANSSILVANISCHE KANTATE,EINE see Veress, Sandor

TRAUMWALD see Tamas, Janos

TRAVAUX DE LA VIGNE, LES see Doret, Gustave

TRAVELIN' MAN see Spevacek, Linda

TRAVELLING MUSICIANS, THE see Henderson, Ruth Watson

TRE CANTI see Lagana, Ruggero

TRE CANTI DI BETOCCHI see Prosperi, Carlo

TRE CITAT AV ULLA ISAKSSON see Hemberg, Eskil

TRE CORI see Pierucci, Armando

TRE FRAMMENTI DI ANACREONTE see Zecchi, Adone

TRE KÄRLEKSDIKTER see Swingle, Ward

TRE KORSLÅTTER see Vea, Ketil

TRE LÅTAR TILL see Broberg, Robert Karl Oskar

TRE SKJEMTEVISER see Volle, Bjarne

TREBLE AND BASS SONG BOOK (BOOK 1)
  *CC21L
  (Whitfield, John B.R.) mix cor BANKS f.s. cor pts, voc sc (T124)

TREBLE AND BASS SONG BOOK (BOOK 2)
  *CC26L
  (Whitfield, John B.R.) mix cor BANKS f.s. cor pts, voc sc (T125)

TREE IN THE WOOD see Specht

TREE OF LIFE see Niimi, Tokuhide

TREE OF THE LONELY SOUL see Estevez, Antonio, Mata Del Anima Sola

TREE TOAD AND LONE DOG see Henderson

TREECE, ROGER
  Holiday Blues
    SATB,perc (gr. III) UNC JP (T126)

TREMBLOT DE LA CROIX, FRANCINE
  A Dos D'oiseau
    3pt jr cor BILLAUDOT (T127)
    3-4pt wom cor BILLAUDOT (T128)

TRENET, CHARLES
  Soleil Et La Lune, Le
    mix cor HUG 8850 (T129)

TRENTACINQUE CANTI POPOLARI ITALIANI see Schinelli, Achille

TRES CANCIONES DE CUNA see Gustavino, Carlos

TRÈS RICHES HEURES, LES see Mermoud, Robert

TRICOTEUSES, LES see Mermoud, Robert

TRINKLIED see Huber, Walter Simon see Schmid, Walter see Winter, Peter von

TRINKSPRUCH see Schnepper, Othmar

TRISTANO, GERARDO (1955-    )
  Il Paesaggio Delle Analogie
    mix cor,acap (text by Sanesi)
    BERBEN BERBEN 3088 (T130)

TRISTE DEPART see Gombert, Nicolas

TRISTEZZA see Zecchi, Adone

TRIUMF ATT FINNAS TILL see Jennefelt, Thomas

TROIS BALLADES see Badings, Henk

TROIS CHANSON DE FRANCE: see Lagger, Oscar

TROIS CHANSONS see Debussy, Claude

TROIS CHANSONS À L'ENCRE DE CHINE see Falquet, Rene

TROIS CHANSONS DE CLÉMENT MAROT see Vaubourgoin, Marc

TROIS CHANSONS DE FRANCE see Canteloube, Joseph

TROIS CHANSONS DE FRANCE see Canteloube, Joseph

TROIS CHANSONS DE MARINS see Aubanel, Georges

TROIS CHANSONS DE MARINS see Boller, Carlo

TROIS CHANSONS DE ROUTE see Henchoz, Emile

TROIS CHANSONS DE SOLDATS TCHÉCOSLOVAQUES see Tichy, O.A.

TROIS CHANSONS DU "JEU DU FEUILLU" see Jaques-Dalcroze, Émile

TROIS CHANSONS, NR.1 see Debussy, Claude

TROIS CHANSONS, NR.2 see Debussy, Claude

TROIS CHANSONS, NR.3 see Debussy, Claude

TROIS CHANSONS POPULAIRES FRANÇAISES see Roland-Manuel, Alexis see Roland-Manuel, Alexis

TROIS CHANSONS POPULAIRES TCHÉCOSLOVAQUES see Tichy, O.A.

TROIS CHANTS GREC see Reuchsel

TROIS COMMÈRES, LES see Henchoz, Emile

TROIS FABLES DE LA FONTAINE see Thiriet, Maurice

TROIS FILEUSES, LES see Indy, Vincent d'

TROIS FILLES EN BLANC see Boller, Carlo

TROIS GRAPPES... see Henchoz, Emile

TROIS IMAGES see Hagiwara, Hidehico

TROIS JEUN'S FILL'S ONT TANT DANSÉ see Lagger, Oscar

TROIS OISEAUX CHANTANTS, LES see Jaques-Dalcroze, Émile

TROIS PENSÉES see Haenni, G.

TROIS PETITS OISEAUX DANS LES BLÉS see Martin

TROIS P'TITS TOURS ET PUIS S'EN VONT see Suter, L.M.

TROLLEY SONG, THE
  (Snyder, Audrey) 1-2pt cor WARNER T6600TC5 (T131)

TROLLS see Crawley, Clifford

TROMMELLIED see Zahler, J.R.

TROST DER NACHT see Stocker, Karl

TROUBLE IS A-COMIN' see Williams

TRUTZLIED see Märki, Ernst

TSCHULIMUNG-LIEDLI see Keller, Hugo

TSUBONOH, KATSUHIRO (1947-    )
  Symphonic Space
    wom cor,orch HUG (T132)
  Tibetan Light
    wom cor HUG (T133)
  To-Myo-Rai-Go
    men cor HUG (T134)
  Trance's Ceremony
    wom cor HUG (T135)
  Voices Stars
    wom cor HUG (T136)

TSUCHIDA, EISUKE (1963-    )
  Komoriuta, Komoriuta Yo
    wom cor HUG (T137)
  Toward Tomorrow
    jr cor,orch HUG (T138)

TU ES LE PAYS see Bron, Patrick

TU ES MON BERGER see Martin

TU N'ES PAS UN GRAIN DE SABLE see Müller, P.

TU TU TU... see Regnart, Jacob

TUCK, DANNY
  Duality
    SATB,org MUSIC SEV. 667 (T139)

TUESDAY GREETING (PEACE GREETINGS) see Stockhausen, Karlheinz, Dienstags-Gruss (Friedens-Gruss)

TUINEN, FEIKE VAN
  Canon
    see Drie Miniaturen
  Drie Miniaturen
    SATB,acap BANK 11.900.027 f.s.
    contains: Canon; Melodie; Ostinaat (T140)
  Melodie
    see Drie Miniaturen
  Ostinaat
    see Drie Miniaturen

TULPE,DIE see Bigler, Rudolf

TUMBALALAIKA
  (Lazar, Matthew) SATB,T solo,pno (med, russian-jewish folksong in yiddish) HAZA HZ-016 (T141)

TURKISH DANCE see Adachi, Hiromi

TURN AROUND, LOOK AT ME see Capehart, Jerry

TURN THE LIGHTS ON see Albrecht, Sally K.

TURN TURN TURN see Seeger, Pete

TURNERLIEDCHEN see Zahler, J.R.

TURTLE DOVE
  (Webb, Merrilee) TB,pno SANTA SBMP 76 (T142)

TVÅ FÅGELKÖRER see Karkoff, Maurice

TVÅ KINESISKA VISOR
  (Öhrwall, Anders) mix cor,acap SVERIG SK 774 (T143)

TVÅ LUSSEVISOR see Cederberg, Anna

TVÅ TRÄD see Holmberg, Leif

TWELVE DAYS OF CHRISTMAS see Henderson

TWELVE DOGS OF CHRISTMAS, THE see Lawrence, Stephen L.

TWELVE MONTHS, THE see Reinhardt, Bruno

TWELVE SONGS OF CHRISTMAS, THE (A MEDLEY OF SEASONAL FAVORITES)
  (Althouse) 2pt cor/SSA ALFRED 11611 (T144)
  (Althouse) SATB ALFRED 11609 (T145)
  (Althouse) SAB ALFRED 11610 (T146)

TWENTY-FOUR FAVORITE NURSERY AND FOLK SONGS *CC24U
  cor,pno KODALY f.s. (T147)

TWILIGHT HOURS, THE see Sacco, P.

TWIST OF THE TONGUE, A see Strommen, Carl

TWO CHRISTMAS SONGS see Minikel

TWO DIFFERENT WORLDS see Frisch, Albert T.

TWO DUETS see Hensel, Fanny Mendelssohn

TWO ELIZABETHAN LYRICS, OP.24 see Kenessey, Stefania Maria de

TWO GREAT SOARING EAGLES see Burritt, Lloyd

TWO HERRICK PIECES see Barrett, Richard

TWO INUIT SONGS see Robinovitch, Sid

TWO ISRAELI FOLK SONGS
  (Gallina) 3pt cor SHAWNEE D-0476 (T148)
  (Gallina) 2pt cor SHAWNEE EA-0204 (T149)

TWO LATIN CHORUSES FROM AMADEUS see Perry

TWO LITTLE DOVES see Manchai Puito

TWO MADRIGALS see Klein, Gideon

TWO MEDIEVAL SONGS see Braun, Yeheskiel, Duo Medii Aevi Cantica

TWO MENDELSSOHN PART SONGS see Mendelssohn-Bartholdy, Felix

TWO-PART BALLATE see Landini, Francesco

TWO SEA SONGS see Vaughan Williams, Ralph

TWO SONGS OF WINTER see Vaughan Williams, Ralph

TYSON
   Feel Good (composed with Scott)
     3pt treb cor,pno BOOSEY-ENG sc
     OCTB6711, cor pts ENB395   (T150)

TYSTNAD see Jansson, Gunnar

## U

ÜBARN GLÅNTÅLBODN  *CCU,Austrian
   (Mulle, Justinus -Glawischnig, Gerhard) mix cor/men cor/wom cor HEYN ISBN 385366 589 6 f.s.   (U1)

ÜBER DIE FELDER see Tamas, Janos

UBI CARITAS see Leavitt, John

UBI CARITAS ET AMOR see Lagger, Oscar
   see Wilson, Thomas

UDSIGTER FRA ULRIKKEN
   (Volle, Bjarne) men cor,pno NOTON N-9241-C   (U2)
   (Volle, Bjarne) 4pt mix cor,pno NOTON N-9141-B   (U3)
   (Volle, Bjarne) 3pt mix cor,acap NOTON N-9141-D   (U4)
   (Volle, Bjarne) 3pt mix cor,pno NOTON N-9241-D   (U5)
   (Volle, Bjarne) men cor,acap NOTON N-9241-C   (U6)
   (Volle, Bjarne) 4pt mix cor,acap NOTON N-9245   (U7)
   see Volle, Bjarne

UEBER DIE HEIDE see Märki, Ernst

UEBERBAUTES LAND see Märki, Ernst

UEBERGANG see Huber, Paul

UEBERMUT see Leuthold, W.

UEDA, AKIRA (1932- )
   Kodomo No Mainichi
     mix cor HUG   (U8)

UF EM BÄRGLI see Märki, Ernst

UHLMANN, OTTO (1891- )
   Lebensart
     men cor,acap MULLES   (U9)

UHR,DIE see Zentner, Johannes

UHRMACHERLADEN, DER see Lischka, Rainer

UKRAINIAN BELL CAROL see Spevacek, Linda

ULLMANN, JAKOB (1958- )
   Voice, Books And Fire I
     voice(s) and any sound-creators [70'] ARIAD 91054   (U10)
   Voice, Books And Fire II(1)
     2 choirs and 2 speakers [45'] ARIAD 94022   (U11)
   Voice, Books And Fire II(2)
     6 choirs and 1 soloist [25'] ARIAD 92010   (U12)

UM KVOLD see Sigurbjörnsson, Thorkell

UMI-FURUSATO NO see Hirayoshi, Kunitake

UMI NO BALLADE see Yuyama, Akira

UMI O MI-NI YUKO see Kawasaki, Etsuo

UN P'TIT TRAIN see Henchoz, Emile

UN VILLAGE SELON MON COEUR see Miche, Paul

UNCHAINED MELODY see Zaret, Hy

UNCHAINED SNOWBIRDS see Rogers

UND DA WIND VERWAHT'S LAB see Mittergradnegger, Günter

...UND ES BIRKNBAMLE LOST MA ZUA
   *CC24U,Austrian
   (Ortner, Sepp-Bünker, Otto) mix cor HEYN ISBN 3 85366 463 6 f.s.   (U13)

UNDER MY COMMAND see Goetze, M.

UNDICI CANTI POPLARI FRIULANI see Anonymous

UNICORN,THE see Lessia see Silverstein

UNION see Barnes, Edward

UNLESS IT'S YOU see Mandel, Johnny Alfred

UNSER LEBEN GLEICHT DER REISE see Krenger, R.

UNSER LEBEN GLEICHT DER REISE (BERSINALIED) see Ammann, Benno

UNSER SCHÖNES LAND see Milde, Friedrich

UNSERE DÖRFER see Boller, Carlo

UNSERE SCHWEIZ see Bovet, J., Notre Suisse

UNSERE ZEIT see Helmschrott, Robert M.

UNTAN NOCK IN DA MULDN (from "Neue Kärntner Chorblätter" Edited By Reinhard Kühr) CCU,Austrian
   (Kahlhammer, Jelle) men cor HEYN ISBN 3 85366 643 4 f.s. neue kärntnerlieder   (U14)

UNTARN BAM BIN I GSESSN (from Chorblätter)
   (Streiner, Hans) mix cor HEYN   (U15)
   (Streiner, Hans) men cor HEYN   (U16)

UNTER DER LINDE see Diener, Theodor

UNTERM AHORNBAUM see Krayenbühl, F.

UNTERM LINDENBAUM see Sturm, Wilhelm

UO NIOU MACHI see Fukushima, Yujiro

UP A LAZY RIVER see Carmichael, Hoagy

UP ON A ROOFTOP see Cable, Howard

UP! QUIT THY BOWER see Richards, [Henry] Brinley

UP WHERE WE BELONG see Sainte-Marie, Buffy

URATA, KENJIRO (1941- )
   Tebako
     jr cor HUG   (U17)
   Toi Tomo E
     mix cor HUG   (U18)

URFER, ALBERT
   Chanson Oubliée
     mix cor HUG 8424   (U19)
     men cor HUG 8425   (U20)
   Il Suffit De Chanter
     mix cor HUG 8660   (U21)
   N'allez Plus Au Bois
     mix cor HUG 8600   (U22)
     men cor HUG 8601   (U23)
   Saute La Brume
     mix cor HUG 8661   (U24)

URLICHT see Berr, José

URSPRUNG DES FEUERS,DER see Sibelius, Jean

URWALDSONG see Schindler, Peter

USE ALL OF YOUR SENSES
   (Rosander, Christine) SATB,acap (gr. III) UNC JP   (U25)

UTSUKUSHII MONO NI TSUITE see Suzuki, Yukikazu

UY, PAUL (1932- )
   Choral Pour La Paix
     mix cor,STB&narrator,pno,horn,trp, trom,perc,strings [60'] CBDM   (U26)

# V

VA-T-EN GUERRE, LE see Pasquier, Marius

VACANCES see Müller, P.

VAE ARIEL! see Zardini, T.

VAGUE DU SOIR, LA see Delmas, Marc-Jean-Baptiste

VALAIS, MON BEAU VALAIS see Parchet, A.

VALDEZ, PELUZA
  Mi Canto A La Nochebuena
    mix cor,pno LAGOS   (V1)

VALLÉE, LA see Pasquier, Marius

VALPARAISO see Aubanel, Georges

VALSE DES FEUILLES, LA see Bovet, J.

VALSE TENDRE see Lang, H.

VANCE, MARGARET
  Ring Out The Bells! (from I Saw Three Ships)
    SATB HERITAGE 15-1035   (V2)

VANITÉS DU MONDE, LES see Gagnebin, Henri

VÄNTA INTE MED ATT SJUNGA see Janunger, Kjell

VÅRFANTASI see Janunger, Kjell

VARGELTSGOTT FÜRS GUATSEIN (from Chorblätter)
  (Streiner, Hans) mix cor HEYN   (V3)
  (Streiner, Hans) men cor HEYN   (V4)

VARIATIONS ON "AH! VOUS DIRAI-JE, MAMAN" see Mozart, Wolfgang Amadeus

VARIATIONS ON FA-LA-LA (from Deck The Halls)
  (Bridwell) cor ALEX.HSE. oct CK253109, sc CK673109   (V5)

VÄRMLANDSVISAN see Sköld, Bengt-Göran

VÅRMORGEN see Nyhus, Rolf

VARSHA see Bhatia, Vanraj A.

VATERLAND, RUH IN GOTTESHAND see Müller, Joseph Ivar

VATERLANDSHYMNE see Barblan, Otto, Hymne À La Patrie

VATERLANDSLIEBE see Märki, Ernst

VATERLANDSLIED see Schmid, Walter

VAUBOURGOIN, MARC (1907-1985)
  Trois Chansons De Clément Marot *CC3U
    mix cor BILLAUDOT f.s.   (V6)

VAUDOISES, LES see Lang, H.

VAUGHAN WILLIAMS, RALPH (1872-1958)
  Acre Of Land, An (from Folk Songs Of The Four Seasons)
    unis cor,inst (easy) OXFORD 343791-0 pts rent   (V7)
  Call, The (from From Five Mystical Songs)
    unis cor,kbd MORN.ST. 50-9912   (V8)
  Come Let Us Gather Cockles
    see Three Gaelic Songs
  Dawn On The Hills
    see Three Gaelic Songs
  Early In The Spring (from Folk Songs Of The Four Seasons)
    SSA,acap (easy) OXFORD 343793-7   (V9)
  God Bless The Master
    see Two Songs Of Winter
  Heart's Music
    mix cor,acap OXFORD 3428083   (V10)
  Jack The Sailor
    see Two Sea Songs
  John Barleycorn (from Folk Songs Of The Four Seasons)
    unis cor&SA,strings&pno/orch OXFORD   (V11)
  Love Is A Sickness
    SATB,acap (med) PRESSER 392-03022   (V12)

VAUGHAN WILLIAMS, RALPH (cont'd.)
  New Commonwealth, The
    mix cor,strings,opt inst OXFORD   (V13)
  Nothing Is Here For Tears
    unis cor,strings&pno/orch OXFORD   (V14)
  O How Amiable
    mix cor,band OXFORD sc 385485-6 B, oct 350154-6   (V15)
  Sun, Moon, Stars, And Man (from The Sons Of Light)
    unis cor,strings,pno OXFORD   (V16)
  Three Gaelic Songs
    mix cor,acap OXFORD f.s.
    contains: Come Let Us Gather Cockles; Dawn On The Hills; Wake And Rise   (V17)
  To The Ploughboy (from Folk Songs Of The Four Seasons)
    unis cor&SA,inst (med) OXFORD 385794-4 pts rent   (V18)
  Two Sea Songs
    TTBB,opt pno (med easy) PRESSER 392-03003 f.s.
    contains: Jack The Sailor; We Be Three Poor Mariners   (V19)
  Two Songs Of Winter (from Folk Songs Of The Four Seasons)
    unis cor&desc,inst OXFORD f.s., ipr
    contains: God Bless The Master; Wassail Song   (V20)
  Wake And Rise
    see Three Gaelic Songs
  Wassail Song
    see Two Songs Of Winter
  We Be Three Poor Mariners
    see Two Sea Songs
  When Icicles Hang By The Wall
    unis cor,pno OXFORD   (V21)

VEA, KETIL (1932- )
  Ertevise
    4pt mix cor,acap NOTON N-9105   (V22)
  Humoreske
    men cor,acap NOTON N-9038   (V23)
  Tre Korslåtter *CCU
    4pt mix cor,acap NOTON N-9108 f.s.   (V24)

VECCHI, ORAZIO (HORATIO) (1550-1605)
  Bergère Sous Les Saules, La
    mix cor HUG 6056   (V25)
  Four-Voice Canzonettas With Original Texts And Contrafacta By Valentin Haussmann And Others, The *CCU, Renaissance
    (Deford, Ruth I.) 4pt cor A-R ED ISBN 0-89578-278-8   (V26)
  Wenn Der Mai Neu Erwachet
    mix cor SCHUL CLS 190   (V27)

VECY LE MAY see Aubanel, Georges

VED NYINGEN see Nyhus, Rolf

VENDANGE, LA see Doret, Gustave

VENDANGES, LES see Cools, Eugène

VENDANGEURS, LES see Ithier

VENERABILIS BARBA CAPUCINORUM see Mozart, Wolfgang Amadeus

VENEZ VOIR S'ENVOLER see Haenni, G.

VENIKI see Brooms

VENT, LE see Boller, Carlo

VENT D'AUTOMNE, LE see Mermoud, Robert

VENT DU NORD, LE see Parchet, A.

VENTE SUR DEMANDE see Aboulker

VENUSBERG see Wagner, Richard

VERANO PORTENO
  (Escalada) SATB (argentine folksong) KJOS 8774   (V28)

VERCKEN, FRANÇOIS (1928- )
  Atelier
    SATB,acap (diff) PRESSER 512-00665   (V29)
  Danse Des Animaux, La
    SATB,acap (diff) PRESSER   (V30)

VERDI, GIUSEPPE (1813-1901)
  Anvil Chorus From "Il Trovatore"
    2pt treb cor,pno,opt perc BOOSEY-ENG MET0001   (V31)
  Choeur Des Hébreux
    [It/Fr] mix cor HUG 7854   (V32)
    [It/Fr] men cor,opt pno/org/orch HUG 7854   (V33)
  Chorus Of The Hebrew Slaves From "Nabucco"
    (Pliska-Dik) SATB BOOSEY-ENG MET0005   (V34)
  Choruses From 'Il Trovatore', 'Nabucco' & 'Aida' *CCU
    mix cor FABER 51482 0   (V35)

VERE LANGUORES NOSTROS see Lotti, Antonio

VERESS, SANDOR (1907-1992)
  Song Of The Season *CC7U
    mix cor,acap ZERBONI 8330 f.s.   (V36)
  Transsilvanische Kantate,Eine
    mix cor,acap ZERBONI 8331   (V37)

VERETTI, ANTONIO (1900- )
  Prière Pour Demander Une Étoile
    cor,1.1.2.1. 2.1.1.0. timp,perc, cel,harp,strings sc RICORDI-IT 131269   (V38)
    cor,acap sc RICORDI-IT 131224   (V39)

VERGÄSSE CHÖNNE see Märki, Ernst

VERGER AU SOLEIL see Gesseney, L.

VERGER DU SOUVENIR see Gesseney, L.

VERGISSMEINNICHT see Bruckner, Anton

VERLASSENE,DIE see Brun, Fritz

VERLIABT SEIN IS KA HEXEREI *CCU, Austrian
  (Inzko, Josef) HEYN f.s. mix cor ISBN 3 85366 447 4; men cor ISBN 3 85366 491 1; wom cor ISBN 3 85366 514 4   (V40)

VERLORNI HEIMAT see Ruprecht, Ernst

VERMAHLIED AN DIE EIDGENOSSENSCHAFT see Schmid, Walter

VERMAHNLIED see Schmid, Walter

VÉRONIQUES, LES see Bovet, J.

VERS LA LUMIÈRE see La Tombelle, Fernand de

VERS LES SENTIERS PLEINS D'ALLÉGRESSE see Clavié

VERS MON VILLAGE see Bovet, J.

VERSCHIEDENE VOLKSLIEDER 1981 (from Kärntner Chorblätter) CCU
  (Mittergradnegger, Günther) mix cor HEYN f.s.   (V41)

VESPERGESANG see Bortniansky, Dimitri Stepanovich

VESTIGIA see Raminsh, Imant

VEUX-TU DE MON COEUR see Broquet, Louis

VIE EST UN RUISSEAU, LA see Mermoud, Robert

VIEILLARD, LE see Haydn, [Franz] Joseph

VIEILLE CHANSON see Apotheloz, Jean

VIEILLES GENS, LES see Mermoud, Robert

VIELLE, LA see Lesur, Daniel see Mermoud, Robert

VIELLE VILLE, LA see Jaques-Dalcroze, Émile

VIENS, DOUX PRINTEMPS see Haydn, [Franz] Joseph

VIENS, MON ÂME, ET CONTEMPLE see Bach, Johann Sebastian

VIENS, NUIT SEREINE see Lang, H.

VIENT LE JOUR DE LA FIANCÉE see Boller, Carlo

VIER CHORSTÜCKE see Killmayer, Wilhelm

VIER GESÄNGE see Schubert, Franz (Peter)

VIER LIEDER see Mendelssohn-Bartholdy, Felix

VIER LIEDER ZUR JAHRESWENDE see Drischner, Max

VIER STÄMME see Ryser, Otto

VIEUX, LES see Jaques-Dalcroze, Émile

VIEUX BOHÉMIEN see Marcel, J.M.

VIEUX BÛCHERON see Hemmerling, Carlos

VIEUX CHALET, LE see Bovet, J.

VIEUX CHALETS, LES see Broquet, Louis

VIEUX GARÇON, LE see Martin

VIEUX JARDIN, LE see Sutermeister, Heinrich

VIEUX LÉMAN, LE see Bovet, J.

VIEUX MÉNÉTRIER see Villermin

VIEUX MOULIN, LE see Delmas, Marc-Jean-Baptiste

VIEUX PAYS, LE see Broquet, Louis

VIEUX POMMIER, LE see Falquet, Rene

VIEUX PONT DU VILLAGE, LE see Miche, Paul

VIEUX TILLEUL, LE see Mermoud, Robert

VIEUX VIGNERON, LE (from Terre Et L'étoile, La)
   mix cor HUG 8844 (V42)

VIGILIE "OB DIE ZÄRTLICHKEITEN ENDLICH ANGEKOMMEN" see Helmschrott, Robert M.

VIGNE DE PRINTEMPS, LA see Boller, Carlo

VIGNE EN FLEUR, LA see Doret, Gustave

VIGNE EST EN FLEUR, LA see Doret, Gustave

VIGNE FLEURIT, LA see Hemmerling, Carlos

VIGNERON DIT À SA VIGNE..., LE see Miche, Paul

VIGNETTES see Boller, Carlo

VIGNOBLES see Bovet, J.

VIL SCHÖNER KUNST UND GABEN see Vollenweider, Hans

VILLAGE, LE see Miche, Paul see Schubert, Franz (Peter), Dörfchen, Das

VILLAGE AU BORD DE L'EAU, LE see Bovet, J.

VILLAGE DE JAPON see Niikura, Ken

VILLAGE DE MÉMOIRE, LE see Falquet, Rene

VILLAGE SELON MON COEUR, UN see Miche, Paul

VILLAGE VOUS DIT: BONJOUR!, UN see Kaelin, Pierre

VILLANELLA see Killmayer, Wilhelm

VILLANELLE see Donati, Baldassare (Donato)

VILLANELLE PRINTANIÈRE see Miche, Paul

VILLEGAGNON see Prado, José-Antonio (Almeida)

VILLERMIN
   Vieux Ménétrier
      4pt mix cor BILLAUDOT (V43)

VIN RADIEUX see Haenni, G.

VINÉTA see Heim, Ignatz

VIOLETTE, LA see Anonymous see Sala, Andre

VIOLETTE DOUBLE, LA see Lagger, Oscar

VIOLONCELLISTE see Normand, Claude

VIOLONEUX, LE see Henchoz, Emile see Martin

VIRELAIS, LES see Machaut, Guillaume de

VISIONARY see Diemer, Emma Lou

VISIT FROM ST. NICHOLAS, A *Xmas
   (Swingle, Ward) SSAATTBB,acap voc pt, pts UNC JP SBS-15X (V44)
   (Swingle, Ward) SATB,5brass voc pt, pts UNC JP SBS-14X (V45)

VISLUMBRE see Nunes, Emmanuel

VITA DUVA see Cederberg, Anna

VITA PERENNIS *Ger
   TTBB,T solo,2.2.2.2. 4.3.1.0. timp, strings [10'] MULLES (V46)

VITRIER, LE see Mermoud, Robert

VITRY, PHILIPPE DE (1291-1361)
   Complete Works *CCU
      (Schrade) OISEAU RE 909 f.s. (V47)

VIVALDI, ANTONIO (1678-1741)
   Fugue
      (Bach; Swingle) SATB,db,drums (gr. III) UNC JP GB-8X (V48)

VIVE LA ROSE! see Delor

VIVE LE MUSCAT see Daetwyler, Jean

VIVIER, CLAUDE (1948-1983)
   Chants
      7pt wom cor TRANSAT. TR001378 (V49)

VIVONS EN CHANTANT see Jaques-Dalcroze, Émile

VLIJMEN, JAN VAN (1935- )
   Inferno (from Dante Alighieri)
      4pt mix cor,3.3.4.3. 2.2.2.1. 2perc,marimba,cym,harp,gtr,mand, 4vln,3vla,2vcl,db [40'] sc DONEMUS (V50)

VOCI see Macchi, Egisto

VOGEL, ROGER CRAIG (1947- )
   Crab,The (from Cats And Bats)
      men cor THOMAS 1C0999392 (V51)

VOICE, BOOKS AND FIRE I see Ullmann, Jakob

VOICE, BOOKS AND FIRE II(1) see Ullmann, Jakob

VOICE, BOOKS AND FIRE II(2) see Ullmann, Jakob

VOICE WITHIN, THE see Hagen, Daron

VOICES OF EARTH see Henderson, Ruth Watson

VOICES STARS see Tsubonoh, Katsuhiro

VOICI LA SAINT-JEAN see Planel, Jean see Sala, Andre

VOICI LE MOIS DE MAI see Boller, Carlo see Sala, Andre

VOICI LE RHÔNE see Daetwyler, Jean

VOICI LES HEURES BRÈVES see Bach, Johann Sebastian

VOIS SOURIRE LA ROSE see Lotti, Antonio

VOIX DE LA FOULE, LES see Rougnon, Paul

VOIX DU LAC, LA see Jaques-Dalcroze, Émile

VOIX DU SOUVENIR, LA see Delmas, Marc-Jean-Baptiste

VOLE AUTOUR DU MONDE see Schubert, Franz (Peter), Heidenröslein

VOLENT NOS COEURS see Wissmer, Pierre

VOLERY, FRANCIS
   Bohémien
      mix cor,acap HUGUENIN CH 2104 (V52)

VOLK
   I Am A Poet
      SATB oct SOUTHERN SC404 (V53)
   Will Ye No Come Back Again
      SSA oct SOUTHERN SC411 (V54)

VOLKSLIEDER AUS ALLER WELT *CCU,folk song
   (Mittergradnegger, Günther) men cor HEYN NR. 38 f.s. (V55)

VOLKSLIEDER AUS ALLER WELT *CCU
   (Mittergradnegger, Günther) men cor HEYN NR. 49 f.s. (V56)

VOLKSLIEDER AUS ALLER WELT *CCU,folk song
   (Anderluh, Anton) mix cor HEYN NR. 106 f.s. (V57)

VOLKSLIEDER AUS ALLER WELT (HEFT 1) *CCU,folk song
   (Anderluh, Anton-Mittergradnegger) mix cor HEYN NR. 107 f.s. (V58)

VOLKSWEISE see Ries, Hubert

VOLLE, BJARNE (1943- )
   Alles Øyne
      SA,pno NOTON N-8903-F (V59)
   Du Ska Itte Trø I Graset
      SA,pno NOTON N-8905-F (V60)
      men cor,acap NOTON N-8905-C (V61)
      3pt mix cor,acap NOTON N-8905-D (V62)
      4pt mix cor,acap NOTON N-8905-B (V63)
   En Kjaerlighedsvise
      4pt mix cor,acap NOTON N-8907-B (V64)
      men cor,acap NOTON N-8907-C (V65)
   En Liten Vise
      men cor,acap NOTON N-8904-C (V66)
      SA,pno NOTON N-8904-F (V67)
   En Liter Vise
      4pt mix cor,acap NOTON N-8904-B (V68)
   Gå Inte Så Hårt I Gräset
      (Janunger) 4pt mix cor,acap NOTON N-8905-S (V69)
   Gjenteleik
      see Tre Skjemteviser
   Hver Tar Sin
      see Tre Skjemteviser
   Myggen
      see Tre Skjemteviser
   Tre Skjemteviser
      4pt mix cor,acap NOTON N-9245 f.s. contains: Gjenteleik; Hver Tar Sin; Myggen (V70)
   Udsigter Fra Ulrikken
      SSA,pno NOTON N-9141-F (V71)

VOLLE, MARTIN
   Songen Er Eit Band Som Bind
      (Volle, Sverre) SSA,acap NOTON N-9025-F (V72)
      (Volle, Sverre) men cor,acap NOTON N-9025-H (V73)
      (Volle, Sverre) 4pt mix cor,acap NOTON N-9025-G (V74)

VOLLE, SVERRE (1938- )
   Den Naesvise Flue
      4pt mix cor,acap NOTON N-9266 (V75)
   Jeg Taenk Te, Jeg Blev
      men cor,acap,Bar solo NOTON N-9137 (V76)

VOLLENWEIDER, HANS (1918- )
   Abendlied
      (Claudius, M.) wom cor,acap MULLES (V77)
      (Keller, G.) wom cor,acap MULLES (V78)
   Alte Schwyzer,Die
      men cor,acap MULLES (V79)
   Bärner Bär,Der
      men cor,acap MULLES (V80)
   Drei Sprüche
      men cor,acap MULLES (V81)
   Föhnnacht Im Meije
      wom cor,acap MULLES (V82)
   Im Schatte
      wom cor,acap MULLES (V83)
   Jägerlied
      men cor,acap MULLES (V84)
   Kapelle,Die
      men cor,acap MULLES (V85)
   Marienlied
      wom cor,acap MULLES (V86)
   Nunni, Nunni, Chindli
      wom cor,acap MULLES (V87)
   Rat
      men cor,acap MULLES (V88)
   Spruch
      wom cor,acap MULLES (V89)
   Stets In Truure Muess I Läbe
      men cor,acap MULLES (V90)
   Vil Schöner Kunst Und Gaben
      men cor,acap MULLES (V91)

VOLVEDORA,LA see Falu

VOM BALKONE see Kreis, Otto

VOM EWIGE BRUNNE see Märki, Ernst

VOM FISCHER UN SIN FRU see Katzer, Georg

VOM GOLDENEN HORN see Rheinberger, Josef

VOM HIMMEL ABE CHUNT E STÄRN see Brun, Fritz see Burkard, Willi

VON ALLEN DEN MÄDCHEN see Silcher, Friedrich

VON DER WATERKANT BIS ZUM ALPENLAND see Mahr, Curt

VON LIEBE UND TREUE see Jugend Singt II

VOORN, JOOP (1932- )
   Goud In Haar Eigen Afglans Staat De Maan
     SATB EXC.MH 19.003.001 (V92)

VOTIVLIEDER FÜR FRAUENCHOR see Einem, Gottfried von

VOTRE PAYS EST TOUJOURS LÀ see Henchoz, Emile

VOUS FUYEZ BIEN LOIN D'ICI see Schumann, Robert (Alexander)

VOUS ME PLAISEZ! see Haenni, G.

VOYAGERS see Cooper, Paul

VRAI MARIN, LE see Alexandrov, Alexander Vasilievich

VRENELI AB EM GUGGISBERG (DUR), 'S see Munzinger, Carl

VRENELI DU GUGGISBERG see Doret, Gustave

VRENELI VOM THUNERSEE, 'S see Müller, Joseph Ivar

VUATAZ, ROGER (1898- )
   A La Surface Des Eaux
     men cor HUG 8503 (V93)

   Automne
     men cor HUG 8270 (V94)

   Berceuse (from Chopin Polonaise)
     eq voices HUG 7464 (V95)

   Cantique
     mix cor HUG 8272 (V96)

   C'est Un Vrai Bateau
     eq voices HUG 7459 (V97)

   Chanson À Boire
     men cor HUG 8363 (V98)

   Chanson De Nos Deux Coeurs, La
     eq voices HUG 8128 (V99)

   Chanson Des Quatre Temps
     mix cor HUG 8127 (V100)

   Coucou, Casse-Cou
     4 eq voices HUG 8358 (V101)

   De Trois Roses
     men cor HUG 8495 (V102)

   Détresse
     men cor HUG 8220 (V103)

   Epitaphe Pour Un Chat
     mix cor HUG 8271 (V104)

   Epithalame
     mix cor HUG 8126 (V105)

   Hymne À La Bannière
     "Lied Vom Kreuz, Das" men cor HUG 7021 (V106)

   Idiote Du Village, L'
     men cor HUG 8219 (V107)

   Incantation
     men cor HUG 7904 (V108)

   Jour S'en Va..., Un
     men cor HUG 8125 (V109)

   Juste Milieu, Le
     men cor HUG 8222 (V110)

   Lied Vom Kreuz, Das
     see Hymne À La Bannière

   Nocturne
     mix cor HUG 8359 (V111)

   O Mon Pays
     men cor HUG 8360 (V112)

VUATAZ, ROGER (cont'd.)
   O Mons Pays
     mix cor HUG 8361 (V113)

   Quand Passent Les Oiseaux
     mix cor HUG 8364 (V114)

   Qui L'eût Cru?
     men cor HUG 8124 (V115)

   Rengaine
     men cor HUG 8122 (V116)

   Rose Et Le Rossignol, La
     eq voices HUG 8129 (V117)

   Sagesse
     men cor HUG 8269 (V118)

   Sorcière, La
     men cor HUG 7678 (V119)

   Temps Des Amours, Le
     men cor HUG 8123 (V120)

# W

WAALER, FREDRIKKE (1865-1952)
   Hamarsangen
     SSA,pno NOTON N-9329-F (W1)
     4pt mix cor,acap NOTON N-9329-B (W2)

   Sangermarsj
     (Bjorå, Olav) 4pt mix cor,acap NOTON N-9367 (W3)

WAAROM see Belcum, Henk Van

WACH AUF, MEIN'S HERZENS SCHÖNE see Oetiker, August

WACHT AUF, IHR LIEBEN VÖGELEIN see Gumpeltzhaimer, Adam

WADE IN THE WATER
   (Hayes) SATB ALFRED 5810 (W4)

WAGNER, DOUGLAS EDWARD (1952- )
   Girl's Garden, A
     SATB HERITAGE 15-1177H (W5)

   Road Not Taken, The (from Robert Frost)
     SATB,pno HERITAGE 15-1103 (W6)

   Shalom, My Friends
     3pt mix cor,pno HERITAGE 15--1029 (W7)
     2pt cor HERITAGE H5882 (W8)

   Single Flower Grows, A (composed with Wagner, Jennifer Anne)
     SATB,pno HERITAGE 15-1036 (W9)

WAGNER, RICHARD (1813-1883)
   Agape Sacra, L' (from Parsifal)
     cor,orch RICORDI-IT (W10)

   Brautchor Aus "Lohengrin"
     mix cor,winds RUNDEL sc ARTIKEL-NR.0127, cor pts ARTIKEL-NR.0127C (W11)

   Chant Des Matelots
     men cor HUG 3624 (W12)

   Choeur Des Pèlerins (from Tannhäuser)
     men cor,opt pno/org/orch HUG 3259 (W13)

   Marcia E Coro (from Tannhäuser)
     cor,orch RICORDI-IT (W14)

   Marcia Nuziale (from Lohengrin)
     cor,orch RICORDI-IT (W15)

   Venusberg (from Tannhäuser)
     wom cor,orch RICORDI-IT (W16)

WAHT DA WIND ÜBAN SEE
   (Kraxner, Walter) HEYN f.s.
     contains: Lieder Für Gemischten Chor (mix cor); Lieder Für Männerchor (men cor) (W17)

WAHT DA WIND ÜBAN SEE *CCU,Austrian
   (Ortner, Sepp-Kraxner) men cor HEYN NR. 63 f.s. (W18)

WAHT DA WIND ÜBAN SEE *CCU
   (Ortner, Sepp-Kraxner, Walter) mix cor HEYN NR. 140 f.s. (W19)

WAILLIE, WAILLIE
   (Cleveland, Michael) SSA WARNER OCT02599 (W20)

WAKE AND RISE see Vaughan Williams, Ralph

WAKE TO THE HUNTING see Smart, Henry Thomas

WAKIN' see Stoloff, Bob

WALDEINSAMKEIT see Oser, Hans

WALDESSEHNEN see Märki, Ernst

WALDKÖNIG see Attenhofer, Karl

WALDNER, GEORG
   Wia Schean Is Mei Hamat *CC16U
     men cor HEYN ISBN 3 85366 264 1 f.s. (W21)

WALESNACHT see Brahms, Johannes

WALK ON see Strommen, Carl

WALKER
   Chinook
     SSA WARCH 35228 (W22)

   Loping Along
     SSA WARCH 35230 (W23)

WALKER (cont'd.)
  Steal Away
    SATB WARCH 26781 (W24)

WALKER, GEORGE THEOPHILUS (1922- )
  Stars
    SATB MMB S940003 (W25)

WALKIN' see Broadley, Sharon

WALL HAS DISAPPEARED, THE see Niimi, Tokuhide

WALLONIE see Delmas, Marc-Jean-Baptiste

WALTER, SAMUEL (1916- )
  Joseph Lieber, Joseph Mein
    SSATB [1'35"] JOED WA2 (W26)

WALTERS, EDMUND
  Bonny Bobby Shafto
    SSA,pno ROBERTON 75325 (W27)

  Johnny Todd
    SA,pno ROBERTON 75330 (W28)

WANDERBURSCHEN'S ABSCHIED see Sturm, Wilhelm

WANDERER,THE see Joplin

WANDERGLÜCK see Schmid, Walter

WANDERLIED
  SA&3pt men cor MULLES (W29)
  jr cor MULLES (W30)
  see Abt, Franz see Güdel, W. see Kägi, Walter see Märki, Ernst see Schmid, Walter see Schumann, Robert (Alexander)

WANDERLUST see Schmid, Walter see Zahler, J.R.

WANDERN see Jaeggi, Oswald see Schmid, Walter

WANDERN IST DES MÜLLERS LUST, DAS see Kupp, Albert

WANDERSPRUCH see Zentner, Johannes

WÄNN DÄS HERZLE SCHNELL PUMPART (from Chorblätter)
  (Streiner, Hans) mix cor HEYN (W31)
  (Streiner, Hans) men cor HEYN (W32)

WAPPENSPRUCH see Kreis, Otto

WÄR GLÖGGELET see Aeschbacher, C.

WAR LAMENT see Blumenfeld, Harold

WAR POEMS see Dijker, Mathieu

WARD, WILLIAM REED (1918- )
  Nothing Else To Do (from Four Old American Songs Of Merriment)
    SATB,pno LAWSON 52754 (W33)

WARM-UPS FOR THE JAZZ-SHOW CHOIR see Shaw, Kirby

WARMER, RANDY
  I'm In A Hurry (And I Don't Know Why) (composed with Murrah, Roger)
    (Baker, Andy) SATB WARNER 4282IC1X (W34)
    (Baker, Andy) SAB WARNER 4282IC3X (W35)

WARUM SEUFZEST DU SO SCHWER? see Doret, Gustave

WAS BRUCHT E RECHTE SCHWYZERMA? see Meister, Casimir

WAS HAB ICH DENN MEINEM FEINSLIEBCHEN GETAN see Silcher, Friedrich

WAS HAN I GSEH IM GARTE see Steiger, F.

WAS HÜLFE ES DIR? see Häsler, Hans

WAS LIEBE IST see Hägler, Paul

WAS SIND DIE JAHRE? see Kreis, Otto

WASHBURN, ROBERT BROOKS (1928- )
  Ode To Freedom
    mix cor,band/orch OXFORD sc 385417-1 B, oct 385420-1 (W36)

WASSAIL SONG see Vaughan Williams, Ralph

WASSERMAN, DER see Schumann, Robert (Alexander)

WASSERSPEIER see Kathedrale

WASURENAGUSA MO KOISHITERU see Nishida, Yumiko

WATER IS WIDE, THE
  (Freed) SSA,kbd (very easy) PRESSER 392-41694 (W37)
  see Matsuoka, Yumiko see Serain, Craig

WATER OF THE TYNE, THE *folk song,Eng
  (Coomes, Douglas) SA,pno LINDSAY (W38)

WATERFALL, THE see Williams

WAY WE WERE,THE
  (Swain, Yern) SSATBB,opt high female solo,acap (gr. III) UNC JP (W39)

WAYFARING STRANGER, THE *folk song,Nor Am
  (Caracciolo, Stephen) SATB DEAN 15-1078 (W40)

WE ARE ONE see Donnelly

WE ARE THE MUSIC see Strommen, Carl

WE BE THREE POOR MARINERS see Vaughan Williams, Ralph

WE CAME TO SING IN JERUSALEM see Burger, David Mark

WE SING FELIZ NAVIDAD see Strommen, Carl

WE WILL SING! see Price

WE WISH YOU A MERRY CHRISTMAS
  (Ames, Morgan) SATB,acap UNC JP (W41)
  see Kirkland, Terry see Somers

WE WISH YOU A VERY HAPPY HOLIDAY see Gould, Raymond

WEARMOUTH, GRAHAM
  Magnetic North
    SATB THOMP.G VEI1151 (W42)

WEATHERS see Bissell

WEBER, CARL MARIA VON (1786-1826)
  Choeur Des Chasseurs (from Freischütz, Der)
    men cor HUG 6289 (W43)
    4pt men cor BILLAUDOT (W44)
    2 eq voices BILLAUDOT (W45)

  Frühlingsahnung
    wom cor,acap MULLES (W46)

  Gebet (from Freischütz, Der)
    mix cor BUTZ 596 (W47)

  Printemps
    men cor HUG 6286 (W48)

WECKRUF see Märki, Ernst

WEDDING DAY see Telfer

WEDDING GIFT see Mechem, Kirke Lewis

WEE DRAPPIE O'T, A *folk song,Scot
  (Shur, Laura) SATB,acap LAWSON 52705 (W49)

WEEDS see Sugino, Yasuhiko

WEEP, O WILLOW see Lekberg

WEEP YOU NO MORE SAD FOUNTAINS see Holman, Derek

WEEPING WILLOW see Joplin

WEGGEFÄHRTEN (HEFT 4) see Klein, Richard Rudolf

WEGGEFÄHRTEN (HEFT 5) see Klein, Richard Rudolf

WEGGEFÄRTEN (HEFT 1) see Klein, Richard Rudolf

WEGGEFÄRTEN (HEFT 3) see Klein, Richard Rudolf

WEHRLI, WERNER (1892-1944)
  Ha An Em Ort Es Blüemli Gseh
    wom cor,acap MULLES (W50)

WEIHNACHTSBOTSCHAFT see Schmid, Walter

WEIN UND ROSEN see Güdel, W.

WEIN UND SANG see Schmid, Walter

WEINACHTSLIED see Hofer-Schneeberger, Emma

WEINE NICHT, MÜTTERLEIN see Graf, Albert

WEISMANN, JULIUS (1879-1950)
  Dem König Folg Ich
  see Drei Männerchöre Op.31

WEISMANN, JULIUS (cont'd.)
  Drei Männerchöre Op.31
    GRAV f.s.
    contains: Dem König Folg Ich; Ich Schell Mein Horn; Jakobitenlied (W51)

  Ich Schell Mein Horn
  see Drei Männerchöre Op.31

  Jakobitenlied
  see Drei Männerchöre Op.31

WEISMANN, WILHELM (1900-1980)
  Ausgewählte Chorwerke
    mix cor,acap PETERS 9644 (W52)

WEISSER FLIEDER see Kreis, Otto

WEIT, WEIT see Stocker, Karl

WEITE FLUR see Kammerer, Imanuel Johannes

WELCKER, MAX (1878-1954)
  Zur (Weltlichen) Hochzeitsfeier, Op. 148 No. 4
    SATB BOHM (W53)

WELCOME, SWEET PLEASURE see Laster, James

WELCOME SWEET SPRING see Riley

WELCOME TO ALL PLEASURES see Purcell, Henry

WE'LL FIND A WAY see Gray, Cynthia

WEM GEB ICH WOHL DIE ROSE? see Doret, Gustave

WENN ALLE BRÜNNLEIN FLIESSEN see Müller-Zürich, Paul see Oetiker, August

WENN DER MAI NEU ERWACHET see Vecchi, Orazio (Horatio)

WENN DIE BETTELLEUTE TANZEN see Butz, Josef

WENN DIE REB' IM SAFTE SCHWILLT see Jensen, Adolf

WENN D'SCHNEEBALLE BLÜEIT see Hofer-Schneeberger, Emma

WENN D'SCHNEEBALLE BLÜEJT see Hofer-Schneeberger, Emma

WENN DU MICH MIT DEM BOOT see Fässler, Guido

WENN FRÜHLINGSTAGE NEU BELEBEN see Silcher, Friedrich

WENN ICH EIN VÖGLEIN WÄR see Silcher, Friedrich

WENN IN STILLER STUNDE see Kupp, Albert

WENN WIR IN HÖCHSTEN NÖTEN SEIN see Lidström, John

WERDIN, EBERHARD (1911- )
  Rhythmische Sprechchöre
    2-3pt cor,opt perc FIDULA 329 (W54)

WE'RE FREE see Rogers

WE'RE IN THIS LOVE TOGETHER see Jarreau,Al

WE'RE THE FUTURE OF TOMORROW see Simms, Patsy Ford

WEST WIND, THE see Christiansen, Paul

WESTERGAARD, PETER (1931- )
  Plot Against The Giant,The (Canatata I)
    wom cor,inst JERONA J3142 (W55)

WESTON, MARK
  Ernest, The Unbelieving Reindeer
    unis cor,opt solo HERITAGE 15-1105 (W56)

  Like A Shepherd
    2pt mix cor,inst WARNER BSC00277 (W57)

  Santa, What You Gonna Get From Me?
    unis cor HERITAGE 15-1010 (W58)

WETTERWEIBCHEN see Kreis, Otto

WEYNANDT
  Soldat Qui Reviens De La Guerre...
    men cor HUG 6619 (W59)

WHALE (AQUA BLUES) see Jennings, Carolyn

WHALES SWIMMING FREE see Coombes, Douglas

WHAT CAN I DO?
    (Johnson) 2pt cor SHAWNEE EA-178
        (W60)

WHAT DO THE STARS DO? see Rosetti

WHAT HATH NIGHT TO DO WITH SLEEP see Holman

WHAT IS BEAUTY see Niles, John Jacob

WHAT SHALL BE DONE FOR SORROW see Sapieyevski, Jerzy

WHAT STRANGERS ARE THESE? see Purvis

WHAT THE WORLD NEEDS NOW IS LOVE see David

WHAT THEN, MY LOVE? see Telfer, Nancy

WHATEVER YOU IMAGINE
    (Schmutte, Pete) SATB WARNER CH9567
        (W61)
    (Schmutte, Pete) SAB WARNER CH9568
        (W62)
    (Schmutte, Pete) 2pt cor WARNER CH9569
        (W63)

WHEELS see Broughton

WHEN AGE AND YOUTH UNITE see Ridout

WHEN CHILDREN SING see Goetze, M.

WHEN GOOD MEN SING TOGETHER see Rodby, Walter

WHEN I AM DEAD, MY DEAREST see Shur, Laura

WHEN I SET OUT FOR LYONESSE see Bissell

WHEN I WAKE IN THE MORNING see Calvert

WHEN ICICLES HANG BY THE WALL see Vaughan Williams, Ralph

WHEN I'M 64 see Lennon, John

WHEN IN DREAMLAND see Spevacek, Linda

WHEN LILACS BLOOM'D see Atteberry, Ron

WHEN ON MY SICK BED I LANGUISH see Purcell, Henry

WHEN THE BUDS ARE BLOSSOMING see Sullivan, [Sir] Arthur Seymour

WHEN THE DAWN APPEARS see Togni, Peter

WHEN THE GOOD TIMES COME AGAIN
    (Chinn, Teena) SATB WARNER 7056WC1X ipa
        (W64)
    (Chinn, Teena) 3pt mix cor WARNER 7056WC3X ipa
        (W65)
    (Chinn, Teena) 2pt cor WARNER 7056WC5X ipa
        (W66)

WHEN THE SAINTS GO MARCHING IN
    SAB WARCH 30166        (W67)
    (Chinn, Teena) SATB WARNER CH95100 ipa
        (W68)
    (Chinn, Teena) 2pt cor WARNER CH95101 ipa
        (W69)

WHEN THE SHOE IS ON THE OTHER FOOT FOR A CHANGE see Henderson, Ruth Watson

WHEN THE STARS BEGIN TO FALL see Linberg, Per

WHEN WILL I BE LOVED see Everly, Phil

WHEN YOUR SMILING (THE WHOLE WORLD SMILES WITH YOU) see Fisher, Mark

WHEN YUBA PLAYS THE RUMBA ON THE TUBA see Hupfeld, Herman

WHERE DO YOU GO SO HASTY? see Gastoldi, Giovanni Giacomo

WHERE EARTH MEETS THE SKY see Gray, Cynthia

WHERE GO THE BOATS see Govedas

WHERE HAVE ALL THE FORESTS GONE? see Grier, Gene

WHERE IS LOVE see Bart

WHERE'ER YOU WALK see Handel, George Frideric

WHEREVER MUSIC LIVES see Estes, Jerry

WHEREVER YOU GO see Estes, Jerry

WHICHER, JAMES
    Man From Okerboker
        unis cor WARCH 35246        (W70)

WHICHER, JAMES (cont'd.)
    Remarkable Tale Of Quentin B. Quail
        unis cor WARCH 34381        (W71)

WHISPERS OF HEAVENLY DEATH see Clausen, Rene

WHITACRE, ERIC
    Go, Lovely Rose
        SATB,acap SANTA SBMP 43     (W72)

    I Hide Myself
        SATB,acap SANTA SBMP 63     (W73)

    With A Lily In Her Hand
        SATB,acap SANTA SBMP 64     (W74)

WHITE
    Daylight And Moonlight
        SATB LAWSON 4-52770         (W75)

WHITE BLOSSOM, A see Blumenfeld, Harold

WHITE BUTTERFLIES see Bray

WHITE KNIGHT'S SONG, THE see Fine

WHITE LAND see Rippentrop, Denice

WHITE MOON, THE see Porterfield, Sherrie

WHITE NIGHT see Crockett, Donald

WHITE SHELL WOMAN, COMPOSITION FOR CHORUS NO. 13 see Mamiya, Michio

WHITE SPORT COAT (AND A PINK CARNATION), A see Robbins, Marty

WHITEHEAD
    Echo Carol
        SATB WARCH 34471            (W76)

WHITER SHADE OF PALE, A see Reid

WHITTAKER, WILLIAM GILLIES (1876-1944)
    Aye She Kaimed Her Yellow Hair
        SSAATTBB BANKS ECS 137      (W77)

WHO CAN I TURN TO?
    SATB WARCH 34815                (W78)
    see Bricusse, Leslie

WHO HAS SEEN THE WIND? see Ebel-Sabo, V. see Porterfield, Sherrie

WHO IS SYLVIA? see Schubert, Franz

WHO KNOWS?
    (New York Voices) SSATB,male solo, perc (gr. IV/gr. V) UNC JP   (W79)

WHO WILL BUY?
    SATB WARCH 34807                (W80)

WHUP! JAMBOREE
    (Shaw-Parker) TTBB LAWSON 4-51065
        (W81)

WHY SO PALE? see Dicks, Ernest A.

WI SHI KOOD see Lyons,Bill

WIA SCHEAN IS MEI HAMAT see Waldner, Georg

WIDE O'ER THE BRIM see Clarke (-Whitfield), [Dr.] John

WIDMANN, ERASMUS (1572-1634)
    Floh,Der
        4pt mix cor FIDULA 6146     (W82)

    Musikalische Kurzweil,Die
        4pt mix cor FIDULA 6145     (W83)

WIEGELE, WAGELE see Lampart, Reinhold

WIEGENLIED see Brahms, Johannes

WIEH, MICHAEL
    Jag Är En Människa I Världen
        (Jehrlander) mix cor,pno SVERIG SK 814        (W84)

WIENER-WALZER see Strauss, J.

WIFE'S SONG,A see Barnby, [Sir] Joseph

WILAN
    Fain Would I Change That Note
        SATB WARCH 34488            (W85)

WILDER, ALEC (1907-1980)
    Blackberry Winter
        (Cross, Dave) SATB,perc (gr. III) UNC JP    (W86)

WILKIN
    One Day At A Time (composed with Kristofferson)
        SATB NOVELLO 090730         (W87)

WILL YE NO COME BACK AGAIN see Volk

WILL YOU BE THERE see Jackson, Michael

WILL YOU STAND BY ME see Cassils

WILLAERT, ADRIAN (ca. 1490-1562)
    A La Fontaine Du Pres
        SSAATB [3'15"] JOED W2      (W88)

WILLAN, HEALEY (1880-1968)
    Fair In Face
        SATB THOMP.G VG594          (W89)

    O Be Joyful
        SATB THOMP.G VG591          (W90)

WILLE see Kreis, Otto

WILLIAMS
    Let There Be Music (composed with Elliot)
        unis cor WARCH 34375        (W91)

    Old Fashioneed Love Song, An
        SATB NOVELLO 090330         (W92)

    Trouble Is A-Comin' (composed with Martin)
        SAB SHAWNEE D-465           (W93)

    Waterfall, The (composed with Martin)
        SATB SHAWNEE A-2012         (W94)

WILLIAMS, ARNOLD
    O Mistress Mine
        SATB BANKS 1127             (W95)

    Topsy-Turvey Land
        2pt cor BANKS 1029          (W96)

WILLIAMSON, MALCOLM (1931-   )
    Love The Sentinell
        SATB WEINBERGER 26998       (W97)

    Musicians Of Bremen, The
        men cor WEINBERGER 26855    (W98)

    Ode To Music
        sc WEINBERGER 26851         (W99)

    Six English Lyrics *CCU
        SATB WEINBERGER 26918       (W100)

    Sonnet
        SATB WEINBERGER 26904       (W101)

    Sweet And Low
        SSA WEINBERGER 26951        (W102)

    Symphony For Voices
        SATB WEINBERGER 26905       (W103)

    Three Choric Hymns *CCU
        SATB WEINBERGER 26953       (W104)

    Young Girl, A
        SATB WEINBERGER 26906       (W105)

WILLKOMMEN, DIE GEHEN EIN UND AUS see Steiner, Luis

WILSON, THOMAS (1927-   )
    Night Songs
        SATB,acap [12'] QUEEN       (W106)

    There Is No Rose
        SATB,acap [5'] QUEEN        (W107)

    Ubi Caritas Et Amor
        TTBarBarB [18'] QUEEN       (W108)

WIND, THE see Schram, Ruth Elaine

WIND HORSE see Takemitsu, Toru

WIND IN LIGHT BLUE see Niimi, Tokuhide

WINDS THROUGH THE OLIVE TREES see Lau

WINFREY, ROBERT
    Let's Build A City
        (Norcott) SATB,pno SCHIRM.G 5048201
            (W109)

WINGED JOY, THE see Mechem, Kirke Lewis

WINGS AS EAGLES see Perder, Kjell

WINK AND A SMILE, A see Shaiman, Marc

WINN, JULIE
    Lullay My Baby
        SATB THOMP.G VA4000         (W110)

WINTER see Bhatia, Vanraj A., Hemant see Stocker, Karl

WINTER, PETER VON (1754-1825)
    Trinklied
        men cor,acap MULLES         (W111)

WINTER AUF DEM LANDE see Dallinger, Gerhard

WINTER CAROL see Porterfield, Sherrie

WINTER CHANGES see Brunner

WINTER LIGHT see Revil, H.

WINTER SONG see Shibata, Minao

WINTER STORE see Henderson, Ruth Watson

WINTER WIND see Ebel-Sabo, V.

WINTER WONDERLAND
   (Porterfield, Sherri) SATB WARNER
    SV9541 (W112)
   (Porterfield, Sherri) 3pt mix cor
    WARNER SV9542 (W113)
   see Winter's Wonderland

WINTERNACHT see Hägler, Paul see Zentner, Johannes

WINTER'S WONDERLAND
   (Schmutte, Pete) WARNER ipa SATB
    C0347C1X; SAB C0347C3X; 2pt cor
    C0347C5X
    contains: It's The Most Wonderful
    Time Of The Year; Let It Snow!;
    Winter Wonderland (W114)

WINTERSONG see Snyder, Audrey

WINZERCHOR see Mendelssohn-Bartholdy, Felix

WIR see Helmschrott, Robert M.

WIR HABEN DREI KATZEN see Rathgeber, Valentin

WIR TANZEN, WIE ES UNS GEFÄLLT see Strauss-König, Richard

WISDOM OF WIND, THE see Rippentrop, Denice

WISE FROGS AND ELETELEPHONY
   unis cor WARCH 34387 (W115)

WISH FOR AN EVERLASTING EARTH, A see Ota, Sakurako

WISHART, PETER (1921-1984)
   New Year Carol
    wom cor BANKS ECS0210 (W116)

WISHING YOU A MERRY CHRISTMAS
   (Schmutte, Pete) WARNER ipa SATB
    C0350C1X; SAB C0350C3X; 2pt cor
     (W117)

WISHING YOU WERE SOMEHOW HERE AGAIN see Lloyd Webber, Andrew

WISSMER, PIERRE (1915- )
   Folle Abeille
    men cor HUG 8213 (W118)

   Saisons
    mix cor HUG 8318 (W119)
    men cor HUG 8317 (W120)

   Volent Nos Coeurs
    men cor HUG 8214 (W121)

WITCHES CHARM see Holman

WITH A LAUGH AS WE GO ROUND see Bennett, [Sir] William Sterndale

WITH A LILY IN HER HAND see Whitacre, Eric

WO SIND DIE QUELLEN? see Kreis, Otto

WOHIN SOLL ICH MICH WENDEN? see Schubert, Franz (Peter)

WOHL IN DEN HOLDEN MAIENSCHEIN see Saladin, O.

WOHLAUF *CC14U,folk song,Ger
   (Lenders, Hans-Günter) 3pt jr cor
    FIDULA 6064 f.s. (W122)

WOHLAUF, DIE LUFT GEHT FRISCH UND REIN see Becker, Valentin E.

WOHLAUF, IHR LIEBEN GÄSTE see Sartorius, Thomas

WOLF, HUGO (1860-1903)
   Dem Vaterland (from Kritische
    Gesamtausgabe, W XI)
    4pt men cor,2+pic.2.2.2. 4.3.3.1.
    timp,perc,strings MUSIKWISS.
     (W123)

   Elfenlied (from Kritische
    Gesamtausgabe, W XI)
    SSAA,S solo,2+pic.2.2.2. 2.0.0.0.
    harp,strings MUSIKWISS. (W124)

   Fest Auf Solhaug, Das (from Kritische
    Gesamtausgabe, W XIV)
    SATB,SB soli,2.2+English horn.2.2.
    4.2.3.1. timp,perc,strings
    MUSIKWISS. (W125)

WOLF, HUGO (cont'd.)

   Feuerreiter, Der (from Kritische
    Gesamtausgabe, W XI)
    SATB,2+pic.2.2.3. 4.3.3.1. timp,
    tam-tam,strings MUSIKWISS. (W126)

   Frühlingschor Aus "Manuel Venegas"
    (from Kritische Gesamtausgabe, W
    XI)
    SATB,3.2+English horn.2.3. 4.3.3.1.
    timp,perc,harp,strings MUSIKWISS.
     (W127)

   Morgenhymnus (from Kritische
    Gesamtausgabe, W XI)
    SATB,2.2+English horn.2.3. 4.3.3.1.
    timp,perc,harp,strings MUSIKWISS.
     (W128)

WOLFE, PHYLLIS ALETA
   Sixty Million Snowflakes
    unis cor HERITAGE 15-1004 (W129)

WONDERFUL DAY LIKE TODAY, A see Bricusse

WONNE DER WEHMUT see Franz

WRIGHT, MAURICE (1949- )
   Fat Man,The (1976)
    mix cor,bsn&trom&vcl (parts
    available by special order) sc
    JERONA JB23690 (W130)

   Of Liberty (1976)
    men cor JERONA JB23712 (W131)
    mix cor JERONA JB23710 (W132)
    wom cor JERONA JB23711 (W133)

WULLUR, SINTA
   Indoratorium I (from Drieduyn-
    Soeroto)
    4pt mix cor,1.1.1.1. 1.1.1.0.
    2perc,2vln,vla,vcl,db [12'] sc
    DONEMUS (W134)

WUNDERLICHE HAST DES LEBENS see Schmid, Walter

WUNDERSAMES WOLKENSPIEL see Hägler, Paul

WURMSER
   Concert Printanier
    4pt men cor BILLAUDOT (W135)

WYSHEITE-FROUEHÄRZLI-TRÖSCHTERLI
   MULLES NR.2, MKKB (W136)

WYTHORNE, T.
   Songes For Three Voyces *CC14U
    (McQuillan, Robert) 3pt cor ANTICO
    AE31 f.s. (W137)

# X

XENAKIS, YANNIS (IANNIS) (1922- )
   Bacchantes D'euripide, Les
    cor,instrumental ensemble SALABERT
    EAS 19143 (X1)

   Knephas
    mix cor,acap SALABERT EAS 18909
     (X2)

   Pour la Paix
    cor,acap SALABERT EAS 17729 (X3)

   Pu Wijnuej We Fyp
    jr cor,acap SALABERT EAS 19074 (X4)

   Sea Nymphs
    mix cor,acap SALABERT EAS 19220
     (X5)

## Y

Y AVAIT DIX FILLES DANS UN PRÉ see Lagger, Oscar

Y ENTONCES COMPRENDIÓ see Nono, Luigi

YA FARAOULE see Hatfield, S.

YA Z'UN PETIT BOIS see Dutilleux, Henri

YAK AND THE TRAIN DOGS see Henderson

YAMAGISHI, MAO (1933- )
  For Female Chorus And Piano
    wom cor,pno HUG (Y1)

YAMAMOTO, HIROYUKI (1967- )
  Metamorphosis I
    wom cor,pno HUG (Y2)

YAMAMOTO, JUNNOSUKE (1958- )
  Ki Rei
    mix cor,pno HUG (Y3)

YAMAMOTO, NAOZUMI (1933- )
  Tokimeki Yokohama
    mix cor,orch HUG (Y4)

YAMATO TAKERU see Saegusa, Shigeaki

YANAGIDA, TAKAYOSHI (1948- )
  Pony Of Star, A
    mix cor HUG (Y5)

YANAI, KAZUMI (1947- )
  Passion, The
    men cor,pno HUG (Y6)

YANCEY, THOMAS LELAND (1932- )
  En Halvvägs Vals
    4pt mix cor,fl,kbd NOTON S-8909-8 (Y7)
  Sommarminnen
    4pt mix cor,kbd NOTON (Y8)

YANOMAMO
    sc WEINBERGER 12248 (Y9)

YARROW, PETER (1938- )
  Puff (The Magic Dragon) (composed with Lipton, Leonard)
    (Leavitt, John) SATB WARNER WBCH9416 (Y10)
    (Leavitt, John) SSA WARNER WBCH9417 (Y11)

YASUGI, TADATOSHI (1951- )
  Honokani Hitotsu
    men cor HUG (Y12)

YATRA TA
  (Treece, Roger) SATB,soli,perc (gr. V) UNC JP (Y13)

YE BANKS AND BRAES see Calvert, Stuart

YE BANKS AND BRAES O'BONNIE DOON see Sköld, Bengt-Göran

YE MARINERS OF ENGLAND see Pierson, Henry Hugo

YE SHALL HAVE A SONG see Porterfield, Sherrie

YEAR'S AT THE SPRING, THE see Kirk see Rosewall, Richard B.

YELLOW see Rainwater, Eric

YERUSHALAYIM see Rappaport, Moshe

YESTERDAYS
  (Treece, Roger-Childs, Billy) SSAA, solo,perc (gr. IV) UNC JP (Y14)

YLIAM see Scelsi, Giacinto

Y'MINAH, Y'MINAH (from Three Palistinian Dances)
  (Hunter) SATB LAWSON 4-567 (Y15)

YO, MAESTRA see Gustavino, Carlos

YO NO TENGO SOLEDAD (ADAGIO) see Gustavino, Carlos

YOGUELI ET VRÉNELI see Bovet, J.

YOU ARE A WINNER
  (Farrell, Jim) SSATB,perc (gr. IV) UNC JP (Y16)

YOU CAN CALL ME AL see Simon, Paul

YOU GOTTA TAKE ME AS AM see Schwartz, Dan

YOU HID YOUR HEART see Sapieyevski, Jerzy

YOU MADE ME LOVE YOU see McCarthy

YOU NEED LOVE see Monk,Thelonius

YOU STOLE MY LOVE see MacFarren, Walter [Cecil]

YOU'LL NEVER GUESS WHAT I SAW
    unis cor WARCH 34388 (Y17)

YOUNG, OVID
  Shining River, The
    SATB HOPE F 1011 (Y18)

YOUNG, ROBERT H. (1923- )
  Echo
    SSATTB,acap GENTRY JG2176 (Y19)

YOUNG DEAD SOLDIERS, THE see Schonthal-Seckel, Ruth

YOUNG GIRL, A see Williamson, Malcolm

YOUR FRIEND SHALL BE THE TALL WIND see Porterfield, Sherrie

YOUR HAND, MY HEART see Ideta, Keizo

YOUR PASSION see Hayashi, Hikaru

YOUR SSA CHOIR see Perry

YOU'RE EVERYTHING see Corea,Chick

YOU'RE MY BEST FRIEND see McPheeters

"YOUTSE", LA see Bovet, J.

YOU'VE GOT A FRIEND see King, Carole

YOU'VE GOT WHAT IT TAKES see Mallow, Monti

YUME THREE SHO see Abiko, Yoshiro

YUMEMITA MONO WA see Kino, Seiichiro

YUYAKE NO UTA see Yuyama, Akira

YUYAMA, AKIRA (1932- )
  Ayame No Uta
    wom cor,pno HUG (Y20)
  Go Phoenix!
    wom cor&jr cor,brass HUG (Y21)
  Ima Ikiru Kodomo March
    jr cor,2pno HUG (Y22)
  Umi No Ballade
    jr cor,pno HUG (Y23)
  Yuyake No Uta
    mix cor,pno HUG (Y24)

## Z

ZAHLER, J.R.
  Ausgang
    wom cor,acap MULLES (Z1)
  D's Geissbuebli
    wom cor,acap MULLES (Z2)
  Fröhliche Wanderung
    wom cor,acap MULLES (Z3)
  Frühling Kommt,Der
    wom cor,acap MULLES (Z4)
  Im Frühling
    wom cor,acap MULLES (Z5)
  Mein Liebes Schweizerland
    wom cor,acap MULLES (Z6)
  O Wie Freun Wir Uns
    wom cor,acap MULLES (Z7)
  Simmentaler Sennenlied
    wom cor,acap MULLES (Z8)
  Sonntag
    wom cor,acap MULLES (Z9)
  Stärnebärglied
    wom cor,acap MULLES (Z10)
  Trommellied
    wom cor,acap MULLES (Z11)
  Turnerliedchen
    wom cor,acap MULLES (Z12)
  Wanderlust
    wom cor,acap MULLES (Z13)
  Zyt Isch Do
    wom cor,acap MULLES (Z14)

ZAHN, DER see Loewe, Carl Gottfried

ZÄHRINGERLIED see Kaelin, Pierre

ZAMBA DE LA CANDELARIA see Falu

ZAMBA DE USTED see Ramirez, Ariel

ZAMBA PARA SARMIENTO see Ficco, Lito

ZANOLINI, BRUNO
  Secondo La Promessa
    cor,perc ZERBONI 8841 (Z15)

ZAPFENSTREICH see Kraehenbuehl, J.G.

ZARDINI, T.
  Vae Ariel!
    4pt mix cor BERBEN BERBEN 1969 (Z16)

ZARET, HY (1907- )
  Unchained Melody (composed with North, Alex)
    (Taylor, Peter) TTBB,T solo,perc (gr. II) UNC JP (Z17)

ZARUBA, ROBIN
  Come Back
    TTTBBB,T solo,acap (gr. IV) UNC JP (Z18)
  Love Will Find A Way
    TTTBBB,acap (gr. IV) UNC JP (Z19)

ZAYADANA see Robinovitch, Sid

ZAZOU ZINZIN, LE see Bezencon, Gilbert

ZBINDEN, JULIEN-FRANÇOIS (1917- )
  A L'émigrant
    mix cor HUG 8406 (Z20)
  Apprenti Forgeron, L'
    men cor HUG 8494 (Z21)
  Au Clair De La Terre
    mix cor HUG 8407 (Z22)
  Banale, La
    mix cor HUG 8405 (Z23)
  Berceuse Pour L'an 2000
    mix cor HUG 8404 (Z24)
  Chanson Pour Ma Mère
    men cor HUG 8403 (Z25)
  Comptine
    mix cor HUG 8062 (Z26)
  Deux Valses, Les
    men cor HUG 8483 (Z27)
  Ferdinand-La-Torpille
    men cor HUG 8064 (Z28)

ZBINDEN, JULIEN-FRANÇOIS (cont'd.)

    Marins D'eau Douce, Les
      men cor HUG 8061 (Z29)

    Pintier, Le
      men cor HUG 8371 (Z30)

    Réminiscence
      men cor HUG 8516 (Z31)

    Saisonniers, Le
      men cor HUG 8408 (Z32)

    Sous Les Noyers
      men cor HUG 8372 (Z33)

    Sur La Lune
      mix cor HUG 8063 (Z34)

    Tira Ma Lyre
      mix cor HUG 8065 (Z35)

ZECCA, GIANNINO (1911- )
    La Fontana
      4pt cor (text by Putelli) BERBEN
        BERBEN 1913 (Z36)

ZECCHI, ADONE (1904- )
    Convivio
      see Tre Frammenti Di Anacreonte

    Io Non Amo...
      see Tre Frammenti Di Anacreonte

    Tre Frammenti Di Anacreonte
      3pt cor sc RICORDI-IT 131992 f.s.
      contains: Convivio; Io Non
        Amo...; Tristezza (Z37)

    Tristezza
      see Tre Frammenti Di Anacreonte

ZEHAVI, ODED (1961- )
    Thy Mornings I Shall Seek
      2pt wom cor,acap ISR.MUS.INST.
        IMI 6999 (Z38)

ZEHN KÄRNTNER VOLKSLIEDER *CCU,folk
    song,Austrian
    (Anderluh, Anton) mix cor HEYN
      NR. 119 f.s. (Z39)

ZENTNER, JOHANNES (1903- )
    August
      wom cor,acap MULLES (Z40)

    Freundeskreis,Der
      men cor,acap MULLES (Z41)

    Gegenwart
      men cor,acap MULLES (Z42)

    Herbst
      men cor,acap MULLES (Z43)

    Maiabend
      wom cor,acap MULLES (Z44)

    Meine Zelle
      men cor,acap MULLES (Z45)

    Morgengruss
      wom cor,acap MULLES (Z46)

    Musica
      men cor&jr cor&wom cor/mix cor,org/
        winds MULLES (Z47)

    Uhr,Die
      wom cor,acap MULLES (Z48)

    Wanderspruch
      wom cor,acap MULLES (Z49)

    Winternacht
      men cor,acap MULLES (Z50)

ZEVENTIEN DAPPERE HOUTEN SOLDAATJES see
    Smaling, Cor

ZIGEUNERLEBEN see Schumann, Robert
    (Alexander)

ZIEGLER, JOSEF W.
    Gesegn Dich Laub, Gesegn Dich Gras
      3pt mix cor BOHM (Z51)

ZIGEUNERLIEDER see Brahms, Johannes

ZIJ SCHOOF DEN LINTELDOEK OPZIJ... see
    Kersters, Willem

ZIMMERMANN, BERND ALOIS (1918-1970)
    Bei Meines Buhlen Haupte *folk song
      mix cor,acap sc SCHOTTS C 47825
        (Z52)

ZINGG
    Schmiede-Lied: "I Isch Nümme Die Zyt"
      (Ummel) wom cor,acap MULLES (Z53)

ZIPP, FRIEDRICH (1914- )
    Fröhlich Wir Nun All Fangen An
      mix cor SCHUL CLS 376 (Z54)

ZIPP, FRIEDRICH (cont'd.)

    Güldne Sonne,Die
      2 eq voices,opt vln/fl SCHUL
        CLS 322 (Z55)

ZONDAG VAN JANUARI see Swerts, Piet

ZORMAN, MOSHE (1952- )
    Little Ones *CC3U
      [Heb] 4pt jr cor,acap ISR.MUS.INST.
        IMI 6968 f.s. (Z56)

ZORTZICO see Albéniz, Isaac

ZUCKER, YOSEF
    Hashkivenu
      SATB,cantor/solo voice OR-TAV (Z57)

ZUCKERSÜSSE STADT, EINE see Diener,
    Theodor

ZUGVÖGEL (HEFT 1) *CCU
    (Sädler, Arthur) 3-4 eq voices FIDULA
      6091 f.s. North European Songs
        (Z58)

ZUGVÖGEL (HEFT 2) *CCU
    (Sädler, Arthur) 3-4 eq voices FIDULA
      6092 f.s. East European Songs (Z59)

ZUGVÖGEL (HEFT 3) *CCU
    (Sädler, Arthur) 3-4 eq voices FIDULA
      South European Songs (Z60)

ZUGVÖGEL (HEFT 4) *CCU
    (Sädler, Arthur) 3-4 eq voices FIDULA
      West European Songs (Z61)

ZUMBA, ZUMBA see Stultz, Marie

ZUNGO *folk song,Afr
    (Brown, Uzee) SATB,opt perc DEAN
      15-1079 (Z62)

ZUR HOCHZEIT see Olpen, Friedrich W.

ZUR KALTEN ZEIT see Gasser, Ulrich

ZUR (WELTLICHEN) HOCHZEITSFEIER, OP.
    148 NO. 4 see Welcker, Max

ZUVERSICHT see Schmid, Walter

ZWEI ALTE KÄRNTNERLIEDER *CCU
    (Mittergradnegger, Günther) mix cor
      HEYN NR. 135 f.s. (Z63)

ZWEI ALTE KÄRNTNERLIEDER *CCU
    (Mittergradnegger, Günther) mix cor
      HEYN NR. 136 f.s. (Z64)

ZWEI EINFACHE WEISEN see Märki, Ernst

ZWEI KURZE WAHLSPRÜCHE see Müller,
    Joseph Ivar

ZWEI LIEBES LIEDER see Jeep, Johann

ZWEI LIEDER see Katz, Paul

ZWEI LIEDER AUS MAN-YO see Hasegawa,
    Tsutomu

ZWEI LIEDER ZUM GEBURTSTAG ODER ZU
    NEUJAHR see Rothschuh, Fritz

ZWEI MADRIGALE see Klein, Gideon

ZWEI TIERLIEDER
    3pt mix cor MULLES f.s.
      contains: Huhn Und Karpfen;
        Panther,Der (Z65)

ZWEI TRINKSPRÜCHE UND GLÜCKWUNSCH see
    Krieger, Fritz

ZWISCHEN TRAUM UND WACHEN see Klein,
    Richard Rudolf

ZWISSIG,A.
    Cantique Suisse
      mix cor HUG 6941 (Z66)

ZWÖI BÄRNDÜTSCHI LIEDER
    SATB,acap MULLES f.s.
      contains: Es Chnöi; Gygechaschte
        (Z67)

ZWYSSIG, ALBERICH (1808-1854)
    Schweizerpsalm: Tritts Im Morgenrot
      men cor,acap MULLES (Z68)

ZYT ISCH DO see Zahler, J.R.

# ARRANGER INDEX

ACCIAI, G.
  Sabbatini, Antonio Luigi
    Canoni Sui Principi Elementari

  Salieri, Antonio
    Scherzi Armonici

ADAMS, BRANT
  Here We Come A-Caroling

ALBRECHT
  St. Nick At Night (Jolly Old St. Nicholas)

ALLAWAY, BEN
  Sainte-Marie, Buffy
    Dream Tree, The

ALTHOUSE
  All Alone At Christmas

  Bricusse, Leslie
    Who Can I Turn To?

  Don't Get Around Much Anymore

  Follow The Drinking Gourd

  He Ain't Heavy, He's My Brother

  Henderson
    Bye Bye Blackbird

  Jingle Bells

  Koehler
    Stormy Weather

  McCarthy
    You Made Me Love You

  Nobody Knows The Trouble I've Seen

  Scarborough Fair

  Still A Bach Christmas (Bach's "Air"- "Still, Still Still")

  Twelve Songs Of Christmas, The (A Medley Of Seasonal Favorites)

ALTHOUSE, JAY
  Barry, Jeff
    Do Wah Diddy Diddy

  Come Follow The Bands

  Darin, Bobby
    Splish Splash

  Favorite Son

  Holland, Brian
    Stop! In The Name Of Love

  Rockin' At The Hop

  Rockin' Christmas Celebration!

  Rodgers, Richard
    My Funny Valentine

AMES, MORGAN
  Berlin, Irving
    They Say That Falling In Love Is Wonderful

  Boogie Woogie Santa Claus

  Cole, Nat (King)
    Straighten Up And Fly Right

  Fum Fum Fum

  I Don't Know Why I Love You Like I Do

  Mandel, Johnny Alfred
    Unless It's You

  Once Upon A Christmas Time

  Santa's Watching

  We Wish You A Merry Christmas

AMFT, GEORG
  Deutscher Männerchor. Heft I

  Deutscher Männerchor. Heft II

  Deutscher Männerchor. Heft III

ANCIRA
  Christmas Memories

ANDERLUH, ANTON
  Alte Kärntnerlieder

  Deutsche Volkslieder

  Frisch Gesungen (I. Teil)

  Frisch Gesungen (Ii. Teil)

  Glück Auf

ANDERLUH, ANTON (cont'd.)
  Mutter Wir Grüssen Dich!

  Österreichische Volkslieder (Heft 1)

  Österreichische Volkslieder (Heft 2)

  Sechs Österreichische Volkslieder

  Sing Mit!

  Tanzlieder Aus Österreich

  Volkslieder Aus Aller Welt

  Zehn Kärntner Volkslieder

ANDERLUH, ANTON- ASENBAUER, ANDREAS
  Setz' Auf Mei Grüans Hüatle

ANDERLUH, ANTON-MITTERGRADNEGGER
  Volkslieder Aus Aller Welt (Heft 1)

ANDERLUH, ANTON -MITTERGRADNEGGER, GÜNTHER
  Kärntens Liederschatz

ANDERLUH, ANTON-WULZ, HELMUT
  Anderluh Männerchorbuch, Das

ANDERSON, JEAN
  Morning Dew, The

ANDERSON, MILTON
  Button Up Your Overcoat

ANDERSON, TOM
  Basie, William (Count)
    One O'clock Jump

  Corea, Chick
    Sea-Crystal Journey

  Ellington, Edward Kennedy (Duke)
    Duke's Place (C Jam BTues)

  Jazzy Old Saint Nicholas

  Kern, Philip
    Sing, Sing, Sing

ANDRIEU
  Chopin, Frédéric
    Marche Funèbre

ARABIAN-TINI
  Like Someone In Love

ARABIANTINI, APRIL
  Bye, Bye Blackbird

ARCH
  Four Jazz Spirituals

ARCH G
  Lloyd Webber, Andrew
    Mr. Mistoffelees And Other Choruses From Cats

  Schwartz
    Choruses From 'Godspell' And 'Children Of Eden'

ARCHER, VIOLET
  Children Singing

ARNOUD
  Bazin, François-Emanuel-Joseph
    Gloire À La France

  Mendelssohn-Bartholdy, Felix
    Chant De L'alouette, Le
    Ma Forêt

  Rameau, Jean-Philippe
    Hymn À La Nuit

BACH; SWINGLE
  Vivaldi, Antonio
    Fugue

BAKER, ANDY
  Everly, Phil
    When Will I Be Loved

  Granada

  Guantanamera (Guajira Guantanamera)

  I'll Take You There

  Some Kind Of Wonderful, (She's)

  Warmer, Randy
    I'm In A Hurry (And I Don't Know Why)

BALZANELLI, ALBERTO
  Isella, César
    Cancion Con Todos

BARNBY, J.
  Men Of Harlech

BARTLETT, IAN
  Boyce, William
    Together Let Us Range The Fields

BAXTER, F
  Shepherdess Of Sadness

BAXTER, FRANCIS
  Hei Tsuki Bushi

  Kiso Bushi

  Soran Bushi

BAXTER, FRANCIS H.
  Four Chinese Children's Songs

  Itsuki No Komori Uta

BELAN, W.
  Mananitas De Mi Tierra

  Piel Canela

BELL, RICK
  Coots, John Frederick
    For All We Know

  Corea, Chick
    You're Everything

BENT, HALLMARK
  Ciconia, Johannes
    Motets And Latin Contrafacta
    Secular Works

BERGER, ERWIN
  Schau, Wia Gliacht Is Da Tåg

BERTALOT
  Allouette

BESIG, DON
  Santa Claus Is Comin' To Town

BIANCONI, L.
  Frescobaldi, Girolamo
    Primo Libro Dei Madrigali, Il

BILLINGSLEY
  Highlights From Blood Brothers

  In The Swing

BILLINGSLEY, ALAN
  Reach Out, I'll Be There

BISSELL
  Song Of Longing

BJORÅ, OLAV
  Waaler, Fredrikke
    Sangermarsj

BØE, BERNT
  Bruramarsj Frå Osre

BONNEAU
  Aliprandi, Paul
    Harmonie Du Soir
    Saint Raphaël

BRADLEY ELLINGBOE
  Ash Grove, The

BRAND, HANS V.D.
  Davids, Louis
    Naar Buiten Met Louis Davids

BRAUN, YEHEZKEL
  Jerusalem Of Gold

  Rain Storm

BRAUN, YEHEZKEL-JACOBSON, JOSHUA
  Dime Rozina

  Don Amadi

  Durme, Durme

  Esta Rakhel

  Morenica

  Nani, Nani

  Por Que Llorax

BRÉARD
  Rouget de l'Isle, Claude Joseph
    Marseillaise, La

BRECHT
  Sauseng, Wolfgang
    Rudern, Gespräche

BREMER, JETSE
  Arise, Arise

  As I Walked Through The Meadows

# ARRANGER INDEX

BRIDWELL
   Nutcracker Jingles

   Variations On Fa-La-La

BRITO, MANUEL CARLOS DE
   Anonymous
      Five Portuguese Villancicos

BROCHART
   Gluck, Christoph Willibald, Ritter von
      Choeur D'Armide

BROOKS, JEANICE
   Castro, Jean de
      Chansons, Odes, Et Sonetz De Pierre Ronsard (1576)

BROWER F
   Rachmaninoff, Sergey Vassilievich
      Three Russian Songs, Op. 41

BROWN, UZEE
   Zungo

BRUN
   Méhul, Étienne-Nicolas
      Chant Du Départ, Le

   Rouget de l'Isle, Claude Joseph
      Marseillaise, La

BUFFA, TODD
   Little Drummer Boy

BURKARD
   Huber, Walter Simon
      Abendlied (Lueged, Vo Bärge Und Tal)

BURKE, HOWARD
   Bach, Johann Sebastian
      Toccata And Fugue In D Minor

BURNELL, MARK
   Burnell, Mark
      Star Spangled Banner

   Morrison, Van
      Moondance

BUSTA
   Einem, Gottfried von
      Votivlieder Für Frauenchor

BUTZ
   Josef
      Hochzeitsmadrigal

   Silcher, Friedrich
      Am Brunnen Vor Dem Tore
      Es Löscht Das Meer Die Sonne Aus
      Hab Oft Im Kreis Der Lieben
      In Einem Kühlen Grunde
      Morgen Muss Ich Fort Von Hier
      Nun Leb Wohl, Du Kleine Gasse
      Rosestock Holderblüt
      Wenn Ich Ein Vöglein Wär

CACAK-LEIPERT
   Am Zirbitzen Droben (Heft 1)

CADWALLADER, REX
   Street Smarts

CAMPIONE, A.
   Balfe, Michael William
      Kilarney

CANNING, ANDREW
   Kind, Glover
      I Do Like To Be Beside The Seaside

CARACCIOLO, STEPHEN
   Wayfaring Stranger, The

CARTER, ALLEN
   Kern, Jerome
      Song Is You, The

CASAGRANDE
   Anonymous
      International Folk

CASAGRANDE, RAMOUS
   Quattordici Canti Popolari

CEDERBERG, ANNA
   Bacharach, Burt F.
      Raindrops Keep Fallin' On My Head

   Geld, Gary
      Sealed With A Kiss

CHALLINOR, F.A.
   Barnby, [Sir] Joseph
      Sweet And Low

   Lully, Jean-Baptiste (Lulli)
      Gentle Night

CHARLES PELLETIER
   En Roulant

   Imprisoned Once At Nantes

CHARLET
   Séparation

CHILDS
   Pick A Bale Of Cotton

   Sweet Betsy From Pike

CHINN-CACAVAS-SNYDER-GILPIN
   Best Selling Pops For Young Voices: Song Kit #15

CHINN, TEENA
   Body And Soul

   Carmichael, Hoagy
      Skylark

   Edwards, Sherman
      See You In September

   Express Yourself

   Forever And Ever

   Forever's As Far As I'll Go

   Gershwin For Girls

   Gummoe, Joe
      Rhythm Of The Rain

   Hall, Dave
      Dreamlover

   Hart, Lorenz
      Isn't It Romantic

   I'll Be There

   I'm Every Woman

   In This Life

   Jazzy Jingle Bells

   Lost And Found

   Merry Christmas, Darling

   Naughty But Nice

   Now And Forever

   On Bended Knee

   On With The Show

   Red Hot Country Boogie

   Red Hot Country Showdown Revue

   Rose, The

   Sharron, Marti
      If I Could

   Snow!

   Stevenson, William
      Dancing In The Street

   Summertime Blues

   Theme From "New York, New York"

   This Is The Moment

   When The Good Times Come Again

   When The Saints Go Marching In

CLAPP, MARTI
   Eruption

CLAUDIUS, M.
   Vollenweider, Hans
      Abendlied

CLEVELAND, MICHAEL
   Waillie, Waillie

COOMBES, DOUGLAS
   Keeper, The

   King Arthur And His Sons

COOMES, DOUGLAS
   Water Of The Tyne, The

COR, ROBERT DEMIER
   Mangwani Mpulele

   May There Always Be Sunshine

CORMIER, ROBERT DE
   Ku-Ku

   Street Of Laredo, The

CRENSHAW, RANDY
   Corea, Chick
      Spain

   Jones, Quincy
      Love Is In Control

   Quiet Place, A

CRENSHAW, RANDY-TERRA NOVA
   'Round Midnight

CRESTANI, M.
   Anonymous
      Europa Unita Canta, L'

CROSS, DAVE
   I Thought About You

   Morrison, Van
      Moondance

   Saxophone Joe

   Shortnin' Bread

   Things Are Gettin' Better

   Time After Time

   Wilder, Alec
      Blackberry Winter

DA ROS
   Melodie Natalizie. Elaborazioni Corali Di Melodie Tradizionali Per Coro Di Voci Pari E Dispari

DEALE, EDGAR M.
   Lark In The Clear Air, The

DEFONTAINE
   Fort, P.
      Ronde

DEFORD, RUTH I.
   Vecchi, Orazio (Horatio)
      Four-Voice Canzonettas With Original Texts And Contrafacta By Valentin Haussmann And Others, The

DELONG, RICHARD
   Come My Way

DICKS, E.A.
   Balfe, Michael William
      Excelsior!

   Bishop, [Sir] Henry (Rowley)
      Home Sweet Home

   Calkin, J. Baptiste
      Chivalry Of Labour, The

   Clarke (-Whitfield), [Dr.] John
      Wide O'er The Brim

   Crouch, Frederick Nicholls
      Kathleen Mavourneen

   Glover, Stephen
      Gipsies' Laughing Trio, The

   Golden Slumbers Kiss Your Eyes

   On The Banks Of Allan Water

   Phillips, Henry
      To Our Next Merry Meeting

   Richards, [Henry] Brinley
      Up! Quit Thy Bower

DIPIAZZA, O.
   Anonymous
      Cantar Friulano
      Dodici Canti Popolari Friulani
      Quattordici Canti Popolari Friulani

DIPIAZZA, ORLANDO
   Antologia Di Canti Popolari

DREWES, HELMUT
   Aber Diandle Im Tål

DREWES, HELMUT-HOPFGARTNER, JOSEF
   Jåhr Is Lei A Wind, Dås

DREWES, HELMUT-MITTERGRADNEGGER, GÜNTHER

   Du Mei Hamat Ghearst Mein

DUCASSE
   Mozart, Wolfgang Amadeus
      Mon Faible C'est Le Vin

DUSI, M.
   Fonseca, Julio
      Mananitas De Mi Terra

## ARRANGER INDEX

DÜSING
  Morse
    Oysters And Clams

DÜSING, DAVID
  Foster, Stephen Collins
    Beautiful Dreamer
    Camptown Races, The
    Oh! Susanna!

EASSON, J. - TORRANCE, W.P.
  Sang Scule

EDENROTH, ANDERS
  Ellington, Edward Kennedy (Duke)
    It Don't Mean A Thing

EDLUND, LARS
  Drink To Me Only With Thine Eyes

EHRISMANN
  Rolli
    I Bi Soldat Und Du Bisch Soldat

EMLEN
  One Man Shall Mow My Meadow

EPSTEIN, ELEANOR
  Ozi VeZimrat Yah

ERB
  Colorado Trail, The

ERIKSSON, GUNNAR
  Hylin, Birgitta
    Sommarn Och Jag

ESCALADA
  Manchai Puito

  Verano Porteno

F.W.WILSON
  Gaudeamus Igitur

FARRELL, JIM
  King, Carole
    You've Got A Friend

  Simon, Paul
    You Can Call Me Al

  Talkin' 'Bout My Baby

  You Are A Winner

FENLON, IAIN
  Arcadelt, Jacob
    Three Madrigals By Jacques Arcadelt

FÉVRIER
  Rameau, Jean-Philippe
    Au Son Du Tambourin

  Schumann, Robert (Alexander)
    Célèbre Rêverie
    Gai Laboureur, Le

FILIPPI, S.
  Antologia Di Canti Popolari Natalizi

FLEET
  Brahms, Johannes
    Zigeunerlieder

  Mendelssohn-Bartholdy, Felix
    There Shall A Star

  Schumann, Robert (Alexander)
    Mailied
    Schön Blumelein

FLIARKOVSKY, A.
  Garden Gate,The

FORSYTH
  Three Zulu Songs

FOUQUE, MARTIN
  Lincke, Paul
    Es War Einmal
    Glühwürmchen Idyll

FOXE, WILFRED
  Pecci, Tomaso
    First Book Of Madrigals For Five Voices (1602)

FRANCIS, G.T.
  All In A Garden Fair

FRANK CLARK
  Mr. Froggie Went A-Courtin'

FREED
  Water Is Wide, The

FUCHS, PETER
  Da Guggu Hät Ja Gölbe Füass

FUNK
  All Aboard!

  Be My Baby Tonight

  Be True To Your School

FUNK, JEFF
  All Aboard!

  Bitten By The Beat

  Calendar Girls

  Christmas Time!

  Ciancioso, Carole
    Christmas Rockin' Eve

  Jennings, Will
    Best Years Of My Life, The

  Lion Sleeps Tonight, The

  McVie, Christine
    Don't Stop

  Masser, Michael
    It's My Turn

  Queen Of Soul

  Roaring '20s

  Robbins, Marty
    White Sport Coat (And A Pink Carnation), A

  Secada, Jon
    I'm Free

  Sweetest Days, The

GAILEY, DAN
  Metheny,Pat
    Lone Jack

GALLINA
  Brahms, Johannes
    Sandman, The

  Music From "Hansel And Gretel"

  Two Israeli Folk Songs

GAND-KREIS
  Eigenössisches Danklied

  Marschlied Des Inf Rg 45

GAND-KREIS-MÄRKI
  Chnabe Vo Chappel,Die

  Petite Gilberte De Courgenay,La

GARDEWEG
  Silcher, Friedrich
    Ach Gott, Wie Weh Tut Scheiden
    Dem Himmel Will Ich Klagen
    Es Fliegt Manch Vöglein
    Es Sass Ein Häslein
    Himmel Lacht, Der
    Ich Ging Einmal Spazieren
    Ich Kann Und Mag Nicht
    Lieben Bringt Gross' Freund, Das
    Mai Tritt Ein Mit Freuden, Der
    Mein Schätzle Ist Fein
    Von Allen Den Mädchen
    Wenn Frühlingstage Neu Beleben

GATES, C.
  Scott, [Lady] John (Alicia Ann)
    Annie Laurie

GILL, RANDALL
  Pretty Saro

GILPIN
  There, I've Said It Again

GILPIN, GREG
  Gershwin, George
    Calp Yo' Hands (Clap Your Hands)

  Get Ready

  One Song

GINSBURG, NED
  Anderson, Leroy
    Syncopated Clock, The

  Best Of Bond:, The

  Heart To Climb The Mountain, The

  Movie Classics: Golden Love Songs Of The '70s

GLICK-HERRINGTON
  Cotton Eye Joe

GOMEZ, EDUARDO
  Berbel, Marcelo
    Quimey Neuquen

  Falu
    Volvedora,La

  Ramirez, Ariel
    Parana En Una Zamba,El

GOMEZ, EDUARDO (cont'd.)
  Sampayo, Anibal
    Ky Chororo

GRITTON
  Lloyd Webber, Andrew
    Memory And Other Choruses From Cats
    Mr. Mistoffelees And Other Choruses From Cats

  Three Carribean Calypsos

GUENTER
  Mendelssohn-Bartholdy, Felix
    Two Mendelssohn Part Songs

GUENTNER
  Dindirin, Dindirindaña

GUENTNER, FRANCIS
  Gastoldi, Giovanni Giacomo
    Hark To The Fanfare Sounding

GUIBAT
  Annie Laurie

  Douce Annie

  Foster, Stephen Collins
    Ma Vieille Maison

HAGEMANN, P
  Purcell, Henry
    Caught In The Act

HALLORAN, JACK
  Foster, Stephen Collins
    Nelly Bly

HÅRD AF SEGERSTAD, B.
  Sjöberg, Birger
    Hos Min Doktor

HARNADY, WALLACE
  Nodle Kangbyon

HARRIS
  Grieg, Edvard Hagerup
    Humoresque

HARRISON
  Musicorum Collegio: Six Fourteenth Century Musicians' Motets

HATCH
  Sleigh Song

HAYES
  Children, Go Where I Send Thee

  Old West Medley

  Wade In The Water

HELLER
  Niggun

HELVEY
  Ding Dong! Merrily On High

HENLEY, ROD
  Fagen,Donald
    Maxine

  Jarreau,Al
    We're In This Love Together

HERMAN
  Haydn, [Franz] Joseph
    Everyone Has His Day

HINDERMANN, PAUL
  Brahms, Johannes
    Liebeslieder - Walzer, Op. 52

HINES
  She Never Told Her Love

HOARE, KRUMMACHER
  Schubert, Franz (Peter)
    Night

HOFFMAN
  Elanoy

  Rodeo

HOOD
  Berlin, Irving
    Alexander's Ragtime Band

HOOGAKKER, WILL
  Smaling, Cor
    Zeventien Dappere Houten Soldaatjes

HUNTER
  Y'Minah, Y'Minah

HUNTER-SHAW
  Bishop
    Home, Sweet Home

# ARRANGER INDEX

IDAR, INGEGERD
  Abba För Damkör

INZKO, JOSEF
  Hån Jå Lei Dih

  In Dar Lercharleitn

  Verliabt Sein Is Ka Hexerei

JACOBSON, JOSHUA
  Jagoda, Flory
    Ocho Kandelikas

  Papir Iz Doch Vais

  Rappaport, Moshe
    Yerushalayim

JANUNGER
  Volle, Bjarne
    Gå Inte Så Hårt I Gräset

JANUNGER, KJELL
  Gånglåt

JEFFERS, RON
  Johnny Aroo'

JEHRLANDER
  Wieh, Michael
    Jag Är En Människa I Världen

JERGENSON, D
  Lily Of Erabu Isle

JOHNSON
  What Can I Do?

JULLANDER
  Tchaikovsky, Piotr Ilyich
    Blommornas Vals

KAHLHAMMER, JELLE
  Es Hausdåch Brat Übar

  Untan Nock In Da Muldn

KAISER
  Taneyev
    Ah, Behold-The Dark Of Night
    Evening
    Ruins Of A Tower, The

KAMP, TOMMY
  Metheny, Pat
    (It's Just) Talk

KARLSEN, KJELL MØRK
  Fem Folkeviser Fra Gausdal

KATT, LEOPOLD
  Jugend Singt II

  Jugend Singt III

KELLER
  Koch
    Am Wellenspiel Der Aare

KELLER, G.
  Vollenweider, Hans
    Abendlied

KERN
  Pat-A-Pan-Fum, Fum

KERN, PHILIP
  Broadway Ladies

KINSALE, HILLARY
  Christmas Toys

  Get Happy

  Tender Shepherd (Count Your Sheep)

KLEEWEIN, OTTO
  De Hamlane Tür

KLEIN, RICHARD RUDOLF
  Stegreifsätze 1

  Stegreifsätze 2

KOSCHAT, THOMAS
  Männerchöre Im Kärntner Volkston
    (Heft 1)

  Männerchöre Im Kärntner Volkston
    (Heft 2)

KRÄHENBÜHL
  Müller, Joseph Ivar
    Vreneli Vom Thunersee, 'S

KRAXNER, WALTER
  Waht Da Wind Üban See

KRENGER
  Abt, Franz
    Wanderlied

  Boesch, Balthasar
    I Dr Frömdi

KRENGER (cont'd.)
  Mendelssohn-Bartholdy, Felix
    Winzerchor

  Munzinger, Carl
    Frühlingsjubel

KRINGS, ALFRED
  Deutsche Lieder

  Englische Madrigale

  Französische Chansons

  Italienische Madrigale

  Musik Und Wein

KÜHR, REINHARD -FUCHS, MONIKA
  Möcht'n Viel Zacharian

KUNC
  Ronsard
    Chanson À Quatre Voix

LAMMERZ
  Silcher, Friedrich
    Ach, Wie Ist's Möglich Dann
    Ännchen Von Tharau
    Drunten Im Unterland
    Ich Weiss Nicht, Was Soll Es
      Bedeuten
    Mir Ist's Zu Wohl Ergangen
    Ohne Dich Wie Lange
    Was Hab Ich Denn Meinem
      Feinsliebchen Getan
    Wenn Ich Ein Vöglein Wär

LANE, PHILIP
  Sullivan, [Sir] Arthur Seymour
    When The Buds Are Blossoming

LARKIN, MICHAEL
  Sally Gardens, The

LARSON, LLOYD
  Mozart, Wolfgang Amadeus
    Sing, Come Sing A Song Of Gladness

LAWRENCE, STEPHEN
  Bird Dog

LAZAR, MATTHEW
  Cuando El Rey Nimrod

  Tumbalalaika

LEAVITT
  Gifts Of Love

  Tell Me It's Not True

LEAVITT, JOHN
  Dvorák, Antonín
    Steal Away

  Gershwin, George
    Man I Love, The

  Magic To Do

  Niles, John Jacob
    What Is Beauty

  Pierpont, James
    Dashing Through The Snow

  Shaiman, Marc
    Wink And A Smile, A

  Yarrow, Peter
    Puff (The Magic Dragon)

LEE, CAROLYN
  Anonymous
    Seven Courtly Love Songs

LEMMERMANN, HEINZ
  Cucaracha, La

  Ol' Texas

  Shalom

LENDERS, HANS-GÜNTER
  Madrigale-Vilanellen

  Wohlauf

LESLIE, HENRY
  Lass Of Richmond Hill, The

LESURE
  Anthologie De La Chanson Parisienne
    Au Xvie Siecle

LEVI
  Eddystone Light, The

LEVI, MICHAEL
  Mermaid, The

LEWIN
  Fi Mi Love

  Rio Grande

  Tambo

LIANI, D.
  Anonymous
    Undici Canti Poplari Friulani

LIEBERGEN
  Buxtehude, Dietrich
    Be Joyful With Singing

LIEBERGEN, PATRICK
  Arcadelt, Jacob
    Sing Out With Joy

  Nola, G. Domenico da
    On This Delightful Day

  Schubert, Franz (Peter)
    Sing Forever

  Sing With Joy Today!

LINBERG, PER
  Sometimes I Feel Like A Motherless
    Child

LIVINGSTON
  Elgar, [Sir] Edward (William)
    As Torrents In Summer

LJUNG, NILS
  Andersson, Benny
    Älska Mej

LOOMER, A
  MacGillivray, Allister
    Song For Peace

LOUGHTON, LYNNETTE-STEED, GORDON
  Gypsy Rover, The

LYONS, BILL
  Earth, Wind And Fire Medley

  Morris, Stevland (Stevie Wonder)
    Creepin'

  Star Spangled Banner, The

MARIE STULTZ
  Simple Gifts

MAROIS, REJEAN
  Herzog
    God Bless The Child

MARTIN
  Mozart, Wolfgang Amadeus
    Alphabet, The

  "Round" And A "Round" We Go!

MARTIN, ROBERT
  Standard On The Braes O' Mar, The

MARVIN, JAMESON
  Fung Yang Kuh Lai

  I Love My Love

  K'ang-Ting Love Song

MATERASSI, M. GIUSTINIANE, IL
  Primo Libro Delle

MATSUOKA, YUMIKO
  Black Is The Color

MCCULLOUGH, JIM
  Bye, Bye Blackbird

MCKENZIE
  Cornyshe, William (Cornish)
    Ah, Robin, Gentle Robin

MCLIN
  Can't You Hear Those Freedom Bells
    Ringing?

MCQUILLAN, ROBERT
  Wythorne, T.
    Songes For Three Voyces

MEADER,
  Coltrane, John
    Giant Steps

MEADER, DARMON
  Now That Love Is Over

MECHELL, HARRY
  Rejected Lover, The

MEREDITH
  Certon, Pierre
    Je Ne Fus Jamais Si Aise

  Purcell, Henry
    Shepherd, Shepherd

# ARRANGER INDEX

MEREDITH (cont'd.)
  Rossi, Luigi
    Dormite, Begl' Occhi

MERRITT, LESURE
  Janequin, Clement
    Complete Chansons

MITTERGRADNEGGER, GÜNTHER
  A Blüah Übarn Himml

  Alpenländische Jodler Und Volkslieder

  Alpenländische Jodler Und Volkslieder

  Alpenländische Volkslieder

  Aufisteig'n - Eineschau'n

  Ausländische Volkslieder 1982

  Cantus Carinthicus

  Chorliederbuch

  Deutsche Volkslied,Das 1978

  Europäische Weihnachtslieder

  Fünf Heitere Alpenländische Volkslieder

  Fünf Heitere Alpenländische Volkslieder Und Jodler

  Kärntnerlieder

  Kleine Chöre U. Ausländische Volkslieder 1980

  Kommt Zum Singen (Heft 1)

  Kommt Zum Singen (Heft 2)

  Lieder Aus Aller Welt

  Lieder Für Feste, Feiern Und Frohes Singen

  Neue Kärntner Lied,Das 1979

  Sechs Heitere Alpenländische Volkslieder Und Jodler

  Stiller Als Eine Wolke

  Verschiedene Volkslieder 1981

  Volkslieder Aus Aller Welt

  Volkslieder Aus Aller Welt

  Zwei Alte Kärntnerlieder

  Zwei Alte Kärntnerlieder

MITTERGRADNEGGER, GÜNTHER-GLAWISCHNIG, GERHARD
  Is Schon Still Uman See

MOORE, DONALD
  I'm Bound Away

  In A Sentimental Mood

  Rockin' Jerusalem

  Siyahamba

MORROW
  Ragged Leevy

MOUCHET
  Handel, George Frideric
    Largo

  Mozart, Wolfgang Amadeus
    Caravane Turque Sur La Marche Turque

  Rameau, Jean-Philippe
    Hymne À La Nuit

  Schubert, Franz (Peter)
    Gais Compagnons

MULLE, JUSTINUS -GLAWISCHNIG, GERHARD
  Übarn Glåntålbodn

MULLE, JUSTINUS- MITTERGRADNEGGER, GÜNTHER
  Aus Der Liedermappe Des Kärntner Lehrerquintetts

  Aus Der Liedermappe Des Kärntner Lehrerquintetts

  Aus Der Liedermappe Des Kärntner Lehrerquintetts

  Aus Der Liedermappe Des Kärntner Lehrerquintetts

MULLE, JUSTINUS- MITTERGRADNEGGER, GÜNTHER (cont'd.)
  Aus Der Liedermappe Des Kärntner Lehrerquintetts

  Aus Der Liedermappe Des Kärtner Lehrerquintetts

NEW YORK VOICES
  Ellington, Edward Kennedy (Duke)
    Caravan

  Meader, Darmon
    Baroque Samba
    National Amnesia

  Now Or Never

  'Round Midnight

  Sassy Samba

  Sign Of Spring

  Soon One Day

  Street Party

  To Dare The Moon

  Top Secret

  Who Knows?

NIGGLI
  Stoessel, Albert
    Chum Übers Mätteli

NORCOTT
  Winfrey, Robert
    Let's Build A City

NOVIKOV, A.
  Mistress

NYHUS, ROLF
  I Skovens Dybe, Stille Ro

OETIKER
  Huber, Walter Simon
    Lueget, Vo Bärge Und Tal

OETIKER, AUGUST
  Schubert, Franz (Peter)
    Im Gegenwärtigen Vergangenes

ÖHRWALL, ANDERS
  Deck The Halls

  Ding, Dong

  Pierpont, James
    Jingle Bells

  Två Kinesiska Visor

OLASO, LUIS MARIA DE
  Alem, Oscar
    Pampa Verde, La

OLIVIERI, L.
  Capo,B.
    Piel Canela

O'NEILL
  Farewell, Lad

O'NEILL, JACKIE
  Never Met A Man I Didn't Like

  Revil, H.
    Winter Light

ORTNER, SEPP-BÜNKER, OTTO
  ...Und Es Birknbamle Lost Ma Zua

ORTNER, SEPP-KRAXNER
  Waht Da Wind Uban See

ORTNER, SEPP-KRAXNER, WALTER
  Waht Da Wind Uban See

OSCARSSON, KJELL
  Sankt Staffan

PACE, DANIEL DI
  Marziali, Jorge
    Cebollita Y Huevo

  Parodi,Tenesa
    Pedro Canoero

PAQUIN-SALERNO, CHRIS
  Ellington, Edward Kennedy (Duke)
    Don't You Know I Care

  Ritenour,Lee
    Bullet Train

  Santa Claus Is Coming To Town

  Silver,Horace
    Peace

PARKER
  To Ladies' Eyes

PARKER-SHAW
  Drink To Me Only With Thine Eyes

PARRY
  Schwartz
    Choruses From 'Godspell' And 'Children Of Eden'

PATRIQUIN, DONALD
  J'entends Le Moulin

PAYNES
  Cape Cod Shanty

PEARSON, A.
  Schubert, Franz
    Serenade

PEROSA, A. - DIPIAZZA, O. - RUSSOLO, G. - NESBEDA, F.
  Anonymous
    Quattro Elaborazioni Corali

PFAUTSCH
  Devil's Nine Questions, The

PFAUTSCH, LLOYD
  Snow-White Messenger, The

PICKARD, WAYLAND
  Star Spangled Banner

PLESCHBERGER, HANS
  Liada Aus'n Liesertal

PLISKA-DIK
  Leoncavallo, Ruggiero
    Bell Chorus From "Il Pagliacci"

  Smetana, Bedrich
    Let Us Join In Celebration From "The Bartered Bride"

  Verdi, Giuseppe
    Chorus Of The Hebrew Slaves From "Nabucco"

POISOT
  Rameau, Jean-Philippe
    En Ce Doux Asile

POORMAN, SONJA
  Martin, Joseph M.
    Day By Day

PORTERFIELD, SHERRI
  Brahms, Johannes
    Wiegenlied

  Jingle Bells Festivo

  Winter Wonderland

POSER, HANS
  Rathgeber, Valentin
    Augsburger Tafelconfect.Das

PRENTICE, FRED
  Songs My Father Sang With Friends

PRICE
  Berlin
    I Love A Piano

  Besig
    Regards To Broadway!

PRINTZ, BRAD
  Foster, Stephen Collins
    Oh! Susanna!

  Hills Of Glenshee

PUGH, DAVID
  Christmas Time Is Here

  Heart Of A Hero

  Old Man's Back In Town, The

RALPH
  Ritchie, Jean
    Let The Sun Shine Down On Me

RAMSETH HOILAND, MELINDA
  Ramseth, Betty Ann
    Slumbertown

RASI, F.
  Madrigali Di Diversi Autori

RAUGEL
  Le Blanc, Didier
    O Doux Baisers Colombin
    On Peut Feindre Par Le Cizeau
    Pour Avoir Ma Fin Assurée
    Quand J'esprouve En Aimant La Rigueur D'une Dame
    Si Tost Que Vostre Oeil M'eut Blessé

## ARRANGER INDEX

RAUGEL (cont'd.)
   Maillard, René
     Amours Perdit Les Traict Qu'il Me Tira

READ
  That Yonge Child

READ, PAUL
  Loesser, Frank
    I've Never Been In Love Before

RENTZ
  At The Foot Of Yonder Mountain

RICE, MARTIN
  Ageless Admonitions

  Schubert, Franz (Peter)
    Drinking Song From The 14th Century

RICE, MARTIN R.
  Hiding In The Foggy Dew

RILLÉ, DE
  Rameau, Jean-Philippe
    Hymne À La Nuit

RINGWALD
  Three American Classics

RISCHE, QUIRIN
  Lincke, Paul
    Berliner Luft
    Schenk Mir Doch Ein Kleines Bisschen Liebe

ROBERT LUCAS DE PEARSALL
  Adieu! My Native Shore

ROBINSON
  Morley, Thomas
    Sing We And Chant It

  Purcell, Henry
    In These Delightful Pleasant Groves

ROBINSON, RUSS
  Mancini, Henry
    Days Of Wine And Roses

RODGERS, THOMAS
  Casey
    Drill Ye Tarriers, Drill

ROFF, J.
  Bach, Johann Sebastian
    Magnolia Petals

  Music Alone Shall Live

ROGALSKI
  Monk, Thelonius
    You Need Love

ROSANDER, CHRISTINE
  Inch Worm

  Use All Of Your Senses

RUBTSOV, F.
  Brooms

RUGGERI
  Froberger, Johann Jakob
    Deux Motets

RUNSWICK
  Gospel Christmas, A

RUSSO, ANTONIO
  Canciones Populares De Todo El Mundo Vol.I

  Canciones Populares De Todo El Mundo Vol.II

SÄDLER, ARTHUR
  Zugvögel (Heft 1)

  Zugvögel (Heft 2)

  Zugvögel (Heft 3)

  Zugvögel (Heft 4)

SAUNDERS
  Gershwin, George
    Fascinating Rhythm
    I Got Rhythm
    Love Walked Right In

SCHMID
  Hiller
    Sonntag

SCHMID, ANTON
  Daham In Mein Häuslan

  Neue Kärntnerlieder Für Gemischten Chor

  Neue Kärntnerlieder Für Männerchor

SCHMID, W.
  Schmid, A.
    Helle Grühling, Der

  Strauss, J.
    Wiener-Walzer

SCHMUTTE, PETE
  Angels Among Us

  Anything Goes!

  Anytime You Need A Friend

  Best Loved Songs Of Rodgers And Hart

  Best Of Garth Brooks:, The

  Best Of My Love

  Bock, Jerry
    Grand Knowing You

  City Scapes

  Collins, Phil
    Hero

  Come See About Me

  Danzig, Evelyn
    Scarlett Ribbons (For Her Hair)

  Everyday People

  Fisher, Mark
    When Your Smiling (The Whole World Smiles With You)

  Gershwin, George
    Someone To Watch Over Me

  Hayes, Isaac
    Soul Man

  I Will Always Love You

  Jackson, Michael
    Will You Be There

  Jam Up!

  Manhattan Melodies

  Most Beautiful Girl In The World, The

  My Guy

  Oh Happy Day

  Porter, Cole
    Night And Day

  Rhythm Escapades

  Rockin' Around The Christmas Tree

  Rusciano, C.D.
    Song For You, A

  Santa's A-Comin'

  Scarborough Fair

  Sleigh Bells!

  This Is It!

  Whatever You Imagine

  Winter's Wonderland

  Wishing You A Merry Christmas

SCHRADE
  Landini, Francesco
    Complete Works

  Machaut, Guillaume de
    Complete Works

  Roman De Fauvel, Le

  Vitry, Philippe de
    Complete Works

SCHRADE, HARRISON, VON FISCHER, BENT
  Polyphonic Music Of The Fourteenth Century

SCHRADER
  Crouch
    Soon And Very Soon

SCHRAM
  All Through The Night

SCHRAM, RUTH
  Capehart, Jerry
    Turn Around, Look At Me

  Moment To Moment

  Movie Magic

SCHRAM, RUTH ELAINE
  Christmas Traditions: A Revue

SHAW
  Calvary

  Carol Of The Birds

  Costeley, Guillaume
    Allon Gay Bergeres

  Hacia Belen Va Un Borrico

  If I Got My Ticket, Can I Ride?

  O Tannenbaum

SHAW AND AVERRE
  Fum Fum Fum

SHAW AND PARKER
  Boar's Head Carol

  Cherry Tree Carol

  Good King Wenceslas

  Holly And The Ivy

  I Saw Three Ships

  Lay Down Your Staffs

  March Of The Kings

  O Sons And Daughters

  Susanni

  'Tis Finished

SHAW, KIRBY
  Fly Me To The Moon

SHAW-PARKER
  Down By The Sally Gardens

  Good-Bye, Fare Ye Well

  Loch Lomond

  Tom's Gone To Hilo

  Whup! Jamboree

SHEEHAN, RAY
  Golson, Benny
    I Remember Cliffor

  Sondheim, Stephen Joshua
    Send In The Clowns

SHUR
  Ding Dong! Merrily On High

  Masters In This Hall

SHUR, LAURA
  John Henry

  Wee Drappie O't, A

SIMMS
  Kumbayah

SKÖLD
  Bellman, Carl Michael
    Träd Fram Du Nattens Gud

  Schumann, Robert (Alexander)
    Om Slaraffenland

SMITH, GREGG
  Drunken Sailor, The

  Gibbons, Orlando
    Silver Swan, The

  Lieben Ringt Gross Freud, Das

  Morgan, J.
    Three Justin Morgan Choruses

  Now I Walk In Beauty

  O Jeanie, There's Naething To Fear Ye

  O Tannebaum

  O Tannenbaum

  Parry, [Sir] Charles Hubert Hastings
    Jerusalem

  Riqui, Riqui . Riquirrán

SMITH SINGERS, GREGG
  Multiple Echoes

SNAPP, DOUG
  Harmon, John
    Harvest

SNYDER
  All My Trials
SNYDER, AUDREY
  Frisch, Albert T.
    Two Different Worlds
  Have Yourself A Merry Little Christmas
  My Unknown Someone
  Once Upon A Time
  Over The Raionbow
  Rodgers, Richard
    Bewitched
  Swing Low!
  Trolley Song, The
SOWASH, RICK
  Elliot, Alonzo
    Hiker's Prayer (There's A Long, Long Trail)
SPECHT
  She's Like The Swallow
SPERBER, STANLEY
  Rebbe,Der
SPEVACEK, LINDA
  David
    What The World Needs Now Is Love
  Handy
    St. Louis Blues
  International Carols, Set 1
STEEL, DAVID WARREN
  Jenks, Stephen
    Complete Works Of Steven Jenks
STEFFEN
  Ries, Hubert
    Sonnenwende
    Volksweise
STERN, HERMANN
  Lasset Uns Singen
STOCKER, D.
  Blow Ye Winds
  Single Girl
STÖLLINGER, HEIDE
  Sillehofer Liederbuch
STRAND, MICHAEL
  Broberg, Robert Karl Oskar
    Beach Party
    Tre Låtar Till
STREINER, HANS
  A Liadle Macht Das Herzle Weit
  A Windschiefes Keuschle
  Båld Scheint A Liacht Von Dar Heah
  Durchn Wintawald Geahn
  Funken Lebensfreude, Einen
  Hätt I Di Nit Ba Mir
  He, Karntna, Geh Leich Ma Dei Liad
  Kleines Land, Ein Schönes Land,Ein
  Lei Liabm, Lei Liabm, Wia A Wind Umaflieagn ...
  Liandlan Sing Ma Überåll
  Untarn Bam Bin I Gsessn
  Vargeltsgott Fürs Guatsein
  Wånn Dås Herzle Schnell Pumpart
STROMMEN
  Sainte-Marie, Buffy
    Up Where We Belong
STROMMEN, CARL
  Afanasieff, Walter
    Hero
  Arlen, Harold
    It's Only A Paper Moon
  Brooks, Garth
    River,The
  Carmichael, Hoagy
    Star Dust
  Garner, Erroll
    Misty

STROMMEN, CARL (cont'd.)
  Gershwin, George
    Embraceable You
    Oh, Lady Be Good!
  Henderson
    Twelve Days Of Christmas
  Hupfeld, Herman
    When Yuba Plays The Rumba On The Tuba
  I Swear
  Jackson, Michael
    Heal The World
  Moon Magic
  Shearing, George Albert
    Lullaby Of Birdland
STUREBORG, HELENE
  Hammarström, Hugo
    Lucia Och Staffan
    Sankta Lucia
STURM, FRED
  If I Only Had A Brain
SUND, ROBERT
  Pim-Pim
    Dalpolska
  Sjöberg, Birger
    Aftontankar Vid Fridas Ruta
SVENSON, ANITA
  Taube, Evert
    Ingrid Dardels Polska
SVESHNIKOV, A.
  Brightly Shines The Moon
SWAIN, YERN
  Way We Were,The
SWINGLE, WARD
  Albéniz, Isaac
    Grana
    Sevilla
    Tango In D Major
    Zortzico
  Anonymous
    Amour De Moi,L'
    Audete, Gaudete
    Cargado De Tantos Males
    Country Dances
    De Punta Y Taco
    El Paisanito
    Music History 101
    Romanza Española
    Saints Fugue
    Suite Québecoise
  Bach, Carl Philipp Emanuel
    Solfeggietto
  Bach, Johann Sebastian
    Aria
    Badinerie
    Bourree
    Canon
    Chorale Prelude
    Fugue In C Minor
    Fugue In D Major
    Fugue In D Minor
    Gigue
    Invention In C Major
    Largo
    Organ Fugue BWV 578
    Preambule
    Prelude In C Major
    Prelude In F Minor
    Prelude No. 9
    Prelude No. 19
    Prelude No. 22
    Prelude No. 24
    Sinfonia
  Bach, Wilhelm Friedemann
    Fruehling,Der
  Beethoven, Ludwig van
    Allegro
    Scherzo
  Beiderbecke
    In A Mist
  Bellman, Carl Michael
    Bellman Suite,A
  Brubeck, David (Dave) Warren
    Blue Rondo A La Turk
  Byrd, William
    Though Amaryllis Dance
  Carmichael, Hoagy
    Up A Lazy River

SWINGLE, WARD (cont'd.)
  Couperin, François (le Grand)
    Couperin,La
  Daquin, Louis-Claude
    Rondo "Le Coucou"
  Debussy, Claude
    Claire De Lune
  Dowland
    Come Again
  Ehrenborg
    Nu Tändas Tusen Juleljus
  Encina, Juan del
    Mas Vale Trocar
  Gascongne, Mathieu
    Je Ne Saurais Chanter Ni Rire
  Gibbons
    Silver Swan,The
  Granados, Enrique
    Andaluza
    Rondalla Aragonesa
  Gruber
    Swingle Bells VII
  Handel, George Frideric
    Air
    Allegro
  Hassler, Hans Leo
    Mein Lieb Will Mit Mir Kriegen
  Henry VIII, King of England
    Agincourt Song,The
    Pastime With Good Company
  Hopkins
    Swingle Bells IX
  Jones
    Farewell, Dear Love
    Sing Us
  Joplin
    Entertainer,The
    Heliotrope Bouquet
    Hotshot
    Mr. Superman
    Satchmo
    Wanderer,The
    Weeping Willow
  Kern, Jerome
    All The Things You Are
  Lassus, Roland de (Orlandus)
    Bon Jour, Mon Coeur
  Lejeune
    Revecy Venir Du Printemps
  Lennon, John
    When I'm 64
  Marcello, Benedetto
    Presto
  Mendelssohn-Bartholdy, Felix
    Andante
    Spinner,The
  Mouton, Charles
    Marche De Limoges, Le
  Mozart, Wolfgang Amadeus
    Allegretto
    Allegro
    Allegro
    Allegro
    Andante
    Fugue
    Menuetto
    Overture To The Marriage Of Figaro
    Romance
    Rondo
    Variations On "Ah! Vous Dirai-Je, Maman"
  Muffat, Georg
    Fugue In D Minor
  Olman
    Oh, Johnny, Oh!
  Ortega
    Pues Que Me Tienes, Miguel
  Othmayr, Kaspar
    Mir Ist Ein Feins Brauns Maidelein
  Passereau
    Il Est Bel Et Bon
  Porter, Cole
    It's All Right With Me

# ARRANGER INDEX

SWINGLE, WARD (cont'd.)
   Rimsky-Korsakov, Nikolai
     Flight Of The Bumble-Bee

   Sarasate, Pablo de
     Romanza Andaluza

   Shaw
     Back Bay Shuffle

   Soler, [Padre] Antonio
     Sonata In D Major

   Swedish Carol Medley

   Swingle Bells I

   Swingle Bells II

   Swingle Bells III

   Swingle Bells IV

   Swingle Bells V

   Swingle Bells VI

   Swingle Bells VIII

   Swingle Bells X

   Telemann, Georg Philipp
     Concerto A Six
     Gugue
     Largo
     Presto

   Tomkins, T.
     O Let Me Live For True Love

   Torme
     Christmas Song,The

   Visit From St. Nicholas,A

TAN
   Chan Mali Chan

   Lenggang Kangkong

   Suriram

TAYLOR, PETER
   Only You

   Zaret, Hy
     Unchained Melody

TELFER
   I'se The D'y

   Petty Harbour Bait Skiff, The

TERRI
   He's Gone Away

THE REAL GROUP
   Ellington, Edward Kennedy (Duke)
     Come Sunday

   Everybody Needs Somebody

   I'm With You

THOMAS
   Light One Little Candle

THOMAS, BERNARD
   Three Parisian Chansons

THOMPSON
   Purcell, Henry
     In These Delightful Pleasant Groves

THOMPSON, DICK
   Leontovich, M.
     Bell Carol

THOMPSON, MILLARD
   Skye Boat Song

TILLEY, A.
   Down By The Fair River

   Grandma's Advice

TINI, A.A.
   Brown, Nacio Herb
     Singin' In The Rain

TORRANCE, W.P.
   Gallant Weaver,The

TREECE, ROGER
   Yatra Ta

TREECE, ROGER-CHILDS, BILLY
   Yesterdays

UGLAND, JOHAN VAREN
   Bach, Johann Sebastian
     Bourree

UMMEL
   Zingg
     Schmiede-Lied: "I Isch Nümme Die Zyt"

VACCARO,J.
   Jessel, Leon
     Parade Of The Wooden Soldiers

VEA, KETIL
   Lord Randall

VETTORI, R.
   Contino, Giovanni
     Madrigali A Cinque Voci - Libro I

VINCENT, CARLOS
   Morales
     De Mi Esperanza

VIOQUE-LORENZO
   Suite En Langues D'oc

VOGEL, R.
   Crab,The

   Owl,The

VOLLE, BJARNE
   Hambe, Alf
     Kajsas Udde

   Skaarset, Ivar
     Mazurka

   Udsigter Fra Ulrikken

VOLLE, SVERRE
   Den Fyrste Song

   Grieg, Edvard Hagerup
     Fola, Fola Blakken

   Hauger, Kristian
     So Ro, Perlemor

   Volle, Martin
     Songen Er Eit Band Som Bind

WAGNER
   Berlin
     Alexander's Ragtime Band

WALTER, LANA
   Lawrence, Stephen L.
     Song For Mother Earth

   Mangwani Mpulele

WARRELL, ARTHUR
   Merry Christmas,A

WEBB, MERRILEE
   Streets Of Laredo

   Turtle Dove

WEBER
   Mozart, Wolfgang Amadeus
     Bald Prangt, Den Morgen Zu Verkünden Aus "Die Zauberflöte"
     Im Früling ("Unsre Wiesen Grünen Wieder"), Kv Anh.262

WELKER
   Grün War Dein Sommer-Kleid

   Katjuscha

WETHERELL,E.
   Along The Shore

WHITFIELD, JOHN B.R.
   Treble And Bass Song Book (Book 1)

   Treble And Bass Song Book (Book 2)

WIESENBERG, MENACHEM
   En Gedi

   Once Upon A Time

   Take Me Under Your Wing

WILBY, PHILIP
   Marianne

   Three North Country Folk Songs

WILLIAM BAUSANO
   Sing We, Dance We On The Green

WILLIAMS
   Patriotic Festival, A

WILSON
   Nystrom, Hampus Huldt
     As The Deer

WULZ, HELMUT
   Alt, Aber Guat

   Anderluh Volksliederbuch,Das

   Bäumlein Stand Im Tiefen Tal, Ein

WULZ, HELMUT (cont'd.)
   Land Und Leut Im Lied

ZADOFF, NESTOR
   Musica Popular Argentina (Volumen I)

   Musica Popular Argentina (Volumen II)

ZECCA
   Anonymous
     E L'üselin Del Bosch... Andremo A Strapà I Selari, L'

ZEGREE
   Strayhorn
     Take The A Train

ZOTTO, G.
   Anonymous
     Cantar Veneto

ZYTOWSKI
   Come, All You Fair And Tender Ladies

# Publisher Directory

The list of publishers which follows contains the code assigned for each publisher, the name and address of the publisher, and U.S. agents who distribute the publications. This is the master list for the Music-in-Print series and represents all publishers who have submitted information for inclusion in the series. Therefore, all of the publishers do not necessarily occur in the present volume.

| Code | Publisher | U.S. Agent |
|---|---|---|
| A COEUR JOIE | Éditions A Coeur Joie<br>Les Passerelles, BP 9151<br>24 avenue Joannés Masset<br>F-69263 Lyon cédex 09<br>France | |
| A MOLL DUR | A Moll Dur Publishing House | |
| A-R ED | A-R Editions, Inc.<br>801 Deming Way<br>Madison, WI 53717 | |
| AAP | Edition AAP (Audio Attic Productions)<br>Aas-Wangsvei 8<br>N-1600 Fredrikstad<br>Norway | |
| ABC | ABC Music Co. | BOURNE |
| ABER.GRP. | The Aberbach Group<br>988 Madison Avenue<br>New York, NY 10021 | |
| ABERDEEN | Aberdeen Music, Inc.<br>170 N.E. 33rd Street<br>Fort Lauderdale, FL 33334 | PLYMOUTH |
| ABINGDON | Abingdon Press<br>P.O. Box 801<br>Nashville, TN 37202 | |
| ABRSM | Associated Board of the Royal<br>   Schools of Music<br>14 Bedford Square<br>London WC1B 3JG<br>England | PRESSER |
| ACADEM | Academia Music Ltd.<br>16-5, Hongo 3-Chome<br>Bunkyo-ku<br>Tokyo, 113<br>Japan | KALMUS,A |
| ACCURA | Accura Music<br>P.O. Box 4260<br>Athens, OH 45701-4260 | |
| ACORD | Edizioni Accordo | CURCI |
| ACSB | Antigua Casa Sherry-Brener, Ltd.<br>   of Madrid<br>3145 West 63rd Street<br>Chicago, IL 60629 | |
| ADAM | D. Adams Music<br>P.O. Box 8371<br>Asheville, NC 28814 | |
| ADD.PRESS | Addington Press | ROYAL |
| ADD.-WESLEY | Addison-Wesley Publishing Co., Inc.<br>2725 Sand Hill Road<br>Menlo Park, CA 94025 | |
| AEOLUS | Aeolus Publishing Co.<br>60 Park Terrace West<br>New York, NY 10034 | |
| AGAPE | Agape | HOPE |
| AHLINS | Ahlins Musikförlag<br>Box 26072<br>S-100 41 Stockholm<br>Sweden | |
| AHN | Ahn & Simrock<br>Sonnenstraße 19<br>D-8 München<br>Germany | |
| AKADDV | Akademiska Druck- und<br>   Verlagsanstalt<br>Schönaugasse 6<br>A-8010 Graz<br>Austria | |
| AKADEM | Akademiska Musikförlaget<br>Sirkkalagatan 7 B 41<br>SF-20500 Abo 50<br>Finland | |
| ALBERSEN | Muziekhandel Albersen & Co.<br>Groot Hertoginnelaan 182<br>NL-2517 EV Den Haag<br>Netherlands | DONEMUS |
| ALBERT | J. Albert & Son Pty. Ltd.<br>139 King Street<br>Sydney 2000, N.S.W.<br>Australia<br><br>J. Albert & Son - U.S.A.<br>1619 Broadway<br>New York, NY 10019 | |
| ALCOVE | Alcove Music | WESTERN |
| ALEX.HSE. | Alexandria House<br>211 Whitsett Road<br>Nashville, TN 37210 | |
| ALFRED | Alfred Publishing Co.<br>16380 Roscoe Blvd.<br>P.O. Box 10003<br>Van Nuys, CA 91410-0003 | |
| ALKOR | Alkor Edition | FOR.MUS.DIST |
| ALLAIRE | Allaire Music Publications<br>93 Gooseneck Point Road<br>Oceanport, NJ 07757 | |

| Code | Publisher | U.S. Agent |
|---|---|---|
| ALLANS | Allans Music Australia Ltd.<br>P.O. Box 4072<br>Richmond East<br>Victoria 3121<br>Australia | PRESSER |
| ALLEN | William Allen Music, Inc.<br>P.O. Box 790<br>Newington, VA 22122-0790 | |
| ALLOWAY | Alloway Publications<br>P.O.Box 25<br>Santa Monica, CA 90406 | |
| ALMITRA | Almitra | KENDOR |
| ALMO | Almo Publications | CPP-BEL |
| ALPEG | Alpeg | PETERS |
| ALPHENAAR | W. Alphenaar<br>Kruisweg 47-49<br>NL-2011 LA Haarlem<br>Netherlands | |
| ALPUERTO | Editorial Alpuerto<br>Caños del Peral 7<br>28013 Madrid<br>Spain | |
| ALSBACH | G. Alsbach & Co.<br>P.O. Box 338<br>NL-1400 AH Bussum<br>Netherlands | |
| ALSBACH&D | Alsbach & Doyer | |
| AM.COMP.ALL. | American Composers Alliance<br>170 West 74th Street<br>New York, NY 10023 | |
| AM. GEHR | American Guild of English Handbell<br>Ringers, Inc. | LORENZ |
| AM.INST.MUS. | American Institute of Musicology | FOSTER |
| AM.MUS.ED. | American Music Edition<br>263 East Seventh Street<br>New York, NY 10009 | PRESSER<br>(partial) |
| AMADEUS | Amadeus Verlag<br>Bernhard Päuler<br>Am Iberghang 16<br>CH-8405 Winterthur<br>Switzerland | FOR.MUS.DIST. |
| | American String Teachers Association<br>see ASTA | |
| AMICI | Gli Amici della Musica da Camera<br>Via Bocca di Leone 25<br>Roma<br>Italy | |
| AMP | Associated Music Publishers | LEONARD-US<br>(sales)<br>SCHIRM.G<br>(rental) |
| AMPHION | Éditions Amphion<br>12, rue Rougement<br>F-75009 Paris<br>France | |
| AMS PRESS | AMS Press, Inc.<br>56 East 13th Street<br>New York, NY 10003 | |
| AMSCO | AMSCO Music Publishing Co. | MUSIC |
| AMSI | Art Masters Studios, Inc.<br>1599 SE 8th Street<br>Minneapolis, MN 55414 | |
| ANDEL | Edition Andel<br>Madeliefjeslaan, 26<br>B-8400 Oostende<br>Belgium | |
| ANDERSONS | Anderssons Musikförlag<br>Sodra Forstadsgatan 6<br>Box 17018<br>S-200 10 Malmö<br>Sweden | |
| ANDPR | Andrea Press<br>75 Travis Road<br>Holliston, MA 01746 | |
| ANDRE | Johann André Musikverlag<br>Frankfurterstraße 28<br>Postfach 141<br>D-6050 Offenbach-am-Main<br>Germany | |
| | Andrea Press<br>see ANDPR | |
| ANDREU | Andreu Marc Publications<br>611 Broadway, Suite 615<br>New York, NY 10012 | MUSIC SC. |
| ANDREW | Andrew's Music<br>4830 South Dakota Avenue, N.E.<br>Washington, D.C. 20017 | |
| ANERCA | Anerca Music<br>35 St. Andrew's Garden<br>Toronto, Ontario M4W 2C9<br>Canada | |
| ANFOR | Anfor Music Publishers<br>(Div. of Terminal Music Supply)<br>1619 East Third Street<br>Brooklyn, NY 11230 | MAGNA D |
| ANGLO | Anglo-American Music Publishers<br>4 Kendall Avenue<br>Sanderstead<br>Surrey, CR2 0NH<br>England | |
| ANTARA | Antara Music Group<br>248 Second Avenue South<br>Franklin, TN 37064 | |
| ANTICO | Antico Edition<br>P.O. Box 1, Moretonhampstead<br>Newton Abbot<br>Devon TQ13 8UA<br>England | BOSTON EMC |

## PUBLISHER DIRECTORY

| Code | Publisher | U.S. Agent |
|---|---|---|
| APM | Artist Production & Management | VIERT |
| APNM | Association for Promotion of New Music<br>2002 Central Avenue<br>Ship Bottom, NJ 08008 | |
| APOGEE | Apogee Press | WORLD |
| APOLLO | Apollo-Verlag Paul Lincke<br>Weihergarten 5<br>6500 Mainz<br>Germany | SCHOTT |
| ARCADIA | Arcadia Music Publishing Co., Ltd.<br>P.O. Box 1<br>Rickmansworth<br>Herts WD3 3AZ<br>England | |
| ARCANA | Arcana Editions<br>Indian River<br>Ontario K0L 2B0<br>Canada | |
| ARCO | Arco Music Publishers | WESTERN |
| ARGM | Editorial Argentina de Musica &<br>  Editorial Saraceno<br>Buenos Aires<br>Argentina | PEER |
| ARIAD | Ariadne Buch- und Musikverlag<br>Schottenfeldgasse 45<br>A-1070 Wien<br>Austria | |
| ARION | Coleccion Arion | MEXICANS |
| ARION PUB | Arion Publications, Inc.<br>4964 Kathleen Avenue<br>Castro Valley, CA 94546 | |
| ARISTA | Arista Music Co.<br>8370 Wilshire Blvd<br>Beverly Hills, CA 90211 | CPP-BEL |
| ARNOLD | Edward Arnold Series | NOVELLO |
| ARS FEM | Ars Femina Ensemble<br>P.O. Box 7692<br>Louisville, KY 40257 | |
| ARS NOVA | Ars Nova Publications<br>121 Washington<br>San Diego, CA 92103 | PRESSER |
| ARS POLONA | Ars Polona<br>Krakowskie Przedmies cie 7<br>Skrytka pocztowa 1001<br>PL-00-950 Warszawa<br>Poland | |
| ARS VIVA | Ars Viva Verlag<br>Weihergarten<br>D-6500 Mainz 1<br>Germany | EUR.AM.MUS |
| ARSIS | Arsis Press<br>1719 Bay Street SE<br>Washington D.C. 20003 | PLYMOUTH |

| Code | Publisher | U.S. Agent |
|---|---|---|
| ARTHUR | J. Arthur Music<br>The University Music House<br>4290 North High Street<br>Columbus, OH 43214 | |
| ARTIA | Artia Prag<br>Ve Smeckkách 30<br>Praha 2<br>Czech Republic | |
| | Artist Production & Management<br>  see APM | |
| ARTRANSA | Artransa Music | WESTERN |
| ASCHERBERG | Ascherberg, Hopwood & Crew Ltd.<br>50 New Bond Street<br>London W1A 2BR<br>England | |
| ASHBOURN | Ashbourne Publications<br>425 Ashbourne Road<br>Elkins Park, PA 19117 | |
| ASHDOWN | Edwin Ashdown Ltd. | BRODT |
| ASHLEY | Ashley Publications, Inc.<br>P.O. Box 337<br>Hasbrouck Heights, NJ 07604 | |
| ASPEN | Aspen Grove Music<br>P.O. Box 977<br>North Hollywood, CA 91603 | |
| ASSMANN | Hermann Assmann, Musikverlag<br>Franz-Werfel-Straße 36<br>D-60431 Frankfurt<br>Germany | |
| | Associated Board of the Royal Schools<br>  of Music<br>  see ABRSM | |
| | Associated Music Publishers<br>  see AMP | |
| | Association for Promotion of New<br>  Music<br>  see APNM | |
| ASTA | American String Teachers Association<br>3839 Riley Avenue<br>Terre Haute, IN 47803 | PRESSER |
| ATV | ATV Music Publications<br>6255 Sunset Boulevard<br>Hollywood, CA 90028 | CHERRY |
| | Audio Attic Productions<br>  see AAP | |
| AUG-FOR | Augsburg Fortress Publishers<br>426 South Fifth Street<br>P.O. Box 1209<br>Minneapolis, MN 55440 | |
| AULOS | Aulos Music Publishers<br>P.O. Box 54<br>Montgomery, NY 12549 | |
| AUREOLE | Aureole Editions | PARACLETE |

| Code | Publisher | U.S. Agent |
|---|---|---|
| AUTOGR | Autographus Musicus<br>Ardalavägen 158<br>S-124 32 Bandhagen<br>Sweden | |
| AUTRY | Gene Autry's Publishing Companies | CPP-BEL |
| AVANT | Avant Music | WESTERN |
| BAGGE | Jacob Bagge | STIM |
| BANK | Annie Bank Muziek<br>P.O. Box 347<br>1180 AH Amstelveen<br>Netherlands | HARMONIA |
| BANKS | Banks Music Publications<br>The Old Forge<br>Sand Hutton<br>York YO4 1LB<br>England | INTRADA |
| BARDIC | Bardic Edition<br>6 Fairfax Crescent, Aylesbury<br>Buckhamshire, HP20 2ES<br>England | PRESSER |
| BÄREN. | Bärenreiter Verlag<br>Heinrich Schütz Allee 31-37<br>Postfach 100329<br>D-3500 Kassel-Wilhelmshöhe<br>Germany | FOR.MUS.DIST. |
| BARNHS | C.L. Barnhouse<br>205 Cowan Avenue West<br>P.O. Box 680<br>Oskaloosa, IA 52577 | |
| BARON,M | M. Baron Co.<br>P.O. Box 149<br>Oyster Bay, NY 11771 | |
| BARRY-ARG | Barry & Cia<br>Srl Lavalle 1145 4A<br>1048 Buenos Aires<br>Argentina | BOOSEY |
| BARTA | Barta Music Company | JERONA |
| BASART | Les Éditions Internationales Basart | GENERAL |
| BASEL | Musik-Akademie der Stadt Basel<br>Leonhardsstraße 6<br>CH-4051 Basel<br>Switzerland | |
| BAUER | Georg Bauer Musikverlag<br>Luisenstraße 47-49<br>Postfach 1467<br>D-7500 Karlsruhe<br>Germany | |
| BAVTON | Bavariaton-Verlag<br>München<br>Germany | ORLANDO |
| | Mel Bay Publications<br>see MEL BAY | |
| BEACON HILL | Beacon Hill Music | LILLENAS |
| BEAUDN | Stuart D. Beaudoin<br>629 Queen Street<br>New Market, Ontario<br>Canada L3Y 2J1 | |
| BEAUT | Beautiful Star Publishing, Inc.<br>4040 West 70th Street<br>Minneapolis, MN 55435 | |
| BECKEN | Beckenhorst Press<br>P.O. Box 14273<br>Columbus, OH 43214 | |
| BEECHWD | Beechwood Music Corporation<br>1750 Vine Street<br>Hollywood, CA 90028 | WARNER |
| BEEK | Beekman Music, Inc. | PRESSER |
| BEIAARD | Beiaard School<br>Belgium | |
| BELAIEFF | M.P. Belaieff<br>Kennedyallee 101<br>D-6000 Frankfurt-am-Main 70<br>Germany | PETERS |
| | Centre Belge de Documentation<br>  Musicale<br>  see CBDM | |
| BELLA | Bella Roma Music<br>1442A Walnut Street<br>Suite 197<br>Berkeley, CA 94709 | |
| BELMONT | Belmont Music Publishers<br>P.O. Box 231<br>Pacific Palisades, CA 90272 | |
| BELWIN | Belwin-Mills Publishing Corp.<br>15800 N.W. 48th Avenue<br>P.O. Box 4340<br>Miami, FL 33014 | CPP-BEL<br>PRESSER<br>(rental) |
| BENJ | Anton J. Benjamin<br>Werderstraße 44<br>Postfach 2561<br>D-2000 Hamburg 13<br>Germany | PRESSER |
| BENNY | Claude Benny Press<br>1401 1/2 State Street<br>Emporia, KS 66801 | |
| BENSON | John T. Benson<br>365 Great Circle Road<br>Nashville, TN 37228-1703 | |
| BERANDOL | Berandol Music Ltd.<br>110A Sackville Street<br>Toronto, Ontario M5A 3E7<br>Canada | |
| BERBEN | Edizioni Musicali Berben<br>Via Redipuglia 65<br>I-60122 Ancona<br>Italy | PRESSER |
| BERGMANS | W. Bergmans | BANK |
| BERKLEE | Berklee Press Publications | LEONARD-US |

## PUBLISHER DIRECTORY

| Code | Publisher | U.S. Agent |
|---|---|---|
| BERLIN | Irving Berlin Music Corp.<br>29 W. 46 Street<br>New York, NY 10036 | |
| BERNOUILLI | Ed. Bernouilli | DONEMUS |
| BESSEL | Éditions Bessel & Cie | BREITKOPF-W |
| BEUSCH | Éditions Paul Beuscher Arpège<br>29, Boulevard Beaumarchais<br>F-75180 Paris<br>France | |
| BEZIGE BIJ | De Bezige Bij | DONEMUS |
| BIB C | Biblioteca de Catalunya<br>Hospital, 56<br>08001 Barcelona<br>Spain | |
| BIELER | Edmund Bieler Musikverlag<br>Thürmchenswall 72<br>D-5000 Köln 1<br>Germany | |
| BIG BELL | Big Bells, Inc.<br>33 Hovey Avenue<br>Trenton, NJ 08610 | |
| BIG3 | Big Three Music Corp | CPP-BEL |
| BILLAUDOT | Éditions Billaudot<br>14, rue de l'Echiquier<br>F-75010 Paris<br>France | PRESSER |
| BIRCH | Robert Fairfax Birch | PRESSER |
| BIRNBACH | Richard Birnbach Musikverlag<br>Aubinger Straße 9<br>D-8032 Lochheim vor München<br>Germany | |
| BIZET | Bizet Productions and Publications | PRESSER |
| BMG RICORDI | BMG Ricordi S.P.A.<br>Via Salamone, 77<br>I-20138 Milano<br>Italy | |
| BMI | Broadcast Music, Inc.<br>320 West 57th Street<br>New York, NY 10019 | |
| | Boccaccini and Spada Editori<br>see BSE | |
| BOCK | Fred Bock Music Co.<br>P.O. Box 333<br>Tarzana, CA 91356 | ANTARA |
| BODEN | Bodensee-Edition<br>Fabrikstrasse 16A<br>D-78224 Singen<br>Germany | |
| BODENS | Edition Ernst Fr. W. Bodensohn<br>Dr. Rumpfweg 1<br>D-7570 Baden-Baden 21<br>Germany<br>see also ERST | |
| BOEIJENGA | Boeijenga Muziekhandel<br>Kleinzand 89<br>NL-8601 BG Sneek<br>Netherlands | |
| BOELKE-BOM | Boelke-Bomart Music Publications | JERONA |
| BOETHIUS | Boethius Press<br>3 The Science Park<br>Aberystinyth<br>Dyfed SY23 3AH<br>Wales | |
| BOHM | Anton Böhm & Sohn<br>Postfach 110369<br>Lange Gasse 26<br>D-86028 Augsburg 11<br>Germany | |
| BOIL | Casa Editorial de Musica Boileau<br>Provenza, 287<br>08037 Barcelona<br>Spain | |
| BOIS | Bureau De Musique Mario Bois<br>19 Rue De Rocroy<br>F-75010 Paris<br>France | |
| BOMART | Bomart Music Publications | BOELKE-BOM |
| BONART | Bonart Publications | CAN.MUS.<br>CENT. |
| BONGIOVANNI | Francesco Bongiovanni<br>Via Rizzoli 28 E<br>I-40125 Bologna<br>Italy | |
| BOONIN | Joseph Boonin, Inc. | EUR.AM.MUS. |
| BOOSEY | Boosey & Hawkes Inc.<br>24 West 57th Street<br>New York, NY 10019-3977 | |
| | Boosey & Hawkes Rental Library<br>52 Cooper Square<br>New York, NY 10003-7102 | |
| BOOSEY-CAN | Boosey & Hawkes Ltd.<br>279 Yorkland Boulevard<br>Willowdale, Ontario M2J 1S7<br>Canada | BOOSEY |
| BOOSEY-ENG | Boosey & Hawkes Music Publishers Ltd.<br>295 Regent Street<br>London W1 R 8JH<br>England | BOOSEY |
| BORNEMANN | Éditions Bornemann<br>15 rue de Tournon<br>F-75006 Paris<br>France | KING,R<br>PRESSER |
| BOSSE | Gustav Bosse Verlag<br>Von der Tann Straße 38<br>Postfach 417<br>D-8400 Regensburg 1<br>Germany | EUR.AM.MUS. |
| BOSTON | Boston Music Co.<br>172 Tremont Street<br>Boston, MA 02111-1001 | |

# PUBLISHER DIRECTORY

| Code | Publisher | U.S. Agent |
|---|---|---|
| BOSTON EMC | Boston Early Music Center<br>see Early Music Shop of<br>New England | |
| BOSWORTH | Bosworth & Company, Ltd.<br>14-18 Heddon Street, Regent Street<br>London W1 R 8DP<br>England | BRODT |
| BOTE | Bote & Bock<br>Hardenbergstraße 9A<br>D-10623 Berlin<br>Germany | PRESSER |
| BOURNE | Bourne Co.<br>5 W. 37th Street<br>New York, NY 10018-6232 | |
| BOWDOIN | Bowdoin College Music Press<br>Department of Music<br>Bowdoin College<br>Brunswick, ME 04011 | |
| BOWM | Bowmaster Productions<br>3351 Thornwood Road<br>Sarasota, FL 33581 | |
| BRCONT.MUS. | British and Continental Music<br>Agencies Ltd. | EMI |
| BRADLEY | Bradley Publications<br>80 8th Avenue<br>New York, NY 10011 | CPP-BEL |
| BRANCH | Harold Branch Publishing, Inc.<br>95 Eads Street<br>West Babylon, NY 11704 | |
| BRANDEN | Branden Press, Inc.<br>17 Station Street<br>P.O. Box 843<br>Brookline Village, MA 02147 | |
| BRASS PRESS | The Brass Press<br>136 8th Avenue North<br>Nashville, TN 37203-3798 | |
| BRATFISCH | Musikverlag Georg Bratfisch<br>Hans-Herold-Str. 23<br>D-8650 Kulmbach<br>Germany | PRESSER |
| BRAUER | Les Éditions Musicales Herman Brauer<br>30, rue St. Christophe<br>B-1000 Bruxelles<br>Belgium | |
| BRAUN-PER | St. A. Braun-Peretti<br>Dreieck 16<br>Postfach 1309<br>5300 Bonn 1<br>Germany | |
| BRAVE | Brave New Music | SON-KEY |
| BREITKOPF-L | Breitkopf & Härtel (Leipzig) | |
| BREITKOPF-LN | Breitkopf & Härtel | |
| BREITKOPF-W | Breitkopf & Härtel<br>Walkmühlstraße 52<br>Postfach 1707<br>D-65195 Wiesbaden<br>Germany | SCHIRM.G<br>(rental) |

| Code | Publisher | U.S. Agent |
|---|---|---|
| BRENNAN | John Brennan Music Publisher<br>Positif Press Ltd.<br>130 Southfield Road<br>Oxford OX4 1PA<br>England | ORGAN LIT |
| BRENT | Michael Brent Publications, Inc.<br>P.O. Box 1186<br>Port Chester, NY 10573 | CHERRY |
| BRENTWOOD | Brentwood Publishing Group, Inc.<br>P.O. Box 19001<br>Brentwood, TN 37027 | |
| BRIDGE | Bridge Music Publishing Co.<br>1350 Villa Street<br>Mountain View, CA 94042 | |
| BRIGHT STAR | Bright Star Music Publications | WESTERN |
| | British and Continental Music Agencies<br>Ltd.<br>see BR.CONT.MUS. | |
| | Broadcast Music, Inc.<br>see BMI | |
| BROADMAN | Broadman Press<br>127 Ninth Avenue, North<br>Nashville, TN 37234 | |
| BRODT | Brodt Music Co.<br>P.O. Box 9345<br>Charlotte, NC 28299-9345 | |
| BROEKMANS | Broekmans & Van Poppel B.V.<br>van Baerlestraat 92-94<br>NL-1071 BB Amsterdam<br>Netherlands | |
| BROGNEAUX | Éditions Musicales Brogneaux<br>73, Avenue Paul Janson<br>B-1070 Bruxelles<br>Belgium | |
| BROOK | Brook Publishing Co.<br>4047 Meadowbrook Blvd.<br>University Heights, OH 44118-3836 | |
| BROUDE,A | Alexander Broude, Inc. | PLYMOUTH |
| BROUDE BR | Broude Brothers Ltd.<br>141 White Oaks Road<br>Williamstown, MA 01267<br><br>Broude Brothers Ltd.-Rental Dept.<br>170 Varick St.<br>New York, NY 10013 | |
| BROWN | Brown University Choral Series | BOOSEY |
| BROWN,R | Rayner Brown<br>2423 Panorama Terrace<br>Los Angeles, CA 90039 | WESTERN<br>COMP.LIB |
| BROWN,WC | William C. Brown Co.<br>2460 Kerper Boulevard<br>Dubuque, IA 52001 | |

| Code | Publisher | U.S. Agent |
|---|---|---|
| BRUCK | Musikverlag M. Bruckbauer<br>"Biblioteca de la Guitarra"<br>Postfach 18<br>D-7953 Bad Schussenried<br>Germany | |
| BRUCKNER | Bruckner Verlag<br>Austria | PETERS<br>(rental) |
| BRUZZI | Aldo Bruzzichelli, Editore<br>Borgo S. Frediano, 8<br>I-50124 Firenze<br>Italy | MARGUN |
| BSE | Boccaccini and Spada Editori<br>Via Francesco Duodo, 10<br>I-00136 Roma<br>Italy | PRESSER |
| BUBONIC | Bubonic Publishing Co.<br>706 Lincoln Avenue<br>St. Paul, MN 55105 | |
| BUDAPEST | Editio Musica Budapest (Kultura)<br>Vörösmarty tér 1<br>H-1051 Budapest<br>Hungary<br>   see also EMB | BOOSEY<br>PRESSER<br>(partial) |
| BUDDE | Rolf Budde Musikverlag<br>Hohenzollerndamm 54A<br>D-1000 Berlin 33<br>Germany | |
| BUGZY | Bugzy Bros. Vocal Athletics<br>P.O. Box 1900<br>Orem, UT 84059 | MUSICART |
| BUSCH | Hans Busch Musikförlag<br>Stubbstigen 3<br>S-18147 Lidingö<br>Sweden | |
| BUSCH,E | Ernst Busch Verlag<br>Schlossstrasse 43<br>D-7531 Neulingen-Bauschlott<br>Germany | |
| BUTZ | Dr. J. Butz Musikverlag<br>Postfach 3008<br>D-53739 Sankt Augustin<br>Germany | |
| CAILLARD | Edition Philippe Caillard<br>5 bis rue du Château-Fondu<br>78200 Fontenay-Mauvoisin<br>France | |
| CAILLET | Lucien Caillet | SOUTHERN |
| CAMBIATA | Cambiata Press<br>P.O. Box 1151<br>Conway, AR 72032 | |
| CAMBRIA | Cambria Records & Publishing<br>P.O. Box 374<br>Lomita, CA 90717 | |
| CAMBRIDGE | Cambridge University Press<br>The Edinburgh Building<br>Shaftesbury Road<br>Cambridge CB2 2RU<br>England | |
| CAMDEN | Camden Music<br>19a North Villas<br>Camden Square<br>London NW1 9BJ<br>England | PRESSER |
| CAMERICA | Camerica Music<br>535 Fifth Avenue, Penthouse<br>New York, NY 10017 | CPP-BEL |
| CAMPUS | Campus Publishers<br>713 Ellsworth Road West<br>Ann Arbor, MI 48104 | |
| CAN.MUS.CENT. | Canadian Music Centre<br>20 St. Joseph Street<br>Toronto, Ontario M4Y 1J9<br>Canada | |
| CAN.MUS.HER. | Canadian Musical Heritage Society<br>Patrimoine Musical Canadien<br>P.O. Box 262, Station A<br>Ottawa, Ontario K1N 8V2<br>Canada | |
| CANAAN | Canaanland Publications | WORD |
| CANT DO | Cantate Domino<br>Editions de musique<br>Rue du Sapin 2a<br>C.P. 156<br>2114 Fleurier<br>Switzerland | |
| CANTANDO | Cantando Forlag<br>Bj. Bjornsonsgt. 2 D<br>N-4021 Stavanger<br>Norway | |
| CANTORIS | Cantoris Music<br>P.O. Box 162004<br>Sacramento, CA 95816 | |
| CANYON | Canyon Press, Inc.<br>P.O. Box 447<br>Islamorada, FL 33036 | KERBY |
| CAPELLA | Capella Music, Inc. | BOURNE |
| CAPPR | Capital Press | PODIUM |
| CARABO | Carabo-Cone Method Foundation<br>1 Sherbrooke Road<br>Scarsdale, NY 10583 | |
| CARISCH | Carisch S.p.A.<br>   see Nuova Carisch | |
| CARLAN | Carlanita Music Co. | LEONARD-US<br>(sales)<br>SCHIRM.G<br>(rental) |
| CARLIN | Carlin Publications<br>P.O. Box 2289<br>Oakhurst, CA 93644 | |
| CARLTON | Carlton Musickverlag | BREITKOPF-W |
| CARUS | Carus-Verlag<br>Wannenstrasse 45<br>D-70199 Stuttgart<br>Germany | FOSTER |

| Code | Publisher | U.S. Agent |
|---|---|---|
| CATAL | Catalana D'Edicions Musicals<br>Laietana, 23 1r.-D<br>08003 Barcelona<br>Spain | |
| CATE | Catena Press<br>67 Marlborough Ave.<br>Glenfield, Auckland 1310<br>New Zealand | |
| CATHEDRAL | Cathedral Music<br>Maudlin House<br>Westhampnett<br>Chichester<br>West Sussex PO18 0PB<br>England | PAVAN |
| | Catholic Conference<br>see U.S. CATH | |
| CAVATA | Cavata Music Publishers, Inc. | PRESSER |
| CAVELIGHT | Cavelight Music<br>P.O. Box 85<br>Oxford, NJ 07863 | |
| CBC | Cundey Bettoney Co. | FISCHER,C |
| CBDM | CeBeDeM<br>Centre Belge de Documentation<br>  Musicale<br>rue d'Arlon 75-77<br>B-1040 Bruxelles<br>Belgium | |
| CCMP | Colorado College Music Press<br>14 E. Cache La Poudre<br>Colorado Springs, CO 80903 | |
| CEL | Celesta Publishing Co.<br>P.O. Box 560603, Kendall Branch<br>Miami, FL 33156 | |
| | Centre Belge de Documentation<br>  Musical<br>    see CBDM | |
| CDMC | Centre de Documentation de la<br>  Musique Contemporaine<br>225 Avenue Charles De Gaulle<br>F-92521 Nevilly-Sur-Seine<br>France | |
| | Éditions du Centre Nationale<br>  de la Recherche Scientifique<br>    see CNRS | |
| CENTO | Centorino Productions<br>P.O. Box 4478<br>West Hills, CA 91308 | |
| CENTURY | Century Music Publishing Co.<br>263 Veterans Boulevard<br>Carlstadt, NJ 07072 | ASHLEY |
| CENTURY PR | Century Press Publishers | |
| CESKY HUD. | Cesky Hudebni Fond<br>Parizska 13<br>CS-110 00 Praha 1<br>Czech Republic | BOOSEY<br>(rental)<br>NEW W |
| CHANT | Éditions Le Chant du Monde<br>31/33, rue Vandrezanne<br>F-75013 Paris<br>France | |
| CHANTERL | Éditions Chanterelle S.A.<br>Postfach 103909<br>D-69 Heidelberg<br>Germany | BÄREN. |
| CHANTRAINE | Éditions Chantraine<br>S.A., 7, Avenue Henri-Paris<br>B-7500 Tournai<br>Belgium | |
| CHANTRY | Chantry Music Press, Inc.<br>c/o Augsburg Fortress Publishers<br>426 South Fifth Street<br>P.O. Box 1209<br>Minneapolis, MN 55440 | AUG-FOR |
| CHAPLET | Chaplet Music Corp. | PARAGON |
| CHAPPELL | Chappell & Co., Inc.<br>1290 Avenue of the Americas<br>New York, NY 10019 | LEONARD-US |
| CHAPPELL-CAN | Chappell Music Canada Ltd.<br>85 Scarsdale Road, Unit 101<br>Don Mills, Ontario M3B 2R2<br>Canada | LEONARD-US |
| CHAPPELL-ENG | Chappell & Co. Ltd.<br>Printed Music Division<br>60-70 Roden Street<br>Ilford, Essex IG1 2AQ<br>England | LEONARD-US |
| CHAPPELL-FR | Chappell S.A.<br>25, rue d'Hauterville<br>F-75010 Paris<br>France | LEONARD-US |
| CHAR CROS | Charing Cross Music, Inc.<br>1619 Broadway, Suite 500<br>New York, NY 10019 | |
| CHARNWOOD | Charnwood Music Publishing Co.<br>12 Barrington Road<br>Leicester LE2 2RA<br>England | |
| CHARTER | Charter Publications, Inc.<br>P.O. Box 850<br>Valley Forge, PA 19482 | PEPPER |
| CHENANGO | Chenango Valley Music Press<br>P.O. Box 251<br>Hamilton, NY 13346 | |
| CHERITH | Cherith Publishing Co. | INTRADA |
| CHERRY | Cherry Lane Music Co.<br>10 Midland Avenue<br>Port Chester, NY 10573 | CPP-BEL |
| CHESTER | Chester Music<br>8-9 Frith Street<br>London W1V 5TZ<br>England | SCHIRM.G |
| CHILTERN | Chiltern Music<br>  see Cathedral Music | |

## PUBLISHER DIRECTORY

| Code | Publisher | U.S. Agent |
|---|---|---|
| CHOIR | Choir Publishing Co.<br>564 Columbus Street<br>Salt Lake City, UT 84103 | |
| CHORAG | Choragus<br>Box 1197<br>S-581 11 Linköping<br>Sweden | |
| CHORISTERS | Choristers Guild<br>2834 West Kingsley Road<br>Garland, TX 75041 | LORENZ |
| CHOUDENS | Édition Choudens<br>38, rue Jean Mermoz<br>F-75008 Paris<br>France | PRESSER |
| CHRI | Christopher Music Co.<br>380 South Main Place<br>Carol Stream, IL 60188 | PRESSER |
| CHRIS | Christophorus-Verlag Herder<br>Hermann-Herder-Straße 4<br>D-7800 Freiburg Breisgau<br>Germany | |
| CHURCH | John Church Co. | PRESSER |
| CIRONE | Cirone Publications<br>P.O. Box 612<br>Menlo Park, CA 94025 | |
| CJC | Creative Jazz Composers, Inc.<br>1240 Annapolis Road<br>Odenton, MD 21113 | |
| CLARION | Clarion Call Music | SON-KEY |
| CLARK | Clark and Cruickshank Music Publishers | BERANDOL |
| CLAS | Classic Artists Publishing | LAURN |
| CLASSV | Classical Vocal Reprints<br>P.O. Box 20263<br>Columbus Circle Station<br>New York, NY 10023 | |
| CLIVIS | Clivis Publicacions<br>C-Còrsega, 619 Baixos<br>Barcelona 25<br>Spain | |
| CMP | CMP Library Service<br>MENC Historical Center/SCIM<br>Music Library/Hornbake<br>University of Maryland<br>College Park, MD 20742 | |
| CNRS | CNRS Editions<br>20-22 rue Saint-Armand<br>F-75015 Paris<br>France | SMPF |
| CO OP | Co-op Press<br>RD2 Box 150A<br>Wrightsville, PA 17368 | |
| COBURN | Coburn Press | PRESSER |
| CODERG | Coderg-U.C.P. sàrl<br>42 bis, rue Boursault<br>F-75017 Paris<br>France | |
| COLE | M.M. Cole Publishing Co.<br>919 North Michigan Avenue<br>Chicago, IL 60611 | |
| COLEMAN | Dave Coleman Music, Inc.<br>P.O. Box 230<br>Montesano, WA 98563 | |
| COLFRANC | Colfranc Music Publishing Corp. | KERBY |
| COLIN | Charles Colin<br>315 West 53rd Street<br>New York, NY 10019 | |
| COLOMBO | Franco Colombo Publications | CPP-BEL<br>PRESSER<br>(rental) |
| | Colorado College Music Press<br>see CCMP | |
| COLUM UNIV | Columbia University Music Press<br>562 West 113th Street<br>New York, NY 10025 | SCHIRM.EC |
| COLUMBIA | Columbia Music Co. | PRESSER |
| COLUMBIA PIC. | Columbia Pictures Publications<br>see CPP | |
| COMBRE | Consortium Musical, Marcel Combre Editeur<br>24, Boulevard Poissonnière<br>F-75009 Paris<br>France | KING,R |
| COMP.FAC. | Composers Facsimile Edition | AM.COMP.AL. |
| COMP.LIB. | Composer's Library Editions | PRESSER |
| COMP-PERF | Composer/Performer Edition<br>2101 22nd Street<br>Sacramento, CA 95818 | |
| COMP.PR. | The Composers Press, Inc. | OPUS |
| COMPOSER'S GR | Composer's Graphics<br>5702 North Avenue<br>Carmichael, CA 95608 | |
| CONCERT | Concert Music Publishing Co.<br>c/o Studio P-R, Inc.<br>16333 N.W. 54th Avenue<br>Hialeah, FL 33014 | CPP-BEL |
| CONCERT W | Concert Works Unlimited | SHAWNEE |
| CONCORD | Concord Music Publishing Co. | ELKAN,H |
| CONCORDIA | Concordia Publishing House<br>3558 South Jefferson Avenue<br>St. Louis, MO 63118-3968 | |
| CONGRESS | Congress Music Publications<br>100 Biscayne Boulevard<br>Miami, FL 33132 | |

# PUBLISHER DIRECTORY

| Code | Publisher | U.S. Agent |
|---|---|---|
| CONSE | Consejo Superior de Investagaciones Cientificas<br>Servicio de Publicaciones<br>Vitruvio, 8<br>28006 Madrid<br>Spain | |
| CONSOL | Consolidated Music Publishers, Inc.<br>33 West 60th Street<br>New York, NY 10023 | |
| CONSORT | Consort Music, Inc.<br>(Division of Magnamusic Distributors)<br>Sharon, CT 06069 | |
| CONSORT PR | Consort Press<br>1755 Monita Drive<br>Ventura, CA 93001 | |
| CONSORTIUM | Consortium Musical | PRESSER |
| | Consortium Musical, Marcel Combre Editeur<br>see COMBRE | |
| CONTINUO | Continuo Music Press, Inc. | PLYMOUTH |
| | Editorial Cooperativa Inter-Americana del Compositores<br>see ECOAM | |
| COPPENRATH | Musikverlag Alfred Coppenrath<br>Postfach 11 58<br>D-84495 Altötting<br>Germany | |
| COR PUB | Cor Publishing Co.<br>67 Bell Place<br>Massapequa, NY 11758 | |
| CORMORANT | Cormorant Press<br>P.O. Box 169<br>Hallowell, ME 04347 | PLYMOUTH |
| CORONA | Edition Corona-Rolf Budde<br>Hohenzollerndamm 54A<br>D-1 Berlin 33<br>Germany | |
| CORONET | Coronet Press | PRESSER |
| COROZINE | Vince Corozine Music Publishing Co.<br>6 Gabriel Drive<br>Peekskill, NY 10566 | |
| COSTALL | Éditions Costallat<br>60 rue de la Chaussée d'Antin<br>F-75441 Paris Cedex 09<br>France | PRESSER |
| COVENANT | Covenant Press<br>3200 West Foster Avenue<br>Chicago, IL 60625 | |
| COVENANT MUS | Covenant Music<br>1640 East Big Thompson Avenue<br>Estes Park, CO 80517 | |
| CPP | Columbia Pictures Publications<br>15800 N.W. 48th Avenue<br>Miami, FL 33014 | CPP-BEL |
| CPP-BEL | CPP-Belwin Music<br>15800 N.W. 48th Avenue<br>Miami, FL 33014 | WARNER |
| CRAMER | J.B. Cramer & Co., Ltd.<br>23 Garrick Street<br>London WC2E 9AX<br>England | CPP-BEL |
| CRANZ | Éditions Cranz<br>30, rue St.-Christophe<br>B-1000 Bruxelles<br>Belgium | |
| | Creative Jazz Composers<br>see CJC | |
| CRES.-NETH | Uitgeverij Crescendo | DONEMUS |
| CRESCENDO | Crescendo Music Sales Co.<br>P.O. Box 395<br>Naperville, Il 60540 | FEMA |
| CRESPUB | Crescendo Publications, Inc.<br>6311 North O'Connor Road<br>#112<br>Irving, TX 75039-3112 | |
| CRITERION | Criterion Music Corp.<br>P.O. Box 660<br>Lynbrook, NY 11563 | |
| CROATICA | Croatian Music Institute | DRUS.HRVAT. SKLAD. |
| CRON | Edition Cron Luzern<br>Zinggentorstraße 5<br>CH-6006 Luzern<br>Switzerland | |
| CROWN | Crown Music Press | BRASS PRESS (partial) |
| | Cundey Bettoney Co.<br>see CBC | |
| CURCI | Edizioni Curci<br>Galleria del Corso 4<br>I-20122 Milano<br>Italy | |
| CURTIS | Curtis Music Press | KJOS |
| CURWEN | J. Curwen & Sons | LEONARD-US<br>SCHIRM.G<br>(rental) |
| CZECH | Czechoslovak Information Centre<br>Besedni 3<br>CS-118 00 Praha 1<br>Czech Republic | BOOSEY (rental) |
| DA CAPO | Da Capo Press, Inc.<br>233 Spring Street<br>New York, NY 10013 | |
| | Samfundet til udgivelse at Dansk Musik<br>see SAMFUNDET | |
| DANE | Dane Publications<br>1657 The Fairway, Suite 133<br>Jenkintown, PA 19046 | |

## PUBLISHER DIRECTORY

| Code | Publisher | U.S. Agent |
|---|---|---|
| DANTALIAN | Dantalian, Inc.<br>Eleven Pembroke Street<br>Newton, MA 02158 | |
| DAVID | E. Henry David Music Publishers | PRESSER |
| DAVIMAR | Davimar Music<br>M. Productions<br>159 West 53rd Street<br>New York, NY 10019 | |
| DAYBRK | Daybreak Productions | ALEX.HSE. |
| DE MONTE | De Monte Music<br>F-82240 Septfonds<br>France | |
| DE SANTIS | Edizioni de Santis<br>Viale Mazzini, 6<br>I-00195 Roma<br>Italy | |
| DEAN | Roger Dean Publishing Co.<br>345 West Jackson Street, #B<br>Macomb, IL 61455-2112 | LORENZ |
| DEIRO | Pietro Deiro Publications<br>133 Seventh Avenue South<br>New York, NY 10014 | |
| DELRIEU | Georges Delrieu & Cie<br>Palais Bellecour B<br>14, rue Trachel<br>F-06000 Nice<br>France | SCHIRM.EC |
| DENNER | Erster Bayerischer Musikverlag<br>Joh. Dennerlein KG<br>Beethovenstraße 7<br>D-8032 Lochham<br>Germany | |
| DESC | Descant Publications | INTRADA |
| DESERET | Deseret Music Publishers<br>P.O. Box 900<br>Orem, UT 84057 | MUSICART |
| DESHON | Deshon Music, Inc. | CPP-BEL<br>PRESSER<br>(rental) |
| DESSAIN | Éditions Dessain<br>Belgium | |
| DEUTSCHER | Deutscher Verlag für Musik<br>Walkmühlstr. 52<br>D-6200 Wiesbaden 1<br>Germany | BREITKOPF-W |
| DEWOLF | DeWolfe Ltd.<br>80-88 Wardour Street<br>London W1V 3LF<br>England | DONEMUS |
| DIAPASON | The Diapason Press<br>Dr. Rudolf A. Rasch<br>P.O Box 2376<br>NL-3500 GJ Utrecht<br>Netherlands | |
| DIESTERWEG | Verlag Moritz Diesterweg<br>Wachterbacher Strasse 89<br>D-60386 Frankfurt-am-Main<br>Germany | |
| | Dilia Prag<br>see DP | |
| DIM | D.I. Music<br>13 Bank Square<br>Wilmslow<br>Cheshire SK9 1AN<br>England | |
| DIP PROV | Diputacion Provincial de Barcelona<br>Servicio de Bibliotecas<br>Carmen 47<br>Barcelona 1<br>Spain | |
| DITSON | Oliver Ditson Co. | PRESSER |
| DOBER | Les Éditions Doberman-Yppan<br>C.P. 2021<br>St. Nicholas, Quebec G0S 3L0<br>Canada | BOOSEY |
| DOBLINGER | Ludwig Doblinger Verlag<br>Dorotheergasse 10<br>A-1011 Wien I<br>Austria | |
| DOMINIS | Dominis Music Ltd.<br>Box 11307, Station H<br>Ottawa<br>Ontario K2H 7V1<br>Canada | |
| DONEMUS | Donemus Foundation<br>Paulus Potterstraat 14<br>NL-1071 CZ Amsterdam<br>Netherlands | PRESSER |
| DOORWAY | Doorway Music<br>2509 Buchanan Street<br>Nashville, TN 37208 | |
| DORABET | Dorabet Music Co.<br>170 N.E. 33rd Street<br>Ft. Lauderdale, FL 33334 | PLYMOUTH |
| DORING | G.F. Döring Musikverlag<br>Hasenplatz 5-6<br>D-7033 Herrenburg 1<br>Germany | |
| DORN | Dorn Publications, Inc.<br>P.O. Box 206<br>Medfield, MA 02052 | |
| DOUBLDAY | Doubleday & Co., Inc.<br>1540 Broadway<br>New York, NY 10036 | |
| DOUGLAS,B | Byron Douglas | CPP-BEL |
| DOVEHOUSE | Dovehouse Editions<br>32 Glen Avenue<br>Ottawa, Ontario K1S 2Z7<br>Canada | |
| DOVER | Dover Publications, Inc.<br>31 East 2nd Street<br>Mineola, NY 11501 | ALFRED |

# PUBLISHER DIRECTORY

| Code | Publisher | U.S. Agent |
|---|---|---|
| DOXO | Doxology Music<br>P.O. Box M<br>Aiken, SC 29802 | ANTARA |
| DP | Dilia Prag | BÄREN. |
| DRAGON | Dragon Music Co.<br>28908 Grayfox Street<br>Malibu, CA 90265 | |
| DREIK | Dreiklang-Dreimasken Bühnenund<br>Musikverlag<br>D-8000 München<br>Germany | ORLANDO |
| DRK | DRK Music Co.<br>111 Lake Wind Rd.<br>New Canaan, CT 06840 | |
| DRUS.HRVAT.<br>SKLAD. | Drustvo Hrvatskih Skladatelja<br>Berislavićeva 9<br>Zagreb<br>Croatia | |
| DRUSTVA | Edicije Drustva Slovenskih<br>Skladateljev<br>Trg Francoske Revolucije 6<br>Ljubljana<br>Slovenia | NEW W |
| DRZAVNA | Drzavna Zalozba Slovenije | DRUSTVA |
| DUCHESS | Duchess Music Corp. | MCA<br>PRESSER<br>(rental) |
| DUCKWORTH | Gerald Duckworth & Co., Ltd.<br>43 Gloucester Crescent<br>London, NW1<br>England | |
| DUMA | Duma Music Inc.<br>580 Alden Street<br>Woodbridge, NJ 07095 | |
| DUN | Dunstan House<br>P.O. Box 1355<br>Stafford, VA 22555 | INTRADA |
| DUNV | Dunvagen Music Publishers, Inc. | SCHIRM.G |
| DURAND | Durand & Cie<br>215, rue du Faubourg St.-Honoré<br>F-75008 Paris<br>France | PRESSER |
| DUTTON | E.P. Dutton & Co., Inc.<br>201 Park Avenue South<br>New York, NY 10003 | |
| DUX | Edition Dux<br>Arthur Turk<br>Beethovenstraße 7<br>D-8032 Lochham<br>Germany | DENNER |
| DVM | DVM Productions<br>P.O. Box 399<br>Thorofare, NJ 08086 | |
| EAR.MUS.FAC. | Early Music Facsimiles<br>P.O. Box 711<br>Columbus, OH 43216 | |
| | Early Music Shop of New England<br>65 Boyston Street<br>Brookline, MA 02146 | |
| | East West Publications<br>see WP | |
| EARTHSNG | Earthsongs<br>220 N.W. 29th<br>Corvallis, OR 97330 | |
| EASTMAN | Eastman School of Music | FISCHER,C |
| EBLE | Eble Music Co.<br>P.O. Box 2570<br>Iowa City, IA 52244 | |
| ECK | Van Eck & Zn. | DONEMUS |
| ECOAM | Editorial Cooperativa Inter-Americana<br>de Compositores<br>Casilla de Correa No. 540<br>Montevideo<br>Uruguay | PEER |
| EDI-PAN | Edi-Pan | DE SANTIS |
| EDUTAIN | Edu-tainment Publications<br>(Div. of the Evolve Music Group)<br>P.O. Box 20767<br>New York, NY 10023 | |
| EERSTE | De Eerste Muziekcentrale<br>Flevolaan 41<br>NL-1411 KC Naarden<br>Netherlands | |
| EGAN | Randall M. Egan & Associates,<br>Publishers, Inc.<br>2024 Kenwood Pkwy.<br>Minneapolis, MN 55405 | |
| EGTVED | Edition EGTVED<br>P.O. Box 20<br>DK-6040 Egtved<br>Denmark | FOSTER |
| EHRLING | Thore Ehrling Musik AB<br>Box 21133<br>S-100 31 Stockholm<br>Sweden | |
| EIGEN UITGAVE | Eigen Uitgave van de Componist<br>(Composer's Own Publication) | DONEMUS |
| ELITE | Elite Edition | SCHAUR |
| ELKAN,H | Henri Elkan Music Publisher | |
| ELKAN&SCH | Elkan & Schildknect<br>Vastmannagatan 95<br>S-113 43 Stockholm<br>Sweden | |
| ELKAN-V | Elkan-Vogel, Inc.<br>Presser Place<br>Bryn Mawr, PA 19010 | |
| ELKIN | Elkin & Co., Ltd | PRESSER |

## PUBLISHER DIRECTORY

| Code | Publisher | U.S. Agent |
|---|---|---|
| EMB | Editio Musica Budapest<br>Vörösmarty tér 1<br>H-1051 Budapest<br>Hungary<br>   see also BUDAPEST | BOOSEY<br>PRESSER |
| EMC | European Music Centre (Holland)<br>Ambacktsweg 42,<br>1271 AM Huizea | |
| EMEC | Editorial de Musica Española<br>   Contemporanea<br>   Ediciones Quiroga<br>Alcalá, 70-28009<br>Madrid 9<br>Spain | |
| EMERSON | Emerson Edition<br>Windmill Farm<br>Ampleforth<br>York YO6 4HF<br>England | EBLE<br>GROVE<br>KING,R<br>WOODWIND<br>PRESSER |
| EMI | EMI Music Publishing Ltd.<br>127 Charing Cross Road<br>London WC2H 0EA<br>England | INTER.MUS.P. |
| ENGELS | Musikverlag Carl Engels Nachf.<br>Auf dem Brand 3<br>D-5000 Köln 50 (Rodenkirchen)<br>Germany | |
| ENGSTROEM | Engstroem & Soedering<br>Borgergade 17<br>DK-1300 Kobenhavn K<br>Denmark | PETERS |
| ENOCH | Enoch & Cie<br>193 Boulevard Pereire<br>F-75017 Paris<br>France | PRESSER<br>SCHIRM.G<br>(rental-partial) |
| ENSEMB | Ensemble Publications<br>P.O. Box 98, Bidwell Station<br>Buffalo, NY 14222 | |
| ENSEMB PR | Ensemble Music Press | FISCHER,C |
| EPHROS | Gershon Ephros Cantorial Anthology<br>   Foundation, Inc. | TRANSCON. |
| ERDMANN | Rudolf Erdmann, Musikverlag<br>Adolfsallee 34<br>D-62 Wiesbaden<br>Germany | |
| ERES | Edition Eres Horst Schubert<br>Hauptstrasse 35<br>Postfach 1220<br>D-2804 Lilienthal/Bremen<br>Germany | |
| ERICKSON | E.J. Erickson Music Co.<br>606 North Fourth Street<br>P.O. Box 97<br>St. Peter, MN 56082 | |
| ERIKS | Eriks Musikhandel & Förlag AB<br>Karlavägen 40<br>S-114 49 Stockholm<br>Sweden | |
| ERST | Erstausgaben Bodensohn<br>   see also BODENS | |
| ESCHENB | Eschenbach Editions<br>28 Dalrymple Crescent<br>Edinburgh, EH9 2NX<br>Scotland | PRESSER |
| ESCHIG | Éditions Max Eschig<br>215 rue du Faubourg Saint-Honoré<br>F-75008 Paris<br>France | PRESSER |
| | Editorial de Musica Española<br>   Contemporanea<br>   see EMEC | |
| | Union Musical EspañOLA<br>   see UNION ESP | |
| ESSEX | Clifford Essex Music | MUSIC-ENG |
| ESSO | Van Esso & Co. | DONEMUS |
| ETHOS | Ethos Publications<br>P.O. Box 2043<br>Oswego, NY 13126 | |
| ETLING,F | Forest R. Etling<br>   see HIGHLAND | |
| ETOILE | Etoile Music, Inc.<br>Publications Division<br>Shell Lake, WI 54871 | MMB |
| EUGANEA | Euganea Editoriale Comunicazioni<br>Via Roma 82<br>I-35122 Padova<br>Italy | |
| EULENBURG | Edition Eulenburg | EUR.AM.MUS.<br>(miniature<br>scores) |
| EUR.AM.MUS. | European American Music Corp.<br>P.O. Box 850<br>Valley Forge, PA 19482 | |
| EVANG | Evagel Press | AMSI |
| EWP | East West Publications | MUSIC |
| EXC.MH | Excellent Music Holland<br>Postbus 347<br>1180 AH Amstelveen<br>Netherlands | HARMONIA |
| EXCELSIOR | Excelsior Music Publishing Co. | PRESSER |
| EXPO PR | Exposition Press<br>325 Kings Highway<br>Smithtown, NY 11787 | |
| FABER | Faber Music Ltd.<br>3 Queen Square<br>London WC1N 3AU<br>England | LEONARD-US<br>(sales)<br>FOR.MUS.DIST.<br>(rental) |
| FAIR | Fairfield Publishing, Ltd. | PRESSER |

# PUBLISHER DIRECTORY

| Code | Publisher | U.S. Agent |
|---|---|---|
| FAITH | Faith Music | LILLENAS |
| FALLEN LEAF | Fallen Leaf Press<br>P.O. Box 10034-N<br>Berkeley, CA 94709 | |
| FAR WEST | Far West Music | WESTERN |
| FARRELL | The Wes Farrell Organization | LEONARD-US |
| FAZER | Musik Fazer<br>P.O. Box 169<br>SF-02101 Espoo<br>Finland | PRESSER |
| FEEDBACK | Feedback Studio Verlag<br>Gentner Strasse 23<br>D-5 Köln 1<br>Germany | BÄREN. |
| FEIST | Leo Feist, Inc. | PRESSER |
| FELDMAN,B | B. Feldman & Co., Ltd. | EMI |
| FEMA | Fema Music Publications<br>P.O. Box 395<br>Naperville, IL 60566 | |
| FENETTE | Fenette Music Ltd. | BROUDE,A |
| FENTONE | Fentone Music Ltd.<br>Fleming Road, Earlstrees<br>Corby, Northants NN17 2SN<br>England | PRESSER |
| FEREOL | Fereol Publications<br>Route 8, Box 510C<br>Gainesville, GA 30501 | |
| FEUCHT | Feuchtinger & Gleichauf<br>Niedermünstergasse 2<br>D-8400 Regensburg 11<br>Germany | |
| FIDDLE | Fiddle & Bow<br>7 Landview Drive<br>Dix Hills, NY 11746 | HHP |
| FIDELIO | Fidelio Music Publishing Co.<br>39 Danbury Avenue<br>Westport, CT 06880-6822 | |
| FIDULA | Fidula-Verlag Johannes Holzmeister<br>Ahornweg, Postfach 250<br>D-56154 Boppard/Rhein<br>Germany | HARGAIL |
| FILLMH | Fillmore Music House | FISCHER,C |
| FINE ARTS | Fine Arts Press<br>2712 W. 104th Terrace<br>Leawood, KS 66206 | ALEX.HSE. |
| FINN MUS | Finnish Music Information Center<br>Runeberginkatu 15 A<br>SF-00100 Helsinki 10<br>Finland | |
| FISCHER,C | Carl Fischer, Inc.<br>62 Cooper Square<br>New York, NY 10003 | |
| FISCHER,J | J. Fischer & Bro. | BELWIN<br>PRESSER<br>(rental) |
| FISHER | Fisher Music Co. | PLYMOUTH |
| FITZSIMONS | H.T. FitzSimons Co., Inc.<br>18345 Ventura Boulevard<br>P.O. Box 333, Suite 212<br>Tarzana, CA 91356 | ANTARA |
| FLAMMER | Harold Flammer, Inc. | SHAWNEE |
| FMA | Florilegium Musicae Antiquae | HÄNSSLER |
| FOETISCH | Foetisch Frères<br>Rue de Bourg 6<br>CH-1002 Lausanne<br>Switzerland | SCHIRM.EC |
| FOG | Dan Fog Musikforlag<br>Grabrodretorv 7<br>DK-1154 Kobenhavn K<br>Denmark | |
| FOLEY,CH | Charles Foley, Inc. | FISCHER,C<br>PRESSER<br>(rental) |
| FORBERG | Rob. Forberg-P. Jurgenson<br>  Musikverlag<br>Mirbachstraße 9<br>D-5300 Bonn-Bad Godesberg<br>Germany | PETERS |
| FOR.MUS.DIST. | Foreign Music Distributors<br>13 Elkay Drive<br>Chester, NY 10918 | |
| FORLIVESI | A. Forlivesi & C.<br>Via Roma 4<br>50123 Firenze<br>Italy | |
| FORNI | Arnaldo Forni Editore<br>Via Gramsci 164<br>I-40010 Sala Bolognese<br>Italy | OMI |
| FORSTER | Forster Music Publisher, Inc.<br>216 South Wabash Avenue<br>Chicago, IL 60604 | |
| FORSYTH | Forsyth Brothers Ltd.<br>126 Deansgate<br>Manchester M3 2GR<br>England | |
| FORTEA | Biblioteca Fortea<br>Fucar 10<br>Madrid 14<br>Spain | |
| FORTISSIMO | Fortissimo Musikverlag<br>Margaretenplatz 4<br>A-1050 Wien<br>Austria | |
| | Fortress Press | AUG-FOR |
| FOSTER | Mark Foster Music Co.<br>28 East Springfield Avenue<br>P.O. Box 4012<br>Champaign, IL 61820-1312 | |

# PUBLISHER DIRECTORY

| Code | Publisher | U.S. Agent |
|---|---|---|
| | Foundation for New American Music see NEWAM | |
| FOUR ST | Four Star Publishing Co. | CPP-BEL |
| FOXS | Sam Fox Publishing Co.<br>5276 Hollister Avenue<br>Suite 251<br>Santa Barbara, CA 93111 | PLYMOUTH<br>(sales)<br>PRESSER<br>(rental) |
| FRANCAIS | Éditions Françaises de Musique | PRESSER |
| FRANCE | France Music | AMP |
| FRANCIS | Francis, Day & Hunter Ltd. | CPP-BEL |
| FRANG | Frangipani Press | ALFRED |
| FRANK | Frank Music Corp. | LEONARD-US<br>SCHIRM.G<br>(rental-partial) |
| FRANTON | Franton Music<br>4620 Sea Isle<br>Memphis, TN 38117 | |
| FREDONIA | Fredonia Press<br>3947 Fredonia Drive<br>Hollywood, CA 90068 | SIFLER |
| FREELAND | Freeland Publications<br>2718 Russell Street<br>Berkeley, CA 94705 | |
| FREEMAN | H. Freeman & Co., Ltd. | EMI |
| FROG | Frog Peak Music<br>Box 1052<br>Lebanon, NH 03766 | |
| FROHLICH | Friedrich Wilhelm Fröhlich Musikverlag<br>Ansbacher Straße 52<br>D-1000 Berlin 30<br>Germany | |
| FUJIHARA | Fujihara | |
| FURORE | Furore Verlag<br>Johannesstrasse 3<br>3500 Kassel<br>Germany | TONGER |
| FURST | Fürstner Ltd. | BOOSEY |
| FUZ | Editions Fuzeau<br>B.P. 6<br>79440 Courlay<br>France | |
| GAF | G.A.F. and Associates<br>1626 E. Williams Street<br>Tempe, AZ 85281 | |
| GAITHER | Gaither Music Company | ALEX.HSE. |
| GALAXY | Galaxy Music Corp. | SCHIRM.EC |
| GALLEON | Galleon Press<br>17 West 60th St.<br>New York, NY 10023 | BOSTON |
| GALLERIA | Galleria Press<br>170 N.E. 33rd Street<br>Fort Lauderdale, FL 33334 | PLYMOUTH |
| GALLIARD | Galliard Ltd.<br>Queen Anne's Road<br>Southtown, Gt. Yarmouth<br>Norfolk<br>England | GALAXY |
| GANDL | G and L Publishing<br>2337 Jersey Street<br>Stevens Point, WI 54481-3123 | |
| GARLAND | Garland Publishing, Inc.<br>717 5th Avenue, #2500<br>New York, NY 10022-8101 | |
| GARZON | Éditions J. Garzon<br>13 rue de l'Échiquier<br>F-75010 Paris<br>France | |
| GEHRMANS | Carl Gehrmans Musikförlag<br>Odengatan 84<br>Box 6005<br>S-102 31 Stockholm<br>Sweden | BOOSEY |
| GEMINI | Gemini Press<br>Music Div. of the Pilgrim Press<br>Box 390<br>Otis, MA 01253 | PRESSER |
| GENERAL | General Music Publishing Co., Inc.<br>145 Palisade Street<br>Dobbs Ferry, NY 10522 | BOSTON |
| GENERAL WDS | General Words and Music Co. | KJOS |
| GENESIS | Genesis | PLYMOUTH |
| GENTRY | Gentry Publications<br>P.O. Box 570567<br>Tarzana, CA 91357 | ANTARA |
| GERIG | Musikverlage Hans Gerig<br>Drususgasse 7-11 (AM Museum)<br>D-5000 Köln 1<br>Germany | BREITKOPF-W |
| GIA | GIA Publications<br>7404 South Mason Avenue<br>Chicago, IL 60638 | |
| GILBERT | Gilbert Publications<br>4209 Manitou Way<br>Madison, WI 53711 | |
| GILLMAN | Gillman Publications<br>P.O. Box 155<br>San Clemente, CA 92672 | |
| GILPIN | Gilpin-McPheeters Publishing | INTRADA |
| GLOCKEN | Glocken Verlag Ltd.<br>12-14 Mortimer Street<br>London W1N 8EL<br>England | EUR.AM.MUS. |
| GLORY | Glory Sound<br>Delaware Water Gap, PA 18327 | SHAWNEE |
| GLOUCHESTER | Glouchester Press<br>P.O. Box 1044<br>Fairmont, WV 26554 | HEILMAN |

# PUBLISHER DIRECTORY

| Code | Publisher | U.S. Agent |
|---|---|---|
| GM | G & M International Music Dealers<br>1225 Candlewood Hill Road<br>Box 2098<br>Northbrook, IL 60062 | |
| GOLDEN | Golden Music Publishing Co.<br>P.O. Box 383<br>Golden, CO 80402-0383 | |
| GOODLIFE | Goodlife Publications | CPP-BEL |
| GOODMAN | Goodman Group<br>(formerly Regent, Arc & Goodman) | WARNER<br>LEONARD-US<br>(choral) |
| GOODWIN | Goodwin & Tabb Publishing, Ltd. | PRESSER |
| GORDON | Gordon Music Co.<br>Box 2250<br>Canoga Park, CA 91306 | |
| GORNSTON | David Gornston | FOX,S |
| GOSPEL | Gospel Publishing House<br>1445 Boonville Avenue<br>Springfield, MO 65802 | |
| GRAHL | Grahl & Nicklas<br>Braubachstraße 24<br>D-6 Frankfurt-am-Main<br>Germany | |
| GRANCINO | Grancino Editions<br>15020 Burwood Dr.<br>Lake Mathews, CA 92370<br><br>Grancino Editions<br>2 Bishopswood Road<br>London N6 4PR<br>England<br><br>Grancino Editions<br>Schirmerweg 12<br>D-8 München 60<br>Germany | |
| GRAS | Éditions Gras<br>36 rue Pape-Carpentier<br>F-72200 La Flèche (Sarthe)<br>France | SOUTHERN |
| GRAV | Editions Gravis<br>Adolfstrasse 71<br>Postfach 1107<br>D-6208 Bad Schwalbach 1<br>Germany | |
| GRAY | H.W. Gray Co., Inc. | CPP-BEL<br>PRESSER<br>(rental) |
| GREENE ST. | Greene Street Music<br>354 Van Duzer Street<br>Stapleton, NY 10304 | |
| GREENWOOD | Greenwod Press, Inc.<br>88 Post Road West<br>P.O. Box 5007<br>Westport, CT 06881 | WORLD |

| Code | Publisher | U.S. Agent |
|---|---|---|
| GREGG | Gregg International Publishers, Ltd.<br>1 Westmead, Farnborough<br>Hants GU14 7RU<br>England | |
| GREGGMS | Gregg Music Sources<br>P.O. Box 868<br>Novato, CA 94947 | |
| | Gregorian Institute of America<br>see GIA | |
| GROEN | Muziekuitgeverij Saul B. Groen<br>Ferdinand Bolstraat 6<br>NL-1072 LJ Amsterdam<br>Netherlands | |
| GROSCH | Edition Grosch<br>Phillip Grosch<br>Postfach 1736<br>D-82145 Planegg Bei<br>München<br>Germany | THOMI |
| GROVEN | Eivind Grovens Institutt for<br>Reinstemming<br>Ekebergveien 59<br>N-1181 Oslo 11<br>Norway | |
| GUARANI | Ediciones Musicals Mundo Guarani<br>Sarmiento 444<br>Buenos Aires<br>Argentina | |
| GUILYS | Edition Guilys<br>Case Postale 90<br>CH-1702 Fribourg 2<br>Switzerland | |
| GUNMAR | Gunmar Music, Inc.<br>see MARGUN | JERONA |
| HA MA R | Ha Ma R Percussion Publications, Inc.<br>333 Spring Road<br>Hutington, NY 11743 | BOOSEY |
| HAMBLEN | Stuart Hamblen Music Co.<br>26101 Ravenhill Road<br>Canyon Country, CA 91351 | |
| HAMELLE | Hamelle & Cie<br>175 rue Saint-Honoré<br>F-75040 Paris Cedex 01<br>France | KING,R<br>PRESSER<br>SOUTHERN |
| HAMPE | Adolf Hampe Musikverlag<br>Hohenzollerndamm 54A<br>D-1000 Berlin 33<br>Germany | BUDDE |
| HAMPTON | Hampton Edition | MARKS |
| HANSEN-DEN | Wilhelm Hansen Musikforlag<br>Bornholmsgade 1,1<br>1266 Copenhagen K<br>Denmark | SCHIRM.G |
| HANSEN-ENG | Hansen, London<br>see CHESTER | |

# PUBLISHER DIRECTORY

| Code | Publisher | U.S. Agent |
|---|---|---|
| HANSEN-FIN | Edition Wilhelm Hansen<br>Helsinki | SCHIRM.G |
| HANSEN-GER | Edition Wilhelm Hansen, Frankfurt | SCHIRM.G |
| HANSEN-NY | Edition Wilhelm Hansen-Chester Music New York Inc.<br>New York, NY | SCHIRM.G |
| HANSEN-SWED | Edition Wilhelm Hansen<br>see NORDISKA | SCHIRM.G |
| HANSEN-US | Hansen House Publications, Inc.<br>1824 West Avenue<br>Miami Beach, FL 33139-9913 | |
| HÄNSSLER | Hänssler-Verlag<br>Röntgenstrasse 15<br>Postfach 1230<br>D-7312 Kirchheim/Teck<br>Germany | ANTARA |
| HAPPY | Happy Music<br>P.O. Box 2842<br>San Anselmo, CA 94960 | |
| HARGAIL | Hargail Music Press<br>P.O. Box 118<br>Saugerties, NY 12477 | CPP-BEL |
| HARMONIA | Harmonia-Uitgave<br>P.O. Box 210<br>NL-1230 AE Loosdrecht<br>Netherlands | FOR.MUS.DIST. |
| HARMS,TB | T.B. Harms | WARNER |
| HARMUSE | Harmuse Publications<br>529 Speers Road<br>Oakville, Ontario L6K 2G4<br>Canada | |
| HARP PUB | Harp Publications<br>3437-2 Tice Creek Drive<br>Walnut Creek, CA 94595 | |
| HARRIS | Frederick Harris Music Co., Ltd.<br>529 Speers Road<br>Oakville, Ontario L6K 2G4<br>Canada | HARRIS-US |
| HARRIS-US | Frederick Harris Company, Ltd.<br>340 Nagel Drive<br>Buffalo, NY 14225-4731 | |
| HARRIS,R | Ron Harris Publications<br>22643 Paul Revere Drive<br>Woodland Hills, CA 91364 | ALEX.HSE. |
| HART | F. Pitman Hart & Co., Ltd. | BRODT |
| HARTH | Harth Musikverlag<br>PSF 467<br>D-04004 Leipzig<br>Germany | |
| HAS | Edition HAS Publishing Co.<br>P.O. Box 1753<br>Maryland Heights, MO 63043 | HENLE |
| HASLINGER | Verlag Carl Haslinger<br>Tuchlauben 11<br>A-1010 Wien<br>Austria | FOR.MUS.DIST. |
| HASTINGS | Hastings Music Corp. | CPP-BEL |
| HATCH | Earl Hatch Publications<br>5008 Aukland Ave.<br>Hollywood, CA 91601 | |
| HATIKVAH | Hatikvah Publications | TRANSCON. |
| HAWK | Hawk Music Press<br>668 Fairmont Avenue<br>Oakland, CA 94611 | |
| HAYMOZ | Haydn-Mozart Presse | EUR.AM.MUS. |
| HAZA | Hazamir Publications<br>35 Garland Road<br>Newton, MA 02159 | |
| | Hebrew Union College Sacred Music Press<br>see SAC.MUS.PR. | |
| HEER | Joh. de Heer & Zn. B.V.<br>Muziek-Uitgeverij en Groothandel<br>Rozenlaan 113, postbus 3089<br>NL-3003 AB Rotterdam<br>Netherlands | |
| HEIDELBERGER | Heidelberger | BÄREN. |
| HEILMAN | Heilman Music<br>P.O. Box 1044<br>Fairmont, WV 26554 | |
| HEINN | Heilmann Publications<br>P.O. Box 18180<br>Pittsburgh, PA 15236 | |
| HEINRICH. | Heinrichshofen's Verlag<br>Liebigstraße 16<br>Postfach 620<br>D-26354 Wilhelmshaven<br>Germany | PETERS |
| HELBING | Edition Helbling<br>Kaplanstraße 9<br>A-6021 Neu-Rum b. Innsbruck<br>Austria | |
| HELBS | Helbling Edition<br>Pfäffikerstraße 6<br>CH-8604 Voketswil-Zürich<br>Switzerland | |
| HELICON | Helicon Music Corp. | EUR.AM.MUS. |
| HELIOS | Editio Helios | FOSTER |
| HENDON | Hendon Music | BOOSEY |
| HENKLE | Ted Henkle<br>5415 Reynolds Street<br>Savannah, GA 31405 | |
| HENLE | G. Henle Verlag<br>Forstenrieder Allee 122<br>Postfach 71 04 66<br>D-81454 München<br>Germany<br><br>G. Henle USA, Inc.<br>P.O. Box 1753<br>2446 Centerline Industrial Drive<br>St. Louis, MO 63043 | |

| Code | Publisher | U.S. Agent |
|---|---|---|
| HENMAR | Henmar Press | PETERS |
| HENN | Editions Henn<br>8 rue de Hesse<br>Genève<br>Switzerland | |
| HENREES | Henrees Music Ltd. | EMI |
| HERALD | Herald Press<br>616 Walnut Avenue<br>Scottdale, PA 15683 | |
| HERITAGE | Heritage Music Press | LORENZ |
| HERITAGE PUB | Heritage Music Publishing Co. | CENTURY |
| HEUGEL | Heugel & Cie<br>175 rue Saint-Honoré<br>F-75040 Paris Cedex 01<br>France | KING,R<br>PRESSER<br>SOUTHERN |
| HEUWEKE. | Edition Heuwekemeijer & Zoon<br>Postbus 289<br>NL-1740 AG Schagen<br>Netherlands | PRESSER |
| HEYN | Verlag Johannes Heyn<br>Friedensgasse 23<br>A-9020 Klagenfurt<br>Austria | |
| HHP | Hollow Hills Press<br>7 Landview Drive<br>Dix Hills, NY 11746 | |
| HIEBER | Musikverlag Max Hieber KG<br>Postfach 330429<br>D-80064 München<br>Germany | |
| HIGH GR | Higher Ground Music Publishing | ALEX.HSE. |
| HIGHGATE | Highgate Press | SCHIRM.EC |
| HIGHLAND | Highland/Etling Music Co.<br>1344 Newport Avenue<br>Long Beach, CA 90804 | |
| HILD | Hildegard Publishing Co.<br>Box 332<br>Bryn Mawr, PA 19010 | |
| HINRICHSEN | Hinrichsen Edition, Ltd. | PETERS |
| HINSHAW | Hinshaw Music, Inc.<br>P.O. Box 470<br>Chapel Hill, NC 27514 | |
| HINZ | Hinz Fabrik Verlag<br>Lankwitzerstraße 17-18<br>D-1000 Berlin 42<br>Germany | |
| HIRSCHS | Abr. Hirschs Forlag<br>Box 505<br>S-101 26 Stockholm<br>Sweden | GEHRMANS |
| HISPAVOX | Ediciones Musicales Hispavox<br>Cuesta Je Santo Domingo 11<br>Madrid<br>Spain | |

| Code | Publisher | U.S. Agent |
|---|---|---|
| HLH | HLH Music Publications<br>611 Broadway, Suite 615<br>New York, NY 10012 | MUSIC SC. |
| HOA | HOA Music PUblisher<br>756 S. Third Street<br>Dekalb, IL 60115 | |
| HOFFMAN,R | Raymond A. Hoffman Co.<br>c/o Fred Bock Music Co.<br>P.O. Box 333<br>Tarzana, CA 91356 | ANTARA |
| HOFMEISTER | VEB Friedrich Hofmeister, Musikverlag,<br>Leipzig<br>Karlstraß 10<br>D-701 Leipzig<br>Germany | |
| HOFMEISTER-W | Friedrich Hofmeister Musikverlag,<br>Taunus<br>Ubierstraße 20<br>D-6238 Hofheim am Taunus<br>Germany | |
| HOHLER | Heinrich Hohler Verlag | SCHNEIDER,H |
| | Hollow Hills Press<br>see HHP | |
| HOLLY-PIX | Holly-Pix Music Publishing Co. | WESTERN |
| HONG KONG | Hong Kong Music Media Publishing<br>Co., Ltd.<br>Kai It Building, 9th Floor<br>58 Pak Tai Street<br>Tokwawan, Kowloon<br>Hong Kong | |
| HONOUR | Honour Publications | WESTERN |
| HOPE | Hope Publishing Co.<br>380 South Main Place<br>Carol Stream, IL 60188 | |
| HORNPIPE | Hornpipe Music Publishing Co.<br>400 Commonwealth Avenue<br>P.O. Box CY577<br>Boston, MA 02215 | |
| HUEBER | Hueber-Holzmann<br>Pädagogischer Verlag<br>Krausstraße 30<br>D-8045 Ismaning, München<br>Germany | |
| HUG | Hug & Co. Musikverlage<br>Limmatquai Postfach 28-30<br>CH-8022 Zürich<br>Switzerland | EUR.AM.MUS. |
| HUGUENIN | Charles Huguenin & Pro-Arte<br>Rue du Sapin 2a<br>CH-2114 Fleurier<br>Switzerland | |
| HUHN | W. Huhn Musikalien-Verlag<br>Jahnstraße 9<br>D-5880 Lüdenshied<br>Germany | |

## PUBLISHER DIRECTORY

| Code | Publisher | U.S. Agent |
|---|---|---|
| HULL | Hullenhagen & Griehl Verlage<br>Ringstrasse 52<br>D-22145 Hamburg<br>Germany | |
| HULST | De Hulst<br>Kruisdagenlaan 75<br>B-1040 Bruxelles<br>Belgium | |
| HUNTZINGER | R.L. Huntzinger Publications | WILLIS |
| HURON | Huron Press<br>P.O. Box 2121<br>London, Ontario N6A 4C5<br>Canada | |
| ICELAND | Islenzk Tónverkamidstöd<br>Iceland Music Information Centre<br>Sidumuli 34<br>108 Reykjavik<br>Iceland | |
| IISM | Istituto Italiano per la Storia della<br>   Musica<br>Academia Nazionale di Santa Cecilia<br>Via Vittoria, 6<br>I-00187 Roma<br>Italy | |
| IMB | Internationale Musikbibliothek | BÄREN. |
| IMC | Indiana Music Center<br>322 South Swain<br>P.O. Box 582<br>Bloomington, IN 47401 | |
| IMPERO | Impero-Verlag<br>Liebigstraße 16<br>D-2940 Wilhelmshavn<br>Germany | PRESSER<br>(partial) |
| INDEPENDENT | Independent Publications<br>P.O. Box 162<br>Park Station<br>Paterson, NJ 07513 | |
| INDIANA | Indiana University Press<br>601 N. Morton Street<br>Bloomington, IN 47404-3797 | |
| INST ANT | Instrumenta Antiqua, Inc.<br>P.O. Box 2804<br>Menlo Park, CA 94026-2804 | |
| INST.CO. | The Instrumentalist<br>200 Northfield Road<br>Northfield, IL 60093-3390 | |
| | Institute Of Stringed Instruments<br>   Guitar & Lute<br>   see ISI | |
| | Editorial Cooperativa Inter-Americana<br>   de Compositores<br>   see ECOAM | |
| INTERLOCH | Interlochen Press | CRESCENDO |
| INTERNAT. | International Music Co.<br>5 W. 37th Street<br>New York, NY 10018 | |
| INTER.MUS.P. | International Music Publications<br>Woodford Trading Estate<br>Southend Road<br>Woodford Green, Essex IG8 8HN<br>England | WARNER |
| | Internationale Musikbibliothek<br>   see IMB | |
| INTERNAT.S. | International Music Service<br>133 W. 69th Street<br>New York, NY 10023 | |
| INTRADA | Intrada Music Group<br>P.O. Box 1240<br>Anderson, IN 46015 | |
| IONA | Iona Music Publishing Service<br>P.O. Box 8131<br>San Marino, CA 91108 | |
| IONE | Ione Press | SCHIRM.EC |
| IRIS | Iris Verlag<br>Hernerstraße 64A<br>Postfach 100.851<br>D-4350 Recklinghausen<br>Germany | |
| IROQUOIS PR | Iroquois Press<br>P.O. Box 2121<br>London, Ontario N6A 4C5<br>Canada | |
| | Islenzk Tónverkamidstöd<br>   see ICELAND | |
| ISI | Institute Of Stringed Instruments,<br>   Guitar & Lute<br>Poststraße 30<br>4 Düsseldorf<br>Germany | SANDVOSS |
| | Aux Presses d'Isle-de-France<br>   see PRESSES | |
| ISR.MUS.INST. | Israel Music Institute<br>P.O. Box 3004<br>61030 Tel Aviv<br>Israel | PRESSER |
| ISR.PUB.AG. | Israel Publishers Agency<br>7, Arlosoroff Street<br>Tel-Aviv<br>Israel | |
| ISRAELI | Israeli Music Publications, Ltd.<br>25 Keren Hayesod<br>Jerusalem 94188<br>Israel | PRESSER |
| | Istituto Italiano per la Storia della<br>   Musica<br>   see IISM | |
| J.B.PUB | J.B. Publications<br>404 Holmes Circle<br>Memphis, TN 38111 | |
| J.C.A. | Japan Composers Association<br>3-7-15, Akasaka<br>Minato-Ku<br>Tokyo<br>Japan | |

# PUBLISHER DIRECTORY

| Code | Publisher | U.S. Agent |
|---|---|---|
| JACKMAN | Jackman Music Corp.<br>P.O. Box 1900<br>Orem, UT 84059 | MUSICART |
| JAPAN | Japan Federation of Composers<br>307 5th Sky Bldg.<br>3-3-8 Sendagaya<br>Shibuya-Ku<br>Tokyo 151<br>Japan | |
| JAREN | Jaren Music Co.<br>9691 Brynmar Drive<br>Villa Park, CA 92667 | |
| JASE | Jasemusiikki Ky<br>Box 136<br>SF-13101 Hämeenlinna 10<br>Finland | |
| JAYMAR | Jaymar Music, Ltd.<br>P.O. Box 2121<br>London, Ontario N6A 4C5<br>Canada | |
| JAZZ ED | Jazz Education Publications<br>P.O. Box 802<br>Manhattan, KS 66502 | |
| JEANNETTE | Ed. Jeannette | DONEMUS |
| JEHLE | Jehle | HÄNSSLER |
| JENSON | Jenson Publications, Inc.<br>7777 W. Bluemound Road<br>Milwaukee, WI 53213 | LEONARD-US |
| JERONA | Jerona Music Corp.<br>P.O. Box 671<br>Englewood, NJ 07631 | |
| JEWISH | Jewish Music Publications<br>2500 NE 135 Street, #111<br>N. Miami, FL 33181-3554 | |
| JOAD | Joad Press<br>4 Meredyth Road<br>London SW13 0DY<br>England | FISCHER,C<br>(rental-partial) |
| JOBERT | Editions Jean Jobert<br>76, rue Quincampoix<br>F-75003 Paris<br>France | PRESSER |
| JOED | Joed Music Publications<br>234 Stanley Park Road<br>Carshalton Beeches<br>Surrey, SM5 3JP<br>England | |
| JOHNSON | Johnson Reprint Corp.<br>757 3rd Avenue<br>New York, NY 10017 | |
| JOHNSON,P | Paul Johnson Productions<br>P.O. Box 2001<br>Irving, TX 75061 | |
| JOSHUA | Joshua Corp. | SCHIRM.G |
| JOY | Joy Music Press | INTRADA |
| JRB | JRB Music Education Materials<br>Distributor | PRESSER |
| JUNNE | Otto Junne GmbH<br>Sendinger-Tor-Platz 10<br>D-8000 München<br>Germany | |
| JUS-AUTOR | Jus-Autor<br>Sofia, Bulgaria | BREITKOPF-W |
| JUSKO | Jusko Publications | WILLIS |
| KAHNT | C.F. Kahnt, Musikverlag<br>Kennedyallee 101<br>6000 Frankfurt 70<br>Germany | PETERS |
| KALLISTI | Kallisti Music Press<br>810 South Saint Bernard Street<br>Philadelphia, PA 19143-3309 | |
| KALMUS | Edwin F. Kalmus<br>P.O. Box 5011<br>Boca Raton, FL 33431 | CPP-BEL<br>(string and miniature scores) |
| KALMUS,A | Alfred A. Kalmus Ltd.<br>38 Eldon Way, Paddock Wood<br>Tonbridge, Kent TN12 6BE<br>England | EUR.AM.MUS. |
| KAMMEN | J. & J. Kammen Music Co. | CENTURY |
| KAPLAN | Ida R. Kaplan<br>1308 Olivia Avenue<br>Ann Arbor, MI 48104 | |
| KARTHAUSE | Karthause Verlag<br>Panzermacherstrasse 5<br>D-5860 Iserlohn<br>Germany | |
| KAWAI | Kawai Gafuku | JAPAN |
| KAWE | Edition KaWe<br>Brederodestraat 90<br>NL-1054 VC Amsterdam 13<br>Netherlands | KING,R |
| KAY PR | Kay Press<br>612 Vicennes Court<br>Cincinnati, OH 45231 | |
| KELTON | Kelton Publications<br>1343 Amalfi Drive<br>Pacific Palisades, CA 90272 | |
| KENDALE | Kendale Company<br>6595 S. Dayton Street<br>Englewood, CO 80111 | |
| KENDOR | Kendor Music Inc.<br>Main & Grove Streets<br>P.O. Box 278<br>Delevan, NY 14042 | |
| KENSING. | Kensington Music Service<br>P.O. Box 471<br>Tenafly, NJ 07670 | |
| KENYON | Kenyon Publications | LEONARD-US |

# PUBLISHER DIRECTORY

| Code | Publisher | U.S. Agent |
|---|---|---|
| KERBY | E.C. Kerby Ltd.<br>198 Davenport Road<br>Toronto, Ontario M5R IJ2<br>Canada | LEONARD-US<br>BOOSEY<br>(rental) |
| KEYS | The Keys Press<br>66 Clotilde Street<br>Mount Lawley<br>Western Australia 6050<br>Australia | |
| KIMM | Kimmel Publications, Inc.<br>P.O. Box 1472<br>Decatur, IL 62522 | HOPE |
| KINDRED | Kindred Press | HERALD |
| KING,R | Robert King Sales, Inc.<br>Shovel Shop Square<br>28 Main Street, Bldg. 15<br>North Easton, MA 02356 | |
| KING'S | King's Music<br>Redcroft, Bank's End<br>Wyton, Huntingdon<br>Cambridgeshire PE17 2AA<br>England | |
| KIRK | Kirkland House | LORENZ |
| KISTNER | Fr. Kistner & C.F.W. Siegel & Co.<br>Adrian-Kiels-Straße 2<br>D-5000 Köln 90<br>Germany | CONCORDIA |
| KJOS | Neil A. Kjos Music Co.<br>4382 Jutland Drive<br>Box 178270<br>San Diego, CA 92117-0894 | |
| KLAV | Klavarskribo<br>Postbus 39<br>2980 AA Ridderkerk<br>Holland | |
| KLIMENT | Musikverlag Johann Kliment<br>Kolingasse 15<br>A-1090 WIEN 9<br>Austria | |
| KNEUSSLIN | Edition Kneusslin<br>Amselstraße 43<br>CH-4059 Basel<br>Switzerland | FOR.MUS.DIST. |
| KNOPF | Alfred A. Knopf<br>201 East 50th Street<br>New York, NY 10022 | |
| KNUF | Frits Knuf Uitgeverij<br>Rodeheldenstraat 13<br>P.O. Box 720<br>NL-4116 ZJ Buren<br>Netherlands | PENDRGN |
| KODALY | Kodaly Center of America, Inc.<br>15 Denton Road<br>Wellesley, MA 02181 | SUPPORT |
| KON BOND | Kon. Bond van Chr. Zang- en<br>Oratoriumverenigingen | DONEMUS |
| KONINKLIJK | Koninklijk Nederlands<br>Zangersverbond | DONEMUS |
| KOPER | Musikverlag Karl-Heinz Köper<br>Schneekoppenweg 12<br>D-3001 Isernhagen NB/Hannover<br>Germany | |
| KRENN | Ludwig Krenn Verlag<br>Neulerchenfelderstr. 3-7<br>A-1160 Wien<br>Austria | |
| KROMPHOLZ | Krompholz & Co.<br>Spitalgasse 28<br>CH-3001 Bern<br>Switzerland | |
| KRUSEMAN | Ed. Philip Kruseman | DONEMUS |
| KUNZEL | Edition Kunzelmann<br>Grutstrasse 28<br>CH-8134 Adliswil<br>Switzerland | FOR.MUS.DIST. |
| KYSAR | Michael Kysar<br>1250 South 211th Place<br>Seattle, WA 98148 | |
| LAAB | Laaber Verlag<br>Regensburgstrasse 19<br>D-8411 Laaber<br>Germany | |
| LAB | Editions Labatiaz<br>Case Postale 112<br>CH-1890 St. Maurice<br>Switzerland | |
| LAGOS | Editorial Lagos<br>Talachuano 638 P.B."H"<br>1013 Buenos Aires<br>Argentina | |
| LAKES | Lake State Publishers<br>P.O. Box 1593<br>Grand Rapids, MI 49501 | |
| LAMP | Latin-American Music Pub. Co. Ltd.<br>8 Denmark Street<br>London<br>England | |
| LAND | A. Land & Zn. Musiekuitgevers | DONEMUS |
| LANDES | Landesverband Evangelischer<br>Kirchenchöre in Bayern | HÄNSSLER |
| LANG | Lang Music Publications<br>P.O. Box 11021<br>Indianapolis, IN 46201 | |
| LANSMAN | Länsmansgarden<br>PL-7012<br>S-762 00 Rimbo<br>Sweden | |
| | Latin-American Music Pub. Co. Ltd.<br>see LAMP | |
| LARK | Lark Publishing | INTRADA |

## PUBLISHER DIRECTORY

| Code | Publisher | U.S. Agent |
|---|---|---|
| LATINL | The Latin American Literary Review Press<br>2300 Palmer St.<br>Pittsburg, PA 15218 | |
| LAUDA | Laudamus Press | INTRADA |
| LAUDINELLA | Laudinella Reihe | FOSTER |
| LAUMANN | Laumann Verlag<br>Alter Gartenweg 14<br>Postfach 1360<br>D-4408 Dülmen<br>Germany | |
| LAUREL | Laurel Press | LORENZ |
| LAURN | Laurendale Associates<br>15035 Wyandotte Street<br>Van Nuys, CA 91405 | |
| LAVENDER | Lavender Publications, Ltd.<br>Borough Green<br>Sevenoaks, Kent TN15 8DT<br>England | |
| LAWSON | Lawson-Gould Music Publishers, Inc.<br>250 W. 57th St., Suite 1005<br>New York, NY 10107 | ALFRED |
| LEA | Lea Pocket Scores<br>P.O. Box 138, Audubon Station<br>New York, NY 10032 | EUR.AM.MUS. |
| LEAWOOD | Leawood Music Press | ANTARA |
| LEDUC | Alphonse Leduc<br>175 rue Saint-Honoré<br>F-75040 Paris Cedex 01<br>France | KING,R<br>PRESSER<br>(rental) |
| LEE | Norman Lee Publishing, Inc.<br>Box 528<br>Oskaloosa, IA 52577 | BARNHS |
| LEEDS | Leeds Music Ltd.<br>MCA Building<br>2450 Victoria Park Avenue<br>Willowdale, Ontario M2J 4A2<br>Canada | MCA<br>PRESSER<br>(rental) |
| LEMOINE | Henry Lemoine & Cie<br>17, rue Pigalle<br>F-75009 Paris<br>France | PRESSER |
| LENGNICK | Alfred Lengnick & Co., Ltd.<br>Purley Oaks Studios<br>421a Brighton Road<br>South Croydon, Surrey CR2 6YR<br>England | |
| LEON S | Stanley Leonard Publications<br>551 Sandrae Drive<br>Pittsburgh, PA 15243 | |
| LEONARD-ENG | Leonard, Gould & Bolttler<br>60-62 Clerkenwell Road<br>London EC1M 5PY<br>England | |
| LEONARD-US | Hal Leonard Music<br>7777 West Bluemound Road<br>Milwaukee, WI 53213 | |
| LESLIE | Leslie Music Supply<br>P.O. Box 471<br>Oakville, Ontario L6J 5A8<br>Canada | BRODT |
| LEUCKART | F.E.C. Leuckart<br>Nibelungenstraße 48<br>D-8000 München 19<br>Germany | |
| LEXICON | Lexicon Music<br>P.O. Box 2222<br>Newbury Park, CA 91320 | ALEX.HSE. |
| LIBEN | Liben Music Publications<br>1191 Eversole Road<br>Cincinnati, OH 45230 | |
| LIBER | Svenska Utbildningsförlaget Liber AB<br>Utbildningsfölaget, Centrallagret<br>S-136 01 Handen<br>Stockholm<br>Sweden | |
| LICHTENAUER | W.F. Lichtenauer | DONEMUS |
| LIED | VEB Lied der Zeit Musikverlag<br>Rosa-Luxemburg-Straße 41<br>D-102 Berlin<br>Germany | |
| LIENAU | Robert Lienau Musikverlag<br>Hildegardstr. 16<br>D-10715 Berlin<br>Germany | |
| LIGA | Liga de Compositores de Musica de Concierto de Mexico, A.C.<br>Mayorazgo No. 129<br>Col. Xoco<br>03330, Mexico, D.F.<br>Mexico | |
| LIGHT | Light of the World Music | INTRADA |
| LILLENAS | Lillenas Publishing Co.<br>P.O. Box 419527<br>Kansas City, MO 64141 | |
| LINDSAY | Lindsay Music<br>23 Hitchin Street<br>Biggleswade, Beds SG18 8AX<br>England | PRESSER |
| LINDSBORG | Lindsborg Press<br>P.O. Box 737<br>State Road 9 South<br>Alexandria, VA 46001 | ANTARA |
| LINGUA | Lingua Press<br>c/o 1st Natl. Bank<br>310 S. Hamel Road<br>Los Angeles, CA 90048-3844 | |
| LISTER | Mosie Lister | LILLENAS |
| LITOLFF,H | Henry Litolff's Verlag<br>Kennedy Allee 101<br>Postfach 700906<br>D-6000 Frankfurt 70<br>Germany | PETERS |

## Publisher Directory

| Code | Publisher | U.S. Agent |
|---|---|---|
| LITURGICAL | Liturgical Music Press<br>St. Johns Abbey<br>Collegeville, MN 56321 | |
| LLUQUET | Guillermo Lluquet<br>Almacen General de Musica<br>Avendida del Oeste 43<br>Valencia<br>Spain | |
| | London Pro Musica Edition<br>see LPME | |
| LONG ISLE | Long Island Music Publishers | BRANCH |
| LOOP | Loop Music Co. | KJOS |
| LORENZ | Lorenz Corporation<br>501 East Third Street<br>P.O. Box 802<br>Dayton, OH 45401-9969 | |
| LPME | The London Pro Musica Edition<br>15 Rock Street<br>Brighton BN2 1NF<br>England | MAGNA D |
| LUCKS | Luck's Music Library<br>P.O. Box 71397<br>Madison Heights, MI 48071 | |
| LUDWIG | Ludwig Music Publishing Co.<br>557-67 East 140th Street<br>Cleveland, OH 44110-1999 | |
| LUNDEN | Edition Lundén<br>Bromsvagen 25<br>S-125 30 Alvsjö<br>Sweden | |
| LUNDMARK | Lundmark Publications<br>811 Bayliss Drive<br>Marietta, GA 30067 | SUPPORT |
| LUNDQUIST | Abr. Lundquist Musikföflag AB<br>Katarina Bangata 17<br>S-116 25 Stockholm<br>Sweden | |
| LYCHE | Harald Lyche<br>Postboks 2171 Stromso<br>N-3003 Drammen<br>Norway | WALTON<br>(partial) |
| LYDIAN ORCH | Lydian Orchestrations<br>31000 Ruth Hill Road<br>Orange Cove, CA 93646 | SHAWNEE |
| LYNWD | Lynwood Music Photo Editions<br>2 Church St. West Hagley<br>West Midlands DY9 0NA<br>England | |
| LYRA | Lyra Music Co.<br>133 West 69th Street<br>New York, NY 10023 | |
| MAA | Music Associates of America<br>224 King Street<br>Englewood, NJ 07631 | |
| MAAS | Kurt Maas<br>Postfach 710267<br>D-8 München 71<br>Germany | |
| MACNUTT | Richard Macnutt Ltd.<br>Hamm Farm House<br>Withyham, Hartfield<br>Sussex TN7 4BJ<br>England | |
| | Mac Murray Publications<br>see MMP | |
| MAGNA D | Magnamusic Distributors<br>Route 49<br>Sharon, CT 06069 | |
| MALCOLM | Malcolm Music Ltd. | SHAWNEE |
| MANNA | Manna Music, Inc.<br>22510 Stanford Avenue<br>Suite 101<br>Valencia, CA 91355 | |
| MANNHEIM | Mannheimer Musikverlag<br>Kunigundestraße 4<br>D-5300 Bonn 2<br>Germany | |
| MANU. PUB | Manuscript Publications<br>see CO OP | |
| MAPA MUNDI | Mapa Mundi - Music Publishers<br>72 Brewerey Road<br>London N7 9NE<br>England | SCHIRM.EC |
| MARBOT | Edition Marbot Gmbh<br>Mühlenkamp 43<br>D-2000 Hamburg 60<br>Germany | PEER |
| MARCHAND | Marchand, Paap en Strooker | DONEMUS |
| MARGUN | Margun/Gunmar Music, Inc.<br>167 Dudley Road<br>Newton Centre, MA 02159 | JERONA |
| MARI | E. & O. Mari, Inc.<br>38-01 23rd Avenue<br>Long Island City, NY 11105 | |
| MARK | Mark Publications | CRESPUB |
| MARKS | Edward B. Marks Music Corp.<br>1619 Broadway<br>New York, NY 10019 | LEONARD-US<br>(sales)<br>PRESSER<br>(rental) |
| MARSEG | Marseg, Ltd.<br>18 Farmstead Road<br>Willowdale, Ontario M2L 2G2<br>Canada | |
| MARTIN | Editions Robert Martin<br>B.P. 502<br>106, Grande rue de la Coupée<br>F-71009 Charnay-les-Macon<br>France | PRESSER |
| MASTER | Master Music | CRESPUB |

# PUBLISHER DIRECTORY

| Code | Publisher | U.S. Agent |
|---|---|---|
| MASTERS | Masters Music Publications<br>P.O. Box 810157<br>Boca Raton, FL 33481-0157 | |
| MAURER | J. Maurer<br>Avenue du Verseau 7<br>B-1200 Brussel<br>Belgium | |
| MAURRI | Edizioni Musicali Ditta R. Maurri<br>Via del Corso 1 (17R.)<br>Firenze<br>Italy | |
| MAYHEW | Kevin Mayhew Ltd.<br>Rattlesden<br>Bury St. Edmunds<br>Suffolk IP30 0SZ<br>England | BRODT |
| MCA | MCA and Mills/MCA Joint Venture Editions<br>1755 Broadway, 8th Floor<br>New York, NY 10019 | LEONARD-US (sales)<br>PRESSER (rental) |
| MCAFEE | McAfee Music Corp. | CPP-BEL |
| MCGIN-MARX | McGinnis & Marx<br>236 West 26th Street, #11S<br>New York, NY 10001 | |
| MDV | Mitteldeutscher Verlag<br>Thalmannplatz 2, Postfach 295<br>D-4010 Halle-Saale<br>Germany | PETERS |
| MEDIA | Media Press<br>P.O. Box 250<br>Elwyn, PA 19063 | |
| MEDICI | Medici Music Press<br>5017 Veach Road<br>Owensboro, KY 42301-9643 | |
| MEDIT | Mediterranean | GALAXY |
| MEL BAY | Mel Bay Publications, Inc.<br>P.O. Box 66<br>Pacific, MO 63069 | |
| MELE LOKE | Mele Loke Publishing Co.<br>Box 7142<br>Honolulu, Hawaii 96821 | HIGHLAND (continental U.S.A.) |
| MELODI | Casa Editrice Melodi S.A.<br>Galleria Del Coroso 4<br>Milano<br>Italy | |
| MENC | Music Educators National Conference<br>Publications Division<br>1902 Association Drive<br>Reston, VA 22091 | |
| MENTOR | Mentor Music<br>13205 Indian School Road<br>Albequerque, NM 87112 | |
| MERCATOR | Mercator Verlag & Wohlfahrt (Gert) Verlag<br>Stresemannstrasse 20-22<br>Postfach 101461<br>D-4100 Duisberg 1<br>Germany | |
| MERCURY | Mercury Music Corp. | PRESSER |
| MERID | Meriden Music<br>The Studio Barn Silverwood House<br>Woolasten Nr. Lidney<br>Gloucestershire GL15 6PJ<br>England | |
| MERIDIAN | Les Nouvelles Éditions Meridian<br>5, rue Lincoln<br>F-75008 Paris 8<br>France | |
| MERION | Merion Music, Inc. | PRESSER |
| MERRYMOUNT | Merrymount Music, Inc. | PRESSER |
| MERSEBURGER | Merseburger Verlag<br>Motzstraße 13<br>D-3500 Kassel<br>Germany | |
| METRO | Metro Muziek<br>Uilenweg 38<br>Postbus 70<br>NL-6000 AB Weert<br>Netherlands | |
| METROPOLIS | Editions Metropolis<br>24, Frankrijklei<br>B-2108 Antwerpen<br>Belgium | |
| MEULEMANS | Arthur Meulemans Fonds<br>Charles de Costerlaan, 6<br>2050 Antwerpen<br>Belgium | |
| MEXICANAS | Ediciones Mexicanas de Musica<br>Avenida Juarez 18<br>Mexico City<br>Mexico | PEER |
| MEZ KNIGA | Mezhdunarodnaya Kniga<br>39, Dimitrov St.<br>Moscow 113095<br>Russia | |
| MIDDLE | Middle Eight Music | CPP-BEL |
| MILL CREEK | Mill Creek Publications<br>P.O. Box 556<br>Mentone, CA 92359 | |
| MILLER | Miller Music Corp. | CPP-BEL |
| MILLS MUSIC | Mills Music Jewish Catalogue | TRANSCON.<br>PRESSER (rental) |
| MINKOFF | Minkoff Reprints<br>8 rue Eynard<br>CH-1211 Genève 12<br>Switzerland | OMI |
| MIRA | Mira Music Associates<br>199 Mountain Road<br>Wilton, CT 06897 | |
| | Mitteldeutscher Verlag<br>see MDV | |

# PUBLISHER DIRECTORY

| Code | Publisher | U.S. Agent |
|---|---|---|
| MJQ | M.J.Q. Music, Inc.<br>1697 Broadway #1100<br>New York, NY 10019 | FOX,S |
| MMB | MMB Music, Inc.<br>Contemporary Arts Building<br>3526 Washington Avenue<br>St. Louis, MO 63103-1019 | |
| MMP | Mac Murray Publications | MUS.SAC.PRO. |
| MMS | Monumenta Musica Svecicae | STIM |
| MOBART | Mobart Music Productions | JERONA |
| MOD ART | Modern Art Music | SON-KEY |
| MODERN | Edition Modern<br>Rhodter Strasse 26<br>D-76185 Karlsruhe<br>Germany | |
| MMM | Modern Musical Methods<br>P.O. Box 245<br>90 South Demarest Ave.<br>Bergenfield, NJ 07621 | |
| MODUS | Mödus Musiikki Oy<br>PL 82, 57101 Savonlinna<br>Finland | |
| MOECK | Herman Moeck Verlag<br>Postfach 143<br>D-3100 Celle 1<br>Germany | EUR.AM.MUS. |
| MOLENAR | Molenaar's Muziekcenrale<br>Industrieweg 23<br>Postbus 19<br>NL-1520 AA Wormerveer<br>Netherlands | GM |
| MONDIAL | Mondial-Verlag KG<br>8 rue de Hesse<br>Genève<br>Switzerland | |
| MONTEVERDI | Fondazione Claudio Monteverdi<br>Via Ugolani Dati, 4<br>I-26100 Cremona<br>Italy | |
| MORAVIAN | Moravian Music Foundation | CPP-BEL<br>BOOSEY<br>BRODT<br>PETERS |
| MORN.ST. | Morning Star Music Publishers<br>2117 59th St.<br>St. Louis, MO 63110-2800 | |
| MOSAIC | Mosaic Music Corporation | BOSTON |
| MÖSELER | Karl Heinrich Möseler Verlag<br>Hoffman-von-Fallersleben-Straße 8-10<br>Postfach 1661<br>D-3340 Wolfenbüttel<br>Germany | |
| MOSER | Verlag G. Moser<br>Kirschweg 8<br>CH-4144 Arlesheim<br>Switzerland | |
| MOWBRAY | Mowbray Music Publications<br>Saint Thomas House<br>Becket Street<br>Oxford OX1 1SJ<br>England | PRESSER |
| MSM | MSM Music Publishers | BRODT |
| MT.SALUS | Mt. Salus Music<br>709 East Leake Street<br>Clinton, MS 39056 | |
| MT.TAHO | Mt. Tahoma | BROUDE,A |
| MULLES | Muller & Schade AG Musikhaus<br>Kramgasse 50<br>CH-3011 Bern<br>Switzerland | |
| MÜLLER | Willy Müller, Süddeutscher Musikverlag<br>Marzgasse 5<br>D-6900 Heidelberg<br>Germany | |
| MUNSTER | Van Munster Editie | DONEMUS |
| MURPHY | Spud Murphy Publications | WESTERN |
| MUS.ANT.BOH | Musica Antiqua Bohemica | SUPRAPHON |
| MUS.ART | Music Art Publications<br>P.O. Box 1744<br>Chula Vista, CA 92010 | |
| | Music Associates of America<br>see MAA | |
| MUS.PERC. | Music For Percussion, Inc.<br>170 N.E. 33rd Street<br>Fort Lauderdale, FL 33334 | |
| MUS.RARA | Musica Rara<br>Le Traversier<br>Chemin de la Buire<br>F-84170 Monteux<br>France | |
| | Musica Russica<br>see RUSSICA | |
| MUS.SAC.PRO | Musica Sacra et Profana<br>P.O. Box 7248<br>Berkeley, CA 94707 | |
| MUS.SB | Music Service Bureau<br>1645 Harvard St. NW<br>Washington, D.C. 20009-3702 | |
| MUS.SUR | Musica del Sur<br>Apartado 5219<br>Barcelona<br>Spain | |
| MUS.VERA | Musica Vera Graphics & Publishers<br>350 Richmond Terrace 4-M<br>Staten Island, NY 10301 | ARISTA |
| MUS.VIVA | Musica Viva<br>262 King's Drive<br>Eastbourne<br>Sussex BN21 2XD<br>England | |
| MUS.VIVA.HIST. | Musica Viva Historica | SUPRAPHON |

## PUBLISHER DIRECTORY

| Code | Publisher | U.S. Agent |
|---|---|---|
| MUSIA | Musia | PETERS |
| MUSIC | Music Sales Corp. Executive Offices<br>225 Park Avenue South<br>New York, NY 10003 | |
| | Music Sales Corp. (Rental)<br>5 Bellvale Road<br>Chester, NY 10918 | |
| MUSIC BOX | Music Box Dancer Publications Ltd. | PRESSER |
| | Music Educators National Conference<br>see MENC | |
| MUSIC-ENG | Music Sales Ltd.<br>Newmarket Road<br>Bury St. Edmunds<br>Suffolk IP33 3YB<br>England | MUSIC |
| | Musica Russica<br>see RUSSICA | |
| MUSIC INFO | Muzicki Informativni Centar-ZAMP<br>Ulica 8 Maja 37<br>P.O. Box 959<br>Zagreb<br>Croatia | BREITKOPF-W |
| MUSIC SC. | Musical Score Distributors<br>611 Broadway, Suite 615<br>New York, NY 10012 | |
| MUSIC SEV. | Music 70, Music Publishers<br>170 N.E. 33rd Street<br>Fort Lauderdale, FL 33334 | |
| | Société d'Éditions Musicales<br>Internationales<br>see SEMI | PLYMOUTH |
| MUSICART | Musicart West<br>P.O. Box 1900<br>Orem, UT 84059 | |
| MUSICIANS PUB | Musicians Publications<br>P.O. Box 7160<br>West Trenton, NJ 08628 | |
| MUSICO | Musico Muziekuitgeverij | DONEMUS |
| MUSICPRINT | Musicprint Corporation<br>P.O. Box 20767<br>New York, NY 10023 | |
| MUSICUS | Edition Musicus<br>P.O. Box 1341<br>Stamford, CT 06904 | |
| MUSIKAL. | Musikaliska Konstföreningen<br>Aarstryck, Sweden | WALTON |
| MUSIKHOJ | Musikhojskolens Forlag ApS | EUR.AM.MUS |
| MUSIKINST | Verlag das Musikinstrument<br>Klüberstraße 9<br>D-6000 Frankfurt-am-Main<br>Germany | |
| MUSIKK | Musikk-Huset A-S<br>P.O. Box 822 Sentrum<br>0104 Oslo 1<br>Norway | |
| MUSIKWISS. | Musikwissenschaftlicher Verlag Wien<br>Dorotheergasse 10<br>A-1010 Wien 1<br>Austria | FOR.MUS.DIST<br>(Bruckner &<br>Wolf) |
| | Muzicki Informativni Centar-Zamp<br>see MUSIC INFO | |
| | Eerste Muziekcentrale<br>see EERSTE | |
| MUZYKA | Muzyka Publishers<br>14 Neglinnaya Street<br>103031 Moscow<br>Russia | |
| MYRRH | Myrrh Music | WORD |
| MYRTLE | Myrtle Monroe Music<br>2600 Tenth Street<br>Berkeley, CA 94710 | |
| NAGELS | Nagels Verlag | |
| NAKAS | H. Nakas-C. Papagrigoriou Co.<br>39 Panepistimiou Str.<br>105 64 Athens<br>Greece | |
| NATIONAL | National Music Publishers<br>16605 Townhouse<br>Tustin, CA 91680 | ANTARA |
| NEUE | Verlag Neue Musik<br>An der Kolonnade 15<br>Postfach 1306<br>D-1080 Berlin<br>Germany | FOR.MUS.DIST |
| NEW HORIZON | New Hrizon Publications | TRANSCON. |
| | New Music Edition<br>see NME | |
| NEW MUSIC WEST | New Music West<br>P.O. Box 7434<br>Van Nuys, CA 91409 | |
| NEW VALLEY | New Valley Music Press of Smith College<br>Sage Hall 49<br>Northampton, MA 01063 | |
| NEW W | New World Enterprises of Montrose, Inc.<br>2 Marisa Court<br>Montrose, NY 10548 | |
| NEWAM | Foundation for New American Music | LUCKS |
| NGLANI | Edition Nglani<br>Box 871<br>Merrifield, VA 22116-2871 | |
| NIEUWE | De Nieuwe Muziekhandel | DONEMUS |
| NIPPON | Nippon Hosu | PRESSER |
| NL | NL Productions Inc. | PLUCKED ST |
| N.LIGHT | Northlight Music Inc. | SCHIRM.G |
| NLS | NLS Music | LAUREN |

| Code | Publisher | U.S. Agent |
|---|---|---|
| NME | New Music Edition | PRESSER |
| NO.AM.LIT. | North American Liturgy Resources<br>Choral Music Department<br>10802 North 23rd Avenue<br>Phoenix, AZ 85029 | |
| NOBILE | Nobile Verlag<br>Aixheimer Straße 26<br>D-7000 Stuttgart 75<br>Germany | |
| NOETZEL | Noetzel Musikverlag<br>Liebigstraße 16<br>Postfach 620<br>D-26354 Wilhelmshavn<br>Germany | PETERS |
| NOMOS | Edition Nomos | BREITKOPF-W |
| NOORDHOFF | P. Noordhoff | DONEMUS |
| NOEDISKA | AB Nordiska Musikförlaget<br>Nybrogatan 3<br>S-114 34 Stockholm<br>Sweden<br>see also HANSEN-SWEDEN | |
| NORGE | Norsk Musikkinformasjon<br>Toftesgatan 69<br>N-0552 Oslo 5<br>Norway | |
| NORK | Norske Komponisters Forlag<br>Gjernesvegen 24<br>N-5700 Voss<br>Norway | |
| NORRUTH | Norruth Music Publishers | MMB |
| NORSK | Norsk Musikforlag AS<br>Karl Johansgaten 39<br>P.O. Box 1499 Vika<br>N-0116 Oslo 1<br>Norway | WALTON |
| | Norske Komponisters Forlag<br>see NORK | |
| | North American Liturgy Resources<br>see NO.AM.LIT. | |
| | Northlight Music Inc.<br>see N. Light | |
| NORTHRIDGE | Northridge Music, Inc.<br>7317 Greenback Lane<br>Citrus Heights, CA 95621 | CPP-BEL |
| NORTON | W.W. Norton & Co., Inc.<br>500 Fifth Avenue<br>New York, NY 10003 | |
| | Norwegian Music Information Center<br>see NORGE | |
| NOSKE | A.A. Noske | DONEMUS |
| NOTEN | De Notenboom<br>Dever 10<br>2550 Kontich<br>Belgium | |
| NOTERIA | Noteria<br>S-590 30 Borensberg<br>Sweden | STIM |
| NOTON | Noton<br>Kolltjernvn. 11<br>P.O. Box 1014<br>N-2301 Hamar<br>Norway | |
| NOVA | Nova Music Ltd.<br>Goldsmid Mews<br>15a Farm Road<br>Hove<br>Sussex BN3 1FB<br>England | SCHIRM.EC |
| NOVELLO | Novello & Co., Ltd.<br>Block 7, Unit 3<br>Vestry Estate, Otford Road<br>Sevenoaks, Kent TN14 5EL<br>England | SHAWNEE<br>MUSIC<br>(sales)<br>G.SCHIRMER<br>(rental) |
| NOW VIEW | Now View | PLYMOUTH |
| | Nuova Carisch s.r.l.<br>Via M.F. Quintiliano, 40<br>20138 Milano<br>Italy | |
| NYMPHEN | Edition Nymphenburg<br>Unterföhring, Germany | PETERS |
| OAK | Oak Publications | MUSIC |
| OCTAVA | Octava Music Co. Ltd. | WEINBERGER |
| OECUM | Oecumuse<br>52a Broad St.<br>Ely, CB7 4AH<br>England | CANTORIS |
| OISEAU | Éditions de L'Oiseau-Lyre<br>Les remparts<br>Boite Postale 515<br>MC-98015 Monaco Cedex | MAGNA D<br>OMI |
| OJEDA | Raymond J. Ojeda<br>98 Briar Road<br>Kentfield, CA 94904 | |
| OKRA | Okra Music Corp. | SEESAW |
| OLIVIAN | Olivian Press | ARCADIA |
| OLMS | G. Olms Verlag<br>Hagentorwall 7<br>D-3200 Hildesheim<br>Germany | |
| OMI | OMI - Old Manuscripts & Incunabula<br>P.O. Box 6019, FDR Station<br>New York, NY 10150 | |
| ONGAKU | Ongaku-No-Tomo Sha Co. Ltd.<br>Kagurazaka 6-30, Shinjuku-ku<br>Tokyo 162<br>Japan | PRESSER |
| OPUS | Opus Music Publishers, Inc.<br>1318 Chicago Avenue<br>Evanston, IL 60201 | |

# PUBLISHER DIRECTORY

| Code | Publisher | U.S. Agent |
|---|---|---|
| OPUS-CZ | Opus<br>Ceskoslavenske Hudobne<br>  Vydaratelstro<br>Mlynske nivy 73<br>827 99 Bratislava<br>Slovakia | BOOSEY<br>(rental) |
| OR-TAV | Or-Tav Music Publications<br>P.O. Box 1126<br>Kfar Sava 44110<br>Israel | |
| OREGON | Oregon Catholic Press<br>5536 NE Hassalo<br>Portland, OR 97213 | |
| ORGAN | Organ Music Co. | WESTERN |
| ORGAN LIT | Organ Literature Foundation<br>45 Norfolk Road<br>Braintree, MA 02184 | |
| ORGMS | Organmaster Music Series<br>282 Stepstone Hill<br>Guilford, CT 06437 | |
| ORION MUS | Orion Music Press<br>P.O. Box 145, University Station<br>Barrien Springs, MI 49104 | OPUS |
| ORLANDO | Orlando Musikverlag<br>Kaprunerstraße 11<br>D-8000 München 21<br>Germany | |
| ORPHEUM | Orpheum Music<br>10th & Parker<br>Berkeley, CA 94710 | |
| OSTARA | Ostara Press, Inc. | WESTERN |
| ÖSTER | Österreichischer Bundesverlag<br>Schwarzenberg Platz 5<br>A-1010 Wien<br>Austria | |
| OSTIGUY | Editions Jacques Ostiguy Inc.<br>12790 Rue Yamaska<br>St. Hyacinthe, Quebec<br>Canada J2T 1B3 | |
| OSTNOR | Ostnorsk Musikkforlag<br>Nordre Langgate 1 B<br>N-9950 Vardo<br>Norway | |
| OTOS | Otos Edizioni Musicali<br>Via Marsillo Ficino, 10<br>I-50132 Firenze<br>Italy | |
| OUVRIERES | Les Éditions Ouvrières<br>12, Avenue Soeur-Rosalie<br>F-75621 Paris Cedex 13,<br>France | KING,R |
| OXFORD | Oxford University Press<br>7-8 Hatherly Street<br>London SW1P 2QT<br>England | |
| OXFORD | Oxford University Press<br>200 Madison Avenue<br>New York, NY 10016 | |
| PACIF | Pacific Publications | INTRADA |
| PAGANI | O. Pagani & Bro, Inc.<br>c/o P. Deiro Music<br>289 Bleeker Street<br>New York, NY 10014 | |
| PAGANINI PUB | Paganiniana Publications, Inc.<br>1 T.F.H. Plaza<br>3rd & Union Avenue<br>Neptune City, NJ 07753 | |
| PAIDEIA | Paideia Editrice | BÄREN |
| PALLMA | Pallma Music Co. | KJOS |
| PAN | Editions Pan<br>Schaffhauserstraße 280<br>Postfach 176<br>CH-8057 Zürich<br>Switzerland | PRESSER |
| PAN AM | Pan American Union | PEER |
| PAN F | Edition Pan of Finland<br>Vihertie 56C<br>01620 Vantaa<br>Finland | |
| PANTONH | Panton<br>Radlická 99<br>CS-150 00 Praha 5<br>Czech Republic | NEW W |
| PARACLETE | Praclete Press<br>P.O. Box 1568<br>Hilltop Plaza, Route 6A<br>Orleans, MA 02653 | |
| PARAGON | Paragon Music Publishers | CENTURY |
| PARAGON ASS. | Paragon Associates | ALEX.HSE. |
| PARIS | Uitgeverij H.J. Paris | DONEMUS |
| PARKS | Parks Music Corp. | KJOS |
| PASTORALE | Pastorale Music Company<br>235 Sharon Drive<br>San Antonio, TX 78216 | |
| PASTORINI | Musikhaus Pastorini AG<br>Kasinostraße 25<br>CH-5000 Aarau<br>Switzerland | |
| PATERSON | Paterson's Publications, Ltd.<br>8-10 Lower James Street<br>London W1R 3PL<br>England | MUSIC |
| PATHW | Pathway Music<br>P.O. Box 2250<br>Cleveland, TN 37320 | |
| | Patrimoine Musical Candien<br>  see CAN.MUS.HER. | |
| PAVAN | Pavane Publishing<br>321 Railroad Avenue<br>Myrtle Point, OR 97458 | INTRADA |

# PUBLISHER DIRECTORY

| Code | Publisher | U.S. Agent |
|---|---|---|
| PAXTON | Paxton Publications<br>Sevenoaks, Kent<br>England | PRESSER |
| PECK | Pecktackular Music<br>3605 Brandywine Drive<br>Greensboro, NC 27410 | |
| PEER | Peer Southern Concert Music<br>810 Seventh Avenue<br>New York, NY 10019 | PRESSER |
| PEER MUSIK | Peer Musikverlag GmbH<br>Muhlenkamp 43<br>Postfach 602129<br>D-2000 Hamburg<br>Germany | PEER |
| PEG | Pegasus Musikverlag<br>Liebig Straße 16<br>Postfach 620<br>D-2940 Wilhelmshaven<br>Germany | PETERS |
| PELIC.C | Pelican Cay Publications | PLYMOUTH |
| PELIKAN | Musikverlag Pelikan | EUR.AM.MUS. |
| PEMBROKE | Pembroke Music Co., Inc. | FISCHER,C |
| PENADES | José Penadés<br>En Sanz 12<br>Valencia<br>Spain | |
| PENDRGN | Pendragon Press<br>R.R. 1, Box 159<br>Stuyvesant, NY 12173-9720 | |
| PENGUIN | Penguin Books<br>120 Woodbine Street<br>Bergenfield, NJ 07621 | |
| PENN STATE | Penn State Press<br>The Pennsylvania State University<br>Barbara Building, Suite C<br>University Park, PA 16802-1003 | |
| PENOLL | Penoll<br>Goteberg<br>Sweden | STIM |
| PEPPER | J.W. Pepper And Son, Inc.<br>P.O. Box 850<br>Valley Forge, PA 19482 | |
| PERF.ED | Performer's Editions | BROUDE BR |
| PERFORM | Perform Our Music<br>Leuven<br>Belgium | PEER |
| PERMUS | Permus Publications<br>P.O. Box 02033<br>Columbus, OH 43202 | |
| PETERER | Edition Melodie Anton Peterer<br>Brunnwiesenstraße 26<br>Postfach 260<br>CH-8409 Zürich<br>Switzerland | |
| PETERS | Edition Peters<br>C.F. Peters Corp.<br>373 Park Avenue South<br>New York, NY 10016<br><br>Edition Peters<br>Postfach 746<br>D-7010 Leipzig<br>Germany<br><br>C.F. Peters Musikverlag<br>Postfach 700851<br>Kennedyallee 101<br>D-6000 Frankfurt 70<br>Germany<br><br>Peters Edition Ltd.<br>Bach House<br>10-12 Baches Street<br>London N1 6DN<br>England | |
| PETERS.K | Kermit Peters<br>1515 90th Street<br>Omaha, NE 68124 | |
| PETERS,M | Mitchell Peters<br>3231 Benda Place<br>Los Angeles, CA 90068 | |
| PFAUEN | Pfauen Verlag<br>Adolfsallee 34<br>Postfach 471<br>D-6200 Wiesbaden<br>Germany | |
| PHILH | Philharmonia | EUR.AM.MUS.<br>(miniature scores) |
| PHILIPPO | Editions Philippo | ELKAN-V |
| PHOEBUS | Phoebus Apollo Music Publishers<br>1126 Huston Drive<br>West Mifflin, PA 15122 | |
| PIEDMONT | Piedmont Music Co. | PRESSER<br>(rental) |
| PILES | Piles Editorial de Musica<br>Archena 33y Yatova, 4<br>Apartado 8.012<br>E-46080 Valencia<br>Spain | |
| PILLIN | Pillin Music | WESTERN |
| PILLON | Pillon Press | THOMAS |
| PIONEER | Pioneer Music Press | MUSICART |
| PIPER | Piper Music Co.<br>P.O. Box 1713<br>Cincinnati, OH 45201 | LIBEN |
| PLAINSONG | Plainsong & Medieval Music Society<br>Catherine Harbor, Hon.Sed.<br>c/o Turner<br>72 Brewery Road<br>London N7 9NE<br>England | |

| Code | Publisher | U.S. Agent |
|---|---|---|
| PLAYER | Player Press<br>139-22 Caney Lane<br>Rosedale, NY 11422 | |
| PLENUM | Plenum Publishing Corp.<br>233 Spring Street<br>New Jork, NY 10013 | DA CAPO |
| PLESNICAR | Don Plesnicar<br>P.O. Box 4880<br>Albuquerque, NM 87106 | |
| PLOUGH | Plough Publishing House<br>Rifton, NY 12471 | |
| PLUCKED ST | Plucked String<br>P.O. Box 11125<br>Arlington, VA 22210 | |
| PLYMOUTH | Plymouth Music Co., Inc.<br>170 N.E. 33rd Street<br>P.O. Box 24330<br>Fort Lauderdale, FL 33334 | |
| PODIUM | Podium Music, Inc.<br>360 Port Washington Boulevard<br>Port Washington, NY 11050 | |
| POLSKIE | Polskie Wydawnictwo Muzyczne<br>Al. Krasinskiego 11a<br>PL31-111 Krakow<br>Poland | PRESSER |
| POLYPH MUS | Polyphone Music Co. | ARCADIA |
| POLYPHON | Polyphon Musikverlag | BREITKOPF-W |
| PORT.MUS. | Portugaliae Musicae<br>Fundaçao Calouste Gulbenkian<br>Avenida de Berna 45<br>P-1093 Lisboa Codex<br>Portugal | |
| | Postif Press Ltd.<br>  see BRENNAN | |
| POST | Posthorn Press | INTRADA |
| POWER | Power and Glory Music Co.<br>6595 S. Dayton St.<br>Englewood, CO 80111 | SON-KEY |
| PRAEGER | Praeger Publications<br>383 Madison Avenue<br>New York, NY 10017 | |
| PRB | PRB Productions<br>963 Peralta Avenue<br>Albany, CA 94706-2144 | |
| PREISSLER | Musikverlag Josef Preissler<br>Postfach 521<br>Bräuhausstraße 8<br>D-8000 München 2<br>Germany | |
| PRELUDE | Prelude Publications<br>150 Wheeler Street<br>Glouchester, MA 01930 | |
| PRENTICE | Prentice-Hall, Inc.<br>Englewood Cliffs, NJ 07632 | |
| PRESSER | Theodore Presser Co.<br>Presser Place<br>Bryn Mawr, PA 19010 | |
| PRESSES | Aux Presses d'Isle-de-France<br>12, rue de la Chaise<br>F-75007 Paris<br>France | |
| PRICE,P | Paul Price Publications<br>470 Kipp Street<br>Teaneck, NJ 07666 | |
| PRIMAVERA | Editions Primavera | GENERAL |
| PRINCE | Prince Publications<br>1125 Francisco Street<br>San Francisco, CA 94109 | |
| PRO ART | Pro Art Publications | CPP-BEL |
| PRO MUSICA | Pro Musica Verlag<br>Postfach 467<br>D-04004 Leipzig<br>Germany | |
| PRO MUSICA INTL | Pro Musica International<br>130 Bylor<br>P.O. Box 1687<br>Pueblo, CO 81002 | |
| PROCLAM | Proclamation Productions, Inc.<br>Orange Square<br>Port Jervis, NY 12771 | |
| PROGRESS | Progress Press<br>P.O. Box 12<br>Winnetka, IL 60093 | |
| PROPRIUS | Proprius Musik AB<br>Vartavagen 35<br>S-115 29 Stockholm<br>Sweden | |
| PROSVETNI | Prosvetni Servis | DRUSTVO |
| PROVIDENCE | Providence Music Press<br>251 Weybosset St.<br>Providence, RI 02903 | |
| PROVINCTWN | Provincetown Bookshop Eitions<br>246 Commercial Street<br>Provincetown, MA 02657 | |
| PROWSE | Keith Prowse Music Publishing Co.<br>138-140 Charing Cross Road<br>London, WC2H 0LD<br>England | INTER.MUS.P |
| PRUETT | Pruett Publishing Co.<br>2928 Pearl<br>Boulder, CO 80301-9989 | |
| PSALTERY | Psaltery Music Publications<br>P.O. Box 111325<br>Dallas, TX 75223 | KENDALE |
| PSI | PSI Press<br>P.O. Box 2320<br>Boulder, CO 80306 | |
| PTM | PTM Music Manuscripts<br>6004 Candlewood Ct.<br>Brooklyn Park, MN 55443 | |

## PUBLISHER DIRECTORY

| Code | Publisher | U.S. Agent |
|---|---|---|
| PURIFOY | Purifoy Publishing<br>P.O. Box 30157<br>Knoxville, TN 37930 | JENSEN |
| PUSTET | Verlag Friedrich Pustet<br>Gutenbergstraße 8<br>Postfach 339<br>D-8400 Regensburg 11<br>Germany | |
| PYRAMINX | Pyraminx Publications | ACCURA |
| QUEEN | Queensgate Music<br>120 Dowanhill Street<br>Glasgow G12 9DN<br>Scotland | |
| QUIROGA | Ediciones Quiroga<br>Alcalá, 70<br>28009 Madrid<br>Spain | PRESSER |
| RAD | Radiant Music<br>1445 Boonville Avenue<br>Springfield, MO 65802 | |
| RAHTER | D. Rahter<br>Werderstraße 44<br>D-2000 Hamburg 13<br>Germany | SCHAUR |
| RAMSEY | Basil Ramsey Publisher of Music | INTRADA |
| RARITIES | Rarities For Strings Publications<br>11300 Juniper Drive<br>University Circle<br>Cleveland, OH 44106 | |
| RAVEN | Raven Press<br>1185 Avenue of the Americas<br>New York, NY 10036 | |
| REAL | Real Musical Publicaciones y<br>   Ediciones, S.A.<br>CTRA, C-501, KM9, 300<br>APDO, De Correos No. 27<br>28670 Villaviciosa De Odón Madrid,<br>Spain | |
| RECITAL | Recital Publications, Ltd.<br>P.O. Box 1697<br>Huntsville, TX 77342-1697 | |
| | Regent, Arc & Goodman<br>   see GOODMAN | |
| REGENT | Regent Music Corp.<br>488 Madison Avenue<br>5th Floor<br>New York, NY 10022 | LEONARD-US |
| REGINA | Regina Verlag<br>Schumannstraße 35<br>Postfach 6148<br>D-6200 Wiesbaden 1<br>Germany | |
| REGUS | Regus Publisher<br>10 Birchwood Lane<br>White Bear Lake, MN 55110 | |
| REIMERS | Edition Reimers AB<br>Box 15030<br>S-16115 Bromma<br>Sweden | PRESSER |
| REINHARDT | Friedrich Reinhardt Verlag<br>Missionsstraße 36<br>CH-4055 Basel<br>Switzerland | |
| REN | Les Editions Renaissantes | EUR.AM.MUS. |
| RENK | Musikverlag Renk "Varia Edition"<br>Herzog-Heinrich-Straße 21<br>D-8000 München 2<br>Germany | |
| RESEARCH | Research Publications, Inc.<br>Lunar Drive<br>Woodbridge, CT 06525 | |
| RESOU | Resource Publications, Inc.<br>160 E. Virginia Street, #290<br>San Jose, CA 95112-5876 | |
| RESTOR | Restoration Press | THOMAS |
| REUTER | Reuter & Reuter Förlag AB<br>Box 26072<br>S-100 41 Stockholm<br>Sweden | |
| RHODES,R | Roger Rhodes Music, Ltd.<br>P.O. Box 1550, Radio City Station<br>New York, NY 10101 | |
| RICHMOND | Richmond Music Press, Inc.<br>P.O. Box 465<br>Richmond, IN 47374 | |
| RICHMOND ORG. | The Richmond Organization<br>11 W. 19th St., Suite 711<br>New York, NY 10011<br>   see also TRO | PLYMOUTH |
| RICORDI-ARG | Ricordi Americana S.A.<br>Cangallo, 1558<br>1037 Buenos Aires<br>Argentina | LEONARD-US<br>BOOSEY<br>(rental) |
| RICORDI-BR | Ricordi Brasileira S.A.<br>R. Conselheiro Nebias 773<br>1 S-10-12<br>Sao Paulo<br>Brazil | LEONARD-US<br>BOOSEY<br>(rental) |
| RICORDI-CAN | G. Ricordi & Co.<br>Toronto<br>Canada | LEONARD-US<br>BOOSEY<br>(rental) |
| RICORDI-ENG | G. Ricordi & Co. Ltd.<br>The Bury, Church Street<br>Chesham, Bucks HP5 1JG<br>England | LEONARD-US<br>BOOSEY<br>(rental) |
| RICORDI-FR | Société Anonyme des Éditions<br>   Ricordi | LEONARD-US<br>BOOSEY<br>(rental) |
| RICORDI-GER | G. Ricordi & Co.<br>Postfach 114<br>D-85618 Feldkirchen Bei München<br>Germany | LEONARD-US<br>BOOSEY<br>(rental) |

| Code | Publisher | U.S. Agent |
|---|---|---|
| RICORDI-IT | G.Ricordi & Co.<br>see BMG RICORDI | LEONARD-US<br>BOOSEY<br>(rental) |
| RIDEAU | Les Éditions Rideau Rouge<br>24, rue de Longchamp<br>F-75116 Paris<br>France | PRESSER<br>SCHIR.G |
| RIES | Ries & Erler<br>Charlottenbrunner Straße 42<br>D-4193 Berlin (Grunewald)<br>Germany | |
| RILEY | Dr. Maurice W. Riley<br>Eastern Michigan University<br>512 Rossevelt Boulevard<br>Ypsilanti, MI 48197 | |
| ROBBINS | Robbins Music Corp. | CPP-BEL<br>PRESSER<br>(rental) |
| ROBERTON | Roberton Publications<br>The Windmill, Wendover<br>Aylesbury, Bucks, HP22 6JJ<br>England | PRESSER |
| ROBERTS,L | Lee Roberts Music Publications, Inc.<br>P.O. Box 225<br>Katonah, NY 10536 | |
| ROBITSCHEK | Adolf Robitschek Musikverlag<br>Graben 14 (Bräunerstraße 2)<br>Postfach 42<br>A-1011 Wien<br>Austria | |
| ROCHESTER | Rochester Music Publishers, Inc.<br>358 Aldrich Road<br>Fairport, NY 14450 | ACCURA |
| RODEHEAVER | Rodeheaver Publications | WORD |
| ROLLAND | Rolland String Reasearch Associates<br>#101 W. Windsor Road #3114<br>Urbana, IL 61801 | BOOSEY |
| RONCORP | Roncorp, Inc.<br>P.O. Box 724<br>Cherry Hill, NJ 08003 | |
| RONGWEN | Rongwen Music, Inc. | BROUDE BR |
| ROSSUM | Wed. J.R. van Rossum | ZENGERINK |
| ROUART | Rouart-Lerolle & Cie | SCHIRM.G |
| ROW | R.D. Row Music Co. | FISHER,C |
| ROYAL | Royal School of Church Music<br>Addington Palace<br>Croydon, Surrey CR9 5AD<br>England<br><br>Associated Board of the Royal Schools<br>  of Music<br>    see ABRSM | |
| ROYAL,TAP. | Royal Tapestry<br>50 Music Square West<br>Suite 500A<br>Nashville, TN 37203 | ALEX.HSE |
| ROZSAVÖ | Rozsavölgi & Co. | BUDAPEST |
| RUBANK | Rubank, Inc.<br>16215 N.W. 15th Avenue<br>Miami, FL 33169 | LEONARD-US |
| RUBATO | Rubato Musikverlag<br>Hollandstraße 18<br>A-1020 Wien<br>Austria | DONEMUS |
| RUH,E | Emil Ruh Musikverlag<br>Zürichstraße 33<br>CH-8134<br>Adliswil - Zürich<br>Switzerland | |
| RUMAN.COMP. | Uniunea Compozitorilor din<br>  R.S. România<br>(Union of Rumanian Composers)<br>Str. C. Escarcu No. 2<br>Bucuresti, Sector 1<br>Rumania | |
| RUND | Musikverlag Rundel<br>Postfach 61<br>D-88428 Rot an der Rot<br>Germany | |
| RUSSICA | Musica Russica<br>27 Willow Lane<br>Madison, CT 06443 | |
| RUTGERS | Rutgers University Editions | JERONA |
| RYDET | Rydet Music Publishers<br>P.O. Box 477<br>Purchase, NY 10577 | |
| SAC.MUS.PR. | Sacred Music Press of Hebrew Union<br>  College<br>One West Fourth Street<br>New York, NY 10012 | TRANSCON. |
| SACRED | Sacred Music Press | LORENZ |
| SACRED SNGS | Sacred Songs, Inc. | WORD |
| SALABERT | Francis Salabert Éditions<br>22 rue chauchat<br>F-75009 Paris<br>France | LEONARD-US<br>(sales)<br>SCHIRM.G<br>(rental) |
| SAMFUNDET | Samfundet til udgivelse af Dansk<br>  Musik<br>Valkendorfsgade 3<br>DK-1151 Kobenhavn<br>Denmark | PETERS |
| SAN ANDREAS | San Andreas Press<br>3732 Laguna Avenue<br>Palo Alto, CA 94306 | |
| SANJO | Sanjo Music Co.<br>P.O. Box 7000-104<br>Palos Verdes Peninsula, CA 90274 | |
| SAUL AVE | Saul Avenue Publishing Co.<br>4172 Fox Hollow Drive<br>Cincinnati, OH 45241-2939 | |
| SNATA | Santa Barbara Music Publishing<br>P.O. Box 41003<br>Santa Barbara, CA 93140 | |

## PUBLISHER DIRECTORY

| Code | Publisher | U.S. Agent |
|---|---|---|
| SAVGOS | Savgos Music Inc.<br>P.O. Box 279<br>Elizabeth, NJ 07207 | |
| SCARECROW | The Scarecrow Press, Inc.<br>4720 Boston Way<br>Lanham, MD 20706 | |
| SCHAUM | Schaum Publications, Inc.<br>2018 East North Avenue<br>Milwaukee, WI 53202 | |
| SCHAUR | Richard Schauer, Music Publishers<br>67 Belsize Lane, Hampstead<br>London NW3 5AX<br>England | PRESSER |
| SCHEIDT | Altonaer Scheidt-Ausgabe | HÄNSSLER |
| SCHERZANDO | Muziekuitgeverij Scherzando<br>Lovelingstraat 20-22<br>B-2000 Antwerpen<br>Belgium | |
| SCHIRM.EC | E.C. Schirmer Music Co.<br>138 Ipswich Street<br>Boston, MA 02215-3534 | |
| SCHIRM.G | G. Schirmer, Inc. (Executive Offices)<br>257 Park Avenue South, 20th Floor<br>New York, NY 10010<br><br>G.Schirmer Rental Performance Dept.<br>P.O. Box 572<br>5 Bellvale Road<br>Chester, NY 10918 | LEONARD-US<br>(sales) |
| SCHMIDT,H | Musikverlag Hermann Schmidt<br>Berliner Straße 26<br>D-6000 Frank-am-Main 1<br>Germany | |
| SCHMITT | Schmitt Music Editions | CPP-BEL |
| SCHNEIDER,H | Musikverlag Hans Schneider<br>Mozartstraße 6<br>D-8132 Tutzing<br>Germany | |
| SCHOLA | Editions Musicales de la Schola<br>  Cantorum<br>Rue du Spain 2A<br>CH-2114 Fleurier<br>Switzerland | |
| SCHOTT | Schott & Co. Ltd.<br>Brunswick Road<br>Ashford, Kent TN23 1DX<br>England | EUR.AM.MUS. |
| SCHOTT-FRER | Schott Frères<br>30 rue Saint-Jean<br>B-1000 Bruxelles<br>Belgium | EUR.AM.MUS. |
| SCHOTT,J | Schott & CO.<br>Kasuga Bldg., 2-9-3 Iidabashi,<br>Chiyoda-ku<br>Tokyo 102<br>Japan | EUR.AM.MUS. |
| SCHOTTS | B. Schotts Söhne<br>Weihergarten 5<br>Postfach 3640<br>D-6500 Mainz<br>Germany | EUR.AM.MUS. |
| SCHROTH | Edition Schroth<br>Kommandatenstrasse 5A<br>D-1 Berlin 45<br>Germany | BÄREN. |
| SCHUBERTH | Edward Schuberth & Co., Inc. | CENTURY |
| SCHUBERTH,J | J. Schuberth & Co.<br>Marienstrasse 13<br>D-99817 Eisenach<br>Germany | |
| SCHUL | Carl L. Schultheiß<br>Postfach 1736<br>D-82145 Planegg Bei München<br>Germany | |
| SCHULZ.FR | Blasmusikverlag Fritz Schulz<br>Am Märzengraben 6<br>D-7800 Freiburg-Tiengen<br>Germany | |
| SCHWANN | Musikverlag Schwann | PETERS |
| SCHWEIZER | Schweizericher Kirchengesangbund<br>Markusstrasse 6<br>CH- 2544 Bettlach<br>Switzerland | FOSTER |
| SCOTT | G. Scott Music Publishing CCo. | WESTERN |
| SCOTT MUSIC | Scott Music Publications | ALFRED |
| SCOTUS | Scotus Music Publications, Ltd. | ESCHENB |
| SCREEN | Screen Gems<br>Columbia Pictures | WARNER |
| SDG PR | SDG Press<br>170 N.E. 33rd Street<br>Ft. Lauderdale, FL 33334 | PLYMOUTH |
| SEAMONT | Seamont International | INTRADA |
| SEESAW | Seesaw Music Corp.<br>2067 Broadway<br>New York, NY 10023 | |
| SELAH | Selah Publishing Co.<br>P.O. Box 3037<br>Kingston, NY 12401 | |
| SELMER | Selmer Éditions<br>18, rue de la Fontaine-au-Roi<br>F-75011 Paris<br>France | |
| SEMI | Société d'Editions Musicales<br>  Internationales | PEER |
| SENART | Ed. Maurice Senart<br>22 rue Chauchat<br>F-75009 Paris<br>France | SCHIRM.G |

| Code | Publisher | U.S. Agent |
|---|---|---|
| SEPT | September Music Corp.<br>250 W. 57th Street<br>New York, NY 10019 | |
| SERENUS | Serenus Corp.<br>145 Palisade Street<br>Dobbs Fery, NY 10522 | |
| SERM | Servant Music | INTRADA |
| SERVANT | Servant Publications<br>P.O. Box 8617<br>840 Airport Boulevard<br>Ann Arbor. MI 48107 | |
| SESAC | Sesac, Inc.<br>10 Columbus Circle<br>New York, NY 10019 | |
| SHALL-U-MO | Shall-U-Mo Publications<br>P.O. Box 2824<br>Rochester, NY 14626 | |
| SHAPIRO | Shapiro, Bernstein & Co., Inc.<br>10 East 53 Street<br>New York, NY 10022 | PLYMOUTH |
| SHATTINGER | Shattinger Music Co.<br>1810 S. Broadway<br>St. Louis, MO 63104 | |
| SHAWNEE | Shawnee Press, Inc.<br>49 Waring Drive<br>Delaware Water Gap, PA 18327-1099 | MUSIC |
| SHEPPARD | John Sheppard Music Press | EUR.AM.MUS. |
| | Antigua Casa Sherry-Brener, Ltd.<br>See ACSB | |
| SIDEMTON | Sidemton Verlag | BREITKOPF-W |
| SIFLER | Paul J. Sifler<br>3947 Fredonia Drive<br>Hollywood, CA 90068 | |
| SIGHT & SOUND | Sight & Sound International<br>3200 South 166th Street<br>Box 27<br>New Berlin, WI 53151 | |
| SUN | D. van Sijn & Zonen<br>Banorstraat 1<br>Rotterdam<br>Netherlands | |
| SIKORSKI | Hans Sikorski Verlag<br>Johnsallee 23<br>Postfach 132001<br>D-2000 Hamburg 13<br>Germany | LEONARD-US |
| SIMROCK | Nicholas Simrock<br>Lyra House<br>37 Belsize Lane<br>London NW3 5AX<br>England | PRESSER |
| SINGSPIR | Singspiration Music<br>The Zondervan Corp.<br>1415 Lake Drive S.E.<br>Grand Rapids, MI 49506 | |
| SIRIUS | Sirius-verlag | PETERS |

| Code | Publisher | U.S. Agent |
|---|---|---|
| SKAND | Skandinvisk Musicforlag<br>Gothersgade 9-11<br>DK-1123 Kobenhavn K.<br>Denmark | |
| SLATKINE | Slatkine Reprints<br>5 rue des Chaudronniers<br>Case 765<br>CH-1211 Genève 3<br>Switzland | |
| SLOVAKA | Slovenska Akademija Znanosti in<br>   Umetnosti<br>Trg Francoske Revolucije 6<br>Ljubljana<br>Slovenia | |
| SLOV.HUD.FOND. | Slovenský Hudobny Fond<br>Fucikova 29<br>811 02 Bratislava<br>Slovakia | BOOSEY<br>(rental) |
| SLOV.MAT | Slovenska Matica | DRUSTVO |
| SMITH PUB | Smith Publications-Sonic Art Editions<br>2617 Gwynndale Avenue<br>Baltimore, MD 21207 | |
| SMPF | SMPF, Inc.<br>16 E. 34th St., 7th Floor<br>New York, NY 10016 | |
| SOC.FR.MUS. | Société Française de Music | TRANSAT |
| | Society for the Preservation &<br>  Encouragement of Barber Shop<br>  Quartet Singing in America<br>    see SPEBSQSA | |
| SOC.PUB.AM. | Society for the Publication<br>  of American Music | PRESSER |
| | Société d'Éditions Musicales<br>  internationales<br>    see SEMI | |
| | Society of Finnish Composers<br>    see SUOMEN | |
| SOLAR | The Solar Studio<br>178 Cowles Road<br>Woodbury, CT 06798 | |
| SOLID | Solid Foundation Music | SON-KEY |
| SOMERSET | Somerset Press | HOPE |
| SON-KEY | Son-Key, Inc.<br>P.O. Box 31757<br>Aurora, CO 80041 | |
| SONANTE | Sonante Publications<br>P.O. Box 74, Station F<br>Toronto, Ontario M4Y 2L4<br>Canada | |
| SONOS | Sonos Music Resources, Inc.<br>P.O. Box 1510<br>Orem, UT 84057 | |
| SONSHINE | Sonshine Productions | LORENZ |

## PUBLISHER DIRECTORY

| Code | Publisher | U.S. Agent |
|---|---|---|
| SONZOGNO | Casa Musicale Sonzogno<br>Via Bigli 11<br>I-20121 Milano<br>Italy | PRESSER |
| SOUTHERN | Southern Music Co.<br>1100 Broadway<br>P.O. Box 329<br>San Antonio, TX 78292 | |
| SOUTHERN PUB | Southern Music Publishing Co., Pty. Ltd.<br>Sydney, Australia | PEER |
| SOUTHWEST | Southwest Music Publications<br>Box 4552<br>Santa Fe, NM 87502 | |
| SPAN.MUS.CTR. | Spanish Music Center, Inc.<br>4 Division Street<br>P.O. Box 132<br>Farmingville, NY 11738 | |
| SPEBSQSA | Society for the Preservation & Encouragement of Barber Shop Quartet Singing in America, Inc.<br>6315 Third Avenue<br>Kenosha, WI 53143-5199 | |
| SPIRE | Spire Editions | FISHER,C<br>WORLD |
| SPRATT | Spratt Music Publishers<br>17 West 60th Street, 8th Fl.<br>New York, NY 10023 | PLYMOUTH |
| ST.GREG | St. Gregory Publishing Co.<br>64 Pineheath Road<br>High Kelling, Holt<br>Norfolk, NR25 6RH<br>England | ROYAL |
| ST.MARTIN | St. Martin Music Co., Inc. | ROYAL |
| STAFF | Staff Music Publishing Co., Inc.<br>170 N.E. 33rd St.<br>Ft. Lauderdale, FL 33334 | PLYMOUTH |
| STAINER | Stainer & Bell Ltd.<br>P.O. Box 110, Victoria House<br>23 Gruneisen Road<br>London N3 1DZ<br>England | HOPE |
| STAMON | Nick Stamon Press<br>4280 Middlesex Drive<br>San Diego, CA 92116 | |
| STAMPS | Stamps-Baxter Music Publications<br>Box 4007<br>Dallas, TX 75208 | SINGSPIR |
| STANDARD | Standard Music Publishing, Inc. | |
| STANGLAND | Thomas C. Stangland Co.<br>P.O. Box 19263<br>Portland, OR 97280 | |
| STEIN | Edition Steingräber<br>Auf der Reiswiese 9<br>D-6050 Offenbach/M.<br>Germany | |
| STILL | William Grant Still Music<br>22 S. San Francisco Street<br>Suite 422<br>Flagstaff, AZ 86001-5737 | |
| STIM | STIMs Informationcentral för Svensk Musik<br>Sandhamnsgatan 79<br>Box 27327<br>S-102 54 Stockholm<br>Sweden | |
| STOCKHAUS | Stockhausen-Verlag<br>Kettenberg 15<br>D-51515 Kürten<br>Germany<br><br>Stockhausen-Verlag, U.S.<br>2832 Maple Lane<br>Fairfax, VA 22030 | |
| STOCKTON | Fred Stockton<br>P.O. Box 814<br>Grass Valley, CA 95945 | |
| STRONG | Stronghold Publications | ALEX.HSE. |
| STUD | Studio 224 | STUDIO |
| STUDIO | Studio P/R, Inc. | CPP-BEL |
| STYRIA | Verlag Styria<br>Schönaugasse 64<br>Postfach 435<br>A-8011 Graz<br>Austria | |
| SUECIA | Edition Suecia | STIM |
| SUISEISHA | Suiseisha Editions | ONGAKU |
| SUMMA | Summa Productions | AMSI |
| SUMMIT | Summit Music Ltd.<br>38 North Row<br>London W1R 1DH<br>England | |
| SUMMY | Summy-Birchard Co.<br>265 Secaucus Road<br>Secaucus, NJ 07096-2037 | LEONARD-US |
| SUOM | Suomen Laulajien JA<br>Soittajien Liitto Fredrikinkatu 61<br>FIN-00100 Helsinki<br>Finland | |
| SUOMEN | Suomen Säveltäjät ry<br>(Society of Finnish Composers)<br>Runeberginkatu 15 A<br>SF-00100 Helsinki 10<br>Finland | |
| SUPPORT | Support Services<br>79 South Street<br>P.O. Box 478<br>Natick, MA 01760 | |
| SUPRAPHON | Supraphon<br>Palckeho 1<br>CS-112 99 Praha 1<br>Czech Republic | FOR.MUS.DIST<br>(rental)<br>NEW W |

# PUBLISHER DIRECTORY

| Code | Publisher | U.S. Agent |
|---|---|---|
| | Svenska Utbildningsförlaget Liber AB<br>see LIBER | |
| SVERIG | Sveriges Körföbund<br>Walton Rosenlundsgatan 54<br>S-116 53 Stockholm, Sweden | |
| SWAN | Swan & CO.<br>P.O. Box 1<br>Rickmansworth, Herts WD3 3AZ<br>England | ARCADIA |
| SWAND | Swand Publications<br>120 North Longcross Road<br>Linthicum Heights, MD 21090 | |
| | Swedish Music Information Center<br>see STIM | |
| SYMPHON | Symphonia Verlag | CPP-BEL |
| TAUNUS | Taunus | HOFMEISTER-W |
| TCAPUB | TCA Publications<br>Teacher-Composer Alliance<br>P.O. Box 6428<br>Evanston, IL 60204 | |
| TELCA | Telca Editions<br>Soar Chapel<br>Penderyn<br>South Wales CF 44 9JY<br>United Kingdom | |
| TEESELING | Muziekuitgeverij van seeseling<br>Buurmansweg 29B<br>NL-6525 RV Nijmegen<br>Netherlands | |
| TEMPLETN | Templeton Publishing Co., Inc. | SHAWNEE |
| TEMPO | Tempo Music Publications<br>3773 W. 95th Street<br>Leawood, KS 66206 | ALEX.HSE. |
| TEMPO P | Tempo Praha | PRESSER |
| TEN TIMES | Ten Times A Day<br>P.O. Box 230<br>Deer Park, L.I., NY 11729 | |
| TENUTO | Tenuto Publications<br>see also TRI-TEN | PRESSER |
| TETRA | Tetra Music Corp. | PLYMOUTH<br>WESL<br>(rental) |
| TFS | Things For Strings Publishing Co.<br>P.O. Box 9263<br>Alexandria, VA 22304 | |
| THAMES | Thames Publishing<br>14 Barlby Road<br>London W10 6AR<br>England | |
| THOMAS | Thomas House Publications<br>P.O. Box 1423<br>San Carlos, CA 94070 | INTRADA |
| THOMI | E. Thomi-Berg Musikverlag<br>Postfach 1736<br>D-82145 Planegg Bei München<br>Germany | |
| THOMP. | Thompson Music House<br>P.O. Box 12463<br>Nashville, TN 37212 | |
| THOMPS.G | Gordon V. Thompson Music<br>see WAR | |
| THORP | Thorpe Music Publishing Co. | PRESSER |
| TIEROLFF | Tierolff Muziek Centrale<br>P.O. Box 18<br>NL-4700 AA Roosendaal<br>Netherlands | |
| TISCHER | Tischer und Jagenberg Musikverlag<br>Nibelungenstraße 48<br>D-8000 München 19<br>Germany | |
| TOA | Toa Editions | ONGAKU |
| TONGER | P.J. Tonger, Musikverlag<br>Postfach 501818<br>50978 Köln<br>Germany | |
| TONOS | Editions Tonos<br>Ahastraße 9<br>D-6100 Darmstadt<br>Germany | SEESAW |
| TOORTS | Muziekuitgeverij De Toorts<br>Nijverheidsweg 1<br>Postbus 576<br>NL-2003 RN Haarlem<br>Netherlands | |
| TRANSAT. | Éditions Musicales Transatlantiques<br>151, avenue Jean-Jaures<br>F-75019 Paris<br>France | PRESSER<br>GENERAL<br>(rental) |
| TRANSCON. | Transcontinental Music Publications<br>838 Fifth Avenue<br>New York, NY 10021 | |
| TREKEL | Joachim-Trekel-Verlag<br>Postfach 620428<br>D-2000 Hamburg 62<br>Germany | |
| TRI-TEN | Tritone Press and Tenuto<br>Publications<br>P.O. Box 5081, Southern Station<br>Hattiesburg, MS 39401 | PRESSER |
| TRIGON | Trigon Music Inc. | LORENZ |
| TRINITY | Trinity House Publishing | CRESPUB |
| TRIUNE | Triune Music, Inc. | LORENZ |
| TRN | TRN Music Publishers<br>111 Torreon Loop<br>P.O. Box 1076<br>Ruidoso, NM 88345 | |

## PUBLISHER DIRECTORY

| Code | Publisher | U.S. Agent |
|---|---|---|
| TRO | TRO Songways Service, Inc.<br>11 W. 19th St., Suite 711<br>New York, NY 10011<br>see also RICHMOND ORG. | PLYMOUTH |
| TROY | Troy State University Library<br>Troy, AL 36081 | |
| TUSKEGEE | Tuskegee Institute Music Press | KJOS |
| U.S.CATH | United States Catholic Conference<br>Publications Office<br>1312 Massachusetts Avenue N.W.<br>Washington, D.C. 20005 | |
| UBER,D | David Uber<br>Music Department<br>Trenton State College<br>Trenton, NJ 08625 | |
| UFATON | Ufaton-Verlag | ORLANDO |
| UNC | UNC Jazz Press<br>University of Northern Colorado<br>Greeley, CO 80639 | |
| UNICORN | Unicorn Music Company, Inc. | BOSTON |
| UNION ESP. | Union Musical Ediciones<br>Carrera de San Jeronimo 26<br>Madrid 14<br>Spain | SCHIRM.G |
| UNISONG | Unisong Publishers | PRESSER |
| UNITED ART | United Artists Group | CPP-BEL<br>PRESSER<br>(rental) |
| UNITED MUS. | United Music Publishers Ltd.<br>42 Rivington Street<br>London EC2A 3BN<br>England | PRESSER |
| UNIV.ALA | University of Alabama Press<br>Box 870380<br>Tuscaloosa, AL 35487-0380 | |
| UNIV.CAL | University of California Press<br>2120 Berkeley Way<br>Berkeley, CA 94720 | |
| UNIV.CH | University of Chicago Press<br>5801 South Ellis Avenue<br>Chicago, IL 60637 | |
| UNIV.CR | University College - Cardiff Press<br>P.O. Box 78<br>Cardiff CF1 1XL, Wales<br>United Kingdom | |
| UNIV.EVAN | University of Evansville Press<br>P.O. Box 329<br>Evansville, IN 47702 | |
| UNIV.IOWA | University of Iowa Press<br>Iowa City, IA 52242 | |
| UNIV.MIAMI | University of Miami Music<br>Publications<br>P.O. Box 8163<br>Coral Gables, FL 33124 | PLYMOUTH |
| UNIV.MICRO | University Microfilms<br>300 North Zeeb Road<br>Ann Arbor, MI 48106 | |
| UNIV.MINN | University of Minnesota Press<br>2037 University Avenue S.E.<br>Minneapolis, MN 55455 | |
| UNIV.MUS.ED | University Music Editions<br>P.O. Box 192-Ft. George Station<br>New York, NY 10040 | |
| UNIV.NC | University of North Carolina Press<br>P.O. Box 2288<br>Chapel Hill, NC 27514 | |
| UNIV.OTAGO | University of Otago Press<br>P.O. Box 56<br>Dunedin<br>New Zealand | |
| UNIV.TEXAS | University of Texas Press<br>P.O. Box 7819<br>Austin, TX 78712 | |
| UNIV.UTAH | University of Utah Press<br>Salt Lake City, UT 84112 | |
| UNNIV.WASH | University of Washington Press<br>Seattle, WA 98105 | |
| UNIVER. | Universal Edition<br>Bösendorfer Straße 12<br>Postfach 130<br>A-1015 Wien<br>Austria | EUR.AM.MUS. |
| | Universal Edition (London) Ltd.<br>2/3 Fareham Street, Dean Street<br>London W1V 4DU<br>England | EUR.AM.MUS. |
| UNIVERH | Universal Songs Holland<br>Postbus 305<br>1200 AH Hilversum<br>Netherlands | GM |
| UNIVERSE | Universe Publishers<br>P.O. Box 1900<br>Orem, UT 84059 | PRESSER |
| UP WITH | Up With People<br>3103 North Campbell Avenue<br>Tucson, AZ 85719 | LORENZ |
| VAAP | VAAP<br>6a, Bolshaya Bronnaya St.<br>Moscow 103670,GSP<br>Russia | SCHIRM.G |
| VALANDO | Valando Music, Inc. | PLYMOUTH |
| VAMO | Musikverlag Vamö<br>Leebgasse 52-25<br>Wien 10<br>Austria | |
| VAN NESS | Van Ness Press, Inc. | BROADMAN |
| VANDEN-RUP | Vandenhoeck & Ruprecht<br>Theaterstrasse 13<br>Postfach 3753<br>D-3400 Göttingen<br>Germany | |

# PUBLISHER DIRECTORY

| Code | Publisher | U.S. Agent |
|---|---|---|
| VANDERSALL | Vandersall Editions | EUR.AM.MUS. |
| VANGUARD | Vanguard Music Corp.<br>357 W. 55th Street<br>New York, NY 10019 | |
| VER.HUIS | Vereniging voor Huismuziek<br>Utrechtsestraat 77<br>Postbus 350<br>NL-3041 CT Ijsselstein<br>Netherlands | |
| VER.NED.MUS. | Vereniging voor Nederlandse Muziekgeschiedenis<br>Postbus 1514<br>NL-3500 BM Utrecht<br>Netherlands | |
| VEST-NORSK | Vest-Norsk Musikkforslag<br>Postboks 4016, Dreggen<br>N-5023 Bergen<br>Norway | |
| VIERT | Viertmann Verlag<br>Lübecker Straße 2<br>D-5000 Köln 1<br>Germany | |
| VIEWEG | Chr. Friedrich Viewweg, Musikverlag<br>Nibelungenstrße 48<br>D-8000 München 19<br>Germany | LEONARD-US<br>SCHIRM.G<br>(rental) |
| VIKING | Viking Press, Inc<br>P.O. Box 4030<br>Church Street Station<br>New York, NY 10261-4030 | |
| VIOLA | Viola World Publications<br>14 Fenwood Road<br>Huntington Station, NY 11746 | |
| VOGGEN | Voggenrieter Verlag<br>Viktoriastraße 25<br>D-5300 Bonn<br>Germany | |
| VOGT | Musikverlag Vogt & Fritz<br>Friedrich-Stein-Straße 10<br>D-8720 Schweinfurt<br>Germany | |
| VOICE | Voice of the Rockies<br>P.O. Box 1043<br>Boulder, CO 80306-1043 | |
| VOLK | Arno Volk Verlag | BREITKOPF-W |
| VOLKWEIN | Volkwein Brothers, Inc. | CPP-BEL |
| WADSWORTH | Wadsworth Publishing Co.<br>10 Davis Street<br>Belmont, CA 94002 | |
| WAGENAAR | J.A.H. Wagenaar<br>Oude Gracht 109<br>NL-3511 AG Utrecht<br>Netherlands | ELKAN,H |
| WAI-TE-ATA | Wai-te-ata Press<br>Dept. of Music<br>Victoria University of Wellington<br>P.O. Box 600<br>Wellington, New Zealand | |
| WALKER | Walker Publications<br>P.O. Box 61<br>Arnold, MD 21012 | |
| WALKER MUS.PRO. | Walker Music Productions<br>643 Oenoke Ridge<br>New Canaan, CT 06840 | |
| WALTON | Walton Music Corp.<br>170 N.E. 33rd Street<br>Ft. Lauderdale, FL 33334 | |
| WARNER | Warner Brothers Publications, Inc.<br>15800 NW 48th Avenue<br>Hialeah, FL 33014<br><br>Warner-Chappell Music<br>810 Seventh Avenue<br>New York, NY 10119 | |
| WAR-CH AUS | Warner/Chapel Music<br>1 Cassins Avenue<br>North Sidney NSW 2060<br>Australia | |
| WATERLOO | Waterloo Music Co. Ltd.<br>3 Regina Street North<br>Waterloo, Ontario N2J 4A5<br>Canada | |
| WEHMAN BR. | Wehman Brothers, Inc.<br>Ridgedale Avenue<br>Morris County Mall<br>Cedar Knolls, NJ 07927 | |
| WEINBERGER | Josef Weinberger Ltd.<br>12-14 Mortimer Street<br>London W1N 7RD<br>England<br><br>Josef Weinberger<br>Oeder Weg 26<br>D-60318 Frankfurt<br>Germany | BOOSEY<br>CANTORIS<br>BOCK |
| WEINTRUB | Weintraub Music Co. | SCHIRM.G<br>(rental) |
| WELT | Welt Musik<br>Josef Hochmuth Verlage<br>Hegergasse 21<br>A-1160 Wien<br>Austria | |
| WESL | Wesleyan Music Press<br>P.O. Box 1072<br>Fort George Station<br>New York, NY 10040 | |
| WESSMAN | Wessmans Musikforlag<br>S-620 30 Slite<br>Sweden | STIM |
| WESTEND | Westend | PETERS |
| WESTERN | Western International Music, Inc.<br>3707 65th Avenue<br>Greeley, CO 80634 | |
| WESTMINSTER | The Westminster Press<br>925 Chestnut Street<br>Philadelphia, PA 19107 | |

## PUBLISHER DIRECTORY

| Code | Publisher | U.S. Agent |
|---|---|---|
| WESTWOOD | Westwood Press, Inc.<br>3759 Willow Road<br>Schiller Park, IL 60176 | WORLD |
| WHITE HARV. | White Harvest Music Publications<br>P.O. Box 1144<br>Independence, MO 64051 | |
| WIDE WORLD | Wide World Music, Inc.<br>Box B<br>Delaware Water Gap, PA 18327 | |
| WIEN BOH. | Wiener Boheme Verlag GmbH<br>Sonnenstraße 19<br>D-8000 München 2<br>Germany | |
| WIENER | Wiener Urtext Edition | EUR.AM.MUS. |
| WILDER | Wilder | MARGUN |
| WILHELM | Wilhelmiana Musikverlag<br>see HANSEN-GER | |
| | William Grant Still Music<br>see STILL | |
| | Williams School of Church Music<br>see WSCM | |
| WILLIAMSN | Williamson Music, Inc. | LEONARD-US |
| WILLIS | Willis Music Co.<br>7380 Industrial Road<br>Florence, KY 41042 | |
| WILLSHIRE | Willshire Press Music Foundation, Inc. | WESTERN |
| WILSHORN | Wilshorn | HOPE |
| WILSON | Wilson Editions<br>13 Bank Square<br>Wilmslow SK9 1AN<br>England | (see DIM) |
| WIMBLEDN | Wimbledon Music Inc.<br>1888 Century Park East<br>Suite 10<br>Century City, CA 90067 | |
| WIND MUS | Wind Music, Inc.<br>153 Highland Parkway<br>Rochester, NY 14620 | KALMUS,A |
| WINGERT | Wingert-Jones Music, Inc.<br>2026 Broadway<br>P.O. Box 419878<br>Kansas City, MO 64141 | |
| WISCAS | Wiscasset Music Publishing Company<br>Box 810<br>Cambridge, MA 02138 | |
| WOITSCHACH | Paul Woitschach Radio-Musikverlag<br>Grosse Friedberger Strasse 23-27<br>D-6000 Frankfurt<br>Germany | |
| WOLF | see WOLFL | WESTERN |
| WOLFL | Wolfland Music Publishing<br>7949 Belton Drive<br>Los Angeles, CA 90045 | |

| Code | Publisher | U.S. Agent |
|---|---|---|
| WOLLENWEBER | Verlag Walter Wollenweber<br>Schiffmannstrasse 4<br>Postfach 1165<br>D-8032 Gräfelfing vor München<br>Germany | FOR.MUS.DIST |
| WOODBURY | Woodbury Music Co.<br>33 Grassy Hill Road<br>P.O. Box 447<br>Woodbury, CT 06798 | PRESSER<br>(rental<br>-partial) |
| WOODWARD | Ralph Woodward, Jr.<br>1033 East 300 South<br>Salt Lake City, UT 84102 | |
| WOODWIND | Woodwind Editions<br>P.O. Box 457, Station K<br>Toronto, Ontario<br>Canada M4P 2G9 | |
| WORD | Word, Incorporated<br>3319 west End Avenue<br>Suite 200<br>Nashville, TN 37203 | |
| WORD GOD | The Word of God Music | SERVANT |
| WORLD | World Library Publications, Inc.<br>3825 Willow Road<br>P.O. Box 2703<br>Schiller Park, IL 60176 | |
| WORLDWIDE | Worldwide Music Services<br>P.O. Box 995, Ansonia Station<br>New York, NY 10023 | |
| WSCM | Williams School of Church Music<br>The Bourne<br>Harpenden<br>England | |
| WYE | WYE Music Publications | EMERSON |
| WYNN | Wynn/Music Publications<br>P.O. Box 739<br>Orinda, CA 94563 | |
| XYZ | Muziekuitgeverij XYZ<br>P.O. Box 338<br>NL-1400 AH Bussum<br>Netherlands | SUNSHINE |
| YAHRES | Yahres Publications<br>1315 Vance Avenue<br>Coraopolis, PA 15108 | |
| YBARRA | Ybarra Music<br>P.O. Box 665<br>Lemon Grove, CA 92045 | |
| YORKE | Yorke Editions<br>31 Thornhill Square<br>London N1 1BQ<br>England | SCHIRM.EC |
| YOUNG WORLD | Young World Publications<br>10485 Glennon Drive<br>Lakewood, CO 80226 | |
| | Yugoslavian Music Information Center<br>see MUSIC INFO | |

| Code | Publisher | U.S. Agent |
|---|---|---|
| ZALO | Zalo Publications & Services<br>P.O. Box 913<br>Bloomington, IN 47402 | FRANG |
| ZANIBON | G. Zanibon Edition<br>Piazza dei Signori, 44<br>I-35100 Padova<br>Italy | |
| ZEN-ON | Zen-On Music., Ltd.<br>3-14 Higashi Gokencho<br>Shinjuku-ku<br>Tokyo 162<br>Japan | EUR.AM.MUS<br>MAGNA D |
| ZENEM. | Zenemukiado Vallalat | BOOSEY<br>GENERAL |
| ZENGERINK | Herman Zengerink,<br>Urlusstraat 24<br>NL-3533 SN Utrecht<br>Netherlands | |
| ZERBONI | Edizioni Suvini Zerboni<br>Via Quintiliano 40<br>I-20138 Milano<br>Italy | BOOSEY<br>(rental) |
| ZIMMER. | Musikverlag Zimmermann<br>Gaugrafenstraße 19-23<br>Postfach 940183<br>D-6000 Frankfurt-am-Main<br>Germany | |
| ZIMMER.PUBS | Oscar Zimmerman Publications<br>4671 State Park Highway<br>Interlochen, MI 49643-9527 | |
| ZINNEB | Zinneberg Musikverlag | LEUCKART |
| | The Zondervan Corp.<br>  see SINGSPIR | |
| ZURFLUH | Éditions Zurfluh<br>73, Boulevard Raspail<br>F-75006 Paris<br>France | PRESSER |

# Advertisements

## Index to Advertisers

| | |
|---|---|
| The American Organist | 158 |
| The Diapason | 161 |
| Music Library Association - NOTES | 159 |
| Sacred Music USA | 165 |
| University of California Press - 19th Century Music | 163 |
| University of California Press - Journal of Musicology | 160 |
| University of California Press - Music Perception | 164 |
| University of Illinois Press - American Music | 157 |
| University of Texas Press - Latin American Music Review | 162 |

# American Music

*A quarterly journal devoted to all aspects of American music and music in America*

If you are interested in Amy Beach, New Orleans jazz, minimalism, Broadway musicals, Charles Ives, ragtime, Martha Graham, AME hymnals, Philip Glass, barbershop, John Coltrane, or the Beach Boys: then *American Music* is for you!

"This first-class quarterly [covers] everything from early jazz to new compositions by John Cage. A section of record reviews provides long, signed reviews of Indian songs, brass music, and string quartets — in short, the whole scope of US music heritage. The book reviews are equally extensive." — *Choice*

Individuals: $32.00 ($39.00 foreign)
Institutions: $48.00 ($55.00 foreign)

Published quarterly by the Sonneck Society and the University of Illinois Press. Complete sets of volumes still available.

Address subscriptions to

**UNIVERSITY OF ILLINOIS PRESS**
1325 South Oak Street, Champaign, IL 61820

# SUBSCRIBE NOW
# TO TODAY'S MOST WIDELY READ
# ORGAN AND CHORAL MAGAZINE

Official Journal of the
American Guild of Organists
Royal Canadian College of Organists
American Pipe Organ Builders Association

*Subscriptions*

| RATES | 1 Year | 2 Years | 3 Years |
|---|---|---|---|
| U.S. | ❏ $42 | ❏ $78 | ❏ $110 |
| Foreign & Canada | ❏ $52 | ❏ $98 | ❏ $130 |

Send check with name and address to:
American Guild of Organists
475 Riverside Drive, Suite 1260
New York, NY 10115

 *New and Forthcoming Books from*
# THE MUSIC LIBRARY ASSOCIATION

**MLA INDEX SERIES:**

No. 25  **Analyses of Nineteenth- and Twentieth-Century Music, 1940-1985**, by Arthur B. Wenk, 1987. ISBN 0-914954-36-9; $29.00.

No. 26  **Opera Performances in Video Format: A Checklist of Commercially Released Performances**, by Charles Croissant, 1991. ISBN-0-914954-43-1; $15.00

No. 27  **A Thematic Catalog of the Works of Robert Valentine**, by J. Bradford Young, 1994. ISBN-0-914954-46-6; $30.00

No. 28  **An Introduction and Index to the Contents of FAMS Bulletin and Pro-Musica Quarterly, 1923-1929**, compiled by Paula Elliot. (to be published in early 1996)

**MLA TECHNICAL REPORTS:**

No. 22  **Collection Assessment in Music Libraries**, edited by Jane Gottlieb, 1994. ISBN 0-914954-47-4; $22.00.

No. 23  **Knowing the Score: Preserving Collections of Music**, compiled by Mark Roosa and Jane Gottlieb, 1994. ISBN 0-914954-48-2; $22.00.

No. 24  **World Music in Music Libraries**, edited by Carl Rahkonen, 1994. ISBN 0-914954-49-0; $24.00.

**SPECIAL PUBLICATIONS:**

**The 1995 MLA Membership Handbook.** $5.00 members/$15.00 non-members. (Available from the MLA Executive Secretary, Richard Griscom.)

**Index/Supplement to the Music Cataloging Bulletin volumes 16-20**, compiled and edited by Betsy Gamble, 1993. ISBN 0-914954-40-7; $22.00.

**Notes: An Index to Volumes 1-50**, compiled by Karen R. Little, 1995. ISBN 0-914954-50-4; $30.00.

Available from library booksellers or from
The Music Library Association, P.O. Box 487L, Canton, MA 02021.
Membership information is also available from the same address.
MLA members receive a 10% discount on all publications.
Institutions requesting billing will be charged for handling.

# THE JOURNAL OF MUSICOLOGY

*A Quarterly Review of Music History, Criticism, Analysis, and Performance Practice*

"A superb publication."
— George Perle

Now in its twelfth year, the **Journal of Musicology** continues to provide some of the most significant research and critical thought in the field.

The **Journal of Musicology** is an indispensable resource both for research and for remaining in touch with new and sometimes controversial turns of musicological thought.

*Subscriptions:* $32.00 Individuals; $70.00 Institutions; $23.00 Students (Outside U.S., add $5.00)

*To order, write:* University of California Press
Journals Division
2120 Berkeley Way #5812
Berkeley, CA 94720-5812

*Or FAX:* 510/642-9917 (Visa/MasterCard only)

# THE DIAPASON

### AN INTERNATIONAL MONTHLY DEVOTED TO THE ORGAN, HARPSICHORD, CARILLON AND CHURCH MUSIC

*Official Journal*
*International Society for Organ History and Preservation*

- Feature articles by noted contributors.
- Reviews of organ, choral and handbell music, books and recordings.
- Stoplists and photos of organ installations.
- Monthly calendar of events.
- Extensive classified advertising section.

**THE DIAPASON** 380 E. Northwest Highway, Des Plaines, IL 60016-2282

NAME _____

STREET _____

CITY _____

STATE _____ ZIP _____

PLEASE ALLOW FOUR WEEKS FOR DELIVERY
OF FIRST ISSUE ON NEW SUBSCRIPTIONS.

❏ $36.00 — 3 YEARS
❏ $27.00 — 2 YEARS
❏ $18.00 — 1 YEAR

**FOREIGN SUBSCRIPTIONS:**
❏ $60.00 — 3 YEARS
❏ $43.00 — 2 YEARS
❏ $28.00 — 1 YEAR

# Revista de Música Latino Americana / Latin American Music Review

**Editor: Gerard Béhague, University of Texas at Austin**

**Latin American Music Review** explores the historical, ethnographic, and socio-cultural dimensions of Latin American music. Each issue contains film, record and video reviews and appear in English, Spanish, or Portuguese.

**Magazines for Libraries,** *"It is interdisciplinary in scope, touching the disciplines of anthropology, sociology, and urban studies. Recommended for academic libraries."*

### Spring/Summer 1996

Puerto Rican Affirmation and Denial of Musical Nationalism: The Cases of Campos Parsa and Aponti Ledée
**Edgardo Díaz Díaz**

Indicios, sociabilización y *performance* en las danzas nocturnas de los wici del chaco argentino
**Miguel A. García**

A presença do Cancioneiro Ibérico na lírica de José de Anchieta: Um enfoque musicológico
**Rogério Budasz**

---

**Subscription rates (one year):**
Individual $22, Institution $38, foreign postage, add $4/subscription
**Single copy rates:**
Individual $13, Institution $24, foreign postage, add $2/copy

**University of Texas Press, Journals Division, Box 7819, Austin, Texas 78713-7819**
Phone # 512-471-4531, Fax # 512-320-0668
*journals@uts.cc.utexas.edu*

# 19TH CENTURY MUSIC

features articles on music history and criticism, analysis, and theory, as well as studies of performance practice, reviews and review articles, and commentary by guest columnists on a broad range of issues.

**Quarterly Subscriptions:** $33 Individuals; $69 Institutions (add $5 for foreign postage).
**Single copies:** $13 Individuals; $26 Institutions

**Send orders and subscription inquiries to:**
Journals Division
University of California Press
2120 Berkeley Way, #5812, Berkeley, CA 94720-5812
FAX: 510/642/9917

# Music Perception

EDITOR: Jamshed J. Bharucha

ASSOCIATE EDITORS
Edward C. Carterette
Robert O. Gjerdingen
W. M. Hartmann
Adrianus J. M. Houtsma
Carol L. Krumhansl
Eugene Narmour
Johan E. F. Sundberg

FOUNDING EDITOR: Diana Deutsch

"*Music Perception* has assumed a dominant position among publications in its field. It publishes a wise balance of experimental work, theoretical papers and reviews from recognized leaders in experimental psychology, music theory and acoustics. If one is skeptical that the cognitive sciences have urgent things to say about music, he should be guided to this journal, fast."

*Robert G. Crowder, Yale University*

"An increasingly important area of music theory is the relationship between theoretical constructs and psychological reality. *Music Perception* therefore comes at a most propitious time, and provides an important opportunity for music theorists and cognitive scientists to meet on common ground."

*F. Lerdahl, Columbia University*

Quarterly. Subscriptions: $49 individuals, $104 institutions (add $6 for foreign postage).
Editorial office: Dept. of Psychology, Dartmouth College, 6207 Gerry Hall, Rm. 201, Hanover, NH 03755.
To order, write:
UNIVERSITY OF CALIFORNIA PRESS, JOURNALS DIVISION
BERKELEY, CALIFORNIA 94720-5812, or FAX: 510/642-9917

## Sacred Music USA

### National Directory and Resource Guide of the Sacred Performing Arts

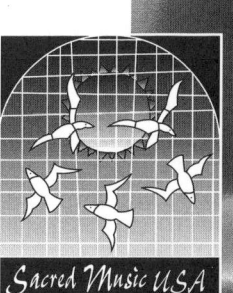

The Single most important resource for the Church Musician!

**Essential**

All the resources you need under one cover.

**Complete**

Complete listings of Music Publishers, Choir Robe manufacturers, Organ Companies, and More!

**Unique**

With a special emphasis on concert series in Churches, Sacred Music USA offers all the resources you need to put together a successful concert series, or to maintain an existing series including: Artists Managers, Publicity/PR, Music Critics, Fundraising, and more!

---

Please send me a copy of the 1995 issue of *Sacred Music USA*. I am enclosing a check or money order for $35.00.

Name _____

Address _____

City _____ State ____ Zip _____

---

**Please make checks payable to Sacred Music Publications**
21346 St. Andrews Blvd., Suite 207 Boca Raton, FL 33433
For information, or to inquire about advertising in the
Sacred Music USA 1996 Edition please call (800) 249-9410